Distant
Friends

Distant Friends

The United States and Russia, 1763–1867

Norman E. Saul

 University Press of Kansas

To Mary Ann
with Love

© 1991 by the University Press of Kansas
All rights reserved

Published by the University Press of Kansas
(Lawrence, Kansas 66045), which was organized by
the Kansas Board of Regents and is operated and
funded by Emporia State University, Fort Hays
State University, Kansas State University, Pittsburg
State University, the University of Kansas, and
Wichita State University

Library of Congress Cataloging-in-Publication
Data

Saul, Norman E.
    Distant friends : the United States and Russia,
  1763–1867 / by Norman E. Saul.
        p.   cm.
    Includes bibliographical references and index.
    ISBN 0-7006-0438-3 (alk. paper)
    1. United States—Relations—Soviet Union.
  2. Soviet Union—Relations—United States.
  3. United States—Foreign relations—1783–1865.
  4. Soviet Union—Foreign relations—19th
  century. 5. Soviet Union—Foreign
  relations—1689–1800. I. Title.
  E183.8.S65S274   1990
  303.48′273047—dc20   90-41807
                                                 CIP

British Library Cataloguing in Publication Data is
available.

Printed in the United States of America
10 9 8 7 6 5 4 3 2 1

The paper used in this publication meets the minimum
requirements of the American National Standard for
Permanence of Paper for Printed Library Materials
Z39.48-1984.

Contents

List of Illustrations

Preface

My interest in Russian-American relations began somewhat by accident: intriguing materials encountered while working on another subject in the Public Record Office in London, a chance meeting with someone whose ancestor had been to Russia. I soon discovered that surprisingly little recent research on Russian-American relations before 1917 had been done on the American side, though Soviet scholars were at work on various aspects of the subject. One other thing was apparent—the existing literature on the subject in English was rather episodic.

After drilling several test wells, I began a systematic investigation of the subject "from our revolution to theirs." As with so many research topics, the deeper I dug the more material I found, much of it quite unexpected. This naturally delayed and complicated the work. The scattered nature of the materials and the limited time and resources available caused further delays. Instead of the one volume I originally contemplated covering the whole period before 1917, I now plan a three-volume study with the first extending up to the purchase of Alaska, the second to the beginning of World War I, and the third from the beginning of that war to the mid-1920s. The result will be a comprehensive treatment of Russian-American relations that is both monographic and synthetic. It is not exhaustive. I have summarized and referred the reader to the more detailed works of other scholars. From my research experiences, stumbling over materials in unlikely places and still finding large gaps in the historical record, I know that more information is to be found, and one goal of this work is to try to bring more to light. My hope is that more trunks will appear out of attics.

Though I was fortunate to gain access for a period to Soviet archives, the story is better covered on the American side. The inadequate or nonexistent cataloging in Soviet libraries and archives and the apparent loss of much material, especially personal papers, as well as my inability to pursue research in the USSR on a regular basis, leave much ground uncovered. There are, thus, the inevitable gaps in knowledge about the roles of persons, places, and things on the Russian side. On the other hand, I have benefited from the work and advice of many Soviet scholars.

The purpose of this study is to present in a chronological and meaningful way what is known about the Russian-American experience through the Russian Revolution. This volume ends with the sale/purchase of Alaska, a climactic event in the relations between the two countries. Much new material is presented here from a variety of collections in the United States and the Soviet Union and from the publications of a large number of Soviet and American scholars. Contemporary journals and newspapers, the rich U.S. diplomatic post records for Russia in the National Archives, as well as the consular and diplomatic correspondence on microfilm, and the Russian diplomatic correspondence that was made available to me in Moscow were of particular importance for my study.

Financial support for the project has been most gratefully welcomed from the International Research and Exchanges Board (Soviet-American scholarly exchange), a National Endowment for the Humanities Travel to Collections grant, a short-term fellowship at the Kennan Institute for Advanced Russian Studies in Washington, and the University of Illinois Summer Research Laboratory. The University of Kansas has been especially supportive of the project with General Research Grants (summer stipends), a sabbatical leave, and a Hall Center for the Humanities Fellowship.

A scholar is always deeply indebted to those who have blazed the paths on the topic. They include from an earlier generation Frank Golder, Anatole Mazour, Max Laserson, Avraam Yarmolinsky, Benjamin Platt Thomas, William Appleman Williams, and Thomas A. Bailey. For the more recent period the list is longer: David Griffiths, Howard Kushner, Glynn Barratt, James Gibson, Raymond Fisher, John Gaddis, George Lensen, Richard Pierce, Robert Allen, Richard Haywood, Patricia Herlihy, Walther Kirchner, Dane Hartgrove, Hans Rogger, and especially Nikolai Bolkhovitinov. I want to thank my colleagues in American history at the University of Kansas—Donald R. McCoy, W. Stitt Robinson, Phillip Paludan, Lloyd Sponholtz, and Rita Napier—for enduring my queries for details and sources and being patient with questions that betrayed a frustrating ignorance of American history. This work could never have been completed without the moral encouragement and helpful advice of John Gaddis, Walter LaFeber, Hans Rogger, Theodore Wilson, Alexander Dallin, Patricia Grimsted, Nikolai Bolkhovitinov, Gennady Kuropiatnik, Robert Ivanov, and my colleague in Russian history, Jay Alexander. Several of the above read part or all of the manuscript at various stages and made many valuable suggestions. They are, of course, not responsible for the final form.

The assistance, kindness, and sympathy of a very large number of library and archive staff members can never be acknowledged enough. A project of this kind also depended heavily on interlibrary loans, microforms, and government documents, as well as rare book and manuscript collections. Work conditions naturally varied widely in these facilities, but I invariably met with cooperation and skilled guidance in obtaining what I needed. To all of these sincere devotees of books and documents go my special appreciation of their role and many thanks. On the other end of the process I am deeply indebted to the secretarial staff of my department—Sandee Kennedy, Terri Rockhold, Ellen Garber, and Jan Emerson—and Pam LeRow for their patience in coping with idiosyncrasies, nurturing my limited literacy in word processing, and shuffling floppy disks into printers to produce a miraculously neat printed copy, only to have it chopped, slashed, and rewritten.

Once the manuscript was assembled, the production and editorial staff of the University Press of Kansas provided for its expert care and feeding. They agreed to my early insistence on placing the notes at the bottom of the pages and endured my many questions and inquiries with good humor and steady encouragement. Cindy Ingham's thorough copyediting raised questions of content as well as of style. Only I can fully appreciate her imprint upon the book.

My family has contributed to this work in many ways. Mary Ann was not only a pillar of support for the whole project but served as the critical first reader for various drafts. Our children, Alyssa, Kevin, and Julia, were graciously tolerant of research trips (such as five months in a Moscow hotel room) and diversions to see yet one more manuscript collection that interfered with vacation plans. They also assisted directly (for only very modest rewards) in reading microfilm and leafing through the endless pages of newspapers and journals. And their own varied and individual activities and career developments created welcome interruptions as well as constant stimulation for my own work. My only regret is that they have moved on to other pastures and will not be as directly involved in future projects.

In the midst of manuscript collections my thoughts would occasionally turn to the efforts and sacrifices made by these representatives of each country: traveling so far from home to quite different social and political environments, often enduring harsh, unfamiliar climates (whether the hot summers of Washington or the cold, damp winters of St. Petersburg), and suffering a variety of illnesses and ailments while obtaining varying, often intangible, rewards. I sensed some of these conditions myself in my own travels to and from the Soviet Union, but they did not approach those of the eighteenth and nineteenth centuries. These men and women on the whole made a real effort, sometimes with personal gain in mind, or as victims of circumstance, but more often than not, they strove to understand the other country and its people. For this—and the words they left behind—I am the most indebted of all. This is their book.

Note on Transliteration and Spelling

For rendering Russian sources into English I have consistently used a simplified Library of Congress transliteration in the Notes and Bibliography. Russian names, however, are more complicated, because so many are already known to English readers in more familiar Anglicized versions, such as Nicholas for Nikolai and Alexander for Aleksandr. I have generally followed a commonsense approach by using the English form for the most familiar names: thus Nicholas I, Grand Duke Constantine, Alexander Herzen, Leo Tolstoy. The least familiar are usually in transliterated form: Nikolai Murav'ev-Amurskii, Pavel Mel'nikov. The same principle applies to names of places. Those in between present the biggest problem, and compromises, resulting more from feel or sense than anything else, have been made (for example, Alexander Bodisko whose last name is spelled Bodisco in contemporary American sources).

A further difficulty is that a number of "Russians" are really German. Rather than Stekl (Russian transliteration), the reader will find Stoeckl, the form most commonly used in English. The reader may at first be baffled by these inconsistencies and incongruities. The goal has been to retain some of the Russian flavor of name and place—but not so as to become burdensome or awkward.

Although the Russian calendar varied from the Western calendar by eleven days in the eighteenth century and twelve days in the nineteenth century, dates are less of a problem than names. Most Russian official documents provide both dates (as 15/27 April 1855), as do newspapers, and both are thus used in the Notes, while the dating in the text is consistently by the Western calendar. There are a few cases—for example, a Russian abroad writing home—in which the calendar is not clear, but just as often are found letters with no date or with just "Saturday" to annoy the historian. Fortunately, none of these are of critical importance.

Abbreviations
Used in Notes

ADM	Admiralty
AVPR	Archive of the Foreign Policy of Russia, Moscow
CaHS	California Historical Society, San Francisco
CGG	Correspondence of the Governor General
CinHS	Cincinnati Historical Society
ConnHS	Connecticut Historical Society
CR	Communications Received
CS	Communications Sent
DIDS	Diplomatic Instructions of Department of State
DPR	Diplomatic Post Records
DUSC	Despatches from United States Consuls
DUSM	Despatches from United States Ministers
FO	Foreign Office
HSP	Historical Society of Pennsylvania
LC	Library of Congress
MaryHS	Maryland Historical Society, Baltimore
MassHS	Massachusetts Historical Society
NA	National Archives and Records Service
NYHS	New-York Historical Society
NYPL	New York Public Library
PRO	Public Record Office
RG	Record Group
RRAC	Records of the Russian America Company
SHSM	State Historical Society of Missouri
SI	Smithsonian Institution
TsGIA	Central State Historical Archive, Leningrad

UCB   University of California, Berkeley
USR   *The United States and Russia: The Beginning of Relations, 1775–1815*
WUTE   Western Union Telegraph Expedition

1

First Contacts for Distant Friends

In the eighteenth century profound cultural, political, economic, and military changes occurred within the "old Europe." In 1700 the cultural and political centers of the "civilized" western world were Paris, London, and Vienna, but they were being challenged by new commercial cities. The age of Enlightenment rose slowly but dramatically from the accumulated imperial and national wealth and knowledge that resulted from more efficient and centralized administration and improved communications. This in turn inspired a new wave of exploration of talent, resources, and territory. In this great expansion of "civilization" both America and Russia emerged as factors that had to be reckoned with in the councils of Europe, especially as potential disruptive elements in the preservation of the balance of power in Europe. Armed conflicts, which tend to dominate the older textbook histories of the century, were provoked by dynastic and national ambitions, by rival colonial policies and consolidations, and by changes in military and naval tactics and strategy. From the abilities and ambitions of Peter the Great and Louis XIV, of Marlborough and Charles XII, military operations assumed a world scale in both scope and cost. Europe had expanded, not only militarily, but with ideas and institutions, to include Russia to the east and those parts of America under European hegemony to the west. British America's Europeanization coincided with the adaptation of western models by the Russian Empire.

This new expansion of Europe may best be symbolized by the famous tour of northern Europe by Peter the Great that culminated with a stay of several weeks in London early in 1698. There he met with William Penn, the colonial entrepreneur, more because of Peter's interest in the Quakers than in America. Nevertheless, two indirect effects can be traced to these first Russian appreciations of an American reality: the impact of religious pluralism represented by American Quaker and Puritan sects on Peter's church policies and his removal of restric-

1

tions on the import of tobacco into the Russian Empire. At Utrecht, in early 1698, Peter agreed to special arrangements for English tobacco merchants in Russia that gave them a virtual monopoly and expanded the market considerably for that colonial American product.[1]

Russia and the Commercial Revolution

While economic growth supported military needs, capital wealth, population increase, and urban development promoted travel and commerce across the Atlantic. North American cotton and tobacco and West Indian products entered Europe in larger and larger amounts, while manufactured goods and materials such as bar iron were exported to the developing colonies. And in the Baltic, where this increased activity was reflected, the Russian conquest of territory from Sweden in the Great Northern War (1700–1721) made possible the founding on that sea of a new capital of the Russian Empire—St. Petersburg. The city was not simply proof of Russia's entry into European political and cultural life. Helped by Peter's mercantilist edicts, it quickly became a vital trading center, augmented and supported by the nearby naval base and commercial port of Kronstadt. It immediately participated in the flourishing Baltic trade, which was nurtured by the enterprising activities of British and Dutch ship captains and middlemen and the enduring vitality of the Hanseatic League. The American colonies were a primary focus of this trade. Economics was, therefore, of first and foremost importance in early Russian-American relations, but intertwined and inseparable from it was politics.

Through the first half of the eighteenth century, direct contact between North America and Russia did not exist, since the colonial empires of North America had mercantilist restrictions that ruled out direct trade with Russia. The Seven Years' War (1756–63), however, acted as a catalyst for a number of striking changes, collectively labeled a commercial revolution. Maritime necessities brought improvements in naval architecture and in shipbuilding techniques, particularly in Britain, and made possible more, larger, faster, and more maneuverable sailing vessels. At the same time the quest for financial resources and the growth of the urban economy led to the development of more sophisticated and competitive banking, insurance, and trading institutions. During and immediately after the war, independent commission merchants and shipowners prospered, with the encouragement of favorable state fiscal policies and more efficient international monetary exchanges.

[1]Eufrosina Dvoichenko-Markov, "William Penn and Peter the Great," *Transactions of the American Philosophical Society*, 97, 1 (February 1953): 12–24; Jacob M. Price, "The Tobacco Adventure to Russia: Enterprise, Politics, and Diplomacy in the Quest for a Northern Market for English Colonial Tobacco, 1676–1722," *Transactions of the American Philosophical Society*, n.s. 51, pt. 1(1961): 19–32.

This window of opportunity permitted the rapid growth of colonial trading centers such as Boston, New York, and Philadelphia, owing in part to the diversion of British and French capital, resources, and shipping for the war effort. The war and commercial expansion also produced a dramatic increase in the demand for "naval stores"—masts, tar, hemp for rope, iron for nails, chains and anchors, and, most important, for large quantities of linen for sailcloth to equip the bigger and more numerous ships. The chief suppliers of this expanding market were the Baltic nations, especially Russia with its enormous hinterland and vast resources of labor and material. The British navy and merchant marine were primary consumers of these goods, but the North American colonial centers, forced into virtual economic independence by the war, were naturally inclined to build their own ships from native timber and then to outfit them with the superior imported materials. At the same time, Russian territorial and economic development spurred the rapid expansion of an internal market for colonial products such as sugar, coffee, dyewoods, spices, tobacco, and cotton.

First Direct American-Russian Contacts

In May 1763 the brig *Wolfe*, owned by Nicholas Boylston, a prominent Boston merchant, dropped anchor at Kronstadt, ending the first recorded direct transatlantic voyage to Russian waters by an "American" ship. The cargo consisted of sugar, indigo, rum, mahogany, and sassafras, all originating in the West Indies. The *Wolfe* returned directly to New England with naval stores purchased in the Russian capital: hemp, iron, and linen cloth—ravensduck and sheeting.[2] This first direct encounter between Americans and Russians received no public notice, Americans at that time being hardly distinguishable from British. Yet the British ambassador to Russia became alarmed and alerted his government to this challenge to home trade supremacy protected by the Royal Navigation Laws, now being overtaken by the commercial revolution. The British governor of Massachusetts was put on guard to interdict this shipping but with no apparent result. Though still relatively few in number, the voyages of the *Wolfe* and of

[2]See Norman E. Saul, "The Beginnings of American-Russian Trade, 1763–1766," *William and Mary Quarterly*, 3d ser. 26, 4 (October 1969): 595–601. The interaction of technological change, commerce, and international relations remains to be thoroughly examined for this period and it especially neglected in both the general literature and in specialized studies on foreign affairs. For important background studies, see R. G. Albion, *Forests and Seapower: The Timber Problem of the Royal Navy* (Cambridge, Mass.: Harvard University Press, 1926); Carl Bridenbaugh, *Cities in Revolt: Urban Life in America, 1743–1776* (Columbia University Press, 1964); for the rise in number and size of ships, Joseph A. Goldenburg, *Shipbuilding in Colonial America* (Charlottesville: University of Virginia Press, 1976); and, especially for eighteenth-century Russia, Arcadius Kahan, *The Plow, the Hammer, and the Knout: An Economic History of Eighteenth-Century Russia* (Chicago and London: University of Chicago Press, 1985).

those that followed, from New York and Philadelphia as well as Boston, illustrated the growing independence of the American colonial ports and their aspirations for economic and political equality with the home country.

Meanwhile, Russia under Empress Catherine II was undergoing a westernization and modernization that would substantially alter international politics. As part of her ambition to make Russia a great power, Catherine sent several young noblemen to train as naval officers on British ships. By coincidence, about the same time that the *Wolfe* was crossing the Atlantic, the British frigate *Coventry* brought Lt. Ivan Seniavin to New York, where he was based until his return to Russia in 1767, allowing him ample opportunity to view the British colonies firsthand.[3] The British trained a number of such young Russian officers, and the Russian navy employed British officers, most of whom had seen service in America. With this help Russia soon acquired a capable fleet, which it proved by making a dramatic voyage from the Baltic to the Mediterranean and surprising the Turks at the Battle of Chesme in July 1770, thereby achieving temporary naval supremacy in the eastern Mediterranean. Like the American colonies, Russia was reaching out into new waters.

Underlying the profitable exchange of commodities between the colonies and Russia were inhumane serf and slave systems. Russia's production of iron, hemp, and sailcloth depended largely on its ability to command peasant labor; America's expansion of sugar, rice, tobacco, and cotton production rested on the backs of more and more imported black slaves. Indeed, the increase in Atlantic commerce and the growth of Russian trade with America in particular helped to preserve and to expand slave labor systems and to worsen the conditions of slavery. Yet this trade also increased communications and the awareness of these conditions, thus provoking serious criticism and challenges to their existence.

A Common Enlightenment

The ideas of the Enlightenment spread by means of the printed word and a growing sense of civilized progress. While Catherine read Montesquieu, corresponded with Voltaire, and flirted with a variety of "improvements" at home, many British-Americans pondered a better future in their scientific and political tracts. Practical techniques and science dominated the initial Russian-American

---

[3]At least seven other Russian naval officer trainees served with the British navy in American waters in the 1760s, but Seniavin seems to have left the best record of his activities and perhaps spent the most time on land. See the annotations and references to Soviet naval archives in *The United States and Russia: The Beginning of Relations, 1765–1815* (Washington, D.C.: Department of State and Government Printing Office, 1980), pp. 12–13. This valuable collection of documents was jointly edited and amply annotated by American and Soviet scholars and published in both American and Soviet editions as part of a joint cultural exchange project, a commendable cooperative effort. Hereafter it will be cited as *USR*.

cultural exchanges. Publications of learned societies, such as the Royal Society in London, the American Philosophical Society in Philadelphia, and the Free Economic Society and the Imperial Academy of Sciences in St. Petersburg, were patronized by progressive courts and by the new urban wealth and provided an international forum for the exchange of ideas. Thus, Americans interested in scientific advances, such as Ezra Stiles and Benjamin Franklin, became acquainted with works of Russian scientists Josias Braun, Franz Aepinus, and Mikhail Lomonosov, while Russians especially followed and commented on the writings of Franklin.[4] Stiles even wrote a letter to Lomonosov in 1765, the first effort at direct scholarly communication, but, owing apparently to news of Lomonosov's death, it was never sent.[5] Before 1776, therefore, knowledge about each area's intellectual and political development was based mostly on serial publications of the societies, independent pamphlets and journals, and such British publications as the *Annual Register*.

At least one North American resident, Peter Allaire of New Jersey, toured Russia before the beginning of the war for independence. However, his close association in St. Petersburg with the British envoy Sir Robert Gunning, and his later loyalist stance, place him more in the "British" category than "American."[6] Americans, indeed, generally had many, more compelling places to travel than to Russia and many new problems to absorb their attention in the early 1770s.

Most contacts were still indirect. The Russian court was provided with detailed information about the rising colonial strife and American animosity toward British rule by the ambassador in London, Count Aleksei Musin-Pushkin. Beginning from 1767, his letters to Catherine II and to Nikita Ivanovich Panin, her chief adviser on foreign affairs, contain enough material for a good contem-

[4]Eufrosina Dvoichenko-Markov, "Benjamin Franklin, the American Philosophical Society, and the Russian Academy of Science," *Proceedings of the American Philosophical Society* 96, 3 (August 1947): 250–58. See also the correspondence between Ezra Stiles and Benjamin Franklin in *USR*, pp. 2, 8–10, and M. I. Radovskii, *Veniamin Franklin i ego sviazi s Rossiei* (Moscow-Leningrad: Nauka, 1958).

[5]The original of the Stiles letter to Lomonosov is in the Franklin Papers at the American Philosophical Society and published in *USR*, pp. 4–8. For another discussion of early Russian-American cultural connections, see N. N. Bolkhovitinov, *The Beginnings of Russian-American Relations, 1775–1815*, trans. Elena Levin (Cambridge, Mass., and London: Harvard University Press, 1975), pp. 117–24. This important study, which along with *USR* provides the foundations for this chapter, should be used with caution in its English edition because of a number of typographical and other errors. Careful scholars will want to refer to the original Soviet edition, *Stanovlenie russko-amerikanskikh otnoshenii 1775–1815* (Moscow: Nauka, 1966). The section on the American revolutionary period is also available in a slightly different form: *Russia and the American Revolution*, trans. and ed. C. Jay Smith (Tallahassee, Fl.: Diplomatic Press, 1976).

[6]*USR*, pp. 25–28. A Russian source, a supplement to the *Kamerfur'erskii zhurnal* for 1778, advertised an American "physicist and mechanic" named Blank demonstrating scientific (magic?) experiments in Moscow.

porary history of the increasing strain between Britain and its colonies.[7] In part, this particular interest in American affairs by certain internationally minded Russians can be attributed to concern about the internal troubles of an important friend and ally. However, they were also attracted to both the practical development of American commercial and natural resources and to the more idealistic experiments with enlightened principles of self-government in the American colonies. Many of the latter were, after all, aristocratic or elitist in concept, following the lines of some of the Russian nobility's political aspirations. Another more official factor was a fear that a disruption in America would spread to great-power conflict in Europe itself, possibly upsetting the balance of power there and affecting Russia's relatively successful expansionist strategy.

The Russian government, however, was in no position to intervene actively, either to help preserve the British Empire or to mediate in favor of greater autonomy for the colonies. In 1774 Russia was just emerging from Catherine's First Turkish War. The long and costly conflict had considerably advanced Russia territorially to the south, and economically into the Mediterranean, but had in turn provoked one of the severest threats of that era to the internal security of imperial institutions and to Catherine personally—the Pugachev Rebellion. The difficult but ultimately successful suppression of this revolt was followed by a series of administrative reforms that diverted Russian attention and resources over the next several years. By the time stability had been restored in Russia, the course for conflict in America had already been set.

Russia and the Beginning of the Revolutionary War

Even before the war was under way, Britain attempted to call in a debt owed for British assistance and support during the Russo-Turkish War and obtain a sizable detachment of Russian mercenaries for service in its American colonies. George III was especially confident of his "Sister Kitty's" favorable response, since Catherine had already tendered a vague offer of help in policing the restless colonies. And Russia's foreign policy under Nikita Panin, the so-called Northern System, was based on a mutual understanding among the nations of northern Europe, especially Prussia but also including Britain, against France and Austria. This, then, might have been a golden opportunity for Russia to confirm Britain's allegiance in gratitude for direct military assistance. Catherine, however, rejected the British request, primarily on the practical grounds that her

---

[7]Bolkhovitinov, *The Beginnings*, pp. 3–4. For excerpts from Musin-Pushkin's reports, see *USR*, pp. 14–19, 28–33. Nikita I. Panin should not be confused with his nephew, Nikita Petrovich Panin, who served Emperor Paul briefly in a similar capacity.

troops, exhausted by six years of war and rebellion, could not be spared.[8] Moreover, she and her ministers were quite aware of French sympathy for the colonies, which could provoke a wider European conflict that Russia could ill afford at the time. But another and perhaps just as important reason for initial neutrality was Catherine's personal dislike of George III and his chief ministers, who she believed had badly bungled American affairs and who deserved to be taught a lesson. Finally, the empress had already committed Russia to naval and commercial expansion in areas where Britain was the dominant power and a potential, if not already real, obstacle. Russians would not be Hessians.

On the other hand, Catherine apparently did not have any personal sympathy for American aspirations for independence, which were widely perceived as part of the ongoing confrontation between Britain and France in the colonial world. Nor did she draw any parallels between the rebellion of British "aristocrats" in America and the destructive revolt of her own peasants in the recent past. The situations were so obviously different. As David Griffiths has clearly shown, the American "revolution" was not regarded by Catherine as a potential threat to herself or to monarchical government in general.[9] Catherine, after all, remained a believer in the principles of a moderate, centrally controlled Enlightenment, which she viewed as having a natural "civilizing" influence in America as they still were having, to some extent, in Russia itself and which were designed to strengthen empires rather than destroy or weaken them. Thus her recorded remarks on American affairs were few and never very consistent. She admired the British but was annoyed with their political and commercial arrogance; she was also personally disgusted with their rulers for being unresponsive to reasonable American claims and for failing in their proper role as "enlightened despots." To Catherine, Americans were Britishers who simply agreed with her assessment.

Although there is no evidence that she was aware of it, the Russian empress would probably have been pleased with John Adams's effort to create a "Model Treaty" in 1776 to chart the new republic's foreign relations. His purpose was to avoid the possibility of commercial and political dominance by either France or Britain; his method was to strengthen the balance of power in Europe by invit-

[8]The British ambassador in St. Petersburg at the time, Sir Robert Gunning, had formed the mistaken opinion, as did the British press, that Russia had made a commitment to provide military assistance. This was clarified in a firm refusal by Catherine in a letter to George III, dated 23 September/4 October 1775, reprinted in *USR*, pp. 33–35. See also Bolkhovitinov, *The Beginnings*, pp. 5–6; William Lee to Robert Nicholas, 24 September 1775, and editor's notes, in *Letters of William Lee, . . . 1766–1783*, comp. and ed. Worthington Chauncey Ford, vol. 1 (Brooklyn: Historical Printing Club, 1891; New York Times and Arno Press Reprint, 1971), pp. 179–80.

[9]David M. Griffiths, "Catherine the Great, the British Opposition, and the American Revolution," in *The American Revolution and "A Candid World"*, ed. Lawrence S. Kaplan (Kent, Ohio: Kent State University Press, 1977), pp. 85–110.

ing all countries to ascribe to the basic principles of free trade. Though printed (and discussed) by the Continental Congress, the Adams project fell victim to more pressing concerns and to policy and personality differences among those Americans who had to carry out diplomatic assignments in Europe. France quickly assumed the dominant position in early American foreign relations.

Russians in America during the War

As French noblemen would join the American cause with more enthusiasm than can be explained by their support of their king's long-term rivalry with Britain, Russians too would be drawn to the commencement of the great American experiment. The first, and evidently the only, Russian subject to serve in the Continental army was Baron Gustavus Heinrich Wetter von Rosenthal, a Baltic (Livonian) German who had killed another nobleman in St. Petersburg. Escaping Russia for America, by September 1776, he was already serving as a surgeon's mate at Fort Ticonderoga. Under the name of "John Rose" he continued his medical practice at Valley Forge and after 1781 was aide-de-camp to Brig. Gen. William Irvine with the rank of major. Visiting his homeland in 1784, Rose/Rosenthal apparently intended to return to the United States, but he changed his mind after he was reprieved for his crime and appointed a marshall of nobility for Livonia. He conducted an infrequent correspondence with the Irvine family until his death in 1830.[10]

At least four other "Russians" were in America during the war years: Vasily Baranshchikov, a wandering adventurer; Zakhar Bobukh, an artisan from Estonia who served with German mercenaries on the British side; Charles Cist, a Philadelphia physician; and Fedor Karzhavin. Of the first three, Cist was the best known, becoming a noted publisher who later served as Public Printer of the United States during the John Adams presidency. He was apparently of German origin and under the name Charles Jacob Sigismund Thiel had served as a court physician in St. Petersburg in the 1760s.[11] The connections of these "Russians" with America were slight and had no political implications.

The experiences of the fourth, Fedor Karzhavin, are on a different level according to the documentary evidence that survives. The son of a prominent St. Petersburg merchant, Karzhavin spent much of his youth in Paris, where he naturally became acquainted with the ideas of the Enlightenment. Returning to Russia, he worked in the early 1770s with Vasilyi Bazhenov, a prominent Moscow teacher and adherent of the Enlightenment who laid the foundations for a classical school of architecture in Russia. After being denied a teaching post in

---

[10]*USR*, pp. 37–39, 84–86 (picture on p. 39); "A Russian in the American Revolutionary Army," San Francisco *Daily Evening Bulletin*, 17 January 1867, citing Dr. William A. Irvine, grandson of the general.

[11]Bolkhovitinov, *Russia and the American Revolution*, pp. 177–79.

French at the University of Moscow, Karzhavin accepted an offer to serve as a guide-companion to a young Russian nobleman who was going abroad to study at Leiden. From there Karzhavin made his way in 1776 to Martinique, where he reputedly helped the French smuggle supplies through the British blockade into the rebelling colonies. This led in turn to extended and somewhat involuntary wanderings along the North American seaboard.

Though Karzhavin visited Boston, New York, and Philadelphia, his most important contacts with Americans were in Virginia during his stays in Williamsburg. In June 1777, he offered his services as an emissary to Russia to John Hancock, president of the Continental Congress.[12] Though apparently not given serious consideration at that time, his proposal may have prepared the ground for the idea of sending a special envoy to Russia that took root by the end of 1779. Karzhavin, according to his own testimony, had since decided that he would not be a welcome candidate at the Russian court because of his nonnoble rank and his known free-thinking and liberal pronouncements.

After further trips between the American states and the French and Spanish West Indies (using Havana as a base) in pursuit of trade, profit, and assistance to the rebel cause, Karzhavin returned to Virginia in 1784. By that time, if not during his earlier visits, he had become involved with freemasonry and acquainted with Carlo Bellini and James Wise, well-known scholars and professors at William and Mary College, and probably also with James Madison, the cousin of the future president, who was a Church of England bishop then serving as president of the college.[13] Through these associations, Karzhavin was presumably known to the most famous Virginians of the time—Washington, Jefferson, and Madison.[14]

Karzhavin spent most of his remaining years in America, from 1784 to 1787, writing various tracts on his travels and on atheism while supporting himself as a translator in the French consulate. He also corresponded from America with some of the more enlightened Russians of that period—Nikolai Novikov, his former employer Bazhenov, the poet Andrei Bukharskii, and the explorer-scholar Gavriil Sarychev.[15] Karzhavin finally left the United States in 1787 and returned to Russia, appropriately on an American ship. Most of his subsequent literary work in Russia involved translations, though he sometimes wrote under

---

[12]Karzhavin to Hancock, 15 June 1777, *USR*, pp. 45–46; S. R. Dolgova, *Tvorcheskii put' F. V. Karzhavina* (Leningrad: Nauka, 1984), pp. 23–28. Karzhavin's journals for 1777 and 1778 are published in the original French in Alexander Nikoliukin, *A Russian Discovery of America* (Moscow: Progress Publishers, 1986), pp. 33–70. See also A. I. Startsev, "F. V. Karzhavin i ego amerikanskoe puteshestvie," *Istoriia SSSR*, no. 3. (1960): 132–39, and Eufrosina Dvoichenko-Markov, "A Russian Traveller to Eighteenth-Century America," *Proceedings of the American Philosophical Society* 97, 4 (September 1953): 350–55.

[13]Bolkhovitinov, *Russia and the American Revolution*, p. 171.

[14]Dolgova, *Tvorcheskii*, pp. 31–33.

[15]Ibid, pp. 33–35.

the pseudonym "A Russian-American." In 1797 he entered government service in the Admiralty College as a translator. During his nine years there, and probably until his death in 1812, it is likely that he spread positive impressions of and information about America and the new American institutions to a wide circle of friends and acquaintances in the Russian capital.[16]

Important contacts were being established in other quarters, most significantly in Paris. Though the Grand Duke Paul, heir to the Russian throne, refused to see American emissary Benjamin Franklin when he passed through Paris in 1781 on a grand tour of Europe, other official Russians were quite receptive to the American commissioners in Europe. Besides Franklin, these included John Adams, Arthur Lee, and Silas Deane. Franklin, however, concentrated on securing and strengthening the alliance with France, which would allow the French foreign minister, Comte de Vergennes, to influence American policy in Europe. Ivan Bariatinskii, the Russian minister in the capital of America's chief ally, was a supportive and encouraging intermediary whose enlightened views led him to sympathize with American aspirations of independence and with the goals of their European agents. The same was true of Dmitri Golitsyn at The Hague, where John Adams would eventually stake out a more independent (as it would seem to Franklin and France) diplomatic position. Both of these Russian ambassadors were in regular communication with the respective American representatives and thus provided Russia and the new republic with the closest equivalent to formal diplomatic relations.[17]

Russia's Declaration of Armed Neutrality

In the meantime, Russia assisted the French and American cause diplomatically by helping to maintain peace between Prussia and France's ally Austria, so that

[16]Ibid, pp. 109–22; Eufrosina Dvoichenko-Markov, "A Russian Traveller to Eighteenth-Century America," pp. 352–55. The extent of Karzhavin's influence and involvement with Russia's "Enlightenment" remains controversial among such Soviet scholars as Bolkhovitinov, Dolgova, and Startsev. See the latter's "Byl li Karzhavin drugom Radishcheva," *Voprosy Literatury*, no. 4 (1971): 170. An autobiographical sketch and survey of Karzhavin's written work was published much earlier by N. P. Durov, "Fedor Vasil'evich Karzhavin," *Russkaia Starina* 12 (February 1875): 272–97. See also *USR*, pp. 45–46, 81–84, 220–22; and Bolkhovitinov, *The Beginnings*, pp. 55–65.

Also worth mentioning is Vasili Baranshchikov of Nizhni Novgorod, who apparently spent some time in the Caribbean during the war. At least he wrote a rather popular, exaggerated account of such a trip in 1787, read by a wide audience of Russians. Barbara Maggs, "Fedor Karzhavin and Vasili Baranshchikov: Russian Travellers in the Caribbean and Colonial America," in *Russia and the World of the Eighteenth Century*, ed. R. P. Bartlett (Columbus, Ohio: Slavica, 1988), pp. 603–14.

[17]For the important role of John Adams as an American representative in Europe, see James H. Hutson, *John Adams and the Diplomacy of the American Revolution* (Lexington: University of Kentucky Press, 1980). A colorful but less reliable account of Americans abroad is Elmer Bendiner, *The Virgin Diplomats* (New York: Alfred A. Knopf, 1976).

France could concentrate on the American war. The widening and intensification of the war nevertheless brought Russia into a more active role, as first France, then Spain, became committed to the American side. Reliance by these countries, as well as by the American states, on neutral shipping provoked greater British interference with the passage of vessels at sea, as they were stopped and searched for rather broadly defined contraband. A general commercial war ensued in which the British had the obvious naval edge. Since the remaining neutrals were concentrated in the Baltic region and Baltic naval products were in great demand, Russia naturally became involved in protecting neutral rights. Catherine saw an opportunity to arbitrate European affairs to Russian advantage.

The empress was also genuinely alarmed by the successes of American privateers, especially Daniel McNeil during the summer of 1778, in capturing British vessels coming from Russia laden with naval stores, thus threatening this highly important export trade. She ordered her Baltic fleet to prepare for protective cruises the following year. Though Russia possessed little significant commercial shipping, Catherine certainly hoped to develop it. With active encouragement from the government, a number of Russians were beginning to seize the opportunities presented by the war and by the demand for Russian products and were venturing into long-distance voyages. The possibilities of direct Russian trade with American ports were considered as early as August 1778 by the Commerce College on the basis of a dispatch from the Russian consul in Bordeaux, Arvid Wittfooth.[18] Although he later reported ships sailing under the Russian flag for American ports in 1782, they were probably Dutch or French in origin and went to French islands in the West Indies. Even so, they illustrate Russia's difficulty in remaining an innocent bystander in a widening and lengthening conflict.

Ironically, when Sir James Harris, the British envoy to St. Petersburg, tried to take advantage of the American privateering to bring Russia more actively into the conflict, his attempt misfired. As a result of mounting annoyances in 1779 about British naval infringements of neutral rights, a more specific grievance against Spain, and exasperation with the initial successes of American privateers, Catherine issued the famous Declaration of Armed Neutrality in March 1780. The document well deserves its reputation, containing at its heart the basis of modern maritime law regarding neutrality at sea:

[18]Bolkhovitinov, *The Beginnings*, pp. 92–94; David M. Griffiths, "An American Contribution to the Armed Neutrality of 1780," *Russian Review* 30, 2 (April 1971): 164–72. The Commerce College report, signed by Alexander Radishchev and three others, is in *USR*, pp. 54–55.

1st. That neutral vessels may navigate freely from one port to another and along the coasts of nations at war.

2nd. That the effects belonging to the subjects of the belligerent powers may pass inviolably on neutral ships, with the exception of contraband merchandise. [the free ships, free goods doctrine]

3rd. That the Empress, as to the specifications of the abovementioned merchandise, adheres to what is stipulated in articles 10 and 11 of her treaty of commerce with Great Britain, extending these obligations to all powers at war. [narrow definition of contraband]

4th. That, in order to determine what is a blockaded port, one ought to characterize as such only those where the attacking power has stationed its vessels sufficiently near in such a way as to render access thereto clearly dangerous. [real as opposed to paper blockade]

5th. That these principles ought to serve as a rule in proceedings and verdicts as to the legality of prizes.

The Anglo-Russian Treaty of Commerce of 1766, referred to in point three, limited contraband to firearms, cold arms such as swords, gunpowder and the materials for its production, and ammunition. These announced principles of maritime neutrality were then "armed" by the statement that followed:

> In proclaiming these, Her Imperial Majesty does not hesitate to declare that in order to maintain them and to protect the honor of her flag, the safety of commerce, and the navigation of her subjects against anyone, she has ordered a considerable portion of her maritime forces to put to sea.[19]

At the same time Catherine reaffirmed Russia's neutrality in the conflict, but the declaration nevertheless represented a triumph of French policy over British, of Vergennes and his ambassador in Russia, the Marquis de Verac, over Lord North and Sir James Harris. Adding to the complexities of the situation at the Russian court, as usual a center of international intrigue, was the emergence of a

[19]*USR*, pp. 79–80. For a discussion of the extensive literature on the armed neutrality, see Bolkhovitinov, *The Beginnings*, pp. 14–16. The best treatment is by Isabel de Madariaga, *Britain, Russia and the Armed Neutrality of 1780* (New Haven, Conn.: Yale University Press, 1963). Her more recent examination of Catherine's reign is also recommended—*Russia in the Age of Catherine the Great* (New Haven, Conn., and London: Yale University Press, 1981)—as well as John T. Alexander's *Catherine the Great: Life and Legend* (New York and Oxford: Oxford University Press, 1989). Madariaga convincingly shows that Catherine was the principal author of the declaration, though this was obscured at the time by court rivalries, the bungled diplomacy of Harris, and the claims of the French. A less accurate assessment that exaggerates the French role is Paul Fauchille's *La Diplomatie française et la ligue des neutres de 1780 (1776–1783)* (Paris: A. Durand et Padone Lauriel, 1893).

power struggle between the pro-Prussian Nikita Panin and Prince Grigori Potemkin, Catherine's enduring favorite and military commander. Potemkin supported closer relations with Austria in order to advance his designs against the Turks and to promote Russia's southern expansion. His so-called Greek Plan would dismember the Ottoman Empire and reestablish a "kingdom" of Byzantium under Catherine's second grandson, appropriately named Constantine.

Catherine's other diplomatic maneuvers of this period also favored the American colonies' fight for independence, though more indirectly. She successfully mediated a peace in 1779 between Austria and Prussia, whose quarrel over Bavaria had threatened to involve France; she thus freed that country for a greater commitment to the American conflict. Next came an unsolicited joint Austrian-Russian offer to Britain of arbitration; its rejection made Britain appear even more isolated. And by the summer of 1780 a League of Armed Neutrality had been formed against Britain and included Russia, Denmark, and Sweden. The Netherlands joined late in the year but immediately had to withdraw when a state of war was declared between it and Britain. Prussia, Austria, Portugal, and the Kingdom of the Two Sicilies eventually participated as well.

Coming as it did at the beginning of new military campaigning and the shipping season, the Declaration of Armed Neutrality created a considerable stir in Britain, in the rebelling states and their allies, and among neutrals, despite the fact that it had little immediate impact on commerce or British maritime behavior. The condition of the Russian naval forces limited their ability to enforce the pronouncement, but there was a definite effect on morale for both sides of the conflict. Although it would be difficult to discern any increased British regard for neutral rights, the declaration did encourage more neutral ships, including a few under the Russian flag, to risk running the blockade into American ports. More important, it caused the American leaders, seconded by Franklin and Adams in Europe, to pay more attention to Russia, which they had heretofore suspected of being pro-British. The Continental Congress, whose privateers were also in violation of some of the principles of the statement but whose suspicions of French intentions had deepened, announced their acceptance of the document. They then approved a mission to Russia, devised by James Lovell and headed by Francis Dana, a proper and staid Boston merchant and protégé of John Adams.

The Dana Mission

Before Dana could be formally designated the American emissary and start on his journey, another person attempted to bring Russia more directly into the fray. Stephen Sayre, a former London banker and sheriff turned international adventurer, had personal grievances against the British for his political and economic misfortunes. Arriving in St. Petersburg in April 1780 and using the name Smith, he undertook to build large merchant ships for direct trade with America and to man smaller free-lance privateers. One of his schemes even involved the Russian occupation of an island off South America to be used as a smuggling base. His first efforts, in partnership with a Russian army officer named Arsen'ev, were thwarted by a mysterious fire. He then apparently participated in an independent attempt to launch an American privateer at Archangel, until Catherine learned of it and ordered it stopped. A few of the ships Sayre sponsored did eventually leave for France in 1782 with vital cargoes of naval stores, which he hoped would be reshipped to America with the help of Adams and Franklin. In general, however, Sayre received little support either from the cautious official American agents in Europe or from the Russians, and his efforts were of no avail.[20]

The idea for a formal American mission to Russia originated in Europe, but the source—whether it came from the American agents, the French government, or even the Russian resident ministers—is not clear. John Adams certainly favored a wider American diplomatic role in Europe, as opposed to Franklin's narrower concentration on France. The proposal was placed before Congress in Philadelphia in December 1780 by Arthur Lee, who had recently returned from Paris.[21] It may also have been his idea to select Dana, who was already in Europe serving as Adams's secretary and liaison with Paris, for the assignment. The official appointment letter sent by Samuel Huntington gave Dana very general instructions—to win Russia over to the American cause, as if that were necessary, and to establish the basis for closer commercial and political ties by illogically offering to join the Russian-sponsored League of Armed Neutrality.[22]

Dana first went to Paris to confer with Franklin and with French Foreign Minister Vergennes, both of whom were obviously mindful of how awkward it was for Russia to receive an emissary from a government at war with Britain, still Russia's official friend and erstwhile ally. Franklin in fact advised Dana to obtain formal acceptance from the Russians before his departure; Vergennes was even more cautious, really hoping to maintain exclusive French control over American policy in Europe. However, they finally gave Dana their reluctant

[20]*USR*, pp. 93–94, 103; David M. Griffiths, "American Commercial Diplomacy in Russia, 1780 to 1783," *William and Mary Quarterly*, 3d ser. 27, 3 (July 1970): 388; John R. Alden, *Stephen Sayre, American Revolutionary Adventurer* (Baton Rouge: Louisiana State University Press, 1983), pp. 122–36.

[21]*USR*, pp. 101–2 n. 1.

[22]For an analysis of court politics in Russia during this period, see David L. Ransel, *The Politics of Catherinian Russia: The Panin Party* (New Haven, Conn., and London: Yale University Press, 1975), pp. 262–89.

support. Resenting the French monopolistic attitude toward American affairs, Adams thought that this was the opportune time to approach Russia directly. He encouraged Dana to proceed immediately to St. Petersburg in a private capacity, and he even assigned his fourteen-year-old son, John Quincy, to accompany him.[23] Dana delayed the start of his mission to await the outcome of another Russian-Austrian effort to intercede in the conflict in the spring of 1781 and the results of the dispatch of commissioners from Philadelphia to London to attempt a direct negotiation of a peace treaty. After these exertions became stalled by British intransigence, Dana departed with the young Adams and a more mature secretary, Samuel Stockton, for St. Petersburg, where they finally arrived in early August 1781.[24]

True to Franklin's warning, Dana could not be received by the Russian court, which still hoped to coax Britain into accepting its mediation. While extending hospitality, it could not receive any American functioning diplomatically until a peace had been signed. Dana was placed in a tenuous situation and obviously lacked the prestige of a Benjamin Franklin, John Adams, or Thomas Jefferson. Yet he was still able to conduct lengthy discussions with Marquis de Verac, the French representative in St. Petersburg—despite his lack of fluency in French— and through him and other sources obtain valuable information on both French and British policies regarding the recognition of American independence. Also with French support he was able to gain entry into high Russian political circles. Dana, however, was personally divided between being "most heartily weary of the old world" and his desire to achieve success. "I confess," he wrote to a Boston friend, "it would be a great mortification to me to return without accomplishing the business of my mission."

One of Dana's major obstacles was the conviction of some influential Russians that the independence of the British American colonies would be detrimental to the empire's commercial interests, that the United States would become a rival in the world market for naval stores. Therefore, in June 1782,

---

[23]*USR*, pp. 98–101.

[24]Adams (Leyden) to Dana, 7/18 April 1781, *USR*, pp. 112–14. Stockton of New Jersey was studying law in London when the war began. He then volunteered his services to the American commissioners, so he had several years of secretarial and courier service on the continent before accompanying Dana. *Letters of William Lee*, 1:528, 657; Dana to Sam Osgood, 2 January 1786, Osgood Papers, New-York Historical Society (hereafter NYHS). Dana in his letter to Osgood claimed expenses for Stockton, while noting he could not do so for the underage Adams. However, this secretary's presence in Russia must remain suspect, since there is no mention of him in the extensive Adams and Dana records of the time. See, for example, the richly annotated *Adams Family Correspondence*, vol. 4 (October 1780–September 1782), ed. L. H. Butterfield and Marc Friedlaender (Cambridge, Mass.: Belknap Press of Harvard University, 1973).

although formally still a private character, Dana managed to circulate anonymously through official channels a long defense of the American cause that stressed the commercial advantages to Russia of American independence.[25] He also cultivated the support of Maksim Alopeus and Petr Bakunin, former secretaries and supporters of Nikita Panin. He failed, however, to budge Russia toward a more active role in the conflict on the American side.

British military defeat at Yorktown, the rising economic costs on both sides, and the pressures for peace through mediation finally brought the war to a formal close by negotiations in Paris early in 1783. The main political reason for Dana's presence in St. Petersburg was thus removed. The man in charge of foreign affairs for the Continental Congress at this time, Robert Livingston, was suitably impressed by the commercial arguments for continuing Dana's mission but was not happy with what he perceived to be the Bostonian's imprudence in contacts with Russians, or with the expense of the venture. Led to believe that any recognition by Russia would involve a commercial treaty that would cost a considerable sum in bribes, he decided to recall Dana early in 1783. Dana hastily abandoned the Russian capital soon after receiving Livingston's instructions—even though Vice Chancellor Ivan Osterman, Panin's successor, was then advising him that the last barriers to full recognition were being cleared away.[26]

Thus, the opportunity was lost to establish formal diplomatic relations with Russia at the same time they were being framed with France and Britain. The reasons on the American side included distrust of Dana's diplomatic tactfulness, the fear of additional expenses coupled with concern for debts already incurred, and a somewhat erroneous but prevalent belief that Russia and America had little economic or political interest in common but were in fact commercial rivals. As if to deny this latter point, Dana, who still hoped to obtain a treaty and the renown associated with it, reported in detail on the resumption of direct

[25]Dana (St. Petersburg) to Thomas McKean (President of the Continental Congress), 4/15 September 1781, *USR*, pp. 123–26, 127n. The quotations are from Dana to James Lovell, 14/25 October 1781, Manuscript and Rare Book Department, Boston Public Library (hereafter BPL). This summary of the Dana mission is based on the excellent article by David Griffiths, "American Commercial Diplomacy in Russia, 1780 to 1783." For a more romanticized view, see William Penn Cresson, *Francis Dana: A Puritan Diplomat at the Court of Catherine the Great* (New York: Dial Press, 1930).

[26]Included in Dana's report to Robert R. Livingston, 17/28 June 1782, *USR*, pp. 152–57. At least two copies have been located in Soviet archives. *USR*, p. 158n. For further discussion surrounding the circumstances of the report, see Bolkhovitinov, *Russia and the American Revolution*, pp. 83–84. Copies of Dana's official and private correspondence are in the Dana Papers, Massachusetts Historical Society (hereafter MassHS).

American shipping to Russia in June 1783.[27] Russia, on its part, was slow in responding to overtures and still very uneasy about giving offense to Britain. Dana departed St. Petersburg on 24 August 1783, and twenty years would pass before Russia would accept an official American representative.

In Dana's defense, the complexities of the situation in St. Petersburg must be noted. First of all, the French, enamored of their diplomatic triumphs on the continent, desired to retain full control of the "American problem." They obviously did not favor a separate Russian-American relationship. But even the French were helpless in the face of a court revolution in St. Petersburg that embraced private ambition, grand national strategy, and complicated court intrigues. Catherine, proud of her larger role in international politics, was being pressured by Nikita Panin and his supporters to accede to a constitutional project and arrangements for the succession to pass to her son Paul. But the empress had a long-standing ambition, intensified by the passage of time, to complete and expand the work of her illustrious predecessor, Peter the Great, whose famous statue (the "Bronze Horseman") had just been commissioned.[28]

Catherine now forged new policies for Russia that veered away from the north and the Atlantic to the south. Her chief assistant and guide in this new orientation was Grigori Potemkin, a former lover with personal charm and demonstrated administrative ability who was still reaping the rewards of a great victory over the Turks ten years earlier. Because of his southern ambitions, Potemkin favored Austria and Britain, not France or Prussia. He also fully supported the absolute autocratic system and opposed any constitutional plans. Both his foreign and domestic policies thus conflicted with the Panin party at court.

The opening for Potemkin's—and Catherine's—designs came with the ascendancy of Aleksandr Lanskoi, an aide-de-camp of Potemkin's, as Catherine's new

[27]Livingston recommended Dana's recall on 15 February, and Dana noted in his journal on 19 February of Osterman's new disposition to receive him. *USR*, pp. 174–75. Congress moved slowly, however. Its act of 1 April, enclosed in Livingston's instruction to Dana of 2 May, "approved" his return "provided he should not be engaged in a negotiation with the Court of St. Petersburg at the time of receiving this resolution." *USR*, p. 176n.

Dana and his mission had a poor "press" at home. Mercy Otis Warren viewed him as Adams's protégé who "had not either the address, the penetration, the knowledge of courts, or of the human character, necessary for a negotiator at the court of a despotic female at the head of a nation of machines, under the absolute control of herself and her favorites." Quoted in Alden, *Stephen Sayre*, p. 131.

[28]Dana to Livingston, 13 June 1783, *USR*, pp. 196–98. For an excellent analysis of Russia's international position at this time, see David M. Griffiths, "The Rise and Fall of the Northern System: Court Politics and Foreign Policy in the First Half of Catherine II's Reign," *Canadian Slavic Studies* 4, 3 (Fall 1970): 547–69.

lover in 1780 and the death of the anti-Russian Maria Theresa of Austria in November of that year. By May 1781, Catherine had formed an alliance with the new Austrian emperor, Joseph II, that included a vague plan formulated between them to partition the Ottoman Empire. Panin, seeing his control over foreign policy shattered and the Northern System replaced by what Catherine referred to as the system of Peter the Great, left court immediately and was removed as chancellor early in 1782, shortly before his death. Dana witnessed during his stay in Russia the triumph of Potemkin, which represented a setback for French and American policy; the concentration of Russian diplomatic activity toward realizing long-sought gains in the Black Sea region, where the Crimea would be annexed in 1783; and the consequences of Catherine's absorption in an intensely personal relationship with Lanskoi. These factors reduced the prospects for closer American-Russian relations in 1783–84.

The Impact of the American Revolution upon Russia

On an official level, the United States retreated during the 1780s from the international connections necessitated by the war for independence and concentrated on internal political and economic matters; likewise, the Russian Empire under Catherine and Potemkin was diverted to other pursuits. However, the unofficial Russian interest in the United States increased dramatically, inspired by a rising appreciation of the wider world, French publications, and the Russian government's own public declaration of 1780. The arguments for the creation of a new independent government based on republican institutions naturally fell on fertile ground among those Russians who had imbibed the nectar of enlightened ideas in the relatively liberal and tolerant atmosphere of the first half of Catherine's reign. Russian interest in the United States was also spurred by the trend, especially promoted by Peter the Great and Catherine, to look to the West for new concepts and possible models for modernization. The two most important Russian publicists of American life and institutions were Nikolai Novikov and Aleksandr Radishchev, who merit distinction also as the empire's foremost advocates of a more humanitarian order for Russia itself.[29]

As an editor and publisher of literary journals since 1769, Novikov was responsible for circulating much information about the new republic by using Russian translations of French works as newspaper articles and commentaries in *Moskovskie Vedomosti* [Moscow Gazette]. A typical example was the publication in September 1782 of a French fable, "The Bluebird in the Field," about a bird that escaped from its cage and would not return to its mistress, even though she

[29]Soviet historians have emphasized the "American view" of Russians. See Bolkhovitinov, *Russia and the American Revolution*, pp. 120–163; and, for a good but popular Western appraisal, Max Laserson, *The American Impact on Russia, Diplomatic and Ideological, 1784–1917* (New York: Collier Edition, 1962).

promised to set it free.[30] Everyone who read it would think of the American colonies. With less literary allusion, Novikov's paper included informational and laudatory pieces on Washington, Jefferson, Franklin, Lafayette, and John Adams. Some were translations of French or American articles, while others were sent directly to Russia by Fedor Karzhavin. Novikov's obvious American partiality did not prevent him from sharply criticizing the survival of slavery and from reporting in detail the difficulties faced by the country after the war and the circumstances of Shays's Rebellion. Novikov's pen eventually was silenced in 1792 by personal financial troubles and by official displeasure, not so much with his "Americanness" as with his Masonic involvement and his satirical comments about the Russian church.[31]

Aleksandr Radishchev's views were more sophisticated and penetrated deeper into the meaning of the American achievement. The writings for which Radishchev, in Soviet eyes, most deserves his reputation as the father of Russian enlightened thought carry an American theme. He included a number of references to the United States in his famous *Journey from St. Petersburg to Moscow*, written in the 1780s, which emphasized such progressive principles as freedom of speech and freedom of the press.[32] Though Radishchev's knowledge about the United States was acquired indirectly and mainly through western European sources, such as Abbé Raynal's *Philosophical History*, it nevertheless was the basis for stirring tributes. Especially notable is the well-known passage from his ode to "Liberty," penned soon after the American victory.

My soul yearns for thee,
For thee, O glorious land,
Where once freedom lay trampled,
Bent under the yoke.
Thou rejoiceth now, while we still suffer!
We all thirst for the same things,
Thy example has revealed the goal,
I have not partaken of thy glory
But, since my spirit is not enslaved,
Let my ashes rest on your shores.

This was the inception of a Russian view of the United States as inspiration and as a model. Radishchev's sharp criticism of the institution of slavery was cast

---

[30]Bolkhovitinov, *The Beginnings*, p. 43.

[31]A. N. Nikoliukin, *Literaturnye sviazi Rossii i SSha: Stanovlenie literaturnykh kontaktov* (Moscow: Nauka, 1981), pp. 56–60; for a recent examination of Novikov's career, which stresses his role as a publicist of enlightened ideas in Russia, see W. Gareth Jones, *Nikolay Novikov, Enlightener of Russia* (Cambridge: Cambridge University Press, 1985).

[32]Nikoliukin, *Literaturnye sviazi*, pp. 61–64; Bolkhovitinov, *The Beginnings*, pp. 51–54.

broadly to include all of the Americas and more particularly Latin America than the United States. Romanticizing further on the just sacrifices required to gain liberty, Radishchev wrote:

> Gaze on the boundless field,
> Where the host of brutality stands effaced:
> They are not cattle driven there against their will.
> It is not a chance that brings courage,
> Nor the crowd—
> Each soldier feels himself a leader.
> He seeks a glorious end.
> O steadfast soldier,
> Thou art and were unconquerable,
> Your leader Washington, is liberty.[33]

There is no doubt that the United States was already achieving a somewhat dreamlike, mystical appeal to influential Russian publicists.

Another Russian man of letters, Nicholas Karamzin, struck a similar chord in his writings from Paris during the 1790s. In an ode to the eighteenth century, his invocation on its greatest men included one Englishman, one Frenchman, one Russian, and two Americans:

> You have redeemed our corrupted mores, and
> Opened a road to the temple of knowledge.
> You gave birth to Voltaire, Franklin, Cook
> To Rumiantsev and to Washington
> Through you, nature's laws were made known to man.[34]

Given the obvious attraction of enlightened Russians to the United States, it is surprising that none made the journey to this new citadel of freedom at this time. Karzhavin, it is true, worked in Petersburg, Virginia, for a few years at the French consulate before returning to Russia, but Rosenthal (alias Rose) immediately went back to his homeland, as did the famous Polish volunteers, Casimir Pulaski and Thaddeus Kosciuszko. Other Russians, however, were reaching the United States in another quarter and for different reasons.

Americans and Russians in the Pacific

The transpacific expansion of Russia evolved from the extension of the Siberian fur industry and from a government-sponsored series of explorations to deter-

[33]Bolkhovitinov, *The Beginnings*, pp. 47 and 50 (translations by Elena Levin). Niko-liukin (*Literaturnye sviazi*, p. 61) probably errs in stating that the "Ode" could not have been written before the summer of 1784.

[34]Bolkhovitinov, *The Beginnings*, p. 133.

mine the maritime frontiers of the empire, the best known being the two voyages of Vitus Bering in the first half of the eighteenth century. After the first recorded sighting of the Alaskan mainland in 1732, occasional Russian vessels in quest of furs or information or both visited those shores. Finally, in 1784, an advance hunting-base was established on the island of Kodiak, the largest and most hospitable of the Aleutian chain. This new Russian presence in America and the sudden increase of Russian ships in the North Pacific in the 1780s was due to the ambitions and exploratory interests of Catherine the Great and some of her subjects, the rapid expansion of the Russian economy, and growing competition with other powers, especially Britain. Above all, it stemmed from the increasing demand for sea otter skins in China. Under the influence of enterprising merchants such as Grigori Shelikhov and hired explorers like Joseph Billings, Russia began a penetration of North America that would continue for many years and provide the basis for another important relationship with the United States.[35]

Americans, too, were drawn to the North Pacific for reasons of commerce and curiosity. One of particular note was John Ledyard of Connecticut, who escaped the Revolutionary War by joining Capt. James Cook's second expedition (1776–80). A few years later, he tried to secure financial backing in England for the purpose of exploring the American North Pacific shores; unable to raise enough support there, he offered his services to Russia. Ledyard belonged to that category of international adventurers of the eighteenth century whose citizenship was chameleonic, but he is credited with being the first "American" to travel deep into the Russian hinterland.

Arriving in the Russian capital early in the summer of 1787, he visited the well-known geographer Peter Simon Pallas and proceeded on his journey beyond Moscow without formal permission. In Irkutsk he interviewed Shelikhov

[35]A substantial literature exists on Russian Pacific-American ventures; my purpose here is to summarize and integrate. Examples are: Frank A. Golder, *Russian Expansion on the Pacific, 1641–1850* (New York: Paragon Reprint, 1971); Raymond H. Fisher, *Bering's Voyages: Whither and Why* (Seattle and London: University of Washington Press, 1977); Glynn Barratt, *Russia in Pacific Waters, 1715–1825: A Survey of Russia's Naval Presence in the North and South Pacific* (Vancouver and London: University of British Columbia Press, 1981); James R. Gibson, *Feeding the Russian Fur Trade: Provisionment of the Okhotsk Seaboard and the Kamchatka Peninsula, 1639–1856* (Madison: University of Wisconsin Press, 1969); Howard I. Kushner, *Conflict on the Northwest Coast: American-Russian Rivalry in the Pacific Northwest, 1790–1867* (Westport, Conn.: Greenwood Press, 1975); and for a good popular account, Hector Chevigny, *Russian America: The Great Alaskan Venture, 1741–1867* (New York: Viking Press, 1965). An excellent edition of the important Russian documents is *The Russian American Colonies, 1798–1867: A Documentary Record*, vol. 3 of *To Siberia and Russian America: Three Centuries of Russian Eastward Expansion*, ed. and trans. Basil Dmytryshyn, E. A. P. Crownhart-Vaughan, and Thomas Vaughan (Portland: Oregon Historical Society, 1989).

and the governor of Siberia, Ivan Iakobi, and went on as far as Yakutsk in search of Billings, who had also been with Cook and was now leading a Russian exploring party across Siberia to the Pacific northeast. Ledyard had succeeded by this time in arousing the suspicions of Russian officials as to his intentions, including the possibility that he was a British spy. He was "arrested" upon his return to Irkutsk and escorted back across the European frontier during the winter. He died in Egypt later the next year on the first leg of an African odyssey. Ledyard's expulsion from Russia has sometimes been cited as evidence of Russian disfavor toward the American "revolution." Such could hardly be the case, since Ledyard was not directly identified with the cause of independence and received a fairly warm reception in Russia considering his unsanctioned wanderings.[36]

An American Admiral in Russia

The Russian contacts of another "American," John Paul Jones, are similar. Of Irish origin, Jones had become an American hero by his gallantry and naval skill in the Revolutionary War. The Continental Congress had largely decommissioned what navy still existed after 1783 and had offered free land to war heroes. Rather than settle down, John Paul Jones sought to continue his naval exploits in different waters. The beginning of hostilities between Russia and Turkey in 1787 provided a new opportunity. With the support of the American minister in Paris, Thomas Jefferson, the Russian envoy in Copenhagen, and Lewis Littlepage, another American adventurer, Jones solicited an appointment in the Russian navy early in 1788. An initial offer was tendered through Jefferson, but Jones did not take it seriously. Finally, Littlepage, who had served as Stanislas Poniatowski's emissary to Russia during the grand imperial passage of Catherine and Joseph II through Kiev in 1787, arranged a breakfast at his apartment in Paris with Jones and the Russian ambassador, and there the "contract" was arranged.[37]

[36]For Ledyard's own account, see his *Journey through Russia and Siberia, 1787–1788: The Journals and Selected Letters*, ed. Stephen D. Watrous (Madison: University of Wisconsin Press, 1966). Two important additional sources on Ledyard are a letter from William Stephens Smith (London) to John Jay, 1 September 1786, and Ledyard (Iakutsk) to Smith, 2 November 1787, in *USR*, pp. 225–26, 238–41.

[37]The literature on the first great American naval hero is extensive, but the best study is still that by Samuel Eliot Morison, *John Paul Jones: A Sailor's Biography* (Boston and Toronto: Little, Brown, 1959). Frank Golder edited a number of relevant documents from Soviet archives in *John Paul Jones in Russia* (Garden City, N.Y.: Doubleday, 1927). For a cautious Soviet interpretation with relevance to more recent times, see Bolkhovitinov, *The Beginnings*, pp. 65–75. On Littlepage, see Nell Holladay Boand, *Lewis Littlepage* (Richmond, Va.: Whittet & Shepperson, 1970), pp. 102–4, 113–15, who discusses the gossip about Littlepage being the prime minister of Poland and a lover of Catherine the Great.

*John Paul Jones. Courtesy Independence National Historical
Park Collection*

Catherine, perturbed by growing British opposition to her expansionist
schemes, was happy to lessen her dependence on British servitors for her navy by
hiring an accomplished sea fighter who was definitely anti-British. This shift in
Russian policy naturally stirred tensions between Jones and the remaining British
officers in the Russian navy. Nevertheless, he arrived in St. Petersburg in May
1788 and was soon dispatched to the Black Sea to serve under Prince/Field Marshal Potemkin as a rear admiral commanding the Black Sea sailing squadron.

Though largely removed from the bothersome presence of British officers, Admiral Jones still found a difficult situation in his new Russian command. In contrast to the relative freedom and independence he had enjoyed in American service, he was now subject to a rigid chain of command and a cumbersome
bureaucracy. Most crucial was his inability to establish a rapport with another
man-about-war, Prince Charles Nassau-Siegen, who had also been employed by
Catherine. Given command of the larger galley flotilla on the Black Sea, he
held seniority over Jones. The enmity between the two naval adventurers went

back to an episode in 1778, when Jones refused to serve under Nassau-Siegen, then in French service. Even the sophisticated Lewis Littlepage, detached from his service to Poniatowski to assist the Russians, failed to effect a working relationship between the two. Jones was also hampered by the poor condition of his ships and Potemkin's strategy of subordinating the naval fleet to the land forces in the Black Sea coastal campaign. Despite these handicaps, the American admiral was respected by the Russian officers under and above him and managed a fairly distinguished performance in beating off a confused Turkish attack on 16 July. His subsequent outspoken criticism of Nassau-Siegen, however, caused Potemkin to ask for his recall to St. Petersburg for the winter.[38]

While still in Russian service, Jones outlined in early 1789 a project of alliance between the United States and Russia based on the Declaration of Armed Neutrality, specifically applying it in the Mediterranean against attacks on commercial shipping by the Barbary corsairs.[39] He also envisaged closer naval cooperation with a substantial American involvement in shipbuilding and naval service in the Black Sea area. Jones was awaiting the outcome of these overtures and a new assignment, when, in the spring of 1789, he was accused of raping a twelve-year-old delivery girl. Jones denied the charge and claimed that he had been framed either by his old rival, Nassau-Siegen, or by a resentful Englishman (as Lewis Littlepage thought).[40] However, this seems problematic, since the risks involved in such an intrigue would seem to outweigh any real gains.

Regardless of the truth, John Paul Jones had few supporters left in Russia. Though the nature and extent of his "crime" remained unproven, the official charges drawn up against him and the associated publicity made his appearance in a Russian uniform no longer tenable. Since incidents of this kind were not uncommon within Russian official circles, one can surmise that the government—and probably Catherine herself—did not defend him as a convenient way of detaching from Russian service a person whose presence was now awkward and embarrassing. Jones was allowed to take an official leave of absence abroad and exited the country at the end of 1789. While passing through Warsaw, Jones, obviously still shaken by his Russian experience, was convinced by an old "American" comrade in arms, Thaddeus Kosciuszko, to consider service in the Swedish navy, which was then involved in a war against Russia.[41] Despite

[38]Morison, *John Paul Jones*, pp. 367–83. See also Curtis Carroll Davis, *The King's Chevalier: A Biography of Lewis Littlepage* (Indianapolis and New York: Bobbs-Merrill, 1961), pp. 180–82. Littlepage acted as an intermediary in Paris in February 1788. He was apparently the first "American" actually to meet Catherine—in Kiev in 1787, while in the entourage of Poniatowski.

[39]Jones to Ivan Osterman, 11 February 1789, USR, pp. 264–67.

[40]Morison, *John Paul Jones*, pp. 174–76; David, *King's Chevalier*, pp. 201–14, 260.

[41]Miecislaus Haiman, *Kosciuszko: Leader and Exile* (New York: Kosciuszko Foundation and Polish Institute of Arts & Sciences in America, 1977), pp. 6–8.

the Polish leader's assistance, the negotiations with Sweden failed, and the admiral made his way to Paris, from where he tried to secure his reinstatement in Russia. Regrettably, the cloud over his career followed him back to Paris, and he died there in 1792 in the course of the French Revolution, the whole depressing Russian episode having perhaps hastened his death.

The Rise of Russian-American Trade

Though nothing came of Jones's plan for close Russian-American commercial and naval cooperation in the Mediterranean and Black seas, more and more American ships arrived at Russia's northern ports. Unfortunately, the data are far from precise or complete. At least five American vessels came to anchor in Russian harbors in 1784, and their numbers steadily increased to over forty in 1795 at Kronstadt alone. One can estimate, on the basis of available evidence, that around four hundred of these voyages, perhaps as many as five hundred, were made before 1800. Still, they carried a small percentage of Russia's total imports and exports and cannot be considered an important element in the total Russian foreign trade—except for the less determinable factor of the additional competition introduced into the northern markets. Whatever was the case for Russia, these voyages were indeed significant to American commercial development.

Details of the American economic stake in the Russia trade are sketchy, since ships rarely hauled goods directly from the United States but picked them up from a variety of intermediate areas such as the West Indies, Portugal, France, Holland, and Britain. Many also arrived in ballast at their Russian destination, the ships having already discharged cargoes at other European ports, most often Hamburg and Copenhagen. The important items in the wide range of goods imported into Russia by American ships were tea, coffee, rice, raw sugar, and indigo but also included silks and satin, fresh lemons and oranges, almonds, figs, raisins, corks for bottles, olive oil, sulfur, cacao, cambric, lumber, and printed books, each commodity varying widely in value from year to year. Exports from Russia were fewer in number and more regular: iron, linen (ravensduck, sailcloth, and sheeting), hemp, cordage, bristles, tallow, flax, and furs. Most of the American voyages originated from Boston and nearby ports with a few from Rhode Island, New York City, and Philadelphia, and many were financed by the largest of the American merchant houses: Crowninshield, Endicott, Peabody, Brown, Osgood, Oliver, Champlin, and Russell. Several, however, were sponsored by smaller houses or independent captains, the expansion of trade with

Russia being a significant result of the rapidly developing commission merchant business.[42]

The typical voyage from New England to the West Indies to western Europe and then into the Baltic to St. Petersburg and back across the Atlantic usually took an entire shipping season and involved many risks, both natural and institutional. The American commerce, being somewhat new and lacking firm foundations, relied on European mercantile establishments for disposing of ships' cargoes, handling exchanges, and buying outgoing goods on the market. Most of these "factories" were of British or German origin and had either branch operations in St. Petersburg or standing relationships with the largest St. Petersburg dealers in foreign trade, such as Blandow, Cramer and Smith, and Cayley. The Americans thus followed the traditional practices of British, German, and Dutch shippers, who were more numerous and more experienced. There was, of course, an element of national competition, though not as pronounced as one might expect, since they all dealt with the same people and markets on shore. The real competition was internal, as American merchants vied with one another to meet the New England and Middle Atlantic demand for Russian products. From the volume of the imports, it can safely be claimed that by 1800 most New England houses and ships were put together with Russian nails, and it would be a rare vessel that did not have sails, tackle, and anchors of Russian origin. As Samuel Eliot Morison concluded: "Not only did this triangular commerce give quick turnover and large profits; it supplied maritime New England with the iron, hemp, and linen duck, which, until replaced by the products of Pennsylvania, Manila, and Lowell, were indispensable to her shipbuilding, fisheries, and navigation. The vessels engaged in it were called 'Russiamen.' "[43]

These Russian products spread easily to all parts of the United States by coastal vessels and by inland routes. Even the presidential household in Phila-

---

[42]Bolkhovitinov, *The Beginnings*, pp. 96–97; *USR*, pp. 281n, 1115. Scattered records are available in both the Peabody Museum and Essex Institute in Salem, in the Champlin Papers at the Rhode Island Historical Society, and in the Brown papers in the John Carter Brown Library in Providence. Some of these are published in *USR*.

[43]*The Maritime History of Massachusetts, 1783–1860*, 2d ed., (Boston: Houghton Mifflin, 1961), p. 155. Another student of early Russian-American trade exaggerated to some extent in making the same point: "Young America, more than we have ever realized, was economically tied to Russia. In 1800, the average American blacksmith used either Swedish or Russian iron if called on to make anything finer or stronger than horseshoes or andirons; and the American sailor, possibly the most important individual in our young economy, thought twice—and twice again—before he took any craft without Russian rigging, cables, and sails beyond the harbor mouth. To an appreciable extent, the American economy survived and prospered because it had access to the unending labor and rough skill of the Russian muzhik." Alfred W. Crosby, Jr., *America, Russia, Hemp, and Napoleon: American Trade with Russia and the Baltic, 1783–1812* (Columbus: Ohio State University Press, 1965), p. 24.

delphia made good use of them, judging from a letter sent by Abigail Adams to her sister: "I also wish you to purchase me a piece of Russia sheeting and sit Nabby to make it. I have not half sheeting enough for these People, which is stout. I also want you to get me a piece of the plain Russia toweling. The sheeting and toweling take a receipt for as thus, 'for the use of the Household of the President of the U.S.' "[44] As Mrs. Adams would have known, the prices fluctuated considerably from year to year. American merchants were handicapped when special problems arose, such as delays in passage or in loading that forced them to spend the winter in Russia. They also faced the vagaries of the Russian climate, arbitrary Customs rulings on import duties, and unexpected competition.

Approaches to More Formal Relations

The main drawback to more regular commerce was the absence of diplomatic or consular representation in Russia to support it. In the period following the failure of the Dana mission, from 1783 to 1792, progress along this line was prevented by the skeletal and skinflint nature of the new republic's foreign service, the ability of experienced merchant houses to perform most of the routine consular services themselves, and Russia's disinterest in developing regular relations. Both countries, moreover, were absorbed in more pressing economic and diplomatic problems. During this period the notion of a closer political connection, which Dana and Jones had promoted in Russia, was kept alive by the Russian and American diplomatic representatives resident in western European countries, particularly in Britain and France. In France, for example, the American minister Gouverneur Morris frequently dined and discussed affairs with Viktor Kochubei, the Russian envoy, and through him was introduced to Semen Vorontsov, Russian ambassador to Britain. They all shared a revulsion to the radical course taken by France in the early 1790s.[45]

After 1792 three additional factors hindered the establishment of direct relations between the two countries. Catherine became more uneasy about the

[44]Stewart Mitchell, ed., *New Letters of Abigail Adams, 1788–1801* (Boston: Houghton Mifflin, 1947), p. 206.

[45]See, for example, the letter of Gouverneur Morris (Paris) to Alexander Hamilton, 10 April 1792, *USR*, pp. 282–83, and some of his diary references beginning with 1 December 1791, in *A Diary of the French Revolution*, ed. Beatrix Cary Davenport, vol. 2 (Boston: Houghton Mifflin, 1939); and Rufus King (London) to Timothy Pickering, 10 November 1798, *USR*, p. 319. On the Russian side: Kochubei (Paris) to Semen Vorontsov (London), 15 January 1791, and Vorontsov to Count Khanykov, June 1795, in *Arkhiv kniazia Vorontsova*, ed. Petr Bartenev, 40 vols. (St. Petersburg: tip. Mamontova, 1870–95), 18:8 and 9:342. For details on the quite active political and social life of Morris in Paris, see Jean-Jacques Fiechter, *Un diplomate américain sous la Terreur* (Paris: Fayard, 1983).

threat of revolt and republican ideas owing to the excesses of the French Revolution and the existence of a Polish rebellion on her doorstep. Consequently, she favored renewing friendly relations with Britain. On the American side considerable sympathy was expressed by all political factions in the Polish struggle against Russian power, mainly because a great "American" war hero, Kosciuszko, and an "underdog" country were involved. This naturally fostered an anti-Russian sentiment in the United States in the mid-1790s. Ironically, the American Lewis Littlepage, again serving as adviser to Stanislas Poniatowski, is credited with supporting the "Russian party" in Poland and helping engineer the second partition of Poland in 1792 with the goal of saving the throne for his patron.[46]

The radical turn of events in France, however, corresponded with a growing American hostility to French meddling in American affairs, especially annoying to President Washington and the "high" Federalists, and that led to an embarrassing diplomatic break with France in 1796. Many American leaders now perceived that foreign relations should be better balanced and organized to cope with the shifting and volatile European scene. More diplomatic and consular agents were now deemed appropriate for the expanding American political and economic interests abroad. The time was ripe for direct connections.

But when John Miller Russell, a Boston shipowner, arrived in St. Petersburg in the summer of 1795, authorized by Congress as American consul, Russia refused to recognize him on the grounds that his reception had not been cleared in advance by negotiation with the British.[47] Catherine at this time was still assiduously catering to British interests, apparently oblivious to the fact that a sovereign nation recently liberated from colonial rule would not want to be shackled by such a condition. Clearly, continental European concerns remained paramount for Russia in the 1790s. Russell, who worked for a time as a partner in the St. Petersburg firm of Bulkley, Russell and Company, also seemed to lack sufficient initiative and commitment to pursue recognition of his appointment. The first real possibility of establishing direct relations after Dana's departure was thus stillborn.

Fresh fears about the security of Russian monarchical institutions also silenced the voices of Novikov and Radishchev and others who had written about America for the small, politically conscious part of Russian society. There was strict censorship, but news still filtered in, partly by way of the rising numbers of American ships' officers and seamen. In addition, scientific exchanges were expanding. In 1789 Ekaterina Dashkova, president of the Russian Acad-

[46]Davis, *King's Chevalier*, p. 282.
[47]Russell (St. Petersburg) to Rufus King, 5 August 1795, *USR*, pp. 291–92. Obviously, Bolkhovitinov errs in stating that Russell never reached his destination. Bolkhovitinov, *The Beginnings*, p. 107.

emy of Sciences, was elected on Franklin's initiative into the membership of the American Philosophical Society, the first Russian and first woman to be so honored. In turn, a few American scholars achieved recognition in Russia. Physicist John Churchman, whose work on magnetism was known in Russia as early as 1788, was added to the honorary ranks of the Academy of Sciences in St. Petersburg in 1795.[48]

Catherine the Great herself initiated a scientific exchange between the two countries in her quest for North American Indian words to include in her ambitious plan for a universal dictionary. Through the Marquis de Lafayette in 1787–88, she obtained responses from Benjamin Franklin and George Washington. The latter was especially interested in the success of the empress's project, and, in general, her effort is credited with provoking the first serious comparative study of Indian languages.[49]

Even so, these contacts were made by remote communication. No person with scientific credentials from one country visited, or was even invited to visit, the other country. Selective, honorary "academic" memberships, however, did increase the mutual appreciation of scientific and practical advances as well as promote the exchange of books and pamphlets. Most significant was the publication in Russia of selections from the works of Franklin, including his *Autobiography* in 1791. Yet the amount of such material remained fairly small, especially in comparison with what each country drew from Britain and western Europe.

Russians in the United States

Two Russians of some distinction did come to the United States in the 1790s. Dmitri Dmitrievich Golitsyn, whose father had known John Adams while serving as Russian ambassador to The Hague, had converted to Roman Catholicism through the influence of his mother and arrived in Baltimore in the fall of 1792 under the name of Schmidt to study at St. Mary's Seminary. A few years after being ordained as a priest in 1795 by Bishop John Carroll, he established a conservative Catholic mission at Loretto in western Pennsylvania, which grew rap-

[48]In her acceptance, Dashkova refers to a letter of May 1788, but the certificate of membership is dated May 1789, the discrepancy apparently due either to Dashkova's carelessness or a publisher's typographical error. Dashkova to the American Philosophical Society, 13 August 1791, *USR*, pp. 281–82. On Churchman's election, *USR*, pp. 290–91, and M. I. Radovskii, "Iz istorii russko-amerikanskikh nauchnykh sviazei," *Vestnik Akademii Nauk SSSR* 26, 11 (November 1956): 93–94.

[49]Mary Ritchie Key, *Catherine the Great's Linguistic Contribution* (Carbondale, Ill., and Edmonton, Canada: Linguistic Research, 1980), pp. 60–69, 139–44.

idly.[50] He was known as Father Augustine, or Augustine Schmett (his mother's maiden name) or Smith, and was sometimes referred to as "Demetrius A. Gallit-zen"). He was the first well-known permanent immigrant from the Russian Empire, but although he acquired a reputation as a superb horseman and for his missionary zeal, he contributed little to Russian-American understanding. His surviving correspondence with relatives in Russia is mostly about financial matters.

A Russian naval officer who would achieve future fame, Lt. Iurii Lisianskii arrived in Halifax in September 1795 on a British frigate. Since the ship was delayed in port for repairs, he decided to tour the eastern United States. Visiting Boston, New York, and Philadelphia during the winter months, he recorded details of the region in his journal and in letters to his brother.[51] Though formally in Russian service (detailed to a British ship), he apparently did not file any official reports on his tour of duty, and his journal, though often cited and prepared for publication in 1913, is still not available in complete form.

The best-known visitor to the United States technically from Russia was Thaddeus Kosciuszko, the Revolutionary War general who had returned to his native Poland only to become embroiled in that country's efforts to maintain an independent existence—and to become one of the first of the Polish "freedom fighters." The author of a new constitutional scheme for Poland, Kosciuszko was a principal advocate of American ideals in Europe and especially in the country that would be largely consumed by the Russian Empire. Following the collapse of the revolt that he led in 1794, and in the face of overwhelming Russian force, he surrendered and was imprisoned by Catherine in Russia. Released not long afterwards by her successor, Paul I, and in poor health, Kosciuszko decided to try to find a new homeland in the United States.[52] He arrived in the summer of 1797, accompanied by his secretary, Julian Niemcewicz, another Polish patriot who achieved fame as a poet-writer and who had also been released from Russian custody. In Philadelphia and elsewhere they were given heroes' receptions.

Apparently because he felt isolated from European politics and hoped for a rebirth of Poland under French auspices, Kosciuszko left the United States rather suddenly in May 1798, never to return, though he carried on from Paris an extended correspondence with Thomas Jefferson and other Americans. Niemce-

[50]Bishop John Carroll to Mariana Golitsyna, 13 December 1792, *USR*, pp. 285–86; Bolkhovitinov, *The Beginnings*, p. 77; and Daniel L. Schlafly, Jr., "Gallitzin, Demetrius Augustine," in *Modern Encyclopedia of Russian and Soviet History*, ed. Joseph L. Wieczynski, 46 vols. (Gulf Breeze, Fla.: Academic International Press, 1976–87), 12:71–74.

[51]A long excerpt from Lisianskii's diary from a typewritten copy in a Soviet archive is in *USR*, pp. 295–307. See also Robert V. Allen, *Russia Looks at America: The View to 1917* (Washington, D.C.: Library of Congress, 1988), p. 11.

[52]Haiman, *Kosciuszko*, pp. 27–32; Bogdan Grzelonski, *Poles in the United States of America, 1776–1865* (Warsaw: Interpress, 1976), pp. 102–5.

wicz, however, stayed behind to travel around the country and write about it; he married a wealthy widow of Elizabethtown, New Jersey, and became an American citizen in 1806. Learning in 1807 of the victories of the French army in central Europe, he decided to leave for Europe and eventually resettled in Russian Poland.[53]

Kosciuszko and Niemcewicz illustrate another feature of the times that was influencing both the United States and Russia—political upheaval in western and central Europe. This was the negative impulse to emigration. Conditions in mostly Germanic-speaking Europe from the time of the Seven Years' War caused large numbers of inhabitants to seek better and safer places to live. The positive side was the attraction of virtually free land in a comparatively stable environment. The movement of these "refugees" to the United States, especially into Virginia, Pennsylvania, and farther west, is a well-known aspect of the American economic, mainly agricultural, advance on the frontier. The same was true of Russia, though to a lesser degree, as people were recruited by Catherine to settle in southern colonies with special privileges near the Black Sea and on the Volga, where they incidentally began to grow tobacco to help solve the shortage during the American war. These Lutheran and Roman Catholic Germans and Dutch and Swiss Mennonites achieved fame in Russia for their agricultural innovations and successes. It was the luck of the draw, one might say, whether a German emigrant ended up in the Shenandoah Valley or along the Volga. Many of the Russian-Germans, after about one hundred years in Russia, moved again, this time settling on the vast virgin lands of the American plains.[54]

Broadening the Base of Relations

Considering the increase in American trade with Russia, the background of Russian assistance to the American cause of independence, and the natural curiosity about the outside world that people of both countries were developing, direct contacts between Russia and the United States were still surprisingly limited before 1800. However, common political and economic interests were already forging the basis for a more intensive diplomatic and political relationship.

On one side, the Russian presence in the North Pacific was definitely becoming more entrenched and substantial. The first clerical mission arrived at Ko-

[53]Grzelonski, *Poles in the United States*, pp. 104–11; Julian Ursyn Niemcewicz, *Under Their Vine and Fig Tree: Travels through America in 1797–1799, 1805 with Some Further Account of Life in New Jersey*, ed. Metchie J. E. Budka, vol. 14, *Collections of the New Jersey Historical Society at Newark* (Elizabeth, N.J.: Grossman, 1965).

[54]For more details on this German migration to Russia, see Adam Giesinger, *The Story of Russia's Germans from Catherine to Khrushchev* (Battleford, Sask.: Marian Press, 1974).

Headquarters of Russian America Company, St. Petersburg–Leningrad. Photograph by the author

diak in 1795, immediately built a church, and started converting natives.[55] The next year the first permanent settlement was established on the mainland. By 1798 the two Russian fur companies operating in the area joined forces and in the following year were officially chartered as the Russian America Company by Emperor Paul with sole rights in the Northwest. These events were little known at the time in the United States and had no discernible effect on Russian-American relations for some years. American ships, however, were quietly venturing into the very same region in larger numbers as an extension of an expanding China trade.[56] New England merchants, limited in access to the British West Indies by the Jay Treaty (1794), were seeking profitable alternatives in the Far East. Some of the "Bostonians" that made the journey carried practical outward cargoes for the natives of the Pacific Northwest to exchange for furs for the China markets, which would then yield Far Eastern commodities (silks, tea, china) for home consumption. By 1799 they were already challenging the British trade there and were perceived by some as a threat to Russian economic interests.

However, the real initiative for direct diplomatic exchange came from another quarter. American commercial expansion into the Mediterranean coincided with a new Russian presence, which was in turn provoked by French military

[55]From the notes of Shelikhov's widow, *USR*, pp. 315–18.
[56]Bolkhovitinov, *The Beginnings*, p. 171.

victories in Italy and finally by the launching of a French campaign to Egypt in 1798.[57] Russia, uncommonly allied with the Ottoman Empire, sent a fleet into the eastern Mediterranean. Access to the Black Sea was now unhindered, making feasible an American commercial expansion into the area. And Russia was clearly interested in that prospect, belatedly confirming John Paul Jones's premise of 1789. The deterioration of Franco-American relations also resulted in a quasi-war at sea, which meant that Russia and the United States were again on the same side of an international military contest, this time centered in Europe and the Mediterranean.

Diplomatic contact actually did exist but was oblique. The American minister in London, Rufus King, first discussed the possibility of direct relations with Russian ambassador Semen Vorontsov in November 1798. Encouraged by his response, King obtained authority from Secretary of State Timothy Pickering to continue the negotiation. Emperor Paul I, who had succeeded his mother in 1796, approved the idea and suggested through Vorontsov in May 1799 that an American mission to conclude a commercial treaty would be welcome in St. Petersburg. His vice chancellor, Fedor Rostopchin, thanked Vorontsov for following up the proposal and even suggested Vorontsov's friend Vasily Lizakevich as the first Russian envoy to the United States.[58] The volatility of Paul's government prevented any immediate result, but King passed the information on to the Department of State, thus clearing the way for a new, more concrete proposal for an exchange of consular and diplomatic agents early in the next century.

Russia in the American Mind

Distances between Russia and the United States were narrowing by virtue of expanding commercial and diplomatic contacts by the end of the eighteenth century. Yet, in terms of mental images and references, the two countries were still very far apart. The attention of each was riveted on France and Britain in foreign relations and on domestic difficulties. In actual fact, very few Americans thought seriously about Russia. For most of them it was an exotic faraway place with strange customs. Many abhorred or were suspicious of an autocratic power that had turned more conservative in the 1790s and had suppressed Polish inde-

[57]See Norman E. Saul, *Russia and the Mediterranean, 1797–1807* (Chicago: University of Chicago Press, 1970), pp. 61–77.

[58]Fedor Rostopchin to S. R. Vorontsov, 18 April 1799 (O.S.), *Arkhiv kniazia Vorontsova*, 8: 209; Rufus King to Thomas Jefferson, 10 November 1798 and 16 March 1799, in Charles R. King, ed., *Life and Correspondence of Rufus King*, 4 vols. (New York: Putnam, 1897), 2:462, 553. The correspondence between King and Vorontsov in London, between King and Pickering, and between Vorontsov and Paul I in 1799 is in *USR*, pp. 327–39.

pendence. They would have accepted John Quincy Adams's youthful impressions of 1782 with little dissent:

> Upon the whole this Nation is far from being civilized: their Customs, their dress, and even their amusements, are yet gross and barbarous: it is said that in some parts of the Empire, the women think their husbands despise them or don't Love them, if they don't thrash them now & then but I do not give this as a fact: in Petersburg they have bathes, where they go pell-mell men and women. they bathe themselves at first in very warm water, and from thence they plunge themselves into the snow, & roll themselves in it. they accustom themselves to this from Infancy, and they think it preserves them from Scurvy.[59]

The young Adams may have betrayed his gullibility and naivety, but the sources available to his countrymen were only marginally better, since Americans were forced to rely on British and French accounts for basic knowledge about Russia.

Americans had plenty of reason to mistrust the bias of the British and French and were finding some of their own channels of information through trade. The very lively state of international relations at the turn of the century also drew American attention to Europe and aroused concern about the preservation of a balance of power. Politics, as well as commerce, required that the United States have relations with—and more intelligence about—Russia.

That empire, however, bound by the legacy of Peter the Great and Catherine, was oriented toward Europe culturally, economically, and politically, especially after the French Revolution. With an ocean and most of a continent between them, with diametrically opposed systems of government and society, Russians and Americans might still have found little in common—were it not for war, commerce, new modes of transportation and communication, the concern for preserving an international equilibrium, and the fact that numerous Russians had political aspirations similar to those of Americans. These factors were drawing the two peoples inevitably but gradually closer together as a new century dawned.

[59]Quoted in Eugene Anschel, ed., *The American Image of Russia, 1775–1917* (New York: Frederick Ungar, 1974), p. 32.

2

War and Peace

At the beginning of the nineteenth century the United States and Russia became caught up in a complex political and military maelstrom provoked by the aftershocks of the French Revolution and the ambitions of Napoleon Bonaparte. Both countries attempted to maintain a detached and uninvolved posture but found that economic, political, and other interests forced their participation. Because of their ambivalence, they failed to achieve a consistent policy, a factor that made their relations with other European powers, and with each other, even more complicated.

The distant quasi-alliance of Russia and the United States against France continued into 1800. However, Catherine's successor, the erratic Emperor Paul I, became increasingly impatient as Austria and Britain failed to cooperate with his strange and idealistic military and political plans. As the newly designated Grand Master of the Order of St. John of Jerusalem, he was particularly annoyed by the British refusal to turn over to him its citadel, the island of Malta, which had been liberated from its French captors by the British navy. He abruptly withdrew from the Second Coalition against France, thus dooming plans for further military concert on the Continent.[1] Late in the year he signed the Declaration of Armed Neutrality of 1800, which, even more than its predecessor of 1780, was aimed directly at Britain and resulted in a reversal of alliances, a peace with France, and a virtual state of war with Britain. This dramatic shift must be credited in part to the successful diplomacy of the great French foreign minister Talleyrand and to the military genius of General Bonaparte. The same is true of a coincidental rapprochement between France and the United

---

[1]For a full treatment of this extraordinary turn in international politics, see Hugh Ragsdale, *Detente in the Napoleonic Era: Bonaparte and the Russians* (Lawrence: Regents Press of Kansas, 1980); Norman E. Saul, *Russia and the Mediterranean, 1797–1807* (Chicago: University of Chicago Press, 1970); and A. M. Stanislavskaia, *Russko-angliiskie otnosheniia i problemy sredizemnomor'ia, 1798–1807* (Moscow: Nauka, 1962).

States. Following the advice of his eldest son, John Quincy Adams, who was now minister to Prussia, President Adams dispatched emissaries to Paris, and late in 1800 they signed a convention that reaffirmed the principle of free ships, free goods, contained in the Armed Neutrality.[2] Ratified first by the Senate early in 1801 and again after Thomas Jefferson became president, the convention was only one of several diplomatic moves that would reestablish, although briefly, a general peace in Europe.

In the meantime, the embargo that Paul I had placed on British shipping stranded in Russian ports a group of American seamen who were serving on those ships. The Russian minister in Berlin, Baron Aleksei Krudener, discussed their plight with Adams and suggested that the best solution would be the presence of an American consul who could handle such problems and assist the increasing numbers of American ships now forcibly independent of resident British merchants. Adams recommended this course of action to Secretary of State James Madison in March 1801, but by the time Madison received it, Paul had been murdered by disgruntled servitors, and Madison doubted whether the new tsar, Alexander I, was amenable to the idea. Urged on by more and more Americans who were trading in Europe, President Jefferson considered appointing Daniel Clark as the first official representative in Russia in the summer of 1801. Finally, early in 1803, Levett Harris of Philadelphia, who had been in Paris with Benjamin Franklin, was formally commissioned as consul for St. Petersburg.[3]

Official and Unofficial American Emissaries

While this protracted, behind-the-scenes process was taking place, Joseph Allen Smith, the son of a South Carolina planter, had already arrived in St. Petersburg after wandering around Europe for several years. He was received by the Russian court in the manner of a special diplomatic envoy because of his prior contacts with Rufus King and Semen Vorontsov in London, which gave his extended sojourn in Russia a semiofficial character—a kind of testing of the waters.[4] Smith's detailed reports to King reveal the warmth of his reception, for

[2]Samuel Flagg Bemis, *John Quincy Adams and the Foundations of American Foreign Policy* (New York: Knopf, 1949), p. 101.

[3]Adams (Berlin) to James Madison, 21 March 1801, in *USR*, pp. 347–48; Madison to William Jones, 13 July 1801, in *The Papers of James Madison: Secretary of State Series*, vol. 1 (4 March–31 July 1801) (Charlottesville: University Press of Virginia, 1986), pp. 408–9; and commission signed by Thomas Jefferson and James Madison, 4 April 1803, in *USR*, pp. 359–60.

[4]Smith (St. Petersburg) to Rufus King (London), 28 September 1802, *USR*, pp. 356–59; George C. Rogers, Jr., ed., "Letters from Russia, 1802–1805," *South Carolina Magazine* 60, 2 (April 1959): 95.

which he felt particularly indebted to Chancellor Aleksandr Vorontsov (Semen's brother) and Count Viktor Kochubei, who were among the new tsar's closest advisers. Writing from Moscow in April 1803, Smith noted:

> The marks of friendship and attention which I received in that city [St. Petersburg] were far beyond what I expected or deserved. I should say no more on this subject if I did not think that they were in many instances directed rather to the country to which I belong than to myself. At the fetes of the Court I was put on a footing with the foreign Ministers, and often, as an American traveller, I found myself more favoured than if I had had a diplomatic character. . . . The Emperor invited me to dine with him "en famille," placed me next to him, and conversed with me some time respecting America and France.[5]

After enjoying the hospitality of the governor of Moscow for over four months, Smith traveled south through Cherkassk and Astrakhan to Persia and left by way of Baku, Odessa, and Constantinople. His letter to King from the last stop stressed the importance of establishing full diplomatic relations but reported that he had avoided direct discussion of the subject while in St. Petersburg.[6]

Levett Harris also met with a cordial reception when he arrived to take up his official duties as consul in October 1803. The rapid increase in American-Russian commercial relations was obviously a determining factor not only in the earlier establishment of partial diplomatic relations but also in the degree of friendship and cooperation that was so quickly achieved. In the year of Harris's arrival and the installment of the first consulate, eighty-four American ships were recorded as leaving the port of St. Petersburg (Kronstadt), the greatest number up to that time, and they were now hauling a significant portion—over 15 percent—of Russia's overseas exports.[7] Counting the other ports, over one hundred American ships visited Russia in 1803. Smith even reported an American ship sailing through the Black Sea to Taganrog that year.

One obstacle to the maintenance of this enlarged American trade with Russia, however, was that much of it consisted of "carrying trade," that is, goods obtained from a third source outside of the United States. President Jefferson was initially opposed to supporting and defending it from British pressures because he believed in the primacy of trade in native products and because at first it relied heavily on the "borrowing" of British seamen. Also, Jefferson was more

[5]Smith (Moscow) to King, 20 April 1803, *USR*, p. 366.
[6]Smith (Constantinople) to King, 22 January 1805, in *Life and Correspondence of Rufus King*, ed. Charles R. King, 4 vols. (New York: Putnam, 1897), 4:437.
[7]Levett Harris to Nikolai Rumiantsev, 25 January 1804, in *USR*, pp. 387–91.

worried at the time about French expansion in America, even briefly contemplating an arrangement with Britain before resolving the matter with the purchase in May 1803 of the enormous territory of Louisiana.

The Russian situation was quite different, since the country was involved in the upheavals in Europe and relied heavily on the carrying trade, ordinarily dominated by Britain, to sustain commerce. Harris was soon engaged in extensive conversation and correspondence with Russia's progressive minister of commerce, Nikolai Rumiantsev, about how the United States could obtain a greater share. He noted that the 84 American ships arriving at Kronstadt in 1803 had brought cargoes equivalent in value to that carried by 166 of the other foreign ships. Yet to further develop this trade, there had to be a breakthrough in the set mercantile patterns controlled by British shippers and German merchants and the provision of an independent mechanism for currency exchanges. Cargoes of cotton, for example, had in most cases been delivered to England, spun into yarn, and then reexported by British ships to Russia. Harris also foresaw an improvement in the American position through the continued industrial advancement of both Russia and the United States.[8] But the real lifeblood of this trade was the naval stores provided by Russia: the coarse linen woven by cheap peasant labor and ideal for sailcloth and sacks; superior Russian iron for anchors, chains, nails, and barrel rings; and the hemp made into the finest rope and tackle. The expansion of the American merchant marine greatly depended upon the purchase of these items and thus was a major impetus to a firmer commercial relationship.

The Russian Court and the United States: Alexander and Jefferson

The economically minded Rumiantsev, the most important and enduring of those Russians who sought closer relations with the United States, complemented a group of "young friends" with liberal inclinations who surrounded the new emperor, Alexander I. One of them, Viktor Kochubei, the minister of the interior, had formed a liaison with Gouverneur Morris while serving as ambassador to France in the early 1790s.[9] The republican virtues of the United States Constitution were a likely subject of their conversations. Prince Adam Czartoryski came from a distinguished Polish noble family and assumed the portfolio

---

[8]Ibid. For Jefferson's views on trade, see Burton Spivak, *Jefferson's English Crisis: Commerce, Embargo, and the Republican Revolution* (Charlottesville: University Press of Virginia, 1979), pp. 7–8, 29, passim.

[9]N. N. Bolkhovitinov, *The Beginnings of Russian-American Relations, 1775–1815*, trans. Elena Levin (Cambridge, Mass., and London: Harvard University Press, 1975), pp. 104–5. Kochubei was also especially hospitable to Joseph Allen Smith. *USR*, pp. 366, 375–76.

for foreign affairs under Alexander I. It was he who formally welcomed Harris and suggested that a more regular commercial agreement or treaty might be best initiated by a letter directly from President Jefferson to Alexander I.[10]

The mutual regard between Jefferson and Alexander was another significant factor in the foundations of early Russian-American diplomatic relations. The original intermediary was Frederic Cesar de La Harpe, the Swiss philosophe who had served as the principal tutor to Alexander from 1783 to 1795 and who revisited Russia from August 1801 to May 1802 to advise the new tsar during a time when a number of liberal reforms were being discussed.[11] Alexander apparently indicated to La Harpe a keen interest in the United States and its new president, with whose writings he was somewhat familiar. After La Harpe returned to Paris in the summer of 1802, he discussed with John Hurford Stone Alexander's desire for a closer relationship. Stone, an English bookseller and friend of the writer Joseph Priestley, then wrote to Priestley in the United States, citing his conversation with La Harpe: "Among the rulers of the day, your President enjoys the greatest respect and benevolence of the Emperor. . . . I am sure that he would be most grateful for information on the internal government of the United States. By this I mean the very mechanism of the government, i.e. the order of relations between the President and his ministers and their offices, between the ministries and the lower organs of the administration."[12] And Priestley enclosed extracts from this letter in his to Jefferson, which resulted in Jefferson, in November 1802, sending through Priestley a reading list on the Constitution specifically for the tsar. This was in turn relayed through La Harpe to Alexander.[13]

Over a year later, in December 1803, La Harpe again noted the value of a study of the American experience while advising Alexander on the settlement and development of new lands in south Russia. He referred Alexander to Jefferson's message to Congress on the Louisiana Purchase and emphasized that all of this new land was "under the patronage of the wise and modest republican Jefferson." Prompted by La Harpe's communications and perhaps also by his conversation with Joseph Allen Smith, Alexander asked La Harpe in July 1803 if he "could arrange for me the closest acquaintance with Jefferson." The Swiss ad-

[10]Harris to James Madison, 17 November 1803, *USR*, pp. 379–80.

[11]Bolkhovitinov, *The Beginnings*, p. 139.; La Harpe to Alexander I, 19 December 1803, *USR*, p. 383.

[12]Quoted in Bolkhovitinov, *The Beginnings*, p. 139. The Jefferson-Alexander I correspondence was first analyzed by V. M. Kozlovskii, "Tsar' Aleksandr I i Dzhefferson: Po arkhivnym dannym," *Russkaia Mysl'*, no. 10 (1910): 79–95. See also N. Hans, "Tsar Alexander and Jefferson: Unpublished Correspondence," *Slavonic and East European Review* 32 (December 1953): 215–25.

[13]Jefferson to Priestley, 29 November 1802, in *USR*, pp. 359–60.

viser again contacted Stone, who, in early 1804, used as intermediary Joel Barlow, a well-known man of letters then living in Paris.[14]

Soon a suitable occasion came for a direct communication. Levett Harris, in the first proof of the advantages of having diplomatic representation in Russia, requested Russian assistance in freeing the American frigate *Philadelphia*, under sequester by the Barbary powers in Tripoli. Chancellor Vorontsov was quick to oblige, using the authority that Russia then possessed of a fleet in the Mediterranean and a formal alliance with the sultan of the Ottoman Empire, who was still suzerain of the region.[15] The frigate was soon released, and, on 15 June 1804, Jefferson wrote Alexander to thank him both officially and personally for his successful intervention.[16] The president also noted the importance of the rising commerce between the two countries and the friendly reception accorded to Harris. Alexander responded in November in a similar tone: "Extremely sensible to the interest which you tell me you take in the well-being and prosperity of Russia, I believe I can no better express how my sentiments towards the United States are reciprocal in this connection than by making the wish that they will long keep at the head of their administration a chief as virtuous as he is enlightened."[17]

A gap then occurred in the correspondence, and Alexander even feared that his November letter had gone astray.[18] Domestic problems in the United States and Russia's participation in the Third Coalition against France no doubt played a part in this hiatus. Jefferson finally renewed communication with a letter of April 1806, in which he called the tsar's attention to one of the international political issues foremost on his mind: a renewed declaration in support of the maritime rights of neutrals.[19] Alexander responded with the vagueness that was a harbinger of the "Holy Alliance" rhetoric of 1815: "I have no illusion about the magnitude of the obstacles which prevent the return of an order of things consistent with the common interest of all civilized nations, and firmly guaranteed against the efforts of ambition and greed. But this goal is too beautiful and too dear to my heart for the difficulties which it presents to be able to dishearten me."[20] Though the correspondence between President Jefferson and

[14]Barlow to Jefferson, 11 February 1804, in *USR*, pp. 393–95.

[15]Documents pertaining to the Russian intercession in the Mediterranean are in *USR*, pp. 396–403. The United States reciprocated by releasing a ship under the Russian flag that had violated its blockade of Tripoli. Capt. Edward Preble (USS *Constitution*) to Levett Harris, 7 June 1804, *USR*, pp. 402–3.

[16]*USR*, pp. 403–5.

[17]Alexander I to Jefferson, 19 November 1804, *USR*, p. 419.

[18]A duplicate, dated 1 September 1805, was sent through Harris. Bolkhovitinov recounts how he unraveled this mystery. *The Beginnings*, pp. 420–21 n. 115.

[19]Jefferson to Alexander I, 19 April 1806, *USR*, p. 438.

[20]22 August 1806, *USR*, p. 458.

Emperor Alexander had no immediate effect upon Russian-American relations, it did serve an important function of familiarization, especially through the transmission of books and other materials, and it prepared the ground for the exchange of formal recognition.

Another American, Joel Roberts Poinsett, who would later have a distinguished diplomatic career and serve as secretary of war in Martin Van Buren's administration, provided more direct service to the cause of early Russian-American understanding. The son of a Charleston physician, Poinsett, like Joseph Allen Smith, was a native of South Carolina. Though only twenty-seven when he arrived in St. Petersburg in November 1806, he was already an experienced traveler as well as intelligent, well read, and ambitious. Because of the impressive recommendations he carried, the precedent established by Smith, and the assistance of Levett Harris, this young American gained quick access to court society. He was the guest at an intimate imperial dinner of twelve and conversed privately and at length on American topics with Alexander I, the empress, and the empress dowager. Alexander invited him to enter Russian service as an officer, but Poinsett wanted to tour the empire before taking up his duties. After a long journey through Moscow to Central Asia, Persia, and the Caucasus, Poinsett returned to St. Petersburg early in 1808. He then decided against staying in Russia. In their last conversation, probably in May 1808, Alexander told Poinsett: "Upon your return to Washington, I beg you will expose to the President the esteem I have for his person and the interest I feel in the welfare of the United States. I hope the good understanding which exists between us at present will long continue. Our commercial interests are the same. The late energetic measures of Congress have given me great satisfaction, and I believe it for the advantage of both to maintain the same system."[21]

Though Poinsett declined the Russian appointment, two American naval offi-

---

[21]Poinsett to John Armstrong (Paris), 8 September 1808, *USR*, p. 534. See also J. Fred Rippy, *Joel R. Poinsett: Versatile American* (Durham, N.C.: Duke University Press, 1935), pp. 20–34; and Charles J. Stillé, "The Life and Services of Joel R. Poinsett," *Pennsylvania Magazine of History and Biography* 12, 2 (1888): 129–64.

Some of Poinsett's papers are in the Historical Society of Pennsylvania (hereafter HSP). For his conversations with the imperial family, see especially his letter to Joseph Johnson of 20 February 1807. Excerpts from letters that no longer survive but were originally published in 1888 are in *USR*, pp. 466–71. On p. 469, Poinsett quotes from one of several conversations with Alexander I: "We cannot create a mercantile marine, and have been hitherto entirely dependent upon England for the transportation of our produce. We now hope the United States will relieve us from this dependence and are therefore anxious to encourage your shipping and to form the closest commercial relations with you. You must say so to your President." And Poinsett's visit was vividly recalled several years later by Russians, perhaps owing to his reputation as "a devil among women." Alexander Hill Everett, Russian journal, 12 November 1809, Everett-Noble Papers, Diaries 1804–33, MassHS.

cers, about whom little is known, did join the Russian forces during the Napoleonic Wars. George Sontag of Philadelphia commanded a ship in the Black Sea fleet before transferring to the army and leading a Russian regiment that followed Napoleon's retreat to Paris. He later became an adjutant to Mikhail Vorontsov in the Black Sea provinces. The other was a Lieutenant Barrett of Boston who served in the Baltic fleet; no other accounts of him have survived.

Meanwhile, prompted by the worldly, progressive outlook of Rumiantsev in particular, Russians were expanding their commercial presence on the seas as never before. Ocean-going Russian merchant ships, though still in relatively small numbers, began sailing out of the Baltic and from Archangel in the north to all parts of the world. Knesofont Anfilatov, a merchant of Slobodsk, was mainly responsible for the voyages of 1806 to the United States. He experimented with vessels built simply of pine, and one of his ships returned intact the following year. Yet his effort reflected Russia's greater confidence and growing ambition, and he considered the undertaking a success. In the course of these new contacts a young Russian named Vasili Apraksin reciprocated the visits of Smith and Poinsett by his extended tour of the United States between 1802 and 1808, supported by the family sales of cordage, and while there he enjoyed the hospitality of several prominent New England merchants.[22] Russian shipping, however, would remain largely insignificant and unprofitable in Russian-American commercial relations.

A Meeting in the Pacific

Much more important from the standpoint of Russian-American relations was the increasing commitment of Russia to an economic and political stake in the Pacific. The primary target of this Russian advance was the sea otter, whose numbers along the immediate Siberian coast had dwindled but whose fine pelts continued to command a handsome price in the Chinese, Russian, and other European markets. The Russian America Company, chartered in 1799, had been given initial encouragement by the imperial family and by leading officials who bought stock in the company, whereupon the Russian presence along the Pacific coast of America advanced rapidly. Part of this phenomenon of Russian economic outreach can be credited to Rumiantsev, one of the largest stockholders, and to other promoters, especially Aleksandr Baranov and Nikolai Rezanov.

The son of a storekeeper in northwest Russia, Baranov served an apprenticeship to a German merchant in Moscow before establishing a successful glass factory in Irkutsk and then entering the fur trade along the Sea of Okhotsk. As a Siberian *promyshlennik* [fur hunter-trader], he attracted the attention of the en-

---

[22]Anfilatov to Rumiantsev, June 1809, *USR*, pp. 567–68. For the limited information on Apraksin, see ibid., p. 356.

*Aleksandr Baranov. Oil by Mikhail Tikhanov (original in
State Historical Museum, Moscow), from* The United States
and Russia: The Beginning of Relations, 1765–1815
(Washington, D.C.: Department of State, 1980)

trepreneur Grigori Shelikhov, who, after several unsuccessful attempts, signed
him to a five-year contract in 1790 to supervise his company's hunting operations in the North Pacific.[23] Reaching Kodiak the next year, Baranov began his
long tenure as "boss" of the colonial territory, establishing a regular administration and building new outposts. These included the one on Baranov Island
(Sitka), soon to become the "capital" of Russian America as New Archangel.

Baranov's rough and practical methods suited the time and place, and he well
deserves the title of "Lord of Alaska" for surmounting such obstacles as hostile
natives, scarce supplies, and the small number of Russian colonists and, above

[23]Hector Chevigny, *Russian America: The Great Alaskan Venture, 1741–1867* (New
York: Viking Press, 1965), pp. 80–81.

all, for acquiring large quantities of furs for the company. Neither he nor any of his successors fully resolved the conflict with the Indians, but he inaugurated the Russian policy of winning over some groups through employment and bribery (and marriage) and attempting to control the others by means of force. He built forts for the protection of hunting parties and did not hesitate to deal ruthlessly with uprisings. Still, his quasi-personal "colonial empire" remained shaky.

Supply was the chief problem, exacerbated by the great distance from Russian sources and by the war that interfered with shipping schedules and Russian naval support capability. American ships, whose pattern of shipping had also been upset by the war, began coming in larger numbers to Baranov's territory. By 1800 he reported that about six of what were generally referred to as "Bostonians" were frequenting the Northwest each year and driving out the British from the area. Their sponsors were primarily interested in the China trade but had discovered that furs (mainly seal, fox, and sea otter skins) were much in demand in Canton, where they could be profitably traded for tea and silks. The furs could be obtained through hunting parties of local Indians or, more often, simply in exchange for items wanted by the natives: spirits, guns, utensils, and trinkets. Baranov was naturally concerned about this development:

> I have told [the Americans] many times that they should not sell firearms and powder to the barbarians, who not only are engaged in continuous bloodshed among themselves but are dangerous even to them, attacking so unexpectedly that many times ships have been captured. This trade in firearms is still more harmful for us Russians, who have settled on these shores. I told them of peace treaties [?] between our Imperial Court and their Republic, but they paid no attention to my arguments saying only: "We are traders, sailing more than fifteen thousand nautical miles in search of profits, and no one has told us that such trading is prohibited."[24]

The American captains often found it more convenient and safer to use the harbors where the Russians were already established and to supply those settlements with basic necessities in return for the furs collected there. Baranov, practical businessman that he was, was soon contracting with the Bostonians to carry furs for the company to China, which was not yet open to Russian ships. Joseph O'Cain, one of the first of the real Bostonians involved in this business by 1803, even hired from Baranov skilled Aleut hunters for joint Russian-American expeditions along the California coast in quest of more sea otters.[25]

Perhaps the best documented and longest of these Bostonian voyages was that of John D'Wolf of Bristol, Rhode Island, who set out from there in August 1804

[24]Baranov to Emel'ian Larionov, 4 August 1800, *USR*, pp. 342–43.
[25]Bolkhovitinov, *The Beginnings*, p. 181. For a more complete analysis of the Bos-

with the schooner *Juno*. After trading along both coasts of South America, he reached New Archangel in the summer of 1805, at a time when the Russian colony was badly in need of an ocean-going ship. The Russians offered him a good price for the *Juno*, including furs, a smaller ship, and a large amount of cash, but he could collect the latter only in St. Petersburg. Making the long overland journey across the North Pacific and Siberia in winter, he reached the Russian capital in 1808 and his home in 1809, around the world by sea and land in five years—the hard way.[26]

The relations between Russians and Americans in the Pacific Northwest were from the beginning a love-hate affair. Although the New England seafarers, such as Joseph O'Cain, Jonathan Winship, and John Ebbets, provided valuable and at times essential services in these early years, they also traded independently with the natives when it seemed more convenient and profitable. Baranov and other officials naturally viewed with growing alarm the American interlopers who were supplying the Indians with arms, including small cannon, which were then used against the Russians. In defense of the American practices, it must be pointed out that Russian jurisdiction was not well defined along these largely uncharted coasts. Moreover, the Russians frequently traded to the natives the same commodities (arms and spirits) about which they complained, especially in meeting ransom demands for captured Russians.[27] Though selective

tonian role in the Northwest, see Mary E. Wheeler, "Empires in Conflict and Cooperation: The 'Bostonians' and the Russian-American Company," *Pacific Historical Review* 40 (1971): 419–41; and James R. Gibson, "Bostonians and Muscovites on the Northwest Coast, 1788–1841," in *The Western Shore: Oregon Country Essays Honoring the American Revolution*, ed. Thomas Vaughan (Portland: Oregon Historical Society, n.d.), pp. 81–119. For the long, rambling report of Rezanov that included information about Winship and O'Cain; see Petr A. Tikhmenev, *A History of the Russian American Company*, ed. Richard A. Pierce and Alton S. Donnelly, trans. Dmitri Krenov, 2 vols. (Kingston, Ont.: Limestone Press, 1979), 2:174–97.

[26]Capt. John D'Wolf, *A Voyage to the North Pacific and a Journey through Siberia* (Cambridge, Mass.: n.p., 1861). D'Wolf's experiences are also of interest for two other incidents: his encounter in the Sea of Okhotsk with a giant albino whale, a story that later made a strong impression upon his young nephew, Herman Melville; and a gay summer party on an island to celebrate his arrival in St. Petersburg, after which two very promising naval officers and explorers who had accompanied Rezanov, G. I. Davydov and N. A. Khvostov, tragically drowned. George Howe, "The Voyage of Nor'west John," *American Heritage* 10, 3 (April 1959): 78–80.

[27]For the complicated interaction between Russians, Americans, and natives, in which Americans sometimes acted as intermediaries with the natives, see Chevigny, *Russian America*, pp. 85–103; and Glynn Barratt, *Russia in Pacific Waters, 1715–1825: A Survey of Russia's Naval Presence in the North and South Pacific* (Vancouver and London: University of British Columbia Press, 1981), pp. 143–62; and for an emphasis on the conflicts provoked, see Howard I. Kushner, *Conflict on the Northwest Coast: American-Russian Rivalry in the Pacific Northwest, 1790–1867* (Westport, Conn.: Greenwood Press, 1975).

documents may give a false impression of the degree of Russian concern about the inroads of the Bostonians, other issues would definitely engender serious diplomatic communication between the two countries.[28]

Another person, with a background quite different from Baranov's, attempted to solve the problems of labor and supply in the Pacific Northwest. Nikolai Rezanov came from an old Russian noble family and received a typical "Guards Regiment" upbringing in the enlightened atmosphere of Catherine the Great's capital, rising to the rank of captain. Thinking of becoming a writer, Rezanov transferred to the civil service and served on the legal staff of the Bureau of Petitions. In 1794 he was selected to supervise a detachment of priests and serfs destined for Shelikhov's American colony. Romance quickly entered the picture (as Rezanov was a true Pushkinesque character). On the long trip across Siberia with Shelikhov he not only became entranced by a grand vision of Russian-America but also fell in love with Shelikhov's daughter, whom he married on the return trip.[29] Upon the sudden death of his father-in-law in 1795, Rezanov inherited through his wife a large stake in the company and with his official connections in St. Petersburg lobbied for a greater government role in the colonial venture. Rezanov was thus the true architect of the creation of the Russian America Company in 1799. Consolidating its monopoly rights was far from an easy task, but he and the company managed to survive the jealousies of rival *promyshlenniki* and intense squabbling among government officers, while Baranov was literally holding the fort in North America.

With the accession of Alexander I, the rise of Rumiantsev, and the appointment of Adm. Nikolai Mordvinov as minister of navy, a new day dawned for Russian interest in the Pacific. Rezanov himself had been caught up in the new progressive spirit and was engaged in government reorganization as procurator general of the Senate. Coincidentally, Capt. Ivan Kruzenshtern, already noted for his naval exploits, was advocating a major Russian commitment to Pacific exploration. Through the initiatives of these individuals, two ships, the *Neva* and the *Nadezhda*, were outfitted for the Pacific early in 1803, during a rare interval of European peace.[30] Under the capable command of Kruzenshtern and Iurii Lisianskii, who had recently concluded his visit to the eastern United States, the expedition pursued the missions of surveying the American possessions and opening trade with China through Canton and also with Japan. Their professional staff included the naturalist Georg Heinrich von Langsdorff. Rezanov, still recovering from the shock of his wife's death soon after childbirth in Octo-

[28]In a volume of company documents covering the period from 1793 to 1809, the problem of American interlopers is never mentioned. Richard A. Pierce, ed., *Documents on the History of the Russian-American Company* (Kingston, Ont.: Limestone Press, 1976).

[29]Chevigny, *Russian America*, pp. 66–75.

[30]Barratt, *Russia in Pacific Waters*, pp. 108–18.

ber 1803, was a late addition. He was placed in overall command and, knowing some Japanese, was designated special Russian envoy to Japan.[31]

Sailing from the Baltic in the summer of 1804, Rezanov suffered considerably through the long sea voyage around South America, barely on speaking terms with the naval commanders. He waited in vain for six months at Nagasaki for recognition by the Japanese, then proceeded to Sitka, where he arrived during the summer of 1805. Afflicted with poor health and left without a serviceable ship, Rezanov reported critically to St. Petersburg on Baranov's domain, referring to it as "the drunk republic."[32] He immediately perceived the danger of Russian dependency on the Bostonians for supplies and ships and, concerned that they would soon take over the colony, sought a solution. Using the ship purchased from D'Wolf and borrowing the best officers available, Rezanov explored along the West Coast, reaching San Francisco Bay in April 1806.

There he was able to purchase a quantity of supplies from the normally recalcitrant Spanish governor at Monterey and discussed with him their mutual concerns about the "American problem." Rezanov also promptly fell in love with the beautiful daughter of Jose Dario Arguello, the commander of the presidio at the entrance to San Francisco Bay. After a formal betrothal of the forty-year-old Russian widower and the sixteen-year-old Conception, Rezanov departed with the food stocks for Sitka, pledging to return in two years. Sadly, on his difficult homeward journey across Siberia, Rezanov contracted a fever and died in Krasnoyarsk in 1807.[33] Conception waited in vain for his return and eventually retired to a convent.

Aside from the operatic potential of Rezanov's exploits, he had definitely cut a Russian path to California. Rezanov also drew upon his experience to recommend to St. Petersburg that a triangular trade be opened with Spanish California and the Sandwich (Hawaiian) Islands. Subsequently, Baranov sent one of his first and most loyal lieutenants, Ivan Kuskov, in 1808 to establish a hunting and supply base in the south. Finding the mouth of the Columbia River already occupied by Americans, Kuskov scouted farther along the coast. In 1812 he returned to start a small settlement, Fort Ross, near Bodega Bay, with about 150

[31]Ibid., pp. 105–6; Chevigny, *Russian America*, pp. 105–14; see also Avrahm Yarmolinsky, "A Rambling Note on the 'Russian Columbus,' Nikolai Petrovich Rezanov," *Bulletin of the New York Public Library* 31, 9 (September 1927): 707–13.

[32]Bolkhovitinov, *The Beginnings*, p. 175. Nevertheless, Rezanov advised the directors in St. Petersburg to send drunkards to solve the manpower problem. His correspondence to the directors is published in Petr Tikhmenev, *Istoricheskoe obozrenie obrazovaniia Rossiisko-Amerikanskoi Kompanii i deistvii eia do nastoiashchago vremeni* (St. Petersburg, 1861–63), vol. 2 (English translation cited above, n. 25). Other reports are in *USR*, pp. 370–75, 443–53.

[33]Barratt, *Russia in Pacific Waters*, pp. 146–51; Bolkhovitinov, *The Beginnings*, pp. 176–79.

Russians and Aleuts. But developing this California base would be slow, and for the time being, with war ravaging Europe and wreaking havoc on normal commerce, Baranov's Russian colony to the north was even more dependent upon visiting Americans. Meanwhile, the United States acquired in 1803 an immense new territory by the Louisiana Purchase that fostered westward expansion and ambitions and, although less noticed, brought American and Russian territories much closer together.

Toward Diplomatic Recognition

War and peace continued to alter world geography. As an interlude of peace had allowed the enterprising Rezanov-Kruzenshtern expedition to reach Japan and sail around the world, so the resumption of war produced tighter British blockades of the continental coast and more stringent commercial decrees from Paris that outlawed British vessels *and* British goods from any French or allied areas. The French extended their interdiction so that any ships or goods that made contact with Britain, even at sea, were considered "contaminated" and therefore "British." For example, an American ship carrying genuine American or Spanish West Indian products that was stopped and checked by a British blockading ship would be considered British. These measures stimulated but also interfered with American trade to the Baltic.

None of the increased Russian-American contacts and complications had produced full official diplomatic recognition, mainly because the leadership of each country was absorbed by internal problems, commercial upheavals, and war. The United States, under Republican leadership and aroused by British maritime practices, leaned toward France (though Napoleon failed to requite), while Russia, concerned about French continental power and Napoleon's eastern ambitions, was allied with Britain. But French military and diplomatic superiority resulted in defeat for Russia, and the Treaty of Tilsit of July 1807 established a Franco-Russian concert on the Continent in opposition to British control of the seas around it. Russian ports were again closed to British shipping, and, coincidentally, Russia and the United States were again on the same side (though the latter, perhaps unwisely, hesitated to seize the opportunity and thus delayed war with Britain by five years).

Historians have long noted the causes of the agreement to exchange ministers: the growth of commercial interests, political circumstances created by the European wars, and the mutual understanding fostered by direct correspondence. It seems probable, however, that political motives were foremost when President Jefferson initiated the idea of diplomatic recognition in the summer of 1807. Both the United States and Russia had become more isolated, the result, respectively, of growing British superiority at sea and French dominance on land. The arrogance of the former, at least in American eyes, was demonstrated by the firing on and searching of an American ship—the *Chesapeake-Leopard* episode.

The wheels of diplomacy, nevertheless, turned very slowly. Jefferson chose to make the move not by a direct letter to Alexander (it was his turn to write) or through Levett Harris, but by instructions to James Monroe, minister in London, and through him by an overture to a special Russian envoy to Britain, Maksim Alopeus. Rumiantsev, now serving as foreign minister in addition to being minister of commerce, was quick to agree, even suggesting the suitability of Harris, whose appointment would have speeded the process considerably. After hearing of the Russian assent, again relayed awkwardly through London, in the late summer of 1808 Jefferson designated as minister to Russia William Short, his former secretary, close friend, and life-long correspondent who may also have contributed to the origins of the exchange while in Paris a few years earlier. Keeping the matter secret on the American side for reasons that are not very clear, Jefferson foolishly sent Short on his way to Europe while delaying his formal nomination to the Senate.[34]

Meanwhile, Alexander I named Andrei Dashkov, an official in the Ministry of Commerce, to a triplet of posts: consul-general for Philadelphia, "chargé d'affaires near the Congress of the United States," and, upon Rumiantsev's advice, "corresponding member of the Russian America Company." Why Russia had waited five years to reciprocate Harris's appointment, especially when it had been so well received, is not completely clear, but Alexander had now gone one step further, though not all the way to a ministerial appointment.

Back in Washington, Jefferson chose to wait until virtually the last minute, and in one of his final acts as president at the end of February 1809, he carried Short's nomination to the Senate, where it was unanimously rejected. The reasons for this public insult to the outgoing president are complex and pertain at least in part to the bad relations that had developed between the president and

---

[34]Alopeus to Andreas Budberg, 9/21 August 1807, *USR*, pp. 486–87; and Jefferson to Short, 29 August 1808, *USR*, pp. 528–29; Forrest McDonald, *The Presidency of Thomas Jefferson* (Lawrence: University Press of Kansas, 1976), p. 158. According to Dumas Malone, Jefferson's primary concern was gaining Russian support for American neutrality principles, and for that reason, he wanted to keep the mission secret as long as possible. *Jefferson and His Time*, vol. 5; *Jefferson the President, Second Term, 1805–1809* (Boston: Little, Brown, 1974), pp. 661–64. For a recent study of policy toward France during this period, see Clifford L. Egan, *Neither Peace nor War: Franco-American Relations, 1803–1812* (Baton Rouge and London: Louisiana State University Press, 1983).

Short's "diplomatic career" began as secretary of legation in Paris under Jefferson in 1785, and their relationship was virtually that of father and son. There may also have been a more private reason, involving a French romance, for Short's appointment and his early departure for Paris. Marie Goebel Kimball, "William Short, Jefferson's Only 'Son,'" *North American Review*, no. 223 (September–November 1926): 471–86.

Congress in his last year. There were also political objections to Short and to the expense of another foreign mission during the harsh economic times created by the embargo, and there was considerable concern about Jefferson's conduct of the whole affair (with Short already on his way to St. Petersburg).[35] The rejection caught Short and Rumiantsev, who were at this time both in Paris, by surprise, but Dashkov nonetheless continued his journey to his American post.

James Madison, who appears to have done little to straighten out matters as secretary of state, attempted to resolve the problem soon after assuming the presidency. He nominated John Quincy Adams, who, as a son of a former president and a New Englander with substantial diplomatic experience, seemed an ideal candidate for minister. Madison also wanted to reward Adams for his support of Jefferson's embargo policies. The new Senate, hostile to those policies, rejected his nomination at first but later relented to the administration's coaxing and approved the appointment on 27 June 1809. This type of conflict—when executive interest in expanding relations with Russia would conflict with Congress—was to recur, but often over other, more personal issues.

On 1 July, Andrei Dashkov and his family reached Philadelphia, and within two weeks he was in Washington waiting to be officially received by the president and Secretary of State Robert Smith. His naive request to address Congress was politely but firmly denied, but on 15 July he dined with the Madisons and members of the cabinet. Dashkov was given the impression that the American leaders had all delayed their usual summer departure from Washington for this reception and wrote enthusiastically to Rumiantsev about his long and friendly private conversation with the president.[36] Dashkov also corresponded with minister-designate Adams and with Thomas Jefferson, whom he visited at Monticello in September, leaving Alexander's last letter written the previous September "to his worthy and noble friend."[37] In lengthy dispatches to Rumiantsev, Dashkov analyzed the domestic politics of the United States and described the many departures of American ships for Europe following the substitution of the Non-Intercourse Act for the embargo. As of 1 March, trade was reopened with all countries except Britain and France, and the act also allowed

---

[35]Short's rejection was "the most mortifying event of his last year in office." Malone, *Second Term*, p. 661. See also John C. Hildt, *Early Diplomatic Negotiations of the United States with Russia*; Johns Hopkins University Studies in Historical and Political Science, vol. 24, nos. 5–6 (Baltimore: Johns Hopkins University Press, 1906), pp. 39–42.

[36]Bolkhovitinov, *The Beginnings*, pp. 197–99; Alexander I to Jefferson, 12 September 1818, *USR*, pp. 538–39; two memoranda of Dashkov to Rumiantsev, dated 24 July 1809, *USR*, pp. 576–85.

[37]Dashkov to Adams, 22 July 1809, and to Jefferson, 2 September 1809, *USR*, pp. 575, 591. For the Boylston professorship, see Donald M. Goodfellow, "The First Boylston Professor of Rhetoric and Oratory," *New England Quarterly* 19, 3 (September 1946): 372–89.

for the resumption of commerce with the first of these powers that rescinded their hostile measures. Dashkov relayed the implication from Madison that Adams would be especially authorized to negotiate a commercial treaty in St. Petersburg. The general recess of the government in Washington for the summer, however, suspended Dashkov's diplomatic business.

John Quincy Adams in Russia

The prospect of a great new revival of commerce hastened the departure of John Quincy Adams for his post. As a senator from Massachusetts from 1804 to 1808, he had supported Jefferson's foreign policy and voted for the Embargo Act, much to the distress of the Federalist party which controlled the state legislature. In the fall of 1808 the legislature elected a new senator ahead of schedule, in effect recalling Adams. Back in Boston, Adams resumed his legal work and his chair as Harvard's first Boylston Professor of Rhetoric (which had been founded in part with profits from the illegal trade of Nicholas Boylston with Russia in the 1760s). In July he presented his last series of lectures at the university, and on 5 August, he and his entourage embarked for the Baltic on the *Horace*, a trading vessel owned by William Gray, a prominent Boston merchant. With him were his wife Louisa Catherine (Johnson) Adams, his young son Charles Francis, his wife's sister Catherine Johnson, his nephew William Steuben Smith (as private secretary), and two black servants. Also making the voyage were a favorite Harvard student and future diplomat, Alexander Hill Everett, and William Calley Gray, the son of the shipowner, both of whom were to serve as additional, unpaid secretaries. Another "secretary," John Spear Smith, nephew of the secretary of state, would join the legation early the next year, and accompanying him would be a young friend of Joel Poinsett's named Jones.[38] Distant and isolated as his new post might be, Adams would certainly not lack for company.

After being delayed in Danish waters, the *Horace* reached Kronstadt on 24 October. Levett Harris met the party and helped them get settled in St. Petersburg. The mission was auspicious from the beginning, with Adams receiving at once a cordial reception from Chancellor Rumiantsev. His audience with Alexander, who was recovering from a foot injury, was postponed until 5 November

---

[38]Charles Francis Adams, ed. *Memoirs of John Quincy Adams Comprising Portions of His Diary from 1795 to 1848* (hereafter *Memoirs*), 12 vols. (Philadelphia: J. B. Lippincott, 1874), 2:3–4; William Steuben Smith, Diary and Letterbook, MassHS; Bemis, *John Quincy Adams*, pp. 153–55. For a more popular account, see Jack Shepherd, *Cannibals of the Heart: A Personal Biography of Louisa Catherine and John Quincy Adams* (New York: McGraw-Hill, 1980), pp. 119–29. Adams cites a number of Americans in Russia; Alexander Hill Everett confirms and adds to the list. Journal, Everett-Noble Papers, MassHS.

John Quincy Adams and Louisa Catherine Adams. Oils by
Gilbert Stuart (originals in the White House), from The
United States and Russia: The Beginning of Relations,
1765–1815 (Washington, D.C.: Department of State, 1980)

but was long and extremely friendly. Everett was also very much impressed by his Russian hosts: "One of the first things that at once delights and surprises an American traveller here is the great respect entertained by the Emperor and Court for our national character."[39]

The main problem that Adams faced, and one that plagued most future American diplomats in Russia, was the cost of living. The new minister received $9,000 annual pay from Congress and a "generous" moving allowance of about the same amount, but St. Petersburg was one of the most expensive cities in the world, and foreign representatives were expected to maintain a style in keeping with their rank and the ostentatiousness of the Russian court. Adams, unlike many of his colleagues, had little in the way of a personal fortune to supplement his salary and allowances and, as a parsimonious New Englander, would not be inclined to use it anyway. As a result, the American mission earned a widespread reputation for frugality, which amused many courtiers but did not seem to bother Alexander I.

Lodging his family in just adequate but still expensive quarters, John Quincy Adams followed the practice of accepting most invitations but issuing few of his own. This was generally regarded as a peculiarity of Americans and explained by his wife's being indisposed by pregnancy or occupied with babies. Moreover, several key diplomatic personages—for example, Rumiantsev and French ambassador Marquis de Caulincourt—were without families. Thus, the New Englander, who looked more like a college professor than a diplomat, dutifully made the rounds of a social circuit that centered on court balls and lavish dinners at the palatial residence of Caulincourt. He especially enjoyed the company of Willem Six, the Dutch (Batavian) minister and Amsterdam financier whom he had previously known in Paris. For good reason his wife was much less enthused about life in the Russian capital than her husband and suffered from loneliness and depression.[40] Moreover, Adams's early complaints to his mother about his expenses affected his mission. Abigail Adams, fearing that the small family fortune might be squandered in St. Petersburg, wrote to Madison requesting the recall and reappointment of her son. So, after little more than a year in St. Petersburg, Adams was granted permission to return home and, in February 1811, was nominated as an associate justice of the Supreme Court by Madison. The president

[39]Everett Journal, p. 23, Everett-Noble Papers, MassHS; Smith, Diary, MassHS; Adams, *Memoirs*, 2:47–58; Adams to Robert Smith, 6 November 1809, *USR*, pp. 605–7.

[40]Much of this is well documented throughout the *Memoirs*, vol. 2, but for a particularly detailed description of an event at the French ambassador's palace, see his letter of 22 March 1811 to his mother, in Worthington C. Ford, ed., *The Writings of John Quincy Adams*, 7 vols. (New York: Macmillan, 1913–17), 5:27–34. And the details of the Adams record are verified by the more colorful and interesting diaries of Alexander Hill Everett, on Willem Six, for example, on pp. 30 and 48, Journal, Everett-Noble Papers, MassHS.

even designated Adams's successor in Russia, Secretary of State Robert Smith, thinking that he might remove a troublemaker from Washington.[41] Though Adams declined in order to stay at his post during his wife's pregnancy, the indefiniteness of his appointment, known also to the Russian court, hampered his work, especially in regard to negotiating a commercial treaty.

For many reasons—his future roles as secretary of state and president, the detailed record he kept in diaries and letters, and the crucial and exciting time of his tenure—John Quincy Adams's period as minister to Russia is very well known. Until his departure for the peace conference in 1814, he remained close to his family and, unlike many of his successors, did not travel into the country. He never visited Moscow, the second capital and still largest city in Russia before its destruction in 1812. He did, however, see more of St. Petersburg than perhaps any other American, covering the city systematically on his frequent walks, visiting churches and cemeteries, accepting invitations to the houses of many Russian nobles and merchants, and touring factories, such as the famous imperial porcelain works and the new textile mill at Aleksandrovsk.[42] Adams also established close working and social relationships with Alexander I and Chancellor Rumiantsev. His anti-British, free-trade stance matched the current mood of the court, and even after the great invasion of June 1812, when Britain and Russia again became allies, Rumiantsev continued to dominate diplomacy in the capital.

The "frequent" informal "conversations" of Adams with Alexander, emphasized by several historians, were, upon close examination of Adams's own records, no more than twelve encounters during walks between December 1810 and April 1812, involving brief chats about such subjects as the weather, the stars, his wife's health, and Charles Francis's command of languages.[43] Adams's reflection on his last such meeting with the tsar on 9 April 1812, however, is revealing: "His manner today was graver and less cheerful than I have usually seen him."[44] Momentous changes were soon in store for both countries.

Much more important for his mission than small talk with the tsar were long

---

[41]A description of the household is in *Memoirs*, 2:193. On the opportunity to return, see Bemis, *John Quincy Adams*, p. 165, and Madison to Adams, 16 October 1810, *USR*, pp. 706–7.

[42]*Memoirs*, 2:111, 353–54, passim.

[43]The claims by Shepherd that "they often met along the Neva or the Fontanka, and discovered a mutual bond" (*Cannibals of the Heart*, p. 152), or by Bemis that "frequently—every few days—John Quincy Adams would meet the Emperor walking unattended on the quay or Admiralty Mall" (*John Quincy Adams*, p. 162) are not supported by Adams's own accounts. Alexander, incidentally, was walking on doctor's orders after the injury to his foot—and most of St. Petersburg society had taken to the sidewalks.

[44]*Memoirs*, 2:356.

conversations with Rumiantsev in the latter's official apartments opposite the Winter Palace, at his town and country estates, and during the various diplomatic dinner parties where they were often seated next to each other. The chief concern of Adams and of his home region was commerce, which also happened to be the favorite subject of the chancellor. Obviously welcoming the sudden increase in American shipping to Russian ports, Rumiantsev hoped that it would become a viable alternative to the British. But he was hampered by the treaty arrangement with France and the subsequent French commercial decrees that composed the "continental system," with which he disagreed but was bound, as an ally, to uphold.[45]

The Continental System and Russian-American Relations

The Non-Intercourse Act of March 1809 released a number of American ships carrying the stockpile of colonial goods that had been diverted to New England by the embargo. Since the embargo still applied to France and Great Britain and to their colonies and occupied territories, these vessels were funneled to remaining neutral ports. Many were initially destined for Tonningen in Schleswig-Holstein, the closest open port on the Continent. Articles were available there for export, while the Russo-Swedish War discouraged voyages to Russian Baltic ports for most of that year. Still attempting to secure cargoes of Russian naval stores in high demand, some ships were caught in the net of Danish privateers in the Sound at the entrance to the Baltic and were taken to prize courts, where they were charged with being stopped by British blockading squadrons, as many of them had been, thereby having their neutrality "contaminated," or with carrying goods of British origin.[46]

One of Adams's first successes in St. Petersburg was, therefore, in securing Russian pressure upon Denmark to obtain the release of most of these vessels,

[45]Adams's conversations with Rumiantsev are recounted in *Memoirs*, for example, 2:206–10. For Rumiantsev's isolated position as Alexander's pro-French foreign minister, see Patricia Kennedy Grimsted, *The Foreign Ministers of Alexander I: Political Attitudes and the Conduct of Russian Diplomacy, 1801–1825* (Berkeley and Los Angeles: University of California Press, 1969), pp. 168–93.

[46]J. N. Tønnessen, *Kaperfort og Skipsfart, 1807–1814* (Oslo: J. W. Cappelans Forlag, 1955), examines privateering in Danish waters, while A. N. Ryan, "The Defense of British Trade with the Baltic, 1808–1813," *English Historical Review* 292 (1959): 443–66, describes the British response. A number of ships' papers for the period are available—for example, in the letterbook for 1809–17 in the Oliver Papers, box 14, Maryland Historical Society (hereafter MaryHS).

George Coggeshall later remembered: "The poor neutral ships were driven from pillar to post, treated with every kind of indignity, and could find no safety in any part of Europe, except in Russia. His Britannic Majesty, so called, was the great sea-robber, while the selfish and unjust Bonaparte, was the great land-robber; so that between them both, the whole world was laid under contribution to support and carry on their

though some were able to buy their way out sooner, given the normal corruption of the times, and continue their voyages. But an abnormal number of American ships were still forced by these delays to spend the winter in Danish or Russian ports, complicating even further the lives of the American consuls there. Britain, in the meantime, had lifted the blockade along the North Sea coast of Europe in hopes that freer access by neutral ships, chiefly American, would result in return cargoes to British ports of the badly needed naval stores being consumed in large quantities by warships and their replacements. It was indeed a time of trial and confusion for American merchants and captains trapped between the British blockade and the French embargoes, between different versions of neutrality and radical commercial changes.

The next year, 1810, more American ships concentrated than ever before in the Russian ports, reaching a total of over two hundred. Already by mid-September, Levett Harris reported that ninety-eight ships had arrived at Kronstadt, fifty-four at Archangel, and several more at other Baltic ports. The large number was due to the closure of Danish ports; the French continental system's strict definition of neutral goods, which affected most of Europe; the backlog of both supply and demand on both sides of the Atlantic, which meant that potentially high profits were worth the added risks; and the success of the protected convoys organized by the British navy in warding off privateers. The effect was that ships flying the Stars and Stripes were suddenly carrying the bulk of Russia's imports and exports.

Problems quickly developed. First, French pressure on Russia to close this big loophole in the continental system grew, especially as the imported colonial goods were soon finding their way across the Russian land frontier into other parts of the French-dominated continent. Miers Fisher, for example, advised a client in the summer of 1810 that the price of coffee "is dependent on demand in Germany where the winter sledge roads take a great deal."[47] The French

devastating wars. The world has been too long gulled and deceived by great names, and dazzled by what military men call glory." *Thirty-Six Voyages to Various Parts of the World, Made between the Year 1799 and 1841*, 3d ed. (New York: George P. Putnam, 1858), p. 101. Coggeshall also describes in detail his stay in Riga through the winter of 1809–10. For other voyages to Russia at this time made by illustrious Americans, see H. A. S. Dearborn, *The Life of William Bainbridge, Esq., of the United States Navy*, ed. James Barnes (Princeton; N.J.: Princeton University Press, 1931); Richard Smith, *Reminiscences of Seven Years of Early Life* (Wilmington, Del.: Ferris Bros., 1884); and Norman E. Saul, "Jonathan Russell, *The President Adams*, and Europe in 1810," *American Neptune* 30, 4 (October 1970): 279–93.

[47]Miers Fisher, Jr., to unknown, 12/24 July 1810, VFM 48, George W. Blount Library, Mystic Seaport; Harris to Robert Smith, 13/25 September 1810, Despatches from United States Consuls, St. Petersburg, vol. 2 (roll 2, Microcopy 81), Record Group 59 (General Records of the Department of State), National Archives and Records Service (hereafter cited as DUSC, St. Petersburg, RG 59, NA).

claimed that many of the ships carried false papers and were really British, that the colonial products were of British origin anyway, and that, if accepting convoy protection was not in violation of the French paper blockade of Britain, the fact that outgoing cargoes would end up in British hands certainly was. There was some truth in all of these charges, although much less than the French claimed. The incoming cargoes were mainly from the United States or from islands of the West Indies not under British control. Most of the ships were also genuinely American, but they were often furnished with sets of false papers to deal with the multiple possibilities of interdiction by British cruisers or French or Danish privateers. Some ships, however, held a phony registry and misused the American flag, and there were enough of them to make the general charge seem valid to the French and to a few greedy Russian officials. As Alexander Hill Everett described the situation at the end of 1809: "A great many American vessels pass up the Baltick that never saw the other side of the Atlantick, beside [sic] these English ships bearing the flags of small states of Northern Germany— Pappenburg, Danzig— . . . so that a bona fide American vessel can scarcely get her cargo through without being compelled to make very considerable presents to every officer concerned in the business."[48] The United States could certainly not absorb all the Russian goods and cargoes. Some were indeed left in British ports, but they also found their way to many other parts of the world, including the Russian colony in the Pacific Northwest.

Adams and Harris thus had to contend with closer Russian inspection of ships and cargoes in 1810 and with Russian customs administrators who saw opportunities in the situation to increase their own individual rewards. This was

---

[48]Alexander Hill Everett to Oliver Everett (brother), 13/25 December 1809, Everett-Noble Papers, Diaries 1804–33, MassHS. Harris counted 114 American ships arriving at Kronstadt by mid-August 1811. To Smith, 7/19 August 1811, DUSC, St. Petersburg, vol. 2 (roll 2, M 81), RG 59, NA. For an overall treatment of the Baltic trade during this period, see Alfred W. Crosby, Jr., *America, Russia, Hemp, and Napoleon: American Trade with Russia and the Baltic, 1783–1812* (Columbus: Ohio State University Press, 1965); and M. F. Zlotnikov, *Kontinental'naia blokada i Rossiia* (Moscow-Leningrad: Nauka, 1966).

These American voyages were not always profitable. For the dire effects upon one prominent shipper, see John H. Reinoehl, "Post-Embargo Trade and Merchant Prosperity: Experiences of the Crowninshield Family, 1809–1812," *Mississippi Valley Historical Review* 42, 2 (September 1955): 229–49, although the author's conclusions (p. 243) are too general and extreme in describing the whole of Russian-American commerce as "an unprofitable stopgap trade that would bring bankruptcy to the merchants whose ships jammed the Russian harbors."

For British opportunism, see M. S. Anderson, "The Continental System and Russo-British Relations during the Napoleonic Wars," in *Studies in International History Presented to W. Norton Medlicott*, ed. Kenneth Bourne and D. C. Watt (London: Longmans, 1967), pp. 68–80. For the New Englanders facing these problems, see John D. Forbes, "European Wars and Boston Trade," *New England Quarterly* 9 (December 1938): 709–30.

especially true at Archangel, the White Sea port, where Samuel Hazard, the departing American consul there, complained:

> Russia is in a great degree still a barbarous country and the persons as well as property of our citizens require constant attention and watchfulness, the more in so remote a city as Archangel where the officers of Government are so despotic in their actions and nearly so in the law. If a vice-consul is appointed, holding his office from the Consul in Petersburg, he must necessarily be some German merchant (for the principal merchants are German) and cannot have the requisite independence, for they are frequently, and always in time of war, engaged in fraudulent trade that they tremble at the sight of the Government officials.[49]

Though ship captains in the Baltic echoed these criticisms of Russian practices, they were better served by Harris's reputation and influence and by able vice-consuls such as William Sparrow at Kronstadt and Christian Rodde at Reval. Even Harris drew complaints for the methods he used and the fees he collected to obtain faster handling of clearances or to free ships of unwarranted charges. He certainly seemed to have no difficulty in living in luxurious apartments and posing, much more than Adams, as an aristocrat who was not above bending the rules. As Edward Wyer, a free-lance merchant-adventurer in St. Petersburg, wrote to a friend in London: "Do you think that *vast* numbers of ships under the American flag, with *spurious papers*, have passed the U. S. Consul's office at St. Petersburg, the Consul of the U. S. at the same time, knowing the property to belong to Englishmen (Thomas Wilson of stocking memory) and others. I do assure you, it is of *great importance* to me, and to my country, that *this fact* should be known."[50] And to another correspondent, Wyer wrote: "Russia is the fit place for such men as *The Illustrious Levitt Harris*. I would recommend him, *never* to return to our *once* happy land, as a prophet is *nothing* in his

---

[49]Samuel Hazard (Antwerp) to Sylvanus Bourne, 17 November 1815, Bourne Papers, section A, Duke University Archives.

[50]Wyer to Thomas Mullet, 6 October 1814, Wyer Letterbook (on microfilm), [NYHS]. Proof abounds of the manipulations that were a necessary part of the business of the time; for example, in a memorandum for Capt. Stephen Collins of the ship *Richmond*, dated 13 July 1809: "We inclose herewith fabricated Documents dated yesterday, which you will carefully conceal while you are at sea, and on your arrival in the Elbe put them with the Vessels Papers to make her Cargo appear the property of David Parish (consul there), which we expect will secure it from seizure." Oliver Papers, box 14, MaryHS.

Abraham Gibson, who became consul-general in 1819, later counted forty-six American ships that came to Russia directly from Britain between 1807 and 1812 in violation of the French decrees to which Russia adhered. Harris-Lewis Law Suit, depositions of 1825, Lewis-Neilson Papers, HSP. John D. Lewis described his trials and tribulations to

own country."⁵¹ Like many Americans, however, Wyer was generally disillusioned with the practices and procedures in the Russian ports. "I dislike *this* country for several reasons, but for *one* more than all the rest. The duplicity of character that you find in all classes of society. . . . To make a figure in society a man must be like the weathercock, and the best talent he can possess is that of *versatility*. Without you have a *little* knavery—*some* folly—and *much* presumption, you had better shut up shop and 'whistle home again.' "⁵² Such was business in Russia. Perhaps what was resented most about Harris was his clout with Russian officials, the fees he charged, his favoritism toward the merchants with whom he was associated, and the superior attitude he demonstrated. Adams, for his part, did not interfere and left the day-to-day commercial matters completely in Harris's hands, while at the same time involving Harris in many of his own activities.

One commercial matter that did demand Adams's attention in 1810 was the problem of duties on sugar. Russia has a prohibitively high tariff on refined sugar, so almost all was imported in a raw form, typically brown sugars. American ships, however, began bringing in sizable quantities of a whitish raw sugar, which the Russians classified as refined, from a new source, Cuba. Adams successfully pressed Rumiantsev to review the ruling, but several ships and their cargoes were held up while the Russian administration slowly reassessed its position and eventually granted the American request in the spring of 1811, much to the consternation of the French ambassador.⁵³

a client: "The voyage was attended with much peril and consequently on my part with great pain and anxiety—the circumstances of having been in England, if known to the Russian govt. would have been attended with condemnation. The danger was that the sailors, or some of them might divulge the fact—they disliked the capt—but luckily for us they were fond of me; here it is proper to mention that the presents I made to them and charged in the accounts were deemed necessary." To Fettyplace and Watson (London), 11 January 1811, John D. Lewis Papers, Rutgers University Archives.

Everett saw the solution in the time, "which I hope is not far distant, when the *American Navy* shall be at least sufficient to convoy and defend American merchantmen." Journal, Everett-Noble Papers, MassHS.

⁵¹Wyer to Joseph Lawrence, 14 November 1814, Wyer Letterbook, NYHS. During Adams's presidency, Wyer served as a confidential courier, carrying instructions to Russia at one point. Aida DePace Donald and David Donald, eds., *Diary of Charles Francis Adams* (Cambridge, Mass.: Harvard University Press, 1964), p. 38 n. 1.

⁵²To Nathaniel Amory, 15 November 1814, Wyer Letterbook, NYHS. Everett was more complimentary in describing Harris as a "gentleman of great discretion and talents who has acquired himself during six years residence here in quality of Consul General a respectable fortune and secured to himself such connexions as will enable him to increase it still further whether he should incline to continue here or to return to America." Journal, Everett-Noble Papers, MassHS.

⁵³For Adams's long conversation on the subject with Rumiantsev, see entry of 9 October 1810, *Memoirs*, 2: 178–85. See also Harris to Smith, 12/24 December 1810, with

Arriving in large numbers in 1810, and even more in 1811 with the continuing absence of the British, American ships brought many Americans to Russia. Ship captains and supercargoes, instead of managing a quick turnaround at Kronstadt, were often forced to spend several weeks, sometimes the whole winter, in a Russian port, during which time they often called at the offices of their Russian representatives and upon Harris and Adams in St. Petersburg. Their American sponsors were also more likely to send business managers to help with the complicated procedures at the European end. They could no longer rely on European, especially British, houses for credit transfers, or on the convenience of unloading incoming cargoes in the familiar surroundings of Antwerp, Hamburg, or Copenhagen.

Encountering difficulties that ranged from the sequestration of an entire ship and its contents, to inordinate delays in the processing of papers, to incidents such as the disappearance of Claude Gabriel, a black cook, from the *President Adams* (he later turned up on the staff of the imperial palace), the American captains sought more professional help on shore.[54] Besides Wyer, Harris, and Hazard, Americans who came to Russia to attend to their own business or to provide onshore services for others included William Slade, Redwood, Coffin (Boston), Bache (New York), Baxter, Richardson (Norfolk), Jones, Salter Shreve (Salem), Graham, Donovan, Osgood (Salem), Waters, Malbone (Rhode Island), Willing (Philadelphia), James Proud (Baltimore), Peter Dobell, Miers Fisher, Jr. (Philadelphia), and Lewis (Philadelphia). Most of them, however, functioned on a temporary or seasonal basis as agents of prominent American shippers or as partners of Russian firms. They also provided information on the Russian market for merchant friends or clients at home. The most enduring of these entrepreneurs was John D. Lewis of Philadelphia (originally from Delaware), who established a firm in St. Petersburg in 1810 that operated for over thirty years. Harris, joined after 1813 by his nephew John Levett Harris, was also associated with the "Russian" firm of Meyer and Bruxner.

By law only Russian subjects could buy and sell goods in the Russian market.

supporting documents, and report of 18/30 May 1811, after a five-month fact-finding tour of northern Russia, DUSC, St. Petersburg, vol. 2 (roll 1, M 81), RG 59, NA.

[54]Capt. Richard Field to Jonathan Russell, 3 August 1810, Jonathan Russell Papers, John Hay Library, Brown University, Providence. For Adams's discussions with Rumiantsev about Claude Gabriel, the "deserter," see *Memoirs*, 2:489. The owners of the vessel were eventually paid $700 compensation by the Russian government—and Gabriel was also given the funds to bring his family from the United States. American servants did not come cheap in Imperial Russia. Another black named Nero Prince, from Gloucester, Massachusetts, also entered imperial service as a valet in 1810. See Mrs. Nancy Prince, *Narrative of the Life and Travels of* (Boston: by author, 1850), p. 16. And John Quincy Adams's servant Nelson, much to the minister's chagrin, also joined the imperial court in 1811, making the total number of blacks from the Boston area in the employ of Alexander I at least three. Adams, *Memoirs*, 2:255.

Foreigners, therefore, could only do business by becoming a subject (most often of Finland) and enlisting in the guild of merchants or, more commonly, by contracting as a silent partner or agent of a Russian firm. Most of these "Russian" firms, however, were long-established but originally foreign companies. For example, in Smith, Cramer and Company, the principal partners were Alexander Smith, from a prominent English commercial family, and Benedict and Sebastian Krehmer (variously, Kramer or Cramer), one of whom was married to an American whose maiden name was Falk and whose two sisters enlivened the American community during the 1809–10 winter. In 1809 the English partner was forced to withdraw; the company became simply Brothers Cramer, and it handled more American business than any other firm.[55] Other prominent houses involved heavily in the American trade included Meyer and Bruxner, Bonar Thompson and Company, John Venning, and Steiglitz and Company. The advantage in having a regular merchant-agent in St. Petersburg, especially during this period, was to facilitate the handling of cargo at the peak of the summer season and to contract for future exports in the winter when prices were lower. Also, as imported goods such as cotton piled up and the market collapsed, American merchants could respond by holding them longer, perhaps moving them to the interior, or reshipping them to other countries.

American Society in St. Petersburg

Presiding loosely over this enlarged American community of busy merchants, ship captains, consuls, diplomats, and occasional visitors, John Quincy Adams and his wife hosted simple New England–style dinners at their home that seem to have been greatly appreciated by most of those stranded in the Russian capital. However, given the environment—and the times—it is not surprising to discover that there were quarrels. John Spear Smith, the son of Sen. Samuel Smith who headed a faction often in opposition to Madison, arrived in early 1810 to join the diplomatic colony. He apparently got along fine with Adams personally but never felt welcome and left late in the same year; he complained to his father about the American minister: "He is an unfortunate appointment for this Court. He has no manners, is gauche, never was intended for a Foreign Minister, and is only fit to turn over musty law authorities. You would blush to see him in society, and particularly at Court circles, walking about perfectly listless, speaking to no one, and absolutely looking as if he were in a dream."[56]

Other, less partisan commentators lend credence to this picture, as do the writings and memoirs of Adams himself, filled as they are with his musings

[55]Tsentral'nyi Gosudarstvennyi Arkhiv Drevnikh Aktov [Central State Archive of Ancient Acts] (Moscow), fond 19, Kronstadt Reports, 1809–12.
[56]John Spear Smith to Sen. Samuel Smith, 9 June 1810, *USR*, p. 666.

about the Bible, weights and measures, the Greek and Roman classics, and contemporary literature—the absent-minded professor at Tsar Alexander's court. Smith, moreover, praised Harris, whom the ship captains and supercargoes often criticized, and it is not surprising that there were episodes of friction between Adams and Harris. These were moderated by a sense of common bonds in a foreign environment and by Adams's diplomatic entourage, especially Alexander Hill Everett. When not accompanying Adams on his rounds, Everett found entertainment in Levett Harris's active social life, which included dinners with merchants and nobility, and at the English Club, founded by Russian nobility in 1770 when the British were more popular as exponents of western sophistication in St. Petersburg. Everett was obviously struck by the wealth and position that Harris had earned in the conduct of American business.[57]

Fortunately, or, as some would claim, unfortunately, the Americans did not live in a closed society. During these years of international upheaval, and even after 1812 when Russia and the United States were technically on opposite sides, Americans were enthusiastically welcomed in St. Petersburg society. The many official dinners and receptions had their informal sides, which was also true even for the great state occasions, such as the funeral of Field Marshal Kutuzov and the many "Te Deums" after 1812 celebrating Russian victories.[58] The court circle was a large one and included the diplomatic establishment, ranking officials, generals and admirals who happened to be in the city, and the higher nobility. Besides Rumiantsev, those who were especially hospitable to Americans included the Empress Dowager Maria Fedorovna, Viktor Kochubei, the Naryshkins, Princess Beloselskii, and Admiral Kruzenshtern; and, outside the court, Benedict Cramer, the merchant who was also a director of the Russian America Company, Baron Pflug, a leading rope manufacturer, Baron Aleksandr Rall (or Roll or Rahl), the court banker, and Dr. Galloway, a Scottish physician who had studied in Philadelphia. The Russians tolerated well the American traits of frugality, plainness of dress, and smattering of the court language, French, and many even seemed to enjoy the opportunity to be at ease with friendly Americans at social occasions and to practice their English. In turn, Americans were impressed with the formality, luxury, and ostentation of Russian society but did not find it particularly to their liking.

[57]Ibid.; Everett diary and letter to Oliver Everett, 13/25 December 1809, Everett-Noble Papers, MassHS; Adams, *Memoirs*, 4:282–84. Paul A. Varg, *New England and Foreign Relations, 1789–1850* (Hanover, N.H., and London: University Press of New England, 1983), p. 79–80, sums up Adams's character upon entering the presidency: "Adams brought an iron will, skill, and good judgement to the office, along with a dour personality. . . . To Adams, seemingly all the world was foreboding, including both men and nations."

[58]For an excellent description of the atmosphere surrounding Kutuzov's funeral on 24 June 1813, see Adams, *Memoirs*, 2:482–84.

Tragedy and illness also stalked the American community in St. Petersburg. John Quincy and Louisa Catherine Adams lost an infant daughter in 1811. Most tragic of all was the case of Miers Fisher, Jr., who arrived in 1809 to begin a promising business relationship with John Venning. The son of a prominent Quaker businessman of Philadelphia, Fisher received special dispensation to marry Elena Gregerovskaia without changing religions. Unfortunately, the day after the wedding, on 5 June 1813, he died as a result of a fall down a flight of stairs. Several months later the widow indicated to James Bayard a desire to join her husband's family and apparently did so, for she died in Cincinnati in 1828.[59] Shortly before this incident, Adams had summed up his own lack of attachment to Russia and Russians: "After my experience of four successive Russian Winters, I believe there is no person accustomed to mild climates, who would not be desirous of an opportunity to assure himself once more that in the changes of the seasons there is such a thing as Summer. We have formed no social attachments that can make us regret the Country; and I have no employments here which can even afford me the consolation of being useful to my own."[60]

The Russian Mission in the United States

On the other side of the Atlantic, the Russian representatives also found life rather tedious in Philadelphia and in the new capital to the south that was still largely open space. Joining the small diplomatic colony in Philadelphia, Andrei Dashkov was forced to journey to Washington to conduct his limited political business with the American government. In fact, at the beginning the only matter of any real importance concerned his efforts to obtain a prohibition on American ships trading with the Indians along the northwest American coast. He blamed his failure on the limited authority vested in the federal government—the first of many Russian vexations with the weak and decentralized American administration—but in the negotiation he was also embarrassed by his inability to answer precisely what territory was claimed in that region by Russia.[61]

Dashkov was more successful with his attack on another flank of Russian-American relations in the Northwest. Prompted by Baranov and instructions from St. Petersburg, the Russian consul-general pursued the matter of sending basic commodities to the colony in America, now made particularly urgent by a

[59]Elizabeth Donnan, ed., *The Papers of James A. Bayard, 1796–1815* (New York: Da Capo Press Reprint, 1971), pp. 461–62 and editor's note (originally published as *Annual Report of the American Historical Association for the Year 1913*, vol. 2); and John Quincy Adams to Alexander Hill Everett, 10 June 1813, USR, p. 970.

[60]To Abigail Adams, 1 May 1813, *Writings of John Quincy Adams*, 4:484.

[61]Dashkov to Rumiantsev, 15 November 1809, USR, pp. 614–17.

Sketch by Pavel Svin'in. Two Indians with a Russian, probably the artist Yarmolinsky. From Picturesque United States of America *(New York, 1930)*

state of war with Britain and the consequent difficulty of supplying the area by Russian ships. In October 1809 Dashkov approached John Jacob Astor, a successful pioneer of the eastern trade whose American Fur Company was just getting established on the West Coast. Astor agreed to dispatch a vessel under Capt. John Ebbets, a veteran of Pacific voyages who had already met Baranov, with specified supplies for New Archangel. Dashkov also encouraged Astor to have Ebbets negotiate a long-term contract directly with Baranov.[62]

Little else is known about other early Russian business or social connections in the United States aside from Dashkov's association with the former traveler to Russia, Joseph Allen Smith.[63] The Russian envoy was assisted in political affairs by an able young Russian diplomat, writer, and artist, Pavel Svin'in, who served first as translator and then as secretary to the legation and who obviously had extra time for travel and writing. Svin'in had already gained public attention for his service as diplomatic attaché to Adm. Dmitri Seniavin during his Mediterranean expedition (1804–7) and as an artist and expositive writer; now he proceeded to apply his talents to his new environment. He first exposed

[62]Astor to Ebbets, 4 November 1809; Astor to Baranov, 4 November 1809; and Dashkov to Baranov, 7 November 1809, *USR*, pp. 601–13.

[63]Petr Poletika to S. R. Vorontsov, 20 July/1August 1819, *Arkhiv kniazia Vorontsova*, ed. Petr Bartenev, 40 vols. (St. Petersburg: tip. Mamantova, 1870–95), 30:442–43.

Americans to basic facts about Russia (*Sketches of Moscow and St. Petersburg*) and then published for Russians a pictorial and descriptive account of life in the United States, chiefly in and around Philadelphia.[64] This was a true pioneering effort considering the rudimentary state of knowledge that existed in each country about the other one, and Svin'in's public contributions, more than the many private letters and diaries written by Americans in Russia, should not be undervalued for arousing curiosity.

Also arriving in 1809 was Aleksei Evstaf'ev, who had earned an excellent reputation as a writer and musician while serving in the Russian embassy in London. Evstaf'ev, usually known by the French "Eustaphiève," served as Russian consul for Boston, the chief port from which ships sailed to Russia. Confined as he was to a more northern location and busy at times certifying outgoing vessels, he like Svin'in became famous for the use of written and spoken word in glorifying Russian military successes in the war, mainly for the Boston audience.[65] Russians clearly seized the opportunity that was presented by a more open, literate society.

One episode did occur in 1810 that brought unfavorable public notice to the Russian mission. Dashkov decided to celebrate the anniversary of Alexander's coronation in March with a grand party, to which many of the Philadelphia elite were invited. As fitting decorations for the occasion, he placed illuminations of imperial regalia, perhaps painted by Svin'in, in the windows of his home. This

[64]Paul Svenin, *Sketches of Moscow and St. Petersburg Ornamented with Nine Coloured Engravings, Taken from Nature* (Philadelphia; Thomas Dobson, 1813); Pavel Svin'in, *Vzgliad na respubliku Soedennykh Amerikanskikh oblastei* (St. Petersburg: F. Drekhsler, 1814), and *Opyt' zhivopishago puteshestviia po Severnoi Amerike* (St. Petersburg: F. Drekhsler, 1815). The latter is a considerably expanded version of the former. Svin'in noted in this later edition (p. 2) that he was offered an opportunity to publish the work in England but refused because he would have to write "against his heart, understanding, and justice, . . . as the politics of England demands." For more on the American edition, see Avrahm Yarmolinsky, *Picturesque United States of America, 1811, 1812, 1813* (New York: Rudge, 1930), and A. N. Nikoliukin, *A Russian Discovery of America* (Moscow: Progress Publishers, 1986), pp. 136–59. For an excellent analysis of early Russian views of the United States, see Robert V. Allen, *Russia Looks at America: The View to 1917* (Washington, D.C.: Library of Congress, 1988), pp. 13–18.

[65]Most of Evstaf'ev's panegyrics were published first as articles, especially in the Boston *Gazette*, and then in book form: Alexis Eustaphieve, *Resources of Russia in the Event of a War with France with a Short Description of the Cozaks*, 2d ed., (Boston: n.p., 1813), and *Memorable Predictions of the Late Events in Europe, Extracted from the Writings of Alexis Eustaphieve, Esquire* (Boston: n.p., 1814). See also Bolkhovitinov, *The Beginnings*, pp. 343–44, and Leo Wiener, "The First Russian Consul in Boston," *Russian Review* 1 (April 1916): 131–40. Evstaf'ev had married a British woman, and his children were "American" cosmopolitans, one daughter becoming the wife of a well-known Italian pianist. The consul himself died in Boston in 1857. Genealogical information in "Yevstafiev, Aleksyei Grigorevich," Yevstafiev Papers, Manuscript Division, New York Public Library (hereafter NYPL).

naturally attracted the attention of passersby. Some in the crowd that gathered became incensed at the prominent display of the Russian crown and made their displeasure known. Dashkov was on the point of removing it when an irate (and probably inebriated) naval officer, a son of a Revolutionary War general, fired two shots through the window into one of the rooms where guests were assembled. Fortunately, no one was injured, and the mob marched off proclaiming victory.[66] At least one observer believed the incident reflected more shame on Philadelphia and its lawlessness than it did on autocratic leanings of the Russian mission.[67]

For a time, Dashkov did not head the mission. Fedor Pahlen, the son of a favorite of Emperor Paul's who had been in charge of foreign affairs during the last and most chaotic year of that tsar's reign, had been designated minister to the United States in early 1809, after news of Short's appointment to the Russian court became known. With the hiatus on the American side, Pahlen's departure was delayed until Adams was ensconced in St. Petersburg; he finally arrived in the United States with his family in June 1810, Dashkov remaining as consul-general.[68] Pahlen's tenure was as uneventful as it was short, for in 1811, after a little over a year, he was transferred to Rio de Janeiro as minister to the Portuguese court, and Dashkov officially assumed the position of minister.

Supplying Russian-America during the War

Reviewing Dashkov's discussions with Robert Smith concerning the supply of Russian-America, Pahlen decided that it was useless to approach the American government again about prohibiting the trade with natives and instead encouraged Astor to regularize a commercial connection. In July 1810 he met in Washington with Astor's agent, Adrian Bentzon, a former Danish governor of the island of Santa Cruz in the West Indies who had been employed by Astor in 1808 and who then married Astor's eldest daughter. Pahlen responded favorably to Bentzon's proposal to negotiate directly with the Russian America Company in St. Petersburg for a long-term, exclusive contract.[69]

Pahlen furnished Bentzon with a passport for his journey in September, but because of the lateness of the season, or Astor's involvement with other affairs, Bentzon did not leave until the following spring. It was not until late August or early September 1811 that the Astor project was presented to the directors of

[66]Adams, *Memoirs*, 2:135–36; Charles Jared Ingersoll to Rufus King, 27 March 1810, *USR*, pp. 644–45.

[67]*USR*, p. 645.

[68]Pahlen to Rumiantsev, 18/30 June 1810, *USR*, pp. 672–73.

[69]Bentzon to Astor, 9 July 1810, and Pahlen to Rumiantsev, 9/21 July 1810, *USR*, pp. 674–79; Kenneth Wiggins Porter, *John Jacob Astor Business Man* (New York: Russell and Russell, 1966), 1:171–79.

the Russian America Company.[70] The circumstances were unusual. Through Albert Gallatin, the influential and brilliant secretary of the treasury, Astor attempted to secure President Madison's support for the project and appropriate instructions to Adams in St. Petersburg. Madison hesitated because of Astor's apparent intention to deny other American ships access to the area, but he did permit the Bentzons (including Astor's daughter) to travel in an official capacity on the frigate *John Adams*, which was already carrying a special envoy to Denmark.[71] Once in St. Petersburg, Bentzon dealt directly with Rumiantsev, as Dashkov and Pahlen had advised, before approaching the Russian America Company. He also kept the purpose of his mission secret, even from Adams.[72] This was the first but certainly not the last American effort to share in the Russian company's American monopoly.

All of this had been set in motion before the results of Astor's first supply contract were known in either New York or St. Petersburg, the distant and awkward communications being an obvious handicap for all concerned. After calling at native settlements along the West Coast, Captain Ebbets arrived at Sitka at the end of June 1810. A comedy of errors followed. First, no translator was available: Ebbets knew only English, Baranov only Russian. This problem was solved two weeks later, when the Russian naval ship *Diana* arrived under command of Lt. Vasilii Golovnin, a veteran of Nelson's campaigns who was just beginning a noted career as an explorer. He and another officer, Pavel Rikord, managed to translate Ebbets's documents. The American captain, however, mistakenly allowed them to see some private instructions that authorized Ebbetts to trade in California instead of New Archangel if it seemed more profitable and ordered him to scout out the defenses of the Russian establishments.[73]

This apparent duplicity on the part of Astor naturally annoyed Golovnin, who became convinced of American ill intentions. Baranov was also upset by it, but he still bought most of Ebbets's cargo and chartered him to transport furs to Canton. A more permanent agreement was prevented, however, because the Americans did

[70]Main Directorate of the Russian-America Company to Rumiantsev, 26 September/8 October 1811, *USR*, pp. 789–91.

[71]Kushner, *Conflict on the Northwest Coast*, pp. 20–21; Porter, *John Jacob Astor*, 1:192–98; Gallatin to Madison, 5 January 1811, *The Writings of Albert Gallatin*, vol. 1, ed. Henry Adams (Philadelphia: J. B. Lippincott, 1879), pp. 494–95.

[72]Bolkhovitinov, *The Beginnings*, pp. 261–64. The memoirs and correspondence of John Quincy Adams contain no reference to Bentzon, though Adams surely knew something about his mission. Rumiantsev appears to have referred to Bentzon's project in conversations with Adams in order to postpone a discussion of boundaries. Rumiantsev to Minister of Finance Dmitrii Gur'ev, 26 October/7 November 1811, *USR*, pp. 801–2. For Astor's original contract proposal, see Astor to Bentzon, 21 January 1811, *USR*, pp. 728–31.

[73]From the memoirs of Golovnin, first published in 1861, from July 1810, *USR*, pp. 682–85.

not provide any advance prices for the commodities required by the colony. Baranov also advised Astor that D'Wolf might already have made a contract in St. Petersburg, illustrating the complications of the distances involved and the excuses that might be made of them. Ebbets sent his first letter to Astor reporting his side of all of these negotiations from Macao in January 1811, obviously not trusting communication through Russian channels or by means of competing ships.[74]

Back in St. Petersburg, the directors of the company considered the proposal brought by Bentzon, probably informed by Golovnin of the details of Ebbets's visit to New Archangel. They objected in particular to the length of contract desired (twenty years) and the right of the American Fur Company to import certain kinds of furs into Russia, a monopoly that belonged to the Russian America Company. Nor did they think it was proper for the two companies to agree independently of their governments on a demarcation line between their respective interests on the northwest coast. Rumiantsev concurred in these sound objections but pushed the company toward an agreement on the other terms that concerned regular supplies, conditions for carrying furs to China, and a mutual understanding not to sell firearms to the Indians.[75] An apparent accord on these matters did not actually go into effect, since Bentzon did not reach New York until March 1812, just before another major shift in international alignments.

Openings and Closings: Political and Commercial
Complications of the War

Russia's position in the contest for power in Europe was attracting a variety of diplomatic-commercial missions. Though Bentzon had the unofficial support of the American government, especially because of Gallatin's friendship with Astor, he carried on his business in a private capacity in St. Petersburg. Courtland Parker, another American, represented a fledgling government in Venezuela and arrived in Russia about the same time as Bentzon to gain Russian support for trade with the new Latin American republic. Parker used Levett Harris as an intermediary and successfully won over Rumiantsev, who did not oppose the formation of republics "of the American type" in the Americas and who had already advocated Russian commercial expansion in South America. Rumiantsev

[74]Baranov to Astor, 27 July/3 August 1810, *USR*, pp. 687–90; Ebbets to Astor, 11 January 1811, *USR*, pp. 720–23.

[75]Report of Main Directorate, 1/13 February 1812; and Rumiantsev to Bentzon, 7/19 February 1812, *USR*, pp. 816–20; Bolkhovitinov, *The Beginnings*, pp. 270–74. As for other episodes of this hectic and complex period, valuable documents have apparently been lost—for example, a letter referred to in other materials from Rumiantsev to the Main Directorate, 24 September/6 October 1811. *Vneshniaia politika Rossii XIX i nachala XX veka: Dokumenty Rossiiskogo ministerstva inostrannykh del*, ser. 1, vol. 6 (Moscow, 1962), p. 711.

raised objections to the continental system regarding the technicalities of ensuring the neutrality of the cargoes. His proposal to grant Parker's request for opening Russian ports to South American trade was rejected, however, by the newly created State Council, whose opinion was accepted by Alexander I.

Shortly after Parker's failure, Levett Harris renewed the petition for Russia's recognition of the South American republics on behalf of Luis Lopez Mendez, a Venezuelan representative to London. This too was defeated in a close vote in the State Council, but Rumiantsev asked Harris to relay to Washington the emperor's friendly sentiments and regrets that he could not officially recognize independent states there until Britain did ("the political state of Europe at this moment prevents His doing more").[76] Rumiantsev continued to focus attention on the South American situation by his instructions to Nikolai Kozlov, appointed consul-general in August 1811, and by the transfer of Pahlen to Rio de Janeiro. The United States, in the meantime, was proceeding in 1811 toward recognition and commercial relations with the new republics by the appointment of Joel Poinsett as commercial agent in South America.

In similarly random, long-distance negotiations, the transfer of technology with military possibilities began. Early in 1810 Robert Fulton, already well known for his steamboat and other inventions, sent pamphlets on his ideas for torpedoes to Dashkov. Almost a year passed before they were forwarded to St. Petersburg. In the fall of 1811, while negotiating with Astor in New York, Pavel Svin'in met Fulton and became interested in the possibility of constructing his steamboats in Russia, particularly for the passage between the Kronstadt port and naval base and St. Petersburg, which was frequently hindered by contrary winds. Encouraged perhaps by Svin'in's contacts with him, Fulton proposed in a letter to Adams in November 1811 to build steamboats in Russia in return for an exclusive patent for twenty years. Repeated in April 1812, the offer was passed on to Rumiantsev the following October and fairly promptly granted by Alexander I for a fifteen-year period, with the provision that the first ship be in service within three years.[77]

Meanwhile, Svin'in presented a comparable proposal on his own initiative directly to Rumiantsev and also publicized Fulton's accomplishments in his writings. Nothing ultimately came of this effort, owing to delays in correspondence, the involvement of each side in war, Fulton's premature death early in 1815, and finally the failure of his heirs to follow up on his plan to send American engineers and mechanics to Russia that year. The publicity given to the enterprise by Fulton, whose last American-built ship was named *The Emperor of Russia*, by

[76]Russell H. Bartley, *Imperial Russia and the Struggle for Latin American Independence, 1808–1828*, Latin American Monographs, no. 43 (Austin: University of Texas Press, 1978), pp. 52–54; Bolkhovitinov, *The Beginnings*, pp. 243–48.

[77]Fulton to Dashkov, 24 February 1810, *USR*, p. 643; Dashkov to Rumiantsev, 4 January 1811, *USR*, p. 719; Adams to Rumiantsev, 19 October 1812, *USR*, pp. 887–89.

Svin'in's writings, and by the reports of a Riga physicist, Joseph Hamel, no doubt sustained Russian interest. A charter was granted to Charles Baird, a St. Petersburg factory owner of Scottish descent, who finally put a steamboat in service between St. Petersburg and Kronstadt in November 1815.[78] International relations and another war cut short the possibility of an early, significant American technological impact on Russia.

The Wars of 1812

Another of the ironies of this period's history is that two countries having mutual and compatible interests and witnessing considerably increased contacts with each other found themselves on opposite sides in the last great stage of the Napoleonic Wars. While Napoleon massed his army on the Russian border, the United States rushed toward a breach with Britain, Napoleon's archenemy. Compounding the irony is the fact that an important cause of this course of events was the astounding ability of American trade in the Baltic to break through the barriers of the continental system. That Russia allowed, and by 1811 even aided and abetted, this development in its own economic interest naturally infuriated the master of most of Europe. And the American success, although often to British benefit, aggravated old jealousies and attracted seamen, some of whom were deserters from or possible draftees for the British navy. The British then claimed the right to search American ships for these "strays" and in the process often "impressed" *bona fide* Americans into British service. When in doubt, might ruled.

The mood of the times certainly played its part. The aura of fatalism, of inevitability, reflected in Leo Tolstoy's great novel can easily be found in the demeanor and words of Tsar Alexander and presidents Jefferson and Madison. Although there were plenty of signs of the approaching storm (unlike the surprises of August 1914, or June 1941), the American break with Britain came with less forewarning to Russia than Napoleon's attack on Russia did to the United States. Both countries would suffer considerably in the war, the United States by sea in the interruption of commerce, Russia on land in the devastation of marauding armies. The economic drain of the wars was also comparable, but Russia's was far more enduring due to the military and political commitments made in pursuing Napoleon to final defeat. The United States could resume its path of progress and expansion from essentially the *status quo ante* and from the security of geographic isolation.

Even before the war between Great Britain and the United States began, Rumiantsev had attempted to soften British policies in an effort to avert a transatlantic conflict. He was handicapped by the absence, still, of direct diplomatic

[78]V. S. Virginskii, *Robert Fulton, 1765–1815* (Moscow: Nauka, 1965; translation published for the Smithsonian Institution and National Science Foundation by Amerind Publishing Co., New Delhi, 1976), pp. 171–91.

Nikolai Rumiantsev. Engraving by Skotnikov (original in Pushkin Museum, Moscow), from The United States and Russia: The Beginning of Relations, 1765–1815 *(Washington, D.C.: Department of State, 1980)*

representation in London and the consequent need to use Swedish intermediaries. Regardless, Russian pressure may have had some influence on the British decision to revoke the Orders in Council on 23 June 1812. They had already served their purpose at any rate, but they were only one of several issues in Anglo-American relations, and their rescission came too late. Congress had declared war on 18 June. Napoleon's crossing of the Niemen into Russian territory on the twenty-fourth then absorbed almost all of Russia's attention and particularly that of Emperor Alexander, who had already joined his armies in the field.

The Russian Mediation Attempt

In September, with Napoleon in control of Moscow and the American war increasing in scale, Rumiantsev approached Adams to determine the acceptability to the United States of a Russian effort to mediate.[79] His main concern was not so much to free British forces for the common struggle against Napoleon but the opposite—to avoid the crippling of American commerce that would result in an even greater British dominance in the Baltic trade than before. Britain might force the former colonies into subjection again, thus destroying the counterbalance of an economically strong United States, which Rumiantsev viewed as in Russia's best long-term interests.

Adams, who disliked the nation's growing warlike posture, was quite receptive to Rumiantsev's idea. In early October he wrote favorably about it to Secretary of State James Monroe, and Rumiantsev instructed Dashkov to present formally Russia's mediation project. Both documents were carried to the United States by the same special courier, John Levett Harris, nephew of the consul.[80] On 27 February 1813, Dashkov officially conveyed the offer to Monroe in Washington. Prodded by Albert Gallatin, who was ever mindful of the deteriorating state of the treasury, the secretary of state indicated his agreement in conversation with Dashkov, and on 11 March he formally accepted mediation.[81] The Russian offer reached London even earlier, but the British, especially cognizant of the mutual interests of Russia and the United States in securing neutral maritime rights, were hardly enthusiastic. Nevertheless, they did not want to offend their only powerful continental ally. The result was British prevarication.

Encouraged by Dashkov and influenced by Astor, Gallatin, David Parish, and Stephen Girard, who were all concerned about the war's disastrous economic effects in the United States, President Madison designated on 23 April a team of negotiators. The membership consisted of Adams, Gallatin, who insisted on going, and James Bayard, a former Federalist senator from Delaware who supplied the bipartisan element; these special envoys were to meet with a similar group of British delegates at a peace conference, which was rashly slated for St. Petersburg. Another goal of the commission, specified in the instructions and of particular concern to the antiwar party in New England, was to complete a commercial treaty with Russia.[82] With Dashkov's help British passes were obtained,

---

[79]Adams, *Memoirs*, 2:401–4; and Adams to Monroe, 30 September 1812, *USR*, pp. 878–80. It is interesting that Adams was surprised by the unusually friendly approaches made to him by Madame de Stael, who was visiting St. Petersburg, and by Lord Cathcart, the new British ambassador, shortly before Rumiantsev's overture. *Memoirs*, 2:399–401.

[80]Adams to Monroe, 17 October 1812, *Writings of John Quincy Adams*, 4:401–2; Rumiantsev to Dashkov, 30 September/12 October 1812, *USR*, pp. 880–82.

[81]Monroe to Dashkov, 11 March 1813, *USR*, p. 937; Dashkov to Rumiantsev, 5/17 March 1813, *USR*, pp. 940–41; see also Kate Caffrey, *The Twilight's Last Gleaming: Britain and America, 1812–1815* (New York: Stein and Day, 1977), pp. 199–200.

[82]Monroe's instructions to Bayard, Gallatin, and Adams are dated 15 April 1813, *USR*, pp. 949–53; Raymond Walters, Jr., *Albert Gallatin: Jeffersonian Financier and Diplomat* (New York: Macmillan, 1957), pp. 258–62.

and the Gallatin-Bayard party was on its way by the end of May. At about the same time, however, the Russian ambassador to Britain, Christoph Lieven, received from Lord Castlereagh a categorical refusal of Russian mediation. This was relayed to Alexander, who was with the army following Napoleon's retreat and preoccupied with immediate military matters.[83]

In the meantime, the strange course of war brought another well-known American into Russian territory, in the wake of the French army in 1812. Joel Barlow, who had earlier acted as an intermediary between Alexander I and Jefferson, arrived in Paris as the new American minister to France in October 1811, seeking a commercial agreement and compensation for confiscated ships and cargoes. His efforts were futile until the following year, when he was summoned to Vilna in a French-occupied part of the Russian Empire by Duc de Bassano, then Napoleon's foreign minister, to negotiate a commercial treaty. Arriving with his nephew on 18 November, Barlow was immediately caught up in the disastrous French pullout from Russia. Provoked by Napoleon's hasty flight from his army and horrified by stories of thousands of dead horses and soldiers littering Russian battlefields with deserted wounded managing to survive for weeks on rotting flesh, he composed one of the most stirring indictments of militarism and tyranny to come from an American pen—directed not against Russia but against Napoleon. His "Advice to a Raven in Russia" concluded:

War after war his hungry soul requires,
State after State shall sink beneath his fires,
Yet other Spains in victim smoke shall rise
And other Moskows suffocate the skies,
Each land lie reeking with its peoples slain
And not a stream run bloodless to the main.

[83]Despite extensive scholarly study, the precise sequence of the British response to the mediation offer remains confused. Castlereagh apparently counted on military and political events in the United States to decide the issue. His letter to Baron Nikolai of 18 November 1812 politely listed British objections to the mediation offer but might not be interpreted as a categorical refusal. This was probably hand-carried by Nikolai to Alexander I. *USR*, pp. 893–94.

French military reverses in Russia might cause the United States to consider direct peace negotiations more seriously, but they would also add weight to Russia's voice in allied calculations. Rumiantsev insisted in his correspondence with Alexander that the mediation effort continue, and Lieven, following instructions from Rumiantsev, repeated the offer to Castlereagh in December. The British minister then seems to have been caught by surprise by the American acceptance and quick dispatch of commissioners and only then issued a "categorical refusal," which was relayed, not to St. Petersburg, but to Alexander I in Germany. Lieven to Nesselrode, 4/16 July 1813, *USR*, pp. 982–83; see also Bolkhovitinov, *The Beginnings*, pp. 311–20.

Till men resume their souls, and dare to shed
Earth's total vengeance on the monster's head,
Hurl from his blood-built throne this king of woes,
Dash him to dust, and let the world repose.

Forced to join the great retreat, ill and suffering from the severe cold and lack of shelter, Barlow died at Zarnowiec, about fifty miles north of Krakow, in late December 1812.[84]

Many other Americans abhorred the carnage of the continental war but were impressed by the consideration and friendship shown to them by Russians in a time of troubles. In keeping with its intercessory role, on 5 March 1813, the day following the inauguration of Madison for a second term and on the anniversary of Alexander's coronation, Dashkov hosted a bipartisan ball in Washington, which, a newspaper reported, "in splendour, taste, and numerous attendance has never been surpassed in this city." In contrast to a similar event in Philadelphia three years earlier, "it was a new and unexpected pleasure to observe that the most distinguished characters of both political parties seemed cordially to unite in expressing their joy at the successes of the Russians, and in testifying great regard for the Russian Emperor."[85] Dashkov was especially pleased by the request of Dolley Madison for a copy of a painting of Catherine the Great that she had admired hanging on his wall.[86]

The American Peace Commission in St. Petersburg

The First Lady's interest in Russian affairs may have grown even more because her only, somewhat dissolute son by a previous marriage, John Payne Todd, was appointed as a secretary to the mission in St. Petersburg. Also accompanying Bayard and Gallatin were Gallatin's sixteen-year-old son James, George B. Milligan, George Mifflin Dallas, who would later be a minister to Russia and hold numerous public offices, and personal servants. After a stormy voyage and stopovers in Gothenburg, Copenhagen, and Reval, they reached St. Petersburg on 21 July to join an already substantial American colony marooned by the war. Adams was appointed to the peace commission, and Levett Harris was added to the list of secretaries. With their prompt official recognition and reception by

[84]Irving Brant, "Joel Barlow, Madison's Stubborn Minister," *William and Mary Quarterly*, 3d ser. 15, 4 (October 1958): 438–51. The first generally available publication of the poem was in Leon Howard, "Joel Barlow and Napoleon," *Huntington Library Quarterly* 2, 1 (October 1938): 49–50.

[85]*USR*, p. 946 n. 2; the newspaper clipping was enclosed with Dashkov to Rumiantsev, 24 March/5 April 1813, which is quoted in *USR*, p. 941 n. 1.

[86]Dashkov to Rumiantsev, 23 March/4 April 1813, *USR*, p. 945; Adams, *Memoirs*, 2:504–5.

the Russian government, the new arrivals were grandly welcomed by St. Petersburg society, no rejuvenated by celebrations of a series of military triumphs and by the return of British merchants and diplomats, headed by Lord Horatio Walpole as ambassador. Prompted by Dashkov, Rumiantsev even offered to pay the expenses of the American delegation, while he tried to nudge the British and Americans closer together and wait for a definitive answer from Britain.

Though socially well received, from the beginning the American mission did not proceed at all smoothly in accomplishing its official goals. Gallatin learned that the Senate had belatedly rejected his nomination on the grounds that he could not hold this appointment while he was still secretary of treasury. Bayard did not get along with Adams and was ill much of the time from dysentery, which he thought was caused by drinking the local water. For his part, Adams seemed depressed by the whole business, and his wife was annoyed at the high style Gallatin, Bayard, and company seemed to be able to afford. Gallatin's son James commented that Adams was "very civil but has a disagreeable manner," adding, as if to explain, "he is from New England, a 'Yankee.' "[87]

The main obstacle they faced, however, was the status of the mediation offer, which Rumiantsev, refusing to take "no" from the British, insisted on renewing. This was supported in a desultory fashion by Alexander I, now mesmerized by the idea of becoming the savior of Europe. However, Count Lieven in London refused to deliver Rumiantsev's message, since he believed the British position had been made quite clear. Rumiantsev's earlier pro-French policies were turned against him by the British and by the military and diplomatic advisers close to the tsar, headed by Count Karl Nesselrode. The first British refusal of mediation, for example, had been sent by Ambassador Lieven directly to Nesselrode at Alexander's headquarters. Though informed of the contents, Rumiantsev still had not received a direct communication either from the British (even though it was he who had made the offer) or from Alexander, whose instructions were becoming even more infrequent and ambiguous.[88] Declining in influence, Rumiantsev nevertheless retained his official rank and titles into 1814. Meanwhile, the American commissioners, informed from a variety of sources

[87]Entry of 23 July 1813, *The Diary of James Gallatin: Secretary to Albert Gallatin, a Great Peace Maker, 1813–1827*, ed. Count Gallatin (New York: Charles Scribner's Sons, 1916), p. 4.

[88]For example, Alexander I to Rumiantsev, 6/18 July 1813, *USR*, p. 984: "I completely approve of your views on the question of the mediation, and I authorize you to act accordingly." Gallatin, while passing through Gothenburg on his way to Russia, had solicited information on the British position from London banker Alexander Baring, who, after consulting with Castlereagh, responded with a clear exposition of the British view. Immediately after its receipt in St. Petersburg, Baring's letter was read to Rumiantsev. Baring to Gallatin, 22 July 1813, *Writings of Albert Gallatin*, pp. 546–52; Adams, *Memoirs*, 2:512–13.

that Britain would not allow a third-party mediation, still waited for new orders, even as both sides across the Atlantic tried to improve their military positions. By the time November arrived in St. Petersburg, Americans and Russians were growing weary of one another. As James Bayard noted in his diary: "Our situation in St. Petersburg has become unpleasant. The Society is in no degree inviting to mere strangers and knowing we shall remain here but a short time the object is not worth the trouble of attempting to cultivate the intimacy of anyone. This bye the bye is not an easy task as the Russians are as cold as their climate in its most frosty season."[89]

Finally, in January 1814, the Americans decided that prolonging their stay was useless, and Gallatin and Bayard began their long, difficult overland journey in midwinter, reaching Amsterdam in March. Before leaving St. Petersburg, Gallatin expressed both his appreciation and frustration to Rumiantsev:

> I cannot leave St. Petersburg without thanking you again, no longer as Minister, but as a simple private citizen, for the civility with which you honored me, and above all for the friendship that you showed to me for America.
>
> The confidence that you inspired in me encourages me at the same time to tell you candidly that it is with a very great regret that I see that we are leaving, not only without having succeeded, but even without having received a definite response from His Imperial Majesty on the decision of England on the subject of mediation. I will not repeat to you what I have already told you, and what I would have never said, if I had not felt it, on the perfect confidence that we have in the Emperor Alexander, whose talents and, above all, virtues form a true historical phenomenon. I could not, however, hide from you that the lack of a response to the Extraordinary Mission of the United States may produce in America an unfavorable effect and have the blame that belongs only on England fall back on the Government of Russia.[90]

[89]European diary, 11 November 1813, *Papers of James A. Bayard*, p. 483. Gallatin's son added: "Our position is a very embarrassing one. We plainly see we are not wanted. Romanzoff is pressing the Emperor to renew his offer of mediation to England." *Diary of James Gallatin*, p. 8.

[90]13/25 January 1814, *USR*, pp. 1045–46. Rumiantsev, on his part, was saddened and disappointed by the mediation failure, expressing to Harris that "he was, life and soul, American" but that he also believed that the American delegation "had shown too much ardour in pursuing peace; that he was sure peace was to be obtained for the United States on terms highly honorable and advantageous to them." Levett Harris to James A. Bayard, 5/17 January 1814, *USR*, p. 1041.

Louisa Catherine Adams noted in her randomly kept diary: "Although we saw but little of the Ministers when they were here yet I miss them most unaccountably[;] they

*Albert Gallatin. Courtesy Independence
National Historical Park Collection*

John Quincy Adams waited in Russia, then received instructions to go to Gothenburg, another projected site for the peace conference. Leaving his family behind, he departed St. Petersburg on 28 April for Reval, where he boarded a ship for the remainder of the journey. Adams, too, regretted the failure of communications but interpreted the British response to Russia as follows: "We will not negotiate with America *under your mediation,* but we ask your good offices to prevail upon America to negotiate with us without it." Adams added, "We never answered the overture contained in it, because although we received indi-

. . . return home very much of disgust for the climate[,] the manners and habits of the Russians[;] they were no favourites here and their manner of living did not contribute to render them comfortable or to conciliate the good will or affection of their countrymen. Public men in general do not pay sufficient attention to this point nor are sufficiently aware that in Foreign Countries (more especially here at St. Petersburg) the Americans who reside have little else to do during a large part of the year but to weigh and measure every trifling error in the character of their ministers which in their own country would pass totally unobserved." Adams Papers, reel 264, MassHS.

rect intimations that it would be made, yet it *never* was actually made."[91] And the war continued another year.

Concluding Peaces

Wandering around Europe and staying out of battle zones, the American peace hunters continued to find their game elusive. In one last effort to secure Russian support, Gallatin and Harris had an audience with Alexander I on 17 June 1814 in London, while he was resting on his military laurels. The tsar expressed his continuing friendship and high regard for the United States, regretted the failure of his mediation efforts, and pessimistically concluded that, in the words of Harris, "we should have to fight it out."[92] After further deliberation in London, Bayard, Gallatin, and Adams, joined by Henry Clay and Jonathan Russell, finally met with a British delegation on neutral ground in a Belgian provincial town and succeeded in early 1815 in bringing their war to a close.

The impact of the Russian mediation offers upon the Treaty of Ghent is difficult to assess. Madison's surprise acceptance and dispatch of commissioners to St. Petersburg may have provoked Castlereagh's sharply negative response, which complicated the situation. The presence of the American envoys in the Russian capital, especially at a time when the emperor was absènt, confounded communications and decision making. On the other hand, the sincere interest Russia demonstrated in ending the war, when its power on the Continent was ascending, no doubt registered with British officials. They could not help feeling some pressure to solve their differences with the United States in order to retain a strong negotiating position on the continent. Above all, with expanded diplomatic and territorial responsibilities, neither the United States nor Britain—nor Russia—could tolerate the financial burdens and commercial costs associated with a longer transatlantic war.

One effect of the whole process of concluding a peace was that more prominent Russians and Americans became acquainted with one another, and this was not limited to interaction with the distinguished American delegation to St. Petersburg. In Paris in 1815, a young American army officer, Winfield Scott, became quite friendly with an equally young and promising Russian officer, Mikhail Vorontsov, who was serving as an aide-de-camp to the tsar. Both would later rise to prominence in their respective countries. Because of continuing enmity between British and Americans, Vorontsov offered Scott a battalion of Russian imperial guards to protect a celebration by the American community in

---

[91]Adams to Monroe, 15 April 1814, *USR*, p. 1062.
[92]Harris (London) to Adams, 21 June 1814, *USR*, p. 1078; Gallatin to Monroe, 20 June 1814, *Writings of Albert Gallatin*, pp. 632–33.

Paris of the victory in the Battle of New Orleans.[93] Though politely refused, the Russian soldiers were on alert in case they were needed, conjuring up a fascinating scenario of disrupted international summitry.

By 1815 the aura of Alexander I and the power of the Russian armies loomed over Europe. Having waged a terrible war to a successful conclusion, Alexander wanted to ensure his own variety of peace on the Continent, one imbued with the principles of sovereign legitimacy and protected by the enduring institutions of church and state. The conservative ideals of faith, honor, law, and charity would preserve western (European) civilization from the corruptive, destructive notions advanced by the Enlightenment, the French Revolution, and Napoleon. The emperor was influenced by his own personal experiences, by ideologues and mystics such as Madam Barbara Krudener, the wife of the Russian ambassador to Prussia who had established a salon in Paris, and by practical politicians such as Talleyrand, Metternich, and Nesselrode. Concerned foremost with the European continent, Alexander left Britain and the United States alone to deal with each other. Perhaps this was in part a diplomatic ploy to gain more leverage vis-à-vis Britain at the Congress of Vienna, where the basic terms of the restoration of the Continent were to be worked out. Americans, who had generally responded favorably to Russia's demonstrations of friendship during their recent struggle, now were disappointed at the apparent lack of Russian interest in the outcome of the proceedings at Ghent.

Americans would, of course, benefit from the *pax Russica* in Europe. With peace firmly established, merchants could count on a secure climate for trade in the Baltic, and ships carrying the Stars and Stripes again appeared in substantial numbers in the Russian ports. But the British had clearly regained their dominant position, and with nearly the whole world now open to trade, the American share in the Russian Baltic commerce would never again reach the heights of 1810 and 1811. The American colony in St. Petersburg that had been nurtured by it largely dispersed. Even the diplomatic presence shrank to a low level. John Quincy Adams assumed a new post after the negotiations at Ghent as minister to Great Britain, while Gallatin was assigned to Paris. The other member of the American troika in St. Petersburg, James Bayard, was designated by President Madison as minister to Russia, but, extremely ill, Bayard sailed for home, dying a week after his arrival. Levett Harris dutifully returned to Russia as chargé d'affaires.

[93]Charles Winslow Elliott, *Winfield Scott: The Soldier and the Man* (New York: Macmillan, 1937), p. 202. Scott's assessment of Vorontsov indicated future friendship toward the United States from this developer of southern Russia: "This young man . . . professes himself to be a warm admirer of the U. States, with whose government and history he is well acquainted." To James Monroe, 28 September 1815, quoted in ibid., p. 202 n. 20.

Diplomatic Squabbles

With both the United States and Russia again preoccupied by their own continents, relations should have continued along docile, uneventful lines, except for
the vagaries of human behavior and the continuing tumult of ideas in the aftermath of the Napoleonic Wars. The calm was abruptly broken in late November
1815 when Nikolai Kozlov, who had succeeded Dashkov as Russian consul-
general in Philadelphia, was charged with raping a twelve-year-old servant girl
and brought before a Pennsylvania court. The situation differed from that of
John Paul Jones in Russia because the alleged crime occurred in a much less tolerant society, the American court system was more complex, and, above all, it
involved an official diplomatic agent of Russia. Dashkov, who still resided in
Philadelphia, denied the charges and called for Kozlov's immediate release on
grounds of diplomatic immunity, claiming that the local police and courts did
not have jurisdiction over cases involving foreign diplomats. When he did not
receive satisfaction, he went public with a circular to all other diplomatic missions.[94]

When the case came before the Pennsylvania court in early 1816, it conceded
the last of Dashkov's claims, referring the issue to the federal level. But federal
courts did not have jurisdiction over crimes such as rape and refused to take the
case. Kozlov was thus free from prosecution, although the minister persisted in
demanding recognition of consular immunity *and* exoneration of the Russian official from all past charges. When neither was granted, he announced in October 1816 that he was ceasing communication with the government in Washington. The Russian government, reacting to the initial incident, declared Harris
persona non grata, which deprived him of social status but allowed him to carry
out his diplomatic functions. The United States then escalated the tension by
charging the Russian consul in Boston, Evstaf'ev, with illegally protecting British property during the recent conflict, a complicated issue that probably would
not have been brought out into the open except for the Kozlov affair and that
resulted in the consul's sudden recall in June 1816.[95]

William Pinkney, an experienced diplomat from Maryland, was quickly
named by Monroe as the second minister to Russia, but he was also given a special assignment to present some old claims against Naples on his way. Although

[94]Hildt, *Early Diplomatic Negotiations*, pp. 92–93; N. N. Bolkhovitinov, *Russko-
amerikanskie otnosheniia, 1815–1832* (Moscow: Nauka, 1975), pp. 32–33.

[95]Hildt, *Early Diplomatic Negotiations*, pp. 93–95; Bolkhovitinov, *Russko-amerikanskie
otnosheniia*, pp. 33–35. Most of the correspondence cited on the affair is between Monroe and Dashkov and between Dashkov and St. Petersburg. Harris's reports from St. Petersburg are strangely reserved. Harris reported to Pinkney, but his dispatches to Washington seem to have been lost. Harris to Pinkney (Naples), 30 July 1816, Despatches
from United States Ministers (hereafter DUSM), Russia, vol. 6 (roll 6, M 35), RG 59,
NA.

this duty delayed his arrival in Russia by six months, it allowed him to collect double travel allowances to help finance his Russian stay. The president, alarmed about the possibility that Pinkney might not be accepted, instructed a close associate of Madison's, Edward Coles, to proceed directly to St. Petersburg in August 1816. After conferring with Poinsett in Philadelphia, Coles sailed on board the *Prometheus*, which became the first American warship to enter a Russian port. Fearing that even this would not be enough to ease Russian feelings, Monroe ordered Alexander Hill Everett, who had been with Adams and was already in Europe, to St. Petersburg, but news of Coles's success reached him before he departed.[96]

Levett Harris also discussed the legal position of consuls in an exchange of notes with Count Ionnes Capodistrias, who shared the conduct of foreign affairs with Nesselrode. He eventually agreed with Harris's claim that consuls were subject to the laws of the nation wherein they reside. Solutions came relatively easy, because Alexander I and his ministers were very much interested in maintaining friendly relations and quite willing to accept the American version of the facts. Most of the matters at issue were settled in St. Petersburg by Coles and Harris in November 1816, before Pinkney's arrival and before news was received of Dashkov's precipitous action. Both Dashkov and Kozlov were eventually recalled, while the charges against Evstaf'ev were conveniently forgotten, and he soon returned to his post in Boston to serve many more years as consul there and in New York. The first serious diplomatic incident in Russian-American relations was thus resolved, and Pinkney could resume his journey from Naples to St. Petersburg.

The Pinkney Mission to Russia

The wars had caused both countries to respect each other's military capacities. As William R. King, who preceded Pinkney to St. Petersburg as his secretary, noted: "The extensive military establishment of the Emperor, which amount[s]

[96]Harris to Monroe, 12 November 1816, DUSM, Russia, vol. 5 (roll 5, M 35), RG 59, NA; Bolkhovitinov, pp. 35–37; Benjamin Platt Thomas, *Russo-American Relations, 1815–1867*, Johns Hopkins University Studies in Historical and Political Science, vol. 48, no. 2 (Baltimore: Johns Hopkins University Press, 1930), pp. 22–24. Edward Coles to John Coles, 7 August and 4 October 1816, Coles Correspondence, HSP; A. H. Everett (London) to Edward Everett, 23 December 1816, Hale Family Papers, vol. 9 (Everett letters), Manuscript Division, Library of Congress (hereafter LC).

Rumiantsev, though retired from office, may have played a role in the settlement of the Kozlov case, for Coles reported to Poinsett that the "prepossessing and general deportment of this old gentleman, and particularly the deep interest he seems to take in the welfare of the United States, and his earnest desire to connect and preserve the most friendly relations with them, could not but make him a great favorite with me." Edward Coles (Hamburg) to Poinsett, 15 December 1816, Poinsett Papers, HSP.

to about one million men, is viewed with suspicion by England, and with something of alarm by the Continental Powers. . . . Under this state of things the growing importance of the United States as a Naval Power, naturally excites the attention of all, but more particularly of Russia, who thinks to see in her a nation likely at no distant day to become the rival of England."[97]

Pinkney finally arrived in St. Petersburg at the beginning of 1817, accompanied by Charles Oliver, also from Maryland. At a New Year's Day reception (13 January, according to the Russian calendar), the new American minister found that Alexander considered relations restored to their former friendly level: "The Emperor conversed with me for half an hour and expressed himself from time to time in the strongest terms of regard for our country and frequently declared his desire to cultivate with us the most friendly relations." Alexander also noted "a striking analogy between the two countries," which would become a refrain in the nineteenth-century Russian-American dialogue.[98] Pinkney also displayed a trait common among many other American visitors to Russia—a deep admiration for the person of the tsar. In a letter to Robert Goodloe Harper, he described Alexander I:

> The Emperor is a remarkably handsome man, and of an admirable address. Everybody justly ascribes to him the Merit of *good intentions*, but he has the additional Merit of knowing how to use the best Means for the fulfillment of those intentions. He is one of the few men in the World who, having been seen at a distance in great enterprizes and establishments, gain by being approached and closely examined. I am mistaken in him if he is not a man of great abilities. He appears to me to have a clear vigorous and cultured mind— to be steady and sagacious in the pursuit of his purposes—to be well read in men as well as books—to be prompt and dexterous in the Managements of affairs—to have the wholesome habit of thinking for himself—to be of a generous, though perhaps somewhat hasty, temper—and in a word to be signally fitted for his high vocation. He has a good opinion and the utmost good will towards our Country.[99]

This flattering portrait of the emperor was similar to those of others who looked for positive changes in Russia. Unfortunately, they would soon be disappointed, as Alexander, in the last years of his reign, became increasingly ill, irritable, and conservative.

The Kozlov episode, though having no lasting effect upon Russian-American

[97]Pinkney to Monroe, 28 January 1817, DUSM, Russia, vol. 6 (roll 6, M 35), RG 59, NA.

[98]King to Monroe, 29 January 1817, ibid.

[99]William Pinkney to Robert Goodloe Harper, 10 August 1817, Pinkney Papers, MaryHS.

relations, came at a crucial time in Anglo-Russian relations. With Dashkov discredited, Russia could not approach the United States persuasively about adherence to the Holy Alliance, giving Castlereagh all of 1816 to solidify Britain's opposition to Russia's objectives. For Russia, good relations with the United States could still offset Britain's seapower and colonial expansion, especially now that Russia's former allies in the Armed Neutrality, the smaller states of northern Europe, had been seriously weakened by the wars. By the time of the Congress of Aix-la-Chapelle in September 1818, the lines were sharply drawn by Britain's refusal to support Russia's goal to maintain the Spanish Empire in the Americas, if necessary by force of arms. Nesselrode attempted to win over the United States to a common effort in South America that would circumvent the British checkmate, but by that time he found its sympathies were with the republican causes in the area. Moreover, American hostility toward Spain over Florida was too strong and deeply rooted. The independence of American policy from both Russia and Britain was thus registered in the international arena.

In the summer of 1817, after the Kozlov affair was settled and a new Russian minister, Baron Diderick Tuyll van Serooskerken, was appointed as Dashkov's replacement in the United States, William Pinkney proceeded with his main task—the negotiation of a commercial treaty. With this he had little success owing to the reluctance of Alexander to enter into any definitive commercial agreements. Pinkney also postponed the matter of settling the demarcation between American and Russian territories along the American northwest coast until the new Russian minister was able to report from Washington. Tuyll, however, was delayed, then reassigned to Portugal instead, and finally replaced by the former counselor to Pahlen and Dashkov, Petr Poletika, who did not reach Washington until May 1819.

The Harris-Lewis Affair

The Pinkney mission to Russia, lasting only a year in residence, still left its impact. Pinkney had brought his own staff: Charles Oliver and William R. King as secretaries, and his son Charles as his assistant. Levett Harris, upset at not being promoted after his long service in Russia, left his consulship in favor of his nephew, John Levett Harris. The bad feelings that had earlier developed between the Harrises and other diplomats and merchants erupted in an incident in the summer of 1817 that raised yet another consular issue between the two countries.

William David Lewis had come to Russia in 1813 to assist his brother John in business and then spent much of his time studying Russian and German and traveling through the country. One day in July 1817, he became incensed at language used by John Levett Harris while charging multiple consular fees (an old

*William David Lewis. From the collection of the Historical
Society of Pennsylvania*

bone of contention) to each consignee of the New England ship of Capt. Isaiah
Bowditch. A few days later, Lewis publicly insulted Harris by striking him
lightly on the nose at the exchange. Harris did not immediately respond as
Lewis expected with a challenge to a duel but instead filed formal charges with
the police and asked the Russian government in repeated letters to Nesselrode
and the governor of St. Petersburg to uphold his honor as a foreign consul; the
Russians refused to intervene on the grounds that it was a private American
matter.[100] Pinkney, who had witnessed the first part of the altercation, was quite

[100]The participants' own accounts of the episode are well preserved: unpublished Wil-
liam Lewis autobiography, Lewis-Neilson Papers, box 54, HSP; John Levett Harris to
John Quincy Adams, 28 July 1817, DUSC, St. Petersburg, vol. 2 (roll 2, M 81), RG 59,
NA; William Pinkney to John Quincy Adams, 1 August 1817, DUSM, Russia, vol. 6
(roll 6, M 35), RG 59, NA; and William D. Lewis to Jonathan Russell, Russell Papers,
John Hay Library, Brown University. In his letter to Adams, Pinkney described Lewis as

embarrassed by the event. Though believing that Lewis was basically in the right, Pinkney regretted the whole episode, especially since it came so soon after the settlement of the Kozlov incident, and referred to it as a "ridiculous and disgusting business."[101]

The Harris-Lewis feud had wider implications because it deprived the United States of the services of two persons with the most intimate knowledge of Russian affairs. It was already common knowledge in St. Petersburg that Levett Harris aspired to be minister to Russia and that William Lewis wanted to be consul. Harris, in fact, had gone to Washington early in 1817 to seek that post. Shortly after the public insult, John D. Lewis wrote to the secretary of state, none other than John Quincy Adams, strongly opposing Harris's appointment and charging him with a variety of corrupt activities in Russia.[102] These accusations became public in the aftermath of the exchange incident in the fall of 1817 through a pamphlet circulated by the Lewises in Philadelphia. Levett Harris then sued William Lewis for libel, and the latter was forced to return to Philadelphia in 1819 to defend himself, as did John Levett Harris. The protagonists finally fought a protracted duel on the beach at Red Bank, New Jersey, in which the younger Harris was wounded in the thigh on the fifth shot, marksmanship obviously not having been part of their Russian experience. The senior Harris, convinced that one of his bitterest opponents was the secretary of state, even appealed to the person who had originally appointed him in 1803, Thomas Jefferson.

The Harris versus Lewis court case that began in 1820 dragged out for seven years through numerous depositions and counterdepositions collected by both sides from merchants and officials in St. Petersburg and the United States. Though Harris's lawyers apparently wanted to stall for a settlement out of court, Lewis persisted with the trial, and a jury finally sided with Harris but awarded only $100 in damages, which Lewis considered his victory.[103] The only American

---

"the young and extremely intelligent and respected American" and, in reference to Harris's appeal to Nesselrode, remarked: "I was not a little vexed to find that this mortifying affair was, after I had shaken it off, returning to me in a circle." He then asked for Harris's recall. For additional background, see Norman E. Saul, "America's First Student of Russian: William David Lewis of Philadelphia," *Pennsylvania Magazine of History and Biography* 96, 4 (October 1972): 469–79. There is also a recently discovered translation of a letter from Harris to St. Petersburg governor-general Masmitinov, of 22 August 1817, Samuel Brown Papers (uncataloged), Filson Club, Louisville.

[101]Pinkney to Adams, 15 August 1817, DUSM, Russia, vol. 6 (roll 6, M 81), RG 59, NA.

[102]John D. Lewis to Adams, 27 July 1817, Miscellaneous Letters of the Department of State (roll 37, M 179), RG 59, NA. And for Adams's opinion of Harris, see *Memoirs*, 4:282–84.

[103]Abraham Gibson (St. Petersburg) to Robert Ker Porter, 11/23 July 1825, Porter Papers, no. 14596, Spencer Research Library, University of Kansas. Documents concerning the trial are in the Lewis-Neilson Papers and the Gilbert Cope Collection, HSP. For

really fluent in the Russian language, William D. Lewis became estranged from his brother in Russia but eventually achieved success as a banker and was later designated Collector of the Port of Philadelphia. Neither Harris, uncle or nephew, would again be involved directly in Russian-American relations, although Levett Harris retained some business interests in St. Petersburg, visited several times, and died there in 1839.[104]

George Washington Campbell's Appointment to Russia

Discouraged by the Lewis-Harris feud, the climate, living costs, his poor health, and Russian apathy toward a commercial treaty, William Pinkney requested his recall and, without waiting for a replacement, departed St. Petersburg in February 1818, leaving behind his son Charles as chargé d'affaires.[105] President Monroe, despite objections from his secretary of state, wanted the next minister to Russia to come from the West to ensure a geographical representation in the diplomatic corps. He first considered the military heroes Andrew Jackson and William Henry Harrison—appointments that would have made for interesting Russian court scenes. After a compromise candidate, William Lowndes of South Carolina, refused the offer, Monroe settled on his old friend George Washington Campbell of Tennessee.

As a vocal leader of the War Hawks in the Senate before 1812, Campbell had to put money where his mouth was when he replaced Gallatin as secretary of the treasury in 1814. Facing serious fiscal problems, he resigned this office by the

the best published source on the trial, based on the miraculous recovery 140 years later of federal documents used in the case, see James Barton Rhoads, "Harris, Lewis, and the Hollow Tree," *American Archivist* 25, 3 (July 1962): 295–314. For contemporary comment on the final verdict: *National Intelligencer*, 20 February 1827.

[104]Abraham Gibson to John Forsyth, 5 October 1839 (no. 30), DUSC, St. Petersburg, vol. 5 (June 1839–December 1842) (roll 4, M 81), RG 59, NA. Both men returned to collect materials for the trial. Charles Pinkney reported in 1823, "Mr. Harris is here leaving no stone unturned to forward his suit against Wm. Lewis." To his mother, 19/31 December 1823, Pinkney Papers, MaryHS.

[105]Pinkney to Adams, 14 February 1818, DUSM, Russia, vol. 6 (roll 6, M 35), RG 59, NA. A person who lived with the Pinkneys during the summer of 1817 described the minister as fastidious, parsimonious, aloof from society, a man who loved to eat and drink and never exercise but who was a conscientious diplomat. Pinkney wrote privately to President Monroe: "Notwithstanding my anxiety to get home, I shall quit this station with some regret. They have been very good to me here. The state of the world too requires that we should have a good stock of prudence at this court; and I feel quite sure that on that score I should never be found deficient. My place, however, will doubtless be supplied by a man much more able and distinguished, and at the same time of equal discretion. You cannot put too much ability and character into this mission. One of the foremost men of our country ought to be selected for it." Good advice for any day. Pinkney to Monroe, 21 January 1818, in Henry Wheaton, *Some Account of the Life, Writings, and Speeches of William Pinkney* (New York: J. W. Palmer, 1826), p. 160.

end of the summer. During that period he shared lodgings with Secretary of State Monroe in Washington, which is when they became close friends.[106] He served again in the Senate from 1815 to 1818. Campbell represents the first of several purely political appointments to the Russian post of men who had no diplomatic experience. Adams, who preferred a worldly easterner, still hoped to retain control of the situation by designating his old protégé of 1809, William Calley Gray, as secretary of legation—"who I hope will accept it, and devote himself heart and sole to the diplomatic career, because he can afford it."[107] Gray, however, resisted Adams's "persuasive call to public duty."[108]

Campbell toured leisurely through New England and northern Europe with his family and a staff of servants before arriving at St. Petersburg in September 1818. Because of the emperor's absence at the Congress of Aix-la-Chapelle, he could not be officially received until the following January. Soon afterwards tragedy struck the Campbells, their three children dying of typhus within a week despite the attendance of court physicians Leighton and Wylie. Though Campbell courageously stayed in St. Petersburg until the summer of 1820, he was obviously depressed and performed little diplomatic business of note.[109] Most of it concerned Spain, which continued to lose ground in the Americas, posing a challenge to the Holy Alliance and Alexander's strong support for "legitimacy." Yet Alexander also wanted to preserve peace, and, after clear opposition to intervention on behalf of Spain was voiced by Britain at Aix-la-Chapelle, he did not press the issue. A token assortment of warships was sold to Spain, but they were not really in a condition to cross the Atlantic by the time they reached Cadiz.[110] The new Russian minister to the United States, Petr Po-

[106]Weymouth T. Jordan, *George Washington Campbell of Tennessee, Western Statesman* (Tallahassee: Florida State University Press, 1955), pp. 87–139; Adams, *Memoirs*, 4:72–76; Monroe to Lowndes, 9 April 1818, William Lowndes Papers, South Carolinian Library, University of South Carolina. Monroe's offer to Campbell was dated 11 April. Campbell Papers, box 1, Manuscript Division, LC.

[107]In response to a criticism of Campbell's appointment, John Quincy Adams noted that better men had declined, and he lamented the lack of sufficient remuneration for American diplomats. To William Plummer, 8 July 1818, *Writings of John Quincy Adams*, 6:380–81.

[108]Adams to William Plummer, 6 July 1818, Manuscript and Rare Book Department, BPL. See also his letter to Gray, 3 August 1818, *Writings of John Quincy Adams*, 6:412–14.

[109]Jordan, *George Washington Campbell*, pp. 137–61; George Washington Campbell diary, Campbell Papers, Manuscript Division, LC. He noted on 17 April 1819, "It is not, by any means certain, that the death of our children is *particularly* to be ascribed to the climate of this place." And John D. Lewis echoed the general sentiment in a letter to John Quincy Adams: "A dispensation of providence so mournful I have never witnessed before." 15 April 1818, in Samuel Brown Papers (uncataloged), Filson Club.

[110]Bolkhovitinov, *Russko-amerikanskie otnosheniia*, pp. 48–53; William Spence Robert-

letika, realized that he had arrived too late to have any effect on American recognition of the independence of some of the former Spanish colonies in South America; he then offered Russian assistance in Madrid to secure the ratification of the treaty negotiated in Washington in 1819 for the annexation of Spanish Florida.[111] Russia was obviously more amenable to American acquisition of Spanish territory than to having it broken up into independent states.

New Pacific Developments

While diplomatic relations between Russia and the United States declined from 1814 to 1820 because of the consular incidents, Dashkov's disgrace, and the vagaries of transatlantic communications, commerce and settlement on Pacific shores continued along haphazard, meandering lines with little control exercised by either government. The Kuskov-Baranov colony at Fort Ross in northern California maintained a tenuous existence against mounting opposition from the local Spanish authorities, who at first had been cooperative. To strengthen the Russian position was the chief goal of another around-the-world expedition, this time headed by Otto Kotzebue, a disciple of Kruzenshtern and another of the Baltic Estonian-Germans who were rapidly achieving fame with their navigational skills and ambition.

The voyage of the *Riurik*, moreover, symbolized the growing naval capability of Russia. It also widened the conflict between the navy and the Russian America Company. Like Golovnin before him, Kotzebue found much to criticize in the company's Alaskan ports where he stopped in 1816 on his way to California. There, in keeping with Russia's official support for legitimacy, he sided with Spanish authorities during negotiations about the Fort Ross colony, agreeing with them, to the consternation of company agents, that the right of settlement should be referred to higher-level Russo-Spanish negotiation.[112] The collapse of Spanish rule came first. Finally, in October 1819, Nesselrode quietly informed Campbell of the existence of a Russian colony on the West Coast.[113]

Kotzebue, in the meantime, sailed on to Honolulu, where he found yet another company venture in progress. Georg Anton von Schaeffer (Sheffer in Russian), a Bavarian surgeon and adventurer, had come to the North Pacific on board a company supply ship at the end of 1814. He had been assigned by Baranov the task of seeking recompense for a company ship that had been stranded in the Sandwich Islands and pillaged by the natives. There he exceeded even the eccentricity and avidity of his master by playing one island king

son, "Russia and the Emancipation of Spanish America, 1816–1826," *Hispanic American Historical Review* 21, 2 (May 1941): 204–9.

[111]Adams, *Memoirs*, 4:373–74.

[112]Barratt, *Russia in Pacific Waters*, pp. 176–84.

[113]Diary entry of 23 October 1819, Campbell Papers, Manuscript Division, LC.

against another and securing favors and lands from all; his main goals were to control the valuable exports of sandalwood and to achieve material or other rewards for expanding Russian jurisdiction in the Pacific. He succeeded briefly in winning the support of King Kamehameha upon his arrival late in 1815 and then secured an even greater influence over Kaumualii on Kauii, promising him the protection of the Russian Empire.

When Kotzebue arrived in November 1816, he found the islands in a state of turmoil with an odd coalition of veteran American ship captains, who used Oahu as a base, and King Kamehameha and his British adviser, John Young, combining against Schaeffer. The latter had long expected the Russian navy to secure his position, but Kotzebue instead made peace with Kamehameha and the Americans, then declared that the islands should remain open ports, but made no effort to straighten out the matter with Schaeffer personally at Kauii. Kotzebue's cooperation with the Americans, coupled with Baranov's disavowal of his agent's mid-Pacific empire scheme, revived Hawaiian opposition to Schaeffer, who was forced to flee the islands in July 1817.[114]

The Hawaiian episode, the navy's meddling in company business, the American ship captains' disregard of Russian jurisdiction, and the retirement and death of Baranov in the summer of 1819 left Russian affairs in the Pacific in a precarious situation. What was most alarming was the growing scarcity of sea otter, the original target of the company's activities in North American waters. Local administrators, left largely to their own devices, continued to seek the practical experience of Americans such as Peter Dobell, who also proposed expansion schemes for Hawaii and was later sent as Russian consul to Manila, and William Pigot, who was engaged to teach modern whaling techniques to the natives.[115] Despite the company's demonstration of some real initiative and effort, none of these projects was really successful.

Russia and the United States Draw Closer

Both countries, in 1820 as in 1812, had more important problems to contend with than whales and sea otter. Even so, the distance between the two countries was becoming much shorter, both physically—as shown by the visit to St. Petersburg of the new American steamship *Savannah* in 1819, after making the first

---

[114]For the full details of this amazing affair, see Bolkhovitinov, *Russko-amerikanskie otnosheniia*, pp. 86–131; and Richard A. Pierce, *Russia's Hawaiian Adventure, 1815–1817* (Kingston, Ont.: Limestone Press, 1976).

[115]Main Office to Baranov, 22 March/3 April 1817, in Raymond H. Fisher, ed., *Records of the Russian-American Company 1802, 1817–1867* (Washington, D.C.: National Archives and Records Service, 1971), p. 22.

transatlantic steamship crossing[116]—and psychologically. Their respective involvement in an age of wars and peaces had produced a much more intimate relationship and understanding. Many Americans, whether for commerce, for adventure, or in order to serve their government, had become familiar with Russia
and passed their knowledge on to others in letters and conversation, for this was
an age of curiosity and of communication. William David Lewis, for example,
wrote long, nearly identical descriptive letters on Russian society and customs to
several influential people in 1816.[117] Representatives of some of the country's
leading families—Adams, Gallatin, Bayard, Poinsett, Dallas, Smith—had been
directly exposed to Russia or Russians. No one could ever accuse John Quincy
Adams as secretary of state, or as president, of being ignorant of Russia.

Despite some additional notoriety in 1818 for becoming too curious about the
dress of a Cherokee chief,[118] Andrei Dashkov confessed to Louisa Catherine Adams upon his departure from Washington that he was "too much of a republican
now to be happy at home" but that he expected changes there along American
lines, to which Mrs. Adams responded from her own experience "that in that
country *they had all to do*" to develop a democracy.[119] And for the more general
public, a captain (or supercargo) who had wintered over at Reval in 1811 published an extended and surprisingly accurate political history of Russia in 1819,
based on manuscripts given to him by August Friedrich Kotzebue, a leading
German romantic writer (and Otto's father) who had relocated in Russia.[120] Certainly both the United States and Russia were receiving more information

[116]Entry of 6/18 September 1819, diary, Campbell papers, Manuscript Division, LC.
The return voyage from St. Petersburg to Savannah in fifty days was considered a technical success—"to use Captain Rodger's own phrase, *neither a screw, bolt, or rope-yarn
parted*, although she experienced very rough weather"—but a financial failure. *National
Intelligencer*, 14 December 1819; see also James P. Delgado, "Steamers to Savannah: The
Origins and Establishment of the New-York and Savannah Steam Navigation Company," *American Neptune* 47, 1 (Winter 1987): 33.

[117]The twenty-page commentary was apparently inspired by Jonathan Russell, then
United States minister to Sweden with whom Lewis carried on an extensive correspondence. Lewis to Russell, 15 August 1816, Russell Papers, John Hay Library, Brown University. A copy presented to Edward Coles was published in *Delaware History* 9 (October 1962): 330–40, and in *The American Image of Russia*, ed. Eugene Anschel (New York:
Frederick Ungar, 1974), pp. 64–77.

[118]J. W. Walker (Oakland, Tenn.) to "Doctor" (Washington), 3 September 1818, Samuel Brown Papers, Filson Club.

[119]L. C. Adams diary, 13 March 1819, Adams Papers, reel 264, MassHS.

[120]*National Intelligencer*, 21 August 1819, and in subsequent issues, concluding 18
September. The identity of the correspondent was not revealed, except that he lived on
a farm not far from Washington. He stated that the manuscript materials were given to
him by Kotzebue when he visited him early in 1811, but nothing of this kind can be
found among the extensive publications of Kotzebue, who was murdered in 1819.

about each other, yet most of it still came from older or secondhand sources, mainly British or German.

As the third minister to Russia, George Washington Campbell, left his post in 1820, everything appeared calm and in good order between the two countries. But the weakening of Spanish power in the Americas and the decline of the Ottoman Empire in the Mediterranean would combine to greatly influence and expand the pace of their diplomatic and commercial relations in the following years.

3

Our Manifest
Destinies

The early 1820s was an active but confused period
in Russian-American relations. Russia, under the now unpredictable leadership
of Alexander I, continued to support the status quo, which meant bolstering
monarchical governments and their colonial extensions against a rising tide of
romantically inspired radical and national oppositions. Meanwhile, the United
States was maturing into a stronger and more confident power. The issues that
were to involve the two countries most directly in the 1820s concerned Spain
and the Russian possessions in America. Above all, Alexander I wanted peace
and order, yet his actions aggravated the problems he aspired to solve.

The American war for independence, the ripple effects of the French Revolution, and the infirmity of Spain after the Napoleonic Wars had led to a number
of rebellions against Spanish authority in the New World. There were fears that
the foremost naval power in the area, Britain, would take advantage of the situation to bolster its position in the Americas and recoup its colonial losses. At the
same time the United States was seeking expansion. In Florida, for example, the
combination of weakened Spanish control, British interference, and Seminole
unrest led to an American military invasion and direct negotiations with Spain.
Alexander hoped to interest the United States in stabilizing Spanish colonial
rule in return for the support of Russia and its continental allies for the ratification of the Onis-Adams Treaty of February 1819, ceding Florida to the United
States.[1] Petr Poletika, the tsar's new minister in Washington, pestered Secretary

---

[1]For the background on Russian policy toward Latin America in the early 1820s, see
especially Russell H. Bartley, *Imperial Russia and the Struggle for Latin American Independence, 1808–1828*, Latin American Monographs, no. 43 (Austin: University of Texas
Press, 1978), pp. 131–44; Ekkehard Völkl, *Russland und Lateinamerika, 1741–1841* (Wiesbaden: Otto Harrassowitz, 1968), pp. 188–221; and Lev Iur'evich Slezkin, *Rossiia i voina
za nezavisimost' v ispanskoi Amerike* (Moscow: Nauka, 1964), pp. 210–56.

of State John Quincy Adams about joining the Holy Alliance and assuming a more conservative role for reestablishing peace and order in the Americas. Adams did not fully trust Poletika's assurances, since reports from Albert Gallatin in France indicated that the Russian minister to Spain, Dmitri Tatishchev, was backing Spain's inclination not to ratify the treaty.[2] With the help of French mediation (or intrigue), however, Tatischchev was recalled by Alexander, who feared that a war between the United States and Spain over Florida might cause irreparable damage to Spanish authority in the rest of America and even provoke a general European war.[3] Spain finally ratified the treaty on 24 October 1820, but since the deadline had expired, the Senate was again called upon for its approval, which it gave in February 1821, two years after the original signing.

The Ghent Arbitration

In the meantime, Britain and the United States were quarreling over interpretations of a provision of the Treaty of Ghent that allowed for restitution of, or compensation for, slaves taken from United States territory at the end of the War of 1812. The United States proposed Russia as the third-party mediator of the dispute, to which Britain felt obliged to agree. Awkwardly, George Washington Campbell was already returning from St. Petersburg, and a new minister had to be appointed to carry out the negotiation. Poletika, to Adams's dismay, suggested Levett Harris again; Henry Clay promoted the candidacy of Jonathan Russell, who had been serving as minister to Sweden; and Richard Rush, the minister in Britain, nominated himself.[4] None of these was acceptable to the secretary of state. With the slave question in mind, Adams suggested to Monroe that Henry Middleton, from a prominent South Carolina planter family, be sent to Russia for the Ghent mediation. The president, however, preferred Joel

[2]Adams, *Memoirs*, 4:446–48, 459; Benjamin Platt Thomas, *Russo-American Relations, 1815–1867*, Johns Hopkins University Studies in Historical and Political Science, vol. 48, no. 2 (Baltimore: Johns Hopkins University Press, 1930), pp. 25–28.

[3]Völkl, *Russland*, pp. 213–14; Bartley, *Imperial Russia*, pp. 135–36; N. N. Bolkhovitinov, *Russko-amerikanskie otnosheniia, 1815–1832* (Moscow: Nauka, 1975), pp. 72–75. In an interview with Campbell in November 1819, Nesselrode expressed considerable concern about United States-Spanish relations: "From his manner as well as from what he said he appeared to feel not only a degree of regret, but some chagrin at the conduct of Spain on this occasion, not unaccompanied with some anxiety for the consequences that might result therefrom;—[he] remarked on the great importance of pursuing peace in the world, and expressed with apparent earnestness his desire to be informed, as soon as I should be advised thereof, the course that my government might take in regard to the business." George Washington Campbell to Albert Gallatin, 7 November 1819, Gallatin Papers, 1820, NYHS. Both Tatishchev's replacement in Spain and Poletika urged upon St. Petersburg the view that events in Spain made colonial independence inevitable. Slezkin, *Rossiia*, pp. 219–20.

[4]Adams, *Memoirs*, 4:401–2, 474–75.

Poinsett, who was also from South Carolina and was known in Russia from his previous visit. Poinsett had Poletika's support as well. Adams was then surprised when Monroe suddenly reversed himself and named Middleton to the office.[5]

Henry Middleton would have the distinction of serving as minister to Russia longer than any other American, perhaps because, unlike most of his predecessors and successors, he had no other serious political ambitions and was able and willing to expend some of his own fortune on his residency. Though he was as novice diplomat, Middleton had served on the House Foreign Relations Committee and had lived several years abroad, mainly in Britain. He also knew Poinsett and had other indirect connections with Russia: William Pinkney was his first cousin, and an uncle had married the daughter of the French sculptor Falconet, who had designed the "Bronze Horseman" statue of Peter the Great for Empress Catherine.[6] Like Adams and Monroe, Jefferson and Gallatin, and Russell and Harris, he belonged to that group of American internationalists who were comfortable and well known in foreign circles.

Passing through London first to discuss details of the slave dispute with Castlereagh, Middleton arrived in St. Petersburg in November 1820, several months after Campbell's departure. Continuity was provided by Charles Pinkney, who had remained as secretary of the legation, and by Abraham Gibson, the New York businessman who had begun a long career as Harris's replacement as consul in 1819. Alexander, unfortunately, was again away from home, this time at the congresses of Troppau and then Laibach for several months, so Middleton could not initiate discussions of the arbitration until after his return in June 1821.[7] In the meantime the Middletons, joined by three daughters, two sons, and a full staff of servants, had settled into the apartments of the wife of Aleksandr Golitsyn, the founder of the Russian Bible Society and an influential, conservative minister of education during these years. They commenced a very active social life in the Russian capital.[8] Mrs. Middleton especially enjoyed the company of Mrs. Speransky, the English-born wife of the reform-minded adviser to the tsar and current governor of Siberia, but she was shocked by certain

[5]Ibid., pp. 474–75, 505. The Adamses and Middletons mixed socially. Mrs. Adams noted in her diary in 1819, "This family is the pleasantest in Washington." Adams Papers, reel 264, MassHS.

[6]Harold E. Berquist, Jr., "Russian-American Relations, 1820–1830: The Diplomacy of Henry Middleton, American Minister at St. Petersburg" (Ph.D. diss., Boston University, 1970), pp. 18–22. Middleton still had qualms about his own suitability, "having little confidence in my fitness in such case on account of my entire ignorance of the language, and little acquaintance with the usages of the nations of the north of Europe," though this deterred few others in this period. To John Quincy Adams, 2 February 1820 (photostat), Henry Middleton Collection, South Caroliniana Library, University of South Carolina.

[7]Berquist, "Russian-American Relations," p. 133.

[8]Ibid., p. 122.

*Henry Middleton, U.S. minister to Russia, 1820–1830. From
the collection of the Middleton Place Foundation, Charleston,
South Carolina*

aspects of Russian behavior: "In regard to the Russians, I believe Mrs. C.
[Campbell] is right—they *appear* polite but they are insincere & as to morality
one would suppose they did not understand the term."[9]

Middleton's diplomatic work was at first confined to the Ghent arbitration.
The argument between the United States and Britain centered on whether the
agreed commitment to compensate for slaves pertained to those taken after the
signing of the Treaty of Ghent or after its ratification, a large number of the disputed slaves having left with British forces in the interval. After Capodistrias's
lengthy conferences with the American and British representatives in St. Petersburg, Alexander accepted the recommendation of his foreign adviser to apply
the clause to the earlier date, that is, in favor of the American position.[10] Other
matters concerning the legitimacy of claims and their amounts were to be referred to a board chaired by the British minister in Washington. Although the
United States was generally pleased by the outcome of the Russian mediation,
another old issue soon revived to disturb the calm in relations between the two
countries.

[9]Mrs. Henry Middleton to Mrs. Henry M. Rutledge, 21 October 1821, Cadwalader
Collection, J. Francis Fisher Section, box 5, HSP.
[10]Berquist, "Russian-American Relations," pp. 160–66.

*The Ukaz of 1821, the Monroe Doctrine, and the Convention
of 1824*

On 16 September 1821, Alexander issued a famous *ukaz*, or edict, regarding the
Russian possessions in America.[11] It had two main points: first, that the territory
under the jurisdiction of the Russian America Company along the northwest
coast extended south to 51° north latitude. This was far south of the main Russian settlement and administrative center at New Archangel (Sitka), located at
57°, but was also considerably north of the new colony at Fort Ross. Of less concern was a similar demarcation to the west along the Aleutian chain. The second important provision was the specific exclusion of foreign ships, not only
from ports and native settlements, but also from all of the coastal region within
this territory and from a zone 100 Italian miles (115 English miles) away from
shore. And by another edict of 25 September, a new charter of the Russian
America Company confirmed its monopoly on fur hunting, fishing, and trading
in this area.[12]

When news of the Russian claims reached the United States in December,
there was an immediate public outcry, especially from New England. William
Sturgis, head of a prominent Boston firm trading in that region, published virulent anti-Russian pieces in local newspapers and in the influential *North American Review*; complaints were then registered in Washington and through Adams
in early 1822 to Poletika, who still did not have direct information from his government on the edicts. Middleton first reported the details of the *ukaz*, and finally Poletika produced an actual copy in February that met with a muted official American protest.[13]

Historians have frequently debated the reasons for and the impact of this re-

[11]The essential parts are quoted in Glynn Barratt, *Russia in Pacific Waters, 1715–1825:
A Survey of Russia's Naval Presence in the North and South Pacific* (Vancouver and London: University of British Columbia Press, 1981), pp. 217–18. For a more complete text,
see *Alaska Boundary Tribunal: The Case of the United States* (Washington, D.C.: Government Printing Office, 1903), app., pp. 25–28; or Basil Dmytryshyn, E. A. P. Crownhart-
Vaughan, and Thomas Vaughan, eds. and trans., *The Russian American Colonies, 1798–
1867: A Documentary Record* [hereafter *RAC*], vol. 3 of *To Siberia and Russian America:
Three Centuries of Russian Eastward Expansion* (Portland: Oregon Historical Society,
1989), pp. 339–51.

[12]*RAC*, pp. 353–66; Glynn Barratt, *Russian Shadows on the British Northwest Coast of
North America, 1810–1890: A Study of Rejection of Defence Responsibilities* (Vancouver:
University of British Columbia Press, 1983), pp. 5–6.

[13]For an emphasis on the American protests, see Howard I. Kushner, *Conflict on the
Northwest Coast: American-Russian Rivalry in the Pacific Northwest, 1790–1867* (Westport,
Conn.: Greenwood Press, 1975), pp. 33–42. Judging from his memoirs, John Quincy
Adams was only mildly disturbed by the anti-Russian publications and would not have
wanted to make an issue of them because of the Ghent arbitration then in progress. He
did, however, dislike Poletika and may have seen this as a way to get rid of him. In St.

markable Russian declaration, since it preceded the Monroe Doctrine by only two years and became involved in its interpretation. Some, especially those writing during the Cold War period, found it to be an obvious example of Russian imperialism.[14] Though Russian America Company officials were increasingly annoyed at American violations of their coastal waters, it is important to place the *ukaz* in its historical context and, therefore, to agree with the more reasoned conclusion of Irby Nichols and Nikolai Bolkhovitinov that it was not intended by the Russian government as an anti-American measure.[15]

The territorial claim should not have appeared unreasonable, considering that the United States had not yet argued for more than a 49° boundary on the North Pacific coast. This line had been agreed upon with Britain in 1818, extending from Minnesota to as far west as the Rocky Mountains. The Oregon Territory beyond was to be open for settlement by both countries but was generally considered limited to below 55°, the line designated as the southern limit of the Russian America Company in the original charter of 1799. However, no colonial settlements actually existed along the coast between the 55° and 51° latitudes. The Russian claim was obviously more antagonistic to the British position in the Northwest, as it would restrict their Pacific access to the area around Vancouver Island, assuming an eventual extension of the 49° boundary with the United States. Americans might have been relieved that the *ukaz* ignored the California colony of the Russians, but the Russian demarcation so far south of their settlements in the Northwest seemed unreasonable to those who were

Petersburg, Capodistrias had little difficulty restraining Middleton from an official audience with Nesselrode on the subject. Bolkhovitinov, *Russko-amerikanskie otnosheniia*, pp. 197–98.

James Madison was one contemporary who decried the alarmist attitude toward both Russia and Britain: "They are certainly both formidable powers at this time, and must always hold a high rank among the nations of Europe. I cannot but think, however, that the future growth of Russia and the stability of the British ascendancy are not a little overrated. Without a civilization of the hordes nominally extending the Russian dominion over so many latitudes and longitudes, they will add little to her real force, if they do not detract from it; and in the event of their civilization, and consequent increase, the overgrown empire, as in so many preceding instances, must fall into separate and independent states." To Richard Rush, 20 November 1821, in *Letters and Other Writings of James Madison* (Philadelphia: J. B. Lippincott, 1867), 3:235–36.

[14]For example, see Thomas A. Bailey, *America Faces Russia: Russian-American Relations from Early Times to Our Day* (Ithaca, N.Y.: Cornell University Press, 1950), pp. 28–33. Bailey's chapter is entitled "The Muscovite Menace." Foster Rhea Dulles, among others, also followed this "hard-line" interpretation in *The Road to Teheran* (Princeton, N.J.: Princeton University Press, 1945).

[15]Irby C. Nichols, Jr., "The Russian Ukase and the Monroe Doctrine: A Reevaluation," *Pacific Historical Review* 36, 1 (February 1967): 13–26; and N. N. Bolkhovitinov, "Russia and the Declaration of the Non-Colonization Principle: New Archival Evidence," trans. Basil Dmytryshyn, *Oregon Historical Quarterly*, 72, 2 (June 1971): 101–26.

already beginning to believe in the inevitability of the acquisition by the United States of all of North America. The Florida annexation treaty, which stipulated a 42° northern boundary for Spanish territory on the West Coast, was thus related, at least psychologically, to ideas of an expanding Pacific territory for the United States and a nonexpanding Russian-Alaska. But the question of an actual boundary line remained confused and unsettled in the absence of clear agreement among the parties concerned.

The extension of maritime jurisdiction to over one hundred miles from the coast was another matter. This was obviously inspired by the directors of the Russian America Company in St. Petersburg. Headed by Adm. Nikolai Mordvinov and other naval officers such as Golovnin, they blamed American poachers and traders for the decline in the company's financial position and the reduction of sea otter stocks, the most important resource of the area.[16] Clearly, by this provision the *ukaz* was directly connected with the renewal of the charter of the company for another twenty years. Alexander, with his mind perhaps on other matters, gave in too readily to company desires, supported as they were by Minister of Finance Dmitri Gur'ev. But he was also following the recommendation of a special committee that included Viktor Kochubei, Mikhail Speransky, and Karl Nesselrode, all of whom were friendly to the United States.[17] Though the maritime claim was made before the opening of coastal whaling and fishing grounds in Alaskan waters, the exaggerated extension was still an affront to the doctrine of freedom of the seas, which Alexander had often supported and which he knew was a sensitive issue to the United States.

That the *ukaz* and especially this latter provision were aimed consciously at the United States was certainly not the intention of the tsar and his foreign policy advisers, for it could easily have had the result of bringing the United States and Britain together against Russia, hardly a Russian objective. The Russian government never publicly acknowledged an error, but it did quickly retreat from the *ukaz*, providing follow-up orders to the squadron sent to enforce it to restrict its activities to the immediate coast north of the 55° north latitude. To satisfy the logical objection that ships were on their way to the area without knowledge of the new law, it was made effective only for those American ships leaving port after 1 July 1822, or, in practice, not until the beginning of 1823. And Nesselrode spoke vaguely of the restricted distance from shore being only a "cannon shot."[18] Moreover, the colonial administrators could not tolerate having their chief source of supplies suddenly cut off and simply ignored their new

[16]Kushner, *Conflict on the Northwest Coast*, pp. 31–34; Anatole G. Mazour, "The Russian-American and Anglo-Russian Conventions, 1824–1825: An Interpretation," *Pacific Historical Review* 14, 3 (September 1945): 303–5.

[17]Bolkhovitinov, *Russko-amerikanskie otnosheniia*, pp. 163–67.

[18]Ibid., pp. 181–82.

instructions, so the *ukaz* was never really put into force before it was replaced by conventions with the United States and Great Britain in 1824 and 1825, respectively. To rectify the damage that may have been caused to Russian-American friendship, a new minister was dispatched to replace Poletika—Baron Diderick Tuyll van Serooskerken, who had earlier been designated for the Washington post but had gone to Brazil instead.[19]

Even more disturbing to American policymakers than possible encroachments in the distant Northwest was the situation of Spain and its disintegrating American empire. Russia, as the leader of the Holy Alliance, fully supported the French intervention against the revolution in Spain that began early in 1820, an action opposed by Britain. The Spanish monarchy was successfully restored by the summer of 1823, but the interval of disorder in Spain had weakened its authority even more in the colonies and confused ideological issues. The result was the rapid growth of newly independent states plagued by unstable and contesting political factions. Russia dreaded these developments for the reasons embodied in the principles of the Holy Alliance, but especially because they threatened the restoration and strengthening of the Spanish throne and because Alexander had a deepening aversion to chaotic and unpredictable situations. But partly in response to the existence of these new governments, the United States followed an opposite course—recognition of the nascent Latin American states—once its own annexation of Florida was secured.[20]

Though the northwest *ukaz* gave some contemporaries, as well as a few later historians, the impression of a two-front Russian assault on the Americas, most of the United States' attention was directed toward the south. It was feared that Spain and its European supporters might try to reassert control there or, perhaps worse, that Britain would move in to preempt such a possibility.[21] Britain

[19]Ibid., pp. 194–96.

[20]Bartley, *Imperial Russia*, p. 143; William Spence Robertson, "Russia and the Emancipation of Spanish America, 1816–1826," *Hispanic American Historical Review* 21, 2 (May 1941): 209–12; and for the relatively mild Russian reaction, see Middleton to Adams, 8/20 July 1822, in William R. Manning, ed., *Diplomatic Correspondence of the United States concerning the Independence of the Latin-American Nations*, vol. 3 (New York: Oxford University Press, 1925), pp. 1866–67. Valuable documentary evidence is provided in "Correspondence of the Russian Ministers in Washington, 1818–1825, Part 2," *American Historical Review* 18, 3 (April 1913): 537–62.

[21]Monroe may also have been influenced by a letter from his special emissary to Europe, George W. Erving, who, in referring to a joint Russian-French-Spanish effort to recover the Spanish colonies, noted: "I am, now more than ever, seriously apprehensive that great trouble will grow out of it,—for nobody 'loves us,'—no, not even the Emperor of Russia, whom we have so incessantly flattered.—And an alliance with G. Britain for this, or any other purpose!—that is most to be dreaded." Erving to Monroe, 23 September 1823, quoted in Stanislaus Murray Hamilton, ed. *The Writings of James Monroe* (New York and London: G. P. Putnam's, 1901), 5:303 n. 1. Adams, however, argued

attempted to obtain American backing for a bilateral declaration opposing European intervention, a project supported by John C. Calhoun, but Adams and Monroe preferred an independent statement, which was embodied in the text of the president's annual message to Congress on 2 December 1823. This outlined the principle of noncolonization—that no further extension of a European power should be allowed in the Western Hemisphere (the Monroe Doctrine).[22] Adams, supported by Gallatin, managed to remove passages from Monroe's draft that would have been especially offensive to monarchical powers such as Russia, but he approved the assertion of noncolonization as an instrument to be used in his ongoing negotiations with both Britain and Russia. However, Adams did not conceive it to be particularly anti-Russian, nor could it have been inspired mainly by the Russian *ukaz*. Although the northwest issue was cited in connection with the declaration of noncolonization (paragraph 7), the context of the other relevant paragraphs (48 and 49) was clearly Latin American.[23]

Adams also wrote Tuyll directly in the same vein but was obviously quite sensible of the additional leverage the statement gave him in resolving the issues of the northwest American coast, since he already knew of the Russian desire to appease American interests with a new agreement. Nor does evidence really support the contention of some historians that the doctrine was the result of a rising spirit of imperialism in the United States, except in a very loose and general sense of symbolizing a growing confidence and diplomatic strength.[24] It placed the United States first among, and as protector of, an increasing number of in-

against overreaction: "I observed to the President that I put very little reliance on anything written by G. W. Erving. It might or might not eventuate as he said; but he knew nothing about the matter more than was known to the world, and had views of his own in whatever he wrote." *Memoirs*, 6:196.

[22]The complete text can be found in *Annals of Congress*, 18th Cong., 1st sess., pp. 12–24. The most important part of the doctrine comes near the end of the message, in the middle of a paragraph that begins with a reference to Spain and Portugal: "We owe it, therefore, to candor, and to the amicable relations existing between the United States and those powers, to declare that we should consider any attempt on their part to extend their system to any portion of this hemisphere as dangerous to our peace and safety. With the existing colonies or dependencies of any European power we have not interfered and shall not interfere. But with the Governments who have declared their independence, we have, on great consideration and on just principle, acknowledged, we could not view any interposition for the purpose of oppressing them, or constraining in any other matter their destiny, by any European power, in any other light than as the manifestation of an unfriendly disposition toward the United States."

[23]George Canning, in order to cover his own policy failures, was one of the first to claim that the Monroe Doctrine was directed against Russia, and this interpretation for years was mainly a British one.

[24]Bolkhovitinov cites especially commercial interest in Latin America, but the United States, both then and later, benefited greatly from open trade with *Spanish* colonies. *Russko-amerikanskie otnosheniia*, p. 220. A recent new appraisal by Ernest R. May, *The Making of the Monroe Doctrine* (Cambridge, Mass., and London: Harvard University

dependent American states and was not in direct opposition to Russian interests, as long as Russia's prior position in the Pacific Northwest was duly recognized.

During this period of intensive political activity in Washington, John Quincy Adams met with the Russian and British ministers on almost a daily basis. Baron Tuyll had finally arrived in April 1823, and the secretary of state apparently liked him much better than his predecessors. However, the main negotiation for the settlement of the northwest problems took place in St. Petersburg between Middleton and, oddly enough, Petr Poletika, who owed his role to the absence of Nesselrode and the resignation of Capodistrias in a dispute over Russia's Greek policy. A joint Anglo-American presentation to the Russian government was first considered, but the American proposals were cast in such a way as to provoke Prime Minister George Canning's rejection. The British saw that removal of trade restrictions was foremost on the American agenda and that "their" boundary concerns might be sacrificed to attain open seas and ports. Anyway, Adams naturally preferred a separate, rather than joint, resolution of the matter.[25]

Middleton now had another important task to perform. Whereas in 1821 the views of the tsar's foreign advisers were secondary to those of the Russian America Company and the naval ministry, the situation was now reversed. American protests over Russian policies in both the Pacific arena and in Spanish America, as well as Monroe's message, no doubt influenced the granting of extraordinary concessions by the Russian government in the Convention of 1824 that was signed in April, after the exchange of a number of drafts.[26] The new agreement effectively abolished the *ukaz* and opened the ports and coasts of the Russian Pacific to American ships. After much discussion, the boundary of the Russian "possessions" in the Northwest was withdrawn to 54°40' north latitude (later to become a battle cry of American political history), the 55° boundary of the 1799 charter being adjusted to miss the southern point of Prince of Wales Island.[27] Alexander I, who by this time was often ill and depressed and spent much of his

Press, 1975) explains the doctrine in terms of domestic politics, especially Adams's quest for the presidency. I find this an interesting but not totally convincing effort to extend modern interpretations of recent foreign policy into an earlier age. Adams and Monroe were rooted in eighteenth-century diplomatic gamesmanship.

[25]Irby C. Nichols, Jr., and Richard A. Ward, "Anglo-American Relations and the Russian Ukase: A Reassessment," *Pacific Historical Review* 41, 4 (November 1972): 447–48, 453–56.

[26]The drafts and correspondence relating to them are in *Alaska Boundary Tribunal*, app., pp. 31–93.

[27]Kushner, *Conflict on the Northwest Coast*, pp. 58–61; Barratt, *Russian Shadows*, pp. 15–17. The Russian tendency to favor the United States on Pacific questions may have been influenced not only by the dependency on American shipping but also by the fact that Americans, especially Peter Dobell and Thomas Barton, performed important roles

time away from the capital and administrative affairs, dutifully followed his foreign advisers' desire to preserve warm relations with the United States. But in return Russia gained two points, the most important of which was a firm recognition of Russia's rights in the Northwest (if not in California). The other was the
American admission, left to be enforced, that trading of firearms, ammunition,
and alcohol to the natives was to be forbidden. The section of the agreement
that conceded the most was limited to a ten-year period, upon Middleton's initiative, to make the open trade provision more acceptable to Russia.

The Russian attitude toward foreign traders in the Pacific Northwest cannot
be fully understood without an examination of population dynamics. By 1825
the Russian America Company had managed to hire and settle only about five
hundred Russians in the new, far-flung colony, mainly on Kodiak and at Sitka.
It therefore relied heavily on native Indian tribes for manpower to hunt and to
man boats and coastal stations. Two of the tribes, the Aleuts and Kodiaks, were
fairly easily controlled and exploited initially because of their island locations,
but they were soon decimated by European diseases and the harsh conditions of
their forced labor. A third tribe, the Tlingits, were more independent and
harder to control but also strategically important because they inhabited the
area around the main administrative center at Sitka. These Indians had been
much more successful than the others in acquiring arms, mainly from American
ships, and thus in resisting full Russian subjugation at the very time that the colonial administration needed to employ more of them to maintain its fur supplies. Complicating the situation was the fact that most of the Russian settlers
were male and they bought wives from the Indians, resulting in a native creole
population that by 1822 exceeded the number of Russians and was generally
more dependent than the Indians on the Russian administration.[28] The Russian
navy was the source of temporary skilled navigators, more reliable ships and
communications, and an armed force, while serving its own purposes of achiev-

as employees of the Russian America Company. Some later Soviet historians would
view this as the result of deliberate American imperialism. See N. A. Khalfin and A. A.
Muradian, *Ianki na Vostoke v XIX veke, ili kolonializm bez imperii* (Moscow: Mysl', 1966),
and A. L. Narochnitskii, "Ekspansiia SSha na Dal'nem Vostoke v 50–70-e gody XIX
veka," *Istoricheskie Zapiski* (Moscow) 44 (1953): 130–76.

[28]For an excellent, scholarly study of the Alaskan population under Russian administration, see Svetlana G. Fedorova, *Russkoe naselenie Aliaski i Kalifornii: Konets XVIII
veka–1867 g.* (Moscow: Nauka, 1971). The total Indian population, including a few hundred Eskimos on the north and west coasts, was probably not more than ten thousand
in the 1820s, though contemporary western gazetteers and encyclopedias usually
guessed at over fifty thousand. While Indians subsequently declined in population, creole numbers grew, thus stabilizing the population of Alaska at around twelve thousand
for most of the nineteenth century. See also James Gibson, "Russian Dependence on
the Natives of Alaska," *Russia's American Colony*, ed. S. Frederick Starr (Durham N.C.:
Duke University Press, 1987), pp. 77–104.

ing exploration bases, gaining practical experience for seamen and officers, and, not least in importance, expanding its Pacific presence.

Thus, the terms of the convention predictably upset the Russian naval establishment, the Russian America Company directors, and their bureaucratic partisans, some even predicting the early demise of the company. Their vociferous complaints prompted an attempt to modify the document so that the trading rights would not apply to the Siberian coast, the Aleutian Islands, or the northwest coast above 57°. In a conversation with Tuyll in December, Adams noted that concessions had been made on both sides, that such a change would involve renegotiating the convention, and that it was probably best not to plant ideas in the minds of the American merchants by drawing attention to a region they rarely visited. Tuyll, who was already concerned about the Senate's ratification, quickly dropped the matter with the consolation that these rights would expire and have to be renegotiated after ten years. The Russian fears that there might be problems in the adoption of the convention proved false, and the Senate approved it in January 1825, with one dissenting vote. Ratifications were exchanged the following November—and the first "treaty" between the United States and Russia thus came into force.[29] The United States obviously gained considerably, but Russia had leverage to use in her negotiations with Britain over their common boundary. Arguing the case for a demarcation farther to the north, 59° or 57°, the British minister in St. Petersburg finally had to settle for the 54°40′ line for the Russian Northwest and an eastern border that kept Russia out of the strategic McKenzie River area.[30]

But what about California? The Fort Ross settlement was not discussed in any of these negotiations—and for good reason. Neither the United States nor Britain wanted to recognize a *Russian* outpost that far south (38°) along the coast. Besides, Russia had no legal claim to "possession," since the site was only leased from Spain, whose New World position Russia was endeavoring to strengthen. The future of California, however, was very much in doubt at the time the *ukaz* was issued and while the conventions were being negotiated in St. Petersburg.

Fort Ross's original *raison d'être* was as a base for hunting sea otter along the California coast. With the stock of these animals sharply reduced in number by the 1820s, the colony shifted toward agricultural pursuits, with a goal of providing supplies of food for the settlements in the Northwest more cheaply and effi-

[29]Adams, *Memoirs*, 6:435–37; Berquist, "Russian-American Relations," pp. 410–13; Tuyll to Nesselrode, 17/29 November 1825, *Vneshniaia politika Rossii XIX i nachala XX veka: Dokumenty Rossiiskogo ministerstva inostrannykh del*, ser. 2, vol. 6 (Moscow: Nauka, 1985), pp. 21–27.

[30]*Alaska Boundary Tribunal*, pp. 40–63; *RAC*, pp. 383–86; Nichols and Ward, "Anglo-American Relations," pp. 451–53; and Mazour, "The Russian-American and Anglo-Russian Conventions," pp. 308–9.

ciently. The location on high ground along a barren coast was far from ideal for this purpose, so farms were soon established to the south along the Slavianskii (now Russian) River and at nearby Bodega Bay, which also provided a more suitable anchorage for ships. A rare insight into the conditions of the Russian colony was provided by a Boston visitor of 1832. He found Fort Ross at that time, if not thriving, at least doing a respectable job of furnishing foodstuffs, and he described substantial but weather-beaten buildings, four hundred acres of wheat, and twelve hundred head of cattle. "Eggs, butter, and milk, may be purchased in abundance cheaply," he reported.[31]

California, in the meantime, became part of the newly independent state of Mexico in 1822, although its remote location and the weakness of the central government gave it considerable autonomy. Mexican-California authorities grudgingly, but not formally, recognized the Russian rights that had been secured from Spain, since they were in no position to challenge them and since they saw some advantage in prospects for expanded trade with the northern power.

As did many early visitors to this region, some Russians also saw a great future for California—under Russian rule. A young naval officer, Dmitri Zavalishin, returned to St. Petersburg in 1824 from a voyage that had included a visit to Fort Ross with a scheme for Russian expansion in that area. Extolling the merits of the riches and climate of northern California, Zavalishin proposed that the Russian America Company take possession of the whole area from the 42° north latitude to the south beyond San Francisco Bay.[32] This plan was supported by admirals Kruzenshtern and Mordvinov, but Zavalishin was also interested in liberal reform and became enmeshed in the secret Northern Society's premature attempt to take control of the government in December 1825. His arrest and Siberian exile cut short his promotion of Russian control over northern California.[33] It is very doubtful that anything would have come of it in any event, for Russian territorial expansion would have challenged not only the Monroe Doc-

---

[31]*National Intelligencer*, 21 May 1833. The "Bostonian," who was making his second visit to the area, also noted that the community of three hundred inhabitants was in dire need of tea and sugar but had no money to buy them. For a scholarly analysis of the Russian effort to supply Alaska from California, see James R. Gibson, *Imperial Russia in Frontier America: The Changing Geography of Supply of Russian America, 1784–1867* (New York: Oxford University Press, 1976), pp. 112–39.

[32]Bolkhovitinov, *Russko-amerikanskie otnosheniia*, pp. 294–98; Völkl, *Russland*, pp. 134–37.

[33]Zavalishin resumed his campaign for a Russian California many years later when he led an almost solo campaign against Murav'ev-Amurskii's policy of colonization of the Amur provinces and the sale of Alaska. Anatole G. Mazour, *The First Russian Revolution, 1825* (1937; reprint, Stanford, Calif.: Stanford University Press, 1961), pp. 249–52.

trine but also the Mexican and American ranches and missions that had already encircled San Francisco Bay and moved north to Sonoma.

Russia, the United States, and Spanish America

The real concern of the United States was not in the West or Northwest but to the south, where Cuba and Puerto Rico, among the last commercially significant Spanish colonies in the New World, were being threatened by a joint invasion from Colombia and Mexico. A sizable French fleet had also appeared on station at Martinique for a possible counterattack on behalf of Spain.[34] These moves raised fears in the United States—in the South about possible imitations of the successful slave revolt on Haiti, and in the North about the disruption and perhaps destruction of the important and lucrative trade with the Spanish West Indies. Lacking any real leverage in Madrid, Henry Clay, as secretary of state in John Quincy Adams's administration, attempted through Tuyll in Washington and Middleton in St. Petersburg to win Russian support for a plan that would acknowledge Spanish control over their Caribbean islands in return for a cessation of hostilities and even recognition of the other newly independent, former Spanish colonies.[35]

The diplomatic initiatives that began in May and June 1825 continued with little progress for over two years because of Spanish reluctance to accept these conditions and Russian hesitation about reversing its policy of nonrecognition. Russian Ambassador Peter d'Oubril was sensitive about pressuring the Spanish government, and Russian diplomacy in Spain was further weakened by the death of Alexander I and the turmoil that followed it. Nevertheless, with the American success in delaying the planned invasion and with Nesselrode's new assertiveness in the summer of 1826, Spain and France were reluctantly pushed by Russia toward an essentially defensive posture, if not all the way to concrete recognition. This effectively preserved the rump of a colonial Spanish empire in the West Indies.[36] John Quincy Adams had also appointed his old "Russian" protégé, Alexander Hill Everett, as minister to Spain in order to strengthen Russian-American cooperation. That favorite stepchild of Tsar Alexander, the Holy Alliance, and the policy of international scope that it sustained were now discarded by Nicholas I, whose thoughts were more and more focused on improving the security of his throne and in a foreign policy narrowed to the Ottoman Empire and traditional Russian goals. On its part, the United States sacri-

[34]Thomas, *Russo-American Relations*, pp. 51–55.
[35]Bolkhovitinov, *Russko-amerikanskie otnosheniia*, pp. 310–19.
[36]Ibid., pp. 321–55; Berquist, "Russian-American Relations," pp. 417–45. Bolkhovitinov's discussion of Russian-American cooperation over Cuba and Puerto Rico is especially well done.

ficed a radical interpretation of the Monroe Doctrine and prestige in the independent republics of Latin America for the retention of Spanish colonies that provided stable, conservative buffers and commercial profits to the south of Florida.

Russia, too, had objectives in Latin America that were distinct from Spanish affairs. Brazil had long been a target for expansion of direct trade with Russia in colonial products. While Rio de Janeiro was the seat of the Portuguese government during Iberian unrest, a high-level Russian diplomatic mission was maintained there, at least equal to that sent to the United States. Tuyll, whose tour of duty in Brazil came between his original appointment to Washington and his actual tenure there, left in May 1821, when Brazil became independent. That country by this time had become the second leading trading partner of Russia in the Americas and an important way-station on the journey to the Pacific Northwest; thus a consulate was established in Rio, headed by German-born scientist and explorer Georg Heinrich von Langsdorff. Langsdorff had been with the Rezanov-Kruzenshtern expedition and had become friends with "Northwest" John D'Wolf. His ambitious plans for the development and exploration of the vast interior of South America in the 1820s were supported by both the Russian and Brazilian governments. Finally, in keeping with the more practical approaches to foreign policy under Nicholas I, Russia recognized Brazilian independence at the end of 1825, though it was not until 1828 that full diplomatic relations were established. Throughout the period, direct trade between Russia and South America continued but on a very modest level.[37]

Another new Latin state that attracted Russian attention was Haiti. Zavalishin, who had not confined his expansionist dreams to California, advocated in 1825 that the Russian America Company establish a base there, similar to Fort Ross, for trade and as support for a more direct route through Central America to the North Pacific.[38] As might be expected, this suggestion received active encouragement from Russian naval authorities in the Baltic who were enamored of the idea of cruises to West Indian naval bases. An ideological concern about sanctioning the Haitian revolution was mitigated by the fact that Russia's continental ally, France, had already recognized the independence of Haiti. However, Zavalishin's fate, the "disfavor" shown toward the Russian America Company after 1824, and Nicholas's interests elsewhere relegated Haiti to the lowest priority.

The growing accord in Russian-American relations during the reign of Nicholas I (1825–55) and in the administrations of John Quincy Adams (1825–29) and Andrew Jackson (1829–37) was also evident in the eastern Mediterranean,

[37]Bartley, *Imperial Russia*, pp. 144–55; *Alta California*, 14 May 1858.
[38]Bolkhovitinov, *Russko-amerikanskie otnosheniia*, pp. 300–303.

where common hostility toward the Ottoman Empire nurtured limited support from both countries for the cause of Greek independence. The Turks indeed had few friends at this time, and the joint French-British-Russian destruction of Turkish naval power in 1827 at Navarino (along the Greek coast) was welcomed almost everywhere. The Russo-Turkish War of 1828–29 that followed, however, revived British fears of a Russian threat to its naval and commercial position in the Middle East and South Asia. The United States was quick to take advantage of the situation by negotiating—with Russian assistance secured by Middleton—a commercial treaty with the defeated Turks in April and May 1830. Russia also helped the United States obtain access to the Black Sea and to another point of entry to the Russian Empire, one that had been briefly developed during the Napoleonic Wars but effectually cut off since 1815. Albert Rhind, one of the negotiators of the Turkish treaty, was formally designated consul for the port of Odessa, but after a brief visit he left his duties in the hands of a prominent local merchant of Greek (Sciote) background, John Ralli.[39]

Changing Missions

By this time Middleton's mission to Russia, which originally was confined to the slave compensation issue, had grown to include the four corners of the world. Unlike the subsequent decades, this was a period of constancy in American diplomatic representation in Russia, although Russian ministers in Washington were frequently changed. After Tuyll's departure in 1825 with the ratified 1824 convention, Baron Apollon Maltits served for over a year as chargé d'affaires. In 1828 yet another "Russian" diplomat of foreign origin arrived—Paul Krudener, the son of the celebrated Madam Krudener who is credited with giving Alexander I the idea of the Holy Alliance. Krudener, though hard of hearing and withdrawn, was highly respected both in Russia and the United States for fostering the accord and bridging relations to the Jacksonian democrats.[40]

Middleton's unusually long tenure in St. Petersburg had led to accusations from president Adams's political opponents that he was a toady to autocracy. There was at least some truth to this. He led the life of a Southern planter in the Baltic metropolis, and with grown sons and daughters, the Middletons cut a notable swath through the congenial court society of the Russian capital. Henry

[39]Ibid., pp. 375–87; Charles Rhind to Department of State, 30 May 1831, DUSC, Odessa, vol. 1 (roll 1, M 459), RG 59, NA; Rhind to John Randolph, 20 September 1830, Diplomatic Post Records (hereafter cited as DPR), Russia, Various Documents Received—Randolph-Clay, vol. 4332, RG 84, NA. The DPR collection contains the materials on file at the various diplomatic posts abroad and is very important for both official and unofficial correspondence of a private and interagency nature.

[40]Francis Ley, *La Russie, Paul de Krüdener et les soulèvements nationaux, 1814–1858 (d'après de nombreux documents inédits)* (Paris: Hachette, 1971), pp. 83–88.

Middleton was the first American representative to attend an imperial funeral and to witness the coronation of a new tsar. For the latter ceremony, he traveled to Moscow in the summer of 1826, leaving his family behind—to one daughter's particular regret. Neither the American government nor even Middleton was willing to pay their expenses.[41]

Apparently bearing in mind the charges against Middleton, Adams appointed Beaufort T. Watts as secretary of legation in 1828. Though also from a wealthy South Carolina family, Watts disliked Middleton's haughty and reclusive demeanor; Middleton, on his part, considered Watts a spy sent by Adams and resented his attempted interference with his diplomatic style. Snubbed socially by Middleton, Watts was also primed by disgruntled merchants such as John D. Lewis, who provided him with reports of Middleton's alleged licentious behavior and use of a calling card with the ostentatious label "Monsieur de Middleton." The secretary returned to the United States to file formal complaints against the minister with Martin Van Buren and Secretary of State Henry Clay.[42] This publicity about luxurious diplomatic living abroad may have damaged the reputation of the Adams administration, but it probably played a very small part, if any, in the failure of his bid for reelection.

The Middletons, obviously, confined their social activities to court and diplomatic functions and, unlike Adams and Pinkney, spurned American merchants and ship captains. Although they were suitably hospitable to special couriers Christopher Hughes and Edward Wyer and visiting American "nobility" such as the socially prominent Van Rensselaers of Albany, they probably had nothing to do with another resident American family of a much different background. Nero Prince, one of the founders of an African Masonic lodge in Boston, had arrived in Russia as the steward of Theodore Staneward in 1810 and then joined the staff of the imperial household, which already included about twenty other black servants, mostly of American origin. Returning home to Massachusetts in 1823 after the death of his wife, he brought back to Russia the next year a second wife, Nancy Gardener, of mixed Indian-black descent, from Salem.[43] The Princes settled first at Kronstadt but were forced to move by the great flood of 1824. Mrs. Prince then began a successful business, furnishing baby linens and children's garments to the imperial family and other elite cus-

[41]Maria Middleton to unknown, 10 August 1826, Cadwalader Collection, box 8, HSP, expressing her disappointment that "our *most stingy* . . . government will not pay our expenses to go there and behave like decent people."

[42]Berquist, "Russian-American Relations," pp. 663–74; Beaufort T. Watts (Washington) to Martin Van Buren, 28 December 1829 and 1 March 1830, Watts Papers, South Caroliniana Library, University of South Carolina.

[43]Allison Blakely, *Russia and the Negro: Blacks in Russian History and Thought* (Washington, D.C.: Howard University Press, 1986), pp. 16–18; Mrs. Nancy Prince, *Narrative of the Life and Travels of* (Boston: by author, 1850), pp. 14–18.

tomers, for which she employed several apprentices and learned both Russian and French. She was also active in the Anglo-American religious community, helping with relief and Bible distribution. She returned to Massachusetts in 1833 for health reasons, and her husband died in St. Petersburg in 1836.[44] Nancy Prince subsequently became a leader in the New England antislavery movement and founded an orphanage in Boston modeled on ones she had seen in Russia.[45]

Another American of note in Russia was Thomas Munroe, who was from a prominent and original Washington family. His father had served as first postmaster for thirty years and as superintendent of the capital city, running unsuccessfully for mayor a couple of times, and was a charter member of the Washington National Monument Board.[46] The son came to Russia in 1822 to seek a military career, attaining the rank of colonel in the imperial army and serving during the Turkish war as aide-de-camp to the tsar while he conducted an important peace mission to Constantinople. Munroe died tragically at Nikolaev on the Black Sea in August 1834.[47] His service reflected yet another aspect of the heightened closeness between Russia and the United States because he was very well regarded by fellow officers and the imperial family.[48] Munroe also led an ac-

---

[44]Prince, *Narrative*, pp. 33–81. On her husband's death, see Gibson to Forsyth, 12/24 September 1836, DUSC, St. Petersburg, vol. 3 (roll 3, M 81), RG 59, NA. Less is known about another American woman, Caroline Harrison, who came to Russia before 1820 as the nurse for George Washington Campbell's children and stayed for over forty years as a governess for noble families in the Moscow area.

[45]Prince, *Narrative*. After working in Boston a while, Nancy Prince became disillusioned and emigrated to Jamaica, where she worked as a Baptist missionary. Ill and destitute, she moved once more to New York in 1843, where she was befriended in her last years by the daughter of her husband's original employer.

[46]Wilhelmus Bogart Bryan, *A History of the National Capital from its Foundations through the Period of the Adoption of the Organic Act*, vol. 1: 1790–1814 (New York: Macmillan, 1914), pp. 345–46; vol. 2: 1815–1878 (New York: Macmillan, 1916), pp. 34, 165, 224.

[47]John Ralli (Odessa) to John Randolph Clay (St. Petersburg), 3/15 September and 28 September/10 October 1834, DPR, Russia, Randolph-Clay 1830–36, vol. 4332, RG 84, NA.

[48]John Lloyd Stephens traveled through Odessa shortly after Munroe's death: "At the time of the invasion of Turkey by the Egyptians under Ibrahim Pacha, Mr. Munroe held the rank of colonel in the army sent to the aid of the sultan. While the Russians were encamped at the foot of the Giant's mountain, he visited Constantinople and became acquainted with the American missionaries, who all spoke of him in the highest terms. He was a tall, well-made man, carried himself with a military air, and looked admirably well in Russian uniform. On the withdrawal of the Russians from the Black Sea, Mr. Munroe was left in some important charge at Nicolaif, where he died in the opening of a brilliant career. I heard of him all over Russia, particularly from officers of the army; and being often asked if I knew him, regretted to be obliged to answer no. But, though personally unacquainted, as an American I was gratified with the name he

tive social life, if one can judge from the care the American consul took in returning a bundle of letters written to him by Princess Natalia Golitsyna.[49]

Also still living in the south of Russia was the Napoleonic Wars' volunteer from the United States, George Sontag. By 1830 he held general rank and was an assistant to the capable and progressive governor-general of "New Russia," Mikhail Vorontsov (Winfield Scott's old friend), even serving as acting governor in his absences. Sontag and his Russian wife—who was reputedly a successful writer from a wealthy Moscow family—and their daughter lived on an estate near Odessa, where by 1835 he had established a farm with an American-style dairy barn and a vineyard of six thousand vines that produced high-quality wines. As one American noted after visiting Sontag's estate that year: "Yankee-like, he was very practical, and bestowed great attention on the cultivation of his large tract of land. I had seen no tillage like it in Russia. It was considered a model farm of that region, and famous for its produce of all kinds. He had just erected a dairy on the American plan, and visitors came daily to inspect it."[50] One can only conjecture what influence this may have had on the many Russian, Ukrainian, and foreign colonists who had recently settled in the area around the Black Sea. At least American enterprise was becoming known in Russia—and not just by the printed word.

had left behind him." *Incidents of Travel in Greece, Turkey, Russia and Poland*, 2 vols. (New York: Harper & Bros., 1838), 2:11–12.

[49]John Randolph Clay (St. Petersburg) to John Ralli (Odessa), 5/17 November 1834, and Ralli to Clay, 4/16 January 1835, DPR, Russia, Randolph-Clay 1830–36, vol. 4332, RG 84, NA. Other papers and effects, forwarded to the family in Washington, have apparently been lost.

[50]Henry Wikoff, *The Reminiscences of an Idler* (New York: Fords, Howard & Hulbert, 1880), pp. 235–36. Wikoff also recounted listening to Sontag's daughter play "Yankee Doodle" and "Hail, Columbia" on the piano while he and her father reminisced about their native Philadelphia. Wikoff's account is supported by the manuscript diary of his traveling companion, Edwin Forrest, in the Pusey Theatre Library, Harvard University, though several pages are missing for these dates. John Lloyd Stephens reported listening to the same tunes at the Sontags' home that year—and being shocked to find an American possessing "*white* slaves." *Incidents of Travel*, 1:264.

Another itinerant American named Codman, perhaps related to the Ropes family, was visiting in Odessa in 1840. Vincent Nolte, *Fifty Years in Both Hemispheres: Reminiscences of the Life of a Former Merchant* (New York: Redfield, 1854), p. 454. Two other wandering Americans might also be mentioned, though relatively little precise information is known about their activities. Both had gained entry into Russian service through Russia's Far Eastern expansion. Peter Dobell was an early nineteenth-century traveler and adventurer who by the 1820s had performed special missions to China and had served briefly as Russian consul in the Philippines. Thomas Barton began work for the Russian America Company in Sitka and Siberia in 1832, perhaps earlier, then settled with his Russian family in the vicinity of St. Petersburg in the 1840s. John Randolph Clay to James Buchanan, 10/22 August 1847, DUSM, Russia, vol. 15 (roll 15, M 35), RG 59, NA.

The Continuing Importance of Trade

The principal Russian-American activity of this period was trade. American ships continued to sail through the Baltic to the port complex of Kronstadt-St. Petersburg, although their numbers never approached that of the unusual and distorted period between 1809 and 1812 when British ships were excluded. About fifty-five to ninety American vessels each year were now involved in the Russian trade, but this represented only a small percentage of the total number of ships arriving at the chief Russian Baltic ports. In 1825, for example, out of 3,903 vessels officially recorded as entering Petersburg port, only 81 were American, about 2 percent. This figure is deceptive, however, since many of the others were smaller Baltic coastal vessels; in fact, these 81 American flagships exceeded the total tonnage of the 211 Swedish ships arriving at Kronstadt that year.[51] A better indication of the volume of American shipping is that it constituted around 10 percent of the total value of foreign goods imported into Russia by sea.

Relative importance is further obscured by the nature of the trade and flaws in the recordkeeping. Iron, for example, was a major Russian export to the United States, consuming 29 percent of the total Russian iron shipments, but much of it entered American ports as ballast to avoid high tariffs. The bulk of the goods brought to Russia on American ships originated outside the United States in the West Indies, while Russian products in this lucrative triangular trade could also end up in the West Indies, after passing through New England ports unrecorded. Many items actually from the United States were shipped to British or continental ports and then reexported to Russia by vessels of other nations, or, in the case of tobacco, carried overland across Germany. Some ships were handled by intermediaries and would leave or enter with false or misleading destinations or points of origin recorded in the customs records.[52] This, too, was a time of corrupt officials, especially in Russia, where a comfortable existence depended on commissions, fees, duties, and bribes and many items going and coming "off the books" or as "captain's privilege."

The exports from Russia to the United States were generally more direct, and the figures, therefore, comparatively more reliable. Still heading the list in value was linen cloth of various kinds—sailcloth, ravensduck (coarse canvas), diaper, and flems—with 90 percent of American linen imports coming from Russia.

---

[51]Bolkhovitinov, *Russko-amerikanskie otnosheniia*, pp. 365–66.

[52]For an excellent discussion of the problems in dealing with the statistical records, see Walther Kirchner, *Studies in Russian-American Commerce, 1820–1860* (Leiden: E. J. Brill, 1975). For a specific example, a note in the shipping records of William Appleman and Company shows a cargo of cotton on the *Ceylon* clearing from New Orleans for Liverpool, but actually going all the way to St. Petersburg. Dexter Papers, Appleman and Company, vol. 146, Baker Library, Harvard Business School.

Hemp was next, followed by iron in the 1820s; by 1829 iron surpassed hemp in the official figures, partly because of an effort to develop a home hemp industry but mostly because of competition from manila and jute in the making of rope. Tallow for candles and bristles for brushes were the other leading commodities carried out of St. Petersburg. Overall, American imports of Russian goods remained relatively stable in dollar value but gradually declined in percentage of total imports—from over 3 percent in the 1820s to around 2 percent by 1840—as a result of the growth and diversification of the American economy and the relative stagnation of the Russian.

The shipment of American goods directly to Russia from the United States rose during the 1820s and 1830s in dollar value but remained fairly stable in percentage of total exports, from .5 to 1 percent. But the import of "American" products indirectly by Russia was increasing significantly from the greater use of middistance entrepôts, such as Liverpool for cotton and Amsterdam and Hamburg for tobacco. In the 1830s Russian imports officially recorded as coming from the United States averaged over 10 percent (valued in rubles). Taking into consideration these factors, the balance of exports and imports was shifting during this period away from Russia; that is, the United States was now more a supplier to Russia than a consumer of Russian products. Since the opening of trade, many American ships had arrived at their Russian destinations in ballast to carry out mainly Russian naval stores. By 1830 the arriving ships were more likely than before to be loaded and their cargoes more valuable.[53]

Without question, American shipping was important for Russia because of the West Indian trade, especially the imports of sugar. In a typical year about twenty ships would come to St. Petersburg directly from the United States, but forty or more would originate in the West Indies, mostly in Havana or Matanzas, loaded with both refined and unrefined sugar, coffee, and dyestuffs. In 1831, for example, American ships handled 75 percent of the total Russian imports of sugar with a value of just under 17 million rubles, while the gross imports by American vessels reached only 21 million, ranking second behind Great Britain, well ahead of France and the Ottoman Empire, and constituting almost 15 percent of the total value of imports into Russia through all ports and across all borders.[54] Such figures show why both Russia and the United States had a com-

[53]This analysis is drawn from Bolkhovitinov, *Russko-amerikanskie otnosheniia*; Kirchner, *Russian-American Commerce*, esp. pp. 53–67, based on both United States and Russian published statistics; and a survey of the diplomatic and consular reports.

[54]Bolkhovitinov, *Russko-amerikanskie otnosheniia*, pp. 370–71. Abraham Gibson, the long-term American consul in St. Petersburg, filed infrequent reports that were mainly summaries of the annual trade—for example, Gibson to Forsyth, 10 July 1837, DUSC, St. Petersburg, vol. 4 (1836–38) (roll 4, M 81), RG 59, NA, with attached printed copy of "General Directions to all Masters of American Ships trading to Cronstadt which

mon interest in a stable and tranquil Cuba—or one under the domination of the United States.

It is difficult to calculate exactly what share of the total Russian imports came from the United States. Probably the overwhelming amount of the considerable and rising imports of cotton and tobacco originated in the United States, but less than 20 percent of the cotton came directly and even less of the tobacco. Adding the amount of American goods reaching Russia through American intermediaries handling the West Indian–Russia trade, direct and indirect, one reaches a figure of about 30 percent of Russia's entire foreign imports. This is an approximate calculation of the total American business transacted with Russia. Of course, ships of other countries were involved in the direct trade between Russia and the United States, and usually a few Russian ships (or those carrying the Russian flag) plied the North Atlantic, but their numbers were quite insignificant in comparison to those of American and British vessels.

Obviously, those in the United States who benefited most from this trade were the merchants and shippers of the Northeast and the cotton and tobacco planters of the South. From all of the available evidence, the Russian trade was an important, perhaps vital part of the American maritime economy in the 1820s and 1830s, as the largest and best ships and most valuable cargoes went to Russian destinations. Much of the prosperity of Salem, Newburyport, Marblehead, Gloucester, and Boston depended on the Russian market, but the network also extended to Providence, New York, Philadelphia, Baltimore, Charleston, Savannah, and other coastal cities.[55]

American ships arriving at the customs zone of St. Petersburg anchored at Kronstadt and used lighters to haul the incoming and outgoing cargoes through the shallow channel to and from the city warehouses. Only one or two ships a year frequented such ports as Archangel in the north, Riga and Reval in the Baltic, or, beginning around 1830, Odessa and other Black Sea sites. This com-

They are Advised to Read with Attention, and Recommend to the Strict Notice of their Mates" (Kronstadt, 1837). Signed by Vice-consul Charles R. Lenartzen, the notice included such information as that loading was permitted on Holy Days but not unloading, and the following warning: "The Customhouse having learned that the Mates of ships, from motives of hospitality, are in the habit of treating the Customhouse-Officers with spirits, requests that the Masters of Ships, will order their Mates and people to abstain from this practice, however well meant; as all treating, or making of presents on the part of the master and crew, are strictly prohibited by law; and if done, the act is at the responsibility of the parties so transgressing." One wonders how much compliance there was, in disregard of this age-old tradition.

[55]The income from the Russian trade cannot be precisely determined, since it was so intertwined with West Indian and even American coastal shipping. However, the heyday of Russian-American commerce corresponded to the period of the construction of the grandest houses in the cities mentioned, and many of them were built by people well known in Baltic circles.

merce with the United States naturally brought profits to foreign trading houses in Russia and stimulated shore-based industries. One important fringe benefit for American ships in the Baltic, which helped mitigate the problems associated with dangerous sailing, unforeseen delays, and unpredictable markets, was the opportunity to be refitted in Russian ports with superior sails and tackle, cheaply and duty-free. John D. Lewis often supervised such arrangements as well as the unloading and loading of cargoes for the majority of American ships. As a result his firm became by 1830 one of the four largest in gross volume handled, listed only behind such stalwarts as Steiglitz and Company, Bonar Thompson, and Clements and Berg, all of which dealt in American business.[56]

Another American, William Ropes, also saw an opportunity at the St. Petersburg end of Russian-American commerce. Originally from Salem, Ropes formed a mercantile partnership in Boston with his brother Hardy that concentrated on trade with China, the West Indies, and South America. Ropes made his first trip to Russia, via Havana, in 1830 and managed the business of several other New England ships with the assistance of the St. Petersburg firms of John Venning and Steiglitz. The next summer he established a direct connection with the Aleksandrovsk textile mill near St. Petersburg, and in 1832 he brought his five children and second wife, Mary Codman Ropes, to take up residency in the Russian capital.[57] Whereas John D. Lewis operated independently—as did most other firms in the foreign trade in St. Petersburg that provided services to a variety of customers—Ropes attended mainly to ships commissioned to him by merchant friends in the Boston area; in this respect he operated the St. Petersburg branch of his own Boston-based company.

One key to Ropes's success was his determination to learn, and have his sons and associates study, the complexities and peculiarities of Russian commercial operations so that they could expedite transactions, obtain the best prices on both ends, and avoid paying fees to Steiglitz. He insisted above all that all members of his large family learn Russian and German. John Venning's return to England in 1830 and the Ropes family's involvement in the missionary activities of

<hr/>

[56]Kirchner, *Russian-American Commerce*, pp. 184–86. Numerous surviving records illustrate how business was conducted in the 1830s. See the John D. Lewis Papers, Rutgers University Library; the Lewis-Neilsen Papers, HSP; Osgood Carney Letterbook and Dabney Papers, MassHS; Ropes Papers, Baker Library, Harvard Business School; and especially a series of letters from Nathan Endicott (Salem) to John D. Lewis (St. Petersburg) in 1838 and 1839, in Nathan Endicott Letterbook, Endicott Family Papers, Essex Institute.

[57]Ropes Papers, box 1 and 2 and case 1, Baker Library, Harvard Business School; obituary of William Ropes, 1869, Essex Institute; *A Memoir of the Life of John Codman Ropes* (Boston: privately printed, 1901).

the Protestant religious community helped to sustain their Russian connection through three more generations, until World War I.[58]

The largest single business transaction of this period does not appear in the commercial records. Realizing the importance of naval power after the Battle of Navarino (1827) and desiring to modernize the long-neglected Russian fleet, Nicholas I sent a naval mission to the United States in the fall of 1829, headed by Adm. Aleksandr Avinov, a veteran of Navarino as well as the Battle of Trafalgar (one of several Russian officers serving in the British navy during the Napoleonic Wars). After inspecting various naval facilities and shipyards, Avinov arranged in New York for the purchase of the steam corvette *Kensington*, described at the time as "one of the most beautiful models in the world; 1440 tons burthen; live oak frame, and cost, when built, between three and four hundred thousand dollars with equipments, . . . and certainly worth two hundred thousand dollars now."[59] Unfortunately, the vessel, carrying the Russian minister Krudener, was dismasted in a storm soon after its departure in September 1830, but it was rescued and towed back to New York harbor with the assistance of Silas Burrows. An awkward delay resulted because New York merchants with a large stake in the Russian trade, such as Samuel Hicks, were reluctant to advance money for repairs, fearing a war over Russian suppression of the Polish revolt and a reaction from the Americans sympathetic to the Poles. In fact, in 1831, American public opinion, especially in New York and Washington, was decidedly anti-Russian, having been stirred up by newspapers such as the Washington *Globe* to support the cause of Polish independence.

Burrows, who had built a thriving trade with Latin America, finally came to

---

[58]From William Ropes's letters to his brother and other relatives, it would appear that almost every New England ship arriving at Kronstadt carried quantities of Bibles and religious tracts in the 1830s. Ropes Papers, box 2, Baker Library, Harvard Business School. See also Harriett Ropes Cabot, "The Early Years of William Ropes and Company in St. Petersburg," *American Neptune* 23, 2 (April 1963): 131–39. The American Tract and Bible Society reported in 1838 that 160,000 pamphlets had been printed in a ten-month period, expressly for distribution in Russia. "The Censor commends the work, noblemen engage in distribution, and no peasant, who can read, refuses a tract." New York *Advertiser and Express*, 10 May 1838.

John Venning's retirement from Russia, where he was deeply involved in missionary activities and prison reform, may have precipitated Ropes's decision to settle there. For Venning's life, see Thulia S. Henderson, *Memorials of John Venning, Esq. with Numerous Notices from His Manuscripts Relative to the Imperial Family of Russia* (London: Knight and Son, 1861; Newtonville, Mass.: Oriental Research Partners Reprint, 1975).

[59]Burrows to Baring Bros. (London), 20 July 1831, in Silas E. Burrows, *America and Russia: Correspondence, 1818 to 1848* (N.p., c. 1848), pp. 74–75. In another letter of the same date to the Barings, Burrows commented: "The merchants here are all mad in relation to the Polish insurrection, or else I am. I determined to accomplish the business at all hazards, and show the Emperor of Russia that he had one friend at least in the United States." Ibid., pp. 78–79.

the rescue, advancing around $60,000 for the repairs and the extra costs in-
volved in sending the *Kensington* on to Russia as a good will gesture. Burrows
had hoped to receive quid pro quo and thereby expand into the Russian market,
but he later regretted that he had offered this service to Russia. His creditors,
annoyed by his aid to the oppressor of the Poles, demanded payment, and he
soon found his whole business collapsing. Though Silas Everett, an associate
whom Burrows sent on board the *Kensington*, reported that Nicholas I visited
the ship upon its arrival at Kronstadt in October 1831 and seemed quite pleased
with it, Everett was unsuccessful in obtaining any monetary redress for this
friendly patron of Russia.[60] The absence of the American minister at the time
certainly did not help. The ship, renamed (ironically) the *Prince of Warsaw*, became the flagship of the Baltic fleet, the first large steam-powered vessel in the
Russian navy.

The Commercial Treaty of 1832

The *Kensington* affair demonstrated a new and more complex aspect of Russian-
American commercial connections. The promotion of a formal understanding
on trade relations was almost as old as the trade itself, being part of the Dana,
Harris, and Adams missions to Russia. The persistent American effort to secure
an agreement was dropped after Pinkney was rebuffed once more in 1817. Convinced that Alexander I was personally opposed to such arrangements, John
Quincy Adams also regarded a formal treaty that might be expensive and only
introduce other problems as no longer necessary to protect American interests.
Moreover, American politicians in the age of Monroe were sensitive to the possible international political commitments that might result from an agreement
with Russia.

In 1821 Middleton had reported that confidential sources at court (possibly
Capodistrias) had been surprised when he had not renewed the proposal for a
commercial treaty, and he interpreted this as a hint that a project would be well
received at that time.[61] Middleton and American policymakers, however, were
busy with other issues concerning the Northwest and Latin America in the

[60]Everett (St. Petersburg) to Burrows, 13 October 1831, in ibid., pp. 96–97. Everett
commented on the visit of Nicholas I: "His Majesty made many inquiries, and evinced
a correct idea of the requisites of a good ship-of-war, and expressed himself highly
pleased with the finish and accommodation of the ship."

[61]Middleton to Adams, 30 August/11 September 1821, DUSM, Russia, vol. 9 (roll 9,
M 35), RG 59, NA; Kirchner, *Russian-American Commerce*, pp. 16–17; and for the reaction of John Quincy Adams, see *Memoirs*, 5:429–31, especially: "Now, the object of this
was apparent, to bring us into a *political* connection with the Emperor. Our squadron
in the Mediterranean was its object. A commercial treaty was the lure. But we were supposed to be anxiously desirous for such a treaty. Our true policy was to be always will-

1820s; particularly in relation to Spanish affairs, a commercial negotiation could easily become embroiled in political issues. By 1830 that danger had definitely receded. It is ironic that the real initiative for a commercial treaty came from the administration of Andrew Jackson rather than from its more internationally minded predecessors and that it followed closely Russia's suppression of the Polish effort to regain independence, which had attracted American sympathies.

Middleton, with years of diplomatic experience in Russia, would have been a logical choice to conduct the negotiation, but for partisan reasons this was not possible. Hence, he retired in the spring of 1830 to tend the elaborate gardens on the family plantation near Charleston, and another Southern slave-owner was sent in his place. But John Randolph of Roanoke, Virginia, was an odd choice to carry out this important assignment. Well known for his eccentricity, irascibility, and oratorical skills, he had been an influential critic in Congress of a series of presidents. Andrew Jackson was indebted to Randolph for his political support and wanted to make use of his name and reputation—but not in Washington.[62] To accompany him and to perform most of the ordinary business, Randolph selected a namesake and son of an old family friend, John Randolph Clay, who, though inexperienced, was as young and healthy as his patron was old and ill.[63]

---

ing and ready to treat of commerce with Russia, and rather desiring it; because that desire would always be received as a mark of esteem and respect; but we can really obtain nothing from Russia of any importance in a commercial treaty. She has no discriminating duties, no colonial monopolies to remove. All the trade between us is carried on in our vessels. She imports from us sugar, coffee, and raw cotton without heavy duties; and all we could possibly obtain would be a trifling reduction of them. For everything thus obtained an equivalent would be exacted, and that would now evidently be political. I knew the Emperor Alexander had a rooted personal aversion to commercial treaties, considering them, as they really were, uncongenial to the policy of Russia. He had always refused to renew the old commercial treaty with Great Britain, and always hitherto declined a treaty with us. If he had now changed his mind, we should soon discover that for any advantage he might be disposed to yield he would claim for equivalent more than it would be worth." Both Alexander and Adams may have been correct in their views, but Adams seems to have forgotten about the tsar's notorious inconsistency.

[62]John M. Belohlavek, *"Let the Eagle Soar!": The Foreign Policy of Andrew Jackson* (Lincoln and London: University of Nebraska Press, 1985), pp. 29–30.

[63]George I. Oeste, *John Randolph Clay: America's First Career Diplomat* (Philadelphia: University of Pennsylvania Press, 1966), pp. 44–45, 52–53. Martin Van Buren had long admired Randolph and wanted to please Virginia politicians, so he talked Jackson into Randolph's appointment to the Russian mission: "Our relations with that government being simple and friendly, little harm would be done if it should turn out that we had made a mistake." Quoted in John Niven, *Martin Van Buren: The Romantic Age of American Politics* (New York and Oxford: Oxford University Press, 1983), p. 240. Biographers of John Randolph skip through the Russian mission, treating it as an aberration: "During his short stay at St. Petersburgh he was thought to be insane, which his speedy

That the administration took Randolph's mission to Russia seriously is verified by the long and painstakingly detailed instructions for the new minister, which Martin Van Buren, now secretary of state, carried personally to the departing ship at Norfolk. Randolph and his party, whose baggage included a coop of chickens and a caged mockingbird, traveled in regal splendor aboard a first-class American warship, the USS *Concord*, commanded by Matthew Perry. Though Randolph hated the navy and sea travel, he attempted to command the ship, making the voyage very disagreeable for both the young captain and the aging politician all the way to Kronstadt, where they landed in early August 1830. Nor was Perry impressed by his audience with the emperor. He also claimed that drinking the Neva water made his crew sick.[64]

Randolph's short residence in St. Petersburg was notable for his impatience, bad moods, and his drawing unfavorable attention to the American mission by allegedly falling to his knees before Nicholas I at a state function.[65] Though he apparently enjoyed the hospitality of Baron Steiglitz and Prince Lieven, his dour appraisal of Russia was remembered and repeated by later visitors: "It is Egypt in all but fertility. The extremes of human misery and human splendour here meet." Randolph also blamed Middleton for not staying to greet and brief him and for leaving affairs in a general mess: "Although I succeed an Anglo-Russian who considers himself very neat, yet an exact description of the house prepared to receive me, the public room excepted, would not be very pleasing to him, or to the reader."[66] In poor health, obviously suffering both mentally and physi-

flight, or hegira, seemed to confirm." Lemuel Sawyer, *Biography of John Randolph of Roanoke with a Selection from his Speeches* (New York: William Robinson, 1844), p. 98. The Norfolk *Beacon*, referring to a three-hour speech that Randolph made in defense of his conduct, put it another way: "We are ready to admit, that not only would our relations with Russia have scarcely gone on better, but they might have 'gone on' much worse, if Mr. R. had remained at St. Petersburgh." As cited in the *National Intelligencer*, 23 November 1831.

[64]Niven, *Martin Van Buren*, pp. 52, 66–70; the original of the instructions, dated 18 June 1830, is in DPR, Russia, Randolph-Clay 1830–36, vol. 4332, RG 84, NA; Samuel Eliot Morison, *"Old Bruin" Commodore Matthew C. Perry, 1794–1858* (Boston and Toronto: Little, Brown, 1967), pp. 104–14; J. R. Clay diary, Randolph Papers, Manuscript Division, LC.

[65]The story was publicized by Washington Irving, who was in London at the time. Oeste, *John Randolph Clay*, pp. 75–77. See also John Randolph to Martin Van Buren, 7/ 19 August 1830, DUSM, Russia, vol. 12 (1830–34) (roll 12, M 35), RG 59, NA.

[66]Whatever else, Randolph was quick with the pen. From London, he wrote to Thomas A. Morton, "This country is in a deplorable condition of splendid misery." John Randolph Correspondence, University of Virginia Library, Manuscripts Department. And obviously already defensive about the criticism circulating about his hasty departure from St. Petersburg, Randolph wrote his daughter: "I had done all that man could do before I left Russia, and in case that I shall not succeed finally, no blame can possibly rest upon me or the Government. Events far beyond human control will have

cally, and disgusted that the Russian government had not wound up the treaty business in a few days, Randolph fled on board a Dutch ship, leaving Clay behind to begin what would become an illustrious diplomatic career.

Randolph retreated to a London climate only slightly more hospitable than St. Petersburg, but he still anticipated returning to Russia in the spring to sign the treaty.[67] However, the Jackson administration now decided to rectify its "diplomatic error" and send a more trustworthy minister—James Buchanan, an able lawyer and congressman from Pennsylvania. Buchanan's mother was quite ill, but he reluctantly agreed in July 1831 to undertake the mission on the understanding that his tenure would be short. Delaying his departure until the spring traveling season, he was able to resume the treaty negotiation only the following summer.[68]

The uproar over the Polish revolt in 1831 and the confused state of affairs in Europe also contributed to the hiatus in the treaty negotiation. Even if Randolph had managed to bring back a satisfactory document from Russia in the spring of 1831, it is doubtful that the Senate—or the Jackson administration—would have been able to approve it because of the rather intense anti-Russian feeling in Washington. This situation was aggravated by the maladroit effort of Dmitri von Osten-Sacken, the Russian chargé d'affaires, to interfere with the hallowed principle of freedom of the press by trying to force the government to censure and silence the virulent anti-Russian stance of the Washington *Globe*.[69] But the Polish cause was a transitory phenomenon to Americans and was no longer making headlines within a few months.

Exactly why a treaty was signed in 1832 that neither side really needed and that would cause both countries difficulties in the future is a curious story. Russia was unhappy about the higher tariffs imposed on American imports of hemp and iron in 1828 (the Tariff of Abominations), and the United States sought reciprocity in tonnage duties assessed in the Russian ports, yet both of these issues were reasonably resolved apart from the treaty. The administration also sought an international maritime code and believed the first step was a "freedom of the

caused our failure." 4 June 1831, Coles Collection, University of Virginia Library, Manuscripts Department.

[67]Randolph (London) to Clay, 15 April 1831, Randolph Papers, letters, vol. 2, Manuscript Division, LC; Randolph to Van Buren, 20 February 1831, DUSM, Russia, vol. 12 (roll 12, M 35), RG 59, NA.

[68]Buchanan to Edward Livingston, 29 June 1832, DUSM, Russia, vol. 12 (roll 12, M 35), RG 59, NA.

[69]For a detailed analysis of the American rallying to the Polish cause, see Jerzy Jan Lerski, *A Polish Chapter in Jacksonian America: The United States and the Polish Exiles of 1831* (Madison: University of Wisconsin Press, 1958); and Joseph W. Wieczerzak, "The Polish Insurrection of 1830–1831 in the American Press," *Polish Review* 6 (Winter-Spring 1961): 53–72.

Karl Nesselrode. Lithograph by Oldermann (original in State Historical Museum, Moscow), from The United States and Russia: The Beginning of Relations, 1765–1815 *(Washington, D.C.: Department of State, 1980)*

seas" agreement with a friendly and powerful state such as Russia. However, Nesselrode opposed its inclusion from the start on the grounds that a bilateral declaration of two governments already in full accord on the issues would be of no purpose, especially since Russia's maritime shipping was minimal. Nevertheless, the Russian minister, like Rumiantsev before him, was cognizant of the growing importance of the United States as a naval and commercial counterbalance to Great Britain, whose power was being perceived more and more as a threat to national interests by political leaders in both countries. Precedents also help to explain the pact, since the United States had recently concluded treaties with the Ottoman Empire and with Austria, Prussia, and Bremen. Perhaps the simplest answer is that once the two countries had begun the process out of mutual friendship and political interest, something had to come of it. Buchanan summarized the American position: "I . . . observed that we wished to conclude this Treaty, more from a desire to be on the best terms with Russia, than from a conviction that we should derive any very great benefits from the Trade. That whilst it would merely employ our Navigation, an interest which I certainly did not mean to disparage, Russia would enjoy nearly all its other advantages."[70]

In the Russian government the conservative-minded minister of finance, Georg Ludwig Kankrin, was strongly opposed to the American terms for a commercial treaty, fearing a reduction in port and customs income which constituted up to 20 percent of Russian state revenues. Mainly for that reason, the first drafts were rejected. Buchanan was encouraged by Nesselrode, however, to resubmit the project with additional arguments that stressed the opportunities that might be realized from the expansion of American trade in the Black Sea region, where the chancellor, not incidentally, had extensive land holdings.[71] Another strong supporter of the treaty and perhaps the person who swayed Nesselrode and finally convinced Kankrin was Ludwig von Steiglitz, the head of the principal foreign trading house of German origin and official banker to the Russian government. Steiglitz had long been a friend to American interests in Russia and was rewarded in 1833 by being named the banking agent of the United States in Russia (actually a position of only nominal importance).[72]

Buchanan was also assisted by Krudener, who had returned to St. Petersburg to

[70]Buchanan to Livingston, 6 August 1832 (no. 6), DUSM, Russia, vol. 12 (1830–34) (roll 12, M 35), RG 59, NA; published in *James Buchanan's Mission to Russia, 1831–1833: His Speeches, State Papers and Private Correspondence* (New York: Arno Press and New York Times, 1970), p. 225.

The best and most thorough discussion of the treaty negotiations is that by Bolkhovitinov, *Russko-amerikanskie otnosheniia*, pp. 397–450. See also Kirchner, *Russian-American Commerce*, pp. 28–33; and Thomas, *Russo-American Relations*, pp. 68–91. Nesselrode was obviously cultivating the United States as a counterweight to Britain. See the notes of his dispatches to Krudener and Bodisko of 1829 and 1837 by Frank Golder, comp. and ed., *Guide to Materials for American History in Russian Archives*, vol. 1 (Washington, D.C.: Carnegie Institution, 1917), pp. 53–63.

[71]Buchanan to Livingston, 6 August and 19/31 October 1832, DUSM, Russia, vol. 12 (roll 12, M 35), RG 59, NA. For Kankrin's simplistic fiscal conservatism, "which concentrates on minimizing expenses and collecting as much revenue as possible from existing sources," see Walter McKenzie Pintner, *Russian Economic Policy under Nicholas I* (Ithaca, N.Y.: Cornell University Press, 1967), p. 77, passim. And for the best treatment of the reign of Nicholas: W. Bruce Lincoln, *Nicholas I: Emperor and Autocrat of All the Russias* (Bloomington and London: Indiana University Press, 1978).

[72]Buchanan to Livingston, 20 December 1832, in *James Buchanan's Mission*, pp. 288–89. On Steiglitz's role as the "Rothschild" of Russia, see Kirchner, *Russian-American Commerce*, pp. 186–89; and Paul H. Emden, *Money Powers of Europe in the Nineteenth and Twentieth Centuries* (London: Sampson Low, Marston & Co., 1937), p. 170. At the time of the banker's death in 1843, John Stevenson Maxwell considered him "the best and most powerful friend we had here." Fragment of letter of 1843, Maxwell Papers, NYHS. Steiglitz has been generally neglected in works on Russian finances—by Pintner, *Russian Economic Policy*, for example.

promote the negotiations. At this point a number of people had a stake in the treaty's completion, and Nesselrode managed to convince the tsar to approve it in December 1832. The treaty basically provided reciprocity in port charges, general civil and trading rights, and most-favored-nation treatment. It was to extend to 1839 and then automatically from year to year, unless one signatory gave a year's notice to discontinue it, a step the United States would finally take almost eighty years later.

The 1832 Russian-American Commercial Treaty, immediately carried to Washington by John Randolph Clay, easily secured Senate ratification in March 1833. The treaty really changed nothing of consequence. The Baltic trade continued much as before and actually with some relative decline, while the anticipated Black Sea expansion never did develop. As American consul in Odessa John Ralli pointed out, the chief export from the region—grain—was not needed in the United States, and there were few sugar refineries or cotton manufactories in that area to utilize American imports. Occasionally an American ship, essentially in the Mediterranean business, would wander into the Black Sea to pick up a cargo—for example, the *Henry*, which in 1833 carried a load of barley from Odessa to New York.

Buchanan saw the treaty through the exchange of ratifications and took leave of St. Petersburg in August 1833 without waiting for his successor. He summed up his Russian experience with advice to Washington:

> We have no foreign Mission which requires so much prudence and caution on the part of the Minister as that at St. Petersburg. This Government is extremely jealous and suspicious, and in general society, no man can tell who are spies of the secret police. Every Minister, and especially an American Minister on his first arrival, is narrowly watched; and if he has not sufficient self command to restrain his tongue, he might do more harm in three months, than a prudent man could repair in as many years. When I say this, I do not mean to intimate that he should ever utter a sentiment not truly American, but merely, that he ought to know when to be silent, as well as when to speak. On the contrary, he should take advantage of every safe opportunity which may present of making an impression in favor of his Country. These will be frequent, if he can acquire the confidence of the Nobility about the Court. Indeed many of them are anxious to obtain information concerning the United States, and our political institutions, provided they can do it with safety to themselves.[73]

Americans in Russia

The American merchants in St. Petersburg—Lewis and Ropes—continued to operate as before. Merging with the cosmopolitan English- and German-

---

[73]Buchanan to Louis McLane, 31 July 1833, DUSM, Russia, vol. 12 (roll 12, M 35), RG 59, NA.

speaking foreign trading community, their social life revolved around the non-conformist Anglo-American and Lutheran churches and their missionary activities. Ropes's daughter Martha was an active leader in the Anglo-American church, and his son Joseph spent a year roaming through the Russian countryside as far as Siberia with William Swan, a young British missionary. Mary, another daughter, married a widowed British merchant, William H. Gellibrand. In 1837 Ropes took on a British partner, Archibald Murielees, who had long resided in Russia, to help his oldest son, William Hooper Ropes, in running the St. Petersburg offices. The son married an Englishwoman, Ellen Hall, and seldom visited the United States.[74]

Judging from the extensive correspondence from Russia preserved by Hardy Ropes, this American family and their friends and associates made a decided impression on St. Petersburg society. Though merchants, they were on good relations with several noble families, and much of their profits and energies were devoted to humanitarian and religious causes, to which even the imperial family subscribed. They supported their Scottish pastor's successful efforts to raise money for a new church building and to expand the distribution of religious tracts printed in Russian. In this latter activity, Joseph Ropes was particularly active. After graduating from the local gymnasium and demonstrating a talent for languages, he continued his studies at the University of St. Petersburg. Completing them with distinction entitled him to the rank of Russian nobility, had he chosen to enter Russian service. Instead he devoted his time and energy to the translation and publication of religious and other materials.[75] In 1840 he joined his brother and George Henry Prince, a cousin from Salem, in the St. Petersburg countinghouse, forcing Murielees to withdraw.

John D. Lewis, though apparently not so religiously inclined, was even more oriented toward England. He had also married an Englishwoman and spent most of the off-season winters in England, where his sons were educated and became citizens. One even became a Liberal member of Parliament during the Gladstone years.[76] Lewis never returned to the United States and eventually retired to England shortly before his death in 1841. His friend, the American con-

---

[74]Louisa Ropes to grandfather, 21 February 1834, and William H. Ropes to Hardy, 30 November 1833, box 2, Ropes Papers, Baker Library, Harvard Business School; Martha Ropes Papers, Essex Institute.

[75]Joseph Samuel Ropes letters to his grandparents, aunts, and uncle, box 2, Ropes Papers, Baker Library, Harvard Business School. Some of his letters for the 1840s were found only in typed extracts. The Ropeses in Boston were closely connected to the Park Street Congregational Church, the American Peace Society, the Bible and Tract Society, the Board of Foreign Missions, and the Codman, Ladd, and Beecher ministerial families. Hardy Ropes Papers, box 3, Ropes Papers, Baker Library, Harvard Business School.

[76]John Delaware Lewis, Jr., born in St. Petersburg in 1828 and educated at Eton and

sul Abraham Gibson, also nearly always spent his winters in England. Even John Randolph Clay followed the trend, marrying Fanny Gibbs, the daughter of a local British physician.[77] In fact, some of these people, such as Lewis, barely fit the designation "American"—just as some longtime resident British in Russia seemed barely British. At least most of the American group were nonconformist, pro-American, and often at odds with British policies.

The scarcity of "genuine" Americans had been noted by Nicholas I in conversation with James Buchanan at his New Year's reception of 1833. "It is evident he places considerable value on the good opinion of the American people. He remarked it was strange, that whilst so many of our vessels entered the Ports of Russia, so few American travellers visited his dominions; and twice expressed a strong desire that we should come and see them as they really were, and not as they had been represented by their enemies."[78] Nonetheless, a definite increase in the American presence in Russia can be identified in the commonplace items in incoming cargoes and in the American-style hospitality and home and church life that tended to prevail in a significant part of the St. Petersburg foreign community. This American enclave was enlivened and reinforced by occasional visitors. With the large Ropes clan in residence, members of prominent New England business families appeared almost every year: Everett, Stevenson, Hooper, Appleton, Fettyplace, Saltonstall, Hubbard, Heard, Carney, Warren, Endicott. And other traveler-adventurers would drop in—for example, in 1835, John Lloyd Stephens and Lt. J. Allen Smith, perhaps the son of the 1805 sojourner of the same name.

Also in the summer of 1835 came Henry Wikoff and his friend Edwin Forrest, who had already earned fame as an actor and had just finished a season of leading tragic roles at Drury Lane in London. Wikoff and Forrest toured the sights of St. Petersburg, which they found very dull—"Philadelphia of a Sunday was lively in comparison."[79] At the imperial summer palace at Tsarskoe Selo, they had the run of the place. Forrest performed an impromptu Othello in the the-

Trinity College, Cambridge, was a lawyer known for his erudite writings and classical scholarship. He served in the House of Commons from 1868 to 1874 and died in 1884. *Dictionary of National Biography*, vol. 33 (London: Smith, Elder, & Co., 1893), p. 188.

[77]Clay to James Buchanan, 15/27 December, Buchanan Papers, box 47, HSP; Oeste, *John Randolph Clay*, pp. 153–55.

[78]Buchanan to Livingston, 14/26 January 1833, DUSM, Russia, vol. 12 (roll 12, M 35), RG 59, NA. Names cited are from diplomatic and consular correspondence and in family letters, Ropes Papers, Baker Library, Harvard Business School.

[79]Wikoff, *Reminiscences*, p. 207. Forrest also provides a clue as to how they managed to see so much: "Knowing nothing could be done without a military title in this stiff soldier government I attached to my passport 'Col. of 68th Reg. Penn. Line,' and wondered if there was such a unit." Diary, 20 August, p. 22, MS thr 131, Pusey Theatre Library, Harvard University.

atre to an astonished audience of peasant caretakers, and he was especially impressed by the large stage and handsomely appointed dressing rooms.[80] The duo also enjoyed the smooth, straight, macadamized highway ("one of the best roads I have travelled," Forrest reported) from St. Petersburg to Moscow, where they found much more to amuse them. The actor was steered to "a certain house where I found some Russian fair ones and disposed of two."[81] The trip farther south to Odessa was less amenable but was rewarded at its end by an introduction through Consul Ralli and George Sontag to Governor-general Mikhail Vorontsov, followed by a visit to Vorontsov's country estate at Yalta and a tour of the new fortifications then being erected at Sevastopol. Wikoff and Forrest were among the first of many Americans who would come to Russia purely for their own curiosity and pleasure.

The most prominent American visitor of the 1830s was Gen. James Tallmadge of New York, who arrived in Russia in July 1836. As a former lieutenant governor of the state, Tallmadge received an audience with the emperor and invitations to court balls. Apparently he had aspirations to be named minister, and Clay was at first supportive. Clay believed that Buchanan's replacement, William Wilkins, "had placed the Legation on a pretty shabby footing and his conduct of course reflected somewhat on me so our national character required a little bolstering which, I am in hopes, the Ex-Vice Governor of the state of N. York may afford."[82] The secretary was disappointed, though, when Tallmadge embarrassed the legation by declining Tsar Nicholas's personal invitation to prolong his stay, on the basis that he had borrowed a court uniform from Consul Gibson and had to return it. "Such candid answers might do in *Dutchess* County N. York but are ill suited to the Dutchess's circle here." But what made Tallmadge's visit especially memorable was his daughter, who, as Clay described her, " 'took' (as the English have it) like wild fire and nothing was talked about during the six weeks they stayed here but 'la belle Americaine.' . . . She was definitely the belle of the Peterhoff *fete* and the Empress, who likes pretty persons, invited her to a number of private parties."[83] Miss Tallmadge left Russia with a

[80]Wikoff, *Reminiscences*, p. 211; Forrest Diary, 22 August, pp. 30–31, Pusey Theatre Library, Harvard University. One biographer of Forrest claimed that the visit to Russia definitely influenced his career: "It is with Russia that he has been fascinated,—its massiveness, its hordes subject to the imperious sovereign will. Everywhere he went, he strove to associate himself with the scene. . . . He was always posing, striking attitudes." Montrose J. Moses, *The Fabulous Forrest: The Record of an American Actor* (Boston: Little, Brown, 1929), p. 133.

[81]Wikoff, *Reminiscences*, pp. 226–30, 238–47; Forrest Diary, 25 August and 2 September, pp. 38, 48, Pusey Theatre Library, Harvard University.

[82]Clay to Buchanan, 12 July 1836, Buchanan Papers, box 48, HSP.

[83]Clay to Buchanan, 6 November 1836 and 23 August 1836, Buchanan Papers, box 49 and 48, HSP.

bracelet from the emperor, a cashmere shawl from the empress, and the adulation of much of St. Petersburg society.

Surprisingly, the Americans, both residents and visitors, had a high regard for the autocratic Nicholas I, often comparing him favorably with their own "democratic" Andrew Jackson. From the limited perspective of St. Petersburg, he seemed to capture the fashionable romantic image of kingship. Typical was Clay's early impression: "Nicholas I is I should judge nearly six feet high and perhaps the finest formed and handsomest man in the Russian empire. He has the true imperial gait."[84] And Nicholas, a keen student of war, returned the favor by admiring the American president and his military bearing.

Unresolved North Pacific Issues

Judging from his few reports, William Wilkins felt bored and isolated during his eighteen-month stay in Russia. His only diplomatic business involved the Convention of 1824 and the "open-close" fourth article that had given Americans virtually a carte blanche on commercial activities in Alaskan waters for ten years—that is, until 1834. The frequent complaints of officials of the Russian America Company and naval officers made the Russian government unwilling to extend these privileges. That was one issue; the other hinged on conflicting interpretations of the convention. The Americans contended that approaches to the coastal areas not settled by the Russians remained open, that Americans still had the right—regardless of any convention—to trade with the Indians along the coast and even to hunt sea otters, and that the closure after ten years specified in Article 4 pertained only to direct access without prior permission to harbors, rivers, and Russian settlements.[85]

At the end of November 1835, and again in early December, Wilkins conferred with Nesselrode on these issues, calling on "consideration of our national good-will and our amicable and disinterested reciprocal intercourse." Perhaps unwisely, he pressed the following reasoning on the Russian chancellor: "In a political point of view the Russian possessions upon the American coast are not considered, in this Capital, as of any importance. The only way in which you can avert collision and difficulties there, will be to throw the entire coast open to the fair commercial competition of the three Powers—the United States, England and Russia. Each strives for the trade and each is jealous of the other. Let the most enterprizing and intelligent carry off the profits."[86]

Wilkins may have been correct in his assessment that the Russian government

[84]Clay diary, 18 December 1830, Randolph Papers, Manuscript Division, LC.
[85]Kushner, *Conflict on the Northwest Coast*, pp. 73–78.
[86]Wilkins to Forsyth, 11 December 1835, DUSM, Russia, vol. 13 (roll 13, M 35), RG 59, NA.

really did not care much either way, but that allowed Ferdinand Wrangell, the influential director of the Russian America Company and a seasoned veteran of the Northwest, to cast the deciding vote. Nevertheless, before there was any diplomatic resolution of the controversy, a test case appeared with the Russian interdiction of an American ship, the *Loriot*, out of Honolulu on a hunting expedition into Russian waters in 1835. A Russian naval ship prevented the captain from taking refuge from a storm in a nearby harbor, forcing a dangerous and costly return voyage to Oahu. The owners then sought recompense from the Russian government for losses sustained in the whole venture on grounds that the Convention of 1824 had been violated. For several years the *Loriot* case intermittently disturbed relations between the two countries, while the Russian position hardened. Martin Van Buren, in his message to Congress in 1838, reaffirmed the United States' right to trade with natives on the coast, but the Russian interpretation was basically upheld in practice, and American ships frequented the northwest coastal areas without permission at their own risk.[87] The problem was exacerbated (or eased, depending on the point of view) by the greater number of American ships coming to these waters in the 1830s for trade (sponsored by prominent Boston merchants such as Joseph Peabody and William Boardman) or in search of whales. The ambiguity concerning maritime jurisdiction and the inability of the Russians to carry out a systematic enforcement with so few naval ships along so much coastline left open many opportunities to ambitious and venturesome captains of American vessels. Although Wilkins's successors in St. Petersburg continued to press the case of the *Loriot* and to ask for either a renewal of the convention or a new understanding on northwest jurisdictions, the company and the Russian government remained obdurate, and direct trade between the two countries along the northwest coast stagnated in the 1840s.

By the 1840s American trade with Alaskan natives had become a by-product of whaling. From the standpoint of the American entrepreneur, whaling was a much more attractive pursuit than conducting business through the unpredictable Russian officials. Since whalers operated so far from home, native labor was vital for hunting and processing. The prohibited relations were further encouraged because furs from the coastal settlements were useful to the crews and a source of additional income, and such miscellaneous New England products as ordinary utensils brought for sale were cheaper and better than those provided by the Russians. Liq-

---

[87]Kushner, *Conflict on the Northwest Coast*, pp. 75–79; Forsyth to Dallas, 4 May 1837, Diplomatic Instructions Department of State (hereafter DIDS), Russia, vol. 14 (roll 136, M 77), RG 59, NA. The United States countered by claiming that the convention did not recognize Russian "possession" of the coast north of 54°40' except where actual settlements existed. Forsyth to Dallas, 3 November 1837, DIDS, Russia, vol. 14 (roll 136, M 77), RG 59, NA.

uor remained in demand and was often used to pay Indian workers. The regular and permissible trade declined, since after 1836 the Russian America Company no longer paid for supplies and services with valuable pelts but with letters of exchange that cut their costs and lowered American shippers' profits considerably. But dependence on Americans also took new forms—for example, with the help of New Englander Thomas Barton, the Russian America Company itself engaged in limited coastal whaling operations in the 1830s with native crews.[88]

The leadership of the company had become more naval-oriented under the administration of men like Adolf Etholin, a Finnish officer who had served with distinction in the Russian navy and who devoted much of his life to the cause of strengthening the Russian position in the North Pacific. He and Ferdinand Wrangell were chiefly responsible for an 1839 agreement to lease to the British Hudson's Bay Company an area along the coast that included the important Stikhine River outlet, in return for annual payments that could be used to purchase supplies. This came as a surprise to the American government. Even the Russian minister in Washington was first informed of it by an incredulous secretary of state: "With J. Forsyth's respects to Mr. Bodisco, this strange information is communicated, with the hope and belief that he will ascertain that it is not true."[89]

This lease and the increased British presence on the coast meant that provisions could be obtained from a much closer and more reliable source than Fort Ross. The California base had outlived its usefulness, and steps were taken to sell the rights to land, now acknowledged by the new Mexican government, and such company properties as buildings and docks to John Sutter, a local rancher and miller and a "new Californian." The contract concluded in December 1841 by Peter Kostromitinov specified a payment to the company of 30,000 piastres (dollars) in four installments. Russian ships still traded regularly with northern California and even furnished the equipment for the first steamboat on San Francisco Bay in 1846.

Commercial Decline and the Rise of Technology

Russian-American trade also declined in the Baltic at this time because of changing circumstances: an increase in shipping competition from Britain and

---

[88]Kushner, *Conflict on the Northwest Coast*, pp. 82–85; Gibson, *Imperial Russia in Frontier America*, pp. 165–72, 199–204; Barratt, *Russian Shadows*, pp. 35–38.

[89]Bodisko to Nesselrode, 18/30 May 1840, f. kants. Vashington 1840, d. 180, ff. 11181, Arkhiv Vneshnoi Politiki Rossii (hereafter AVPR), Moscow. Bodisko developed what he considered to be a special friendship with President Tyler, who "hoped to see these two great nations always united in interests and following constantly the same policy" and who invited the Russian minister to his summer mountain retreat in Virginia in 1843. Bodisko to Nesselrode, 18/30 July 1843, f. kants. Vashington 1843, d. 171, AVPR.

Scandinavia, higher duties on imported sugar to protect the development of a Russian sugar beet industry, the decline of the market for furs, and the entry of cheaper alternatives to Russian products into the American market. As Abraham Gibson reported in 1844:

> Since 1837 the export trade to America has been constantly and gradually diminishing in amount, especially for the main articles, namely bar iron, hemp, sail cloth, ravensduck and flems; and as I see no good reasons why it should not continue to diminish, but on the contrary do see reasons why it should, I apprehend that within ten years time it will be of so limited an amount as to become of very trifling importance to what it was a few years ago.[90]

Reduced demand for imports of Russian goods would naturally lower voyage profits and diminish the attractiveness of the long journey to Kronstadt.

The traditional commerce between the two countries may also have been hurt by the decrease in the business of John D. Lewis, in much greater proportion than the overall decline, his withdrawal in 1841, and the departure of William Ropes (Senior) in 1837. Ropes and Company remained in the Russian business, with the St. Petersburg office managed by William Hooper Ropes and George Prince, but they handled chiefly their own ships, perhaps discouraging other Boston-area merchants from striking out on their own in that quarter. Another explanation for the downturn is simply that greater successes could be achieved elsewhere, especially in voyages to China and in whaling, which drained ships, capital, and seamen from New England, especially after 1840.

Certainly there were still profits to be made in the Russian trade. This is obvious from the respectable number and increased size of American ships, though it is difficult to discern a deliberate commercial plan. These Russia-bound vessels were often registered with appropriate names—*Cronstadt, Neva, Baltic, Kutuzov, Czarina, Moscow, Peterhoff, Riga,* and *St. Petersburg.* Most of them made only one or two voyages to the Baltic, but a few made ten or more. The *Czarina*, a Ropes ship, set the record, normally making two complete voyages to St. Petersburg in one season, thanks to the Ropes company's practice of bringing West Indian cargoes to Boston for reshipment. The *Czarina* would start out from Boston in February or March, usually stopping at Charleston before reaching Havana, where

---

[90]Abraham Gibson to John C. Calhoun, 1/13 August 1844, DUSC, St. Petersburg, vol. 6 (roll 6, M 81), RG 59, NA. For the development of the beet sugar industry in the 1830s, see V. K. Yatsunsky, "The Industrial Revolution in Russia," in *Russian Economic Development from Peter the Great to Stalin*, ed. William L. Blackwell (New York: New Viewpoints, 1974), pp. 119–20. The decline of the sailcloth industry in Russia as the result of falling exports caused particular concern in the 1830s. N. S. Kiniapina, *Politika Russkogo samoderzhaviia v oblasti promyshlennosti (20-50-e gody XIX v.)* (Moscow: MGU, 1968), pp. 55–58.

it would unload Russian and New England products and rice from South Carolina and pick up a cargo of sugar, coffee, and logwood for St. Petersburg. An-
choring at Kronstadt just after the ice cleared in May, it would, with the help of
its own local agents, manage a quick turnaround taking iron and hemp for Boston, where another cargo of mainly West Indian products—but often including
items of New England manufacture, such as Franklin stoves—would be loaded,
and the *Czarina* would sail again for St. Petersburg. The second Russian cargo
would then reach the home port by late December.[91] Another Ropes ship, the *St.
Petersburg*, was captained by a veteran Baltic-American sailor, William Hooper
Trask, and had the distinction of being the largest commercial vessel (814 tons)
ever to enter a Russian port when it arrived at Kronstadt in 1841 with 1.5 million pounds of cotton, direct from Mobile.[92]

Problems in the Baltic trade inspired investigative reporting from ministers
and consuls. George Mifflin Dallas, who succeeded his brother-in-law Wilkins
as minister, was a lawyer and former senator from Pennsylvania. He brought his
family and established a ministerial residence congenial to St. Petersburg society
for the first time in over fifteen years, since Henry Middleton's tenure. Dallas
also had the advantage of prior experience in Russia, as a secretary to the peace
commissioners of 1813–14. He definitely enhanced the prestige of the American
mission; one distinguished visitor in 1838 was his nephew Alexander Dallas
Bache, president of Girard College and a scientist-educator in the tradition of
his great-grandfather Benjamin Franklin. Aside from family connections and social achievements, Dallas's remonstrances about renewing the privileges of the
Convention of 1824 and his efforts to promote tobacco and cotton trade raised
the visibility of the United States at the Russian court.[93]

A later minister, Charles Stewart Todd of Cincinnati (the first "midwestern"
appointee to Russia) was equally active in spurring the development of agricultural trade. With local Russian encouragement, he promoted the sending in

[91]The *Czarina*, a 218-ton brig, was in the Baltic service for at least fifteen years. The
ship had several captains during this period, but one, Isaac Thayer, commanded six
voyages. After 1844, however, the ship was diverted to a Boston-New Orleans-Rio de Janeiro route. This information is compiled from logbooks and the annual consular reports from St. Petersburg. Several logbooks of the *Czarina* survive but are scattered:
1832 at the Essex Institute, Salem; 1834–35 in the Manuscript Division, NYPL; 1837–
39 and 1844 at the Baker Library, Harvard Business School.

[92]Consular note, 1841, DUSC, St. Petersburg, vol. 6 (roll 6, M 81), RG 59, NA. The
St. Petersburg was offered for sale to the Russian government for 90,000 silver rubles but
was refused. The vessel was also the largest ever to leave Boston harbor at that time.
Winifred Trask Lee, ed., *Miss Louisa Lord's Diary of a Voyage on the Ship 'St. Petersburg' in
the Year 1840* (New York: Ivy Press, 1875), p. ii.

[93]Dallas to Forsyth, 6 October and 12 December 1837, DUSM, Russia, vol. 13 (roll
13, M 35), RG 59, NA; John M. Belohlavek, *George Mifflin Dallas: Jacksonian Politician*
(University Park and London: Pennsylvania State University Press, 1977), pp. 70–74.

1845 of the first shipload of tobacco direct from the United States to Russia. But in an early example of aid defeating trade, Todd, as a newly elected member of the Russian Agricultural Society, also engineered the dispatch of seeds of the best American tobacco varieties, "with an explanation, as full as practicable, of the mode of cultivating each."[94] Russians, or rather Volga Germans, would soon be growing the leading types of American tobacco, in addition to Turkish, and thereby producing a large quantity of this product domestically.

Perhaps the most dramatic event of this period came in July 1837, when the USS *Independence*, bringing Dallas to Russia, arrived at Kronstadt during an imperial naval review. Nicholas I soon came on board in undisguised incognito—that is, informally and unofficially in the trail of Nesselrode and Prince Aleksandr Menshikov, the minister of navy—for a full inspection of the American warship. The American vice-consul at Kronstadt, Charles Lenartzen, who was to meet Dallas, recognized the emperor. As Dallas described the scene, "He separated himself from the rest, peered actively throughout the ship, spoke inquiringly [in good English] to a number of the seamen, and accidentally coming across my infant daughter, took her in his arms, expressed great delight at her beauty, and repeatedly kissed her."[95] Nicholas I may not have been well versed in American political behavior, but he was apparently the first and only tsar to publicly kiss an American baby.

And he was rewarded for his effort. After the departure of the Russian inspection team, Commodore John B. Nicolson ordered a booming forty-one-gun salute, the first such formal recognition accorded a Russian ruler by an American

[94]Charles S. Todd to Brantz Mayer, 1/13 July 1844, Mayer-Roszel Papers, MaryHS; Todd to James Buchanan, 15/27 September 1845, DUSM, Russia, vol. 14 (roll 14, M 35), RG 59, NA; Gilderoy Wells Griffin, *Memoir of Col. Chas. S. Todd* (Philadelphia: Claxton, Remson, and Haffelfinger, 1873).

[95]George Mifflin Dallas, *Diary of George Mifflin Dallas*, ed. Susan Dallas, (Philadelphia: J. B. Lippincott, 1892), p. 8. Nicholas later explained: "I took your ship on the moment of her arrival, in her sea-trim; I did not want to see her dressed up. . . . I never have seen a nobler vessel." Ibid., p. 11. The imperial visit is also described by M. S. Stokes, a naval officer on board: "He examined everything about the ship minutely and asked a great many questions of the sailors (speaking English very well), he was pleasant in his manners and showed that shrewdness and information for which he is celebrated." To James Gwyn, 10 August 1837, no. 298, folder 4, James Gwyn Papers, Southern Historical Collection, University of North Carolina, Chapel Hill.

Also on board the *Independence* was Chaplain J. C. Webster, who, "having been sent by an associate in the United States whose object is to improve the temporal and religious condition of our mariners," sought permission to preach regularly on board an American ship at Kronstadt or at his lodgings. The Russian government, however, wanted additional information, which apparently discouraged the pastor from establishing a residence in Russia. Webster to Dallas, 23 August 1837, Dallas to Rodofinikin, 28 August 1837, and Rodofinikin to Dallas, 25 September 1837, in DPR, Russia, Miscellaneous Sent, Dallas 1837–39, vol. 4479, RG 84, NA.

naval vessel. This was followed by the raising of the American flag on the imperial yacht and what was reported to be an unprecedented number of additional
forty-one-gun salutes from several nearby Russian warships, "producing as much
uproar and as dense a smoke as could well be endured by three of the senses. As
the centre and pivot of the operation, the occupants of the American frigate experienced unfeigned delight."[96] More consequentially, after the air had cleared,
Russian naval officers inspected the *Independence* from stem to stern and pro-
fessed themselves to be quite impressed, both with its equipment and the profi-
ciency of the crew.

That Americans had mastered and were even leading in certain areas of mechanical and military technology in the first half of the nineteenth century was
not news to Nicholas I and Russian administrators. They had already examined
such innovations as the exploding shells of Joshua Shaw and the naval cannon
of Robert Beale. Information about American advances, especially in the sphere
of transportation and communication, was widely circulated around Russia by
progressive journals; Pavel Svin'in, who had known Robert Fulton in the
United States, was a particularly active publicist. After Fulton's abortive negotiations with Russia, Robert Stevens of Boston proposed in 1817 to build a large
oceangoing steamship for Russia at a cost of over $100,000. The price was con-
sidered too high for a country still recovering from the Napoleonic Wars,
though Russian officials were very impressed by the steamship *Savannah* when it
visited St. Petersburg in 1819. Finally, as previously mentioned, Admiral Avinov
negotiated the ill-fated purchase of the corvette *Kensington* in 1830. The following year another large steam corvette—the *United States*, built by Henry Eck-
ford, the best-known American naval architect of the time—arrived at Kronstadt from New Orleans and was offered for sale, but the Russians demurred,
and the ship was eventually sold to the Ottoman Empire.[97] Even so, these overtures prepared the way for a closer naval relationship.

The Kamchatka Project

After his visit to the *Independence* in 1837, Nicholas I dispatched another naval
mission to the United States. Arriving in late 1838, Capt. Johann Von Schantz

---

[96]*National Intelligencer*, 23 September 1837, citing anonymous letter of 4 August from
Kronstadt.

[97]James A. Field, Jr., *America and the Mediterranean World, 1776–1882* (Princeton,
N.J.: Princeton University Press, 1969), pp. 151–53; Gibson to Van Buren, 4/16 August
1830, DUSC, St. Petersburg, vol. 2 (roll 2, M 81), RG 59, NA; Adams, *Memoirs*, 8:258–
59; Buchanan to Livingston, 12 June 1832, DUSM, Russia, vol. 12 (roll 12, M 35), RG
59, NA; Don Steers, *Silas Enoch Burrows, 1794–1870: His Life and Letters* (Chester,
Conn.: Pequot Press, 1971), p. 26. On the *Savannah*, see *National Intelligencer*, 14 December 1819.

(Ivan Fon Shants) of Finnish background, Captain Pypin, and Lieutenant Sha-
riubin toured shipyards and port facilities on the East Coast, finally signing a
contract on behalf of the Russian government with George L. Schuyler and the
John H. Brown Shipyards in New York for the building of a first-class steam frigate. The design was a combined effort of Brown, Von Schantz, and Schuyler's
brother Robert, with engines modified from Lighthall's Patent Half Beam and
uniquely adapted to burn hard coal—"after our own ideas," as George Schuyler
noted.[98]

The construction of the *Kamchatka* for the Russian navy attracted considerable attention among area residents and in the national press at its various stages:
the public casting of the ten-ton engine cylinders in Jersey City; a grand ceremony accompanying the launch on 24 November 1840 that was witnessed by
ten thousand people; and the trial run to Sandy Hook the following summer.
The *Kamchatka* project was also a milestone in American industrial history, for
it was by far the largest vessel constructed in the United States up to that time.
The hull and rigging upon launch weighed just over 1,000 tons, but by the time
the engines, boilers, guns, and other furnishings were added, along with water
and 700 tons of anthracite coal, displacement reached 2,468 tons (with an official registry of 1,787 tons), perhaps the largest warship of its day. Though the design followed the lines of the *Great Western*, built in England, the many new
technological features included a triangular cylinder placement to power the
600-horsepower engine.[99] All who saw this nautical wonder were impressed by
its size, power, beauty, and lavish interior accouterments. The total expenditure
passed $450,000, counting cost overruns approved by the Russian officers super-
vising construction. In addition, the Russian shipbuilding project broke the
British monopoly over construction of large steamships and was promptly followed by orders from the Spanish government for two similar vessels.

The final cost of the *Kamchatka* exceeded the advances from Russia, so, in order to avoid delays, the necessary supplementary funding was provided by the
Schuylers and guaranteed by the Russian minister in Washington and by the
Russian officers involved.[100] In order to ensure repayment, George Schuyler and
his father-in-law Col. James A. Hamilton embarked on the *Kamchatka* on 1 October 1841 with a full American crew, headed by Joseph Scott as chief engineer.
The colonel was not without political clout, being a son of Alexander Hamilton

[98]George L. Schuyler, *Letter to the Hon. W. Gwin, Member of Congress from Mississippi,
concerning the Steam Ship Kamschatka* (New York: Charles S. Francis, 1843), pp. 3–6.

[99]New York *Herald*, 25 November 1840; 2 December 1840; 30 January 1841; 17 June
1841; 10 July 1841 (full-column description); 16 August 1841; Bodisko to Nesselrode,
17/29 June 1840, f. kants. Vashington 1840, d. 180, ff. 11434, AVPR.

[100]Bodisko to Nesselrode, 19/31 August 1841, f. kants. Vashington 1841, d. 195, ff.
1921, AVPR.

and having served President Jackson briefly as acting secretary of state. While stopping over in Southampton, reports of steam leaks on voyage engendered rumors that the engines were a complete failure, which Schuyler attributed to insufficient time for thorough trials and to British jealousy.[101]

Upon arrival at Kronstadt, and contrary to Schuyler's understanding, a Russian naval crew took over the ship on the perhaps legitimate pretext of securing adequate berthing before the harbor froze. There was an unforeseen technical difficulty: The vessel was too large to enter the military port at Kronstadt and had to anchor in the commercial harbor instead. In addition, the emperor's plan to inspect the vessel on arrival was thwarted by a snowstorm. With the help of Baron Steiglitz and Hamilton's uniformed presence, Schuyler was able to collect the full $55,089.42 that was owed and even managed to avoid the usual payoffs to the various officials involved.[102]

Scott remained behind as supervising engineer for a busy summer of trials in 1842. On its first trip the *Kamchatka* carried Grand Duke Alexander across the Baltic to pick up the king of Prussia for a visit to St. Petersburg. On another voyage the tsar himself sailed on the new flagship and proclaimed that he was fully satisfied with its performance. The *Kamchatka* remained in Russian service for many more years, and Scott and Schuyler maintained that in speed and fuel efficiency it surpassed all of its contemporaries.[103]

Americans Help Build Russian Railroads

The improvement of Russia's internal transportation system was a topic of considerable discussion in the 1830s. The railroad age had indeed dawned in Great Britain and the United States and was working its way eastward across Europe. An Austrian (Prague-born) professor of mechanics, Franz Anton Von Gerstner, had some modest successes in his homeland and visualized great opportunities for railroads in the vast expanses of Russia. He convinced the tsar to build a "trial" line of about fifteen miles from the capital to the site of the imperial summer palace at Tsarskoe Selo, with a short extension to the pleasure park at Pavlovsk. This first Russian railroad opened for business with imported British

[101]"Indeed, I think much credit is due to the builder engaged in fitting up the Kamschatka in every department, that, hurried off as she was without trial, no other than this trifling difficulty presented itself." Schuyler, *Letter to Hon. W. Gwin*, p. 8.

[102]James A. Hamilton, *Reminiscences of . . . or Men and Events, at Home and Abroad during Three Quarters of a Century* (New York: Charles Scribner & Co., 1869), pp. 318–22.

[103]Ibid., pp. 324–29; Schuyler, *Letter to Hon. W. Gwin*, pp. 9–15; Charles S. Todd to Daniel Webster, 10/22 December 1841, DUSM, Russia, vol. 14 (roll 14, M 35), RG 59, NA.

locomotives in April 1838. By this time there were proposals to construct additional railroads and, above all, to link the two main cities, Moscow and St. Petersburg—a plan promoted by an influential Moscow entrepreneur named Aggei Abaza.

With the intention of advancing this project, Von Gerstner left Russia in 1838 on a technological reconnaissance tour that would take him to the United States. American transportation achievements were already well known to readers of the Russian periodical press, and the canal bridge then being constructed over the Potomac attracted particular interest. A pair of engineering experts, Colonels Nikolai Kraft and Pavel Mel'nikov, who had already inspected European facilities (and found the British very secretive), followed the Austrian professor to the United States in 1839. Von Gerstner unfortunately became sick and then died in 1840 in Philadelphia, but the two officers remained in the country for over a year looking at all kinds of transportation and related factories and sites. They conferred with a number of railroad manufacturers and engineers with the intention of supplementing Von Gerstner's work. Since Kraft was ill much of the time and confined himself to New York, the inspection visits were left to Mel'nikov, who filed detailed reports about his American experience upon his return to Russia and thereby received most of the credit for the mission's success.[104]

The year of Mel'nikov's return, 1840, thus marked a turning point in Russian industrial history and also in Russian-American relations. Von Gerstner, who probably would have continued to dominate Russian railroad engineering and kept it in a European context, had left the scene. Gen. Karl von Toll, the superintendent of ways and communications and, ironically, an arch-opponent of railroads, was ill (and died in 1842). Stiff opposition remained from conservative quarters, especially from Minister of Finance Kankrin, on grounds of expense, since costly improvements had just been made on the St. Petersburg–Moscow post road.[105] Others feared that a railroad would put peasant carters out of work or saw dangers from industrialization in general. However, in March 1841, the proponents of railroad construction, led by Mel'nikov, Abaza, Steiglitz, and Aleksandr Bobrinskoi (a grandson of Catherine the Great), persuaded Nicholas

[104]For the story of the early development of railroads in Russia, see Richard Mowbray Haywood, *The Beginnings of Railway Development in Russia in the Reign of Nicholas I, 1835–1842* (Durham, N.C.: Duke University Press, 1969).

Nesselrode to Bodisko, 17 May 1839, f. 206, op. 1, no. 162, Tsentral'nyi Gosudarstvennyi Istoricheskii Arkhiv [Central State Historical Archive] (hereafter, TsGIA), Leningrad; Mel'nikov's memoirs, "Svedeniia o Russkikh zheleznykh dorogakh," are in f. 446, op. 12, no. 4, TsGIA, and were edited by M. Krutilov as "Nachalo zheleznogorozhnogo stroitelstva v Rossii (iz zapisok P. P. Mel'nikov), *Krasnyi Arkhiv*, 99, 2 (1940): 127–79.

[105]Haywood, *Railway Development*, pp. 208–11.

*George Washington Whistler. Courtesy of the Freer Gallery of
Art, Smithsonian Institution, Washington, D.C.*

to appoint a special committee headed by Gen. Alexander Beckendorff, one of
the tsar's favorites and a neutral on railroad advances, specifically to study proposals for the Moscow–St. Petersburg line.[106]

The committee, transformed into a commission, examined Mel'nikov's technical reports and finally recommended that construction begin. Nicholas was
convinced especially of the military advantages of such a line, and his *ukaz* issued in February 1842 established a formal Construction Committee, under the
nominal presidency of his son, Grand Duke Alexander. Also approved was the
suggestion that the American expert who had impressed Mel'nikov the most,
George Washington Whistler, be contracted as "consulting engineer"—in reality,
the chief superintendent of construction.

Whistler was an original "army brat," born at the frontier outpost of Fort
Wayne, Indiana Territory, in 1800 and educated in engineering at West Point.
He also taught mathematics there for a few years before he joined the Baltimore
and Ohio Railroad in 1829 and was sent to observe railroad operations in Britain. He thus had several years of experience in railroad construction and equipment manufacturing, including the management of the locomotive plant of the

[106]Ibid.; Mel'nikov, "Svedeniia," pp. 75–76, f. 446, op. 12, no. 4, TsGIA.

Lowell Locks and Canals Company. Whistler had just finished laying a track over the Berkshires in Massachusetts (later the New York Central line), which was considered a particularly difficult engineering feat, when the Russian representative first visited him in October 1839 at his headquarters in Springfield.[107]

After the cumbersome bureaucratic decisionmaking process was concluded in Russia, Abaza secured the help of the energetic American minister Todd for the formal imperial blessing on the arrangement with Whistler.[108] The offer to come to Russia finally reached him at his Stonington, Connecticut, home, two-and-a-half years after Mel'nikov's contact, by way of another Russian military emissary, Capt. John Bouttatz (Ivan Butats). After consulting with the Russian minister, Secretary of State Daniel Webster in Washington, and such relatives as William H. Swift, chief engineer for the city of New York, Whistler departed for Russia in June 1842 with a contract that paid $10,000 per annum, plus expenses. He would devote the next seven years, the remainder of his life, to building the Russian railroad.[109]

Several crucial decisions awaited the American engineer and his chief Russian colleagues—Mel'nikov, who was in charge of the northern half of the project, and Gen. Peter Kleinmichel, the new superintendent of ways and communications who had the advantage of being a favorite of the tsar. First was the width of the track to be laid. Believing strongly that the existing Tsarskoe Selo line was too wide (six feet), Whistler argued for a compromise of five feet, which was four inches wider than the most common gauge in Britain and the United States but was being used in certain "rougher" areas such as the American South. This "wide" gauge would allow the employment of large cars and provide a smoother

[107]C. S. Todd to Colonel Abert, 13/25 June 1842, Todd Papers, Filson Club; Griffin, *Memoir of Todd*, pp. 79–80; Mel'nikov, "Svedeniia," p. 198, f. 446, op. 12, no. 4, TsGIA. Todd reported that Nicholas I expressly invited Whistler to his and the empress's twenty-fifth wedding anniversary celebration and that he expected Whistler would be conferred general rank. For an excellent outline of the building of the St. Petersburg-Moscow railroad and American involvement with it, see William L. Blackwell, *The Beginnings of Russian Industrialization, 1800–1860* (Princeton, N.J.: Princeton University Press, 1968), pp. 279–323. Richard Haywood is producing a seminal study of the project.

[108]George L. Vose, *A Sketch of the Life of and Works of George W. Whistler* (Boston: Lee and Shepard, 1887), pp. 11–15; Whistler to George Barnes, James Barnes Papers, NYHS; Locks and Canals Company Papers, Baker Library, Harvard Business School; Charles E. Fisher, *Whistler's Railroad: The Western Railroad of Massachusetts*, Railway and Locomotive Historical Society Bulletin no. 69 (Boston, 1947), pp. 8–56; and Edwin R. Clark, *Early Locomotive Building in Lowell, Massachusetts*, Railway and Locomotive Historical Society Bulletin no. 7 (Boston, 1924), pp. 31–33.

[109]W. H. Swift to J. G. Swift, 24 April and 30 April 1842, Whistler-Swift Papers, Manuscript Division, NYPL; Todd to Gen. Aleksandr Chernyshev, 13/25 August 1843, DPR, Russia, Miscellaneous Sent, Todd 1841–46, vol. 4480, RG 84, NA.

ride. It became the standard for Russia, making the railroads of that country distinctive from most others.[110]

Another question concerned the route. In this case, Russian authorities ruled against the commercial interest in reaching as many populated points as possible and in favor of the emperor's vision of a fast, safe connection between the two capitals—virtually a straight line. The rails would parallel the recently improved post road and thus simplify the hauling of men and materials during construction. Because of obstacles such as large swamps that could not be bypassed, this shorter route was probably more expensive and time-consuming to build; a myth even gained currency that Nicholas I simply drew a line with a ruler on a map. At least the survey was relatively easy; by the summer of 1843 Whistler had brought over as associates William Crane and R. G. Fairbanks, with their huge steam-powered pile-driving and excavating machines, and construction had commenced with as many as fifty thousand Russian workmen (peasants and soldiers) engaged at one time.[111] Whistler described the scene in a letter to Swift:

At times I fancied myself flying about in the staff of Field Marshall Koutouzoff in the very teeth of the enemy—all cuts and embankments assumed the shape of fortifications—all was hurry and bustle—at any turn we were met by small parties of cavalry—couriers were going in all directions—with all the glitter of helmets and rattle of spurs and sabres . . . and executed with the rapidity of true Napoleonic tactics . . . at the expense of many a horse left to die by the side of the route.[112]

[110]"Report Made by George Washington Whistler to His Excellency the Count Kleinmichel on the Gauge of the Russian Railway," St. Petersburg, 9 September 1842, Manuscript Division, NYPL; Haywood, *Railway Development*, pp. 229–30 n. 91; and Richard Mowbray Haywood, "The Question of a Standard Gauge for Russian Railways, 1836–1860," *Slavic Review* 28, 1 (March 1969): 72–80; Blackwell, *Russian Industrialization*, p. 285.

[111]"Fairbanks is astonishing the natives with pile driving machines and excavators." John Stevenson Maxwell to his uncle, 6 May 1843, Maxwell Papers, NYHS. And Todd reported that thirty-one thousand men (soldiers?) were employed in 1844, then fifty thousand in 1845. To Buchanan, 5/17 September 1845, DUSM, Russia, vol. 14 (roll 14, M 35), RG 59, NA; Blackwell, *Russian Industrialization*, pp. 291–92. And for the story about Nicholas's prowess as a railroad surveyor: Richard Mowbray Haywood, "The 'Ruler Legend': Tsar Nicholas I and the Route of the St. Petersburg-Moscow Railway, 1842–1843," *Slavic Review* 37, 4 (December 1978): 640–50.

[112]Whistler to W. Swift, 28 October 1844, Whistler-Swift Papers, Manuscript Division, NYPL. Whistler's long letter of 4 April 1844 is especially descriptive of the problems he faced in beginning railroad construction in Russia. For a popular account of his life in Russia, see Albert Parry, *Whistler's Father* (Indianapolis and New York: Bobbs-Merrill, 1939).

And soldiers too, for hidden behind this account was the Russian contractors' preference for hand, virtually slave, labor over the new American machines.

The enormous task of laying a track through over five hundred miles of largely uninhabited swamps and forests turned out, like many such projects, to be even more costly than the critics had claimed. And, naturally, there were delays well beyond the expected date of completion. Moreover, the rails only created a foundation. For the whole system locomotives, rolling stock, stations, and yards were required. Following the advice of Whistler and Mel'nikov, and assuaging fears that the railroad would result in increased unemployment, the decision was made to build this equipment in Russia. Though more expensive than direct purchase from abroad, this would have the advantage of establishing a base of production and expertise in Russia for the future.

Mel'nikov was again quick to recommend American contractors. At the time of his visit to the United States a contest was under way among Philadelphia and Baltimore manufacturers of locomotives on the number of cars that could be pulled by single large engines. The leading contenders were William Norris, whose plant outside Philadelphia was probably the largest in the United States at the time and who actively pursued Russian contracts through a detailed bid in 1840 and visits to the country; the Joseph Harrison–Andrew Eastwick Company of Philadelphia, which had recently perfected a new boiler construction; and Ross Winans, a former New Jersey horse breeder and chief supplier to the Baltimore and Ohio Railroad.[113] Winans's new eight-wheel-drive "camel back" engines (with upright boilers), first manufactured at leased plants in Philadelphia, were apparently winning, though Norris was securing some European orders. After an unusually swift negotiation, however, the award of a twelve-year contract went to a new partnership of Harrison, Eastwick, and Winans, probably the result of Whistler's previous business arrangements with both Harrison and Winans.[114] The American firm had at their disposal the state-owned foundry (the

[113]Philadelphia *Public Ledger*, 15 May 1839 and 2 January 1841. Norris's bid to build two hundred locomotives at $8,000 per locomotive and tender is detailed in his letter of 27 May 1840 to Mel'nikov and Kraft, enclosed in Bodisko to Nesselrode, 1 October 1840, f. kants. Vashington 1840, d. 195, AVPR. By 1861 Norris Brothers had built more locomotives than any other American firm. Only after the Civil War were they surpassed by the Baldwin Works, which actually took over the original Norris factory in 1873. C. H. Caruthers, *The Norris Locomotive Works*, Railway and Locomotive Historical Society Bulletin no. 10 (Boston, 1925), pp. 28–46. G. B. Duncan, in writing a reference for Norris from London, noted how much stir was being created there by "the Emperor's preference for American artisans." To C. S. Todd, 22 September 1843, Todd Papers, Cincinnati Historical Society (hereafter CinHS).

[114]The relationship with Winans went back at least to 1829. Whistler to J. G. Swift, 16 February 1829, Whistler-Swift Papers, Manuscript Division, NYPL. Whistler was also involved in a business venture with an old Russia hand, William D. Lewis. Whistler to Lewis, 27 June 1839, Madigan Collection, Manuscript Division, NYPL. Ironi-

*Joseph Harrison, Jr. From the collection of the Historical Soci-
ety of Pennsylvania*

largest in Russia) at Aleksandrovsk, a few miles up the Neva from St. Petersburg.
There "Harrison, Winans, and Eastwick" were to build 162 locomotives and
5,300 cars for $3 million during the first five-year period of the contract.[115]

Joseph Harrison, Jr., Andrew Eastwick, and Ross Winans's sons, Thomas De-
Kay and William L., arrived in Russia during the summer of 1843 to begin the
big and expensive job of equipping their plant with machinery imported from
Britain and the United States and hiring skilled mechanics, at first primarily
American ones. From the beginning the unskilled Russian crew of around four

cally, the Winans locomotives that Whistler obtained for the Western Railroad proved
unsatisfactory. The eight-wheel drive gave the twenty-two-and-half-ton engine better
traction, but the tall smokestack on the vertical boiler had to be shortened to go under
bridges, thus decreasing its power. Ultimately, bridges were raised, but the days of upright boilers were numbered. Fisher, *Whistler's Railroad*, pp. 41–45.

[115]C. S. Todd to Upshur, 27 December/8 January 1844, DUSM, Russia, vol. 14 (roll
14, M 35), RG 59, NA. Samuel F. B. Morse thought in 1839 that he was negotiating a
contract through Russian agent Peter Meyendorff in Paris to provide a telegraph line,
but the Russians feared at the time that such a communications system would under-
mine the government. Morse to Joseph Henry, 24 April 1839, *The Papers of Joseph
Henry*, vol. 4, ed. Nathan Reingold (Washington, D.C.: Smithsonian Institution Press,
1981), p. 211.

hundred presented problems, with the American managers becoming especially annoyed at the large number of Russian religious holidays. The work force soon grew to over sixteen hundred men, counting those in the machine shops in Moscow.[116] After a year and a half in Russia, Harrison, who led the organization of the project, was still uncertain that it would be lucrative: "It is impossible to tell what we shall do in our business here, it all moves on favourably as far as its mechanical execution is concerned, how far it will be profitable is another matter, but we hope it may pay us for exiling ourselves so long from our homes—this yet remains to be seen."[117] He and William Winans remained in Russia for several years to supervise the plant, living in substantial houses that flanked the main gate of the factory. They also negotiated—without Eastwick—an advantageous supplemental repair and maintenance agreement. By 1847 they were producing "a mile of cars a month."[118]

Once Whistler's family arrived in 1843, the American presence in Russia exceeded that of any earlier time and challenged the still-larger British and German communities. Much information is known about the social life of the American "mechanics" from Anna McNeill Whistler, whose prodigious letter writing and detailed journals complemented posterity's natural desire to preserve the legacy of this famous mother. Along with providing details of her husband's flute playing (he was known as "Pipes" because of it) and her stepdaughter Deborah's considerable vocal and piano skills, she doted especially on her two young sons, Willie and Jamie—for example, describing how they would be stationed outside their summer dacha on the Peterhoff road to hand out religious tracts to passing soldiers. Jamie (James Abbott [later McNeill] Whistler) was, at the age of eight, already demonstrating artistic talent and in 1845 entered drawing classes at the St. Petersburg Academy of Fine Arts.[119]

These warm familial scenes, however, were saddened by homesickness, illness,

[116]Maxwell to his parents, 22 May 1844, Maxwell Papers, NYHS; Whistler to J. G. Swift, 19 December 1845, Whistler-Swift Papers, Manuscript Division, NYPL; Philadelphia *Public Ledger*, 6 August 1847. Maxwell also described how soldiers would have to be stationed at the doors to prevent workers from taking things. "Every morning a dozen or so are flogged." The American employers were not known for their humanity. For another firsthand but more varnished account of these American manufacturing endeavors, see Joseph Harrison, Jr., *The Iron Worker and King Solomon*, 2d ed. (Philadelphia: Lippincott, 1869).

[117]Joseph Harrison to Charles [Naylor?], 21 March/2 April 1846, Joseph Harrison Letterbook no. 1 (1844-50), HSP. Charles Naylor described Harrison as "one of the most eminent machinists in our Country and has a reputation almost unrivalled, as a builder of steam-engines, and is, besides, one of the best of men." To Todd, 28 March 1843, Todd Papers, CinHS.

[118]Philadelphia *Public Ledger*, 6 August 1847.

[119]On the distribution of religious tracts, see the entry of 4 July 1844 in Anna Whistler Journals, 1844, Manuscript Division, NYPL. They are summarized and elaborated

and death. The Whistlers lost their favorite son, Charlie, on the voyage over, and a year later, a Russian-born baby, John Bouttatz Whistler. John Stevenson Maxwell, the secretary of legation from New York who lived in their house, fell critically ill and endured a long convalescence under the Whistler roof.[120] Finally, with the railroad nearly complete after many frustrating delays, "Pipes" (or "Whistler," as Anna called him) succumbed to cholera and died in April 1849, leaving his widow to preside over an ambitious brood of children. George William Whistler, Whistler's oldest son by his first wife, had joined his father in the railroad project, stayed to work at Aleksandrovsk, and married Ross Winans's daughter. He "retired" to Frankfurt in the 1860s with considerable wealth and died in Brighton, England, in 1872. Though living abroad, he was reported to be the largest private investor in United States bonds during the Civil War.[121] Thus, indirectly, Russian railroad money helped finance the Northern cause.

Military, Diplomatic, and Other Missions

News of American activities in Russia and of the building of the *Kamchatka* attracted considerable attention in the press and brought a number of other

upon by Parry, *Whistler's Father*, and in a complementary volume by Elizabeth Mumford, *Whistler's Mother* (Boston: Little, Brown, 1939). Neither author had used, however, the important Maxwell correspondence, and a new, scholarly study of the Whistler family should be done.

[120]The Whistlers and Maxwell lived in the relatively comfortable house formerly occupied by Dallas and belonging to Count Aleksei Bobrinskoi, a grandson of Catherine the Great whom Maxwell described as "a left-handed cousin of the emperor." To his mother, 5 February 1843, Maxwell Papers, NYHS. The legation secretary obviously became quite attached to the Whistler family. In a letter to his uncle (25 February 1843, ibid.) Maxwell wrote, "The Major [Whistler] is very popular here, much to the annoyance of the three thousand John Bulls who have grown fat and saucy on the idea that has generally prevailed here, that nobody but themselves could do any thing for Russia."

But Maxwell was sympathetic to the situation of Anna Whistler, who found herself in a society divided into rival groups, "whose sole amusement seems to be to slander and abuse each other. . . . I really do pity any well educated American lady who has to make a residence here and especially one who has a husband whose professional reputation excites the jealousy and envy of many about him. Major Whistler is a person of so much judgement, so much principle and such good temper that it would be difficult for the most wicked to obtain the slightest advantage over him, and I have strong confidence that he will not only finish his work with great honour to himself, but also leave a character behind him that will do honour to his Country." To his mother, 30 September 1843, ibid. And on Anna Whistler: "I never knew a lady so generally beloved by those with whom she was surrounded than this one" (15 October 1844, ibid.). But Maxwell's infatuation with Whistler's daughter Deborah may have colored his opinions. Deborah, however, soon married a visiting British physician in St. Petersburg and subsequently raised a family in England. Her half-brother's lovely portrait of her playing the piano is in the Taft Museum in Cincinnati.

[121]Obituary, Pennell-Whistler Papers, vol. 34, f. 55, Manuscript Division, LC.

American visitors to Russia. Some came simply to visit friends or out of curiosity or on government assignment, but most sought to benefit from the apparent inclination of the Russian government to throw business toward Americans. In 1840 Secretary of War Joel Poinsett, himself an old Russia hand, directed a special military commission, consisting of ordnance officers Maj. William Wade and Maj. Alfred Mordecai, that included Russia in its tour of European military schools and fortifications. Thus the parade of Russian military agents to the United States was finally reciprocated by this first official army visit from the United States. As it happened, the military tour coincided with the temperance mission to Russia of Presbyterian missionary Robert Baird of New York and, ironically, with an overture to Nicholas I from William Ladd, president of the (Quaker) American Peace Society of Philadelphia. In his introductory note, Ladd claimed that the society "has always considered the Holy Alliance . . . as indicating a new era of the world favorable to the cause of permanent and universal peace."[122] Russians at this time and later would have a mixed image of the United States as professing peace while technologically geared for war.

Churchill Cambreling, longtime congressman of New York, had a brief tenure as minister to Russia in 1841, after which the diplomatic post passed to the eccentric Charles S. Todd, who had served under William Henry Harrison in the War of 1812 and supported his election. Coming to Russia without his family, he was assisted by able secretaries—first, the future historian John Lothrop Motley. Motley accepted the appointment with the intention of studying Russian and gathering material for a history of the country, but sickness, the climate, and lack of money got the best of him, and he left after a short stay to devote his talents to more congenial settings. John Stevenson Maxwell replaced him. The already-active American society in the Russian capital was further enlivened in 1842 when Mrs. Stephen Van Rensselaer and her son and two daughters paid a second visit to St. Petersburg and were presented at court along with J. Sontag Haviland of Philadelphia, the nephew of the now-deceased General Sontag of the Russian service. The number of Americans pressing their demands on the Russian court for official hospitality was certainly growing.

The year 1843 bustled with Americans visiting Russia. Besides those in residence—Whistler, Todd, Maxwell, Ropes, Prince, and Fairbanks; Harrison, Winans, and Eastwick, and their mechanics—the community included the competing locomotive manufacturer William Norris of Philadelphia; Joseph Slocum of Syracuse, who gave plowing demonstrations and hoped for lucrative contracts to modernize Russian agriculture on the American model; William Jenks, who was attempting to sell his much-acclaimed carbines to the Russian army; Joseph

[122]William Ladd to Nicholas I, 18 April 1840, enclosure in Bodisko to Nesselrode, 16/28 May 1840, f. kants. Vashington 1840, d. 180, ff. 11180, AVPR.

Charles S. Todd, U.S. minister to Russia, 1841–1846, from the Collections of the Library of Congress

Merrill, a merchant from Mobile; Gerard Ralston, a bookseller; and Dr. Brewster, a dentist who came to fix the emperor's teeth. The first American journalist to cover Russia was Erastus Brooks, representing the New York *Express*.[123] Even Sylvanus Thayer, longtime superintendent of West Point, paid a visit to his old friend Whistler in 1844. A mix of such travelers was the typical pattern for the 1840s. Though this was the most "liberal" period of Nicholas I's conservative reign, bureaucratic obstacles, Russian finances, basic conservatism, and inadequate capital—separately or in combination—prevented any other Russian-

[123]Derived from American and Russian diplomatic reports and the Whistler, Todd, and Maxwell papers. According to Maxwell, Slocum especially made a nuisance of himself—"a real Yankee, cool, shrewd and calculating, with the usual newspaper education." To his mother, 9 September 1843, Maxwell Papers, NYHS. Jenks on the other hand had been courted by Russian agents, and his carbines were eventually adopted for the Russian army.

American ventures from duplicating the great successes of Whistler, Harrison, or Winans.

By the 1840s the Russian presence in the United States was also enhanced in stature and not only by the building of the *Kamchatka*. In fact, in 1840, after the Dallases had left Russia and while the Mel'nikov and Von Schantz missions were still engaged in American inspections, there were probably more Russian visitors in the United States than Americans in Russia for the first and only time. This was perhaps opportune, since one of the biggest and most publicized social events of Washington, D.C., that year was the marriage on 9 April of the fifty-four-year-old Russian minister, Alexander Bodisko, to a sixteen-year-old Georgetown schoolgirl, Harriet Brooke Williams, who to many observers was as young and beautiful as the minister was old and ugly.[124] The ceremony drew much press attention, the New York *Herald* gushing over it:

> This was thought to be one of the prettiest scenes of the kind ever witnessed. The lovely bride, surrounded by her train of eight young ladies all beautiful and blushing as the roses they carried; bright eyes were flashing on fresh and blooming faces; while everyone looked happy. Mr. Bodisco wore his splendid court dress; a coat almost of entire silver, decorated with several orders. The foreign ministers [including the British ambassador!] of his train also wore their uniforms.[125]

The guests at the magnificent dinner at Bodisko's stately Georgetown house (still standing at 3322 O Street) included Pres. Martin Van Buren, Vice-pres. Richard Johnson, Henry Clay, Gen. Winfield Scott, Sen. James Buchanan, Sen. Thomas Benton (whose daughter was a bridesmaid), Secretary of State

[124]Maxwell, who met the minister in St. Petersburg, described Bodisko as "a dandy in dottage . . . his mouth is toothless, his breath horrible and the *tout ensemble* justifies the opinion of those who considered him the ugliest man in the United States. . . . Concealing his decrepitude in the make of his habiliments, illuminating his [face] with a smile skin deep, and yet deep enough to erase the wrinkles, assuming a manner that seems as natural as it is condescending . . . , the old fellow becomes the admiration of the Washington ballrooms and wins the love of a pretty damsel of sweet seventeen." To his mother, 1 January 1844, Maxwell Papers, NYHS.

[125]New York *Herald*, 13 and 20 April 1840; for an interesting account of the wedding by one of the bridesmaids, see Jessie Benton Fremont, *Souvenirs of My Time* (Boston: D. Lothrop and Company, 1887), pp. 7–33, whose description (p. 20) of the groom agreed with Maxwell's: "He was a short and stout man with a broad Calmuck-face, much wrinkled, and furred across by shaggy whiskers which joined into the mustache over a wide mouth with rather projecting teeth; a shining brown wig curled low over shaggy eyebrows and restless little eyes, while his manner was at variance with all my ideas of dignity." For the impact of this marriage on life in the city of Washington, see Constance McLaughlin Green, *Washington: Village and Capitol, 1800–1878* (Princeton, N.J.: Princeton University Press, 1962), pp. 149–50.

John Forsyth, the entire diplomatic corps, and many other dignitaries. A grand reception there a few nights later created a massive traffic jam, since it was open to all without invitation. The *Herald's* Washington letter described the scene:

> The green house was open with the orange trees, with sweet smelling blossoms. . . . In one of the balcony rooms was hung from the ceiling an enticing swing; the seat was a soft velvet cushion, and the cords red silk; . . . we hear that the new bride has forty-six new and splendid dresses, of satin, of thule, of crepe, and of muslin; eight new bonnets, several sets of jewelry, and everything that can delight a young lady. . . . Much champagne was drunk in toasts to "Nicholas and Martin."[126]

A few days later President and Mrs. Van Buren hosted a formal dinner at the White House for the Bodiskos.

For the remaining fourteen years of Bodisko's term as minister in the United States, his family's goings and comings to Saratoga, Newport, or St. Petersburg for the summers were diligently reported in the national press. The birth of twin boys thirteen months after the wedding, and later of three more children, silenced the tongues wagging about the age differential and enhanced the minister's image as a jovial, likable family man, as well as a socially active and skilled diplomat—a nineteenth-century Anatoly Dobrynin.

Other members of the Russian legation staff also tended to meld into the American scene. Krudener had started the trend by marrying Julie Fulton of New York, while a long-term secretary, George Krehmer, was reported to be dating the daughter of the secretary of state (McLane or Forsyth). Eduard Stoeckl, another secretary and Bodisko's eventual successor, was well known for adapting to local customs and also married an American. These and other members of the diplomatic corps, including Bodisko's two nephews, Boris and Vladimir,

[126]Bodisko to Nesselrode, 18/30 May 1840, f. kants. Vashington 1840, d. 180, ff. 11181, AVPR. Anna Whistler was not impressed by Harriet Bodisco either, when she came with her husband for tea at the Whistlers' in 1844: "Mrs. Bodisco spoke in raptures of the uninterrupted season of pleasure she has participated in at this dissipated court, and said she should never wish to return to her native land if she had her own relatives here—no society in America she says—she must have lost relish for what is rational and intellectual and sincere!" Anna Whistler Journals, 26 February 1844, Manuscript Division, NYPL.
    The Russian minister subsequently gave lavish weekly entertainments, which featured among other things gambling at whist. A story circulated that after losing over $1,000 on one such occasion, he announced to the assemblage: "Ladies and gentlemens! It is my disagreeable duty to make the announce that these receptions must have an end, and to declare them at an end for the present, because why? The fund for their expend, ladies and gentlemens is exhaust, and they must discontinue." Benjamin Perley Poore, *Perley's Reminiscences of Sixty Years in the National Metropolis*, vol. 1 (Philadelphia: Hubbard Bros., 1886), p. 299.

stayed for many years in the United States and continued to associate with Americans when back in Russia. Aside from Consul-general Evstaf'ev in New York, who was setting a record for diplomatic tenure, the other consuls in American port cities were American citizens, a few such as Haviland in Philadelphia having Russian family connections.

Making a journey to the United States on private business or as a tourist was rare, however, for a Russian; visits were usually coupled with an official mission. For example, Sergei Lomonosov, the Russian minister to Brazil, as well as Aleksandr Medem, his successor, toured the country on the way to their post. In addition, there were military agents, who were more interested in meeting officers, businessmen, and inventors and in seeing the sights of the country than in socializing with politicians in Washington. But in general Russians had much less opportunity to acquire firsthand knowledge about the United States than Americans had about Russia. Paris, Italy, the spas of central Europe were simply more to the taste of the Russian aristocracy—and did not require an uncomfortable sea voyage.

Forming Perceptions

Exposure to Americans in Russia did provide Russians with some impressions, though it is difficult to assess the total impact. First of all, the Americans were an odd lot. There were eccentric ministers like Randolph and Todd, the ardent "missionary" families like the Ropeses and Whistlers, retired military or self-styled colonels like Van Rensselaer, Hamilton, and Tallmadge, promoters like Slocum, Jenks, and Norris, and curiosity seekers and adventurers like Stephens and Wikoff. Clearly the Russian desire to gain information about the United States and the American social openness made communication with them easier than with other foreigners. In other words, Russians were more likely to seek out Americans among their foreign guests and more willing to talk openly and directly with them. Even so, contacts were limited by typical American deficiency in foreign languages (very few could manage any Russian and most could not speak French or German). The number of Russians really exposed to Americans was small and confined largely to the court and to those with foreign experience; to official publicists such as the newspaper editor Nikolai Grech, who showed Buchanan around Moscow; or to retired naval officers such as Ivan Kruzenshtern, who still in the 1840s could regale American visitors with stories of his adventures going back to eighteenth-century expeditions. Nonetheless, Americans could have an impact far greater than their numbers when the exposure included the imperial family and such important officials as Mel'nikov (who later as minister of ways and communications kept George Washington

Whistler's Bible by his bedside)[127] and Prince Mikhail Vorontsov (whose chief assistant in governing the southern provinces for many years was George Sontag).

Such encounters of Russians with Americans did have some limitations in conveying an understanding of the United States. Wikoff related a revealing conversation with Vorontsov over the nature of the American government while they sailed between Yalta and Odessa.

> He asked me many questions concerning the United States, and seemed anxious about their destiny.
>
> "It is a strange experiment," he said, "to put a government in the hands of the masses. It may answer in your case, where you have the continent pretty much to yourselves; but in Europe, split up as we are into various States, with conflicting interests and large standing armies, a democratic government strikes me as impossible. You change your executive and legislature at short intervals, and, as both must represent the momentary views of the electors, a consistent policy must be out of the question."

Wikoff responded by emphasizing the ability of democratic elections to find the common interest. The prince replied:

> You have a system of slavery supported by the South and condemned by the North. These opposite views are founded on antagonistic interests, and how is a collision sooner or later to be avoided?

The discussion continued along the lines of how conflict is resolved between majority and minority views, with the prince stressing the dominance of party interests.

> "Against that danger," I rejoined, "we have, in the United States the protection of a free press, which enlightens the popular mind and checks political manoeuvres."
>
> "As far as I can see," returned the Prince, "your press is simply the organ of party, and all its comments on passing events are coloured by party prejudice. It seems to me quite under the control of your politicians, and cares little for the general interests."

Wikoff then argued the case for a better educated and wiser common people.

> "You are quite right," declared the Prince; "all depends on your people, who are said to be shrewd and practical beyond most others. If they discountenance legislation that benefits one section to the detriment of another—if

[127]Mel'nikov, "Svedeniia," p. 198, f. 446, op. 12, no. 4, TsGIA.

they restrain the politicians from involving them in dangerous disputes with one another—if they prevent their passions being inflamed by gaudy rhetoric—then all may go well. But this is expecting too much of human nature, at least such human nature as exists on this side of the Atlantic."[128]

Apparently such conversations were not uncommon between Russians and Americans. Though they might betray a fundamental difference in political outlook, it was not one that seriously disturbed the development of close, friendly relations. These amicable disputes also demonstrated a genuine Russian interest in contemporary American life and issues.

The American Ideal

By 1820 many Europeans were disillusioned with the course of events: They felt the aftershocks of a terrible war and perceived a return to *status quo ante bellum* in spirit as well as in dynastic boundaries and a general absence of progress on the Continent, which seemed to be suffocating under the umbrella of the Holy Alliance. By contrast the United States appeared dynamic and progressive, moving ahead in economic and political terms, even militarily victorious. The result was a series of books describing or predicting the fall and decline of Europe and the rise of the United States. Americans such as the publicist Alexander Hill Everett and "Continentalists" such as C. F. von Schmidt-Phiseldek were foremost in propagating this wax-and-wane imagery.[129]

Progressive Russians agreed with this assessment of Europe, but few were yet willing to recognize an American ascendancy. In the first place, they saw the possibility, even the inevitability, of a Russian exception in Europe's decline. As they searched widely for ideas to revitalize Russian society, the rising United States was a natural magnet. It was convenient most of all as a symbol or shorthand for political contrast, safer and less controversial to apply than French or British political examples. Foreign ideas, including a number inspired by the United States, thus fermented in Russian society, whether among polite com-

---

[128]Wikoff, *Reminiscences*, pp. 246–49.

[129]Alexander Hill Everett, *Europe: or a General Survey of the Present Situation of the Principal Powers with Conjectures* (Boston: O. Everett, 1822); C. F. von Schmidt-Phiseldek, *Europe and America, or the Relative State of the Civilized World at a Future Period*, trans. Joseph Owen (Copenhagen: Bernhard Schlesinger, 1820; facsimile reprint, with postscript by Thorkild Kjaergaard; Copenhagen: Royal Danish Ministry of Foreign Affairs, 1976). For an interesting discussion of the changing perceptions of the United States and Russia during this period, see Geoffrey Barraclough, "Europa, Amerika und Russland in Vorstellung und Denken des 19. Jahrhunderts," *Historische Zeitschrift* 203, 2 (October 1966): 280–315.

pany in the Crimea or within the secret societies that emerged after 1815; they would culminate in a serious challenge to the Russian autocracy in December 1825. As the Russian search for inspiration broadened after 1820, the United States received particular attention.

This new generation of Russian radicals in the early 1820s focused on finding the leadership for change, one of their most obvious shortcomings. The American example was especially admired. Kondraty Ryleev, the poet-clerk of the Russian America Company and a leading dissenter, once remarked that Pavel Pestel, chief spokesman for the Southern Society of the Decembrist movement, "was more like Bonaparte than Washington," obviously meaning that the American leader was the preferable hero image.[130]

Pestel himself described what had turned him toward a radical course of action before the commission that investigated the causes of the Decembrist revolt: "I was led from a monarchic-constitutional outlook to a republican one chiefly by these facts and considerations: the works, in French, of Destutt de Tracy made a great impression on me. All newspapers and books were so full of praise of the increased happiness of the United States of America, ascribing this to their political system, that I took it as clear proof of the superiority of the republican system of government."[131] This is clear indication that information about the United States inspired Russian programs for change, though Pestel believed that the more centrally directed strategies of the French radicals would be most effective for reforming Russian institutions and society.

The more moderate Decembrists of the Northern Society, led by Nikita Murav'ev, borrowed ideas of federalism from the American Constitution for their projects of political reform. A plan to divide Russia into thirteen geographic units that would send representatives to a federal bicameral legislature obviously owed much to an American model, but there were important differ-

---

[130]Bolkhovitinov, *Russko-amerikanskie otnosheniia*, pp. 504–5. Bolkhovitinov and other Soviet historians, at least those writing during periods of relative peace and friendship, stress the American influences upon Ryleev, Murav'ev, and other Decembrists. See also A. I. Startsev, *Amerika i russkoe obshchestvo: Korni istoricheskoi druzhby russkogo i amerikanskogo narodov* (Tashkent: Gosizdat, 1942), pp. 11–21. For contemporary bragging about American influences on the Decembrists, see *National Intelligencer*, 14 September 1826.

[131]Quoted in Glynn Barratt, *Voices in Exile: The Decembrist Memoirs* (Montreal and London: McGill-Queen's University Press, 1974), p. 148. A friend of Pestel's recalled a conversation in which Pestel emphasized the American model of leadership for a Russian revolution. The more cautious friend replied, "Let's suppose that Washingtons and Franklins are found amongst us; even so, our society isn't ready for that revolution." Ibid., p. 112. For studies of the Decembrists that emphasize their liberal, "American" leanings, see Mazour, *First Russian Revolution, 1825*; and Dmitri von Mohrenschildt, *Toward a United States of Russia: Plans and Projects of Federal Reconstruction in the Nineteenth Century* (Rutherford, N.J.: Fairleigh Dickinson University Press, 1981), pp. 21–23.

ences. For example, the individual states were not allowed separate constitutions but would operate under a common standard provided in the federal constitution. The main contrast, however, was that the Russian blueprints did not guarantee the individual rights that were fundamental to the American Enlightenment. This missing cornerstone, compounded by the confusion that arose from mixing French and American ideological programs, largely explains the failures of Pestel, Ryleev, and Murav'ev. Nor was there a suitable vehicle, such as a constitutional convention, to sort out their differences. The Russian political extremists of that and later generations were far more elitist than the American Founding Fathers because of their class origins (nobility), philosophical education (intelligentsia), and the conditions for debate (police control and censorship) in which they were forced to pursue their goals.

Growing and maturing rapidly in the first half of the nineteenth century, the educated public in Russia had an opportunity to learn about the United States from the periodical press. Public craving for facts is obvious from the contents of such journals as *Istoricheskii, Statisticheskii i Geograficheskii Zhurnal* [Historical, Statistical and Geographical Magazine], *Otechestvennyia Zapiski* [Fatherland Notes], and *Dukh Zhurnalov* [Soul of Journals], all starting publication just after the Napoleonic Wars. Almost every issue contained information about the United States, but *Dukh Zhurnalov*, a sort of *Reader's Digest* of foreign periodicals, developed a particular focus on the transatlantic world—apparently one reason it was closed by the censor in 1820. Editors such as Pavel Svin'in of *Syn Otechestva* [Son of the Fatherland] and Nikolai Polevoi of *Moskovskii Telegraf* [Moscow Telegraph] were especially quick to publish material about the United States or about Americans in the 1830s.[132]

Although Svin'in's own sympathetic, firsthand portrait of the United States continued to have a wide readership in Russia, Petr Poletika, from an old Ukrainian family, followed in his footsteps with a more critical, but also more political, analysis, based on his observations as Russian minister. In his second chapter on population, Poletika demonstrated a keen insight into the complex American problem of racial differences:

[132]Bolkhovitinov has thoroughly analyzed the "American content" of *Dukh Zhurnalov* in *Russko-amerikanskie otnosheniia*, pp. 451–91; see also, Ia. A. Ivanchenko, "Promyshlennoe razvitie SShA v 20-30e gody xix v. v otsenke russkoi pechati," *Amerikanskii Ezhegodnik 1982* (Moscow: Nauka, 1982), pp. 229–53. For Svin'in's continuing influence on the Russian perception of the United States, see A. N. Nikoliukin, *Literaturnye sviazi Rossii i SShA: Stanovlenie literaturnykh kontaktov* (Moscow: Nauka, 1981), pp. 137–52. The most important of Svin'in's Russian contributions is contained in Avrahm Yarmolinsky, *Picturesque United States of America 1811, 1812, 1813* (New York: Rudge, 1930). The key excerpts can be found in A. N. Nikoliukin, *A Russian Discovery of America* (Moscow: Progress Publishers, 1986), pp. 136–59.

Slavery, however ameliorated it may be by the operation of laws and customs, is an absolute evil; because it is in the nature of slavery, as in every other usurpation of right or abuse of power, to retard civilization by cramping the development of the moral faculties with which the Supreme Being has endowed mankind. This evil assumes a character, dangerous in another way, in a country, where civil liberty is incessantly invoked—where every thing is done in its name and for its perpetuation. . . . The inconvenience of slavery is the more serious, as nature herself has placed an eternal barrier between the two classes, which, in the United States, stand towards each other in the relation of master and slave. The difference of colour and conformation of face, oppose insurmountable obstacles to their gradual emancipation.[133]

Russian readers could easily substitute "serfdom" for "slavery" and "Russia" for the "United States," one reason no doubt for the difficulty Poletika had in publishing this work in Russian. But, unlike many other European commentators, Poletika also considered the situation of the free black population.

Like their brethren in slavery, the free blacks and mulattoes are not only exiled from the society of whites, but excluded from all participation of power, by virtue of common usage; for the law does not recognize any difference of colour, nor does it establish any distinction except that of master and slave. Consequently it is very natural that the hostility existing between free blacks and whites, should be more inveterate than that of slaves towards their masters, the former being completely subjected to their control; for the free blacks knowing the delights and advantages of liberty, and living in the midst of free men, must frequently experience those mortifying and humiliating sensations that disdain and contempt never fail to inspire.[134]

[133][Poletika, P. I.], *A Sketch of the Internal Condition of the United States of America and of Their Political Relations with Europe, by a Russian, translated from the French by an American with Notes* (Baltimore: E. J. Coale, 1826), pp. 29–30. It is perhaps worth noting that the publisher was the Russian vice-consul for Baltimore. Excerpts in Nikoliukin, *A Russian Discovery*, pp. 160–79. See also Bolkhovitinov, *Russko-amerikanskie otnosheniia*, pp. 534–36.

After visiting Poletika in 1838, George Mifflin Dallas recorded a decidedly negative impression: "Mr. Poletika remembers but little of our country, has, perhaps, never been its friend, and is wholly ignorant of the real character of its recent history. He meddled with more art and success than candour in formating the treaty of 1824, by which Mr. Middleton has entailed upon the relations of Russia and America an embarrassing, if not incurable, source of strife." *Diary*, p. 118.

[134]S. D. Poltoratskii, "Poletika, Petr—bibliograficheskie zametki, 1815–50," Poltoratskii Collection, 41.11, Manuscript Division, Saltykov-Shchedrin State Public Library, Leningrad; "Poletika," *Russkii biograficheskii slovar'*, vol. 13 (St. Petersburg, 1913), pp. 328–29.

Poletika's treatise was published abroad in French and American editions. Although a Russian translation was announced, only excerpts were printed, first in *Journal de St. Petersburg* in 1825, then a few chapters in *Literaturnaia Gazeta* [Literary Gazette] in 1830, which may partly account for that journal ceasing publication immediately afterward. For direct political details of the United States, therefore, Russians had to rely primarily on foreign works that managed to slip through the censorship screen or were smuggled into the country.

Such, for example, was the case of Alexis de Tocqueville's *Democracy in America*, which was of considerable importance in shaping the image of the United States for a generation of Russian radicals, including Alexander Herzen, Michael Bakunin, and Nicholas Chernyshevsky. Harsh assessments of the United States, in fact, were often deemed even more dangerous than favorable ones, since they focused on the shortcomings of the great American experiment, such as the continued existence of slavery, thus again inviting comparisons with Russian serfdom. Criticism of the United States in these contexts could double as criticism of Russia, but because of the smokescreen of censorship and police surveillance, it is not easy to discern to what degree these ideas were absorbed.

A case in point is Alexander Pushkin's long review article in 1836 on *A Narrative of the Captivity and Adventures of John Tanner during Thirty Years Residence among the Indians*. Though Tanner's work was set mainly in British Canada, Pushkin used it as a vehicle to critique United States social and political development. The severe and unfair treatment (depicted by Tanner) of the Indians and blacks by the white settlers and their new "republican" government led Pushkin to denounce the tyranny of American "social democracy" and, by inference, the autocratic tyranny of Russia, which engaged in similar practices toward its population. In this he was obviously influenced by the first two volumes of Tocqueville's work.[135] Pushkin thus began a trend that would continue within the Russian intelligentsia to this day: While sharply critical of existing social and political circumstances in their own country, they doubted that the "democratic" institutions and processes of the United States could produce a harmonious, just society.

In any event, straight facts and political discourse still did not satisfy the general readership in Russia. Given the literary and romantic proclivities of the emerging intellectuals in Russia and the problems censorship presented for editors and writers, it is no surprise that Russian publishing emphasized American literature rather than explicit political or social commentary. The Russian audience, denied an opportunity to debate fully and openly the virtues and evils of American society, à la Tocqueville, had an unusually extensive familiarity with

[135]J. Thomas Shaw, "Pushkin on America: His 'John Tanner,' " in *Orbis Scriptus: Dmitrij Tschizewskij zum 70. Geburtstag*, ed. Dietrich Gerhardt et al. (Munich: Wilhelm Fink Verlag, 1966), pp. 738–56.

the American scene through poetry and fiction. Part of the fascination with the United States thus had nothing to do with politics but was stirred simply by the different, even exotic, settings of the North American continent portrayed by writers.

Washington Irving was the first American author to earn substantial public notice in Russia, partly because the name Washington was widely recognized (Russian journals even initially referred to him as Irving Washington) but also because his works easily lent themselves to translated excerpts in the periodical press. Moreover, Irving's reputation was enhanced in some Russian eyes by his association and correspondence with Dmitri Dolgorukov, a diplomat from a famous princely house and son of a well-known poet who was a friend of Pushkin's. Irving and Dolgorukov became acquainted in the 1820s while serving at respective diplomatic posts in Spain. That connection, combined with the Russian desire for the exotic and romantic, may explain why Irving's *Alhambra* (the notes for which he made while traveling with his Russian friend) was especially popular in its several Russian editions. Judging from both published and manuscript references, "Rip Van Winkle" became a stock term in literary and political conversation, although what was perhaps Irving's best and most "political" work, the Knickerbocker *History of New York*, remained untranslated into Russian until the 1850s.[136] Soviet scholars have amply demonstrated Irving's influence upon Pushkin, Gogol, and other Russian writers of this satirically minded and historically framed generation.

An American author of much greater renown and of more importance for his graphic portrayals of American life was James Fenimore Cooper. "Discovered" already in the 1820s, especially by Polevoi, and published in Polevoi's *Moskovskii Telegraf*, Cooper was most productive during the period of close Russian-American relations and the upsurge of Russian literary awareness in the 1830s and 1840s.[137] As a result, his best-known books—*The Last of the Mohicans*, *The Deerslayer*, and *The Pathfinder*—were published in Russian translation within months of the first English editions and required repeated printings. Americans

---

[136]Nikoliukin, *Literaturnye sviazi*, pp. 181–203. Alexander Hill Everett, the U. S. minister to Spain, may have inaugurated Irving's Russian connection; certainly he was interested both in Irving's literary career and in Russia. Washington Irving (Granada) to A. H. Everett (Madrid), 15 March 1828, Autograph file, Houghton Library, Harvard University; and Irving (Seville) to Everett, 15 April 1828, Everett-Peabody Papers, box 1, MassHS.

[137]For early excerpts from the work of "Irving Washington," see *Moskovskii Telegraf*, no. 4 (February 1825): 297–306, and no. 5 (March 1828): 28–50. About the same time, Polevoi was emphasizing the comparative poverty of Russian literature. Donald Fanger, *The Creation of Nikolai Gogol* (Cambridge, Mass.: Harvard University Press, 1979), p. 25.

traveling in Russia could converse on Cooper almost anywhere—with the empress and officials in the capital, or among the nobility in the provinces.[138]

Cooper's popularity in Russia can be credited in part to the enthusiasm with which literate Russians absorbed the romantic movement in philosophy and the arts as well as in literature. They were, therefore, also attracted to the novels of Sir Walter Scott, and comparative reviews, in which Cooper usually came out on top, appeared frequently in the Russian "fat" journals of the period. One of the best known of the literary critics and editors of this era, Vissarion Belinsky, was especially interested in the American author's natural and "positive" heroes and their battles against the evils of civilization.[139] Upon reading *The Pathfinder* in 1840, Belinsky wrote to a friend, "What a wonderful artiste! I am proud to have known him for a long time, yet this gem of a story—I will admit—has by far surpassed all the efforts of my feeble imagination."[140] He even defended one of Cooper's later novels, *Bravo*, that was incongruously set in Italy, after it was panned by most other Russian and European reviewers.

Like Irving, James Fenimore Cooper also had firsthand contact with Russians. While living in Paris in 1826 and 1827, he and his wife were frequent guests at the salon of Praskovia Golitsyna, where, incidentally, in November 1826, Cooper and Scott first met.[141] Princess Golitsyna, the daughter of one of Catherine the Great's most enlightened courtiers, Andrei Shuvalov, was by the Coopers' accounts an impressive woman and intellectual patronness. It was she apparently who inspired Cooper's plan to visit Russia in 1829. Although he never fulfilled that intention, Cooper continued to correspond with the Golitsyns, even offering to present fragments of George Washington's farm journal to her autograph-collecting daughter-in-law, Mariia Golitsyna, a granddaughter of the famous Field Marshal Suvorov.[142]

---

[138]In the summer of 1837, George Mifflin Dallas had a lengthy discussion with the empress about *The Spy*, *Pioneer*, and *The Last of the Mohicans*. *Diary*, p. 13. And Wikoff conversed with Russians in the South in 1835 about Cooper's works. Wikoff, *Reminiscences*, p. 240.

[139]I. M. Popova, "F. Kuper v otsenke V. G. Belinskogo," *Pisatel' i literaturnyi protsess: Sbornik nauchnykh statei*, vol. 6 (Dushanbe: Tadzhikskii gos. univ., 1979), pp. 61–72; A. K. Savurenok, "Roman Fenimora Kupera 'Bravo' v otsenke russkoi kritiki 1830-kh godov," *Russko-evropeiskie literaturnye sviazi: Sbornik statei k 70-letiiu so dnia rozhdeniia akademika M. P. Alekseeva* (Moscow-Leningrad: Nauka, 1966), pp. 122–26. Nikoliukin, *Literaturnye sviazi*, pp. 292–94; *Moskovskii Telegraf*, no. 13 (1831): 110.

[140]Quoted in Nikoliukin, *A Russian Discovery*, p. 205. Belinsky's favorable review of a Russian translation appeared in *Otechestvennyia Zapiski* in 1841.

[141]M. P. Alekseev, ed., *Neizdannye pis'ma inostrannykh pisatelei XVIII-XIX vekov iz Leningradskikh rukopisnykh sobranii* (Moscow-Leningrad: Nauka, 1960), p. 268; Nikoliukin, *Literaturnye sviazi*, pp. 262–63. M. A. Golitsyn had been a governess to Alexander Pushkin, thus providing another coincidental Russian-American literary link.

[142]Alekseev, *Neizdannye pis'ma*, p. 270. The Washington manuscript has not been located either in Cooper's papers or in the fairly extensive Golitsyn archive.

In 1829 another famous American writer claimed to have journeyed to Russia but apparently did not. The appearance of Edgar Allen Poe's works in Russia lagged behind other European countries, though Poe had achieved some recognition by the 1840s with the translation of "The Gold Bug" and later had a major influence on such prominent Russian writers as Fedor Dostoevsky. Contemporary Russian critics were not as receptive to Poe, however, and he was seldom treated as a genuine American writer. Poe's own account, penned in 1842, of a visit to Russia in the 1820s was repeated by his biographers and his later followers in Russia, even leading to general acceptance of his description of a conversation between himself and Alexander Pushkin.[143] Though no real proof exists of such travels, it is interesting to speculate on Poe's claim: Of all the places he might have gone, or people he might have seen, for whatever reason—why Russia? why Pushkin?

Besides a widespread awareness of American literature, some Russians may also have had a limited exposure to native American art through the efforts of George Catlin to peddle his Indian sketches and paintings in Russia, with minister Churchill Cambrelling and industrialist Joseph Harrison acting as intermediaries.[144] He also presented Nicholas I with a portfolio of sketches during the tsar's visit to England in 1844, for which Catlin was rewarded with a handsome gift of diamond rings. Certainly American Indian lore fascinated Russians, many of whom were surprised upon meeting Americans to discover that they were "white" rather than "red."

In the area of the physical sciences there were only a few direct contacts. In 1833 James Thal, an astronomer from St. Petersburg, visited the Boston area, where he met with Nathaniel Bowditch, Joshua Quincy, and several faculty members at Harvard. Thal brought letters and books from the leading Russian scholars in the field—Otto Struve, Friedrich Adelung, and Andrei Ostrogradskii—and returned with similar scientific materials.[145] With the growing in-

[143]Poe's own story, given wide circulation, included a rescue from a St. Petersburg jail by American minister Henry Middleton, who, still living at the time, neither confirmed nor denied it. See Nikoliukin, *Literaturnye sviazi*, pp. 327–46, and Joan Delaney Grossman, *Edgar Allan Poe in Russia: A Study in Legend and Literary Influence* (Wurzburg: Jal-Verlag, 1973), pp.23–24.

[144]Marjorie Catlin Roehm, ed., *The Letters of George Catlin and His Family: A Chronicle of the American West* (Berkeley and Los Angeles: University of California Press, 1966), pp. 198, 319, 412. Harrison was the most important patron and collector of Catlin's art (with Russian money?), acquired by the Smithsonian Institution in 1879. Lloyd Haberly, *Pursuit of the Horizon: A Life of George Catlin, Painter and Recorder of the American Indian* (New York: Macmillan, 1948), p. 178.

[145]James Thal (Moscow) to Nathaniel Bowditch, 14/26 January 1834, Bowditch Correspondence (doc. 203), Manuscript and Rare Book Department, BPL; N. N. Bolkhovitinov, "V arkhivakh i bibliotekakh SShA: Nakhodki, vstrechi, vpechatleniia," *Amerikanskii Ezhegodnik 1971* (Moscow: Nauka, 1971), pp. 329–41.

terest in scientific advancements in the 1840s, exchanges of books, maps, and mineral and cereal samples expanded, mostly between government agencies, libraries, and museums and a few individuals such as Thal, Struve, Joseph Hamel, and Charles Kramer.

The initiative for these contacts came from both sides, and they were quite varied. In 1844, for example, John Mears of Boston, "aware of the interest the Emperor takes in anything which relates to improvements in agriculture," sent him a "Boston Centre Draught Plough," manufactured by Prouty and Company, for which Mears received a handsome reward: "The medal, which weighs fifteen ounces, is on one side stamped with a fine likeness, in bold relief, of the Emperor Nicholas. . . . The medal is of elegant workmanship, and the reception of such a token of the Emperor's appreciation must be exceedingly gratifying to our young and enterprizing fellow-citizen."[146]

This burgeoning of scientific and technological activities occurred in both countries. The famous Pulkovo observatory near St. Petersburg was built during this period; in Washington, D.C., the new National Institution for the Promotion of Science was established, and among its chief supporters were Joel Poinsett, John Quincy Adams, and Russian minister Bodisko.[147] The founding of the Smithsonian Institution in 1845 strengthened interest in scientific exchanges and may have prompted the 1846 expedition to the United States of two Russian army engineers, Baron Alexander Wrangell and Lieutenant Pfeifer, "to procure information respecting the mining and uses of anthracite."[148] This led to a rich donation of Russian minerals to Walter Johnson of Philadelphia, who was a leading American scientist and educator, chemist for the Smithsonian, and the first secretary of the American Association for the Advancement of Science.

Though prominent American authors were well acquainted with Russians and seriously considered visiting the country, Russian writers seldom if ever met Americans and only toyed with the idea of traveling to that faraway place. This was one reason why Russian literature was scarcely known in the United States—in contrast to the Russian familiarity with American literature. The exposure to Russian works was mostly confined to a few copies of British translations and occasional poems in newspapers and periodicals. The only real American "expert" in the first half of the nineteenth century was William David Lewis, who introduced the readership of Philadelphia newspapers to samplings of Russian poetry, which were later collected in a book of very limited circulation. James Gates Percival, a Yale graduate from Connecticut, pursued an amateur interest in foreign languages and after 1830 concentrated on Russian. He was especially attracted to Adelung's scholarly study of languages, and he sold

[146]*National Intelligencer*, 17 June 1845.
[147]Ibid., 7 January 1841.
[148]"Mineral Wealth of Russia," ibid., 30 December 1848.

translations of Russian poetry to a number of New England publications. Writing under the name of "Talvj" (derived from her maiden name, Therese Albertina Louisa von Jakoban), Therese Robinson was the first to produce a scholarly study of Slavic literature from its inception.[149]

Essentially, American knowledge of Russian literature during the first half of the century was rudimentary. Yet Americans were exposed to numerous political and social commentaries on Russia, ranging from the travel accounts of John Stephens, to the banquet addresses given by prominent Americans who visited Russia and recounted their impressions, sometimes receiving broad press coverage.[150] Much of the general material about Russia was of British origin and was marred by a distinct anti-Russian tone. As a result, the published information on Russia was often distrusted by Americans for being colored by a British or French bias.

The *North American Review*—especially the essays of Alexander Hill Everett—the *American Annual Register*, and the many anti-British newspapers tried to redress the balance and set the record straight. For the most part, however, Americans had to rely on quite fragmentary evidence, such as letters from visitors in Russia that were passed around to relatives and friends, the "correspondence" columns that filtered in news from Russia through London, Paris, Rome, and other western European cities, and the pieces of gossip derived from the small Russian diplomatic community in Washington. Despite the obvious handicaps of reporting accurately on the political and social character of Russia, surprisingly sophisticated attempts were made. Some were inspired, no doubt, by that sense of duty that often motivates the first citizens of the country; an example is John Quincy Adams' long and favorable description of Russian affairs in the Balkans for the *American Annual Register for the Years 1827–9*.

[149]On Lewis's background, see Chapter 2, and Norman E. Saul, "A Russian 'Yankee Doodle,' " *Slavic Review* 33, 1 (March 1974): 46–54. The compilation of Russian poetry was published privately by Lewis under the title: *The Bakchesarian Fountain, by Alexander Pooshkeen, and Other Poems, by Various Authors, Translated from the Original Russian by William D. Lewis* (Philadelphia: by author, 1849); Avrahm Yarmolinsky, ed., *Pushkin in English: A List of Works by and about Pushkin* (New York: New York Public Library, 1937), pp. 5, 8; Nikoliukin, *Literaturnye sviazi*, pp. 359–60; Talvj, *Historical View of the Languages and Literature of the Slavic Nations; with a Sketch of Their Popular Poetry* (New York: Putnam, 1850); Albert Parry, *America Learns Russian: A History of the Teaching of the Russian Language in the United States* (Syracuse, N.Y.: Syracuse University Press, 1967), pp. 28–33.

[150]*National Intelligencer*, 23 November 1831, citing the Lynchburg *Virginius*: "We have heard some of the outlines of the speech of Mr. Randolph on Monday last; but they do not come in a shape sufficiently precise to authorize a specific mention of them. It may not be improper to say, however, that he gave an account of his mission to Russia, which must have been interesting, considering the length of time he tarried at St. Petersburgh."

Circulating widely throughout the country, the *National Intelligencer* came the closest to being an official American newspaper. It provided its readers in the 1830s with a fairly correct and comprehensive history of Russia. "Tacitus" (William Darby) began by condemning the neglect of the subject and the reliance on slanted British publications: "But even with the aid of continental writers, our literature is still not simply barren of facts on the modern Northern nations, but such facts as we have in our books, especially respecting Russia, are, in a peculiar manner distorted."[151] Tacitus stressed that "Russia had more European than Asiatic principles in her primitive organization, and that her connexions with Europe commenced with her existence [with emphasis on the Varangian origin of the Russian state], was renewed by the introduction of Christianity, and was never really broken from the age of Ruric to the present time."[152]

Tacitus was especially critical of the assumption that western Europe was inherently superior to Russia. Above all, he believed that peace was essential for the progress of both:

> In justice to opinion long since recorded in the *National Intelligencer*, I must again repeat, that every consideration of sound policy, every rational induction from history, and in particular the history of the last half century, calls upon the governors and governed in Western Europe to avoid war with Russia, and await the gradual but sure infusion of liberal-thinking, and free institutions amongst the Sclavonic nations—a course of things in actual operation, and which *may* be retarded, and certainly *cannot* be accelerated by war.[153]

Also of interest is his depiction of early Russian-American relations:

> The armed neutrality was the first great national act on the part of Russia which exhibited the hatred of Great Britain, and real cordiality has never since been, perhaps never can be, restored between these rival powers. It is not by any means creditable to our national good sense, that British and French clamor against Russia is so commonly repeated and acceded to in the

[151]*National Intelligencer*, 19 June 1839. Darby is best known for his geographical and statistical yearbooks but certainly deserves attention for his other work. Born in Kentucky early enough to have been a friend of Daniel Boone, he spent most of his later life in eastern Ohio and western Pennsylvania. His writings for the *National Intelligencer* range from reminiscences of his work as a surveyor and mapper of Louisiana after the purchase and of his service with Andrew Jackson's military expeditions in the area to commentaries on constitutional issues and on foreign affairs from the 1820s until his death in 1854. The longest were devoted to detailed histories of European countries; those of 1839 on Russia were also published separately as *The Northern Nations of Europe, Russia and Poland* (Chilicothe, Ohio: by author, 1841).

[152]*National Intelligencer*, 21 August 1839.

[153]Ibid., 22 October 1834.

United States. The facts are, that as long as Russia stands a great Eastern Power, any serious collision with the United States will be avoided by both France and Great Britain. Russia is, from both position and power, the only real and natural ally the United States can have in Europe. That alliance, in point of fact, commenced with the armed neutrality, and continues and must continue, without any documentary parchments to secure the compact or express its conditions.[154]

Opinions of this kind drew from one reader the accusation that the writer was a member of the Russian legation staff, which the editor firmly denied. Tacitus was a retired American, living several hundred miles from Washington, who never had any connection with any diplomatic post: "Of philosophic mind and deeply read in history, he presents the fruits of his knowledge to his countrymen for their instruction, free from any bias, national or political."[155] He was later identified in the paper as William Darby, a geographer and publisher of statistical treatises, from the Kentucky-Ohio region.

Another mysterious American, "G. S.,"[156] writing from the Kuban in Russia, supported Tacitus's plea for a better understanding of Russia:

> Do not imagine that I speak with any too favorable words or feelings of Russia. I know this country *well*. I have seen her thoroughly in *all her parts*. The whole nation stands before the civilized world in a light which should entitle it to its warmest sympathy and regard. But this sympathy is not given in Europe.
>
> It is from America and from Americans that an impartial view of Russia should come, if from any quarter. With seven thousand miles of land and water between us, we have nothing to fear from her political advancement, and can look calmly at her progress, without the ridiculous imagination that her next step will be to devour us. . . .
>
> My travels here have been *patient labor*. I know what a mass of incorrect information in regard to Russia is abroad in the world, and I know the difficulty, the extreme difficulty to a foreigner, of learning anything there but the

[154]Ibid., 10 September 1839.

[155]Ibid., 16 October 1839. Darby also contributed to the *Saturday Evening Post*, presented lectures in Washington and elsewhere, and served several years as political editor of the Pittsburgh *Advocate and Advertiser*.

[156]The identity of "G. S." remains unknown. The likely candidate is George Sontag, but he had not left the United States just two years before, as the author states. Perhaps it was an American named Codman from Marblehead (a relative of Ropes?), whom Vincent Nolte met in Odessa in 1840 and who had received special favors from the government. Nolte, *Fifty Years in Both Hemispheres*, p. 454.

most partial and imperfect, I will say ridiculous, information in regard to her. I have taken great pains, *working hard*, by learning the language, and by studying thoroughly all her institutions, to make myself *well* acquainted with her. . . .

There is no work upon Russia—and I have seen more than sixty, in English and French—that is not filled with errors, from beginning to end! . . . But we are so deluged by books of travel, written by persons who have *never seen*, or have, at most, merely flown through the country which they describe.[157]

Tacitus, like other astute observers in succeeding generations, could only say "Amen" to this, but he thought "G. S." had gone too far in defending Russian military campaigns in the Caucasus and suggested that he should visit Afghanistan and report on the oppression there.[158] But other readers believed Tacitus betrayed his own plea for objectivity in his defense of the partitioning of Poland. At least he had stimulated a lively discussion on rather complex issues involving Russia.

That Americans were really interested in Russia is shown by the fact that the travel account of John Lloyd Stephens, one of the first by an American, went through five printings in 1838. The Marquis de Custine's famous critique of Russia in 1839, however, seems not to have received much attention, even after an English edition was finally available to the American public in 1843. Probably because of its suspected bias, newspapers and journals virtually ignored it.[159] Most Americans who read it and knew something about Russia would doubtless have agreed with an Englishman who went to Russia specifically to test Custine's conclusions: "M. de Custine's 'Russia in thirty nine' has made a great sensation in Europe, and has been almost universally read. In spite of the egotism, vanity, superficialness, and disregard of truth which pervade the whole book, if we could manage to leave out the stories of individuals, politics, and the writer's own deductions and absurd inferences, we should find perhaps the best picture of the present state of Russia that has been given to the world."[160]

Thanks to the pioneering work of Darby, Stephens, and others, Americans could form quite different but not necessarily conflicting views about Russia. During his travels in 1835, Stephens found that "to an American Russia is an interesting country. True it is not classic ground; but as for me, who had now travelled over the faded and wornout kingdoms of the Old World, I was quite

---

[157]*National Intelligencer*, 2 October 1839.

[158]Ibid., 19 October 1839.

[159]For more on the contemporary reaction to Custine both in Europe and the United States, see George F. Kennan, *The Marquis de Custine and His "Russia in 1839"* (Princeton, N.J.: Princeton University Press, 1971).

[160]Richard Southwell Bourke Mayo, *St. Petersburg and Moscow: A Visit to the Court of the Czar* (London: Henry Coburn, 1846), p. 69.

ready for something new. Like our own Russia is a new country, and in many respects resembles ours."[161]

For most Americans this was the standard perception, reinforced by the often-
quoted passage in Tocqueville's *Democracy in America*, which also dates to 1835:

> There are, at the present time, two great nations in the world which seem to
> tend towards the same end, although they started from different points: I al-
> lude to the Russians and the Americans. Both of them have grown up unno-
> ticed; and whilst the attention of mankind was directed elsewhere, they have
> suddenly assumed a most prominent place amongst the nations; and the
> world learned of their existence and their greatness at almost the same time.
>
> All other nations seem to have nearly reached their natural limits, and only
> to be charged with the maintenance of their power; but these are still in the
> act of growth; all the others are stopped, or continue to advance with extreme
> difficulty; these are proceeding with ease and with celerity along a path to
> which the human eye can assign no term. The American struggles against the
> natural obstacles which oppose him; the adversaries of the Russian are men;
> the former combats the wilderness and savage life; the latter, civilization with
> all its weapons and its arts: the conquests of the one are therefore gained by
> the ploughshare; those of the other by the sword. The Anglo-American relies
> upon personal interest to accomplish his ends, and gives free scope to the un-
> guided exertions and common-sense of the citizens; the Russian centers all
> the authority of society in a single arm: the principal instrument of the
> former is freedom; of the latter servitude. Their starting-point is different, and
> their courses are not the same; yet each of them seems to be marked out by
> the will of Heaven to sway the destinies of half the globe.[162]

In general Tocqueville's account of the United States had a much greater impact
in both countries than did Custine's contemporary portrait of Russia.

Echoing Tocqueville, Platon Chikhachev described his impressions of the
United States for a Russian audience from travels in the mid-1830s, the same
time that Stephens was touring Russia:

> During my stay in North America I often thought of my country.
> The wealth of resources with which each of these two states has been en-
> dowed by providence, the stability of the basic principles upon which their

[161]Stephens, *Incidents of Travel*, 1:258.

[162]Alexis de Tocqueville, *Democracy in America*, rev. ed., 2 vols. (New York: Colonial
Press, 1900), 1:441–42.

prosperity is built, and, finally, the youth of their population, keen-witted and full of life, often led me to compare them to each other, and long reflection has further confirmed me in my conviction.

Leaving aside their political sphere of activity, one may affirm that Russia and the United States are two states before whom there is opening up a most promising future. The geographical position of both is simple and continuous: the motive forces of popular activity although different in essence, are young and powerful. Having emerged only recently into the light of history, they have already secured for themselves a place in the future, moving with a firm and stately tread towards their goal.

Whatever may be the political future of these people, who should indeed be called a people rather than a state, whatever their talk about slavery and the individual claims of the provinces may lead to, a huge field of action stretches before them. . . .

. . . if the New World has been blessed by heaven as regards its physical structure, if it is endowed with rivers such as the Mississippi, the Ohio, the Missouri and the St. Lawrence, on which reign industry and the spirit of enterprise, there is another land on the other side of the globe that is no less blessed, and there can be no doubt that the Volga, with its numerous tributaries forming a chain as it were, that links the Caspian and the Baltic, the Dnieper and the Dvina, the Black Sea and Riga, the Niemen and the Vistula . . . are all worthy rivals of the rivers of America. Is not our steppe the same as their prairie? . . .

Everything is identical in this geographical comparison: the same gigantic size, the same majesty in proportion, the same natural advantages for the construction of transport systems—the Allegheny Mountains and the Urals both mark the beginning of broad expanses of level land suitable for railways and farming; everything depends only on the degree to which men are prepared to work.[163]

In 1839, not long after leaving the presidency, Andrew Jackson expressed a similar but more alarming picture of Russian-American relations, seeing Russia as a future rival: "I do not apprehend war with Great Britain for a long period. The next great war we have will be with Russia." When reminded of the current amity that existed between the two countries, the former president responded, "True, but a growing absolute monarchy and a thriving democratic government are naturally antagonistic. It is easy to find pretexts for war; our vicinity to her North-western Pacific possessions will suffice." And what would be the result?

[163]Platon Chikhachev, "On Shipping and Lakes in North America (Extracts from Travel Notes), in Nikoliukin, *A Russian Discovery*, pp. 202–4.

"We will beat them, sir; we can whip all Europe with United States soldiers."[164] If reported accurately, Jackson's comment might still be dismissed as the whimsical mutterings of a bad-tempered former president, except that it probably reflected a fairly common chauvinistic view in frontier America—and conservative Russia—that would harbor the seeds of future conflict.

What is obvious from a perusal of the pages of the *National Intelligencer* and other major American newspapers and journals is that there was an audience for material on Russia, and journalists were responding to it on the whole with surprisingly honest and forthright news, information, and editorial discussions. Considering the obstacles, basic details and their interpretations were as well balanced and sophisticated in the first half of the nineteenth century as they probably ever would be, thanks especially to widespread American literacy and open curiosity.

To many observers then and since, the United States and Russia were following parallel paths toward realization of national goals. One objective was territorial, taking in and assimilating vast stretches of seemingly open land in the North American continent and in Asia, respectively. Both countries also looked south for economic and political reasons: Russia, to gain control of the outlet from the Black Sea and to restrain an old enemy, the Ottoman Turks; the United States, to exclude European powers from the Caribbean and Central and South America and to establish hegemony. In each case they confronted entrenched western European powers, chiefly Britain and France, thus creating an as-yet ill-defined bond of geopolitical mutual interest.

Romantic idealism was also part of the picture. As manifest destiny to many Americans meant not simply territorial acquisition but a triumph of the republican spirit of the United States, so a growing number of Russians perceived a national-imperial mission in civilizing indigenous peoples and protecting and advancing other Slavic groups and Orthodox Christians. But there were also divisions in the messianic impulses that had wider implications. While Americans would divide over slavery, especially the exportation of a slave economy to new territories, Russians would clash over the autocratic nature of their state and the direction of reform. The dispute over the latter became the cardinal feature of the Slavophile-Westerner debate of that generation—whether Russia should look outward to the West for inspiration, as Peter the Great had, or whether it should stress the uniqueness and viability of its own historic institutions and society. In both countries, dynamic romanticism fostered agitation, violence, and instability and encouraged an exaggerated sense of self-confidence and messianism, of manifest destiny.

[164]James Parton, *Life of Andrew Jackson*, vol. 3 (Boston: James R. Osgood, 1876), p. 634.

The period from 1820 to 1845 laid the foundations for the more intimate interaction between the two countries that would follow. One important new development—Russia's search for technological guidance from the United States—would be a permanent element of the Russian-American relationship. Through romantic lenses, each perceived the other as a young, changing, expanding nation, which, though with far different constitutional histories and practices, shared certain visions: among them, respective continents to conquer, tame, and develop; and a desire on the part of many vocal elements of both populations to improve their economic, social, and political circumstances. Their respective and separate paths toward territorial expansion and internal reform, however, would be difficult and bloody.

4

Entente

The close relations and the sense of understanding that prevailed between Russia and the United States in the middle of the nineteenth century were based on some complex factors that are not easy to rank in importance. Most frequently cited are the perception of a common enemy (Britain and, to a lesser degree, France); the lack of substantial points of disagreement; and parallel, basically nonconflicting territorial and economic expansion.[1] Not to be omitted certainly is the historical record of friendship and assistance, as well as the mutual sense of complementary progress and development. Taken together, these reasons still fail to explain completely the phenomenon of a growing entente between the large and expanding democratic republic of North America and the equally expansive autocratic empire of Eurasia at midcentury.

Hostility toward, or fear of, Britain, for example, doubtless played a role in the relationship but should not be overemphasized. Though rivalries existed, Britain was also the chief trading partner of both countries. The times of greatest cooperation between the United States and Russia coincided with limited Russian rapprochement with Britain—such as around 1832, and again in 1844 with the historic visit of Nicholas I to Britain. And many of those Americans who had the most intimate involvement with Russia—Whistler,[2] Ropes, Gibson, Winans,

[1] The best analytical works in this respect are those by John Lewis Gaddis, *Russia, the Soviet Union, and the United States: An Interpretive History* (New York: John Wiley and Sons, 1978), pp. 1–26; Benjamin Platt Thomas, *Russo-American Relations, 1815–1867,* Johns Hopkins University Studies in Historical and Political Science, vol. 48, no. 2 (Baltimore: Johns Hopkins University Press, 1930), pp. 108–21; and Frank A. Golder, "Russian American Relations during the Crimean War," *American Historical Review* 31, 3 (April 1926): 462–76.

[2] The father of George Washington Whistler had fought in the Revolutionary War—on the British side—before joining the American army after the peace, and there were still a number of Whistler relatives in England. Biographical notes by Anna Whistler, vol. 34, pp. 5–9, Pennell-Whistler Papers, Manuscript Division, LC.

and Lewis—were also confirmed Anglophiles, while progressive-minded Russians who were quick to demonstrate their friendship to Americans were often admirers of Britain and France as well. Business, science, education, and liberal crusades such as abolition drew leading citizens of European and American nations together in common cause. There is no question, however, that in the 1840s increased friction with Britain over Oregon and Cuba led to a rise in American Anglophobia at the same time that Britain was experiencing a growing Russophobia for ideological and imperial reasons. Britain's fears were especially fired by the "Eastern Question"—the threat posed to the weakening Ottoman Empire and to British interests in the Middle East and South Asia by Russian military and naval superiority and by rising national consciousness among its Christian subjects in the Balkans. Both trends, however, were rather specific responses to particular situations and hardly sufficient to support a long-term understanding between the United States and Russia.

The absence of disruptive points of friction between the two countries may be considered more a result than a cause of good relations. In fact, there were a number of brooding tensions. By the 1840s Russia and the United States had become the chief competitors in grain sales to western Europe. The rapid increase in the number of American whaling vessels in the North Pacific was leading to more incidents, clear violations of Russian sovereignty, and reciprocal fears of aggression that in other circumstances could have resulted in diplomatic conflict, even war. And as Russia was becoming more defensive about its relatively backward social and political institutions in reaction to industrial change and liberal aspirations in western Europe, the United States was gaining self-assurance as the citadel, at least morally and symbolically, of democratic ideals. The liberal foundations of Jacksonian democracy and the "America first" aspects of manifest destiny would appear to be irreconcilable with the conservative credo of the reign of Nicholas I—"autocracy, orthodoxy, nationality." Though the foreign interests of the two countries were quite separate and relatively independent of each other, there were overall similarities. Russia looked southward into the Balkans and the Ottoman Empire, pushed by Slavophile messianism and the Russian army and restrained by the cautious "German" Karl Nesselrode and his diplomatic staff; meanwhile, the United States gazed on Cuba, a long-cherished target of expansionists that was kept distant by the slave–free soil rivalry. For the United States and Russia, territorial gain and economic interest in the Pacific were secondary considerations but rising in importance by 1850.

Both countries were thus expanding territorially and economically, and though for the time being they did not actually covet the same places, it is normally the nature of one aggrandizing empire to fear and regret the success of another and perceive potential if not actual areas of conflict. In the balance-of-power equation, third parties such as Britain and France were natural variables, as alliances could—and did—easily shift. But beyond all these elements, one must still look for other factors, perhaps more subtle in operation, that brought the two countries together.

Diplomatic Transitions

The "entente" between Russia and the United States can certainly not be credited to the skills of American diplomacy. After George Mifflin Dallas's departure from St. Petersburg in 1839, Washington was represented in Russia by a series of eccentric persons with little or no foreign experience. The parsimonious and solitary Charles S. Todd rivaled John Randolph in becoming a laughingstock of the Russian capital.[3] His well-intentioned blundering was mitigated by the presence of John Stevenson Maxwell as his secretary and then by the return of John Randolph Clay, who capably filled the seventeen-month gap between Todd and his replacement, Ralph Ingersoll. This congressman from Connecticut had dallied several months in western Europe and then managed to write only fourteen inconsequential dispatches during his year's tenure in St. Petersburg (May 1847 to June 1848). Clay, the veteran diplomat who possessed the best knowledge of Russia at the time, was inexplicably reassigned to Peru. Ingersoll's secretaries were his even more inexperienced son, Colin, and a young student, Henry Shelton Sanford, who was later prominent as a diplomat and Florida land speculator. All three escaped Russia and the cholera epidemic before the summer of 1848, leaving absolutely no one of official character in St. Petersburg (Abraham Gibson, the aging consul-general, being typically absent). Colin Ingersoll returned in September to endure the fortunately brief tenure of Arthur P. Bagby.[4]

The Polk administration, even with the presence of former diplomat George Mifflin Dallas as vice-president and James Buchanan as secretary of state, was responsible for some of the worst appointments in the history of American foreign

[3]One story that circulated about Todd concerned his conversation with a lady-in-waiting at an imperial reception in the Winter Palace. In his bad French with a Kentucky accent, he mispronounced the word for year, so that an explanation of his travels came out: "I was an ass in Paris, part an ass in London, almost an ass in Germany, and I am two asses here." To which the lady reportedly responded, "And you will be an ass wherever you go." Charleston *Mercury*, 12 August 1853. An English resident also probably had Todd in mind when he wrote that American diplomats "are rather dandified and walk with a mincing gait." Robert Harrison, *Notes of a Nine Years' Residence in Russia, from 1844 to 1853 with a Notice of the Tzars Nicholas I and Alexander II* (London: T. Cautley Newby, 1855), p. 31.

[4]The tenures and gaps are calculated from the diplomatic reports, DUSM, Russia, vols. 14–15 (rolls 14–15, M 35), RG 59, NA. On Sanford, see Joseph A. Fry, *Henry S. Sanford: Diplomacy and Business in Nineteenth Century America* (Reno: University of Nevada Press, 1982), pp. 8–11.

relations. Senator Bagby of Alabama had been a loyal supporter of the administration in Congress and an advocate of a second term for Polk. He was thus rewarded, much to his and everyone else's surprise, with a late appointment to the
Russian court. Preceded by a substantial consignment of diplomatic liquor, he
arrived in August 1848 in an alcoholic stupor and sobered up briefly in December for a long-postponed audience with the emperor. His condition annoyed
straight-laced resident Americans such as Anna Whistler: "We are all mortified
by the conduct of our new minister, tho' few of us have seen Mr. Bagby. The position of our young secretary, Mr. Ingersoll, is rendered extremely embarrassing."[5] Edward Wright, eventually a secretary to Bagby's successor, was even more
critical: "If Bagby had been actuated by some higher motive than *money-making*,
when he came abroad, do you suppose he would have lain a drunken sot at a
cheap hotel?"[6] The tendency of American presidents to appoint political cronies
purely for the title, monetary reward, and the opportunity to travel has never
promoted the national interest.

Bagby, probably assisted by Colin Ingersoll, still managed in his fifth—and
last—formal communication to report accurately on the Russian role in sup-
pressing the Hungarian revolt in 1849: "The ostensible and avowed object of
aiding Austria in the pending struggle with Hungary, as you will perceive from
the Imperial manifesto, is to put down the spirit of revolt in the latter country—
the real and ultimate object, is to arrest the march of liberal principles in this
section of Europe, and thereby assure the present tranquillity, and the future security of the Russian empire, and government."[7] Though the United States
might have been better off with no one in St. Petersburg than with Bagby, his
departure produced another hiatus in relations. Despite the growing attention

[5]Anna Whistler's postscript of 5 December 1848 to her enfeebled husband's letter to
Joseph Gardner Swift, Whistler-Swift Papers, Manuscript Division, NYPL. For Bagby's
connection with Polk, see Allan Nevins, ed., *Polk: The Diary of a President 1845–1849*
(New York: Capricorn Edition, 1968), pp. 7, 132–33; and John M. Martin, "The Senatorial Career of Arthur Pendleton Bagby," *Alabama Historical Quarterly* 42, 3–4 (Fall
and Winter 1980): 155–56, who noted that "monetary arrangements associated with
the position made it possible for him to resolve some of his financial problems." The
minister's conduct got back to Washington through various channels—for example, Silas Burrows to John Clayton, 15 June 1849, in Don Steers, *Silas Enoch Burrows, 1794–
1870: His Life and Letters* (Chester, Conn.: Pequot Press, 1971), p. 84.

[6]Edward H. Wright to his mother, 8 November 1850, in "Letters from St. Petersburg,
1850–1851," *Proceedings of the New Jersey Historical Society* 82, 2 (April 1964): 85.

[7]Bagby to Clayton, 14 May 1849, DUSM, Russia, vol. 15 (roll 15, M 35), RG 59,
NA. The judgment of Bagby by his contemporaries in Russia may be unduly harsh. It is
apparent from his long, sentimental letters to his wife that he was homesick, depressed,
obsessively fearful of cholera, and concerned about finances, but by March he seemed
to be recovering his composure (or sobering up). Letters of 15 January, 21 March, 15
April, and 16 May 1849, Bagby Papers, State of Alabama Department of Archives and
History, Montgomery.

in the United States to the European situation, there was a fifteen-month gap before Neill Brown, a former governor of Tennessee, arrived.

In contrast to Bagby, Brown was sober to a fault. As his secretary, Edward Wright, described him: "Mr. Brown you know is a quiet man, bent on making money and living on air if possible; while most of the other Ministers have their wives with them, live in fine style and entertain a great deal, and as a consequence are much courted by the natives."[8] This highlights one dilemma of an "ordinary" American in Russia: maintaining an effective diplomatic presence without a knowledge of French and without sufficient means. As Brown himself explained: "I regard my style of living as a medium one. It would be difficult to reduce it with respectability, and difficult to exceed it without bankruptcy. With my family here my expences would absorb my whole salary and probably exceed it. . . . A man without a fortune is compelled to measure his steps."[9]

Yet there were some obvious advantages in the fresh and direct reporting about Russia made by relative novices in foreign affairs. Many later Russian and Soviet "experts" would echo Brown's critical assessment of Russia:

A strange superstition prevails among the Russians, that they are destined to conquer the world, and the prayers of the priests in the church are mingled with requests to hasten and consummate this "divine mission," while appeals to soldiery founded on this idea of fatality, and its glorious rewards, are seldom made in vain. To a feeling of this sort has been attributed that remarkable patience and endurance, which distinguish the Russian soldier in the midst of the greatest privations.

Russia occupies, and will continue to occupy, a commanding position in every struggle against popular rights. And though other governments, its allies, and subordinates, may seem to be most active, yet they are but puppets on the stage. The motive power is the man behind the scenes, and that man is the Emperor of Russia. He is the formidable antagonist of the people. He is the modern Philip of Macedon, strong in resources both mental and physical, but still more powerful in his position, and impelled by a hostility to free institutions, that admits of no compromise and yields to no relaxation.[10]

[8]Wright to his sister, 30 November 1850, in "Letters from St. Petersburg," p. 90. Obviously, Wright did not find the minister a pleasant companion: "The Governor honestly despises balls, dinners, and opera; not because he dislikes such amusement, for he is utterly ignorant of their enjoyment, but because he considers them nothing but fashionable folly—and he is resolved to show his independence." But he added a measure of agreement, "There is NOTHING that fills a stranger with such a feeling of loneliness as a visit to this same city." To his sister, 1 November 1850, ibid., p. 78.
[9]Brown to A. O. P. Nicholson, 25 October 1850, Miscellaneous Papers, NYHS.
[10]To Daniel Webster, 28 January 1852 (no. 15), DUSM, Russia, vol. 15 (roll 15, M 35) RG 59, NA.

And after a long discussion of the minimal impact American press sympathy for the Hungarian rebel leaders had on friendly Russian-American relations, Brown concluded parenthetically, "I still believe there has been some *winter about the palace*."[11]

Though Brown stayed at his post almost three years, counting summer vacations in western Europe, another change of administrations in Washington produced another long vacancy at the legation in St. Petersburg from June 1853 through March 1854—an important period in international relations that witnessed the beginning of the Crimean War. At least part of the delay, however, was due to the desire of the new minister, Gov. Thomas Henry Seymour of Connecticut, to postpone his departure until after the conclusion of a state legislative session.

The consul-general's office was in no position to pick up the slack during the long diplomatic gaps. Abraham Gibson was accustomed to spending protracted "leaves" in England and left consular affairs in the hands of an assistant, Abraham Van Sassen, who was principally occupied as a chief partner of a leading St. Petersburg trading house. Though negligent of his duty, Gibson was still upset when he was summarily dismissed in 1851 after serving nearly thirty-two years in this office: "It only remains for me to express my regret that after so long and faithful a service, I should have been removed without any previous intimation from the Government, or any evidence of respect for my public official conduct and character."[12] Such were the rewards one could expect as an American career foreign-service officer in the nineteenth century. Gibson's removal was followed by the death in 1852 of the longtime vice-consul at Kronstadt, Charles R. Lenartzen. These openings were filled in a makeshift fashion by short-term appointments of local American businessmen, such as William L. Winans, who were naturally more interested in their own enterprises.

Fortunately for the course of Russian-American relations during this period, the story of the Russian mission in the United States sharply contrasted with its American counterpart. With security of tenure, substantial support from the Russian government, and possessing a private fortune wisely invested in both the United States and Russia, Alexander Bodisko continued to build his reputation and exploit his position as dean of the diplomatic corps in Washington. The lavish entertainments at his Georgetown "palace," at his nearby country estate, or at Newport in the summer received ample newspaper coverage and were fondly anticipated by the high personages of each new administration. He still visited regularly with family and officials in St. Petersburg, maintaining his connections there and improving his knowledge of Russian court politics. Following

[11]To Webster, 29 February 1852 (no. 16), ibid.

[12]Gibson (London) to Webster, 3 March 1851, DUSC, St. Petersburg, vol. 10 (roll 6, M 81), RG 59, NA.

is a typical news report on one such departure: "Speaking our language with the fluency of his own, he has mingled with ease and without ostentation with our citizens, and, by the urbanity and frankness and liberal hospitality which have distinguished him, he has won the warm regard of all; a sentiment which was doubtless strengthened by the fact of his having formed among us and with us the dearest and tenderest of ties [his marriage]. The best wishes of our community attend him and his estimable and lovely lady."[13] The American press seemed to delight in the rare constancy that Bodisko provided to the Washington scene, such as at Zachary Taylor's inauguration: "At the head of the corps was M. Bodisco, whose well-known figure, erect, military, and covered with glittering orders, attracted the attention of all observers."[14]

Bodisko also kept a full staff of secretaries—Eduard Stoeckl, Konstantin Katakazi, and Charles Krehmer—two of whom would serve as ministers to the United States over the next seventeen years. To complete the entourage were his American wife, five children, two handsome (and single) nephew-aides (Boris and Vladimir), and an international staff of fifteen to twenty domestic servants. When Bodisko died suddenly in January 1854, both houses of Congress scheduled formal eulogies. Senators and congressmen joined the cabinet, presidents past and present, and the whole diplomatic corps in paying their respects at the funeral, which was said to rival that of President Taylor four years earlier in splendor and attendance.[15]

But even Bodisko's lengthy seventeen-year tenure as minister could not match that of the veteran consul Aleksei Evstaf'ev, who at his retirement in 1857 had completed over forty-five years as consul-general in Boston and New York, perhaps an all-time record. Augmenting the continuity and bolstering the potential strength of Russian consular affairs were a number of prominent American businessmen, who served as vice-consuls in several American port cities, the most

[13]*National Intelligencer*, 19 September 1843.

[14]Ibid., 6 March 1849.

[15]A resolution in the Senate to adjourn formally for Bodisko's funeral was withdrawn because opposition on grounds of lack of precedent would have led to an awkward recorded vote. A typical funeral description follows: "The funeral of Mr. Bodisco yesterday, in Georgetown, furnished strong testimony of the respect and regard entertained for the deceased by all ranks and classes of persons among us. The array of carriages was unusually large even for the funeral of one of high official position, and great numbers of private citizens identified themselves with the occasion. The body was conveyed in an open hearse in a coffin of the best material, but plain and unornamented, followed on foot by Mrs. Bodisco, her children, and the remaining members of the family and suite of the deceased, all the way from the residence on 2nd street to the cemetery on the heights." Ibid., 26 January 1854. For another contemporary report, see Edward Everett diary, 25 January 1854, Everett-Noble Papers, MassHS. The granite shaft that marks the gravesite in Oak Hill Cemetery was cut and sent from Russia. John Clagett Proctor, *Proctor's Washington and Environs* (Washington: by author, 1949), p. 171.

important of which, after New York, Boston, and Philadelphia, were Baltimore, New Orleans, Mobile, Charleston, Savannah, and San Francisco.

As one might expect from such a stable and experienced diplomatic corps, the Russian legation in Washington kept its government very well informed. In fact, the dispatches of Bodisko and his secretaries provide a unique contemporary account of the course of American political and economic affairs, and they included a large number of press clippings, comments on American views of Russia, and character sketches of the personalities in each new administration in Washington. The reporting about the Mexican War was especially full and detailed and carefully followed in St. Petersburg by Nicholas himself, as is evident from the notations in his own hand on the original documents. Could the following observation of Bodisko's have made the tsar less cautious regarding the mounting imbroglio over the "Eastern Question"?: "There is no doubt that in spite of the [Mexican] war the United States is singularly prosperous, but, though commercial activity is immense, this country prospers entirely from the force of circumstances and national energy."[16]

Bodisko, for all of his American connections, did not hesitate to criticize or to show exasperation in his observations of the American scene. He was particularly annoyed after 1849 by the apparent American enthusiasm—"without control and without decency"—for visiting Hungarian political refugees. After objecting vainly to Secretary of State John Clayton, Bodisko reported, "The great majority of Americans are of complete ignorance of all that concerns the institutions and order of things in Europe and believe blindly all of the absurdities published in the journals."[17] He was also perturbed by the tendency of Ameri-

[16]Bodisko to Nesselrode, 2/14 December 1847, f. kants. Vashington 1848, d. 184, AVPR. I am indebted to an archivist at the Archive of the Foreign Policy of Russia in Moscow for identifying the handwriting of Nicholas I on the margins of Bodisko's dispatches. Bodisko noted in another message that the Mexican War was lessening the impact of the European events of 1848 in the United States. To Nesselrode, 1/13 June 1848, ibid.
The emperor also demonstrated his interest in the American war to Ingersoll in St. Petersburg, observing, "in a rather sprightly manner, that the United States had heretofore been at peace while Europe was fighting—but now our relative condition was somewhat changed, we were engaged in a war while Europe was quiet." Ingersoll to Buchanan, 3 June 1847, DUSM, Russia, vol. 15 (roll 15, M 35), RG 59, NA. Ingersoll also reported: "Our war with Mexico excites great interest on this side of the Atlantic, and the first question put to me wherever I go among intelligent men, is, whether I have any late news of the movements of our army. However misinformed the Europeans are on other subjects connected with our country, the information here in regard to our progress in Mexico is remarkably accurate, and never fails to be promptly transmitted from one continent to the other." To Buchanan, 22 November 1847, DUSM, Russia, vol. 15 (roll 15, M 35), RG 59, NA.
[17]Stoeckl to Nesselrode, 4/16 September 1849, f. kants. Vashington 1849, d. 190, AVPR.

cans "to suit their own vanity with exaggerated claims of their own wealth and success."[18] And the Russian minister was especially provoked when American congressmen and officials complained about other countries' violations of agreements but, confronted by similar objections regarding American conduct, made excuses based on the weakness of the central government and the restrictive powers granted to the individual states.[19] What disturbed him most, however, was the lack of continuity produced by changing administrations, amply illustrated by the state of appointments to Russia. Sometimes, during visits to St. Petersburg, he even found himself conducting the United States' diplomatic affairs. Despite his criticism and reservations, Bodisko was basically "American" and deserves at least some credit for the reservoir of goodwill that existed between the two countries by the 1850s.

Public Perceptions

In the period before the Crimean War, Russia easily won the contest for diplomatic reporting, yet access to general information about the other country was much greater in the United States. Bodisko might well complain that the United States was ignorant about European affairs, but Americans certainly had opportunities to learn about Russia in more detail and with more varied interpretations than ever before. Indeed, Americans were being drawn increasingly to Europe by music, art, and literature, by the beginnings of regular steamship communication, and by politics. This is illustrated in a superficial way by the faddish musical craze of the 1840s for the polka and the mazurka, both associated with eastern Europe—Russia as well as Poland and Hungary. Gabriel Korponay, a former Austrian army officer and Hungarian émigré, introduced fashionable New York society to these dances and to Slavic and Hungarian folk songs, first at Niblo's Gardens and then in Newport and Washington in 1844.[20]

Details of life in Russia were furnished to the American public by a host of new books. Though the Marquis de Custine's sour account of his visit in 1839

---

[18]Ibid.

[19]Bodisko to Nesselrode, 16/28 September 1851, f. kants. Vashington 1851, d. 147, AVPR. In the same dispatch, the Russian minister observed that "the American government does not have authority sufficient to restrain the deranged instincts of the minorities."

[20]Korponay's remarkable conquest of New York society began in May 1844. Of prominent nobility and claiming to have been a student of the Hungarian ballet-master Falk, Korponay introduced the United States to the polka and the mazurka, dances that had already become the rage on the continent. With the famous French ballerina Desjardins as his partner, he dominated the New York entertainment scene during the summer of 1844, then in August moved on to Saratoga. There and at Newport a host of prominent ladies and gentlemen (such as former president Martin Van Buren) were

had been dismissed by most American critics as an exaggerated and untrustworthy French view, it had stimulated an interest that led readers to the work of Johann Kohl, who being German was considered less biased and more reliable, to John Barrow's *The Life of Peter the Great*, and to John Stevenson Maxwell's *The Czar, His Court and People*. Maxwell's book, already in its third edition by 1850, was written expressly "to remove the prejudice which has been created by foreigners against the Czar and of causing him to be seen in his true greatness and goodness, the best and noblest Sovereign which a kind Providence permits to reign"—and was partially financed by former minister Todd.[21]

The expanded distribution of newspapers and popular illustrated journals, such as *Harper's New Monthly Magazine*,[22] whetted the appetite for knowledge of "exotic" regions such as Russia. And William Darby, the veteran free-lance historian for the *National Intelligencer*, now writing under his own name, led the way in appealing for more openness about that country.[23] Not to be ignored are the public lecture series (such as those of Darby, Robert Baird, and Bayard Taylor that focused on Russia) and the new vogue in historical panoramas, the Battle of Borodino of 1812 being especially popular. Publicity about American business successes in Russia, such as the visit of Nicholas I in March 1847 to the train factory managed by Harrison, Winans, and Eastwick, also attracted favorable attention to Russia.[24]

among his pupils. Proceeding down the East Coast during the winter, Korponay's career climaxed when he superintended the inaugural ball in Washington in March 1845. In reading newspaper accounts of these events, one begins to wonder if the polka craze did not play some role in James K. Polk's surprise election as president. New York *Herald*, 28 May, 5 June, 10 August, 18 August, and 27 August 1844 and 14 February and 13 March 1845.

[21]Maxwell (Boston) to Charles S. Todd, 25 November 1847, Todd Papers, box 1, f. 8, Filson Club. The works cited are: Johann Georg Kohl, *Russia and the Russians in 1842* (Philadelphia: Carey & Hart, 1843); John Barrow, *A Memoir of the Life of Peter the Great* (New York: Harper & Bros., 1839); John S. Maxwell, *The Czar, His Court and People: Including a Tour in Norway and Sweden*, 3d rev. ed. (New York: Baker and Scribner, 1850).

[22]The anonymous author of "Recollections of St. Petersburg," *Harper's New Monthly Magazine* 4, 22 (March 1852): 447–57, neatly penetrated the facade of imperial Russia (p. 451): "St. Petersburg is certainly the most imposing city, and Russia is the most imposing nation in the world—at first sight. But the imposing aspect of both is to a great extent an *imposition*. The city tries to pass itself off for granite, when a great proportion is of wood or brick, covered with paint and stucco, which peels off in masses before the frosts of every winter, and needs a whole army of plasterers and painters every spring to put it in presentable order."

[23]*National Intelligencer*, 21 July 1853.

[24]Eyewitness accounts of the tsar's visit are in Whistler to Swift, 8/20 April 1847, Whistler-Swift Papers, Manuscript Division, NYPL; and Joseph Harrison to R. G. Fairbanks, 12/24 March 1847, Joseph Harrison Letterbook, 1844–1850, HSP. One of these may have been the source of the newspaper articles that Bodisko sent back to St. Peters-

While the revolts of 1848 sparked renewed interest in a Europe that seemed to be coming around to an American way of thinking, the Russian army's role in the suppression of the Hungarian uprising in 1849 aroused sharply negative feelings toward Russia. This hostility was fueled by the world tours of notable Hungarian exiles such as Louis (Lajos) Kossuth in the early 1850s and by the publicity surrounding the liberation of Martin Koszta from Austrian captivity by an American warship, which severely strained American-Austrian relations.[25] Riding a wave of American enthusiasm for liberal European causes, Kossuth spoke to large audiences around the country in December 1851 and July 1852, while many newspapers poured invective on European despotism. But the effectiveness of anti-Russian tirades was limited by their extremism, for not many Americans could accept the charges that Russia was about to seize Cuba and planned to cut off all American commerce from Europe, especially with the genial Bodisko skillfully handling the Washington politicians. The initial American reaction to the repression of the Hungarian revolution did show, however, that American public opinion could still shift quickly against Russia whenever such a stance was taken up by a popular political movement—in this case, Young America.

The debate about Russia was intensified by the entry into the fray of a book by a Baltimore attorney and aspiring politician, Henry Winter Davis, in 1852. Entitled *The War of Ormuzd and Ahriman in the Nineteenth Century*, the book traced the rise of Russian power in the recent past, emphasized the stifling of liberal revolts in 1831, detailed the Hungarian suppression of 1848-49, and predicted an inevitable conflict between the United States and Russia. No doubt inspired by the Young America spirit and Kossuth's speeches, Davis sounded more like a Cold Warrior of a century later, proclaiming

> that this power [Russia] must from necessity, on principle, and by inclination, be devoted to the ruin of all free governments: that it is absolutely inconsistent with the existence of the English monarchy and the American Republic as free popular representative governments; and that they will be compelled sooner or later to defend by force of arms their freedom and independence against the intrigues, the diplomacy, the legislation, the hostilities of the despotic powers of Europe. . . .

burg in the form of clippings: Bodisko to Nesselrode, 2/14 May 1847, f. kants. Vashington 1847, d. 126, AVPR.

[25]For Kossuth in the United States, see Donald Spencer, *Louis Kossuth and Young America: A Study of Sectionalism and Foreign Policy, 1848-1852* (Columbia: University of Missouri Press, 1977), and John H. Komlos, *Kossuth in America, 1851-1852* (Buffalo, N.Y.: East European Institute, 1973). For a succinct account of the "Kossuth craze," see Thomas A. Bailey, *A Diplomatic History of the American People*, 10th ed. (Englewood Cliffs, N.J.: Prentice-Hall, 1980), pp. 270-72.

The only alternatives are war, in Europe, now, with allies—and war hereafter, on our soil, without allies.

Davis continued to press his argument that the United States must be prepared to fight what Ronald Reagan would term an "evil empire" because of its irreconcilable opposition:

The dictatorship of Russia . . . is not to be looked for in the shape of an actual government—but of an invisible power operating through diplomatic forms, and supported by military power—speaking through the voice of domestic rulers words she has put there—and standing guaranty for the enforcement of whatever they may resolve. . . . It is animated by one spirit and policy. Its great object is the extinction of liberty in the world: and on this is founded its claim and its hope of universal empire.[26]

Since the Kossuth sensation had died down, most of the press quickly turned to attack Davis's work. Roger Pryor of the Washington *Union* termed it "a very wild and silly book."[27] The Charleston *Mercury* echoed: "The fundamentable [sic] idea of the book is so absurd a fiction, that no effort of ingenuity or power of eloquence could clothe it in a plausible garb." Each provided detailed rebuttals based on the historical friendship between the two countries.[28] The Albany *State Register* forwarded what was ostensibly the moderate, "Whig" point of view:

Russia, though in all that pertains to governmental institutions is in perfect antagonism to the United States, . . . to all our notions and axioms of human liberty, is a great and prosperous nation, presenting an example of progress unequalled in all Europe. In her rapid growth and advancement in power her only parallel can be found in our own country. . . . Despotic as she be, the arts of civilization have kept pace with the growth of her power. . . .

Antipodes in all that pertains to government as the Americans and Russians are, yet there is that in the history of both that naturally excites sympathy and fellowship of feeling. Both are young, both of modern origin, but recently admitted among the nations of the earth, and both speeding onward and upward in their career of renown, while the other Powers of the world are

---

[26]Henry Winter Davis, *The War of Ormuzd and Ahriman in the Nineteenth Century* (Baltimore: James S. Waters, 1852), pp. 276, 340. Ironically, Davis, as a prominent Republican congressman, would present a toast to the officers of the Russian fleet visiting Washington during the American Civil War. Bernard C. Steiner, *Life of Henry Winter Davis* (Baltimore: John Murphy, 1916), p. 232.

[27]*National Intelligencer*, 28 May 1853.

[28]*Charleston Mercury*, 24 May 1853.

stationary, or retrogressing. . . . We honor Russia, not for her despotism, not for her institutions of government, but because, like that of our own eagle, her course is upward, with an eye undazzled by the brightness and a wing unwearied by the flight.[29]

Waxing less poetic, William Darby in his column, "The Question of the Day," also stressed the diversity of institutions and commonality of interests: "There is . . . in one respect a strong resemblance. Each is so situated in regard to foreign nations as to have great powers of annoyance, if disposed to use it, while no external danger can seriously menace either, except its worst enemy that exists in its own bosom."[30] He concluded this series, and his own long career as a public educator of two generations of Americans about world affairs, by expressing hopes that Russia would come to its senses and settle differences with the Turks. Finally, Darby delivered a philosophic caution to his readers: "On history the mental vision ought to be unobscured by prejudice, and I have as far as possible removed from before me all false media. . . . We of the United States can say or think no worse of European despotism than do Europeans of our freedom, which they regard as licentiousness."[31] The uproar over the treatment of Hungarians was thus serving to thoroughly air American perceptions of Russia.

Like Davis and Darby, the Reverend Horatio Southgate lacked firsthand experience of Russia, but that did not prevent him from writing authoritatively on its current international involvements. Southgate claimed that "the Government of Turkey is as pure and more exceptionable a despotism than that of Russia, and that hundreds, and thousands, and millions of our fellow-Christians sigh and groan there under a bondage which their fathers have felt for centuries." Constantinople is, he added, "the sewer of Europe, into which the offscourings of European cities, refugees from justice, blackguards, gamblers, and murderers, are poured in reeking profusion."[32] A Russian presence could certainly do no harm, as far as Southgate and many other Americans of missionary bent were concerned. For some what was even worse than Russian expansion was the prospect that Catholicism would triumph there.

Adam Gurowski, a Polish Slavophile formerly resident in St. Petersburg, had lived since 1847 as an exile in the United States. In 1854 he contributed a bal-

[29]Quoted in the *National Intelligencer*, 28 May 1853.

[30]*National Intelligencer*, 7 July 1853.

[31]*National Intelligencer*, 21 July 1853. These were apparently Darby's last thoughts for the American public. He was seventy-eight and died the next year. His biography is yet to be written.

[32]Rt. Rev. Horatio Southgate, *The War in the East* (New York: Pudney and Russell, 1854), p. 23. George Ditson was another American who presented a favorable view of Russia's expansion to the south from his travel experience of 1847. George Leighton Ditson, *Circassia or a Tour to the Caucasus* (New York: Stringer and Townsend, 1850).

anced depiction of Russia, which was, he claimed, in transition away from Russian-centered despotism. He emphasized that private enterprise was growing in Russia and that Russian army officers were being drawn closer to the people through the military settlements in the countryside and had even sympathized with the Hungarians in 1849.[33] In a book also published in 1854, Randal MacGavock described his journey through Russia in 1851 and stressed the American contributions to Russian technical progress, which included the first permanent iron bridge over the Neva in St. Petersburg, built by Joseph Harrison. MacGavock concluded, "Although Russia is an extraordinary country, and her cities present innumerable attractions, yet the many annoyances that fetter the stranger at every step render it intolerable for an American who is permitted to move about at full liberty in his own happy country."[34] MacGavock, nevertheless, viewed Russia overall as progressing and developing in the American direction.

Change in Russia was also the focus of a private communication of Neill Brown that reflected the emerging American consensus about Russia:

> This is indeed, a great and growing empire and rapidly advancing in all the elements that make up strength and wealth. . . . An American looking at these developments, is apt to carry his speculations, beyond the cherished objects of their creation. He sees in the final result, the elevation of the masses and the promotion (I should say the beginnings) of popular liberty. Another such reign as the present—vigorous and enterprising—will change the condition of the Russian people for the better, whatever mischief it may do to the balance of the world. It will follow as consequence without being intended.[35]

[33] Adam Gurowski, *Russia As It Is* (New York: Appleton and Co., 1854), p. 105; Andrzej Walicki, "Adam Gurowski: Polish Nationalism, Russian Panslavism and American Manifest Destiny," *Russian Review* 38, 1 (January 1979): 19. Much of Gurowski's book appeared in columns in the New York *Tribune* during 1853 and early 1854, thus perhaps reaching an even wider audience. See, for example, "Recollections of the Court of Russia," which appeared in the issue of 26 January. The book was out by April, according to a two-column favorable review printed in the *Tribune* on 12 April. George Templeton Strong observed in his diary, 17 April 1854: "Though Gurowski's vaticinations do not amount to a great deal, I used to hear him talk precisely the same talk which is written down and elaborated in *Russia As It Is*, hour after hour, and used to be bored thereby." *The Diary of George Templeton Strong*, ed. Allen Nevins and Milton Thomas, vols. 1–2 (New York: Macmillan, 1952), 2:169.

[34] Randal W. MacGavock, *A Tennessean Abroad or Letters from Europe, Africa, and Asia* (New York: Redfield, 1854). The letters were first published in 1851 in the *Daily Nashville Union*. MacGavock met Neill Brown and his wife while traveling through England and France in the summer of 1851, and they suggested that he visit Russia. During his journey he was accompanied by William Johnstone of South Carolina. Herschel Gower, *Pen and Sword: The Life and Journals of Randal W. McGavock* (Nashville: Tennessee Historical Commission, 1959), pp. 56–58, 222, passim.

[35] Brown to Webster, 28 January 1852, DUSM, Russia, vol. 15 (roll 15, M 35), RG 59, NA.

A number of prominent Americans visited Russia in the years just before the Crimean War, the most illustrious being Sen. Stephen A. Douglas, whose earlier pronouncements on Russia had been extremely negative. Arriving after Brown's departure, he secured with the help of Stoeckl audiences with Nicholas I and Grand Duke Alexander. Douglas appeared to agree with the sentiments of the tsar, who, he recounted later, "considered there were but two proper governments on earth, the one where all the people ruled, and the other where only one man ruled—the American and Russian Governments—the other powers were *mongrels*, and were destined to be absorbed by one or the other of these 'two' Governments."[36] Destinies separate but quite manifest.

The sense of this common bond between the two countries was also noted by a neutral observer of the United States, Lady Emeline Stuart-Wortley, in 1853:

> There are but few Russian visitors here it seems; but I am very much struck by the apparent *entente cordiale* that exists between Russia and the United States. There seems an inexplicable instinct of sympathy, some mysterious magnetism at work, which is drawing by degrees these two mighty nations into closer contact. Napoleon, we know, prophisied that the world, ere long, would be either Cossack or Republic. It seems as if it would first be pretty equally shared between these two giant powers. . . . Russia and the United States are the two young, growing, giant nations of the world—the Leviathans of the lands![37]

She betrayed her British bias in noting the primary difference between the two countries—that Russia was aggressive toward its neighbors and constantly fomenting discord between them and other powers, while the United States was basically peaceful and concerned chiefly with internal development. Nevertheless, "Russia is determined to be on the best possible terms with the United

[36]"Senator Douglas Abroad," New York *Times*, 11 November 1853. See also Robert W. Johannsen, *Stephen A. Douglas* (New York: Oxford University Press, 1973), p. 382, for a brief sketch of the trip. Other prominent Americans who visited Russia in 1853 included Cornelius Vanderbilt, Rev. John Overton Choules, and the black tragedian Ira Aldridge (as far as Warsaw). Choules, *The Cruise of the Steam Yacht North Star* (London: James Blackwood, 1854).

[37]Lady Emeline Stuart-Wortley, *Travels in the United States* (London: Richard Bentley, 1851), pp. 287–88. H. W. Ellsworth, the U.S. minister to Sweden, later reported a conversation he had with Nicholas I in 1849 in which the tsar predicted a war between Russia and France and England and then a second contest between constitutional and unlimited monarchies, with Turkey on Russia's side. "But a third, and still mightier contest is approaching, in which the world will be involved—a struggle between what is called tyranny in any form, and freedom. Into this struggle your nation will be forced from its present policy, *and compelled to take a leading part*. It will be a struggle such as history never has recorded." Hartford *Daily Times* (with underlining), 11 January 1856, citing the Indianapolis *Journal*.

States at any rate."[38] Many influential molders of public opinion in the United States followed Lady Stuart-Wortley in perceiving a growing community of interests and a political convergence of the two countries, some with alarm but most positively. Both countries seemed to need each other psychologically as well as for other, more practical reasons.

Commercial Changes

Few of these observers paid much attention to what was still the most important, continuous, and harmonious Russian-American activity—trade. The volume of commodity exchange increased slightly from 1835 to 1853 but proportionately less than the growth of Russia's overseas trade and the sharper rise of American foreign trade. The dollar value of United States exports to Russia remained a little less than 1 percent of that of all exports, and the proportion of Russian imports coming from the United States dropped from around 10 percent in 1838 to 2.5 percent in 1851. The direct trade of both countries with Britain was much larger. For example, in 1853 American imports from Britain were worth almost $116 million, while those from Russia were only $2.45 million. That year Russia imported goods valued at 27.8 million rubles from Britain and 3.8 million from the United States. But the indirect trade is again difficult to decipher. In 1853 Russia imported cotton worth 12 million rubles, and most of it still came from Britain—60 percent of whose cotton exports originated in the United States.

Among the imports to Russia arriving on American ships, West Indian sugar retained first place, but after peaking at a total of over 50 million pounds in 1850, it began a sharp decline, caused by competition from Russian sugar beet production, to just under 18 million pounds in 1853, never to recover its former position. Meanwhile, the Russian imports of raw cotton soared, reaching 9 percent of total imports, second only to sugar in value. The quantity of raw cotton coming into European Russia in 1853 was ten times that of 1835, while imports of cotton cloth dropped by 80 percent over the same period.[39]

Direct imports of cotton from the United States rose even faster, from only 688,000 pounds in 1845 to over 17 million in 1853, one-fourth of the total. Typical of the new Yankee clippers, built in Maine but sailing out of New Orleans,

[38]Stuart-Wortley, *Travels*, p. 289.

[39]William H. Ropes to Webster, 31 December 1851, DUSC, St. Petersburg, vol. 10 (roll 6, M 81), RG 59, NA; Walther Kirchner, *Studies in Russian-American Commerce, 1820–1860* (Leiden: E. J. Brill, 1975), pp. 53–62; A. Semenov, *Statisticheskiia svendeniia o manufakturnoi promyshlennosti v Rossii* (St. Petersburg: Glazunov, 1857), pp. 102–3; M. L. de Tegoborski (Ludwig Tengoborskii), *Commentaries on the Productive Forces of Russia*, vol. 2 (London: Longman, Brown, Green, and Longmans, 1856; New York: Johnson Reprint, 1972), pp. 206–7.

were the *George Green*, captained by its owner St. Croix Redman, and the *Golden Eagle* under Nathaniel Thompson. The latter, an impressive ship of 1,273 tons registry, carried 5,090 bales of cotton (2,309,576 pounds) on its maiden voyage in 1853.[40] These new vessels of 1,000 tons and over were spurring longer, direct voyages to Russia and capturing a larger share of the Russian cotton import trade for the American flag.

Tobacco followed a similar course, with the number of cigars arriving directly from Cuba and the United States on American ships rising from only 670,000 in 1847 to nearly 3 million in 1853—not counting the large number that entered unrecorded under "captain's privilege." Tobacco thus compensated for some of the sugar decline.[41] Logwood, coffee, and rice continued to be important items carried by American ships, but the number and variety of other goods increased, especially books and machinery. The 713-ton *Strelna* of Boston in 1853 brought sperm oil, olive oil, clockworks, nuts, tortoise shell, books, and 2,027 pounds of machinery to Russia.[42] The latter was undoubtedly connected with the American railroad business, as many of the wheels for the locomotives and cars manufactured by Harrison, Winans, and Eastwick were cast in the United States.

The character of the Russian exports to the United States also changed. Although hemp, iron, and sailcloth remained the principal items, they declined in relation to the total volume of trade. Obviously, other sources of these products were now available: sisal from the Yucatan, iron from a rising native industry, and, most significantly, the replacement of linen sailcloth by homemade cotton canvas.[43] As with the imports, the variety of Russian exports also broadened: for example, reindeer and oxen tongues, tea, soap, wool, rhubarb, books, malachite, isinglass, felt, tooth elixir, bristles, horse manes, and chromium ore.[44] Nevertheless, the trade balance continued to shift in favor of the United States, and the gap would grow as those huge Yankee clippers were unable to fill the space left by unloaded bales of cotton, especially with products that could be sold in the

[40]Ropes to Marcy, 20 July 1853, DUSC, St. Petersburg, vol. 8 (roll 5, M 81), RG 59, NA.

[41]Gibson to Buchanan, 31 December 1847, DUSC, St. Petersburg, vol. 7 (roll 5, M 81), and Ropes to Marcy, 31 December 1853, vol. 8 (roll 5, M 81), RG 59, NA. On the suffering inflicted upon the Russian linen industry by the decline of sailcloth exports, see N. S. Kiniapina, *Politika Russkogo samoderzhaviia v oblasti promyshlennosti (20-50-e gody XIX v.)* (Moscow: MGU, 1968), p. 55.

[42]Ropes to Marcy, 31 December 1853, DUSC, St. Petersburg, vol. 8 (roll 5, M 81), RG 59, NA.

[43]Ibid., and Ropes to Webster, 31 December 1851, vol. 10 (roll 6, M 81), RG 59, NA. Note: The consular records for this period are not in good chronological order and have a number of gaps.

[44]Statistical report enclosed in Ropes to Marcy, 31 December 1853, DUSC, St. Petersburg, vol. 7 (roll 5, M 81), RG 59, NA.

ports of the American South. Though American shipping was now almost entirely confined to the port of Kronstadt-St. Petersburg, ship and cargo origins and destinations in the United States were much more diverse, with New Orleans beginning to rival Boston and certainly surpassing it in the total tonnage of direct trade. Despite important movements in Russian-American trading patterns after 1820, the value of trade, both direct and indirect, increased gradually by 1853 but less than the overall commercial growth of both countries.

The St. Petersburg–Moscow railroad project was another vital economic link between the two countries that was sustained through the middle of the century. The Harrison, Winans, and Eastwick management of the Aleksandrovsk factory had become a model of industrial success in Russia, owing to its monopoly contract to build the many locomotives and cars needed for the Moscow–St. Petersburg line. Though a number of American mechanics were at first employed in supervisory capacities, additional needs were met more conveniently by hiring technicians from other countries, especially Sweden.[45] Also for reasons of expediency, machinery was imported for the railroad from Britain as well as from the United States, a decision possibly influenced by the tendency of the American managers to summer in Britain. Not all of the supplies were absorbed by Aleksandrovsk. Repair shops were also established at the Moscow end under the direction of Robert O. Williams of New York.[46]

The most publicized event in the course of the whole enterprise was the visit of Nicholas I to the Aleksandrovsk factory in March 1847, during which he rode a short distance on a completed section of track.[47] Finishing the whole line, however, was delayed by shortage of funds and labor problems; these frustrations may have contributed to George Washington Whistler's inability to fight off his fatal illness early in 1849.

Meanwhile, the railroad project spawned several other business connections. Silas E. Burrows came to Russia in 1847 with plans to install a Morse-system telegraph line, though his main purpose was to collect on the "loan" made back in 1831 that allowed the Russian naval ship *Kensington* to continue its journey to Russia after

[45]Maxwell indicates that as many as sixty Swedish "mechanics" were hired by the American managers. *The Czar, His Court and People*, p. 127.

[46]MacGavock was probably the first American tourist to travel the full length of the Moscow–St. Petersburg railroad and describes meeting Williams on the train during the summer of 1851. *A Tennessean Abroad*, pp. 381–82.

[47]The event was reported in a number of American newspapers. One article, entitled "The Triumph of American Mechanics," was relayed by Bodisko back to St. Petersburg with a Russian translation. Bodisko to Nesselrode, 2/14 May 1847, f. kants. Vashington 1847, d. 126, AVPR. See also J. Leander Bishop, *A History of American Manufactures from 1608 to 1860*, vol. 2 (Philadelphia: Edward Young & Co., 1868; reprint, New York: Augustus M. Kelley, 1966), pp. 525–26.

being damaged by storms. Failing in the latter endeavor, Burrows inadvertently opened the way for Charles H. Robinson, who was actually in contention with Morse over patent rights to telegraph apparatus, and it was Robinson who finally inaugurated the first long-distance lines in Russia.[48] Another American, Henry Evans, served as the resident superintendent of the government cordage works near St. Petersburg, which was the principal supplier of rope for the imperial navy.

In addition to building trains, Joseph Harrison also constructed the first permanent iron bridge over the Neva in the capital city, at considerable cost to himself. Completed in 1850, the bridge was a memorial to American mechanical achievement and a present to the tsar, who awarded Harrison the Imperial Cross of St. Anne for his efforts. He and his partners need not have worried about financial losses, however, since they reaped vast profits from the Russian business—more than 10 percent of the total $40 million cost of the railroad was paid to the American company. Whistler, though obviously less financially rewarded, was still able to send his young sons to England to continue their general and artistic educations. Shortly before his death, he had even decided to accept the tsar's offer to remain in Russia after completion of the railroad to supervise the construction of a large service and repair facility at Kronstadt for the new steam warships.[49] Maj. Thompson Brown, superintendent of the New York and Erie Railroad, was hired to replace Whistler and to see the railroad to its final completion in 1851, but Minister Kleinmichel and his Russian engineers essentially usurped his role and left him little to do. By that time the Winans brothers and Harrison had negotiated a lucrative supplemental contract for the repair and service of all of the equipment on the railroad, which, given the climate, terrain, and shoddy conditions of Russian government operation, provided plenty of business. That the agreement supplied even more income was made fully evident to the American public by Winanses' ostentatious palaces in

[48]Burrows to Nesselrode, 23 June/5 July 1847, and Burrows to C. H. Robinson, 27 June/9 July 1847, in Steers, *Silas Enoch Burrows*, pp. 68–73; Burrows (New York) to Charles S. Todd, 30 April 1847, Todd Papers, CinHS.

Despite his failure to obtain repayment of the 1830 debt, Burrows remained a loyal friend of Russia: "No American can visit Russia without coming to the conclusion, that the Emperor's government is as well calculated for the happiness of his subjects, as ours is for the citizens of the United States." To Spofford and Tileston, 26 January 1848, in Steers, *Silas Enoch Burrows*, p. 76. But apparently many found his presence tedious or obnoxious: "His two recent visits at St. Petersburg were by no means pleasant to the Americans residing there, or acceptable to the Russian Government." H. W. Ellsworth (Stockholm) to Clayton, 25 April 1849, DUSM, Sweden and Norway, vol. 8 (roll 8, M 45), RG 59, NA.

[49]Whistler to Swift, 31 January/12 February 1849, Whistler-Swift Papers, Manuscript Division, NYPL. This was apparently George Washington Whistler's last letter.

and around Baltimore and Newport and by Harrison's renowned collection of art in Philadelphia.[50]

Pacific Affairs

As American business ventures in Russia and regular Atlantic and Baltic steamer services drew Russia and the United States closer together across the Atlantic, significant developments were also occurring in the Pacific through a similar linkage of business and trade. The Russian America Company became less dependent on American shippers after its 1839 lease of the Stikhine coastal strip to the Hudson's Bay Company, which was paid for in goods and services, such as the conveying of furs to China. In addition to that source, needed supplies were accessed through the more regular arrivals from the Baltic and from one company vessel a year calling in San Francisco Bay. In 1845 Captain Zarembo, vice-governor of the Alaskan colony, finally worked out with Manuel Castro, prefect of Mexico, a means to collect the overdue payment for the sale of the Fort Ross privileges, but the Mexican War intervened.[51] Bodisko, acting on behalf of the Russian company, then obtained from the American government, as the new sovereign of California, a commitment to uphold the Mexican agreement. After he half-jokingly advised Secretary of State James Buchanan that it should be worth $30,000 to the United States "to avoid a pretext for the Russian America Company to return to California and recommence agricultural and commercial operations," a settlement for payment was eventually made through the services of two influential local agents, John C. Fremont and William A. Leidesdorf.[52] The obligation was secured almost simultaneously with the discovery of gold on the new territory. In fact, the pressure to satisfy the Russian de-

---

[50]Miscellaneous scrapbooks (printed copy of 23 August/3 September 1850 contract in box 20), Winans Papers, MaryHS; L. W. Sagle, *Ross Winans*, Railway and Locomotive Historical Society, Bulletin no. 70 (Boston, 1947), p. 17. Thomas DeKay Winans's Baltimore mansion was named "Alexandrovsky" and was modeled after the factory near St. Petersburg, complete with smokestack and two ten-foot cast-iron eagles at the gate, made in Russia. It was torn down in 1914, but Ross Winans's suburban estate, "Crimea," survives in a Baltimore public park. In contrast, the family's Newport residence was named "Shamrock Cliffs." Miscellaneous materials, Winans Papers, MaryHS. Nathan Appleton quoted an 1852 letter of his mother's from Baltimore: "This morning we have been to see the most superb house in the country, built by a gentleman of the name of Winans, who has been employed by the Russian government in the construction of railroads and cars, and has made an immense fortune." *Russian Life and Society* (Boston: Murray and Emery, 1904), p. 99.

[51]Nesselrode to Bodisko, 13/25 June 1847, f. kants. Vashington 1847, d. 126, AVPR.

[52]Bodisko to Nesselrode, 12/24 February 1848, f. kants. Vashington 1848, d. 184, AVPR.

mand for payment may have been an important motivation for John Sutter to construct a water-powered sawmill, at which site the first substantial quantity of California gold was found in the fall of 1848.[53]

At the very time that throngs of Americans were embarking for California to seek their fortunes, Russia was moving into new Pacific ventures. Since the inception of the Russian America Company, very little had been done to improve communications by land with Russia or to develop the Siberian coast. Now a new governor of Eastern Siberia, Count Nikolai Murav'ev, instigated the sending of a Russian expedition to the mouth of the Amur River to test its navigability. The middle and upper reaches of this river formed the boundary between Russia and Manchuria and Mongolia, but the lower part passed through disputed territory. Since China had been weakened by the Opium Wars and increased foreign intervention, Murav'ev became concerned about possible British acquisition of this area.[54] With the support of Minister of Navy Aleksandr Menshikov, a special exploring vessel, the *Baikal*, was built at Helsingfors and set sail in the summer of 1848 under the command of Capt. Gennadii Nevel'skoi. Arriving at the Kamchatka outpost of Petropavlovsk in May 1849, Nevel'skoi explored the mouth of the Amur, proving it was passable to ships. He then claimed that the territory already belonged to Russia (though it was not formally recognized as such by China until 1860—and then vaguely).[55]

Another reason to strengthen the Russian presence in these waters was the appearance in the 1840s of large numbers of American whaling ships in the Sea of Okhotsk, some of which would call at points along the Kamchatka and Siberian coasts for water and to barter for goods. As had been the case earlier in Alaskan waters, the Americans were received with mixed feelings. There was natural resentment about the clear violations of the Convention of 1824 and of Russian sovereignty, but having American supplies available at the Russian administrative centers, especially at the newly established one near the mouth of the Amur at Nikolaevsk, was a genuine godsend to the Russians and an incentive for further settlement, just what Murav'ev desired. And the American interest in opening Japan to traders spurred the Russians to a similar overture, even as an American naval presence in Japan convinced them to consolidate the

---

[53]Bodisko to Nesselrode, 28 November/10 December 1848, f. kants Vashington 1849, d. 190, AVPR.

[54]Murav'ev to Minister of Interior, 14/26 September 1848, and to Nicholas I, 18/30 March 1850, in Ivan Barsukov, ed., *Graf Nikolai Nikolaevich Murav'ev-Amurskii—po ego pis'mam, offitsial'nym dokumentam, razckazam sovremennikov i pechetnym istochnikam (materialy dlia biografii)*, vol 2 (Moscow: Sinodal. tip., 1891), pp. 35, 55.

[55]G. Nevel'skoi, "Obzor rezul'tatov deistviia russkikh na servero-vostochynkh predelakh Rossii i uchastiia ofitserov nashego flota v dele vosprisoedinneniia pri-amurskago kraia k Rossii," *Morskoi Sbornik* 72, 6 (June 1864): 35–39. For the text of Nevel'skoi's instructions from Murav'ev, see *RAC*, pp. 475–78.

Russian position on the island of Sakhalin.[56] One of the American whalers, Matthew Turner, pointed out another resource for the Russians to develop by discovering rich cod-fishing grounds in the Sea of Okhotsk.

The scarcity of ships and manpower again was the most serious Russian problem. To alleviate this, Murav'ev tried to obtain the assistance of the naval ministry and the Russian America Company. Influenced by Adm. Pavel Rikord, who had been interested in Japan for many years, and Vice-adm. Evfimii Putiatin, Menshikov dispatched an expedition under the latter's command in the summer of 1852. The Russian America Company, which had already sent one ship, the *Nikolai I*, and a few men to the Amur-Sakhalin area in 1850, was ordered to turn over its new workhorse, the *Menshikov*, to Putiatin.[57] Murav'ev may have hoped by involving the company to obtain control over it and its territory, and the company suspected that possibility. The company, however, protected by its charter of monopoly privileges in the North Pacific, obviously had other fish to fry.

The fortunes of the Russian America Company fell sharply in the 1840s because of a number of factors—a depressed market for furs, decline of the Indian population from disease, usurpation of native labor by American whaling vessels in return for supplies, loss of uninsured cargoes, and unimaginative leadership. According to the company's own records, revenues dropped from over 1,235,000 rubles in 1842 to only 717,000 in 1849.[58] A move to repair its situation began with the purchase of new ships, made especially urgent by the loss in 1845 of its workhorse, the brig *Chichagov* (built in the United States in1824), near the company's Siberian base of Aian.[59] In 1848 a fine three-masted ship, also from

[56]Nevel'skoi, 'Obzor rezul'tatov," p. 41; A. I. Alekseev, I. N. Argentov, and A. A. Grigorov, *Kostromichi na Amure* (Iaroslavl: Verkhne-volzhskoe izd., 1979), pp. 22–53. The latter is a good biography of Nevel'skoi based on family archives in Kostroma.

[57]Murav'ev to Prince Menshikov, 21 February/5 March 1851, in Barsukov, *Murav'ev-Amurskii*, 2:88; T. M. Batueva, "Iz istorii ekspansii amerikanskogo kapitala na russkom dal'nem vostoke (50-60-e gg 19 v.)," *Trudy Irkutskogo gos. univ. im. A. A. Zhdanova*, (seriia istoricheskaia) 59, 2 (1970): 171.

For Russian activities in the Far East at this time, see the works of George Alexander Lensen, especially *The Russian Push toward Japan, Russo-Japanese Relations, 1697–1875* (Princeton, N.J.: Princeton University Press, 1959); and on Perry, Samuel Eliot Morison, *"Old Bruin" Commodore Matthew C. Perry, 1794–1858* (Boston and Toronto: Little, Brown, 1967), and Arthur Clarence Walworth, *Black Ships Off Japan: The Story of Commodore Perry's Expedition* (New York: Alfred A. Knopf, 1946).

[58]*Otchet Rossiisko-Amerikanskoi Kompanii glavnago pravleniia za odin god, po 1 ianvaria 1843 goda* (St. Petersburg: tip. Fishera, 1843), p. 6; *Otchet . . . po 1 ianvaria 1850 goda* (St. Petersburg, 1850), pp. 4–5. I am indebted to the Saltykov-Shchedrin State Public Library in Leningrad for a nearly complete file of the Russian America Company's annual reports, most of which are summarized and reviewed by the financial newspaper, *Kommercheskaia Gazeta*, available at the University of Helsinki Library.

[59]*Otchet . . . po 1 ianvaria 1846 goda* (St. Petersburg, 1846), p. 34.

an American yard, was purchased in the Sandwich (Hawaiian) Islands and re-named the *Kniaz Menshikov*, and at Sitka a new steamship, the *Baranov*, was launched for coastal communications. Also in 1848 the *Akhta*, a large clipper ship, was leased from the Hudson's Bay Company to bring supplies from Kron-stadt, and the newly built *Nikolai I* was purchased in New York, reaching New Archangel by way of Kronstadt and the Amur in 1850.[60] The Russian America Company thus began the second half of the century with a relatively fresh fleet that consisted mostly of the finest American-built ships.

Commercial expansion was the company's primary goal at this time, with a concentration first on the new whaling and shipping centers on Oahu and Maui in the Sandwich Islands. In return for forest products and salted fish, sup-plies could be obtained more cheaply there than from the Hudson's Bay Com-pany or Kronstadt. The same also applied to the booming settlements around San Francisco Bay, now under American control. The veteran ship *Okhotsk*, for example, carried an assortment of forest products and bar iron, in demand as building material, to San Francisco in late 1848 under the supervision of Martin Klinkovstrem, another of the company's several employees from Finland. It brought back to Sitka basic supplies, half of the payment for Fort Ross, and news about the discovery of gold. In anticipation of a market opportunity, the *Menshikov* was immediately dispatched from New Archangel with a cargo of var-ious kinds of goods and a detachment of gold miners led by engineer Mikhail Doroshin. Arriving in California on 14 January 1849, Russians thus were among the very first of the "Forty Niners."[61]

The sharp increase in prices in San Francisco enabled the company to realize a profit of 125,000 rubles, one-seventh of its 1849 revenue, on the cargo of the *Menshikov*, many of the items having apparently lain unused for years in com-pany storehouses.[62] The *Alta California* advertised:

> For sale on *Menshikov* and store erected at Montgomery and Sacramento Sts: boots and shoes, ready made clothes of all kinds for men, such as pea-jackets, woolen clothes, cloaks, mantles for ladies, caps, gum, elastic, coats, morning gowns, etc., good blankets, also Russian duck, shirts, powder, muskets, pis-

[60]*Otchet . . . po 1 ianvaria 1849 goda* (St. Petersburg, 1850), pp. 18–21.

[61]*Alta California*, 18 January 1849; *Otchet . . . po 1 ianvaria 1850 goda* (St. Petersburg, 1850), pp. 32–33; *Moskovskiia Vedomosti*, 4 May 1850.

[62]*Otchet . . . po 1 ianvaria 1850 goda*, pp. 32–33. About the same time as news of the gold rush reached Russia, an influential conservative journal was providing its Russian readers with a fascinating account of a Russian visit to California at the beginning of the Mexican War. A. I. Markov, "Russkie na Vostochnom okeane," *Moskvitianin*, no. 8 (April 1849): 205–22; no. 9 (May 1849): 17–60; no. 10 (May 1849): 91–111; no. 14 (July 1849): 63–96; no. 16 (August 1849): 147–70. For an account of another extended Rus-sian visit to California in 1850, see *Moskovskiia Vedomosti*, 21 and 25 September 1850.

tols, different kinds of knives, combs, needles, shovels and pickaxes, different kinds of beads for Indians, muscatel wine, porter, cigars, bear skins, metal spoons, forks, earrings, shot, flour, hats, iron pots, tin cups and a large assortment of other articles.[63]

What more could a gold miner want?

Meanwhile, Doroshin had "struck it rich" on the Yuba River, obtaining between February and April 1849 over eleven pounds of pure gold nuggets and a substantial quantity of dust. Most of the proceeds went toward the purchase in San Francisco of a new three-masted ship, the *Shelikhov*, for around $50,000.[64] On its first return voyage for the company, it carried another cargo that reflected the growing needs of the burgeoning center of gold-rush activity:

> For sale cargo of the Ship *Shelikhov*, Russian America Co.,: 133 piles and spars from 15 to 28 feet long, and from 6 to 12 inches diameter, suitable for wharf-building, pickled salmon, potatoes, tallow candles, copper sheeting, assorted iron and copper nails, a very superior assortment of sail cloths and other kinds of Russian linen, window glass, boots and shoes, ropes and cordages of different kinds, iron crowbars, Russian soap, smoking tobacco, bearskins, a large quantity of leather bags, fit for any kind of packages, besides many other articles. For particulars apply on board the said vessel.[65]

Not all of these items, however, could be sold because of a rush of imports then coming through the Golden Gate.

From their experience in California the directors of the Russian America Company learned that it was possible to sell almost any colonial or imported goods. Because of price variations, additional time might be needed for satisfactory returns, but the extraordinary instability in the market meant that European and American goods could be bought cheaply at times for the company's own use. To realize these possibilities would require replacing Russia's first and rather inactive consul, William Montgomery Stewart, and basing a permanent agent in San Francisco. Petr Kostromitinov, the last manager of the Fort Ross colony, was designated.[66] While these changes were being made, the California economy was quickly outstripping the Russian capability of competing effectively. With such distractions for the Russian America Company in California, it is not surprising that Murav'ev was unable to obtain its assistance in his Amur-Sakhalin schemes.

The Russian America Company, meanwhile, did not ignore by far the most

[63]*Alta California*, 8 March 1849.
[64]*Otchet . . . po 1 ianvaria 1850 goda*, p. 34.
[65]*Alta California*, 10 December 1849.
[66]*Otchet . . . po 1 ianvaria 1850 goda*, pp. 35–36.

lucrative business of the North Pacific—whaling. It tried in the 1830s and 1840s to reap some profit from native coastal whaling with the help of American whaler Thomas Barton, but with little success. What was produced was mainly for home consumption. Then, in 1850, the company organized a subsidiary, the Russo-Finnish Whaling Company, in conjunction with a society of shippers from the port of Turku in the Russian Grand Duchy of Finland.[67] The first whaling vessel of this company, the *Suomi*, did not reach the Pacific until 1851. Despite breakdowns and poor results, whaling operations continued for a number of years, even after the sale of Alaska. This activity also illustrated that the Russian America Company, in spite of its economic difficulties, was becoming a multinational and multifaceted enterprise.

Events in the Pacific were watched closely in Washington, as much by Russian diplomats as by American government officials. Bodisko was quick to report on the discovery of gold in California and to point out the irony of finding it on formerly Russian-controlled territory, but he also saw an advantage in that it increased the likelihood of collecting the payment still due.[68] However, it was Eduard Stoeckl, acting as chargé d'affaires during the minister's absences, who outlined the full potential for Russia of the developments in California. Noting in the summer of 1849 that the wave of emigration to California was bringing in a more settled and commercial population, Stoeckl detected important opportunities there for the fortunes of the Russian America Company:

> The new activity that the commerce and navigation is destined to take in the Pacific Ocean will have, it is hoped, a happy influence on our possessions in North America. The relations that exist between them and California have already increased and new objects of exchange will augment their commerce. . . . A new sphere of activity is now open to the Russian America Company; it will undoubtedly profit from it and give our possessions in the Northwest a much greater importance than they have had until now.[69]

After interviewing Secretary of State Clayton the following March, Stoeckl repeated his optimism: "The relations between our possessions in America and California are becoming day by day more frequent and the commerce which is being established between them promises the most beneficial results for our colonies."[70]

[67]*Kommercheskaia Gazeta*, 12 and 31 January 1852.
[68]Bodisko to Nesselrode, 22 November/4 December 1848, f. kants. Vashington 1848, d. 184, AVPR.
[69]Stoeckl to Nesselrode, 31 July/12 August 1849, f. kants. Vashington 1849, d. 190, AVPR.
[70]Stoeckl to Nesselrode, 6/18 March 1850, f. kants. Vashington 1850, d. 138, AVPR.
[71]Stoeckl to Nesselrode, 24 December 1849/5 January 1850, ibid.

This new state of affairs highlighted the possibilities for trade expansion between the two countries in the Pacific, bringing them even closer together and mitigating especially the negative influences of the Russian army's suppression of the Hungarian revolt in 1849. Bodisko and Stoeckl both supported the growing American interest in Cuba and Nicaragua, which was, ironically, being promoted especially by those most friendly to the Hungarian cause (thereby allowing the Hungarian situation to be conveniently forgotten in the rage of a new quest). The Russian envoys emphasized the benefits of an American-sponsored canal through Nicaragua for Russian communications with the North Pacific in their reports to St. Petersburg.[71] They also actively encouraged Matthew Perry's efforts to open Japan to commerce in 1853. At the same time they attempted to nullify the advantages that the Hudson's Bay Company had in trading directly with Alaskan ports by declaring a policy that allowed the ships of all nations into those waters, thus renewing de facto the Convention of 1824 with the United States.[72]

Affairs in the Pacific reinforced the union of Russia and the United States against British expansion in areas extending from the Caribbean to the Sea of Japan, where Admiral Putiatin tried to cooperate with an overly suspicious Commodore Perry in forcing trade agreements upon Japanese authorities. In 1853 Bodisko's nephew Vladimir was sent on a special mission from Washington to California, the Sandwich Islands, and the Far East with orders for Putiatin to collaborate with the Americans.[73] Stoeckl was recalled to St. Petersburg to receive instructions and a new appointment as consul-general for the Sandwich Islands, from which position he was to have overall direction of Russia's growing Pacific commercial interests. These moves seemed to show that Russia was mounting a Pacific offensive and considered the area connected to the United States. All of this did not, of course, go unnoticed by the British or the French. To the American minister in Paris Louis Napoleon gave his advice that the United States should be concerned about the growth of Russian influence in the Far East, to which the minister responded "that we did not find in it the oc-

---

[72]Stoeckl to Nesselrode, 19/31 March 1850, ibid.

[73]Bodisko's mission was, in part, to coordinate Russian support for Perry's expedition to Japan. Brown to Marcy, 10 March 1853, DUSM, Russia, vol. 15 (roll 15, M 35), RG 59, NA; George Lensen, *Russia's Japan Expedition of 1852 to 1855* (Gainesville: University of Florida Press, 1955), pp. 1–6.

[74]RAC Directory to Rudakov, 30 October 1853 (O.S.), Russian America Company Records (hereafter RRAC), Correspondence of the Governors General, Communications Received (hereafter CGG, CR), vol. 19 (roll 19, M 11), RG 261, NA. Draft instructions to Stoeckl, undated, f. kants. Vashington 1854, d. 167, AVPR. Stoeckl arrived back in New York in December 1853 on his way to Honolulu, but when Bodisko died in January, he assumed the role of chargé in Washington and was designated minister

casion for unusual anxiety or distrust as the Russian power was far more enlightened than that which prevailed or was likely to prevail."[74]

Not by accident, the leading newspaper of San Francisco, the *Alta California*,
echoed the Russian view of developing Pacific markets with the help of a
strengthened American presence. A series of articles expressed the predominant
anti-British feeling; for example, in a long column in March 1851, entitled
"Commercial Supremacy of the Pacific Coasts," the paper predicted that San
Francisco would become the base from which American ships would dominate
the whole ocean: "The Yankee, with his clipper ships—with his steamers—with
his enterprise, his skill, his unceasing activity—will defeat his great rival; and, after establishing a successful trade with all his neighbors on the coast, he will
then see opening before him, in tempting colors, that great Oriental trade,
which has contributed so much to the proud commercial supremacy of Great
Britain."[75] At least for the moment, Russians as well as Americans were quite receptive to such romantic views.

In the meantime, Kostromitinov arrived in San Francisco early in 1852 by way
of Honolulu as agent of the Russian America Company with special instructions to develop markets for Russian products, especially salted fish.[76] Californians, however, had another commodity in mind that could be procured from
the Russian north. In the late summer of 1851 the schooner *Exact*, chartered by
Nathaniel Crosby of Portland and captained by Isaiah Folger of San Francisco,
arrived at Sitka to obtain a cargo of ice, a product now much in demand in the
bustling urban center of San Francisco and on the hot Panama steamers.[77] Not
blessed with a handy natural supply produced by cold winters, the California
coast relied upon imports brought from Boston around Cape Horn, which commanded, of course, a high price, often as much as a dollar a pound. It had never
before occurred to the Russian company managers that they might realize some
benefit from an item that plagued their northern location, but they responded
eagerly to the American idea—although, since it was in late summer, nothing
could be done immediately.

the following year. Stoeckl to Nesselrode, 5/17 January 1854, ibid. On Louis Napoleon's
advice and the American response, see Robert M. McLane to Marcy, 22 February 1855,
Marcy Papers, vol. 57, Manuscript Division, LC.

[75]*Alta California*, 27 January 1852.

[76]Capt. Nikolai Rozenberg, Chief Administrator, RAC (New Archangel), to Peter
Kostromitinov, 10/22 September 1851, RRAC, 1802–67, CGG, Communications Sent
(hereafter CS), vol 32 (roll 57, M 11), RG 261, NA; Thomas Vaughan, "Introduction,"
in *The Western Shore: Oregon Country Essays Honoring the American Revolution*, ed.
Thomas Vaughan (Portland: Oregon Historical Society, 1976), p. viii.

[77]Crosby was the great-grandfather of Bing and Bob. See also *Otchet . . . po 1 ianvaria
1853* (St. Petersburg, 1853), pp. 20–25; Rozenberg to Directors, 10/22 September 1851,
RRAC, CGG, CS, vol. 32 (roll 57, M 11), RG 261, NA.

Back in San Francisco the secret of Alaskan ice leaked out and quickly a veritable ice rush was on. In April 1852 the *Bacchus* delivered the first shipload of 250 tons for the Pacific Ice Company.[78] Since all of this occurred while Kostromitinov was making his way aboard a chartered ship, the *Pandora*, to Hawaii and then by means of the *Menshikov* to San Francisco, he was surprised to find his job of expanding commerce with Alaska already well advanced by enterprising Americans. Selling the contents of the Russian "ice box" was not that easy. First of all, there was competition: one group sought ice from the Fraser River area of the Hudson's Bay Company territory, while another reached eastward to mountain lakes. The Russian administration in Alaska, too, was wary of a prospective scramble for ice that could resemble a smaller version of the gold frenzy. Besides, for such a business to be really profitable, considerable capital investment was needed for icehouses at both ends, cutting and handling equipment, and ships for transportation.

With the encouragement and assistance of Kostromitinov, a group of prominent San Francisco businessmen organized in early 1853 the American Russian Commercial Company. They immediately sent men and equipment to Sitka to construct the large icehouses and to supervise the wintertime cutting and storing, bought out the competing companies, and thus commenced an intensive Russian-American business association in the Pacific.[79] The president of this new company was Beverley C. Sanders, a former Baltimore merchant who had come to San Francisco in time to be on the ground floor of the gold-associated business boom. By 1852 he had become president of the gas company, a partner in a savings bank, and, most important, Collector of the Port. In 1853, mindful of the expansion of trade with Alaska to other products and of security for the ice business, he departed San Francisco on a long journey to St. Petersburg to negotiate a formal contract with the directors of the Russian America Company.[80]

[78]*Alta California*, 18 April and 23 April 1852. Rozenberg to Kostromitinov, 6/18 March 1852, RRAC, CGG, CS, vol. 33 (roll 58, M 11), RG 261, NA.

[79]The arrangement with the American Russian Commercial Company was worked out independently in San Francisco to the satisfaction of the Russian directors. Rudakov to Directors, 31 December 1852/11 January 1853, RRAC, CGG, CS, vol. 33 (roll 58, M 11), and Directors to Rudakov, 11/23 November 1852, RRAC, CGG, CR, vol. 20 (roll 20, M 11), RG 261, NA. The complicated communications are at times difficult to follow because of the distances involved and the changes occurring in the management of affairs in Alaska. Rudakov was filling in temporarily between Rozenberg and Voevodskii. In their 11 November letter, the directors in St. Petersburg informed the office in New Archangel that Beverley Sanders, the president of the San Francisco company, was "especially recommended by our representative in Washington." One can see how far a reference had to travel.

[80]*By-laws of the American Russian Commercial Company, Organized May, 1853* (San Francisco: O'Meara and Painter, 1855), Bancroft Library, University of California,

Preparations for War

All of this Russian-American commercial activity in both the Pacific and Atlantic spurred a reawakening of interest in naval technology and exploration in both countries, demonstrated first by appropriations for education and research. Also, with international tensions building in the eastern Mediterranean, Nicholas I was suddenly concerned with modernizing the long-neglected Russian navy. Serving as an agent of Russian interests, a Danish officer by the name of Moller even enticed Cornelius Vanderbilt to sail to Russia aboard his new steam "yacht," the *Northern Star*, in the summer of 1853 in hopes of obtaining a contract for the building of warships.[81] Though no agreement was reached, the visit, attended by much official fanfare, may have inspired the naval contacts between the two countries that followed.

Emerging as a leader of the new naval-technological emphasis on the American side was the eminent astronomer and hydrographer, Matthew F. Maury. His publications had already drawn the notice of Russian officers, and some of them had been translated for the naval journal *Morskoi Sbornik*, which began publication in 1848. In May 1853 Nicholas I delegated Capt. Aleksei Gorkovenko, the future director of the Russian Hydrographical Institute, to attend an international meteorological congress in Brussels, presided over by Maury, who then invited his Russian colleague to visit the United States. Gorkovenko arrived at Norfolk in October 1853, "for purpose of examining all that relates to the progress of naval constructions in the navy and the merchant service of the Union."[82] In reality, the Russian agent was investigating the possibilities of ship purchases, traveling to Charleston to discuss the matter with the firm of Page and Allen before concentrating on New York.

The premier shipbuilder in that city, William H. Webb, had already been contacted by Russian authorities in 1851 and 1852 about the construction of a ship similar to the *Kamchatka*. In the summer of 1853 Webb also journeyed to Russia, where on 12 September he signed a contract with the naval ministry for the

Berkeley (hereafter UCB). For additional information on Sanders, see Norman E. Saul, "Beverley C. Sanders and the Expansion of American Trade with Russia, 1853–1855," *Maryland Historical Magazine* 67, 2 (Summer 1972): 156–70, based on Sanders's papers then in the possession of a descendant. For the Russian side of the negotiations with Sanders and a full text of the "treaty," f. 18, op. 5, f. 1355, TsGIA.

[81]Brown to Marcy, 14 May 1853, DUSM, Russia, vol. 15 (roll 15, M 35), RG 59, NA; M. I. Radovskii, "Iz istorii russko-amerikanskikh nauchnykh sviazei," *Vestnik Akademii Nauk SSSR* 26, 11 (November 1956): 95.

On the Moller-Vanderbilt affair, see the New York *Daily Tribune*, 14 July 1855; unaccountably, even more details are in the *Daily Cincinnati Gazette* of 16 July 1855.

[82]Bodisko to Marcy, 8 October 1853, Notes from the Russian Legation in the United States to the Department of State, vol. 4 (roll 3, M 39), RG 59, NA; V. N. Ponomarev, "Russko-amerikanskie otnosheniia v gody krymskoi voiny, 1853–1856," *Istoricheskie Zapiski* (Moscow) 110 (1984): 269.

building of a major warship. Within weeks the New York press was reporting that a 100-gun, 3,000-ton battleship was to be built for Russia by the Webb Shipyards.[83] Another Russian naval mission, led by Gen. Mikhail Grinval'd (Grunwald), Russia's leading naval architect at the time, and accompanied by captains Firstein and Sokolov, was soon on its way to the United States to make final arrangements and to superintend the construction. Arriving in New York apparently with Stoeckl at the end of December 1853, the naval troika stayed at the Astor Hotel. By February they had aroused considerable interest and alarm because of rumors circulated by a pro-French newspaper, *Courrier des États-Unis,* that their mission was really to charter privateers to prey upon the merchant shipping of any hostile powers.[84] After having investigated and concluded that this information was false, the New York *Herald,* somewhat tongue in cheek, described its effects:

> Had a spent bombshell fallen amongst us it could not have created greater consternation than did this important revelation. It was of course followed by a decline in public securities, and an immediate rise in the *Courrier's* circulation.
>
> The startling announcement . . . has, it appears, not only thrown the Foreign Office into confusion, but it has also disturbed the domestic relations of one of our principal hotels. At the Astor House, where the Russian officers were staying, the whole order of things in that well regulated establishment is upset, all foreigners being looked upon with suspicion—and treated by the ladies—as privateers. Although the gentlemen in question have left on a visit to the Portsmouth navy yard, it is difficult to calm the susceptibilities that have been aroused by the report that they are still inmates of the house. One hears nothing on every side but inquiries as to which is Mr. Grunwald and which is Mr. Sokolov? So much for attempting to sail under false colors.[85]

[83]Norfolk *American Beacon,* 31 October 1853; New York *Herald,* 29 December 1853; G. P. R. James (British consul in Norfolk) to Crampton, 13 March 1854, Foreign Office Paper 5/594, Public Record Office, London (hereafter FO, PRO). Webb recounts his contract negotiations in New York *Times,* 25 January 1863.

[84]"Russo-American Privateers," New York *Herald,* 20 February 1854; "The Russian Agents and Their Mission to This Country," ibid., 21 February 1854. "General" Mikhail Grinval'd was Russia's leading naval engineer and the designer of many capital warships in the 1830s and 1840s.

[85]"The Privateers at the Astor House," New York *Herald,* 25 February 1854. The Baltimore *American and Commercial Advertiser* (22 February 1854) also dismissed the claim that the Russian visitors were involved in such activities, pointing out that these roles were normally assumed by consuls long resident in the country and familiar with its practices: "They came here several months ago, long before a general war was thought probable, or even possible, to superintend the construction of a vessel built by Mr. Webb, and to learn from our ship-builders those great improvements which make the Ameri-

The *Herald* was correct in clearing the Russian naval mission of any effort to involve the United States more directly in a rapidly developing war situation in the Levant. Though the delegation's purpose was certainly connected to the heightened tension in Europe involving the naval powers, it was cautiously limited in scope, at least initially, and only coincident to the outbreak of war.

The Eastern Question

The Eastern Question referred to the problem of the relative decline of the Ottoman Empire and the concurrent rise of national consciousness among its subject peoples, many of whom were Slav and/or Orthodox Christians. The situation was exacerbated by the personal ambitions of subordinate Ottoman administrators such as Mehemet Ali of Egypt, and there had already been a series of diplomatic and military ventures in the eastern Mediterranean by the European Great Powers in the first half of the nineteenth century. Russia's longstanding interests in the fate of the subject Christians, a secure outlet from the Black Sea, and territorial acquisitions to the south were being intensified by the rising foment in the Balkans, the growing importance of the Black Sea grain exports, and the maintenance of diplomatic and military prestige. Meanwhile, Britain continued to harbor fears that Russian expansion into this area, either directly or indirectly, would threaten Britain's lifeline to India and naval dominance in the Mediterranean—fears that were aggravated by such incidents as the destruction of the Ottoman fleet at Navarino in 1827 and by a spreading Russophobia at home.[86]

That this general state of affairs would lead to a breakdown of the Concert of Europe and the first large-scale war between European powers since 1815 was the result of changing circumstances that brought certain personalities to the

can vessels the first of the world." The British minister in the United States also did not believe any arming of privateers was going on, but he asked all consuls to be on the watch. Crampton to Clarendon, 12 and 26 June 1854, FO 5/596, PRO.

[86]For the background on Britain's antipathy toward Russia, see John Howes Gleason, *The Genesis of Russophobia in Great Britain: A Study of the Interaction of Policy and Opinion* (Cambridge, Mass.: Harvard University Press, 1950). The literature in English on the Crimean War is immense, but it concentrates mainly on diplomacy and on the allied side, a notable exception being John Shelton Curtiss, *Russia's Crimean War* (Durham, N.C.: Duke University Press, 1979). Other valuable recent studies include Alan Dowty, *The Limits of American Isolation: The United States and the Crimean War* (New York: New York University Press, 1971); Ann Pottinger Saab, *The Origins of the Crimean Alliance* (Charlottesville: University of Virginia Press, 1977); and Paul W. Schroeder, *Austria, Great Britain, and the Crimean War: The Destruction of the European Concert* (Ithaca, N.Y.: Cornell University Press, 1972). An excellent reappraisal is by Norman Rich, *Why the Crimean War?: A Cautionary Tale* (Hanover, N.H., and London: University Press of New England, 1985). Material in Russian is equally uneven. Probably the best is still Evgenyi Tarle, *Krymskaia voina*, 2d ed., 2 vols. (Moscow: Nauka, 1950).

fore. The most important were the rise to power of Napoleon III in France in the wake of the Revolution of 1848; the ascendancy of the more militant and anti-Russian Viscount Palmerston (Henry George Temple) as British prime minister; the return of the bellicose Stratford de Redcliffe (Stratford Canning) to the post of British ambassador at Constantinople; and the rise in influence of more ag-gressive *Russian* advisers to the tsar, with the consequent decline of the peace-oriented "Germans" such as foreign minister Karl Nesselrode and veteran diplo-mats Philipp Brunnow (London) and Peter Meyendorff (Vienna).[87] The overall effects were an aggressive and hostile stance by the "Western Powers" and seri-ous misperceptions of the shifting international scene by Russian leaders, most notably by the stubbornly autocratic Nicholas I himself.

The chain of events that ended in war began with the Revolution of 1848, fol-lowed by national disturbances in the Balkans, Russian intervention, and pro-tection being given to Hungarian refugees by Ottoman authorities. Russian and Austrian demands for extradition were countered by a British naval demonstra-tion that stiffened Ottoman resistance, resulting in a brief international crisis in October and November 1849. This setback to Russian influence in Constanti-nople encouraged further French penetration into the Ottoman Empire, a pol-icy promoted especially by the new emperor of the French, Napoleon III, who was seeking diplomatic or military gains comparable to those of his illustrious namesake in order to consolidate his recent domestic triumph in France. An is-sue soon presented itself in a squabble between Roman Catholic and Greek Or-thodox monks over privileges in the Holy Land, which was still under Ottoman jurisdiction. In early 1852 the French managed to persuade the Turkish govern-ment to grant the Roman Catholics control over certain churches, a victory that naturally annoyed Russia.

Nicholas I, who had vacillated throughout his reign between a policy of main-taining the Ottoman Empire as the best of possible alternatives and a carefully prearranged dissolution and partitioning among the Great Powers, now veered toward this latter, "final" solution. The tsar had surmised from his meeting with Prime Minister Lord Aberdeen (George Hamilton-Gordon) during the visit to England in 1844 that he could now count on the support of Britain—an impres-sion that he believed had been reinforced by conversations with British Ambas-sador Hamilton Seymour early in 1853. By dispatching a high-level mission to Constantinople, headed by Minister of Navy Menshikov, Nicholas hoped to re-solve the dispute quickly to the satisfaction of Russian interests. At the same time, however, Lord Palmerston, the British cabinet member who most feared

---

[87]The latter view was presented to the American public on the pages of the New York *Tribune* by Adam Gurowski, the Russian-Polish emigré, who also associated Bodisko with the "German" or peace party. See also Bodisko to Nesselrode, 10/22 July 1853, f. kants. Vashington 1853, d. 156, AVPR.

that Russia would gain a permanent upper hand in Ottoman affairs, arranged to have de Redcliffe, Britain's leading Turkish expert and Russia-hater, sent back to the Ottoman capital as ambassador. What followed was a series of political intrigues and diplomatic maneuvers that culminated in a stubborn and angry Menshikov demanding even more concessions. When they were rejected with British encouragement, the Russian envoy departed, effectively breaking off diplomatic discourse.

Military action came next. In the summer of 1853, Nicholas ordered the occupation of the Danubian principalities of the Ottoman Empire as hostages for a Turkish agreement; in response, the British and French engaged in naval demonstrations at the straits. The Ottoman government, thus backed by the visible military presence of these powers, declared war on Russia in October—at the very time that the Gorkovenko naval mission was arriving in the United States. None of the Great Powers really wanted war, but they were driven along by events, national pride, and obstinate leaders. A good initial showing by the Turkish army was succeeded by an overwhelming Russian naval victory at the end of November at Sinope, which encouraged the further intervention of France and Britain. They formally allied and declared war on Russia in March 1854.

The United States and the Beginning of the Crimean War

During these crucial months Russian-American relations were in an embarrassing state of flux. The United States was caught without a minister or even a secretary of legation in St. Petersburg; only an acting consul was there. The illness and death of Bodisko in January handicapped the normally stronger Russian diplomatic mission. Konstantin Katakazi, the second secretary who was temporarily in charge, favored implicating the United States by encouraging American merchant vessels to load cargoes for Russia; if they were then stopped by the British, the United States might be provoked into the war.[88] Eduard Stoeckl's instructions for his new assignment in the Pacific may have included assistance to the Grinval'd mission to buy warships and a more subtle investigation of possible American involvement in a European war. However, he had already concluded in January that the United States would remain strictly neutral and that the many British consuls on guard would make arming of Russian corsairs in these friendly ports impractical.[89] He soon arrived in Washington to provide more stability and experience and to act as chargé d'affaires, but the ministerial

[88]Nesselrode to Bodisko, 28 November/10 December 1853, ibid. Katakazi to Nesselrode, 25 January/6 February 1854, f. kants. Vashington 1854, d. 167, AVPR.

[89]Stoeckl to Nesselrode, 10/22 March 1854, f. kants. Vashington 1854, d. 167, AVPR. Stoeckl waited several weeks in New York and presented his credentials as chargé to Marcy only on 27 March. *National Intelligencer*, 28 March 1854.

succession was kept in doubt for several months with rumors that Count Aleksandr Medem, a former Russian envoy to Brazil who had toured the United States in 1851, would be named.[90] Thomas H. Seymour, the Democratic governor of Connecticut and new American minister to Russia, meanwhile, delayed his departure for St. Petersburg to await events and receive additional instructions.

Because of its rapid economic and territorial expansion, the United States was predisposed to become involved in certain ways in the Crimean War. Politically and economically, the nation was striking a much more aggressive and active posture in foreign affairs after the gains of the Mexican War. With the presidency of Franklin Pierce, a former general and old Jacksonian, came the dominance of the Young America faction in the Democratic party, led by George Soulé, the new minister to Spain; George N. Sanders, consul in London; Sen. William McKendree Gwin of California; and Attorney General Caleb Cushing, the most influential member of the Pierce administration to support a militant foreign policy. Their promotion of the annexation of Cuba, removal of British control over a route to California along the Central American coast at Greytown, settlement of the Canadian fishing rights controversy in favor of the United States, and general opportunism—to take advantage of a European conflict to realize expansionist goals—could easily have caused war between Britain and the United States in the eruption of the crisis over the Eastern Question.

The avoidance of direct military participation by the United States was due to the relative caution and conservatism on all sides, especially of Pierce himself, his Secretary of State William L. Marcy, and the British leaders Palmerston and Clarendon. Also, the main theatre of war was fortunately confined to the Black Sea area, which was hardly of vital interest to the United States. Still, it was a close call. Britain had forestalled a likely American casus belli by announcing at the beginning its adherence to the basic principles of freedom of the seas and neutral rights—only for the duration of the war. Moreover, early in 1854 Congress and the press were absorbed in a pressing domestic debate over the Kansas-Nebraska question, which reopened the "compromise" over the slave issue in the territories. In addition, a vocal group of liberals, merchants, and abolitionists, centered in New England, opposed Russia and sided with Britain for commercial and ideological reasons. Americans, in any case, were not to be idle bystanders in the conflict in which most of Europe was now to become embroiled.

In administration circles and generally, opinion was at first balanced: Traditional hostility toward Britain, disgust with Turkish suppression of Christianity, an aversion to the new "autocratic" government of France, and friendly rela-

[90]This was reported as fact in several American newspapers, for example, Baltimore *American and Commercial Advertiser*, 27 April 1854.

tions with Russia were matched by annoyance about Russia's initial military steps (the occupation of the Principalities and the Battle of Sinope) and by concern about preserving the profitable trade with Britain.[91] But this was before the British and French declarations of war. By March other factors had come into play: a fear that the balance of power in Europe would be changed in ways detrimental to American interests, especially those in the Caribbean and Central America; a belief that Russia was definitely the underdog fighting against a coalition of Great Powers; a sense that Russia was basically in the right in defending the interests of the Christian population of an oppressive and antiquated Ottoman Empire; and, finally, an incident—the seizure of part of the cargo of an American merchant ship, the *Black Warrior*, in a Cuban harbor—that heightened American animosity toward the "old imperial powers" of Europe.[92] Though the autocratic system of Russia had few advocates in the United States, its cause attracted more sympathy from Americans than the "designing and threatening" imperialists of Britain and France. Although they are not easily separated, a coalition of political strategists, idealists, and opportunists had definitely laid the groundwork in the previous decades for a friendly neutrality that bordered on a quasi-alliance between Russia and the United States.

[91]Katakazi to Nesselrode, 25 January/6 February 1854, f. kants. Vashington 1854, d. 167, AVPR. One interesting American reaction to European events is that of George Templeton Strong: "Prospect of war in Europe is increasing. Hurrah for the Czar! His *casus belli* is nonsense and he knows it, but any quarrel's good enough that will rid Europe of the olive-skinned infidels and aliens that have squatted in Constantinople for 400 years." He also at first relished the idea of a general European conflict. "Should the ultimate triumph of Russia introduce a new element . . . into the social life of the Old World, shattering and destroying all its present organizations, the disruption may well prove a blessing." But then he had at least one qualm: "But Englishmen are our brethren in race, speech and culture, after all. I wish they were fighting on the other side." Entries for 17 August 1853, 17 April 1854, and 26 November 1854, *Diary*, 2:128, 169, 198.

[92]In a series of dispatches in March personally carried to St. Petersburg by Vladimir Bodisko, Stoeckl outlined the change in American sentiment, citing his conversations with Marcy and several newspaper articles—in particular, one entitled "An American View of the Eastern Question" in the Washington, D.C., *Union*, written by an unidentified retired senator and statesman who was well known to Stoeckl (George Mifflin Dallas?). Stoeckl to Nesselrode, 10/22 March 1853, f. kants. Vashington 1854, d. 167, AVPR. Marcy's biographer claims that the secretary of state was strictly neutral while Pierce was pro-Russian. Ivor Debenham Spencer, *The Victor and the Spoils: A Life of William L. Marcy* (Providence, R.I.: Brown University Press, 1959), pp. 290–92. This was certainly not the impression Stoeckl was relaying to St. Petersburg in March. Marcy even told the Russian diplomat that he was recalling Perry's squadron from Japan for possible deployment in the Baltic. To Nesselrode, 10/22 March f. kants. Vashington 1854, d. 167, AVPR. For an excellent pioneering discussion of diplomatic relations at the time (though marred by an erroneous assessment of Stoeckl's inexperience), see Golder, "Russian American Relations," pp. 462–76.

Of special importance in this relationship was the North Pacific, where Russia had a vast, thinly populated territory that was poorly defended and exposed and where Russian-American connections had recently expanded. Alarmed about the British declaration of a blockade of Russia's Pacific coastline, Stoeckl conferred around 20 March with Senator Gwin of California and Secretary of State Marcy.[93] Recalling his conversation with Beverley C. Sanders in New York and encouraged by Gwin, Stoeckl urged a plan upon Nesselrode in St. Petersburg and directly to Kostromitinov in California—that the Russian America Company make a temporary sale of its ships to the American Russian Commercial Company, which could then use them under a neutral flag to supply not only Alaska but also the Siberian coast. Stoeckl also favored arming corsairs on the open Pacific, with letters of marque provided by the Russian company. "With the interests of some American capitalists united with our interests, it is extremely probable that any attempt of our enemy on the Russian settlements in America would produce a great impression in San Francisco," he wrote to Nesselrode.[94]

At about the same time, Stepan Voevodskii, the company's chief administrator at Sitka, suggested to Kostromitinov that the whole territory be temporarily signed over to the American Russian Commercial Company—in effect, that the Russian America Company seek the protection of the American flag. Within a month Marcy was confiding to Stoeckl, in the presence of President Pierce, that the United States still wanted to remain neutral, "but God knows if this is possible," and that the British attitude "has considerably Russified us."[95] By coincidence, the Pierce administration was considering at that moment a project for the annexation of the Sandwich Islands and may have seen the Turkish imbroglio as an excellent opportunity for American expansion in the Pacific.

The other Russian agents in the United States were also active in pursuing American absorption into the war but were obviously hampered by lack of instructions and funds. By April several requests for letters of marque had been received in Russian consular offices in New York, New Orleans, and San Francisco, and William Aspinwall, a prominent passenger-ship owner, offered to sell

[93]Stoeckl to Nesselrode, 10/22 March 1854, f. kants. Vashington 1854, d. 167, AVPR. Gwin was specially introduced by Stoeckl in his dispatch, as if this was the first of what would be several meetings between the two.

[94]Stoeckl to Nesselrode, 10/22 March, ibid., AVPR. No direct evidence could be found to confirm Roy Nichols's claim that "sometime during these weeks [April 1854], Marcy went to the Russian minister and told him that if the rumored desire of Russia to sell Alaska were real the United States would buy." Roy Franklin Nichols, *Franklin Pierce: Young Hickory of the Granite Hills* (Philadelphia: University of Pennsylvania Press, 1931), p. 329. If it happened, it must have been in August, when Thomas Cottman returned, but then both Marcy and Gwin were absent from Washington.

[95]Stoeckl to Nesselrode, 8/20 April 1854, f. kants. Vashington 1854, d. 167, AVPR.

the pride of his Pacific steamers, the *Golden Gate*, to Russia for $500,000 and two others for $200,000 each. Stoeckl thought that with these vessels armed, Russia could drive the British from the Pacific, but the money did not come. Webb still planned to build the large Russian warship but not without a substantial payment in advance, since delivery during the war was problematic. Marcy wrote Seymour privately: "Mr. Webb is a very estimable man, and one of our most distinguished ship builders. He desires very much to build a ship for the Emperor, thinking, by doing so, he could add to his professional reputation, which is now very high."[96] No doubt he thought also of profits from future contracts.

In hopes of resolving these financial issues and simultaneously encouraging American direct trade with Russia, Katakazi was dispatched to New York and Boston in May to find a suitable middleman. John P. Schepeler, a naturalized American citizen who was the son of a prominent Riga merchant and representative of the house of Steiglitz in New York, agreed to act as official Russian banker, initially just to supply Russian-America but also for possible future arms purchases. Stoeckl believed it was too late, however, to use Schepeler as an intermediary for Katakazi's plan of provoking the British capture of an American merchant ship, though he still hoped to issue letters of marque through Kostromitinov to American vessels to operate against the British in the Pacific.[97] As yet, Russia was being suitably cautious in its initiatives toward the United States.

But as war, and perhaps a long one, settled in, Russia's naval weakness and vulnerability in the Baltic became obvious. Projects for more direct military assistance quickly came forward. In March the Russian naval agent Grinval'd returned to St. Petersburg with Wesley Smith, a New York businessman. They expected to complete arrangements to furnish timber worth $300,000 that would enhance Russia's own shipbuilding capability. The New York *Herald* reported that accompanying them were people connected with "Taylor's submarine armor and Colt's submarine battery," who intended to produce a new instrument of war: "The plan, we understand, is this:—A portable torpedo, of sufficient power to sink a man-of-war, is to be carried under water by a man encased in submarine armor. He fastens the battery to the bottom of the ship, and returns to the shore, when by means of an electrical wire, the battery is fired, and the

[96]Marcy to Seymour (private), 17 May 1854, Seymour Papers, box 858, Connecticut Historical Society (hereafter ConnHS); Stoeckl to Nesselrode, 8/20 April 1854, f. kants. Vashington 1854, d. 167, AVPR. Stoeckl was enthusiastic about the possibility of acquiring these steamships but warned that supplying them with coal would be a problem.

[97]Stoeckl to Nesselrode, 6/18 May 1854, f. kants. Vashington 1854, d. 167, AVPR.

ship is blown up."[98] Nothing more is known of this early effort to secure American technical assistance, and when Smith reached St. Petersburg, his protracted discussions with the Russian government centered on the supply of coal rather than wood. With the British navy blockading the Baltic and ship timber considered contraband, Russian priorities had changed.

American Missions to Russia

After the arrival of the new American minister, Seymour, the focus of American involvement in the Crimean War shifted to St. Petersburg. Having had plenty of time to prepare and to realize the importance of his mission, Seymour, a bachelor, took with him an able staff that included R. Augustus Erving as secretary, Col. Richard J. Haldeman as attaché, and two recent Yale graduates, Daniel Coit Gilman and Andrew Dickson White, who would later make their impact on American higher education as presidents of Johns Hopkins and Cornell (respectively). The minister and his entourage journeyed through London, Paris (where White remained behind to perfect his French), and Berlin to gain a better understanding of the European situation. Gilman commented in a letter to his mother that "it was really laughable to see what a sensation this party of Americans created" on its tour.[99]

The resident American community, headed by William H. Ropes, his cousin George Prince, William L. Winans, George William Whistler, and their families and employees, was augmented by the new and larger diplomatic mission as well as by several other Americans who descended on the Russian capital for various reasons. It was obvious to all that extensive direct British commerce with Russia had been suspended by the advent of war. But American interests were also threatened by the declaration of a blockade of the Russian Baltic ports. In addition to Wesley Smith and Beverley Sanders, who had waited in western Europe for Seymour's arrival, Arthur Cunningham, a merchant-shipper from Boston, came to oversee the departure of vessels that had reached Russian ports before the blockade and the arrival of ships already in passage to Russia when the war began. Both objectives were accomplished without serious incident, though fear of British interference did force most other American ship captains to seek a neutral, usually Prussian, port to unload their Russian cargoes for transshipment over land. The Russians also encouraged Cunningham to promote future voyages and to consider the possibility of transporting arms and munitions.

The Russian authorities also received Beverley Sanders with open arms. The

[98]"Help for Russia—Curious Movement," New York *Herald*, 7 April 1854; Seymour to Marcy, 8 May [corrected later to 13 May] 1854, DUSM, Russia, vol. 16 (roll 16, M 35), RG 59, NA.

[99]Gilman to his mother, 4 April 1854, Gilman Papers, Milton Eisenhower Memorial Library, Johns Hopkins University.

obvious vulnerability of the Russian-American territories during a war with the British had been greatly diminished by a surprising neutrality agreement concluded in May between the Hudson's Bay Company and the Russian America Company. Although guaranteed by the British government, this "treaty" pertained only to their respective North Pacific colonies and not to ships at sea. Therefore, the problems of British interdiction of Russian supply routes in the Pacific and obstruction of the coasts remained.

The Russian America Company and government leaders viewed Sanders as a potential savior and readily agreed in June to his immoderate proposal for a twenty-year monopoly over the marketing of products of the company's territories—chiefly ice, fish, coal, and lumber—not only in California but all over the Pacific Ocean. Although the arrangement was restrictive, the company was consoled because the term of the contract extended well beyond 1862, the current end of the company's charter. By its approval of Sanders's plan, the government seemed to be guaranteeing a renewal of the company's monopoly. What the Russians received was Sanders's agreement to act as agent for the supply of the Russian-American territory and Siberian coastal outposts for the duration of the war. Funds were granted for the purchase of a first-class steamer to carry interport communications and provisions under the American flag, while other Russian ships in American ports were to be fictitiously sold to the American Russian Commercial Company and used to supply Alaska. In the process of these deliberations, the San Francisco businessman, dressed up in a colonel's uniform, was grandly received by the tsar and various government officials, most particularly by the new minister of navy, Grand Duke Constantine. Apparently the grand duke even seriously considered expanding this enterprise to the purchase of American ships in San Francisco, manning them with sailors sent overland to the Siberian coast.[100]

The Cottman "Mission"

While Sanders was enhancing Russian-American cooperation in the Pacific, another remarkable American on the Petersburg scene, Thomas Cottman, may have been working as an agent for another alternative—the temporary or permanent sale of Russian-American territories to the United States. Since this strange episode in Russian-American relations during the Crimean War has often been cited as groundwork for the eventual purchase of Alaska, it deserves as thorough an examination as the limited sources will allow.

[100]The details are in Saul, "Beverley C. Sanders." Writing in 1863, Jomini claimed that the use of privateers in the Pacific was much discussed in St. Petersburg: "At bottom, it was the only weapon at our disposal against the naval superiority which England so rigorously exerted against us." *Diplomatic Study of the Crimean War* (London: W. H. Allen, 1882), 2:77–78.

Originally from the East Bay (Worcester) area of Maryland, Cottman received a medical education before moving about 1830 to Ascension Parish (Donaldson-ville), Louisiana, where he practiced medicine and superintended his wife's large plantation and many slaves. In the winter of 1853–54 he set off for Europe to place his daughter in school in Paris. Whatever his motivation for going on to Russia early in 1854, Cottman was greeted by the desperate Russians at the commencement of the war as a semiofficial ambassador, a role he played to the hilt, to the annoyance of other American arrivals such as Seymour and Sanders. Cottman is even reported to have ridden beside the emperor at an important military review, and he was conferred officer rank as a surgeon in the Russian army. Daniel Gilman observed Cottman's ascendancy at the Russian court:

One American has been making a great sensation here—a Dr. Cottman of Louisiana. . . . He has offered his professional services to the Russian army and they have been accepted. . . . The American Minister has not given him a single introduction but the Dr. being a person of good address, great tact, and unusual shrewdness, has been leading a remarkable life. No one of the legation has seen half as much as he. His remarkable offer "to serve without pay, merely from motives of humanity" has made a great sensation here, everybody is talking about it, the doctor has been courted and feted, he has been daily with the highest surgeons of the Empire, he has met Count Nesselrode and the other ministers of the various departments, and yesterday he had an hour interview with the Emperor by whom he was introduced to the Empress and several members of the Royal Family.

On the whole his history is most remarkable and I presume no one of any nation ever saw in so short a time so much of the Russian Court.[101]

Though little other direct evidence is available on Cottman's 1854 sojourn in Russia, a brother-in-law, writing to other relatives, quoted excerpts from an April letter of Cottman's from St. Petersburg:

The idea of Tom Cottman, squaring himself off in the "palais d'Hiver" in familiar colloquy with the Emperor of all the Russias as though it were Henry Doyal [a neighboring Louisiana planter]. As to the ladies here I believe they are the most intelligent in the world. . . . You will find it strange but it is nev-

[101]Gilman to his mother, 10 April 1854, Gilman Papers, Johns Hopkins University; see also "A Marylander in the Russian Service," Baltimore *American and Commercial Advertiser*, 15 July 1854; and Seymour to Marcy, 26 June 1854, Marcy Papers, box 50, Manuscript Division, LC.

ertheless true that I sport the double-headed eagle on my coat with the other insignias of a Russian Captain. It is my intention to remain in service here for awhile and go down to Roumelia and from thence to Paris and take Memé [his daughter] home.[102]

Cottman's timely arrival and his excellent knowledge of French—and perhaps some of his Young America expansionist convictions—apparently led him into frank conversations, probably with Grand Duke Constantine, about Russia's vulnerable American territories. All of this must have occurred, however, before the neutrality agreement with the Hudson's Bay Company was known.

Cottman left Russia around the end of June on what people came to believe was a special mission to the United States to tender an offer to sell Alaska, though he was also pursuing a railroad construction project at the same time. Considering the obvious lack of secrecy and the publicity surrounding his objectives, one might suspect that the whole affair was a scheme hatched by Cottman and a few Russians such as Grand Duke Constantine and Count Murav'ev, the governor of Eastern Siberia, who happened to be in St. Petersburg at the same time as Cottman. A year earlier Murav'ev had privately advocated the cession of Alaska—in order to concentrate Russian resources on the Amur region. Now the same suggestion might be used as bait to secure greater American support and possibly to provoke direct involvement in the war—or at least ward off British seizure of the territory. Cottman's contacts with George Sanders, a notorious expansionist, in London add credence to some American acquisitional goal.

In any event, the Cottman "mission" created a sensation in the summer of 1854 and promoted to the general public for the first time the idea that Russia might sell—and the United States might buy—Alaska. When Cottman passed through Paris, newspapers began sensationalizing his purported goal. Under the heading "Proposed sale of Russian America to the United States," the pro-Russian New York *Herald* proclaimed:

It is now beyond a doubt that Russia desires to sell. Her motives—being in brief a knowledge of her naval inferiority, and a desire to concentrate her forces around the vital parts of the empire—are too obvious to require comment or explanation. Having to choose between seeing Sitka captured by the British, or selling it to the United States, Nicholas has very naturally preferred the latter, and no one can question the propriety of his decision.[103]

[102]H. B. Trist to Browse (his son), 26 May 1854, Wood Trist Papers, Southern Historical Collection, University of North Carolina.
[103]"Proposed Sale of Russian America to the United States," New York *Herald*,

But a Maryland newspaper had been following closely the unusual activities of its native son and voiced more caution about the prospects of this acquisition.

> The advantages that would result to the United States from the possession of Russian America do not, with our present knowledge of the subject, strike us as of remarkable importance. . . . As the Czar, however, is disposed to sell it cheap, these inducements, with our mania for the acquisition of territory, may prove sufficient, and if the British cruisers do not anticipate us, we may soon be in possession of territory from which we can take a telescopic view of Asia, and in virtue of our sovereign rights regulate the navigation of Behring's straits and the Arctic ocean. We are happy also to say that this proposed addition to our soil will not excite the prejudices of the North, even the *Tribune* has no fears of slavery going there.[104]

After Cottman's landing in New York at the beginning of August was attended by more fanfare, the paper became more sanguine, foreshadowing the national debate of 1867.

> The Russian envoy [Cottman] seems to have seized every opportunity to make his mission to this country the subject of the utmost publicity. In Paris he communicates freely with an American newspaper correspondent, in London he corresponds with ex-consul Sanders, and his arrival at New York is signalized by another semi-official publication of the object of his mission joined with a laudation of the Emperor that, to say the least, disgusts by its fulsomeness. . . In fact, it looks as if the Czar had been studying some of our national peculiarities, and was determined to humbug us on an enlarged scale. We think this Russian mission will reward examination by the discovery of ulterior purposes in which it will neither advance the interests nor honor of this country to become involved. We certainly can find some worthier object than autocratical Russia on which to bestow our sympathies, and a better purpose to devote our spare millions to than the purchase of ice-bound, befogged Sitka.[105]

25 July 1854. For the possible roles of Gwin and Murav'ev in the Cottman affair, see Hallie M. McPherson, "The Interest of William McKendree Gwin in the Purchase of Alaska, 1854–1861," *Pacific Historical Review* 3, 1 (March 1934): 29–33. Cottman may have known Gwin a few years earlier when Gwin was active in Louisiana politics.

[104]"What Russia Proposed to Sell," Baltimore *American and Commercial Advertiser*, 28 July 1854.

[105]"Arrival of the Russian Envoy," ibid., 4 August 1854. On his way home through Paris, Cottman consulted with U.S. Minister John Y. Mason, but though he discussed his projects for railroads, he apparently did not discuss the sale prospect: "Dr. Cottman

Even the *Herald* had difficulty accepting Cottman's repetition of Nicholas's refrain that republican institutions were fine for the United States but not suited for Russia. The paper condescended to quote the London *Times*: "That the American government would think it part of their natural and traditional policy to buy any part of their continent offered to them on reasonable terms, we can easily understand; but we do hope and trust that Dr. Cottman is not the fairest possible representative of his country on the question of Cossack and republican government, of appropriation of "the right of geographical position," and the points discussed with the Czar."[106] Oddly, the diplomatic correspondence on both sides nearly ignores the reports about Cottman. According to Stoeckl, Cottman wanted to refute the stories about his mission but was counseled not to do so by Marcy.[107] For his part, the Russian diplomat publicly denied that Russia had any intention of selling any territory, but he did add in a private dispatch that he thought Cottman might be useful to Russia. Regardless, the good doctor disappeared mysteriously from the public scene as quickly as he had entered it (though he apparently considered returning to Russia the next year).[108]

has spent some time at St. Petersburg, and has without doubt, been most kindly received and treated by the Emperor. He can give you some very interesting information. . . . He is very intelligent, but ardent, and in regard to Russia, enthusiastic." Mason to Marcy, 8 July 1854, Marcy Papers, box 51, Manuscript Division, LC.

[106]"The Czar—The Yankees—and Doctor Cottman," New York *Herald*, 4 September 1854.

[107]H. B. Trist wrote another son: "Your Uncle T. *entre nous*, is something of a visionary character, but you should not accustom yourself to speak lightly of him, as he entertains a high regard for you and Browse and talks about taking you to St. Petersburg with him should he make another visit to the capital of the Czars (not Tsar as you have it)." To Bringier, 25 November 1854, Southern Historical Collection, University of North Carolina. Apparently Bringier also considered traveling to Russia, since his father later advised him to go and get back before Sevastopol falls, "for we are generally Russians." To Bringier, 4 April 1855, ibid.

[108]August was a poor time for an American response. Senator Gwin, who is credited by many with inspiring the idea, was in California climbing mountains and running for reelection. Stoeckl, who was vacationing at Newport, denied to the local press that Russia had any intention of selling the territory, that it was most likely "a hoax invented in England." "The Sale of Sitka," Baltimore *American and Commercial Advertiser*, 5 August 1854, quoting the Newport *News*.
  Marcy and Gwin did ask Stoeckl about the alleged offer to sell in early September, when all three had returned to Washington. Stoeckl again blamed the British press for the story and "responded to them that we never had any such intention." Privately, Stoeckl attributed the sudden American interest to the likelihood that the Russian possessions were about "to acquire great prosperity." Stoeckl to Seniavin, 24 August/5 September 1854, f. kants. Vashington 1854, d. 167, AVPR. The whole affair continued to intrigue the press. Over two years later, the New York *Times* (6 October 1856) reminisced about Cottman and his disappearance from the public eye. "He had come to Russia because he loved her, sympathized in her causes and hated her enemies. He was the first foreigner of distinction—the first far removed from the Russian frontier—who had used

Was this Alaska sale project of 1854 seriously contemplated by Russia as a way to seal American support in the war against Britain and France? Or was it simply an idea pursued by Southern expansionists, represented by Cottman, Gwin, and George Sanders, to preserve a balance of free and slave states, with the acquisition of Alaska being the concomitant of their real goal, Cuba?[109] More likely, unofficial exploratory discussions on both the Russian and American sides were simply exaggerated by a sensationalist press made nervous by war. Clearly, there is no contemporary official evidence of any serious consideration of the sale or purchase of Alaska by the respective governments, but the publicity supplied by Cottman and the American and European press did prepare the way diplomatically and popularly for a genuine pursuit of such a plan some years later.

Mediation and Arms

In the meantime, back in Washington, the United States government initiated another, more definite project to address Russia's naval weakness—mediation. At the end of June or early July, Marcy met with Stoeckl to discuss the possibility that the United States might arbitrate the dispute between Russia and Britain and France. Marcy had already received indications of French refusal, and the Russian chargé, who believed that Attorney General Caleb Cushing was behind the offer, doubted that Britain would accept because of American partiality toward Russia. Moreover, the secretary of state warned Stoeckl not to relay any information until he had the president's approval, Pierce having already left Washington for the holiday. On 12 July, Marcy resumed the discussion with Stoeckl and Katakazi, who was on the verge of leaving for St. Petersburg, noting, "Russia rendered this same service to us once and it is only just that we repay our debt."[110] Though Katakazi believed anti-British local politics was involved (the Irish vote) and Soviet historians later guessed at economic motives,[111] the rationale seems to have been to put the allies more on the defensive through added diplomatic pressure. Their refusal might also shift public opinion toward Russia and in support of a tougher American policy for acquisi-

such language; and just then, when all Europe seemed uniting against Russia, it could not fail to produce its effect. The fact is, Cottman was more Russian than the Russians themselves. . . . Old Suwarrow himself was never more ultra-Russian than was Cottman, (with the reserve that Cottman was never seen to eat raw salt pork nor tallow candles)."

[109]Golder, "Russian American Relations," pp. 467–69.

[110]In explaining the mediation offer, Marcy told Katakazi just before his departure for St. Petersburg: "Russia rendered us the same service once, and it is only just that we repay this debt." Katakazi to Nesselrode, 2/14 July 1854, f. kants. Vashington 1854, d. 167, AVPR.

[111]B. P. Polevoi, "Popytka amerikanskogo posrednichestva v Krymskoi voine," in *Problemy istorii etnografii Ameriki* (Moscow: Nauka, 1979), pp. 43–54.

tions in the Caribbean. As in the case of the erstwhile purchase/sale of Alaska, neither side expected much to come of this proposal of mediation. In St. Petersburg, Nesselrode took the conservative view that a Russian acceptance would only be a sign to its enemies of military weakness, and he officially refused to make a commitment until the allies had responded positively.[112]

With mediation thus at an impasse, but having done honor to the idea, the United States turned to a more pressing concern—the achievement of a maritime neutrality agreement. Since both Russia and the United States were in full accord on the basic principles of neutral rights at sea—free ships make free goods—a simple "treaty" was quickly drawn up and signed in Washington on 22 July 1854.[113] Though the allies naturally abstained, this bilateral agreement was a forerunner of the Declaration of Paris of 1856, which was a breakthrough in international law of the seas.

Once recognition of long-sought maritime rights of neutrals was achieved—formally by Russia and as accepted policy by Britain and France for the duration of the conflict—the United States was content to let the war proceed in hopes of realizing gains, commercially and territorially, from the distraction of the European countries. Cuba, still a key objective, eluded American grasp. The October Ostend Manifesto had declared the nation's intention of buying or taking the island, yet American diplomacy in Spain failed to prepare the ground for any purchase, and Marcy's conviction that the war would provide a better opportunity stalled a direct military seizure.[114] But one important motive behind the Pierce administration's calculated and cautious support for Russia remained the peaceful annexation of Cuba.

Individual Americans would try to reap profits more directly by war contracts with Russia. Wesley Smith returned from St. Petersburg in August 1854 with plans to ship up to 7,500 tons of coal the next spring at $20 per ton, including freight.[115] In September, Stoeckl, while visiting New York, discussed the purchase of war matériel with two inventors: Morin, who designed incendiary rockets, and Nathan Roosevelt, who built fireships. With the threat of a British fleet advancing on Kronstadt and other Russian Baltic ports in mind, Stoeckl promised to pay both men the expenses of their trips to Russia for further negotia-

---

[112]Nesselrode to Stoeckl, 10/22 September 1854, f. kants. Vashington 1854, d. 167, AVPR, and Stoeckl to Nesselrode, 25 October/6 November 1854, f. kants. Vashington 1854, d. 168, AVPR; Dowty, *Limits of American Isolation*, pp. 125–27.

[113]The text and correspondence relating to the treaty are found in David Hunter Miller, ed., *Treaties and Other International Acts of the United States of America*, vol. 6, 1852–55 (Washington, D.C.: Government Printing Office, 1942), pp. 796–808.

[114]Dowty, *Limits of American Isolation*, pp. 120–22.

[115]Stoeckl to Seniavin, 25 August/5 September and 23 September/5 October 1854, f. kants. Vashington 1854, d. 167, AVPR.

tions.[116] More important was an interview with arms manufacturer Samuel Colt, who promptly dispatched two thousand of his best pistols to Hamburg, where they were acquired by Russia through German intermediaries. Colt also told Stoeckl he could send up to five thousand more at three pounds sterling each to a neutral Belgian or Prussian port.[117] He and his associate Edward Dickerson then left for Europe, where they would peddle arms to both sides. Similarly, Lammot Du Pont was involved in selling gunpowder to the participants. The total impact of all this for the Russian war effort is not exactly clear, since much of the business was conducted secretly outside of diplomatic channels, and the items were smuggled in through third parties. Though the Colt pistols would have been carried only by officers and would have minimal battlefield effect, they could have been significant in terms of morale.

In any event, it is certain that direct American involvement with Russia was soaring. Seymour was obviously quite occupied with the comings and goings of various visiting Americans—from a naval officer (L. B. Elliot) volunteering for Russian service and to a longtime congressman (Charles F. Mercer) touring Europe. For his old hometown friend Colt, the minister summoned up his best influence and arranged appointments with Nesselrode (on 8 November) and with Nicholas I (on 11 November) and a grand dinner with the elite of Russian-American society.[118] Even pistols required imperial audiences.

Perhaps the most interesting of this "second wave" of visitors in 1854 was Taliaferro P. Shaffner from Louisville, Kentucky. An experienced telegrapher, he had superintended telegraph construction in the Middle West, which had included the laying of submarine cables across the Ohio and Mississippi rivers. Shaffner also

[116]Stoeckl to Seniavin, 2/14 September 1854, ibid.

[117]Ibid. Colt was no stranger to Russian arms contacts.

[118]Elliot acted as an official Russian courier, while Mercer came out of curiosity and friendship for Russians he met during his travels. Seymour to Seniavin, 13/25 July 1854, Seymour to Nesselrode, 14/27 September 1854, Seymour to Seniavin, 21 October/2 November 1854, Nesselrode to Seymour, 30 October/11 November 1854, DPR, Russia, vol. 4532, RG 84, NA. In a letter published over the initials "C. D. M.," Mercer described his reception in Russia: "I have heard and seen at two large dinner parties, one German and the other American, . . . more of the country I am in, than I did of Prussia in Berlin, France in Paris, or the three great cities of Italy in all my much longer visits to any of them." Baltimore *American and Commercial Advertiser*, 15 November 1854.

Andrew Dickson White's letters provide many details of the gay social life of wartime St. Petersburg: the beauty of the American ladies such as Mrs. (Alexander) Bodisko and Mrs. Nottbeck (nee Elizabeth Langdon); the large organ in the middle of the Solov'ev house that Seymour rented, with which White could make the whole building and adjoining street reverberate; winter troika rides; museum visits; festive dinners and receptions. See, for example, White to his mother, 16 November and 28 December 1854, reel 2, White Papers, Department of Manuscripts and University Archives, John M. Olin Library, Cornell University (hereafter Cornell).

served from 1850 to 1853 as president of the line from St. Louis to New Orleans. In early 1854 he joined with Samuel Morse and Cyrus and Matthew Field for a project to sink a cable crossing the Atlantic Ocean. But with the outbreak of the Crimean War, Shaffner saw an opportunity to secure contracts for war-related communication needs in Russia and to try to sell a plan for a telegraph line through Siberia as part of a grandiose, round-the-world communications system.

Like Cottman and Sanders, once in Russia, Shaffner soon found himself involved in other activities. After his first visit in September and October 1854, he went to England to purchase wire, galvanic batteries, and other materials to detonate explosives underwater.[119] Under his supervision these items were collected in the United States early in 1855 and reshipped through Bremen to Russia. At this point, Shaffner seemed to be playing a double or triple game, pursuing with Morse and the Field brothers the project for a transatlantic cable by way of Newfoundland, Greenland, Iceland, and Norway, while also informing a British agent of his activities in Russia. To advance his ambitious schemes, he returned to Russia with Matthew Field and stayed to tour the country with his wife and young son for most of 1855, putting on airs in his "blazing attire" of a colonel's uniform.[120] By now his telegraphic and submarine enterprises had expanded to include ventures for constructing railroads from Moscow to Odessa

[119]Stoeckl, citing a conversation with Shaffner, to Nesselrode, 12/24 December 1854, f. kants. Vashington 1855, d. 227, AVPR. Shaffner, however, did not get along well with Stoeckl. Shaffner to Seymour, 23 January 1855, Seymour Papers, box 858, ConnHS. For Shaffner's own recollections in later claims against Cyrus Field and Samuel Morse, see his letters to Morse, 2 May 1856, Morse Papers, reel 18, Manuscript Division, LC, and to the editor, 29 September 1858, New York *Times*, 4 October 1858.

[120]Shaffner's flattering appraisal of Russian telegraph operations was published in *Shaffner's Telegraph Companion, Devoted to the Science and Art of the Morse American Telegraph* (New York: Pudney and Russell, 1855), pp. 383–422; on providing information to the British agent, J. Savile Lumley (British attaché) to Crampton, 24 March 1855, FO 5/620, PRO. And Maj. Alfred Mordecai, a reliable observer, noticed the attention that the Shaffners received from official circles during the summer of 1855. At a military review on 18 July, Shaffner's son, dressed in a Continental army uniform, was called to the empress's box, "where he was much noticed and caressed by them all, and I saw the Emperor leaning from his horse to speak to him." Mordecai's letters to his wife in diary form, entry of 18 July 1855, Mordecai Papers, vol. 2, Manuscript Division, LC.

Augustus Erving, Seymour's secretary, revealed to White on 1 October that "Shaffner is still here constantly making contracts and maturing his vast schemes" and that he had stayed up two nights copying papers for him. White Papers, reel 2, Cornell. And White reflected a few months later: "Shaffner's life in Russia would fill a book and a comical book too. Still as I have said, he is a good fellow, and if he makes a fortune out of the Dutchess Marie's iron-works will deserve it. Especially for the risks he ran of tripping himself up and breaking his neck over his sword which with full American Colonels uniform he used to wear although he was, I think, never even a militia colonel." White (Berlin) to his mother, Clara Dickson White, 9 January 1856, ibid.

and from Moscow to Warsaw.[121] In the process he had, not surprisingly, also become an active and visible publicist for the Russian cause.

Also in 1855, two well-known artillery experts, Robert Earle and Sen. Charles T. James of Rhode Island, came to Russia by special invitation to improve Baltic defenses. These and other American efforts to sell arms or military inventions to Russia may have had a greater psychological than military benefit overall, but judging from the reactions of the London press and the activities of agents in the United States, the British were extremely concerned about them. Moreover, the total American contribution to the military support of Russia was probably greater than has been generally recognized in the past.

The best indication of substantial arms shipments from the United States to Russia during the war concerns the cargo of the *Samuel Appleton* of Boston, which arrived at Baltic Port (in Estonia) in April 1855, apparently while the allied blockading squadron was not on station. The ship was stopped by a British cruiser, however, on its homeward voyage, and the manifests allegedly showed that the ship had carried 50,000 rifles and 100,000 revolvers.[122] Though the quantity appears overstated and the actual evidence is circumstantial, the supercargo of the vessel was Arthur Cunningham of Boston, who was implicated in other munition shipments to Russia. Cunningham's departure from the United States in February was soon after the arrival of a special Russian agent, Capt. Otto Lilienfeldt, whose mission was unquestionably to purchase arms.[123]

[121]Seymour to Seniavin, 6/18 February 1855, and Seymour to Nesselrode, 30 May/11 June 1855, DPR, Russia, vol. 4532, RG 84, NA; on Shaffner's negotiations for the railroad contract, f. 1272, op. 1, no. 5, TsGIA. The biographers of Cyrus Field, in giving him chief credit for the successful laying of an Atlantic cable, dismiss Shaffner's role and fail to mention their Russian ventures. For example, Samuel Carter III, *Cyrus Field: Man of Two Worlds* (New York: Putnam's, 1968), p. 117.

[122]Seymour to Marcy, 26 April 1855, DUSM, Russia, vol. 16 (roll 16, M 35), RG 59, NA. A detailed account of the British inspection of the *Samuel Appleton* was published in the American press; see, for example, "Landing of Arms in Russia," Hartford *Daily Times*, 2 July 1855. The British consul in Boston investigated and thought that the report was correct. "It has in fact been communicated to me lately, and through a respectable source, that a plan for the shipment of arms from this country for Russia is now organizing and may have been going on for some time past." Edward A. Grattan to Clarendon, 3 July 1855, FO 5/628, PRO.

[123]Nesselrode to Stoeckl, 24 December/5 January 1855, f. kants. Vashington 1854, d. 168, AVPR. Leaving Russia in early January, Lilienfeldt reached Washington on 20 February. Stoeckl to Nesselrode, 10/22 February 1855, f. kants. Vashington 1855, d. 227, AVPR. Charles Rackelwicz, a former New York harbor policeman, seems also to have been involved in arms arrangements for Russia during visits to St. Petersburg. White described him as "one of the oddest sticks imaginable. He is a bluff hearty old sea captain and hardly able to hold his own against the land sharks of St. Petersburg." To his mother, 25 January 1855, White Papers, reel 2, Cornell. This character also prompted White to comment, "To tell the truth there have been some pretty hard specimens of America here within the last year," and to relate a story about American sailors causing

Very few American ships, however, called at Russian ports during the war, most preferring to use neutral harbors such as Antwerp, Hamburg, Bremen, or Memel. The American consul in Hamburg reported, for example, that the number of American ships arriving at that port increased to thirty a year in 1855 from a prewar average of eight, and most carried cargoes destined for Russia. He noted that "several American vessels from New York and Boston have brought large quantities of saltpetre, brought from English ports to the United States and thence reshipped for Russian use to this port."[124] There is verification of a shipment of gunpowder arranged by Beverley Sanders on the *William Penn* from San Francisco to Petropavlovsk on the Kamchatka coast.[125]

According to Russian records, Colt sent five thousand revolvers early in 1855 in two shipments through Antwerp and Berlin and accepted an order for five thousand more. He also shipped machinery for making carbines concealed in bales of cotton and addressed to William L. Winans in St. Petersburg.[126] In February, Shaffner routed explosive devices and equipment from England through Bremen expressly for Grand Duke Constantine and under the care of Captain Elliot.[127] He also took with him through that port a number of arms samples in March 1855, such as the new Sharp repeating carbines.[128] Some of these shipments—including a quantity of the Colt revolvers—were intercepted and turned back at the Prussian border. Colt, for one, was not deterred from signing a new contract with Lilienfeldt in August for fifty thousand rifles.[129] What must be remembered is that American arms manufacturers probably did an even larger business with Russia's enemies, though probably the most valuable American service to the allies was providing chartered shipping to the Crimea.

Likewise, the most important American assistance to Russia was in furnishing essential raw materials, though the coal that Smith had planned to ship was not vital and, in fact, ultimately came from German sources instead. A shortfall in imported sugar from the United States could be adjusted to, now that the Russian Empire produced more than a third of its needs from Ukrainian sugar

a scandal climbing the statue of Peter the Great and sitting behind him on the horse. To his mother, 28 December 1854, ibid.

[124]Bromberg (Hamburg) to Seymour, 4 August 1855, DPR, Russia, vol. 4532, RG 84, NA.

[125]Saul, "Beverley C. Sanders," pp. 165–66; Kostromitinov to Voevodskii (chief administrator at Sitka), 10/22 December 1854, RRAC, CGG, CR, vol. 21 (roll 21, M 11), RG 261, NA.

[126]Stoeckl to Nesselrode, 11/23 January and 16/28 January 1855, f. kants. Vashington 1855, d. 227, AVPR.

[127]Stoeckl to Nesselrode, 28 December/9 January, 24 January/5 February 1855 and 28 February/12 March 1855, ibid.

[128]Stoeckl to Nesselrode, 2/14 May and 12/24 September 1855, ibid.

[129]See Joseph Bradley, *Guns for the Tsar* (DeKalb: Northern Illinois University Press, 1990).

beets.[130] Supply of cotton, however, was another matter; the Russian textile industry had rapidly expanded in the 1840s, and Russia did not yet grow any of its own cotton. Even though progress in the Russian spinning and weaving enterprises had reduced dependence on imports of English yarn, most of the raw cotton, mainly from the United States, had been carried by British ships. Their sudden withdrawal naturally worried Russian officials, and they assiduously tried to develop alternative suppliers, primarily American. Stoeckl, the economist Ludwig Tengoborskii, and other Russian agents stimulated direct trade at every opportunity and with some success, judging from the notices of ships leaving from Southern ports such as New Orleans and Charleston with cargoes for Russia.[131] Most of these ships arriving at European ports were carrying, not weapons or other contraband, but unadulterated bales of cotton. The war was proving to be a boon to American shipping and commerce—and especially the Southern economy.

Interference in American Affairs

Other individuals and enterprises in the United States prospered from the war. If one were to believe the charges leveled by Britain and Russia against each other, considerable sums were expended in intelligence activities, in attempts to sway public opinion, and in recruitment efforts. There was certainly some truth to the accusations, though exaggerated rumors were rampant. British agents did keep a close watch on the activities of Russians in the United States and paid willingly for inside information. In the process they uncovered the negotiations by the naval mission of Firstein and Sokolov, which remained in the United States throughout the war, to purchase submarine equipment from the Nautilus Submarine Company in New York.[132] An espionage plot, allegedly hatched by Elliot, to send spies to England "for the purpose of destroying by fire the vessels of war in progress of construction at Deptford and Woolwich Dock Yards and if possible the buildings of these naval establishments," received so much publicity that it was probably scrapped.[133] And while British consuls searched for evidence of arms shipments to Russia, agents of both countries actively sought the latest

---

[130]Tegoborski, *Commentaries on the Productive Forces of Russia*, 2:46–57.

[131]Stoeckl listed eleven ships leaving New Orleans during the summer of 1854 with cotton intended for Russia; most of them declared Cork or Cowes as their destination but in reality headed for Baltic ports. Stoeckl to Nesselrode, 2/14 July 1854, f. kants. Vashington 1854, d. 167, AVPR.

[132]J. Savile Lumley (British attaché) to John Crampton (British minister), 7 May 1855, FO 5/621, PRO.

[133]Barclay (British consul in New York) to Clarendon (secret), 27 January 1855, FO 5/625, PRO.

in American arms developments—for example, the new mortar inventions of Bishop.[134]

Buying the press was a common charge, but evidence of it is fragmentary. Stoeckl subsidized with small payments Adam Gurowski, who wrote for the New York *Tribune*, but that paper was pro-Russian to begin with. Gurowski also wrote *A Year of the War*, published in February 1855, which pleased the Russian minister enough that he sent several copies to St. Petersburg.[135] A British consul bragged that he had "kept straight" the Philadelphia *Inquirer*,[136] but, again, support cannot be found for either side's claim that the other spent large amounts of money to influence the press. Obviously, in the early stages of the war, the Russians were annoyed about the dependence of American writers on British and French sources. By 1855 the British were clearly frustrated by the veering of most newspapers to the Russian side, reflecting concerns that an allied victory would cause a shift in the balance of power detrimental to American interests.

The combatants also grew increasingly uneasy in 1855 about recruitment activities in the United States. The British were disturbed about rumors of a Russian plot to instigate an Irish revolt by promoting that cause with money and transportation for an invasion force of Irish immigrants into their homeland. The vehemently anti-British speeches of Irish nationalists, spurred by the war, certainly did nothing to assuage these fears,[137] though there is no evidence that Russia ever seriously considered playing the "Irish card" during the war (perhaps realizing its own vulnerability to the same trump regarding Poland). The advocates of independence for Ireland no doubt enjoyed seeing the British expect the worst, even though they actually lacked organization and were scattered around the country.

Although only a few resident Poles offered their services to the anti-Russian

[134]Crampton to Clarendon, 12 and 26 March 1855, FO 5/620, PRO.
[135]Stoeckl to Nesselrode, 10/22 February 1855, f. kants. Vashington 1855, d. 227, AVPR.
[136]The British consul in Philadelphia reported on the press as follows: "I regret to say that the general pro-Russian feeling here, caused by the continued tone of the Govt. press, still obtains. The South are, as ever, our bitter opponents." He added that all papers were pro-Russian except the *National Intelligencer*, the New York *Courier*, and the Philadelphia *Inquirer* "(which as Mr. Crampton is aware I have kept straight)." George Mathew to Hammond (War Office), 15 January 1855, FO 5/628, PRO.
[137]Barclay (British consul in New York) to Clarendon, 24 July 1855, FO 5/625, PRO. The consul in Cincinnati, after his implication in a recruitment scandal, became obsessed about the Irish threat from the Middle West. "We have now a clear cut case of conspiracy for promoting an insurrection in Ireland and supporting it by an armed force from the United States, to be transported in vessels provided by Russian agents." Although the British minister cautioned him about trying to make a case in court, Rowcroft went ahead and suffered public ridicule. Rowcroft to Crampton, 30 October 1855, and Crampton to Clarendon, 3 December 1855, FO 5/624, PRO; Cincinnati *Daily Enquirer*, 12 January 1856.

coalition,[138] British recruitment efforts in the United States were very visible. One of the earliest and most active of these programs occurred in Louisville and Cincinnati, beginning in January 1855. Its promoter was Gabriel Korponay, the Hungarian adventurer who had led the United States into the polka world in 1844. After serving in the Mexican War and as an artillery instructor at West Point, Korponay resigned from the army with the intention of returning to Hungary in 1849. He failed to leave before the revolution there was suppressed and so resumed his career as a dance instructor in Louisville. Harboring an understandable resentment against Russia and perhaps bored with teaching Americans how to dance, Korponay volunteered in January 1855 to organize an immigrant (mainly German) detachment from Louisville and Cincinnati for the Crimea with the help of the British vice-consul and another Hungarian emigré, "Captain" Poshner.[139] A specially designated British recruiting agent, Joseph Howe, agreed to pay him $18,000 to include bounties for six hundred recruits delivered to Halifax for embarkation. Korponay himself would receive the rank of colonel in this "Nova Scotian" regiment. Charles Rowcroft, the British vice-consul in Cincinnati, was instructed to support him in this endeavor and to oversee recruitment in that city.[140]

All might have gone smoothly except that the organizational meetings were infiltrated by members of the United Irish Society, which informed the local press and called in the police. Rowcroft, Poshner, and several other leaders were arrested and tried in well-publicized court proceedings.[141] Korponay, however, es-

---

[138]The British neglected potential Polish recruits, but at least one, F. A. Okelomski, who had served as a topographic engineer in the Russian army before emigrating in 1835, offered himself and thirty other Poles to fight against Russia. W. Morton Dyer (British consul in Mobile) to Crampton, 7 May 1855, enclosing Okelomski's statement of 6 May, FO 5/621, PRO. Not only were the Poles scattered about the country, but most of the approximately fifteen hundred refugees were from Austrian and Prussian Poland and more resentful of those "occupying" powers than Russia. Bogdan Grzelonski, *Poles in the United States of America, 1776–1865* (Warsaw: Interpress, 1976), pp. 129–30.

[139]Rowcroft to Clarendon, 12 January 1855, FO 5/629, PRO. Korponay to Rowcroft, 11 and 20 January and 14 February 1855, FO 97/34, PRO.

[140]Howe to Korponay (copy), 6 April 1855, FO 5/629, PRO. Korponay may also have hoped to gain British support for the release of his brother from prison in Hungary. For more on Howe and the British recruitment efforts, see J. Bartlett Brebner, "Joseph Howe and the Crimean War Enlistment Controversy between Great Britain and the United States," *Canadian Historical Review* 11, 4 (December 1930): 300–327, and Charles Calvert Bayley, *Mercenaries for the Crimea: The German, Swiss, and Italian Legions in British Service, 1854–1856* (Montreal and London: McGill-Queen's University Press, 1977).

[141]Rowcroft to Clarendon, 1 July 1855, FO 5/629, PRO. The full details of the recruitment, as exposed by a grand jury investigation, are in the Cincinnati *Daily Enquirer*, 12, 13, 14, and 15 July 1855. It ended with bond set at $2,000 for the British consul. "Mr. Rowcroft then contended that the entire proceedings had been irregular, that he felt

caped, having already led an advance guard of recruits into Canada. The trial dragged on for over a year, and with Poshner turning state's evidence against him, Rowcroft became convinced of an Irish-Russian conspiracy:

> It is true, that, the restless Irish population in this country are always making public harangues on the subject of emancipating Ireland from British rule; but in the present case, the circumstance of England being at war with Russia, and, that, probably, England would have more than the country of Russia in arms against her, gave a new significance to the Irish Movement in this country. The cry was, that, the difficulty of England which was to furnish Ireland's opportunity *had* arrived; and that *now* was the time when the insurrecting Irish at home and the hostile Irish abroad might unite to strike the blow, which was, in the language of the conspirators, "to uproot and overthrow British Government in Ireland."[142]

The whole affair caused considerable damage to Anglo-American relations, for what many considered to be direct violations of the neutrality law of the United States. Similar but less extensive recruitment attempts were exposed in New York and Philadelphia. Other consuls as well as the British minister John Crampton were implicated, and the suspicious death of Rowcroft added a final touch of mystery. Russia could delight in British discomfiture as American public opinion shifted even more decidedly in the Russian direction as a result of these clumsy efforts to penetrate the neutrality blanket that covered the American people, unassimilated immigrants and all.

The American Military Commission to the Crimean War

The American government also pursued a professional interest in the war. Not satisfied with second- and thirdhand accounts of the military activity, the War Department decided in the summer of 1854 to send a team of military observers

himself alone, but that he should ever uphold the rights of his government, and had no fear whatever of prisons. He concluded by saying that he came to this country to cultivate peace between two great nations, and he thanked God that the conspiracy, as shown to exist among the witnesses, did not originate with the American people." Cincinnati *Daily Enquirer*, 15 July 1855.

[142]Rowcroft to Clarendon, 10 March 1856, FO 5/653, PRO. Brebner, "Howe and the Crimean War," pp. 324–26. Rowcroft's death was reported as sudden and unexplained, some British sources claiming that Irish societies were responsible. Obviously suffering mental anguish, he may have taken his own life. "The Mysterious Death of the Late Consul Rowcroft of Cincinnati—Suspicions of Foul Play," New York *Daily Times*, 27 October 1856; Cincinnati *Daily Enquirer*, 23 September 1856. But another view was that the ship had just been painted and that the fumes may have contributed to his death. "The Late Consul Rowcroft—The Real Cause of His Death," New York *Evening Post*, 13 November 1856.

to the battlefronts.[143] The special commission that departed for Russia in the spring of 1855 consisted of Maj. Richard Delafield (engineering), Maj. Alfred Mordecai (ordnance), and Capt. George B. McClellan (cavalry). Though McClellan is certainly the best known of the three because of his Civil War prominence, Delafield was actually the senior officer and later rose to the post of chief of engineers. Mordecai, one of the few American Jews of officer rank, was the most important in terms of his knowledge of Russia (which he had previously visited in 1840), his powers of observation, and his writing skills.

Reaching St. Petersburg on 19 June 1855, the three officers were promptly received by Nesselrode and the new tsar, Alexander II. They attended reviews, visited Kronstadt and other military installations in and around the capital, and socialized with most of the American community. Judging from Delafield's direct communications to Secretary of War Jefferson Davis—as well as individual summary reports published after their return and private letters—the American military observers were clearly impressed by the Russian capability of sustaining military action and saw valuable lessons for the United States:

> Everything indicated resources, ability, and enthusiastic determination to meet whatever crisis could come to pass. Confidence in their ability to defend the city of St. Petersburg was unbounded. . . . It is in our power to inspire our citizens with like confidence, and our enemy with like respect for our strength and power of resistance. It is only for the people and Congress to will it *in time.* The example of Russia is a lesson every way entitled to our study and imitation.[144]

Mordecai especially admired the character of the Russian soldier:

> The Russian soldier is remarkable for physical qualities, well adapted to his profession: an athletic form, broad shoulders, small waist, erect, muscular frame, little encumbered with fat; accustomed to a life of labor, and to be nourished by the most simple diet; add to these qualities, and to the aptitude before mentioned, the habit of implicit obedience to superiors, and the strong religious sentiment which leads to blind and enthusiastic devotion to the Em-

[143]Seymour to Marcy, 9/21 June 1855, DUSM, Russia, vol. 16 (roll 16, M 35), RG 59, NA.

[144]Maj. Richard Delafield, *Report on the Art of War in Europe in 1854, 1855 and 1856* (Washington, D.C.: George W. Bowman, 1860), pp. 35-36. Most of Mordecai's interesting letters to his wife are in the Library of Congress, but an important one is not: 29 June 1855, no. 847, f. 85, Southern Historical Collection, University of North Carolina. For Delafield's official weekly reports to Jefferson Davis in June and July, see Letters Received by the Office of Adjutant General (main series), 1822-60 (roll 513, M 567), RG 94, NA.

peror, as the head of both Church and State, and to unquestioning submission to the delegated authority of the officer. Such are the principal elements of the military character of the Russian soldier.[145]

McClellan, who was sick through much of the visit, had a less sanguine view of the Russian army, which he found filled with "vagabonds, thieves, gipsies [sic], dissipated men, . . . condemned to serve. Yet, mingled with these worthless characters are many good men, in fact, the latter predominate, and the influence of rigid discipline soon converts the others, at least into good soldiers, if not into good men."[146] His Army of the Potomac a few years later would not be much different.

During their six-week sojourn in Russia, the American army officers inspected arsenals and officers' schools, saw the other sights of St. Petersburg and vicinity, and made several visits to the Hermitage and a quick trip to Moscow. Their active social life entailed dinners nearly every evening with Russian officials or with American residents such as Winans and Seymour. Mordecai's private descriptions indicate that all three were gratified by their reception in Russia: "Everywhere that we appear in uniform the greatest attention and civility are shown to us—in fact, our big epaulettes and our gray hair makes us (Del and me) pass for generals by which title we are often saluted and guards turn out and present arms whenever we drive by them."[147]

While waiting for permission to travel to the Crimea, the officers entertained themselves around the capital. Mordecai disliked the city itself—"In another latitude St. Petersburg would be a pest house of intermittent and malignant fever"[148]—but enjoyed the Hermitage and the imperial summer palaces at Tsarskoe Selo and Pavlovsk: "It is such a surprise and pleasure to find so much luxury and beauty in the midst of such a waste."[149] Moscow also earned words of praise, especially when viewed in July from Sparrow (now Lenin) Hills: "No view

[145]Maj. Alfred Mordecai, *Military Commission to Europe in 1855 and 1856, Report of Major Alfred Mordecai of the Ordnance Department* (Washington, D.C.: George W. Bowman, 1860), p. 21.

[146]George B. McClellan, *Report of the Secretary of War Communicating the Report of Captain George B. McClellan* . . . (Washington, D.C.: A. O. P. Nicholson, 1857), p. 75. To his brother, McClellan was much more succinct in appraising the Russian cavalry: "It is superb." To John McClellan, 4 July 1855, McClellan Papers, microform reel 3, Manuscript Division, LC. Unfortunately, McClellan's surviving diary of the mission (reel 67) begins only in September, after leaving Russia.

[147]Mordecai to his wife (in the form of a diary), 3 July 1855, Mordecai Papers, vol. 2, Manuscript Division, LC.

[148]Ibid., 1 July 1855. McClellan, on the other hand, found St. Petersburg "truly a magnificent city." To his brother, 20 June 1855, McClellan Papers, microform reel 3, Manuscript Division, LC.

[149]Ibid., 9 July 1855.

of a city which I have ever beheld bears the slightest comparison with this. The foreground is formed by a beautiful sweep of the river at your feet, enclosing an extensive plain of gardens, with two or three large monasteries interspersed, beyond which the city lay glistening in the setting sun (for here the sun does set) its white walls and green roofs surmounted by a forest of gilded and many coloured domes and spires."[150] Back in St. Petersburg, the officers were exasperated by delays. Nonetheless, Mordecai reflected in a letter to his wife the admiration that was the theme of the mission's findings: "It must be admitted that we have been very forcibly impressed with all that we have seen of government operations, and have formed a vast idea of the power and resources of this empire as they are now developing themselves—all that I can say convey but a faint notion of what I see and feel on this subject."[151] Unable to proceed to the Russian front in the Crimea for the official reason that requests of other neutral observers had already been denied, the commission left Russia early in August and traveled by way of Berlin, Vienna, and Trieste, arriving at British camps in the Crimea in October.[152]

It would be difficult to determine to what extent the commission's detailed reports on the Crimean War affected the organization and training of the United States Army and, subsequently, the strategy and tactics of either the Northern or Southern army in the Civil War without a thorough examination of American military operations before and after the Crimean War. Certainly military adaptation and change is an evolving process that takes many factors into consideration. It is possible that one war influenced the other in negative ways, that lessons were applied even though the two conflicts differed logistically—the Crimean entailing a large amphibious operation and, for the Russians, defensive operations far from the governmental center.

Moreover, the American military observers, deprived of access to the Russian side of the battlefields, examined mainly the background preparations, stressing in their reports the Russian emphasis on military authority, the chain of command, simplicity of arms, and thorough training. As Mordecai summarized the Russian experience in a letter to the secretary of war, "In the organisation of the Russian Empire, as you are well aware, every other interest may be considered as subordinate to the military power."[153] He also stressed esprit de corps and training as prerequisites for combat effectiveness, "especially the Cossacks who form a very large proportion of [the cavalry], and who are as distinguished for their fine persons and handsome features, as for their wonderful dexterity in horse-

---

[150]Ibid., 22 July 1855.

[151]Ibid., 24 July 1855.

[152]Ibid., 4 September, 11 October, passim.

[153]Mordecai to Jefferson Davis, 20 August 1855, Letters Received by the Office of Adjutant General, (roll 513, M 567), RG 94, NA.

manship." For the ordinary soldiers, Mordecai found austerity in food, housing, and clothing the order of the day.[154]

Both McClellan and Delafield would have an opportunity to put to use what they learned directly onto American battlefields. Mordecai, after serving as commandant of the army's Watervliet (New York) arsenal, retired from service at the beginning of the Civil War because of a conflict of family interest (he was from the South, his wife from the North); they spent the war years in Philadelphia.[155]

American Medical Assistance

Another group of Americans had much better success in reaching the Russian front, though some to their regret. About thirty-five American doctors came to Russia during the war to gain surgical experience, for adventure, because of sympathy for the Russian cause, out of humanitarian concern, and perhaps for the money. Of these at least twenty-four actually performed surgery in the war zone; others worked in the St. Petersburg area in the north, and a few returned home without actually entering service.[156] Many had been students in Paris. The first wave in the summer of 1854 had been contacted by Dr. Thomas Cottman, of Alaska-sale fame, who learned of Russian needs during his visit. Through Mikhail Cherptovich and Andrei Budberg, the Russian ministers in Brussels and Berlin, respectively, arrangements were made for the reception of American, as well as German and Dutch, physicians. The contracts provided for a 334-ruble bounty and 668 rubles a year, plus lodging, firewood, a servant, and other expenses.

The initial contingent consisted of Charles F. Henry from Mobile, Courtenay King from Charleston, William J. Holt from Augusta, Georgia, and Isaac Draper from Massachusetts. In July 1854 they traveled directly from Brussels through Vienna and Jassy (Rumania) to Odessa, where they immediately began treating

[154]Ibid.

[155]Ibid.; Robert D. Abrahams, *The Uncommon Soldier: Major Alfred Mordecai* (New York: Farrar, Straus and Cudahy, 1958), is a popular and semifictional portrayal of Mordecai. Clearly the commission fulfilled its goal of collecting information, as George Mifflin Dallas, then minister to Britain, noted: "Our travelling military commissioners, Messrs. Delafield, Mordecai, and McClellan, took pot-luck with me yesterday. . . . They are not talkative men; but I thought I could discern that they are going home full freighted with a large mass of useful information." To Marcy, 28 March 1856, in *Letters from London, Written from the Year 1856 to 1860*, ed. Julia Mifflin (London: Richard Bentley, 1870), 1: 3.

[156]The contributions of the volunteer surgeons were well known at the time from the substantial number of their letters published in various newspapers and later from the articles by Eufrosina Dvoichenko-Markov, "Americans in the Crimean War," *Russian Review* 13, 2 (April 1954): 137–45, and Albert Parry, "American Doctors in the Crimean War," *South Atlantic Quarterly* 54, 4 (October 1955): 478–90.

casualties of the Battle of Alma.[157] By the end of the year they were carrying an even heavier surgical load, operating under primitive conditions in an army hospital in Simferopol, just behind the Russian lines in the Crimea.

At least eight American doctors commenced their service in Russia during 1854, six of them in the Crimean area, two (Draper and Turnipseed) transferring to field hospitals in the heart of besieged Sevastopol.[158] Throughout 1855, other physicians came from all parts of the United States, including California. At least twenty of them hailed from Southern states, nine from Maryland alone. Charles Ross Parke of Bloomington, Illinois, was one of the last to leave the country in September 1855, arriving at the end of October at the Simferopol hospital, where he found seven others (Holt, Read, Stoddard, Johnson, Smith, Eldridge, and Marshall) still at work.

Surgery, even well behind the battle lines, was not without danger. Denwood T. Jones and Charles Deininger had died of cholera just before Parke's arrival and were buried in the same grave in Simferopol; their compatriots contributed to the erection of a large marble monument. Holt soon became gravely ill. No wonder Parke noted in his diary, "All have the blues and think of going home."[159] And Courtenay King, who had kept his hometown apprised of his activities in letters published in his father's newspaper, the Charleston *Courier*, had been the first to die—of typhus—on 14 March.[160] Most of the early arrivals met a similar fate, sacrificing their lives attending to the Russian war casualties. One of the saddest cases was that of Henry Clark, who came to Simferopol in November with Hank, Weems, and Hart, the last group of American doctors to head for the Crimea. Pious and abstemious, Clark became the butt of practical jokes in the American company, Read even threatening once to inject him with vodka. But after a terrible attack of typhus, he died on 18 January 1856 and was buried beside Jones and Deininger.[161]

By this time the remaining "American Florence Nightingales" were spending as much time doctoring themselves and taking care of the affairs of the deceased

[157]Charles F. Henry (Simferopol) to Seymour, 10 March 1855, Seymour Papers, box 858, ConnHS; William Joseph Holt Journal, Holt Papers, South Caroliniana Library, University of South Carolina.

[158]For newspaper accounts, see the Baltimore *American and Commercial Advertiser*, 4 and 25 August 1854; Journal of Isaac Draper (Sevastopol), 1 January to 13 February 1855, Holt Papers, South Caroliniana Library, University of South Carolina.

[159]"Diary of Charles Ross Parke, M.D., during His Trip to Russia and His Medical Service in the Russian Army," 26 October 1855, Manuscript Division, LC.

[160]John Ralli (Odessa) to Marcy, 1/13 April 1855, DUSC, Odessa, vol. 2 (roll 2, M 459), RG 59, NA. Ralli, the long-term American consul of Greek origin, was praised by all concerned for his services to the American doctors in his region.

[161]Parke Diary, 28 November 1855 and 18 January 1856, Manuscript Division, LC. Parke rationalized the practical joking among the homesick Americans: "So we go bobbing through the world, we must have some fun or we would die of ennui."

as they did treating the Russians. Understandably, there were often strained relations with the hospital administrators and other doctors, especially the German and Dutch surgeons, who had also been especially recruited for the war.
One altercation led to the arrest and jailing of Stoddard for beating a German
doctor named Boudler.[162] Released after two weeks of hassling with authorities,
Stoddard, haggard and ill, finally secured permission to leave the country. He
suffered through a painful, wearying journey across Russia in midwinter and finally struggled into Berlin, where he died in a few days, one of the last of the
eleven American Crimean War casualties.[163]

For the survivors, the assessments of their experience in Russia were varied:
Some could not get away fast enough, while others found solace in their humane work, enjoyed the company of Russian friends, and lingered after the war
to tour the country, consider further employment there, or return on another
occasion. John Morton of Nashville, one of the last to leave the theater of war,
reported from Sevastopol:

> A man naturally feels a little lonesome here when he is by himself in a place
> like this, with no other American. I am the only man left. Those who have
> been here are either dead or left for home. When I arrived here I found two
> American physicians, but they left soon after. They were not well pleased,
> and before I saw anything of the benefits to be derived by being here they
> prejudiced me a great deal against the place; but I feel it was their own faults,
> in fact I know it was, if they had anything to complain of.[164]

Others such as Henry F. Bostwick of Baltimore (who was talked into coming by
Stoeckl), George H. Oliver of Boston, and Timothy C. Smith of Vermont were
stationed more comfortably in Odessa, where they had ample time to socialize

[162]Ibid., 30 October 1855; Petition of 5 November 1855, Holt Papers, South Caroliniana Library, University of South Carolina; J. B. Stoddard to Seymour, 2 November
1855, Seymour Papers, box 858, ConnHS.

[163]From Berlin, White described Stoddard's death on 22 January 1856 and that Stoddard believed he had been poisoned by the German doctors. To his mother, 23 January
1856, White Papers, reel 2, Cornell. See also Ralli to Seymour, 19/31 March 1856, DPR,
Russia, vol. 4481, RG 84, NA.

Besides Stoddard, Clark, King, Henry, Jones, and Deininger, the United States lost
A. Addison Marshal, William Hart, Isaac Draper, Charles Nickels, and McMillan,
making a total of eleven. One source adds I. B. P. Hank to the list. Parry, "American
Doctors," p. 490. Naturally, the death rate was of great concern to those remaining:
"The mortality amongst the American surgeons in the Crimea is truly alarming. We
may with propriety ask ourselves, are none of us to reach our homes, and who shall be
the next victim?" But Parke also noted, "I am satisfied that this great mortality is partly
occasioned by the carelessness or ignorance of our Superior Doctors." Parke Diary, 6
and 17 March 1856, Manuscript Division, LC.

[164]National Intelligencer, 27 September 1855, borrowing from the Nashville Gazette.

and learn some Russian. Despite the real hardships of trying to save lives in wartime Russia, most of these doctors would have agreed with Parke's diary comment, "Tis only necessary to say I parted reluctantly with my numerous Russian friends whose kindness to myself and fellow Americans cannot be forgotten."[165] Many of those who returned to the United States soon found their well-practiced surgical skills in demand by both sides of another war.

Other Americans in Russia

Since the war had excluded many Englishmen from service in Russia (though most long-term residents were less affected), more Americans came to fill that vacuum.[166] This was especially true of the American railwaymen in Russia. In 1850 William L. Winans, Joseph Harrison, Jr., and Thomas DeKay Winans formed a new partnership, bought out Andrew Eastwick, and negotiated a twelve-year renewal of their lucrative contract with the Russian government. Joined by "Uncle" William R. Winans and Harrison's son Samuel, they enlarged their operations to handle additional military traffic on the St. Petersburg–Moscow line and to engage in war production. The exact nature of the latter is only partially documented. Members of the Winans family and Samuel and Joseph Harrison made several trips in and out of Russia during the war for business purposes.[167] William L. Winans, now the chief manager of the Russian operations, was also cloaked with diplomatic status as acting consul in St. Petersburg. Records do indicate that the company had considerable success in routing materials from Britain to the United States and on to Russia during the war, while its explicit military activities included adapting ships of the Baltic fleet to screw propulsion, building small auxiliary ships and around fifty sizable gunboats, and, by the fall of 1855, operating a gun foundry.[168]

The expansion called for additional personnel, and one who responded was

[165]Parke Diary, 22 April 1856, Manuscript Division, LC; Bostwick (Odessa) to Seymour, 10 January 1856, Seymour Papers, box 858, ConnHS. Another doctor wrote to Seymour, "Several Americans myself among the number were begged to remain in service—but altho' having the most kindly feeling toward the government—none of us felt disposed to be longer in connection with those who are placed in authority—and who for the most part are ignorant of the meaning of the word gentleman." Smith (Odessa) to Seymour, 19/31 August 1856, Seymour Papers, box 860 (misfiled, to be placed in box 858), ConnHs.

[166]Henry Mills Haskell came from Boston in the summer of 1855 to preach at the Anglo-American chapel in St. Petersburg. A young, recently ordained minister, he was greatly appreciated by the American community but died suddenly at the end of October. Boston *Daily Journal*, 5 March 1855; Hartford *Daily Courant*, 19 July 1855; Seniavin to Seymour, 30 December/11 January 1856, DPR, Russia, vol. 4481, RG 84, NA.

[167]Entries in Thomas Winans Diary for 1854, Winans Papers, box 19, MaryHS; Seymour's requests for couriers' passports, DPR, Russia, vol. 4481, RG 84, NA.

[168]London *Times*, 11 December 1854 and 12 January 1855; details of Russian gun-

Nicholas K. Wade of Pittsburgh's Knap and Wade Cannon Foundry, a company well-known in the United States for its casting of large guns for fortifications. Wade came to Russia early in 1856 to superintend a large ordnance plant in the St. Petersburg area, but he left as soon as the war was over.[169] Winans and Harrison also hired about fifteen American mechanics from Baltimore and Philadelphia, including George Hamblin, Francis Pratt, John Peacock, John Lehr, Edward Brown, and Herman Eckleman, all of whom arrived by September 1855.[170] Some were to stay in Russia several years working for Winans, Harrison, and Winans. Another American who also reached Russia in 1855 was initially connected with the American manufacturers. Gaun M. Hutton had operated the Alta foundry and sawmill in San Francisco during the height of the gold rush. Perhaps inspired by the activities of Beverley Sanders and the increasing contacts with Russians in the Pacific, Hutton went to Russia, where he married a daughter of William L. Winans, worked for him, succeeded him as acting vice-consul in 1856, and later established a large hardware business in Moscow, which he ran for many years.[171]

Obviously, the Crimean War broadened Russian-American relations in many ways and drew the two countries closer together than ever before, politically, economically, and culturally. In general, the people of each country felt no fear of the other, but on the contrary perceived a sense of common mission, common purpose. There were, however, exceptions to this rule, and some saw mutual interests ending one day in an expansionist conflict that would be particularly intense because of the ideological differences between the two countries. Matthew Perry, for example, predicted a rivalry and future estrangement over the Far East. In a paper for an American Geographical and Statistical Society meeting on 6 March 1856, he wrote:

> To me it seems that the people of America will, in some form or other, extend their dominion and their power, until they shall have brought within their

boats built during the war are in William L. Winans to Thomas Winans, 11/23 March 1859, William L. Winans Letterbook, Winans Papers, box 18, MaryHS. During a visit to the Aleksandrovsk plant, White went on board one of the gunboats and described it as strongly built, about seventy feet long, with three huge guns. To his mother, 5 May 1855, White Papers, reel 2, Cornell.

[169]Philadelphia *Public Ledger*, 25 January 1856; Baltimore *American and Commercial Advertiser*, 22 January 1856.

[170]G. Olney to Seymour, 25 August 1855, Seymour Papers, box 858, ConnHS; Erving to White, 1 October 1855, White Papers, reel 2, Cornell; "Mechanics for Russia," *National Intelligencer*, 11 August 1855.

[171]Hutton to Franklin Pierce, 24 December 1856, DUSC, St. Petersburg, vol. 8 (roll 5, M 81), RG 59, NA; *Alta California*, 2 January 1852. Hutton was considered rather odd and unsociable by at least some of the resident Americans. Erving to White, 1 July 1855, White Papers, reel 2, Cornell.

mighty embrace multitudes of the Islands of the great Pacific, and placed the Saxon race upon the eastern shores of Asia. And I think too, that eastward and southward will her great future aggrandizement (Russia) stretch forth her power to the coasts of China and Siam: and thus the Saxon and the Cossack will meet once more, in strife or in friendship, on another field. Will it be friendship? I fear not! The antagonistic exponents of freedom and absolutism must thus meet at last, and then will be fought that mighty battle on which the world will look with breathless interest; for on its issue will depend the freedom or the slavery of the world—despotism or rational liberty must be the fate of civilized man. I think I see in the distance the giants that are growing up for that fierce and final encounter; in the progress of events that battle must sooner or later be inevitably fought.[172]

This surprisingly astute prognosis of a future clash of titans was probably influenced by Perry's own experience of his race with Putiatin to open Japan to trade. Practically unnoticed at the time, Perry's perception of the Russian threat would be tellingly evoked by later historians.[173] But for the time being, and for several more years, Russian-American relations were guided by the "spirit of Crimea."

American Sympathy for Russia

The steady flow of Americans to Russia coincided with a growing public sentiment in favor of Russia in the United States. Newspapers that had been neutral or anti-Russian at the beginning of the war reflected this transition in 1855 throughout the country, but especially in the South and Midwest. As a Baltimore editor noted, the main reason was a fear that a quick and decisive victory by the allies would be detrimental to American interest:

There is in this country no real or substantial sympathy for Russia or its purposes; but there is an increasing fear of British and French interference in our affairs, a constantly growing dread that we are not to be left unmolested in tracking out our own path to empire and power. It is the patriotism of our people, their love for their own country that induces them to magnify every danger that threatens it, and which leads them to feel and to say that for fear

---

[172] *A Paper by Commodore M. C. Perry, U.S.N. Read before the American Geographical and Statistical Society, at a Meeting held March 6th, 1856* (New York: D. Appleton and Company, 1856), p. 28.

[173] Although they reported Perry's emphasis on "extending commercial enterprises" and noted that the paper was read by a Dr. Hawks with Perry present, the New York newspapers failed to mention this passage. New York *Daily Tribune*, 7 March 1856, and *Daily Times*, 7 March 1856. The *Herald* did not cover the meeting at all. For later historians' emphasis on Perry's comment, see Morison, *Perry*, p. 429, and Walworth, *Black Ships Off Japan*, pp. 129–30.

of the two probable courses of England and France towards us, after they have brought Russia to terms, they desire to see that success achieved by such sacrifices and at so great a cost of blood and treasure as will restrain any desire they may have to turn either their arms or diplomacy against us.[174]

American manifest destiny thus clearly influenced public opinion about the conflict. Alarm at the prospect of an Anglo-French combination encroaching on American affairs in the New World heightened natural sympathy toward the underdog, as the more militarily advanced European powers seemed to be ganging up on Russia. After the British bombardment of the Sveaborg island-fortress on the Russo-Finnish coast in July, the Hartford *Daily Times* complained:

It is a very bad sign when great nations make a prodigious noise over a very small success in war. When they exaggerate and by dint of loud puffing and obstreperous glorification, magnify a trivial affair into an important triumph, it shows that they are hard driven for substantial victories, and strive to drown the complaints of a dissatisfied public, by raising an awful clatter and din over nothing.[175]

In general, Americans relished the allies' difficulties and their inability to bring the war to a quick, successful conclusion. The press, in its detailed accounts of the siege of Sevastopol, reflected the cheers of readers for the stubborn Russian defenders.

Oddly, however, there were no American journalists reporting from Russia, except for free-lancers such as Daniel Gilman. Newspapers relied on material taken from the British and French papers, on other sources, including their own, in the allied capitals, on interviews of travelers to Russia, and on letters from Americans in that country. The American physicians thus contributed to the pro-Russian feeling as their letters and other reports were disseminated throughout the country. The death of Nicholas I and the accession of a potentially more liberal ruler, Alexander II, bolstered the American conviction that Russia was in the right. No wonder then that when rumors of the fall of Sevastopol in July proved to be false, celebrations were held in a number of cities, though the Winans denied that this was the purpose of a brilliant illumination staged by them in Baltimore.[176]

When Sevastopol finally did succumb to the allies, American sentiment con-

---

[174]Baltimore *American and Commercial Advertiser*, 6 February 1855. For other studies of the press during the war, see L. Jay Oliva, "America Meets Russia: 1854," *Journalism Quarterly* 40, 1 (Winter 1963): 65–69, and Horace Perry Jones, "Southern Opinion on the Crimean War," *Journal of Mississippi History* 29, 2 (May 1967): 95–117.

[175]Hartford *Daily Times*, 14 September 1855.

[176]Hartford *Daily Courant*, 24 July 1855.

tinued to support Russia, as the Cincinnati *Daily Enquirer* explained: "Nations in their alliances are always governed by *interest*—never by feeling or love. . . . It is because we are an *American* in our feelings and desires that our sympathies are with Russia in this contest. We are not blind to the fact that it is from England and France that our country meets with the greatest opposition in all measures designed to add to our national aggrandizement." Even so, George Washington's dictum of no entangling alliances was still valid "and most certainly [we] would not desire to see it violated for the purpose of having any understanding with the great despotism of Russia, yet, in the present state of our relations with the Western powers—the possibility of a rupture with them—all clearsighted and patriotic Americans will rejoice to see her giving the Allies such severe blows as will preclude them from turning their attention to affairs across the ocean for some time to come."[177] Many Americans were therefore disappointed by Russia's agreeing to peace negotiations early in 1856.

That "isolationist" Americans would be so interested in a conflict so far away was partly attributable to the rapidly expanding number of newspapers and greater literacy. Even the small-town midwestern weeklies carried extensive coverage of the war. Supplementing the newspapers were new pictorial journals, such as *Frank Leslie's Illustrated Newspaper*, which featured articles on Alexander II, St. Petersburg, and the war in its first issues. This was also a time of traveling lecturers, with the Reverend Robert Baird, who had visited Russia a few years earlier, being especially noted for his many pro-Russian speeches.[178] Daniel Gilman developed a similar theme in public appearances, having returned from St. Petersburg in early 1855 after a brief stint as one of Seymour's secretaries. Other speakers were Horatio Southgate, Andrew Foster, and Bayard Taylor, the latter alone presenting over a hundred talks in the winter of 1855–56, many of them focusing on Russia and the Near East.[179]

The war also nurtured extreme, anti-Catholic views, of which Charles Boynton, a Presbyterian minister in Cincinnati, is most representative. In an 1855 Fourth of July oration, he summed up this position:

What Russia is in the East, America is in the West; the hated and dreaded foe of the Papacy. The same powers that fear the progress of Russia, and seek to cripple her in this war, are also they who fear our rapid advance, and who actually threaten it, interrupt it, and every reason which has sent those armies and fleets into the Crimea and the Baltic may also operate to send them

[177]Cincinnati *Daily Enquirer*, 29 November 1855.

[178]*Frank Leslie's Illustrated Newspaper*, 23 February 1856, p. 161; Norfolk *American Beacon*, 14 and 20 March 1854; New York *Herald*, 3 and 15 April 1855.

[179]Hartford *Daily Times*, 28 February 1856, on Gilman; New York *Herald*, 20 January 1855, on Foster; Hartford *Daily Times*, 26 November 1855, on Taylor, for examples.

hither on a similar errand; for as Russia threatens the Papacy and troubles France and England with her southeastern progress, so our Protestant nation is equally threatening to the Pope, and our *south-western* march is equally annoying to those who are struggling to so hold the balance of power, both *East* and *West*, as to rule even us, themselves.[180]

The contest was awakening attitudes that were far from ideal national traits and, ironically, that resembled Old World biases and prejudices often condemned by the United States. No wonder some British were amused and Americans embarrassed by the "hypocrisy" of friendship and understanding between a "supreme" autocratic power and the "most" democratic republic.

The American perception of Russia was a complex phenomenon not explainable solely in terms of a common Anglophobia, since that, for commercial and cultural reasons, was moderating at the time in both countries, despite the political rivalry. As Boynton exemplifies, antipathy toward France and the papacy was running especially high in the United States in the 1850s; missionary and church leaders also stressed the oppressive character of Turkish rule. Moreover, the United States was pursuing expansionist policies that were drawing the nation much more into European balance-of-power considerations. Finally, the dichotomy between liberal democracy on the one hand and autocratic tyranny on the other was less evident (or at least considered less significant) at the time than it was in hindsight. The parallel of slavery with serfdom was perhaps more obvious.

An exceptional view was offered by Andrew Dickson White, who, after leaving Seymour's service in the summer of 1855, wrote privately to his mother and his friend Gilman from Berlin and critically assessed Russia:

There is also much talk here [in Berlin] regarding the present attitude of our country in relation to the war in Europe and of the American love for Russia. This latter I cannot understand. A short journey in the tsar's dominions is a grand curative for such predilections. I am bound in common gratitude to make all due acknowledgement of kind treatment in Russia and I am free to say that some of the popular traits please me. But the nation is the last in the

---

[180]Rev. Charles B. Boynton, *Address before the Citizens of Cincinnati: Delivered on the Fourth Day of July, 1855* (Cincinnati, Ohio: Cincinnati Gazette Company, 1855), p. 16. Boynton's book, *The Russian Empire: Its Resources, Government, and Policy by a "Looker-On" from America* (Cincinnati, Ohio: Moore, Wilstock, Kemp & Co., 1856), expands further on this theme: "It is not entirely a misnomer to call Russia a Democracy governed by an Emperor—England a Constitutional Monarchy, under the despotism of an aristocracy" (p. 336); "the true despotism which threatens the power of the world dwells not in Russia, but in Western Europe, with the Papal Church as the ecclesiastical center of power" (p. 375).

world for *our* love or *our* alliance. The whole governmental system is the most atrociously barbarous in the world. There is on earth no parallel example of a polite society so degraded, of a people so crushed, an official system so unscrupulous. In St. Petersburg is hypocrisy, in Moscow idolatry, and corruption everywhere. Why should we like them? In their hearts they despise us. Their whole ideas are the very reverse of ours. The soldiery is everything—real worth is nothing. A petty lieutenant living on stealings from his regiment looks with contempt on the learned Professor or the merchant prince. I could fill a good sized book with instances of flagrant corruption and oppression—and of which in many instances Americans were the victims which came under my immediate notice. . . . It angers me to read such rascally stuff as is put forth by Cushing and his Company of knaves and fools at Washington. I have even had the thought of printing a long letter or two or three short ones on this subject. I verily believe that I could raise a great breeze but—it is only the fear of mortally offending Gov. Seymour that deters me. . . . I have never ceased from the beginning of the war to wish for the success of the Allies. This of course I could not express in letters which were no doubt often opened by the police. If I seemed to express a dislike to the English it was at their too frequent substitution of brag for work, of petty attacks here and there for a grand blow which last year would have been everything. I almost hated them for their mismanagement. . . . I hope my friends were not led by my letters to think me a bigoted Russian lover and one of the crowd which is ever manifesting a petty hate of the "British."[181]

Russians in the United States

At least a hundred Americans visited Russia during the Crimean War, but, strangely, only White published anything as substantial as articles or books—and his were mostly later reminiscences. For some it was no doubt the result of the secretive nature of their business. The same might be said of the much smaller number of Russians in the United States, yet two—Golovin and Gurowski—produced books in English on their observations. Most of the Russians were connected with the legation in Washington or the consulates in New York and San Francisco, either on special assignments or directly—as in the cases of Stoeckl, Katakazi, Bodisko, Evstaf'ev, and Kostromitinov and their families. Firstein and Sokolov of the original naval mission remained throughout the war and were joined by Capt. Ivan Shestakov and Capt. Stepan Lesovskii, both

[181]White (Berlin) to his mother, 4 November 1855, White Papers, reel 2, Cornell; and the same to Gilman, 5 November 1855, to which he added the suggestion that they collaborate on a book. Gilman, spending Christmas with White's family, hinted his disagreement but was too busy with lectures to respond at length. Gilman to White, 25 December 1855, ibid.

of whom would assume key roles in the future rebuilding of the Russian navy.[182] Army captain Otto Lilienfeldt was assisted by at least two other officers in arranging arms purchases. A venturesome German-American and former New York harbor policeman named Charles Rackelwicz assisted Lilienfeldt and acted as a secret Russian courier, making at least three trips between New York and St. Petersburg during the war. Like so many others, he dabbled in other ventures and brought to Russia a number of sewing machines on his last visit.[183] Understandably, only fragmentary, and sometimes contradictory, information is available about these rather surreptitious activities.

The best-known Russian visitor of the period was Joseph Hamel (Iosef Gamel'), born in the Volga German colony of Sarepta. A self-educated scientist, economist, and writer, Hamel came on a vague educational mission for the tsar early in 1854 and spent the war years touring the country and visiting various American institutions. Starting in the Boston area, he inspected Lowell factories, Harvard University, and the Perkins School for the Blind. Hamel then proceeded to travel over a large part of the country and was among those invited to witness the first attempt to lay an Atlantic cable, along with Matthew Maury, Samuel Morse, and other distinguished Americans. On his departure after over two years sojourn, one paper commented:

> The celebrated Russian traveler Dr. Hamel, who was at one time the tutor of the present Emperor of Russia, and who for the last two years has been in this country visiting our institutions, having achieved the purpose for which he came, departs tomorrow in the *Atlantic* for his own home. . . . At all our fairs, cattle shows, school examinations, school openings, trial trips, ship launches, great castings, etc., as well as our anniversaries, and all lesser and greater celebrations of all our public institutions, the Doctor's face had become quite familiar. Our institutions were carefully studied by him in order to give a thorough knowledge of American enterprise in science, art or public charity.[184]

Undoubtedly the Russian government was paying his expenses and received reports on his visit. Although he planned to return to the United States in 1857, he became ill and died in 1861, apparently without recording his American experiences for posterity.[185]

[182]In denying London reports that Russians were swarming over the United States, the New York *Tribune* (12 November 1855) guessed that there were not more than fifty Russians in the country—an underestimation.

[183]Erving to White, 1 October 1855, White Papers, reel 2, Cornell.

[184]Cincinnati *Daily Enquirer*, 27 May 1856. For additional information on Hamel's visit, see Boston *Evening Transcript*, 25 March 1854; New York *Herald*, 5 August 1854.

[185]Hamel (St. Petersburg) to Seymour, 1 June 1857, Seymour Papers, box 859, ConnHS.

Adam Gurowski, though a Polish emigré, can also be counted among the "Russians" in the United States, since he spent several years as a resident promoting the Russian cause in his books and articles for the New York *Tribune* while being subsidized by the Russian legation. His *Russia As It Is* was especially successful in attaching a more benign, humane face to a country that many Americans might still view as the colossus of tyranny. This was certainly an unusual approach for a Pole, but he was trying both to support himself financially and to establish literary credentials. Moreover, Gurowski had close connections at the Russian court and in literary circles, and his brand of pan-Slavism specified a crucial leadership role for Russia, one perhaps the United States could help bolster.

Ivan Golovin, on the other hand, was an independent traveler and dissident critic of the Russian government. He arrived in July 1855, wandered for almost a year around the country, and published a book, consisting of a series of pompous letters written to various people in Europe, including Tocqueville, Victor Hugo, and Louis Blanc. Golovin proposed "to show that the United States are pursuing a wrong way in their politics and morals, falsely interpreting their destination, and losing sight of the principles which presented at their formation."[186] His account, nevertheless, is mainly descriptive, finding fault with the lack of dignity shown by public officials, the nefarious influence of religion, and the opportunism of Americans (selling gunpowder to both sides). Though opposing Russian serfdom, he observed that he would not be an abolitionist in the United States—yet he predicted the end of slavery over attempts to extend it to Kansas and Nebraska.[187] In passing, Golovin noted that the brother of Napoleonic hero Gen. Aleksei Ermolov had settled in Newport and that he discovered a Russian exile named Vsevelovskii residing in New Orleans. Golovin and perhaps these other Russians seem to have been isolated from the mainstream of Russian dissidence led by Alexander Herzen, now based in London.

The War Atmosphere in the United States

Aside from the occasional exchange of barbs in the press, Russians, British, and French continued for the most part to mix freely and peacefully in the United States during the war. The controversies over recruitment in New York, Philadelphia, and Cincinnati were exceptions caused mainly by the involvement of such third parties as Irish, German, and Hungarian immigrants. One place where expansionist and nationalist tempers were likely to flare up was California. There American assistance to Russia was more open and obvious: the ficti-

[186]Ivan Golovin, *Stars and Stripes, or American Impressions* (New York: Appleton and Co., 1856), p. iv.
[187]Ibid., pp. 100–103.

tious sale of ships of the Russian America Company to the American Russian Commercial Company so the latter could continue to supply the colony under a neutral flag; the shipment of gunpowder and other essential supplies to Siberia; and the protection offered to a Russian warship in San Francisco harbor.

A mixture of many, recent immigrants on the West Coast under a rather loose system of law and order encouraged friction. French consul Dillon also raised the level of tensions in 1854 by claiming the right to have his flag saluted. His arrest and plea of immunity created a diplomatic incident. However, its local impact did not approach the climax of excitement reached on 26 November 1855, when the French and British consulates in San Francisco decided to stage a giant celebration to commemorate the fall of Sevastopol. In a big tent in South Park a huge feast was assembled, complete with a cake in the shape of the Malakov Tower (a major Sevastopol defensive point just taken by the allies) and twenty-five hundred bottles of claret.[188] A large crowd assembled and grew restless through a long, bellicose speech by the French consul. When George Aiken, the British consul, attempted to follow, a disturbance broke out, apparently motivated by boredom and impatience and by the positioning of the British and French flags high on the cake tower. There were also problems in serving the barbecued ox fast enough. Suddenly, a witness reported, "all was noise and turmoil. From cutting the cake it came to tearing and beating it."[189] And the crowd degenerated into "throwing pieces then loaves of bread, bones, roast ducks, and pieces of roast pork and roast beef. Soon a general charge was made on the tender Malakoff and down it went. Different Britishers, Frenchmen, and Sardinians then rushed forward with their respective flags to plant them upon the ruins.[190] The pavilion "resembled the wreck of some gigantic ship, with the tattered remnant of sails dangling amid shattered spars and crushed ribs. The lamps prepared for the evening's banquet were all shattered, tables trampled to fragments, red claret spattered with sanguinary streams about the place, and the work of several days was destroyed."[191]

The next day, once the populace had recovered, a more dignified counterdemonstration marched to the Russian consul's house and applauded a touching speech delivered from the balcony by Kostromitinov's seven-year-old son (who spoke excellent English). The Russian flag was then carried to the *Zenobia*, a ship actually owned by the American Russian Commercial Company, where it was raised with great fanfare and given a full twenty-one-gun salute, to the consternation of the British and French consuls.[192]

[188]*Daily Alta California*, 27 November 1855.
[189]Ibid.
[190]*National Intelligencer*, 1 January 1856, quoting the San Francisco *Chronicle*.
[191]*Daily Alta California*, 27 November 1855.
[192]*National Intelligencer*, 1 January 1856; "Serenade to the Russian Consul," San Fran-

Aside from these almost comic episodes, it would appear that Russian-American relations during the Crimean War, though eventful, were characterized by several missed opportunities. Russia never capitalized on the considerable sympathy and goodwill prevalent at the height of the war in 1855 or took advantage fully of the American technical and military expertise available. To some degree this can be explained by the inability of Russia to break from traditional and conservative moorings, in particular a concentration on Europe in foreign policy matters. Thus peace between the warring parties was concluded at Paris in March 1856, without reference to any American agenda, and Russia received a major, though temporary, setback to its southern ambitions. At the same meeting the Declaration of Paris, an international accord on maritime law, was indeed partly inspired by long-standing American pressure for recognition of neutral rights ("free ships, free goods"), which had been given special publicity by the Russian-American "treaty" of July 1854. Even though its ban on privateering kept the United States from joining, the Declaration of Paris was a turning point in the law of the seas.

One success that the United States did achieve in Europe through the practice of "offensive neutrality" was the elimination of the Sound dues, a sum exacted by the Danish government from merchant ships for the right of passage through Danish waters into the Baltic Sea. Taking advantage of the weakened, defensive posture of Denmark as it tried to maintain neutrality between the allies and Russia, President Pierce simply announced in December 1855 that the United States would no longer honor this traditional duty, much to the annoyance of the European powers.[193]

For the United States, the most notable lost chance was the failure to acquire Cuba or any other territory, even though the door had been opened by the Ostend Manifesto and many Americans initially had great hopes for territorial expansion as a result of a European conflict. Still, the Monroe Doctrine was reasserted, and the sphere of American influence was definitely spread in every direction. Britain was constrained by the war from guaranteeing Spanish control in Latin America, and this mollified many Americans. Though Russia "lost" the war, the fact that it was a limited one and a balance of power in Europe was preserved eased American fears. In the face of serious domestic issues—such as the free state–slave state balance, "Bleeding Kansas," and rising Northern opposition to the possible extension of Southern slavery into the Caribbean—American expansionism abated, and the acquisition of more territory would wait for another, later opportunity, ironically to be provided by Russia.[194]

cisco *Evening Journal*, 27 November 1855.

[193]Emanuel Halicz, *Danish Neutrality during the Crimean War (1853–1856): Denmark between the Hammer and the Anvil* (Odense: Odense University Press, 1977), pp. 176–80.

[194]For an excellent analysis of the controversy over Southern expansion, see Robert

Whereas in the Napoleonic era the United States was a small, relatively insignificant backwater, by the middle of the century it was clearly in a central international position, no longer geographically and emotionally removed from European politics. In addition, the United States was becoming much more technically involved with Europe, symbolized by joint participation in world expositions and congresses, steamship line operations, and intercontinental telegraphic projects. As a leading Russian Slavophile, Konstantin Aksakov, observed in the first issue of a new journal in 1856, "It is impossible not to notice that the more flourishing condition of the finances of the North American states gives them a full capability to participate in the affairs not only of America but of the whole world."[195] Russia, on the other hand, while still militarily formidable, had lost its Napoleonic luster as the "savior of Europe." After being for so long an integral part of the European concert, Russia was becoming more isolated and outcast. With the supremacy and alliance of France and Britain enhanced through the Crimean victory, the conditions for close Russian-American relations seemed not only to remain but actually to grow stronger in the wake of the Crimean War.

During the war itself, the United States had supplied Russia with firearms, gunpowder, cotton, and basic necessities, the latter especially vital to Siberia and Alaska. Technical and medical assistance was promised and given. Above all, however, the American support was most important for morale, contributing to a sense that Russia was not completely alone, that it had a friend who belonged not to the ranks of the fading European powers such as Spain but to the up-and-coming nations of the world. This association with the United States may also have encouraged, at least in spirit, the historically crucial movement for progress and reform in Russia that followed the war and may have inspired the interesting (albeit brief period) of development and cooperation that occurred between the end of the Crimean War and the beginning of the American Civil War.

E. May, *The Southern Dream of a Caribbean Empire, 1854–1861* (Baton Rouge: Louisiana State University Press, 1973).

[195]*Russkaia Beseda*, no. 1 (1856): 27.

5

Interlude

The five-year period from the signing of the Treaty of Paris in March 1856 to the beginning of the American Civil War was one of the most active in the history of Russian-American relations. The level of contacts between the two countries that had developed during the European struggle was not merely sustained but actually rose between 1856 and 1861. Building on the foundations of prewar and wartime friendship, more American businessmen and travelers sojourned in Russia than ever before. In commerce, an expansion and positive change in direction were also anticipated as a result of technological advances. The escalation of interest in the Pacific and the Far East by both governments, and even more by many individual citizens, widened the vista of mutual cooperation in an area that had already attracted their attention, especially in the course of the war. Cultural understanding also matured, as each country prepared for serious internal upheavals and reforms. Above all, books, newspapers, and periodicals increased their coverage of the other country for the general improvement of knowledge and the enhancement of the perception of international kinship.

This greater reciprocal interest may at first glance seem surprising, considering that both countries were engrossed in domestic tensions. However, a definite parallelism existed in those internal matters, especially in the respective abolition movements, and that fostered contact. In addition, Russia was beginning to show a new aspect of change and liberality that did much to remove the former stigma of the stiff, conservative autocracy of Nicholas I. Soon after assuming the throne in 1855, Alexander II removed the favorite ministers and generals of the previous reign, such as Petr Kleinmichel, who had been overly cautious and at times obstructive in meeting the challenges of a changing world.

The Crimean War had not been a total disgrace, and, in fact, the Russian army had performed credibly in the defense of Sevastopol until its fall in Sep-

Alexander II. Engraving by J. C. Buttre from Loubat's Mission to Russia, *1866*

tember 1855 and in the capture of Kars a few months later. However, Alexander II had little enthusiasm for a conflict that demonstrated Russian vulnerability and weakness and was willing to settle for terms that removed Russian naval power from the Black Sea. His manifesto announcing the peace hinted at the internal betterment to follow, but the new tsar remained tentative and reliant on the vast governmental administration built up by his predecessors. Even though an important voice for change, Grand Duke Constantine, was elevated in influence and was able to lead a substantial lobbying effort, the movement toward such reforms as freeing the serfs was slow. In foreign affairs the seventy-six-year-old Nesselrode, who had replaced Rumiantsev in 1814, was succeeded as minister by Alexander Gorchakov, an envoy to various European countries since 1822. Alexander II's caution and Gorchakov's experience and temperament combined to make continuity in policy natural. Their goals were to preserve peace while Russia regained military and economic strength, to concentrate dip-

Alexander Gorchakov. Engraving by J. C. Buttre from Loubat's Mission to Russia, *1866*

lomatically on Europe to restore Russia's position in the balance of power, and to take advantage of opportunities for territorial expansion. The United States would figure in this plan, but not as much as might be expected after the important support rendered during the war.

The Seymour Mission

Thomas H. Seymour, the former governor of Connecticut who had initially accepted his appointment as minister to Russia in 1853 with reluctance, remained at his post through most of 1858, well into the Buchanan administration. Though having no prior diplomatic experience, he performed his tasks well and successfully kept on good terms with the Russian government. As his hometown newspaper bragged: "Governor Seymour was exceedingly popular at the court of Russia. He is not only highly respected, but he is personally liked by the Emperor and his Ministers. This, of course, gives him an influence far greater than could be wielded by some other man, less personally popular."[1]

Seymour lived quite comfortably in a fine house on the Neva near the famous

[1]Hartford *Daily Times*, 8 October 1855.

Thomas H. Seymour, minister to Russia, 1854–1858. Cour-
tesy Connecticut Historical Society

iron bridge built by Joseph Harrison. It even contained a large organ with which
Andrew Dickson White enjoyed shaking up the whole neighborhood.[2] Seymour
had lost the services of his bright and eager, but not wholly dependable, initial
staff—White, Gilman, Haldeman, and Erving (who with his family suffered one
of the perils of those times, going down with a ship that disappeared in the Atlantic). As a result, he relied on Josiah Pierce of Maine, a relative of the former
president who performed very capably as secretary and companion for the
bachelor-minister during his last three years. Usually reticent and business-like
in his official dispatches, Seymour reflected in one 1857 missive on his longer-
than-average tenure in Russia: "It is now three years since I came to this city.
During all the time I have been here, I have received many proofs, both from the
late and present Emperor, of the kind feeling entertained for us by their Majes-
ties. There is a strong desire felt at this juncture, not only by those high in authority, but by a large class of the citizens of this country, that there may be an

[2]Seymour to Lydia Sigourney, 25 October 1856, box 2, Hoadley Papers, ConnHS;
White to his mother, 28 December 1854, reel 2, White Papers, Cornell.

increased intercourse between them and the people of America."³ James Buchanan, upon entering the White House in 1857, informed Seymour privately
of what he already must have known—that it was the custom of a new administration to change appointments to the foreign missions and that he already had
two hundred applications for such jobs. But Seymour remained at his post for
another year and a half. At a touching farewell audience with the emperor, Seymour received as a personal gift from him a stunning malachite table, which was
forwarded to the Connecticut Historical Society for safekeeping.⁴ The minister
observed nostalgically to Lewis Cass, the secretary of state: "I leave Russia with
some regrets—I quit the diplomatic station with pleasure. Russia is a country
worthy of the study of the historian and political economist. That my successor
will do much towards making you better acquainted with its history and resources, I am fully assured in my own mind."⁵ And then Seymour, rather than
return quickly to Connecticut, set off on a two-month tour of the country,
which took him to Kazan and down the Volga to Saratov, Astrakhan, and the
Caspian Sea.⁶

The Coronation

After the conclusion of the peace, the climactic event of 1856 was the coronation of the new tsar, Alexander II, already overdue because of the war. At the
month-long ceremonies in Moscow in August and September, the United States
was represented by more than a minister for the first time. "Colonel" Samuel
Colt, his recent bride, and her brother Richard Jarvis and sister Hetty joined
Seymour as members of the official party.⁷ (Colt was obviously in attendance for

³Seymour to Lewis Cass, 21 March/2 April 1857, DUSM, Russia, vol. 17 (roll 17, M 35), RG 59, NA.

⁴Mary I. Pierce to Mary Atkinson Coburn, 20 February 1859, Autograph file, Houghton Library, Harvard University. The Connecticut Historical Society has no re- cord of the whereabouts of the table today, although a number of other Seymour me- mentos of Russia are held in its collections.

⁵Seymour to Cass, 5/17 July 1858, DUSM, Russia, vol. 17 (roll 17, M 35), RG 59, NA. Toward the end of his tenure, Seymour may have become somewhat jaded by Rus- sian society. A visitor reported in her diary on 8 July, "He [Seymour] scarcely looked human so bloated was he by high living if not by pure drunkenness." Frances (Beall) Knight Diary, 1858, John Knight Papers, 17-B, Manuscript Department, William R. Perkins Library, Duke University (hereafter Duke).

⁶Seymour (Kazan) to Henry Barnard, September 1858 (no day given), Barnard Pa- pers, ConnHS.

⁷Hartford *Daily Courant*, 15 September 1856. About the grand reception at St. Pe- tersburg on 14 August the newspaper quipped: "The flower of the English nobility only were presented at the same time. . . . It was a crack time; but the aristocracy of Europe

business reasons as well as for pleasure.) Another famous American entrepreneur, Samuel F. B. Morse, also appeared in St. Petersburg at this time in quest of pecuniary satisfaction for the Russian adoption of his telegraph system and was invited to attend the coronation (but apparently did not).[8] Several other Americans also made the trip to Moscow to observe the festivities, most of whom demanded a considerable amount of Seymour's time. They included William Shaw Campbell, United States consul in Rotterdam and Morse's attorney; William H. Appleton, the publisher; Henry Dexter, a San Francisco businessman; Charles and James Ward; Gen. George McWillie Williamson of South Carolina; Henry Sparks; and Captain Oglesby. Three other prominent Americans—merchant George Francis Train; reformer Dorothea Dix; and Philip Kearny, Mexican War hero and future Civil War general—visited Russia during the summer of 1856 but did not stay for the ceremony. By one count, 121 Americans came to Russia in 1856, twice as many as in any previous year.[9]

The American press was not directly represented at the coronation gala but copied instead the detailed coverage provided by William Howard Russell for the London *Times*. For British amusement, Russell quoted an alleged conversation between Colt and Grand Duke Constantine at a formal reception: "'Well,' said the Colonel, 'You are the most democratic Grand Duke I ever met!' 'How is that, Colonel?' asked the Grand Duke. 'Why, you shook hands with me, and you are the first Grand Duke that has done that yet,' was the reply. His Imperial Highness smiled, and did not seem to know how to take the remark."[10] The *Times* also noted, however, that of all the foreign delegations present only the British and American ones included women (with the addition of the Saxon minister's wife). At the grand coronation ball especially, "Mrs. Colt and Miss Jarvis grace the American embassy by their presence."[11]

Of the extravagance in general at least some Americans were even more critical than the London *Times*. Its New York namesake commented:

found themselves mated by plain Yankees. Probably the Colt party kept up their end of the stick."

Andrew White later recounted guiding Colt around the Hermitage and finding under some rubbish a lathe allegedly used by Peter the Great along with some unfinished specimens of his work. "The development and Overthrow of the Russian Serf-System," *Atlantic Monthly* 10 (October 1862): 539.

[8]Copy of Morse's petition to Alexander II, 26 July 1856, Morse Papers, reel 18, Manuscript Division, LC; Morse (London) to Cass, 25 May 1857, Miscellaneous Letters of the Department of State, 1 April–31 May 1857 (roll 157, M 179) RG 59, NA.

[9]Walther Kirchner, *Studies in Russian-American Commerce, 1820–1860* (Leiden: E. J. Brill, 1975), p. 183.

[10]London *Times*, 12 September 1856; copied by Baltimore *American and Commercial Advertiser*, 29 September 1856.

[11]London *Times*, 19 September 1856.

In another portion of our journal will be found a gorgeous picture of this grand entry of buffoonery and of the betinseled mummers who took part in the pageant, written for the London *Times* by that brilliant historian of the war, Mr. Russell, whose pen, so gloriously employed in recounting the valor of heroes, we are sorry to see soiled in such a story of absurd and savage pomp. A million of pounds, it seems wrung from the sinew-sweat of a million people, has been expended, besides no end of war of artillery, clashing of bells, and braying of trumpets and "awe-struck multitudes," in the preliminaries to placing with due propriety a cap with half a dozen diamonds on it, on the head of a rather fat, amiable, and middle-aged young man. The ancient triumphs of barbarian powers, we are told, pale their ineffectual fires before the spendors of this awful entry into Moscow.[12]

With all of its pomp and circumstance, the coronation obviously disrupted the normal routine of the Russian government and prevented any significant policy shifts for several months.

American Business in Russia

Morse left St. Petersburg with only verbal assurances regarding payment for the deployment in Russia of his "patented" telegraphic system, as Russia awaited the outcome of Morse's negotiations with other European countries. Colt's attendance at the coronation was recognized by a contract to supply Minnie rifles to the Russian army, but the agreement was subsequently rescinded, resulting in a counterclaim and an arbitration overseen by Stoeckl in the United States in 1857.[13] The original contract was then replaced with an even more lucrative business deal which provided for the manufacture of Colt-style revolvers in Russia with machinery and designs supplied by Colt.[14] The "colonel" must have thought well of the new arrangement, since he sent an assortment of fancy weapons to Alexander II in 1858: "The case, which is of rosewood, lined with silk velvet, contains two large calibre rifles (56 and 44), a holster pistol, breech attachment, belt pistol, and pocket pistol. These arms are highly finished, elegantly engraved, and gold mounted."[15]

The business traffic through St. Petersburg that required Seymour's services was now coming and going in a variety of directions. In the summer of 1856, two newcomers from California arrived with their minds set on seizing the initiative in Siberian-American trade and economic development. Bernard Peyton,

[12]New York *Times*, 25 September 1856.
[13]Philadelphia *Public Ledger*, 25 October 1857; Stoeckl to Gorchakov, 7/19 October 1857, f. kants. Vashington 1857, d. 183, AVPR.
[14]New York *Times*, 11 October 1858.
[15]Charleston *Mercury*, 11 August 1858.

originally from Charlottesville, Virginia, but more recently involved in the ice market in San Francisco, had come to explore the possibilities of an expanded trade in the Russian Far East.[16] Perry McDonough Collins may also have gained some experience in the Alaska-California business before setting out for Russia, but he was better armed than Peyton, carrying a special appointment from Washington as "commercial agent" for the Amur region.[17]

In St. Petersburg, Collins and Peyton joined forces and received Seymour's aid in securing introductions to Grand Duke Constantine and Count Murav'ev, the governor of Eastern Siberia, before heading across the continent. In Irkutsk they met Capt. William H. Hudson, also from California, who had just delivered the steamer *America* (ordered for Russia by Beverley Sanders in 1854), after a harrowing journey around South America to Nikolaevsk on the Amur. Hudson reached St. Petersburg in February 1857 and obtained assistance from Seymour for his voyage home. Though Peyton turned back at Irkutsk to find a quicker passage to the United States, Collins continued down the Amur and arrived in the United States in the summer of 1857, spreading the story of Siberian riches. Peyton soon abandoned his Russian interests to become a successful gunpowder manufacturer in California, while Collins would achieve notoriety for his active pursuit of Siberian-American development in the years to come.

Clearly, though, the largest American business venture in Russia was still that of Winans, Harrison, and Winans, engaged in the building and repair of locomotives and rolling stock for the Russian railroads, mainly the St. Petersburg–Moscow line. The operation was now almost entirely in the hands of William L. Winans, one of the original partners, and his two assistants, George William Whistler (son of the first superintendent of construction, half-brother to the artist, and husband to Winans's sister) and Gaun M. Hutton.

The second contract of August 1850 that was to last twelve years had been amended by a series of written subagreements.[18] After the war the Russian government, believing that the terms were greatly to the advantage of the American company, attempted to alter them and thus cut its mounting transportation expenses. The officials were also unhappy with the frequency of repairs, their high cost, and the complaints of Russian workers at the Aleksandrovsk plant about working conditions and wages; the Americans did not have any better reputation than other manufacturers in Russia for the treatment of their em-

[16]See Norman E. Saul on Peyton, "An American's Siberian Dream," *Russian Review* 37, 4 (October 1978): 405–20.

[17]Seymour to Marcy, 29 November/11 December 1856, DUSM, Russia, vol. 17 (roll 17, M 35), RG 59, NA.

[18]John Appleton to Seward, 25 May/6 June 1861, DUSM, Russia, vol. 18 (roll 18, M 35), RG 59, NA.

ployees.[19] The government, however, had little choice but to go along with the contract, especially in a coronation year, if rail service between Moscow and St. Petersburg was to be maintained.

By 1857 the business arrangement between Winans and the Russian government had become so complicated and filled with charges and countercharges that Winans asked for the assistance of John H. B. Latrobe, a prominent Baltimore attorney and friend of his father's, after meeting him at the opera in Paris. Latrobe agreed to spend the winter in St. Petersburg for a handsome $60,000 retainer.[20] Adjusting well to his new position, he later described his wealthy patron: "Few men have more, in Society, . . . [and] a more thorough man of business I have never met with. He deserves the place he has . . . most unquestionably."[21] Latrobe's letters to his wife during his five-month employment in the Russian capital reveal few details of the legal business, but apparently Winans felt his investment was worthwhile. Meanwhile, the American press continued to boast about the success of Winans, Harrison, and Winans: "These gentlemen have accumulated, in a few years, almost fabulous fortunes, and their contract holds good for several years to come. The terms are immensely in their favor, and it is said that the Government has offered them a very large sum to cancel it, but the proposition has been refused."[22] Winans added to the luxurious furnishings of the Aleksandrovsk residences and reported, in a private letter from his Brighton (England) summer home in November 1860, that the business in St. Petersburg was still doing quite well. [23]

In early 1861, however, the Russian government began withholding payments on a repair subagreement of November 1859 that totaled over one million rubles. This also seemed to presage nonrenewal of the main contract expiring the next year. Appeals of the American minister through the Ministry of Foreign

[19]Winans, Harrison, and Winans to Appleton, undated (enclosed in ibid.), DUSM, Russia, vol. 18 (roll 18, M 35), RG 59, NA.

[20]William L. Winans (Brighton) to Latrobe, 19 September 1857; and Latrobe to Winans, 20 September 1857, Latrobe Papers, Russian Correspondence 1857–58, MaryHS.

[21]Introductory notes, ibid.

[22]Account book, 1858, box 7, Winans Papers, MaryHS.

[23]William L. Winans (Brighton) to Thomas DeK. Winans, 7 November 1860, William L. Winans Letterbook 1858–59, Winans Papers, box 18, MaryHS. The brothers also faced internal problems with suits against another Winans, Uncle William R., who had borrowed money from them, and against Harrison in an effort to force him to sell his share. Thomas DeK. Winans (Baltimore) to Joseph Harrison, 9 March 1860, Thomas Winans Letterbook no. 3 (1859–62), Winans Papers, box 18, MaryHS. The latter suit followed an unsuccessful bid to buy out Harrison for 240,000 pounds sterling. William L. Winans (St. Petersburg) to Harrison, 29 December/9 January 1859, and to Thomas Winans, 23 December/4 January, 7/19 January, and 14 April 1859, William L. Winans Letterbook, box 18, Winans Papers, MaryHS.

Affairs were in vain, and the matter under dispute (government authority to test and reject repaired engines) was referred to the courts.[24] Winans thought that a primary cause of the government's new coolness was its consideration of the idea of selling the state railroad to private interests, and he was clearly dismayed by the thought of losing the business.

Raising Ships at Sevastopol

The largest of the new American enterprises in Russia during this period was directly related to the Crimean War—the raising of the fifty or so ships of the Russian Black Sea fleet that had been intentionally sunk to block the entrance to the harbor of Sevastopol. They were now obstacles to the peacetime use of this important naval base and port. John E. Gowen, a Boston submarine armormaker and supplier, had already earned an international reputation for salvage work with the raising of the American steam frigate *Missouri* at Gibraltar a few years before and had even been approached by the British during the war about the possibility of clearing an entryway into Sevastopol by sea. He arrived in St. Petersburg during the summer of 1856 and then journeyed on to the Black Sea to inspect the site and to negotiate a contract with naval authorities at Nikolaev.[25] Although Russia was denied warships on the Black Sea by the Treaty of Paris, the navy realized that the port needed to be reopened and that the potential monetary gain from the salvage could relieve their hardpressed treasury. The agreement with Gowen, concluded in October, provided for a fifty-fifty split of all materials recovered with Gowen furnishing all of the necessary equipment, labor, and supplies (except for gunpowder, which, as contraband, could not be imported privately into Russia.)[26]

Gowen returned with his family the following May, preceded by supplies and assistants, such as Samuel F. Holbrook of Boston, to help him direct the operations at Sevastopol. Soon two other American companies, the Boston Submarine and Wrecking Company and the Marine Exploring Company of Philadelphia, were competing for the same business. For reasons that are not very clear, Gowen combined with the Philadelphia company, while the other group, headed by William Lane and C. G. Lundborg, went on to Constantinople to ne-

[24]Winans, Harrison, and Winans to Appleton, 27 February 1861, and Tolstoy to Appleton, 10/22 May 1861, DPR, Russia, Notes Received, vol. 4500, RG 84, NA.

[25]John Ralli (Odessa) to Seymour, 30 April/12 May 1857, DPR, Russia, Notes Sent and Received, vol. 4481, RG 84, NA; Charleston *Mercury*, 12 February and 10 November 1856; New Orleans *Commercial Bulletin*, 15 December 1854.

[26]Ralli to Cass, 30 September/12 October 1858, DUSC, Odessa, vol. 2 (roll 2, M 459), RG 59, NA, recounting the history of the salvage expedition. See also Alexandre Tarsaidze, *Czars and Presidents* (New York: McDowell, Obolensky, 1958), p. 160, citing Gowen papers in private hands.

gotiate with the Turks about raising the vessels sunk by the Russians at Sinope at the beginning of the war.[27]

Encountering delays in obtaining specialized machinery and problems with strong westerly winds that inhibited diving, Gowen's company nevertheless managed to bring to the surface a substantial number of guns, chains, and anchors during the first summer. He employed over two hundred "Russians," one hundred Greeks (possibly as divers), and a supervisory crew of about thirty Americans.[28] The latter took up a collection to celebrate the Fourth of July in 1857 with, according to one eyewitness, "a goodly number of Russian officers also joining in the festivities. A large pavilion was erected by order of Colonel Gowen, the interior of which was handsomely decorated with American and Russian flags."[29] Another source reported that the Russians contributed their own twenty-five piece brass band and a separate string orchestra.[30]

Difficulties in the work of the company continued, however, as the largest and most valuable vessels proved to be so deeply mired in mud that it was impossible to raise them intact.[31] Relations with the "Russian" work force were also disturbing. One of the American crew reported:

The harbor is full of sunken ships of the largest class, which lie in every direction; some with their masts only sticking up, and some with the hull partly exposed. . . . Our men impose on the Russians most shamefully, striking them whenever they get the chance. This day I told the ship's company that if any one of them struck one of my men, he would have to strike me, and so he will, for they are harmless fellows and dare not strike back, being serfs. To see the petty tyranny they (our men) practise here, ill-treating these men, it is enough to make a man hang his head, and wish he had been born a dog or a hog.[32]

Gowen's sister, married to one of his foremen, also reacted negatively to the local scene, finding that the commander of the port had two nursing girls, two table girls, and eight other servants, "so his young wife does not have to lift her hand to do the least thing." And the workers "are the most indolent set of

[27]Ralli (Odessa) to Cass, 1 July 1857, DUSC, Odessa, vol. 2 (roll 2, M 459), RG 59, NA; *National Intelligencer*, 29 August 1857; Philadelphia *Public Ledger*, 8 July 1857; Philadelphia *Evening Bulletin* 24 July 1857.

[28]Ralli to Cass, 30 September/12 October 1858, DUSC, Odessa, vol. 2 (roll 2, M 459), RG 59, NA.

[29]*National Intelligencer* 29 August 1857, citing the Boston *Courier*.

[30]"The American Divers at Sebastopol," Philadelphia *Public Ledger*, 28 August 1857.

[31]New York *Herald*, 4 January 1858.

[32]Philadelphia *Public Ledger*, 28 August 1857.

people I ever saw . . . , look[ing] as much worse as our Irish people as you can possibly imagine."[33]

Still, American salvagers achieved modest success in 1858, most notably raising on 23 June the seventy-four-gun steamer *Turk*, which needed only minor repairs to be fully fit for service. Two other steamers, two brigs, one schooner, one yacht, and one cutter were also brought to the surface whole by the end of the summer, while several other ships were broken up and raised in pieces.[34] Because those that remained would be more difficult to tackle, the Russian authorities agreed to renegotiate in the interest of clearing the harbor as soon as possible: Gowen could now sell everything he raised and could provide his own gunpowder, but failure to complete the work in two years (from November 1858) would result in the loss of all his machinery, worth an estimated $200,000.[35]

Even with this simplified contract, there were still problems—with Customs over the duty-free import of machinery and supplies, with local authorities on leaving the harbor bottom absolutely clean of debris, and with the navy about having to disable the cannon permanently before exporting them.[36] Regardless, the company was reported to be prospering, and Gowen was able to obtain an extension beyond the 1860 deadline.[37] Upon completion of the work, Gowen remained in Russia to operate a line of steamers on the Kuban River and by 1863 had leased a large tract of land near Baku on the Caspian Sea, becoming one of Russia's earliest oil-field developers.[38]

Other American ventures in Russia were of more limited scope and duration. Gowen's chief of transportation, D. C. Pierce, contracted to haul railroad ties from the Caucasus to Feodosia for the new lines being laid in the south of Rus-

[33]Mary I. Pierce (Sevastopol) to Mary Atkinson Coburn, 8 February 1858, Autograph file, Houghton Library, Harvard University.

[34]Pierce to Coburn, 5 September 1858, ibid.; "Another Russian Man-of-War Raised," Philadelphia *Public Ledger*, 12 August 1858.

[35]Pierce to Coburn, 5 September 1858, Autograph file, Houghton Library, Harvard University; Ralli to Cass, 30 October/11 November 1859, DUSC, Odessa, vol. 2 (roll 2, M 459), RG 59, NA; Pickens to Gorchakov, 1/13 January 1860, DPR, Russia, vol. 4483, RG 84, NA.

[36]Holbrook to Ralli, 5 and 19 February 1860, enclosed in Ralli to Cass, 4/16 March 1860, DUSC, Odessa, vol. 2 (roll 2, M 459), RG 59, NA; Pickens to Ralli, 1 June 1860, DPR, Russia, vol. 4483, RG 59, NA. The minister in St. Petersburg, asked to intercede for Gowen, advised: "If every little particular form is not fully complied with, the officers under this military government, will take nothing on faith, and will stand upon *form* as particular as substance." Pickens to Gowen, 2 July 1860, DPR, Russia, vol. 4482, RG 84, NA. Gowen responded with more detailed complaints about the Customs officials at Sevastopol. To Pickens, 6/18 July 1860, ibid.

[37]T. C. Smith (Odessa) to Seward, 18 October 1862, DUSC, Odessa, vol. 3 (roll 3, M 459), RG 59, NA.

[38]Smith to Seward, 17 October 1863 and 12 March 1864, ibid.

sia.[39] Taliaferro Shaffner was back in Russia in 1857 to renew his bid to build railroads. He also hoped to reactivate a lease on a factory owned by the Prince and Princess Leuchtenberg for the manufacture of "galvano-plastique" (telegraph wire) but had no success.[40] Shaffner, at this stage of his colorful but erratic business career, was still pursuing the ambitious scheme for a telegraph connection encircling the globe by means of the shortest possible submarine cable distances—from Newfoundland to Greenland to Iceland to Scandinavia (thus bypassing Britain) and through Russia to Alaska and the North American West Coast. He later claimed that Cyrus Field, backed by a group of American and British capitalists, stole his plans and altered them for a more direct transatlantic cable.[41] By 1859, and after the failure of the first cable, Shaffner's alternative project of a Bering Sea cable route (to connect New York with London via Siberia) was being revived in Russia by Perry Collins.

Among the other American proposals for Russia was the bid by Virginia abolitionist John Minor Botts to build drydocks. A renegade Hungarian-American named Laslo Chandor came to Russia armed with a recommendation from Sen. William H. Seward of New York and a plan for the gaslighting of Moscow. The American consul in Moscow, Francis Claxton, alleged that Chandor was involved in numerous swindles along with another naturalized American, Auguste Wilhelm. Chandor, however, claimed that Claxton was only seeking revenge for not being allowed into the deal.[42] Finally, spurred by the Crimean

[39]Ralli to Cass, 19/31 December 1860, ibid.

[40]Shaffner to Kleinmichel, 30 September 1855, f. 1272, op. 1, no. 5, TsGIA.

[41]Shaffner claimed that the Field brothers, Cyrus and Dudley, plotted against him with the help of the British, who resented his assistance to Russia: "My zeal for the welfare of Russia during the war caused the capitalists of England to abandon me, occasioning me heavy losses." Cyrus Field, then, was hired to develop parallel cable schemes: "To do this, he fabricated statements and got up false oaths and affidavits to prove that I was a Russian spy. The whole police of England was on the watch for me. In the Canadian Parliament he claimed that I was a Russian spy, and defeated me there, in a law for my telegraph by Greenland to St. Petersburg." Shaffner to Alexander II, n.d., copy enclosed in Shaffner (Washington) to Pickens, 24 August 1858, DPR, Russia, Miscellaneous Sent, vol. 4482, RG 84, NA. The original was apparently forwarded to the Russian foreign office. Pickens to Tolstoy, 3/15 September 1858, ibid., in which the minister mentions he had met Shaffner in Washington before his departure. See also Philadelphia *Public Ledger*, 5 October 1858, in which Shaffner is quoted, "I claim to have given Mr. Cyrus W. Field the first idea of an Atlantic telegraph."

[42]Botts's whirlwind tour of Europe was observed critically by the American press. See, for example, the Baltimore *Sun*, 8 February 1858. The same paper later (25 February) summarized his trip: "He is reported to have made a large fortune by his tour. It is also stated that the Emperor of all the Russias held a review of sixty thousand troops for his special honor, gratification and pleasure." For Chandor, see Claxton to Seward, 5 October 1860, Seward Papers, indexed correspondence, reel 60, Rush-Rhees Library, University of Rochester (hereafter Rochester); and Pickens to Cass, 5 July 1860, with enclosure (Claxton [Moscow] to Pickens, 1 July 1860); and Appleton to Cass, 29 Novem-

War experience, a number of other Americans came to Russia to sell military inventions. The most successful was Lewis Broadwell, who had a new method for producing breech-loading fortress guns and who was employed for several years by the Russian Ministry of War.

All of these Americans descending on Russia taxed the capacities of the American legation, which was headed first by Seymour and then by Francis Pickens, a former congressman from South Carolina. Like Seymour, Pickens was inexperienced in world affairs upon commencing his appointment, but unlike his predecessor, he had a complex family to care for. Twice widowed, the fifty-year-old Southerner had married the young and beautiful Lucy Holcombe of Marshall, Texas, shortly before leaving the United States. She quickly won the special attention of the imperial family, especially after she became pregnant. The empress even assisted with the birth of the Pickenses' daughter and provided her with the name "Douschka."[43] Two older daughters from his previous marriages accompanied them, but one soon captured the heart of the secretary who served Pickens, John E. Bacon, also a planter from South Carolina. The pair departed Russia in December 1859, leaving the minister with a personnel

ber 1860, with enclosure (Claxton to Chandor, 15 December 1859), DUSM, Russia, vol. 18 (roll 18, M 35), RG 59, NA.

[43]When the Pickenses honeymooned in New Orleans before their departure, a South Carolina paper beamed, "The fascinating and brilliant Lucy Holcombe has become Mrs. Pickens." Charleston *Mercury*, 11 May 1858. Lucy was about twenty-five when she married the fifty-two-year-old Pickens. An earlier fiancé had died in the Quitman expedition to Cuba, about which she had published a book. Jack Thorndyke Greer, *Leaves from a Family Album* (Holcombe and Greer), ed. Jane Judge Greer (Waco: Texian Press, 1975), pp. 51–58. The Russian mission was another step in her illustrious career, and by all accounts she was a great success in St. Petersburg. Pickens himself recorded one such conquest: "Until lately Lucy has been going with much company and at a large Ball, the Emperor singled her out and led her to the stand reserved for the imperial family, and which is high above the general room for the dancers, and stood they two alone, conversing for near half hour. He insisted on her speaking in French, and she said she had only been accustomed to speak French in the family in private, and she was not used to speak French as might be required for royalty. He immediately replied, all in French too, that he had no doubt it would always be difficult for her republican tongue to speak the language required by royalty, then he said she represented a great and beautiful country and etc. It was very marked and not known before to happen to a foreigner, at least lately. Soon afterwards it was perceived, all the courtiers and maids of ceremonies paid Lucy especial attention." Pickens to Mrs. E. D. Holcombe (Lucy's mother), n.d., in ibid., p. 57.

The Russian experience was no doubt good practice for the fame she would achieve as a supporter of the Confederacy during the Civil War, and the imperial family might have been shocked to learn that in 1861 Lucy sold the jewels they gave her to support a Confederate brigade from South Carolina, appropriately named the "Holcombe Legion." She was also the only woman whose picture appeared on Confederate currency. Ibid., pp. 58–61.

crisis.[44] The growth of the United States consular service in Russia, for which Seymour was mainly responsible, had also increased the administrative burdens on the minister and his staff. The situation was far from a happy one, especially since Pickens was understandably anxious about affairs at home. He asked for his recall and returned to the United States late in the summer of 1860 to become governor of South Carolina and one of the South's most astute political leaders during the Civil War. His replacement in Russia for the brief remainder of Buchanan's presidential term was John Appleton, an assistant secretary of state who had apparently accepted the position mainly for the travel opportunity.

Judging from the diplomatic post records, all of the ministers and their staffs for this period, regardless of personal circumstances, did a creditable job keeping up with the burgeoning American presence in Russia. The direct diplomatic business between the two countries was reduced to issues pertaining to the neutrality convention attached to the Treaty of Paris. All maritime nations were invited to join, but the United States refused, considering the terms unsatisfactory on two counts: A neutral flag should protect all goods except the contraband of a belligerent power, and a blockade should be more narrowly defined. As Pickens formulated it to Gorchakov, "No blockade ought to be enlarged so as to cover by construction, extended coasts, without the actual presence of men of war."[45] And the United States still opposed the outlawing of privateering. Although Russia was sympathetic to the American position, it was not inclined to reopen the question with the other powers in the uncertain period just after the Crimean War.

The Russian Mission in the United States

Eduard Stoeckl, the Russian minister to the United States, was also very busy during these years. Like his predecessor, Stoeckl had married an American (Elizabeth Lee from Massachusetts), but lacking the wealth and social position of Bodisko, he maintained a modest residence at 146 G Street, a few blocks from the White House. His staff was similarly centrally located in the capital: Vladimir Bodisko and his family at 51 Pennsylvania Avenue, and Robert Osten-Sacken at Mrs. Nicolson's boardinghouse on the corner of Pennsylvania and Twenty-second Street. To compound the "German" flavor of the Russian diplomatic staff, Baron Nottbeck, a Baltic German who had married the grand-

[44]Pickens to M. L. Bonham, 14 April 1860, Bonham Papers, South Caroliniana Library, University of South Carolina, asking Bonham (his congressman) to intercede with the State Department about his need for a secretary.

[45]Pickens to Gorchakov (copy), 28 July/9 August 1859, enclosed with Gorchakov's reply of 18/30 August in Pickens to Cass (private), 31 August 1859, DUSM, Russia, vol. 18 (roll 18, M 35), RG 59, NA.

*Eduard Stoeckl, Russian minister to the United States, 1854–
1868. From the collections of the Library of Congress*

daughter of John Jacob Astor, replaced Evstaf'ev as consul-general in New York
in 1857, and several naturalized German-Americans were appointed to other
ports—for example, Ferdinand Wolff at Galveston and August Kohler for Baltimore.[46] Foreign Minister Nesselrode may have retired from his post in St. Petersburg, but his "German" legacy was alive and well in the United States.

Once again, stability and familiarity characterized the Russian mission. For
many years, Stoeckl and his staff were frequent guests at the political and social
salons of Washington and at the summer watering holes to the north. During
one such visit to New England, the Boston *Herald* reported:

> Mr. Stoeckl, the Russian minister to the United States, with his wife (an ac-
> complished daughter of Massachusetts) is now stopping at Newport. We un-

[46]Stoeckl to Cass, 1 June and 3 December 1857, Notes from the Russian Legation in
the United States to the Department of State, vol. 3 (roll 3, M 39), RG 59, NA; Stoeckl
to Marcy, 29 March and 12 November 1856, ibid.

derstand, says the New York *Evening Post*, that his success in fusing with some of our most popular institutions is a not unfrequent subject of self congratulations, and that he jocosely boasts that during the fifteen years when he was an *attache* of the legation, he was also a member of a Washington fire company, and "run wid de lantern."[47]

For all of his social climbing, Stoeckl was also an assiduous supporter of close relations, never passing up an opportunity to report American sympathy to Russia. When Stoeckl presented his credentials as envoy extraordinary (a promotion) in the closing days of the Pierce administration, he related the following as the president's gracious response:

> Our policy is eminently pacific. We seek peace with all nations. On this point our interests and tastes are coincident.
>
> But besides the consideration of general policy, there are strong special reasons why the Government and people of the United States should cultivate and maintain the most friendly relations with the Emperor and people of Russia. It may perhaps be regarded as somewhat remarkable that during the period of our national existence, no circumstance has occurred to chill for a day the sentiments of good will between the two nations. Russia has never interfered with our affairs. She has never even suggested intervention except as our friend. . . . I can anticipate nothing but continuance of these relations, which it were hardly possible to improve.[48]

Stoeckl's travels provided excuses for other meetings with American heads of state. Immediately after his return from St. Petersburg in May 1859, he met with James Buchanan and heard him echo the usual friendship refrain: "You are the only power that has never been jealous of the progress we have made as a nation in accomplishing what we call our manifest destiny. You also have your own manifest destiny and far from colliding with you with hostility and jealousy, we applaud your expansion and the extension of your power."[49] Since the president was personally acquainted with the Russian scene and could ask about old friends there, the official relationship with the Russian legation was no doubt facilitated, but that did not stop Stoeckl from reporting the negative side of Buchanan's presidency—his favoritism and general ineffectiveness as a leader.[50]

The Russian minister and his staff actively cultivated the influential politicians in Washington, expressly for purposes of information and leverage. For ex-

[47]"A Diplomatist 'Running with the Machine,' " Boston *Herald*, 29 July 1857.

[48]Enclosure in English, in Stoeckl to Gorchakov, 11/23 February 1857, f. kants. Vashington 1857, d. 183, AVPR.

[49]Stoeckl to Gorchakov, 17/29 May 1859, f. kants. Vashington 1859, d. 206, AVPR.

[50]Stoeckl to Gorchakov, 9/21 April 1858, f. kants. Vashington 1858, d. 185, AVPR. Many Americans agreed with Stoeckl's assessment—for example, William L. Marcy:

ample, in early 1858, in a communiqué about United States policy in the Pacific, Stoeckl referred to Sen. William McKendree Gwin of California as a man "with whom I am intimately acquainted."[51] He did not, however, see eye to eye with Gwin on some of the senator's projects. Gwin's ardent promotion of a railroad to the West Stoeckl believed to be too grandiose because of the expense and the difficulty of crossing "vast deserts infested by Indians." "Few people believe seriously in the realization of this gigantic project," he added, betraying his personal conservatism and the fact that, despite his long tenure, he never ventured west of the Blue Ridge Mountains.[52]

High-placed connections, nevertheless, helped the Russians when dealing with some complex cases left over from the Crimean War. A claim by Samuel Colt for losses incurred in the cancellation of his contract for rifles was submitted by agreement of both parties to a committee of arbitration consisting of the attorney for both sides and Col. Samuel Cooper, who was selected by Secretary of War J. B. Floyd. The decision was in favor of Russia, but this did not discourage "the richest man in New England" from transacting further business with Russia.[53]

The Perkins Affair

Another contract dispute, however, would be a thorn in the side of Russian-American relations for many years. In the summer of 1855, Stoeckl negotiated with Benjamin W. Perkins for the shipment of ten thousand pounds of gunpowder to Russia. After the powder was acquired and loaded on a chartered ship at Boston, the Russians decided that it was not really needed and refused to pay for it. Perkins sustained a considerable loss but had already agreed to a new deal, negotiated by Russian army agent Otto Lilienfeldt, to supply thirty-five thousand rifles. He then proceeded to fulfill this second "contract," apparently in the belief that it would lend support to his claims on the first.[54] But the war sud-

"My knowledge of the qualities of Mr. Buchanan's mind never allowed me to hope that he would display much skill in managing the personal affairs of the government, but he has gone beyond the limit fixed by my apprehensions, in his maladroitness." "Diary and Memoranda of William L. Marcy," *American Historical Review* 24, 4 (July 1919): 652.

[51]Stoeckl to Gorchakov, 30 January/11 February 1859, f. kants. Vashington 1858, d. 185, AVPR.

[52]Stoeckl to Gorchakov, 8/20 February 1859, f. kants. Vashington 1859, d. 106, AVPR.

[53]Stoeckl to Gorchakov, 27 May/8 June and 15/27 September 1857, f. kants. Vashington 1857, d. 183, AVPR.

[54]Stoeckl to Gorchakov, 11/23 June 1858, f. kants. Vashington 1858, d. 185, AVPR; Appleton to Cass, 22 September 1860, DUSM, Russia, vol. 18 (roll 18, M 35), RG 59, NA.

denly ended, the second order was declared void by Russia, and Perkins was again left holding the bag with obligations to other parties and the likelihood of financial ruin. Perkins certainly bore some responsibility since, infatuated with the idea of quick profits, he made unbacked commitments and, most of all, did not secure the arrangements in writing.

Efforts to settle the matter resulted in Lilienfeldt's brief arrest, a temporary out-of-court settlement that netted Perkins only $200, and a continuing volley of charges.[55] Lilienfeldt and Stoeckl claimed that their agreements were only oral, that there were no written, binding contracts, and that consequently no legal basis for supporting Perkins's claim existed. For his part, Perkins argued that, considering the circumstances and nature of the business, the oral agreements were binding and should be honored. Nonetheless, Russia might have settled in favor of Perkins but for several factors: It could have set a dangerous precedent that could be abused by others (the excessive cost of other orders placed in the United States only now being realized), and officials were put off by the bellicose manner in which the case was presented. Resolution was also awkward because Stoeckl, as a principal party, would have nothing to do with it. He argued that Perkins was demanding $400,000 only to extort a settlement of $5,000 to $6,000, and he even hinted that if American officials continued to press the issue, no further arms purchases would be made from the United States.[56]

In 1860, after Perkins had died, the case was presented again by John Appleton in St. Petersburg with attorney Joseph B. Stewart representing Perkins's widow. The Ministry of Foreign Affairs was no more sympathetic to the case than Stoeckl had been, again on the basis of a lack of written proof. Appleton reported to Washington: "In respect to the alleged contract for powder, Mr. [Ivan] Tolstoy (Gorchakov's chief assistant) appears to think it almost incredible that an undertaking involving so large an expenditure, should have been entered upon without a formal and written contract; and for this single reason he dismisses this branch of the case."[57] More formally, the claim was rejected by the Russian Senate, the highest court of the country.

With the backing of Seward the suit was brought up again early in the Lincoln administration with Caleb Cushing and William Ewarts now serving as Perkins's attorney. Stewart continued as intermediary, asserting to the newly appointed minister to Russia: "I never participated in a more just demand in my life—Nor did I ever witness a more disreputable abandonment of contracts on the part of any person, high or low, than marked the conduct of M. de Stoeckl,

[55]"Arrest of a Russian agent," Cincinnati *Daily Enquirer*, 21 June 1856.

[56]Appleton to Tolstoy, 1/13 December 1860, copy enclosed in Appleton to Cass, 13 December 1860, DUSM, Russia, vol. 18 (roll 18, M 35), RG 59, NA.

[57]Joseph B. Stewart (Washington) to Cassius Clay, 5 November 1861, DPR, Russia, vol. 4500, RG 84, NA.

the Russian Minister Resident here and Capt. Otto Lilienfeldt, when they found the war in the Crimea would likely close and they chose to leave Perkins to get his Powder and Guns purchased for Russia on their word, off of his hands the best way he could."[58] In another letter, however, he admitted that the amount of loss to Perkins and his associates was greatly exaggerated and was actually about $130,000, still a considerable sum.[59] The dispute would continue to bedevil Russian-American relations through subsequent administrations.

American Ships for the Russian Navy

More and favorable public attention centered on the construction activity at the lower end of Manhattan Island on the East River. The William H. Webb Shipyards were finally beginning to build warships for the Russian navy that had first been discussed before the Crimean War. Capt. Ivan Shestakov, a later naval minister, arrived in May 1857 to supervise the projects.[60] The first was the construction of a steam corvette specifically for Grand Duke Constantine's planned expansion of the Russian Pacific fleet. Christened the *Iaponets* [Japanese], this ship was built to navigate the shallow waters of the lower Amur River, was 214 feet in length with a displacement of 1,400 tons, and was outfitted with full rigging and with two oscillating engines of 300 horsepower, at a total cost of $250,000. Launched already by November 1857, the *Iaponets* conducted trials on the Hudson in preparation for its voyage to the Far East accompanied by a second, smaller corvette, the *Manzhur*, that had been assembled at a Boston shipyard.[61]

The most extensive Russian-American naval project, however, was the construction of a sizable steam frigate, named the *General-Admiral* in honor of Constantine, to serve as the flagship of the Russian Baltic fleet. The keel was laid at the Webb yards on 21 September 1857, the grand duke's thirtieth birthday, in an elaborate ceremony staged by Shestakov and attended by Mayor Fernando Wood, Stoeckl, Nottbeck, several Russian naval officers, and other invited guests.[62] The company employed an additional hundred workers and remained busy through the financial panic of October.[63] Exemplifying the considerable media attention given the enterprise, the New York *Herald* reported in March:

[58]Stewart to Clay, 17 February 1862, ibid.
[59]Ibid.
[60]Stoeckl to Gorchakov, 27 May/8 June 1857, f. kants. Vashington 1857, d. 183, AVPR.
[61]*National Intelligencer*, 19 November 1857; "The Russian Corvette *Japanese*," *Frank Leslie's Illustrated Newspaper*, 1 May 1858, p. 345.
[62]Stoeckl to Gorchakov, 15/27 September 1857, f. kants. Vashington 1857, d. 183, AVPR.
[63]"The Ship Yards," New York *Herald*, 10 October 1857.

The entire frame of the Russian frigate building by Mr. W. H. Webb at the foot of Sixth Street, East River, is now raised, showing the immense vessel in all her proportions. The iron diagonal truss framing, composed of the longest iron bars ever rolled, is also in place, affording an excellent opportunity to those who wish to examine this method of strengthening vessels. The frigate is pierced for 72 guns, and is intended to mount an unusual heavy battery of eight and nine inch shell guns.[64]

The launching took place as scheduled exactly one year after the keel was laid and "drew one of the largest crowds together that probably ever assembled upon any similar occasion"—about fifty thousand, according to one source. Dodsworth's band was stationed on a large platform amidships and played the Russian national hymn as the ship went down the runway.[65] At a cost of over $1 million, with about 7,000 tons displacement and reaching over 300 feet long and 50 feet wide, the *General-Admiral* was by far the largest vessel built in the United States and reportedly the largest wooden ship constructed anywhere at the time. The United States thus contributed to Russian naval revitalization after the Crimean War, while adding considerably to an international reputation for American shipbuilding.

After outfitting during the winter, the *General-Admiral* cruised up the Hudson in May 1859 and, as Stoeckl noted, continued to attract the curious: The ship "excites the interests of thousands of people who come to see it daily. They agree that this is the most beautiful ship which has ever been launched by American shipyards, and has done a great honor, as much to Mr. Webb who had been its architect, as to the Russian officers who, with indefatigable diligence, supervised the construction up to the most minute details."[66] The *General-Admiral* steamed across the Atlantic in June 1859 in the unprecedented time of eleven days, under command of Captain Comstock with a crew of over two hundred other American officers and seamen. Shestakov and Webb were among the distinguished passengers, arriving at Kronstadt on 14 July amid even more fanfare.[67] According to a press report from St. Petersburg: "Grand Duke Constantine went on board of her soon after her arrival, examined her minutely, and is said

[64]"The New Russian Frigate," ibid., 21 March 1858.

[65]New York *Times*, 22 September 1858; Stoeckl to Gorchakov, 8/20 September 1858, f. kants. Vashington, 1858, d. 185, AVPR. That evening Shestakov and his wife hosted a dinner at Delmonico's with a number of dignitaries, including Gen. Winfield Scott, as guests. Lt. N. Mozhaiskii (who was present), "Spusk fregata 'General-Admiral,' " *Morskoi Sbornik*, no. 1 (January 1859): 277.

[66]*Frank Leslie's Illustrated Newspaper*, 21 May 1859, p. 390.

[67]Stoeckl to Gorchakov, 17/29 May 1859, f. kants. Vashington 1859, d. 206, AVPR. Stoeckl also made a point of emphasizing that no contract problems had occurred and relations between Shestakov and Webb were quite cordial.

"Launch of the General-Admiral," Harper's Weekly, *October 2, 1858*

to have expressed himself highly pleased with the *tout ensemble* of this splendid vessel. She certainly does credit to the American shipyards, and will take her place as the model ship of the new Russian steam navy."[68]

More than thirty Americans resident in St. Petersburg paid tribute to Webb at a ceremony presided over by George H. Prince, the Ropes agent.[69] Separately, Grand Duke Constantine and Adm. Nikolai Metlin, director of the naval min-

[68]"Our St. Petersburg Correspondence," New York *Herald*, 15 August 1859.
[69]Ibid., 1 September 1859.

istry, reaffirmed their high estimation of the ship to its American builder.[70] And, appropriately, Captain Shestakov became the first Russian commander of the *General-Admiral*. Since Russia had deliberately chosen an American shipyard, the frigate and the attendant ceremonies dramatically demonstrated the closeness of Russian-American relations.

Commercial Transitions

Purchases of ships by contract were not counted in the official figures of trade between the two countries. Even if they had been, the volume would still have been proportionally lower than in the early years of the nineteenth century. The nature of the trade had also changed. At the time, however, optimism reigned about the prospects for expansion of Russian-American commerce after the Crimean War. Seymour noted in a dispatch of May 1856: "Our trade with Russia may be said to have only just begun. For several years previous to the late war, it languished, for want of some kind of stimulus, since the war it has shown much activity, and now, though not what it should be, the appearances indicate a change for the better. Whatever we gain in the way of direct trade at the present time, between Russia and the ports of the United States, will, I am inclined to believe, be a permanent gain."[71] Articles published in the American press echoed that sentiment, for example: "Thus, in many particulars, a wider field is opening to American enterprise, skill and activity, and this with a nation possessing vast resources, and wishing to become our commercial pupil and customer. This interchange of courtesies and commodities can be politically and commercially advantageous."[72]

Sensing the need for information and coordination, Seymour pushed Washington for more and better-paid consuls:

[70]Adm. Nikolai Metlin to Webb, 18/30 January 1860, copy in Tolstoy to Pickens, 2 February 1860, DPR, Russia, vol. 4483, RG 84, NA. Pickens reported that Grand Duke Constantine

> expressed great warmth towards the people of the United States, and particularly for the manner in which our naval officers had received him on the *Wabash* last winter in the Mediterranean. He also expressed great satisfaction with the magnificent sixty-four gun screw ship, recently built by Mr. Webb of New York for the Russian Navy etc., and said he hoped the friendship of the two Governments would be perpetual. He said many things very complimentary of the American Navy.

Pickens to Cass, 23 September 1859, DUSM, Russia, vol. 18 (roll 18, M 35), RG 59, NA. Perhaps the grand duke's recommendation helped Webb win contracts to build two slightly smaller ships for the Italian navy.

[71]Seymour to Marcy, 16/28 May 1857, DUSM, Russia, vol. 17 (roll 17, M 35), RG 59, NA.

[72]Charleston *Mercury*, 16 May 1856, quoting the New York *Tribune*.

Our trade with the chief ports on the Gulf of Finland . . . has been considerable during the present season, and the prospect is certainly favorable for a fair increase of our trade in future. It will need encouragement however, of one kind and another, and a good set of Consuls, properly paid for their services, can do something to place it on a respectable footing.

I presume it will not be controverted that, at a time like the present when we have it in our power to take advantage of some of the changes which the late war has brought about, it is important that we should have active commercial agents, at every point where an avenue can be opened for increasing direct trade with Russia. The Consul of a country is its commercial representative and can do much towards promoting its commercial interests.[73]

The minister also faced a crisis from a new requirement that all consuls must be American citizens; moreover, he was for a time unable to secure a permanent replacement for the crucial St. Petersburg post. The United States could no longer make free use of the talents of practicing merchants such as Lenartzen at Kronstadt, Rodde at Reval, and Ralli at Odessa. William L. Winans, who had filled in temporarily as acting consul in St. Petersburg, returned to his own business. His place was taken by Gaun Hutton, who was associated with Winans. Finally, in May 1857 Caleb Croswell assumed the full-time duties of consul in St. Petersburg.[74]

In the meantime and in fulfillment of Seymour's wishes, Francis Claxton arrived early in 1857 to open the first American consular office in Moscow, the second city of the empire. He immediately began an intensive study of Russian and became the first official American appointee to Russia to master the language. At about the same time Perry McDonough Collins was designated commercial agent for the Amur region in the Russian Far East, but it was naturally much later before he reached his remote destination. Though Stoeckl assured his superiors that this new appointment was commercial and not at all political, they refused to recognize Collins. Russian officials were mainly concerned that they would have to grant reciprocal privileges to other countries, especially Britain—a consideration that American authorities could easily understand and support.[75]

[73]Seymour to Marcy, 3/15 July 1856, DUSM, Russia, vol. 17 (roll 17, M 35), RG 59, NA. The most detailed analysis of American commercial prospects in Russia was submitted by Acting Consul Hutton in a sixty-page dispatch of November 1856, in which he stressed the opportunity for Americans that existed in Russia after the Crimean War. Hutton to Marcy, 17/29 November 1856, DUSC, St. Petersburg, vol. 8 (roll 5, M 81), RG 59, NA.
[74]Seymour to Cass, 8/20 May 1857, DUSM, Russia, vol. 17 (roll, M 35), RG 59, NA; Croswell to Cass, 5 June 1857, DUSC, St. Petersburg, vol. 9 (roll 5, M 81), RG 59, NA.
[75]Seymour to Marcy, 1/13 November 1856, DUSM, Russia, vol. 17 (roll 17, M 35), RG 59, NA; Claxton to Cass, 2 October 1857, DUSC, Moscow, vol. 1 (roll 1, M 456), RG 59, NA, in which Claxton reported on the advantages of speaking Russian and

Brooke B. Williams, Aleksandr Bodisko's brother-in-law, initially accepted an appointment to the consular post at Reval with the apparent motive of visiting his sister but was then replaced by Charles A. Leas of Baltimore, one of the Crimean War surgeons.[76] Another doctor in that war, Timothy C. Smith, took charge of the long-established consulate in Odessa, quickly becoming knowledgeable about Russian commercial affairs in the south. Thus, by 1859 the United States had a network of capable consuls in Russia reporting in detail on the Russian scene and particularly on the outlook for increased trade.

Hutton, who had advanced in five years from Baltimore merchant to San Francisco iron founder to a Winans administrator, provided some of the best arguments and optimistic forecasts on Russian-American trade. He observed a continuing trend toward larger American ships handling Russian cargoes: "Although the number of American vessels arriving here, is much smaller than twenty or thirty years ago, yet I find on examination, that their total tonnage has increased." Noting that the average capacity of ships had gone up 2.3 times in sixteen years, he added, "It is true that the trade has not, thus far, increased in proportion to the increase of our general commerce—but in view of the liberal abatements now about to be made in the tariffs of both countries, and the great extension to be soon given to the Rail-Road system in Russia—we may reasonably expect a marked and more rapid increase."[77] Both Russians and Americans counted on this considerable growth in direct trade resulting from the residual hostility toward Britain from the Crimean War. That, in fact, did happen, though not to the degree that Hutton and others had hoped, since the British proved quite adept at recapturing their former dominance of the Russian trade.

The size of the American vessels continued to rise sharply, and several weighing over 1,200 tons entered the Baltic. The largest on record for this period, owned by the Pattens of Bath, Maine, was the *Assyria*, which hauled cotton from New Orleans in 1858, but even larger cargoes (4,700 bales) were carried by the *Golden Eagle*. Like so many of these new Yankee clippers, both were built and owned in Maine but sailed out of New Orleans or Mobile. By 1860 some of these ships had been transferred to Southern owners, such as St. Croix Redman of New Orleans, thus decreasing further the old triangular trading pattern anchored in New England.

that after only a few months he had

> made sufficient progress to be able to speak it indifferently well, and with the aid of a dictionary to write and read it; this knowledge has enabled me to address myself to the manufacturers of Moscow and vicinity, none of whom speak French or English, and I have strenuously endeavoured to promote a direct trade between them and the United States.

[76]Williams (Georgetown) to Cass, 29 October 1858, and Leas (Baltimore) to Appleton, 7 February 1859, DUSC, Reval, vol. 1 (roll 1, M 484), RG 59, NA.

[77]Hutton to Marcy, 1 March 1857, DUSC, St. Petersburg, vol. 8 (roll 5, M 81), RG 59, NA.

The number of American ships arriving at St. Petersburg also rose again, nearing fifty in 1859. By far the most came from New Orleans, while a few were involved in trade with third countries, such as bringing coal to Russia from Newcastle.[78]

Hutton discovered that the increased size and number of ships exacerbated another problem that had plagued American consuls in Russia—administering to the needs of stranded sailors. Those from eight ships that wintered there in 1856–57 because of an early freeze he found to be a mixed and unruly lot, and he had great difficulty keeping them under control.

> I regret to say that the conduct of the men has caused much trouble and anxiety. The breaches of the peace especially, have been numerous, serious, and several times fatal. . . . Now these miscalled American seamen, have been, this winter, the most disorderly and troublesome. In comparing them with . . . Germans, Swedes, Danes, Dutch, etc. who are wintering here . . . the latter appear of a better class, and much more orderly.

Hutton continued, reflecting back over that irksome winter:

> I think it should be held as a *general rule*, that the men are bound to obey and respect their officers *so long as they are under pay*, and whether on board ship or not. The seamen when on shore presume on being foreigners, and the local authorities consider them to be, in a great measure at least, under the special protection and control of their consuls. Last autumn, Mr. Wilkins [agent at Kronstadt], with the chief of the Police at Cronstadt, and myself, had to escort three American Captains to the landing, to prevent an assault upon them by some of their own seamen.[79]

But he later noted one positive feature of the affair:

> I had intended to give a further account of the eight American vessels and their crews which wintered at Cronstadt, but conclude that the subject may as well rest. Yet in the midst of regrettable disturbances between the English and American sailors, I observed one fact worthy of notice. The Swedish, Norwegian and Danish sailors always promptly rallied to the support of our men, and prevented them from being overwhelmed by numbers. The feeling so energetically expressed, may, in case of future possible events, become of considerable national importance.[80]

[78]Croswell to Cass, 26 October 1857, DUSC, St. Petersburg, vol. 9 (roll 5, M 81), RG 59, NA.
[79]Hutton to Cass, 7/19 May 1857, ibid.
[80]Hutton to Cass, 6 July 1857, ibid.

The Russian government was also taking some measures to facilitate trade between the two countries. By 1859 a momentous project was under way to dredge a deeper channel into St. Petersburg so that large vessels could dock and exchange cargoes in the mainland harbor without having to transfer them to lighters. Although one incentive was to convert Kronstadt entirely into a naval base, the new channel would also favor the bigger American vessels.[81] In addition, as the American consuls reported, customs clearances were becoming easier (and authorities more cooperative about the usual shore-leave incidents). In this relatively liberal period of Russian history, passport regulations had eased, allowing for freer entry and exit of both foreign and native merchants. John Schepeler, the semiofficial Russian shipping agent in New York, and Ivan Tolstoy, the assistant minister of foreign affairs, as well as a number of private citizens, were especially active in courting American business.

In other ways, however, the times mitigated against commercial expansion. Russia was suffering financially both from the Crimean War and from the preparations for reform. On the one hand, a prevailing liberal spirit supported free trade, which favored competition especially in the foreign markets and thus a resumption of the British dominance. On the other, a rising national consciousness protected the Russian internal markets and promoted self-sufficiency.[82] As an example of the latter, the Russian government preferred to subsidize the construction of railroads by Russian corporations, as opposed to construction by the state, which had been the method used for the St. Petersburg–Moscow line. Few American businessmen could dispute this policy, even though it severely limited the possibilities of seeking contracts in the manner of Shaffner or Sanders. Of 119 Russian stock companies established by 1859, 80 came into existence after 1855 and several involved railroads.[83] The age of American-style capitalism appeared to have dawned in Russia.

[81]Seymour to Marcy, 23 January/4 February 1856, DUSM, Russia, vol. 16 (roll 16, M 35), RG 59, NA. Seymour apparently valued highly Schepeler's contributions to Russian-American trade: "I am in hopes he will visit Washington on his return, and get a chance to converse with you about our trade with Russia. You will find Mr. Schepeler well acquainted with the subject in all its bearings, and, being a man of much intelligence, I am convinced his conversation will interest you." Seymour later reported that Schepeler's departure had been delayed "on account of his detention by business which I believe to be of importance to the American trade here." To J. A. Thomas, 9/21 April 1856, ibid.

On the dredging of the St. Petersburg–Kronstadt channel, see Croswell to Cass, 20 February 1859, DUSC, St. Petersburg, vol. 10 (roll 5, M 81), RG 59, NA.

[82]For surveys of Russian economic development at this time, see Alfred J. Rieber, *Merchants and Entrepreneurs in Imperial Russia* (Chapel Hill: University of North Carolina Press, 1982); William L. Blackwell, *The Beginnings of Russian Industrialization, 1800–1860* (Princeton, N. J.: Princeton University Press, 1968); and Peter Gatrell, *The Tsarist Economy, 1850–1917* (New York: St. Martin's Press, 1986).

[83]N. S. Kiniapina, *Politika Russkogo samoderzhaviia v oblasti promyshlennosti (20-50-e*

If there is one phrase that could describe the nature of Russian-American trade, it would be the same one often applied to the antebellum South— "Cotton is King." There was a rapid rise in shipments of cotton from the United States to Russia between 1856 and 1860, attributable primarily to the steps taken on both sides to promote direct trade, the larger and more efficient American ships, the similarity of the American and Russian textile operations and their cotton-type requirements, and the new expansion of that industry, especially in and around Moscow. Two Southern politicians, John Claiborne and John Minor Botts, made separate visits to Moscow to foster the cotton trade.[84] Partly as a result of these efforts, in 1857, 870,397 poods (1 pood equaling 36 pounds) of cotton, about 45 percent of total cotton imports, entered Russia via American shipping.[85] The next year the value of cotton brought directly from the United States reached 7,779,221 rubles, out of total exports of 9,367,460 rubles from that country to Russia, or about 80 percent.[86]

Second in rank was sugar, but it was now far below its former prominence in the Russian-American trade of the 1840s, mainly because of the rapid advance of the sugar beet industry in Russia and the changing patterns of New England shipping. Sarsaparilla, rice, and logwood were also significant. Small quantities of a wide variety of goods completed the list. For example, the *W. S. Lindsay*, a large Yankee clipper coming straight from New York in 1859, brought 3,244 bales of cotton, 4,175 boxes of logwood extract, 86 boxes of leather cloth, 20 tons of rice, 60 barrels of resin, 8 parcels, 1 case of books, and 1 box of natural history specimens.[87]

Tobacco, also deemed promising for direct shipment because of the growth of Russian consumption, encountered a double obstacle—the influence of a few controling merchants and Russian tastes. Claxton, the consul in Moscow, reported that, to his surprise, Russia actually exported considerably more leaf tobacco in volume than it imported.[88] However, "the tobacco is of an inferior quality when compared with Kentucky or Cuban production but serves well to mix with those brands, it therefore finds a market in Hamburg and Bremen where it is 'doctored' and then finds its way back to this market as prime Maryland and Ken-

gody XIX v.) (Moscow: MGU, 1968), p. 82. See also New York *Times*, 18 November 1858, on Russian industrial progress.

[84]Hutton to Marcy, 17/29 November 1856, DUSC, St. Petersburg, vol. 8 (roll 5, M 81), RG 59, NA; Claxton (Moscow) to Howell Cobb, 8 January 1858, DPR, Moscow, Miscellaneous Letters, vol. 4225, RG 84, NA.

[85]Hutton to Marcy, 17/29 November 1856, DUSC, St. Petersburg, vol. 8 (roll 5, M 81), RG 59, NA.

[86]Croswell to Buchanan, 5 March 1858, DUSC, St. Petersburg, vol. 10 (roll 5, M 81), RG 59, NA.

[87]Croswell to Cass, 27 May 1859, ibid.

[88]Claxton to Cass, 10 August 1859, DUSC, Moscow, vol. 1 (roll 1, M 456), RG 59, NA.

tucky leaf."[89] These operations were directed by two merchant houses consisting of five partners, all of whom had become very wealthy from their monopoly.[90]

Claxton also found that Russian custom did not fit well with American manufacture of tobacco products, concentrating as it did on cigar production and pipe tobacco:

> Tobacco is more universally used in Russia than in any European country, not only does the practice of smoking prevail amongst the men, and both sexes of the lower classes, but ladies of refinement and position very generally indulge in the luxury both in private and public, their presence is therefore no restraint as *elsewhere*, and the consumption of smoking tobacco in the form of 'papiros' (paper cigarettes), is universal, unremitting, and enormous. Cigars are comparatively but little used, never by females, and principally by the gentlemen after dinner; at all other times, from the moment of rising, to the hour of retiring the 'papiros' is being smoked. In public gardens and promenades, at the theatre between the acts, and even at public balls and private parties a room is reserved for the smokers—slight indications of the prevalence of the habit. Snuff is not in much use, and is taken principally by the soldiers and the lower orders.[91]

Many boxes of Cuban and American cigars still entered Russia as personal effects or as "captain's privilege" and were probably frequently used to smooth the way through Customs and in other commercial or social transactions.

American agricultural implements, a new import into Russia, seemed to have future potential, especially at Reval where the consul Charles Leas led an effort to bring in American models with the help of Assistant Minister of Foreign Affairs Ivan Tolstoy.[92] Both thought that the prospect of sales of these labor-saving machines was very favorable, if only landowners could be made aware of the American manufactures. Leas reported to Washington:

> Since the construction of railroads has been inaugurated in this country, the price of labour has greatly increased, from which, and other causes, agriculturists have commenced to direct their attention to machinery as a means of labour. And as comparatively nothing was known of the capacity of America to furnish machinery suited to the purposes desired, attention was most naturally directed to their neighbours, the English and Germans, for a supply. That is to say, the people of this country have for a long time known, that the

[89]Ibid.

[90]Hutton to Marcy, 17/29 November 1856, DUSC, St. Petersburg, vol. 8 (roll 5, M 81), RG 59, NA.

[91]Claxton to Cass, 10 August 1859, DUSC, Moscow, vol. 1 (roll 1, M 456), RG 59, NA.

[92]Leas to Cass, 4 September 1860, DUSC, Reval, vol. 1 (roll 1, M 484), RG 59, NA.

Americans are an ingenious and inventive people, but as to what kind of machines, or the prices thereof, they have remained comparatively ignorant, nor did they know how they were to be gotten from so great a distance, without involving a cost, far beyond their real value. But I am happy to inform you that a new state of affairs is dawning.[93]

Inspired by Leas, the marshal of nobility of the Estonian province, Baron Ernst Ungern-Sternberg, set off late in 1860 on a mission to the United States.[94] From there he sent back samples of agricultural implements, which Leas, with the assistance of another American from St. Petersburg, exhibited at an agricultural fair during the summer of 1861. "And the result was all that could be desired, the nobility (who are the exclusive landowners in this Province) were perfectly delighted, not only with the working of the machines, but with the cheapness of the prices, at which American machines could be delivered in this country."[95] Thanks to promotion by Leas, Claxton, and other consuls, orders were soon rolling in for shipments through free agents such as Chandor and from G. H. Gray (of Boston) for his hardware business in Moscow.

Though the long-standing triangular trade—New England, West Indies, Baltic—had virtually disappeared, a modest direct interchange between Boston and St. Petersburg continued, especially that managed by Ropes and Company, whose business flourished during this period.[96] The Boston cargoes were typically diverse and included railroad car wheels (for Winans), agricultural machinery, sewing machines, hand spikes, leather belts to drive machinery, clocks, and black walnut, white oak, and mahogany woods, as well as larger quantities of cotton, logwood, and rice. Shipments from Russia were more of a problem, however. Although direct exports from the United States to Russia rose to their highest percentage (almost 2 percent of total exports in 1859), imports from Russia declined to their lowest levels (.25 percent in 1859), not counting the war years.[97] The dollar value of exports from the United States to Russia in 1857 was $4,474,842, while imports from Russia totaled only $1,519,420; in 1859 the respective figures were $5,587,385 and $877,835, the reverse of the ratio of the early nineteenth century.[98]

[93]Leas to Seward, 25 October 1861, ibid.
[94]Leas to Cass, 13 December 1860, ibid.
[95]Leas to Seward, 25 October 1861, ibid.
[96]Seymour to Cass, 11/23 November 1857, DUSM, Russia, vol. 17 (roll 17, M 35), RG 59, NA.
[97]See the excellent tables compiled by Kirchner, *Russian-American Commerce*, pp. 53–54.
[98]"Trade of Russia and the United States," Boston *Post*, 15 January 1858; *Vestnik Promyshlennosti* 8, 5 (March 1860): 112–13. The importation of jute and manila, for example, began in 1843 and quickly (1845) surpassed imports of European hemp. By 1857 the ratio was six to one in favor of the Philippine and East Indian products, much to

This imbalance further weakened the basis for the triangular trade and meant that many of the great ships carrying cotton returned in ballast or took on cargoes of wheat, tallow, and hemp for a British port such as Bristol. The crux of the problem was the relative decline in demand for the traditional Russian exports to the United States—sailcloth, hemp, and iron. Linen sails had been largely replaced by cotton canvas (even in Russia), with a resulting crisis for that industry. Hemp for rope was in competition with sisal and jute, and native iron production was pushing aside imports.[99] The alternative products of Russian export, mainly grains such as wheat, rye, and oats, were also being marketed abroad by the United States. Though some quantities of hemp, rough linens, bristles, feathers, and horsehair continued to be exported to the United States, the few Ropes ships could usually handle all of this demand.

Consuls such as Hutton and Croswell promoted markets for American goods in Russia, but failed to tackle the other half of the trade problem—an imbalance that was limiting the growth of direct shipments of American goods to Russia. Nor was this the complete picture, for there was still the indirect trade to consider. Though both Russians and Americans thought that British and German intermediaries impeded trade and raised costs, in many ways they were an important adjunct, facilitating commerce and especially American sales. If all the figures were available for the indirect shipments of American goods to Russia— cotton and tobacco, the ship construction contracts, the Winans money transfers, and other business ventures—the ratio of the United States' gain at Russia's expense would probably be on the order of twenty to one for the 1850s.

Russia and the United States in the North Pacific

Another area underreported in the official statistics was the Pacific, where a significant expansion of both American and Russian activities was occurring. The commercial outlook there would have appeared even more booming if the figures had included all of the whales caught in Russian waters that entered the American market in the form of oil and bone—a business that reached its zenith in the early 1850s and was easily the largest economic enterprise in that region. The incidents on Russian shores involving trade with the Indians, deserted or stranded sailors, shipwrecks, and illegal hunting were irritating to local authorities and the consuls and ministers who had to deal with them, but they did not disturb the general harmony between Russia and the United States, even in the Pacific where frontiers were still elastic and modern commerce just blossoming. The tremendous development of the California economy was an important factor in Russian-American North Pacific relations that would culminate with the

the concern of the Russians. *Kommercheskaia Gazeta*, 30 August 1858, p. 597.

[99]Kiniapina, *Politika Russkogo samoderzhaviia*, p. 55.

sale of Alaska. California furnished the model and in some ways the spirit for ideas, ventures, and changes. But the Crimean War had been the catalyst that pulled the two countries together, more so in the Pacific because of the very real dependency of Russia upon the United States for supplies.

Beverley Sanders and the small group of San Francisco businessmen who formed the American Russian Commercial Company provided the foundation for a direct California-Alaskan partnership that proved especially useful during the war years. The initial basis of the relationship was ice brought from New Archangel and Kodiak for the growing population of San Francisco. The Americans supplied the capital and expertise for equipment and icehouses, the construction of which proceeded through 1855 and 1856 under the direction of Angus McPherson and Alonzo Coy. But the American company's main wartime activity under Sanders's direction was to outfit the Russian colony with its basic needs—at a cost.

The American Russian Commercial Company thus became a major shipping firm operating the Russian America Company's vessels—the *Nikolai I*, *Kamchatka*, and *Menshikov*—under the neutral American flag. Two new ones were obtained: the *Cyane*, purchased especially for coastal communication and supply in the Northwest; and the *Astoria*, a first-class steamship bought for the Russian company by Sanders in New York in 1855. In addition, the American company's own large sailing ship, the *Zenobia*, served as the workhorse for hauling ice and provisions. Other vessels, such as the *Lucas*, were chartered as needed. The departures and cargoes of these ships depended upon the requests of the administrators in Alaska and the approval of the local Russian consul, Peter Kostromitinov, without any involvement of the faraway directors of the Russian America Company.[100]

The same was true of the requisitions for supplies. The chief administrator in Alaska, Captain Voevodskii, appealed directly to Sanders or through Kostromitinov for shipments of gunpowder, needed for defense as well as for hunting. Worried about the possible loss of control over the native population because of scarce powder and low food stocks, the Russians ordered extensively from California during 1855 and 1856. Judging from the manifests, they obviously provided well for their own needs with little thought of conservation or rationing:

Zenobia, cleared San Francisco January 5, 1856, for Sitka: 546 chests tea, 250 barrels crushed sugar, 40 quarter casks sherry, 2,218 barrels rye flour, 80 kegs

---

[100]Voevodskii to Sanders and Brenham, 18 February/2 March 1855; and Voevodskii to Main Office, 6 June 1855, RRAC, CGG, CS, vol. 36 (roll 60, M 11), RG 261, NA; and Main Office to Voevodskii, 25 May 1855, RRAC, CGG, CR, vol. 21 (roll 21, M 11), RG 261, NA. The *Cyane* was renamed the *Kodiak* and the steamer *Astoria* became the *Aleksandr II*, when they were turned over to the Russian America Company.

butter, 25 barrels flour, 90 boxes candles, 83 boxes soap, 61 bales tobacco, 10 bales calico, 25 bales sheeting, 10 bales domestics, 3 bales blankets, 14 bags coffee, 200 bags potatoes, 9 cases and 2 barrels merchandise, 7 barrels whiskey, 1 roll belting. Value $48,042.

Cyane, cleared March 26, 1856, from San Francisco to Sitka: 104 bundles iron, 1 box gin, 35 barrels syrup, 7 barrels whiskey, 10 barrels vinegar, 21 barrels butter, 1 barrel oil, 3 barrels glue, 180 boxes soap, 200 boxes candles, 10 cases cheroots, 25 kegs pickles, 1 pipe gin, 35 quarter casks wine, 400 bales sugar, 9 casks, 1 bundle, and 52 bales tobacco, 1 case, 3 hogshead, 8 crates, and 31 cases merchandise, 99 bales cotton goods, 8 cases and 1 bundle stationery, 5 boxes raisins, 35 cases oil, 21 cases Italian paste, 10 cases frames, 11 cases mustard, 15 buckets wine, 8 mats spices, 20 bags and 4 barrels nuts, 1,280 barrels grits and meal.

Lucas, cleared San Francisco on April 11, 1856, for Kodiak: 40 quarter bags flour, 12 barrels whiskey, 6 cases and 4 barrels wine, 33 bags vegetables, 80 bundles shingles, 2 launches, 2 chain cables, 15 cases fried meats, 20 barrels beef, 28 packages assorted groceries, 11 half barrels butter, 4 barrels bread, 1 roll lead, 2 kegs nails, 6 bags shot.

Nikolai I, cleared San Francisco on July 12, 1856, for Sitka: 73 barrels brandy, 84 casks butter, 299 boxes candles, 394 boxes soap, 80 bales hay, 100 bags oats, 50 bags barley, 50 bags potatoes, 6 barrels molasses, 18 barrels rice, 100 quarter bags flour, 40 bales tobacco, 10 cases clothing, 5 grindstones, 34 quarter casks, 21 buckets, and 4 cases wines, 15 bundles and 73 bars iron, 28 kegs nails, 2 live oxen, 2000 bricks, 15 bales cotton goods, 1 bale hosiery, 18 packages hardware, and 4 cases crockery.

Although information is not available about the cargo for the second sailing of the *Zenobia* on 1 April and about several shipments to the Amur region, it is obvious from these lists that the Russian colony was amply supplied with both basic and luxury goods from the United States.[101]

By this time, Sanders was no longer involved in California-Alaska economic and political affairs. In November 1855 the Sanders and Brenham Savings Bank failed. The causes stated publicly were related to a federal suit against Sanders for $48,000 in arrears on his accounts as Collector of the Port, which Sanders

[101]*Daily Alta California*, 7 January, 26 March, 11 April, and 12 July 1856. Partial lists of cargoes for 1855 are similar with a few additional items such as oranges, champagne, and lime juice. Gunpowder was apparently not included in the published manifests, for obvious reasons.
The orders from Sitka were fairly specific; for example, one from January 1855 requested 3,000 casks of strong spirits—rum, cognac, brandy, or whiskey—as well as 20 dozen rum glasses, and 50,000 Manila cigars. Voevodskii to Main Office, 24 January 1855, RRAC, CGG, CS, vol. 36 (roll 60, M 11), RG 261, NA.

claimed was carried over from his predecessor. The year 1855 was marked by a number of bank failures, and Sanders and Brenham had already withstood one run several months earlier.[102] Sanders's Russian business may have been a secondary cause: Investors might have lost confidence because of the economic climate, the news of the fall of Sevastopol, and the risks involved in transporting gunpowder.[103] With his financial base destroyed, Sanders was replaced temporarily by Henry Dexter as president of the American Russian Commercial Company. Within a few months Joseph Mora Moss, who had founded with Sanders the San Francisco Gas Company, took charge of the business, while Dexter journeyed to Russia for the coronation. Moss and the Russian-born Charles Baum were the company's chief officers for the duration of its operations, beyond 1867.

Under these circumstances it was not easy for either side to keep accurate and up-to-date accounts. Although the ships carrying supplies to the north usually returned with cargoes of ice, fish, coal, or lumber, the sales of these items barely covered the costs of the capital investment being made by the partnership in equipment, icehouses, and manpower. Some furs were also sent to San Francisco, but because these had to be sold through Lobach and Schepeler in New York, they required costly transshipment, only to fetch very low prices in the end.[104] When the returns were finally in for the war years, the directors of the Russian America Company in St. Petersburg were naturally quite upset. For 1856 alone the charges for supplies purchased in California reached $158,500, of which $75,000 was for items ordered after the peace.[105] They were also unhappy that the price for the *Cyane*, which joined the company's fleet in 1856 as the *Nakhimov*, had been $30,000 rather than the $18,000 that was originally authorized. The main office then instructed its overseer in Alaska to restrict purchases in California and not to accept any foreigners as workers without prior approval.[106] Stepan Voevodskii was recalled, and Capt. Johann Furuhjelm (Ivan Furugelm), the former commander of the Aian post and a naval officer of Finnish origin, was appointed to the chief administrative position at Sitka.

The Crimean War had also taken its toll on the Russian America Company, not so much by any threat of occupation or additional military costs, since it was practically undefended, but by the disruption of its trade that forced it to rely on California for both markets and supplies. This, and the approach of the expiration of its twenty-year monopoly charter at the end of 1861, prompted the

[102]Voevodskii to Sanders, 6/18 January 1855, and Voevodskii to Main Office, 30 September 1855, ibid.

[103]Voevodskii to Main Office, 20 September 1855, ibid.

[104]*Daily Alta California*, 6 November 1855.

[105]Main Office to Voevodskii, 16 December 1857, RRAC, CGG, CR, vol. 22 (roll 22, M 11), RG 261, NA.

[106]*Daily Alta California*, 3 September 1856.

company to double its efforts to restore its economic viability. But the dilemma the directors faced, given a stagnating fur industry caused by both declining demand and scarcity of animals, was how to accomplish this without becoming even more dependent upon American markets and intermediaries.

To the company's credit, it tried. There was a renewed focus on expanding and improving the now-established but as-yet-unrewarding ice trade, which required large, wooden sailing ships. The *Tsesarevich* was sent from the Baltic in 1856 to help with transport, and in 1858 a Yankee clipper of 1,089 tons, the *Coeur de Lion*, was purchased in Hamburg specifically to haul ice and as an alternative to the ships of the American Russian Commercial Company. This was a fine vessel, as a San Francisco paper boasted after its maiden voyage:

> The clipper ship *Coeur de Lion*, now lying at Lombard Dock, is one of the finest modelled and finished ships which we have ever seen in this port. In every place she has visited her fine lines, neat finish, finely proportioned spars, etc., have attracted universal attention, and been the theme of praise by seafaring men, both American and foreign. She is the last ship built by George Raynes, Esq., of Portsmouth, N. H., and considered the best of the splendid fleet constructed by him.[107]

The *Tsaritsa*, as the ship was rechristened, was the largest single capital investment made by the Russian company, exceeding the cost even of a new first-class steamer, the *Grand Duke Constantine*, and it promised a substantial savings in freight charges on the San Francisco ice runs.

In addition, Captain Furuhjelm went to his post in 1859 by way of California with the express purpose of negotiating an annulment of the "Sanders Treaty." The Russian company by that time had realized that the management advantage was entirely with the Americans because of their ability to keep (and juggle) the accounts. The principal reason for the partnership—to obtain timely Ameri-

---

[107]The *Coeur de Lion* had already attracted considerable attention when it arrived at San Francisco on 19 June 1854, on its maiden voyage around the world: "She is very sharp forward, her bow ornamented with a full length figure of the Lion hearted Richard, whilst the stern is rounding and pleasing in its proportions. Forward she has a forecastle below the main deck for the accommodation of the men, and aft a poop cabin forty feet long, divided into two apartments, flanked on either side by large and commodious state rooms. She is owned by Wm. F. Parrot, of Boston, and commanded by Geo. W. Tucker, and will proceed from this port to the East Indies." *Alta California*, 21 June 1854. The ship was delivered to Kronstadt by the same captain four years later. Undated list, with notation "sold to the Russian American Company," DUSC, St. Petersburg, vol. 10 (roll 6, M 81), RG 59, NA. For more construction details and a lovely color painting, see Ray Brighton, *Clippers of the Port of Portsmouth and the Men Who Built Them* (Portsmouth, N. H.: Portsmouth Marine Society, 1985), pp. 54–58.

can capital—had now been served. In the interests of improving their share of the proceeds, the Russian company was even willing to release its own government from the twenty-year commitment it had made by countersigning the Sanders compact, thus losing a legal point in its approaching battle for charter renewal. Furuhjelm successfully made an agreement with the American Russian Commercial Company that basically provided for short-term cash-and-carry arrangements, with prices of commodities and freights to be negotiated periodically by the managers of the two companies.[108] These changes allowed the Russian ice income to double, grossing about $23,000 in 1860.

Selling about four thousand tons in an average year to San Francisco, where Moss and his partners handled the retail trade, the Russian company could use the profits to buy valuable supplies directly from San Francisco without costly exchanges of currency and for relatively prompt delivery. Other problems arose, however: The main source of ice shifted to Wood Island, near Kodiak, far from the administrative center at Sitka where provisions were most needed; warm winters at times left little ice to sell—for example, in 1856, when some ships carrying goods from San Francisco returned there empty; competition appeared from another company, headed by Bernard Peyton, that bought ice carved out from the territory of the Hudson's Bay Company, ironically from the area leased from the Russian company;[109] and unanticipated shipping misfortunes occurred. In 1858 the *Zenobia* was wrecked in San Francisco Bay (though with ice aboard, it remained afloat for several days). Another venerable ice ship, the *Kodiak*, this one belonging to the Russian America Company, sank near Kodiak in 1860. The following year the *Tsaritsa* was pulled by a tug onto rocks as it was leaving Sitka harbor and lost its cargo; out of service for most of a year, it underwent expensive repairs in San Francisco.[110] After the *Tsaritsa* disaster, Furuhjelm wrote that this "ruins all of his plans" to gross $50,000 a year from the ice trade.[111]

[108]Main Office to "the honorable board of the American Russian Commercial Company," 31 October/12 November 1856, complaining of contract (copy), RRAC, CGG, CR, vol. 21 (roll 21, M 11), RG 261, NA; Main Office to Voevodskii, with Furuhjelm's instructions, RRAC, CGG, CR, vol. 22 (roll 22, M 11), RG 261, NA; *Kommercheskaia Gazeta*, 8 January 1860. For a naval inspector's commentary on the ice business, see P. N. Golovin, "Obzor russkikh kolonii v Severnoi Amerike," *Morskoi Sbornik* 57, 1 (January 1862): 107, 124–25, 188 (also published separately).

[109]*Daily Alta California*, 16 March and 6 October 1855.

[110]On *Tsaritsa*, Furuhjelm to Main Office, 4 April 1861, RRAC, CGG, CS, vol. 43 (roll 63, M 11), RG 261, NA. On the *Zenobia*, San Francisco *Daily Evening Bulletin*, 30 April and 1 May 1858; and *Daily Alta California*, 1 May, 1858; and on the *Kodiak*, Furuhjelm to Main Office, 22 June 1860, RRAC, CGG, CS, vol. 42 (roll 63, M 11), RG 261, NA.

[111]Furuhjelm to Kostromitinov, 4 April 1861, RRAC, CGG, CS, vol. 43 (roll 63, M 11), RG 261, NA. The *Tsaritsa* would survive this misfortune and the Russian America Company itself. After many years in the South Pacific, it entered Swedish service in

The Russian America Company tried to develop other resources in their territory to meet its higher expenditures. Coal was first extracted by mining engineer Doroshin in 1854 on the Kenai Peninsula, and some was sold in San Francisco. With ice unavailable, the *Lucas* returned to San Francisco in the summer of 1856 with 500 tons of coal.[112] The company employed Furuhjelm's brother Hjalmar to expand mining operations to the level of several thousand tons a year, but the coal was poor-quality lignite that could not compete with that mined at Bellingham Bay (Oregon Territory) or brought from more distant sources. Even the company's ships found Sakhalin Island coal more suitable and cheaper.[113] Labor was another problem, and the Russian America Company was later criticized for using soldiers, who were supposed to be defending the territory, as miners.[114]

Whaling at first appeared to hold some promise for the company, given the natives' experience in off-shore whaling and the contemporary growth of the industry. An initial trial by the *Suomi* in 1851 had been marginally lucrative for the Russo-Finnish Whaling Company, the joint venture of Finnish merchants and the Russian America Company. Two more ships, the *Aian* and the *Turku*, were sent out from the Baltic but were stranded in Siberian ports during the war at considerable loss. The *Greve Berg* was added to the small Russian whaling fleet in 1857, and the company, on its own initiative, encouraged coastal hunting by the Indians, with the result that small quantities of whale oil could be shipped out each year.[115] The company's profit, if any, was apparently circuitous: Wages given to the native laborers increased their ability to buy more of the company's controlled, imported goods at high prices. The obstacles blocking any substantial direct gains from whaling were insurmountable: Whales were scarce by 1857 because of overhunting by the huge American fleets; the main whaling grounds—the Sea of Okhotsk—were actually farther from Sitka than the chief American whaling base on Maui; neither Russians nor Finns were familiar with the industry; and the company had poor access to central markets for whale oil.

The Amur Region

The Russian America Company also suffered from the growing opposition of the central government to its monopoly position, signaling a rocky road ahead

the Baltic, where it sank during World War I, having sailed on many different seas for over sixty years. Brighton, *Clippers of the Port of Portsmouth*, p. 58.

[112]*Daily Alta California*, 20 September 1856; *Kommercheskaia Gazeta*, 13 January 1859, p. 22.

[113]*Daily Alta California*, 12 January 1858.

[114]Kostlivstev's report, f. 398, op. 24, no. 9196, d. 1860, TsGIA.

[115]Memorandum, 18 April 1860, RRAC, CGG, CR, vol. 23 (roll 23, M 11), RG 261, NA; *Vestnik Promyshlennosti* 2, 4 (April 1859): 4–5.

for charter renewal. In 1856 its Siberian and Sakhalin outposts were transferred to the jurisdiction of the governor-general of Eastern Siberia, Nikolai Murav'ev. The following year, the naval ministry stopped paying its half of the salaries of the naval officers assigned to the company.[116] Behind these moves was a concerted effort by Murav'ev and Grand Duke Constantine to strengthen Russia's economic and naval position in the nearer Far East—that is, around the mouth of the Amur River and the territory to the south referred to as the Amur region (Amuria), or Maritime Provinces. Russian expansion into this sphere was stimulated by a combination of factors—the opening up of Japan by treaty in 1855, continuing instability in China, activities in the area by other Great Powers, especially Britain, and the obstruction of Russian influence and naval development in the Black Sea region by the Treaty of Paris.

Finally, a more progressive administration in St. Petersburg realized the potential of steamship navigation for the Amur River system. The first steamer, the *America*, was sent from New York by Sanders and arrived at the Amur in August 1856, after nearly being stopped by the British in Rio de Janeiro.[117] However, it was primarily an oceangoing ship unsuitable for the river itself. Two river steamers, constructed under the supervision of Capt. Petr Kozakevich, were dispatched from Philadelphia in 1856 in sections aboard the *Europa*, though unloading and assembling them in the shallow waters at the mouth of the Amur proved especially difficult, as Thomas Norton, the mechanic from the *America* who was in charge, discovered.[118] Appropriately named the *Amur* and the *Lena*, they were expected to ply over two thousand miles of the river under their American captains. The commander of the *Amur*, John H. Barr of San Francisco, quickly established a reputation for expert river navigation; he was also adept at superintending the new repair and engineering shops at Nikolaevsk, the machines for which were imported from San Francisco.[119] Another river steamer drawing only two feet was launched at this facility by an American

[116]Main Office to Furuhjelm (Aian), 25 May 1856, RRAC, CGG, CR, vol. 21 (roll 21, M 11), RG 261, NA; and 20 February 1861, RRAC, CGG, CR, vol. 23 (roll 23, M 11), RG 261, NA.

[117]New York *Times*, 29 January 1857; Trousdale to Marcy, 13 February 1856, DUSM, Brazil, vol. 23 (roll 25, M 121), RG 59, NA.

[118]"Interesting from Kamaschatka," *Daily Alta California*, 16 September 1857; N. Nazimov, "O puti po reke Amur v 1857 godu," *Vestnik Imperatorskago Russkago Geograficheskago Obshchestvo* 5 (1857): 25–27; and on conferring the award to Norton: f. 1325, op. 1, no. 716, TsGIA.

[119]"News from the Amoor River," *Daily Alta California*, 13 November 1857. Barr was also apparently a leader of the American community, for he read the "Declaration of Independence" at a Washington's birthday party at Nikolaevsk in 1859. New York *Herald*, 20 April 1859. His services to Russia were officially recognized with a gold medal and a decoration. Murav'ev-Amurskii to Grand Duke Constantine, 4 September 1858, f. 1265, op. 7, no. 188, TsGIA.

named Berlin.[120] Obviously, at the beginning Russia was relying heavily on American assistance in order to develop transportation in the Amur area.

Anxious to establish a claim to the territory through settlement and administrative bases, the Russians encouraged American merchants to bring supplies and operate stores, which was relatively easy since a number of them were already familiar with these waters. Among the first were William H. Boardman of a Boston merchant house whose focus since the eighteenth century had been the Far Eastern trade; William Burling of San Francisco; Matthew Turner, a gold prospector turned ship captain; and Charles Baum, a native of St. Petersburg who had settled in California as a merchant. All of them had helped supply Petropavlovsk and Aian during the Crimean War, and they were soon joined by one of the leading San Francisco merchant-shippers, Charles Wolcott Brooks.

Reaching Nikolaevsk, the new Amur port located twenty-five miles up the river from its mouth, was a real challenge for oceangoing ships because of contrary winds, river currents, shallow waters, and meandering channels. The harsh climate also limited access to less than four months a year. The town, moreover, resembled a makeshift camp and lacked basic amenities. An officer of the *America*, returning on the Russian storeship *Dvina*, reported that "since the time of our landing in Russia we have been most cruelly treated, and forced to sell our clothing or starve, as we were unable to eat Russian food. . . . The most of us are nearly naked, being compelled to throw away shirts, blankets, etc."[121] However, this account was contradicted by another source, and other reports commended Russian hospitality at Nikolaevsk. The varying reactions were at least partly due to an influx of new people, mostly military or naval, as Nikolaevsk replaced Petropavlovsk, which was more exposed and had sustained heavy damage and pillaging during the Crimean War, as the administrative center. The population of Nikolaevsk was reported to be over two thousand by 1858 with consequent developmental and governmental problems.[122]

Officials and private citizens also encouraged civilian settlement in the Amur Valley, one of the first efforts being led by Murav'ev's adjutant, Mikhail

[120]Collins to Cass, 20 September 1859, DUSC, Amoor, vol. 1 (roll 1, T 111), RG 59, NA.

[121]New York *Times*, 29 January 1857, quoting the San Francisco *Herald*. One of the best sources on Russian-American finances in California during this period is none other than William Tecumseh Sherman. See Dwight L. Clarke, *William Tecumseh Sherman: Gold Rush Banker* (San Francisco: California Historical Society, 1969), pp. 154, 195–96, 253.

[122]"From the Russian Possessions," *Daily Alta California*, 22 November 1858; Capt. Bernard Whittingham, *Notes on the Late Expedition against the Russian Settlements in Eastern Siberia* (London: Longman, Brown, Green and Longmans, 1856), p. 138. An eyewitness account of the British destruction by the cabin boy of a whaler is in Henry Hiller Papers, Mystic Seaport.

Volkonskii, son of a famous Decembrist exile.[123] Mennonites from the Ukraine, well known for their industry and agricultural successes, sent a scouting party and were planning to move there—to Murav'ev's delight—and inducements were also offered to foreigners, especially Americans, to settle in the area.[124] Early in 1860 a San Francisco ship captain, J. C. Devries, returned from Nikolaevsk to recruit colonists for a tract of land over one thousand miles up the river.[125] By 1858 the river base of Blagoveshchensk, situated more favorably than Niko-laevsk for internal trade and agriculture, was founded at the junction of the Ussuri with the Amur.

Coordinating this naval build-up and investment of resources in a region that was relatively unexplored and so distant from the Russian capital was obviously not easy. One newspaper reported that Murav'ev was "almost continually en route between the Amoor and St. Petersburg, [where he] has frequent conferences with the Grand Duke Constantine."[126] It is clear that these two officials were the architects of Russia's Amur expansion drive, but Constantine was often away on naval cruises and Murav'ev liked to frequent Paris (with his French wife) as a respite from Irkutsk. Moreover, what had been accomplished along the Amur still lacked firm legal foundation. So, having secured de facto occupation of the Amur, they next pursued, through diplomatic negotiation with China, outright possession for Russia. In assisting them, Foreign Minister Gorchakov enlisted American aid, noting to Seymour that China "*was a power which could only be coerced by fear, or by arguments addressed to its fears.*"[127]

Japan was another mutual concern and received similar treatment. In the summer of 1857, Adm. Evfimii Putiatin, veteran of the attempt to open Japan for Russia in 1853, was sent through Siberia to command the new Pacific steam squadron assembled at Nikolaevsk. Aboard the flagship *America* he set sail for China by way of Nagasaki, where he found that Capt. Konstantin Pos'et had al-

[123]P. F. Unterberger, *Primorskaia oblasti 1856–1898 gg.: Ocherk* (St. Petersburg: Kirshbaum, 1900), p. 47.

[124]Murav'ev-Amurskii (St. Petersburg) to Siberian Committee, 1860, in Ivan Barsu-kov, ed., *Graf Nikolai Nikolaevich Murav'ev-Amurskii—po ego pis'mam, offitsial'nym doku-mentam, razckazam sovremennikov i pechetnym istochnikam (materialy dlia biografii)*, vol. 2 (Moscow: Sinodal. tip., 1891), p. 296, on Mennonite inspection team of 1859.

[125]"Americans Invited to the Amoor Valley," *Daily Alta California*, 28 January 1860. As usual the newspaper exaggerated the opportunities for development of the region, comparing the Amur with the Mississippi: "Prairies of vast extent open out at many points, trees being always thickly interspersed with the open spaces. No country on the earth surpasses these wooded plains in the richness of their grasses. Nowhere do cattle thrive better. The cereal grains can be cultivated almost everywhere, though very little attention has yet been paid, except to rye, which makes the bread of the peasantry."

[126]New York *Herald*, 27 December 1857.

[127]Seymour to Marcy, 17/29 May 1856, DUSM, Russia, vol. 17 (roll 17, M 35), RG 59, NA (underlining in original).

ready laid the groundwork for a commercial treaty with Japan in cooperation
with the first American minister to that country, Townsend Harris. Returning
the next summer, Putiatin completed the negotiation with the help of Harris
(and the attendance of two American warships) that formally inaugurated diplomatic relations between Russia and Japan. The United States and Russia thus
assisted each other in establishing a strong presence in that country.

In May 1858 Murav'ev took advantage of the weakness of China during its
conflict with Britain and France and won concessions from the regional commander at Aigun (on the right bank of the Amur near Blagoveshchensk). Russia obtained the right of passage on both the Amur and the Ussuri rivers and
possession of the left (north) bank of the Amur from Aigun to the sea. However,
this "Aigun Treaty" left the important territory between the Amur and the Ussuri under a vague, shared administration. About the same time at Tientsin, Putiatin, abetted by American envoy William B. Reed, secured for Russia the same
commercial privileges in China as the other western powers had. A subsequent
agreement concluded in 1860 in Peking resolved the Far Eastern border in favor
of Russia. China ceded to Russia full rights to all of the territory yet in dispute
or under technical joint administration between the Ussuri and the coast and
from the mouth of the Amur south along the shore to the Gulf of Tartary, where
Fort Vladimir Vostok (Vladivostok) had just been established. This seemed to
set the permanent border with China in this region; nevertheless, over a hundred years later, during a time of especially tense Sino-Soviet relations and while
major military clashes were occurring along this border, the People's Republic of
China would challenge the legality of these "treaties."

The Collins Mission

This new commercial and political activity in the Far East naturally attracted
the attention of Americans, especially those in California who seemed to have
their eyes glued on the western horizon. An early enthusiast was Perry McDonough Collins, a former army officer who had moved from Hyde Park, New
York, to New Orleans and then to Sonoma, north of San Francisco, where he
practiced law, dabbled in real estate, and opened a bank. In 1856 he set out on
the journey around the world that would make him famous. What initially motivated this venture is not exactly clear; perhaps he had learned about new opportunities in the Russian Far East from the local press and from others who
had already been there, especially those with Lt. John Rodgers's exploring
squadron. Collins indicated in a letter to President Pierce that the Crimean War
had called his attention to Russia's advances, "at which time it was first made
known the vast strides she had recently made toward the *re-annexation* of the
Amoor country." He also emphasized that "it is a country of vast resources and

considerable trade, and that the commerce may be made very advantageous to the United States."[128]

Following Sanders's example, Collins traveled from San Francisco to Washington, where he conferred with Stoeckl and, with the help of Sen. William McKendree Gwin, obtained an appointment as "United States Commercial Agent for the Amur." Setting off across the Atlantic, he arrived on 17 May 1856 in St. Petersburg, where he encountered more than the usual obstacles and delays regarding his status:

> The difficulty seems to rest in the fact that the "Amoor" has been hitherto, and is now, a *secret* country, consequently not open to foreign commerce, and the question has to be now acted upon for the first time, (my appointment being the first from any foreign nation to that country) by the Government of Russia whether it is politic to open this country to other nations. There would be no difficulty, if only the United States was concerned, but in opening it to us, other nations (particularly England) would be admitted under reciprocal clauses in commercial treaties.[129]

Collins, with Seymour's backing, then asked simply for permission to travel to the area but had to await Murav'ev's return from Paris for a decision. In his subsequent conference with Murav'ev in August at the governor's St. Petersburg residence, he found Murav'ev very supportive of his plans and enthusiastic about the future of the Amur. Assured of necessary papers and assistance, Collins linked up with Bernard Peyton, another Californian bent on making a fortune in Siberia, and journeyed on to Moscow. There they visited with Sergei Volkonskii, the Decembrist long exiled in Irkutsk, and others, such as Prince

---

[128]Collins (Washington) to Pierce, 29 February 1856, DUSC, Amoor, vol. 1 (roll 1, T 111), RG 59, NA; Stoeckl to Gorchakov, 10/22 December 1856, f. kants. Vashington 1857, d. 183, AVPR. Collins's book, *A Voyage Down the Amoor: with a Land Journey through Siberia, and Incidental Notices of Manchooria, Kamschatka, and Japan* (New York: D. Appleton and Company, 1860), was dedicated to Murav'ev and was widely read. For a later version, edited by Charles Vevier, see *Siberian Journey Down the Amur to the Pacific, 1856–1857* (Madison: University of Wisconsin Press, 1962), and, for additional details of Collins's life, see Vevier's introduction, pp. 10–13.

The well-known traveler and lecturer Bayard Taylor had also planned to make this trip across Siberia in 1857: "He contemplates returning home by the route across Northern Asia, Siberia and Mantchouria to the mouth of the Amour, whence he will take ship for Oregon or California." Baltimore *American and Commercial Advertiser*, 11 July 1856.

[129]Collins (St. Petersburg) to Marcy, 24 July 1856, DUSC, Amoor, vol. 1 (roll 1, T 111), RG 59, NA; Seymour to Collins, 31 October/12 November 1856, DUSM, Russia, vol. 17 (roll 17, M 35), RG 59, NA.

Aleksei Golitsyn, who were well informed about the area.[130] In mid-December he and Peyton departed on the long, cold trek with members of Murav'ev's suite through Nizhni Novgorod, Kazan, and Tomsk to Irkutsk. They arrived on 7 January 1857 and, to their surprise, met Captain Hudson, traveling through Siberia from the other direction after delivering the *America*.[131]

Collins's reports back to Washington in his "official" capacity were filled with details of the region and optimism about its potential for American business. During the winter, he and Bernard Peyton were wined and dined by Murav'ev and other officials and merchants in Irkutsk and at Kiakhta, the nearby trading center on the Chinese border.[132] The governor had originally intended to accompany Collins down the Amur in the spring but then decided to postpone his trip until the next year, when Grand Duke Constantine planned to descend the Amur and sail across the Pacific to the United States. That summer Collins continued his journey with Johann Furuhjelm (who spoke English fluently) of the Russian America Company, reaching Nikolaevsk by July. After several weeks at the mouth of the Amur, Collins made his way across the Pacific with stops in Japan and Honolulu before landing in San Francisco at the end of November, almost two years after his departure.[133] By February 1858 he was back in Washington to file with Secretary of State Cass a detailed report of his travels, which, under the sponsorship of Senator Gwin, was subsequently read into the *Congressional Record* and published separately.[134]

The "junket" of Collins was covered by the press in a manner that resembled a modern publicity campaign. The emphasis was on the vast riches of the Amur

[130]Bernard Peyton (Moscow) to his wife, 2 December 1856, Peyton Letters (typescript copies, location of originals unknown), Manuscript Division, NYPL.

[131]Collins (Irkutsk) to Marcy, 31 January 1857, DUSC, Amoor, vol. 1 (roll 1, T 111), RG 59, NA.

[132]Collins (Irkutsk) to Marcy, 5 March 1857, ibid.; Peyton (Irkutsk) to his wife, 5/17 January 1857, Peyton Letters, Manuscript Division, NYPL. Peyton's private letters supplement Collins's official and public ones, though Peyton was obviously bored with Collins's pomposity. On the occasion of a grand dinner given to them by Murav'ev on 25 January, Peyton observed: "Everything was going on swimmingly and I said to myself 'now if Collins will only keep quiet and not make a speech our fortunes are made.' He is possessed of the erroneous idea that whenever and wherever one's health is drank he must make a speech and has thereby made himself ridiculous several times. I had rather contain the demon spirit that entered the hogs and impelled them down the mountain side into the sea." And after Collins replied to Murav'ev's toast to "America and Russia" with a lengthy oration, "I experienced the pangs of death. At the conclusion of his remarks, Mouravieff leaned across the table and kissed him, tho' he had not understood a word." Peyton (Irkutsk to his wife, 18/30 January 1857, Peyton Letters, Manuscript Division, NYPL.

[133]Collins (Sonoma) to Cass, 17 December 1857, DUSC, Amoor, vol. 1 (roll 1, T 111), RG 59, NA.

[134]Collins (Washington) to Cass, 8 March 1858, ibid.

region, the special and repeated invitations by Russia to American enterprise, and Collins's individual accomplishments. His official commission from Washington, even though unrecognized by Russia, gave him and his mission greater scope and influence. As outlined in a letter to Seymour from Moscow, Collins's chief goal was to establish a continuous line of communication by steamers on the Amur, Lake Baikal, and other Siberian streams, with a railroad to connect Lake Baikal with the Amur—all to serve the purpose of developing resources and markets by means of American skill and enterprise.[135]

Other Russian-American Pacific Connections

Although Collins was not alone in pursuing Russian-American transpacific projects, the exploits of other people were less well known. For example, Bernard Peyton also left California for St. Petersburg and Siberia about the same time as Collins, but he went westward across the Pacific and through Canton, Calcutta, and Cairo. Originally from Virginia, Peyton had joined the business rush to California, becoming a merchant-shipper in San Francisco (Fernandez and Peyton). He also competed with the American Russian Commercial Company by importing ice from the Hudson's Bay Company territory. His rival bought him out to preserve its monopoly over Russian (Alaska) ice, and it was probably this money that financed Peyton's trip to Russia. Intentionally reticent about his plans, Peyton arrived in St. Petersburg two months after Collins, about whom he commented in a private letter to his wife:

> There is a gentleman here named Collins—appointed Am. Consul at the Amoor River, who made application two months ago for permission to proceed overland to the Pacific. He has not received an answer. That however is because he made his request thro' the United States Ambassador. Now I have nothing to do with the Ambassador—except to go to his house to read the newspapers—and will have an answer and be gone from the Country while Collins is still sucking his thumbs under ministerial auspices.[136]

Nevertheless, Peyton joined Collins in Moscow, and they traveled together to Irkutsk and Kiakhta. While Collins waited for the Amur to thaw, Peyton, in a hurry to get home, retraced his steps to St. Petersburg and then crossed the At-

---

[135]Collins (Moscow) to Seymour, 5/17 November 1856, DPR, Russia, vol. 4481, RG 84, NA.

[136]Peyton (St. Petersburg) to his wife, 8 August 1856, Peyton Letters, Manuscript Division, NYPL. See also Saul, "An American's Siberian Dream," pp. 405–20. Collins never mentions Peyton in his official correspondence, leaving the impression that he is traveling completely alone. An obscure reference in his book led a later editor to misidentify Peyton as John Lewis Peyton, a well-known traveler. Vevier, *Siberian Journey*, pp. 3, 52.

lantic, reaching California several months ahead of Collins. Peyton's project involved simply reversing the flow of supplies into Siberia, which now moved overland through European Russia. Peyton's route would take goods from the United States over the Pacific through the Amur basin:

> There is in the southern part of Siberia a large district of fertile—well culti-vated country—with a population of half a millon of white people who are supplied with foreign goods from Petersburg—thirty five hundred miles off, requiring two years for transport. Their furs and other productions are likewise carried over the same road to a market. Those people are rich and consume largely of foreign goods even at the enormous prices they have to pay for transportation. The Amoor River emptying into the Pacific north of China is nearly as long as the Mississippi, navigable as high as the rich district I speak of.[137]

Nothing, however, came of this plan, since by the time Peyton reached California in August 1857, several others were already very much involved in this same trade.[138]

First and foremost among them was Boardman, who is not known to have ever visited the region himself. Well established in the "Eastern trade," he had extended it to the Russian possessions even before the Crimean War. During that conflict he ran supplies into Petropavlovsk with the help of Harrison G. O. Chase, and he sent George S. Cushing to open a factory-store at Nikolaevsk that was the largest and most permanent of the early establishments there. Stoeckl asked him once if this business was profitable, and according to the minister, Boardman replied, "Not very, but I keep to these affairs because they are 'out of the way business.' "[139] That was probably an understatement.

[137]Peyton (London) to his wife, 9 September 1856, Peyton Letters, Manuscript Division, NYPL. He apparently also talked with Seymour about his plans, as the latter wrote privately to Cass: "Mr. Peyton would be able to give you, as the result of his personal observations much information not to be found in books, not only interesting, but of possible utility to the advancement of our commerce with Northern Asia." Seymour to Cass, 9/21 April 1856, DPR, Russia, vol. 4481, RG 84, NA.

[138]The financial crisis of 1857 may also have hindered the follow-up to grand plans. Peyton prospered nonetheless. He returned to California as superintendent of the California Powder Works at Santa Cruz. A merger of this operation with the Du Pont enterprises was sealed with the marriage of his son (also Bernard) to Anne Du Pont and ensured his descendants a prominent position in that financial empire. See Norman B. Wilkinson, *Lammot Du Pont and the American Explosives Industry, 1850-1884* (Charlottesville: University Press of Virginia, 1984), pp. 251-52; and Leon Rowland, *Annals of Santa Cruz* (Santa Cruz, 1947), p. 154.

[139]Stoeckl cited this as an example of the "adventurous spirit" of Americans, as "they

Perry Collins revealed his high respect for Boardman's business acumen by appointing first Cushing and then Chase as his "vice-commercial-agents for the Amur." However, he contended that San Francisco was the more logical American base for trade to the Amur area than distant Boston:

> San Francisco is naturally the point from whence the Amoor commerce will be most advantageously prosecuted on our side. Of course ships may sail as they have already from Boston, Philadelphia and New York to the Amoor; or may from any other point, but, San Francisco laying nearly opposite and also convenient, the direct trade will naturally concentrate there—two commercial houses have already been established by San Francisco merchants, also two from Boston at the Amoor, showing the fact of a trade already springing up.[140]

The San Francisco merchant who became most actively involved at this time was Otto Esche, who had previously operated a shipping business in South America. A Hamburg bark, the *Oscar*, cleared San Francisco in his name in May 1857 with a large and assorted cargo that included a substantial quantity of whiskey, wine, and other spirits; basic commodities such as flour, beans, salt, olive oil, candles, matches, coffee, and "groceries"; such practical construction needs as nails, spikes, bricks, window glass, and cement; furniture, clothing, agricultural implements, and a pool table and piano.[141] Sailing on the *Oscar*, Esche himself visited the Amur, where he chartered the Russian brig *Conrad* for a shipment of Siberian beef and hams, hempseed, and Japanese beans and returned to San Francisco by way of Shanghai.[142] Encouraged by the friendly Russian reception and initial profits, Esche went back to Nikolaevsk in 1858 to journey all the way up the river with his associate Henry Jacoby, reaching St. Petersburg in early January 1859. The accounts of their trip were published in a number of

see in our Asiatic possessions new countries to exploit for their commerce. The difficulties do not discourage them, and they spare neither their energy nor their capital in surmounting them." Stoeckl to Gorchakov, 30 January/11 February 1858, f. kants. Vashington 1858, d. 185, AVPR.

[140]Collins (Washington) to Cass, 6 March 1858, DUSC, Amoor, vol. 1 (roll 1, T 111), RG 59, NA. The other Boston merchant involved in the trade was Henry Pierce, whose agent at Nikolaevsk was F. A. Hall. San Franciscans also expected an Asian destiny: "From the lights now before us, it is pretty evident that at no distant day San Francisco will monopolize the greater portion of the trade of Eastern Siberia, Mongolia, and Mantchouria. The population of these regions cannot be far short of ten or twelve millions. They are in want of almost every thing, except breadstuffs." "The Siberian Trade," *Alta California*, 27 December 1858.

[141]*Daily Alta California*, 12 May 1857.

[142]Ibid., 11 and 13 November 1857, and "Some Account of the Amoor River," San Francisco *Evening Bulletin*, 13 November 1857.

American newspapers, again with an emphasis on progress and opportunity for Americans in the area.[143]

Before departing on his long passage back to San Francisco, Esche consigned one of the most unusual Siberian exports to the United States on board the schooner *Caroline E. Foote*. About thirty Bactrian camels had been collected at Nikolaevsk by Correns, Esche's agent, in the fall of 1859. Only about half survived the winter and the voyage to San Francisco, but the remainder created a sensation when they landed in July 1860.[144] This was not the first importation of camels into the United States, since the army was experimenting in Texas with some brought from the Ottoman Empire. Nor were they a particularly valuable cargo; Collins noted earlier that they could be purchased for $22.50 a head along the Amur. However, after a second shipment augmented their number to about thirty, the camels' presence in California certainly did more to publicize the new trade with Russian Asia than any other item. There were demonstrations and exhibitions in the city and newspaper discussions about their usefulness for carrying supplies to mining camps through desert and mountain terrain. The camels were then auctioned off at the San Francisco Bay District Fair in October.[145]

Russia's Far Eastern Policies

The expansion of Russian-American activities in the Amur region was thus spurred by adventurous American enterprise and optimistic projections of profits and success on the one hand and by an aggressive Russian administration on the other. The Russian effort was spearheaded by Grand Duke Constantine and Count Murav'ev-Amurskii, who in 1858 had been granted the special title in recognition of his contribution to the Amur annexation. Their support staffs included Adm. Evfimii Putiatin, Gen. Mikhail Korsakov (Siberian Cossack commander), Egor Kovalevskii (head of the Asiatic department in St. Petersburg), Capt. Gennadii Nevel'skoi (Amur explorer), Adm. Petr Kosakevich (governor of Nikolaevsk), Berngardt Struve (Murav'ev's assistant and publicist), and Aleksandr Shelikhov (another Murav'ev assistant). A key figure in the formation of policy was, of course, Prince Alexander Gorchakov, the foreign minister. The physical distances involved, conflicting information about the condi-

[143]Pickens reported in detail on the Esche-Jacoby trip. Pickens to Cass, 10 January 1859, DUSM, Russia, vol. 18 (roll 18, M 35), RG 59, NA. Details of Esche's career are found in *Daily Alta California*, 28 July 1860.

[144]"Tartar Camels for the North American Deserts," *Daily Alta California*, 27 July 1860.

[145]Collins to Cass, 6 March 1858, DUSC, Amoor, vol. 1 (roll 1, T 111), RG 59, NA. *Alta California*, 3 and 10 October 1860. On Correns's role, see "From the Amoor River," *Alta California*, 12 December 1859.

tion of travel and commerce on the Amur, an approaching crisis for the Russian America Company concerning its charter renewal, and the concentration of most of Russian officialdom on preparing for extensive internal reforms—all these circumstances made development and coordination of policy difficult, to say the least.

While invariably Russian officials endorsed American initiatives in the region and seemed pleased with the results, they also at times worked at cross-purposes. In his first meeting with Francis Pickens in the summer of 1858, Gorchakov aggressively pursued American cooperation and assistance in the Far East:

> He desired also to impress me with the idea that it was the earnest desire of his Government that we should act together in our Chinese negotiations, with cordiality and mutual understanding. I replied that I knew it was the desire of my Government that such should be the case, and then further said, that we had no peculiar interest in the war that Great Britain or France might be involved in with China, and that I understood such was the case as to Russia, and that I hoped therefore we would feel together in opening, by commercial treaties with China, such advantages in Commerce and Trade as would benefit all parties.[146]

But Murav'ev-Amurskii followed contradictory policies. He encouraged American economic involvement in the Far East and in Siberia, advocated the application of principles of free trade in developing the area, but also condoned the granting of exclusive privileges to Russians.

For example, both Murav'ev-Amurskii and Gorchakov lent support to the effort of a group of Siberian merchants to form early in 1858 the Amur Company, chartered by the government with monopoly rights to trade along the Amur.[147] Collins, who returned to Russia in August 1858, saw this development as limiting American opportunities in the area and was especially chagrined to learn that the new company was buying vessels in western Europe rather than in the United States for its Far Eastern business.[148] News of this apparent restriction of

[146]Pickens to Cass, 22 October 1858, DUSM, Russia, vol. 18 (roll 18, M 35), RG 59, NA.

[147]Memorandum of conversation with Murav'ev, 5/17 January 1858, enclosure in Pickens to Cass, 14/26 January 1858, DUSM, Russia, vol. 17 (roll 17, M 35), RG 59, NA.

[148]Collins to Cass, 20 September 1859, DUSC, Amoor, vol. 1 (roll 1, T 111), RG 59, NA. Chase was reporting at the same time from Nikolaevsk "that the Amoor Co's operations here up to the present time, are of very little importance, and their doings principally have been, the erecting of magazines, purchasing of houses, preparing of places for the putting together of the steamboats to arrive." Chase to Collins, 7/19 September

the Siberian market was probably one cause of some slackening of American initiative at the time and may account for the failure of Bernard Peyton, for one, to follow up on his project for California-Siberian trade.

Though initially well capitalized by stock subscribers at 3 million rubles, the Amur Company ran counter to the current fashion of free trade and seemed ultimately to have only the lukewarm backing of the central government and of Murav'ev-Amurskii. Regardless, it soon met with almost complete disaster after sinking most of its resources in four new ships, only one of which survived the long voyage to its Pacific destination. Within a few years of its founding the company was in liquidation.

Another barrier to policymaking was a difference in objectives between Murav'ev-Amurskii and Grand Duke Constantine. While the former continued to work for internal progress in Siberia through increased settlement and the development of the Amur waterway, the naval minister emphasized the establishment of naval stations along the coast, a policy that was independent of Amur commercial successes. The staff officers who supported this position—such as the grand duke's Far Eastern naval representative, Admiral Putiatin—waged an effective publicity campaign, arguing that the improvement of coastal stations should have priority over resources for the Amur River or Siberia. In an unusually colloquial letter, written from St. Petersburg late in 1859, Collins insightfully grasped the behind-the-scenes turmoil over Russian expansion policy:

> It cannot be disguised that there is considerable rivalry and jealousy between Count Putiachin and Count Mouravieff Amousky, in which there is perhaps a little personal bitter mixed. Some think (the old ones) that Captain, Major, Colonel, Governor General, Lieutenant General, now Count Mouravieff Amoorsky, has gone ahead rather fast, and that the Amoor projects are too much used for personal aggrandisement, therefore they would check the Amoor Count. That Count P. in his Pie-Ho treaty should have looked more after Chinese Sea Ports being an Admiral (this was natural enough) than after land ports, particularly the Amoor, seems to be admitted, leaving Mouravieff not yet Count to shift upon the Amoor for himself. But General Mouravieff,

1859, ibid. And Collins, from St. Petersburg, noted: "But while the Amoor Co. is stumbling over its true interests with all of its favorable privileges, private enterprise is slowly but surely making headway in the solution of the real difficulty which bars the way to the development of our commerce at the Amoor. . . . It only arises from the miserable stupidity of its management here and at Irkutsk that as yet next to nothing has been done in comparison with what should have been accomplished with its means and outlay. But most undertakings of this nature are badly managed in Russia because of the want of alacrity in commercial transactions, and the great number of employees who are generally pensioned upon such enterprises and who succeed pretty surely in leeching the concern of nearly all vitality in a very short period." Collins to Cass, 1 May 1860, DUSC, Amoor, vol. 1 (roll 1, T 111), RG 59, NA.

now Count, in virtue of his Igoon [Aigun] Treaty, was not to be left in the lurch, and with new diplomatic and some little fighting power, while Count P. was reposing in France or England on his Pie-Ho laurels; pushes down the Amoor and out to Sea, whips to the Yellow Sea, pushes his courier up to Pekin and . . . steams off to Jeddo, surveys and takes possession of all the country, seas, harbours, rivers and coasts not to be found on Chinese or Japanese maps; . . . flashes along the borders of the Amoor, and may be looked for here within a month fighting the battles of Young Russia with progress in one hand and commerce in the other against those who stand firm in the old paths and will not give way to any bold novelties—It is to be seen which will conquer.[149]

The principal forum for the quite-active debate in Russia was the journal of the naval ministry, *Morskoi Sbornik*. The controversy was set in motion in 1859 with a strongly anti-Amur article by Dmitri Zavalishin, the Decembrist exiled in Chita who, forty years earlier, had campaigned for Russian expansion in California. He stressed the most negative aspects of the area and argued for a concentration of Russian resources on Siberia proper and the American territory. He was countered by Dmitri Romanov, a strong supporter of Amur development, who criticized Zavalishin for relying on inferior secondhand sources and emphasized the value of exploiting the potential of the Amur by using the latest technology—steam-powered riverboats, a permanent, modern naval presence, and telegraphic communications.[150]

By 1863 a more reasoned argument was advanced by Dmitri Afanas'ev, who, from a four-year residence in Nikolaevsk, admitted that conditions were far from ideal and that the town could still be likened to a rough mining camp. However, he justified the initial Russian position there by the necessity of preventing the British from taking it.[151] Now the best must be made of the possession, and proper development would take time. The navy, Afanas'ev continued, must be the prime instrument of Russian authority, so the coastal bases such as Vladivostok must take precedence over projects for the inland river. Like others, he disapproved of Russian reliance on the American commercial expansion for the Amur trade, noting that the objects of import were often of poor quality—

[149]Collins to Cass, 20 November 1859, DUSC, St. Petersburg, vol. 11 (roll 11, M 81), RG 59, NA.

[150]D. Afanas'ev, "Amurskii krai i ego znachenie," *Morskoi Sbornik* 69, 11 (November 1863): 58; Leon Rozental', *Ocherk deiatel'nosti aktsionernykh obshchestv v techenie 1862 i 1863 g.* (St. Petersburg: tip. "Obshchestvennaia Pol'za," 1865), table 2; D. Romanov, "Amur," *Morskoi Sbornik* 47, 6 (May 1860): 173–87.

[151]Afanas'ev, "Amurskii krai," pp. 3–86.

"the trash of Hamburg and San Francisco"—and he recommended that the navy promote trade with Japan and China instead.[152]

Murav'ev-Amurskii was at a disadvantage because of his distant location, lack of direct connections with the royal family, and his reputation of being too independent of St. Petersburg. Perhaps he was also being held responsible for the Amur Company debacle. In any event, the hero of Russian Far Eastern expansion relinquished his post as "dictator" of Siberia in 1861 for a more comfortable life of exile in Paris. The position was assumed by his loyal and obedient but less ambitious lieutenant, General Korsakov. This changing of the guard was accompanied by a Russian naval buildup on the coast, centered on the new base of Vladivostok. The navy seemed to have won the round.

American optimism concerning Amur regional development also had shifted by 1860. In 1858 the *Alta California* could still rhapsodize about it:

On the confines of the northeastern shore of Asia, the work of colonization has been commenced, and Russia is launching out untold millions to build up new strongholds, and strengthen her commercial power. The valley of the Amoor, and the plains of Manchooria are about to become the theatre of colonization upon an extended scale, boasting a huge, thriving and industrious population.[153]

Though this promise remained the dominant theme in the American press, other appraisals began to surface. The same newspaper published an account of a visit by American missionary V. D. Collins (apparently not related to Perry McD. Collins) to Nikolaevsk, which he described as

a town of convicts and soldiers, excepting, of course, the higher classes. . . . I would recommend no one to go to the Amoor, either for business, sightseeing, or pleasure. The town is built of logs, and situated on the northern bank of the river, on the margin of a pine forest that stretches away over the dark mountain. As you have already published a part of Mr. Mc-Collins report on the Amoor country, I will add nothing more, except to say that all Americans in Nicolaifsky consider said report much too flattering.[154]

This sentiment was repeated by the semiofficial American agent in Nikolaevsk, who stressed in a report to Perry Collins "the want of an efficient, and sufficient population, of the right sort, to rapidly develop the resources of the

[152]D. Afanas'ev, "Nikolaevsk na Amure," *Morskoi Sbornik* 75, 12 (December 1864): 109–12. For another critique, see A. Michi, *Puteshestvie po Amuru i Vostochnoi Sibiri . . .* (St. Petersburg: Vol'f, 1868).

[153]"Russia and Her Progress," *Alta California*, 12 November 1858.

[154]"A Visit to the Amoor River," *Alta California*, 7 May 1860.

country." He also noted that "the trade of the place has not of late been so particularly satisfactory and encouraging to Americans as . . . appears to have been
generally expected in the United States."[155] Collins, meanwhile, had turned his
attention elsewhere. Hoping to capitalize on the initial failure of a transatlantic
cable, he was promoting his own telegraphic project, to connect the two continents by way of the Amur and the Bering Straits, thus establishing direct communications between the eastern United States and Russia and western Europe
through Siberia.[156]

The Russian America Company under Pressure

The ascendancy of Grand Duke Constantine and the navy in the Russian Far
East continued, but it was not immediately consolidated. The tsar's brother was
very much involved in the preparations for the serfs' emancipation and was often away from St. Petersburg on extended cruises with Baltic naval squadrons in
the Mediterranean. Moreover, he still faced a significant obstacle to his plans to
concentrate Russian strategic development on the Vladivostok base and a
Japan-Korea-China orbit—the Russian America Company and its determination to secure a charter renewal and additional resources for Alaska. Already by
December 1857, Grand Duke Constantine had declared his opposition to the
company, and he began pressing for the abolition of its privileges from that
date. He engineered a transfer of government jurisdiction over the company
from the Ministry of State Domains to the economy-minded Ministry of Finance and then instigated the sending of an inspection team, consisting of
Capt. Pavel Golovin of the navy and Sergei Kostlivstev of the Ministry of Finance, through the United States to Alaska. They were clearly charged with
finding all possible negative and critical points about the functioning of the
company. Several weeks in bustling San Francisco, where they stayed with Kostromitinov and were entertained by Joseph Mora Moss and Senator Gwin, certainly provided them with a convenient sharp contrast to the Russian establishments in North America.[157]

The Russian America Company was especially vulnerable during this period

[155]Chase (Nikolaevsk) to Collins (St. Petersburg), 20 February/3 March 1860, DUSC,
Amoor, vol. 1 (roll 1, T 111), RG 59, NA.

[156]Collins (St. Petersburg) to Cass, 1 May 1860, ibid. For one of the first press reports
of the Collins telegraph enterprise in Russia, see "Russia and the United States," an editorial in *Alta California*, 22 December 1859, predicting that "a direct communication
would be obtained between St. Petersburg and New York."

[157]Golovin, "Obzor russkikh kolonii v Severnoi Amerike," pp. 19–192. Supporting
letters to his family were edited by a friend, Voin Rimskii-Korsakov (brother of the com-
poser): "Iz putevykh pisem P. N. Golovina," *Morskoi Sbornik* 66, 5 (May 1863): 101–82,
and 6 (June 1863): 275–340. These have been handsomely edited and translated by
Basil Dmytryshyn and E. A. P. Crownhart-Vaughan, as *Civil and Savage Encounters: The*

Grand Duke Constantine. Engraving by J. C. Buttre from
Loubat's Mission to Russia, *1866*

of reform in Russia for its treatment of the Indian population of its territory. Though some enlightened steps had been taken upon the initiative of such leaders as churchman Ivan Veniaminov (Archimandrite Innokentii), they were focused primarily on the expanding creole population and on religion and education, which usually meant Russianization. The Tlingit Indians, however, continued to resent the presence of the Russian administration and its efforts not only to exploit them but also to integrate them into a western society. Under Furuhjelm's superintendency, the company was making important new investments in its commercial operations and attempting to respond to criticisms of native conditions. Unfortunately, these efforts were limited by the personnel and resources available and came too late to erase what was a fairly dismal record of achievement over the course of many years. The company also suffered from a run of bad luck; for example, not only did submerged rocks severely dam-

Worldly Travel Letters of an Imperial Russian Navy Officer, 1860–1861 (Portland: Oregon Historical Society, 1983). Golovin, who was to serve on the review committee, died shortly after returning to St. Petersburg.

age the pride of its shipping fleet, the *Tsaritsa*, as it was being towed out of Sitka harbor with a full load of ice in April 1861, but the calamity was witnessed and carefully recorded by the navy-finance inspection team.[158]

Moreover, the initiatives taken by the company contributed to its dependency on the United States—for the ice trade, for supplies, for ship repairs, and even for the purchase and shipping of tea from China, its most lucrative business. Since the early 1850s the latter had been handled by the Augustine Heard Company of Boston from its offices in Shanghai and other China ports. Wishing to expand this enterprise, Augustine Heard, Jr., visited St. Petersburg with his London agent in September and October 1859 and met with the directors of the company headed by Adm. Adolf Etholin. He found Etholin optimistic about future increases in tea sales in Russia but desperately wanting to extend the company's Asian trade. As Heard reported back to the home office:

> He is very anxious to do something on ice. The Company have houses, machines and all the paraphernalia of the business, and can undersell probably any others. Their idea is to supply Hongkong, Manila, Singapore, Calcutta, etc., proceeds to be remitted to us: but I don't exactly understand the way the ships would have to be managed, or what ships would be employed. . . . Meanwhile take measures for getting information from the above places. A little done in that way would be appreciated by the Company.[159]

Heard had identified a basic company weakness—shipping—but he was more sanguine about the possibilities of selling Russian-Alaskan timber in China. As one step in the direction of increased Alaska-China trade, he pursued and obtained the Russian consulship in Shanghai for his brother.[160]

Considering this new Pacific activity, the continuing American expansionist mood, and the rising of a reform spirit in Russia, it is surprising that the selling or buying of Alaska did not stir more attention, especially since the idea had already surfaced during the Crimean War through the "Cottman mission." Grand Duke Constantine, reacting to the financial costs of holding Alaska dur-

[158]Golovin to family, 31 March/12 April 1861, in Rimskii-Korsakov, "Iz putevykh pisem," pp. 305–6.

[159]Augustus Heard, Jr. (St. Petersburg), to Augustus Heard, Sr. (Boston), 30 September 1859, Heard Collection I, HM-12 (Letters Received, 1853–59), Baker Library, Harvard Business School.

[160]Heard, Jr. (London), to Heard, Sr., 24 October 1859, ibid. The extensive Heard Papers have been very little used by scholars. With the decline of the fur market by the 1850s, the monopoly of tea imports by sea was the most important economic privilege of the Russian America Company, one that also drew the ire of Russia's free traders. This was only a wholesale privilege, however, the retail operations being mostly in the hands of the Borisovskii brothers of Moscow. *Vestnik Promyshlennosti*, no. 2 (1859): 113–14.

ing the war and pursuing his own interests in an economical, modern, and strategically concentrated navy, raised the issue at the end of 1857. However, the Americans and Russians most directly involved, such as Moss, Heard, Collins, Boardman, Esche, Furuhjelm, and Kostromitinov, had everything to gain from the continuation of the existing territorial and trade arrangements. After that, the leaders of both countries, including the grand duke, became absorbed in domestic matters. In the meantime, the company's twenty-year charter was set to expire at the end of 1861. The directors in St. Petersburg prepared their case with a draft of a new charter to be reviewed by a special committee, but no action was taken while the Golovin-Kostlivstev inspection mission was still at work.

Meanwhile, at the beginning of 1860, the first direct official discussions about the possibility of a jurisdictional change for Russia's American possessions occurred in Washington, apparently initiated by Senator Gwin and President Buchanan.[161] They formally asked Stoeckl if the Russian government would consider ceding the territory. Acting Secretary of State John Appleton also interviewed Stoeckl "very confidentially" on behalf of the president and mentioned a figure of $5 million. In his report on these conversations, the minister made clear his own position in favor of such a transaction, noting that the company flourished no more now than twenty years ago, that the territory was too far north to attract settlers, that the direction of affairs was in the hands of "foreigners" living in St. Petersburg, and, most important, that a sale would add a new preponderance to the American Pacific position vis-à-vis Great Britain.[162]

Gorchakov's response was that any decision must await the return of the in-

---

[161]The subject of Russian America rarely came up in Stoeckl's dispatches. Once in 1857, the minister saw President Buchanan about a rumor that Brigham Young was threatening to move the Mormons to Canada or Alaska. The president, Stoeckl reported, thought the idea was amusing, and when asked if they would come as conquerors or peaceful settlers, he responded: "It is up to you to decide that question. As far as we are concerned we would be happy to be rid of them." Stoeckl advised his government that while the whole thing was premature, "if realized we would be faced with the alternatives of resisting with force or renouncing part of our territory." Stoeckl to Gorchakov, 20 November/2 December 1857, f. kants. Vashington 1857, d. 183, AVPR.

[162]Stoeckl to Gorchakov, 23 December/4 January 1860, f. kants. Vashington 1860, d. 195, AVPR. Gwin was a noted expansionist, but his precise role in the affair remains unclear in his memoirs and to historians. See Hallie M. McPherson, "The Interest of William McKendree Gwin in the Purchase of Alaska, 1854–1861," *Pacific Historical Review* 3, 1 (March 1934): 28–38. Nor do the memoirs of Gwin's Japanese private secretary reveal anything about his interest in purchasing Alaska. "Joseph Heico [sic], a Christianized Japanese," *Frank Leslie's Illustrated Newspaper*, 1 May 1858, and Joseph Heco, *The Narrative of a Japanese: What He Has Seen and the People He Has Met in the Course of the Last Forty Years* (Yokohama: n. p., n. d.), 1: 145–68. Intriguing, though, is the trip Mrs. Gwin made to St. Petersburg and Moscow in 1858 and her close association with the Pickens family. New York *Times*, 2 September 1858.

spection team and the report of the committee on the charter renewal but that personally he saw no political advantage to the proposal and thought the amount offered was, in any event, too little.[163] When Stoeckl relayed this to Gwin, the latter noted, "For my part I am disposed to offer a much larger sum and I would be supported by my colleagues from California and Oregon, but I am not sure of the agreement of other states of the Union which do not have any direct interest." According to Stoeckl, Gwin also said that the rationale for such an acquisition "would be the prospect of augmenting in the Pacific region the power and influence of the United States to the detriment of England."[164] In the minister's opinion the main impediments would be finances and the general hostility of Congress to the president; therefore, further discussions would probably have to wait until after the next national election. By that time the United States government was preoccupied with internal strife, and Gwin was no longer on the scene in Washington. Nevertheless, the exchanges in 1860 smoothed the way for a relatively easy and simple negotiation on the sale/ purchase of Alaska in 1867.

Another background factor in the preparation for the territorial shift was the readiness with which the United States accepted Russian expansion in the Far East, despite Matthew Perry's earlier warnings. This is a typical contemporary press reaction:

And thus we find ourselves standing face to face upon the shores of the Pacific, the two dominant nations at present possessing powerful States upon the northern portion of these waters. The future is pregnant with vast results, that are to flow out of the commercial relations of the two powers on this ocean. The prophecy of Hertzen, that "between the shores of Asia and North America the ocean would ere long teem with the merchant ships of the world," approaches its fulfillment. The two great nations of the two hemispheres are marching on, each in the fulfillment of its separate destiny, each the antipodes of the other, in its political and social organization, though strangely similar in their career, along the great highway that nations are traveling in the fulfillment of their individual destinies.[165]

---

[163]Gorchakov to Stoeckl, 14 May 1860 (secret), f. kants. Vashington 1860, d. 195, AVPR.

[164]Stoeckl to Gorchakov, 30 August/11 September 1860, ibid.

[165]*Alta California*, 12 November 1858. The New York *Times* was even more unrestrained: "The truth is, Asia is as certainly the theatre of a Russian manifest destiny, as is America for the people of the United States. It is a question simply of time, when that grandest of the five leading divisions of the world will be a Russian province." "The Russians on the Amoor," 6 October 1858.

Thus Americans were willing to see a manifest destiny comparable to their own employed by Russia.

American Perceptions of Russia

The theme of a commonality of interests pervaded both public and private perceptions in Russia and the United States. In a dialogue with Grand Duke Constantine at the end of 1857, John H. B. Latrobe struck this chord again:

> *Latrobe*: We are the only peoples who have a future. The old nations of the world can expect to be no greater than they are. This creates a sympathy, Your Highness.
> *Constantine*: What else?
> *Latrobe*: We are nations of great extent, a consciousness that creates a common feeling.
> *Constantine*: True, what else?
> *Latrobe*: Neither of us are satisfied. We both want more territory, they say.
> *Constantine*: But, don't you think we have, both of us, got enough?
> *Latrobe*: In America, Your Highness, enough means a little more.

At which the grand duke laughed, and they chatted on about the importance of good relations between the two countries.[166] Similar conversations apparently occurred frequently whenever Russians and Americans met.

"Mark Random" (perhaps Bayard Taylor), writing from St. Petersburg for the New York *Times* in 1858, observed:

> An American cannot fail to be most favorably struck with a first view of Russia and the Russians. . . . Indeed Americans have every reason to congratulate themselves upon the cordial friendship entertained for them and for their country in Russia, and by none is this kindly feeling more unmistakably manifested than by the Imperial family and the high functionaries of the Court and Government.[167]

[166]Russian Correspondence, Latrobe Papers, box 2, MaryHS.
[167]"St. Petersburg," New York *Times*, 2 September 1858. Russian hospitality could sometimes get the best of Americans. Lieutenant Habersham told of a friendly reception on the Kamchatka coast: "I never again wish to attend a dinner at Ayan, with 'Old Fryback' as the host;—at any rate, not until some cure for apoplexy is discovered, or the Russians lose some of their relish for fraternizing with Americans." A. W. Habersham, *My Last Cruise: Where We Went and What We Saw* . . . (Philadelphia: J. B. Lippincott, 1878), p. 461.

But only a few of the many American visitors to Russia published their impressions, though some, at least, were mindful of the need for Americans to know more about that faraway country, especially to counter the negative views of it coming out of Britain. As the American minister Seymour noted:

> Hitherto, Russia has been better known to Great Britain than to almost any other Government, except perhaps that of Prussia. The consequence has been that England, through her Consuls and merchants in Russia, has controlled, to some extent, the foreign trade of this country. The time has come when we should take what Britain may have lost by plunging into a hasty if not unnecessary war with Russia. The more then we add to our knowledge of Russia, by means of books, and of maps especially, the better we shall be enabled to enter upon a new and wider field of Commerce with her than we have heretofore had. Whatever objects of Art, which the Genius of this country has produced, we may secure for our public institutions, will show, if they show nothing else, that Russia is not the barbarous nation which her late adversaries have represented her to be.[168]

The most important source of information about Russia for Americans was the newspapers. While Seymour apparently did little himself to broaden American knowledge of Russia, his successor, Francis Pickens, wrote for the Edgefield, South Carolina, *Advertiser*. Culled of any controversial or negative items, these reports were picked up by other newspapers. In one undated note, accompanied by definite instructions that it not be published, Pickens made an interesting comparison between Russia and his own part of the United States:

> The highest classes of Russians are very hospitable and kind, and are as warm in their kindness as our Southern planters although so far North. The reason is that their domestic institutions are patriarchal like ours, as contradistinguished from the feudal system. The former produces kindness and more cordial relations in society, the latter more warlike and haughty. The most cordial people I have met in Europe are the nobility and higher classes of Russia. Perhaps this is somewhat owing too to my being American as they are fond of Americans and dislike English. For instance, the Grand Duke Constantine who is the most powerful man in Russia next to the Emperor, is as casual,

---

[168]Seymour to Marcy, 2 December 1856, DUSM, Russia, vol. 17 (roll 17, M 35), RG 59, NA.

heated, and unaffected in his conversations with me as if he were a Southern planter.[169]

Lucy Pickens, who wrote for a Memphis newspaper, offered a woman's point of view on Russian and European society. In a letter to her sister, she recorded her distaste for the social formalities:

The miserable emptiness of European society is beyond belief. Dress, the opera and ball, is literally *all*. If you advance an idea, you are looked at with a kind of well-bred disgust. . . . There is nothing real in European life but its hollowness. No deference is paid to a woman, because she is a woman, no regard is paid to any goodness, beauty or wit she may possess—unless she has rank or fortune. One who has had the happiness of living always in God's favored land, America, can form an idea of the *pettyness* of men and women abroad, covered as they are with titles and diamonds. I have received great kindness myself, but it does not blind me to the real state of people and things.[170]

In another letter, Mrs. Pickens enlarged on the personal impact these Russian attitudes had on her:

You will doubtless find me changed in many respects—I am no longer handsome, tho' I pass for a great beauty at Court—The Emperor and Grand Dukes dance with me now and then (but not with *any* other minister's wife that I know of) and of course other people would court and admire me. . . . In a Society like this, where the existence of virtue is *not believed* in by men, mine has not been a position free from incidents but I have conducted myself with such prudence that my husband tells me, he loves me more for my dignity and goodness, than for my beauty and intellect.[171]

Another American writing from the Crimea, who was probably connected with the Gowen enterprise at Sevastopol, found Russian society, at least in the provinces, surprisingly equal for men and women:

[169]Undated fragment on legation paper, Pickens Papers, South Caroliniana Library, University of South Carolina. A version of this found its way to the Edgefield *Advertiser*, 11 August 1858: "All Russia, on the other hand, is Asiatic in its social institutions, based upon a system contradistinguished from the feudal by its patriarchal features, which tend more to develop private attachments and home virtues. . . . The higher class are extremely kind, familiar, and hospitable—more like the people of our own South than any I have ever seen. Although they live in so cold a country, they are warm and genial."

[170]Lucy Pickens to her sister, 20 December 1859, Pickens Papers, South Caroliniana Library, University of South Carolina.

[171]Lucy Pickens to her sister, 13 April 1860, ibid.

There are many, perhaps, who suppose, from what they have read of Russia, that the manners, customs and social society of the Russians would be far from agreeable to an American; but such is not the fact; for in no country that I have ever visited have I seen more politeness and refinement than exists in the respectable circles of Sebastopol. Although there are many points where etiquette differs from ours, yet, rather than diminishing, it adds to the sociability of the company. For instance, it might possibly shock the sensibilities of an American lady to be told that, during the recess of a ball, the ladies retire to their apartment (where no gentleman dares enter), light their paper cigars, smoke away, and chat most merrily. Also, at the dinner table, after the dessert, ladies, as well as gentlemen, smoke their cigars and take their glass of wine, and while the smoke is curling up, their beautiful black eyes shine with additional lustre.[172]

Aside from the many newspaper articles, which were mostly anonymous, Americans learned from public lecturers, the most important being Bayard Taylor, who included Russia on his honeymoon tour of Europe in 1858. He then undertook in New York in November a series of lectures on Russia that stressed its unique and exotic character, a mix of East and West. One on Moscow, in which he compared the city to "a turbaned Oriental smoking his pipe on an Arctic block of ice," drew such a large audience that it had to be moved from Clinton Hall to the Cooper Institute. "The ancient city, he said, would always reflect the character of the people—would always be the illuminated index of the country."[173] By the end of the month he was orating on the same subject in Baltimore and early the next year had reached San Francisco, as part of his normal presentation of over a hundred talks a year throughout the country.[174] Another resource for information about Russia was to be found in the new vogue in epic panorama exhibitions, with those featuring the siege of Sevastopol still attracting immense crowds in 1859.[175] At a minimum, exposure to the popular media provided Americans with a basic background for understanding Russia and perhaps whetted the appetite for something more. A few Americans, such as poet

[172]"Etiquette of the Crimea," Baltimore Sun, 7 January 1858.

[173]"Bayard Taylor on Moscow," New York Times, 2 November 1858. Taylor's new wife, who was German, had a sister married to an astronomer who worked at the Pulkovo observatory near St. Petersburg.

[174]"Bayard Taylor's Lecture," Baltimore Sun, 1 December 1858. One hopes that his lectures were more interesting than his book, Greece and Russia (New York: Putnam, 1859); Adam Gurowski, while emphasizing the growing popularity of public lectures in the United States, thought Taylor's were very superficial. "Pis'mo iz Ameriki," Vestnik Promyshlennosti 7, 1 (January 1860): 20–27.

[175]"The Russian War," Baltimore Sun, 7 January 1858, and "Panorama of the Russian War," ibid., 21 November 1859.

Bayard Taylor. Engraving by H. B. Hall from a photograph by Mathew Brady, from Views A-Foot *(New York: Putnam's, 1879)*

Henry Wadsworth Longfellow, were even moved to attempt to learn the language.

Obviously the physical attributes of Russia attracted as much attention as social customs. An American, "Alethe," highlighted for a New Orleans audience the exotic appeal of St. Petersburg: "I am aware that many on our Mississippi (and surely none are more enlightened) regard this city as semi-barbaric. And yet here, strange to say, the Orient and Occident meet in unrivaled splendor, not only in the pride and pomp of wealth and power, but in the might and mystery of art, science and intellect."[176]

But certainly not all American visitors were so impressed. One wrote in frustration of the "Potemkin village" effect:

> I was greatly disappointed with my first view of St. Petersburg. From the extraordinary accounts I had so often read of its magnificence, I was certainly led to expect something infinitely more grand. . . . It is true that in one tab-

[176]New Orleans *Daily Picayune*, 17 October 1858.

leau are assembled a number of splendid buildings, such as few capitals afford; but if within the same space were collected all the finest public buildings in London, with all the advantages of the great extent of ground and clear atmosphere, enabling the visitor to obtain an unobstructed view of their various beauties, it would be easy to guess which would present the most imposing appearance; added to which it must be recollected that the edifices in St. Petersburg are, for the most part, only of brick and stucco. That this assemblage of all that is splendid in the city gives it at first sight a magnificent *ensemble* I do not deny; but, like everything Russian, the showy facade only hides what is mean behind.[177]

A third perspective—that of Russia as a progressing, modernizing country, both socially and economically—was often presented to the American public and was especially evident on the topic of Siberia and the Amur. Although a common view was that the two countries were evolving comparably, this was sometimes used to contrast the respective societies to the benefit, of course, of the United States. One example is a thoughtful editorial from the Baltimore *American and Commercial Advertiser* at the time of the coronation:

Here are two mighty empires both looking far forward into futurity—both occupying prominent positions in their respective hemispheres, and resembling one another in the extent of their territory and in undeveloped resources rich in the promise of much greatness and grandeur yet to come. How similar in some respects, yet what opposites in others. Both are running the same course but the motives that propel each are as different as it is possible for them to be. We move forward by the aggregation of individual energies united in the pursuit of a common purpose, yet each having its own object in view. In Russia we behold the thoughts, feelings and strength of millions subject to one man who concentrates in a single will the power of a multitude of minds. Here the spirit of freedom gives its impetus to progress and works out its ends with an activity never before witnessed. On the other hand, the intense force of the despotic principle, ruling by obedience, presses onward with resistless power. The objects aimed at are equally diverse. . . . We make internal improvements because they are profitable. . . . But our autocratical contemporary gives a secondary importance to these things. He discovers that railroads are capital for transporting troops and munitions of war—that locomotives are much more powerful and serviceable than horses. He constructs railroads,

[177]"Sketches of the City of St. Petersburg," *Frank Leslie's Illustrated Newspaper*, 7 February 1857. John F. Heard wrote to his brother "Gus" (Augustine Heard, Jr.), 21 October 1861: "I was never so much disappointed in any place in my life as with St. Petersburg—its like a second hand French place—gaudy and tinsel." Heard Collection I, GM-1, Baker Library, Harvard Business School.

therefore, and employs locomotives for military purposes. Cronstadt will be united to Sevastopol, the Baltic sea to the Caspian, St. Petersburg brought near to Odessa, and the hissing of the steam engine be heard along the barren steppes of Southern Russia, and perhaps in the ravines of the Circassian mountains, or by the shores of Amoor river—because thereby power may be concentrated and diffused with rapidity and effect. Russia is destined to be great; so are, also, the United States. A Republic and an Empire, they are contending, in their own ways, for the same goal of national pre-eminence; but with us the glory of one is the glory of all, and the humblest citizen has both part and profit in the realization of the task; with Russia, success means nothing but the concentration of greater power and more abundant resources in the hands of a despotic ruler—a vast, terrible and impassive autocracy, the grandeur of which the people may contemplate, perhaps have pride in, but not share.[178]

In 1859 the noted American political economist Henry Carey visited Russia, where he was already well known and much admired through translations of his writings. Carey expounded an optimistic view of industrial advance through tariff protectionism and an incentive-based agriculture with land owned by its workers. But his observations, as described in another American editorial, revealed his doubts about the ability of Russia to inaugurate significant social change through serf emancipation and at the same time to develop the economy:

We question whether Russia is not to be hampered in some of her great undertakings by the want of money. Her resources are indeed vast, but there is a limit beyond which even she cannot afford to push her great enterprises and reforms. It is intimated, on pretty good authority, that it will be very difficult, if not impossible for her to complete the works which she has already begun. The emancipation of the serfs, for instance, threatens to be accompanied with an enormous expense. Mr. H. C. Carey, who has just been to Russia, expresses the fear that the Emperor has advanced too rapidly with this laudable undertaking. It is proposed, Mr. Carey says, to create a debt of a thousand millions of roubles to overcome the obstacles in the way of emancipation. Whether the sum is stated correctly or not, it cannot be doubted that this great reform must necessarily be attended with an expenditure which will interfere seriously with the construction of many railroads, and the clearing of rivers in Central Asia. In order to rival England in eastern trade, Russia must

[178]"Internal Improvements in Russia," Baltimore *American and Commercial Advertiser*, 26 September 1856. Carey's visit was widely covered. See New York *Herald*, 15 August 1859.

bend her energies, not only to opening highways for her commerce, but also to placing her productive powers on a level with those of Great Britain. That cannot be done in a day or a year. The Emperor, with great wisdom, is striving to develop the resources of his land, and to bring his subjects upon a higher plane of civilization. But we must not expect that his great work will be completed at once, or without his meeting many and fearful obstacles.[179]

Carey's assessment did, in fact, have merit, and this recognition of the difficulties of coupling social and political reform with economic progress in Russia would be repeated at later times—especially in the 1980s. Moreover, Foreign Minister Gorchakov responded in the same tone of caution to Latrobe's insistence on the importance of economic advances, mainly railroad construction, being accompanied by the alleviation of social and political evils such as serfdom: "It is to be abated here in Russia. But there are a great number of difficulties in the way. It must be a thing of time—there are so many interests to deal with; we must proceed very cautiously indeed. Yes, yes, I think it will be brought about."[180] Perestroika, Gorchakov-style.

An agreeable characteristic of Russian-American relations during this period that seemed most rewarding was the frank and honest person-to-person conversations such as those that Latrobe recorded. Though at times severe criticism of the respective societies might be voiced, very rarely was any personal dislike or rebuke expressed. On the contrary, at the various official and social occasions that sprang from visits and joint ventures—in Sevastopol and Nikolaevsk, in New York and San Francisco—Americans and Russians harmonized well together. Perhaps typical was a stopover of the Russian Pacific squadron at San Francisco late in 1859:

The Opera House presented a gay spectacle last evening, being dressed with Russian and American flags, in honor of the visit of Admiral Popoff, the Russian consul (Mr. Kostromitinoff), and the officers (about twenty in number) of the Russian squadron now in our harbor. The opera of "The Crown Diamonds," was given by the New Orleans Opera Troupe, and to a full and fashionable house. The guests, dressed in full uniform, entered shortly before

[179]"Russian Progress," Providence *Journal*, 18 October 1859.
[180]Latrobe to his wife, 10 December 1857, Russian Correspondence, box 2, Latrobe Papers, MaryHS. Gorchakov also said: "Russia needs development. The world does not know her capability. They are ignorant of her productions even. In her development she will do much that the world is not prepared for. The Russians themselves scarcely know the capability of their own country. But development is slow. . . . The rest of the world, the English, for instance, they talk, they diplomatize. Their action is in notes and correspondence. Russian development is in deeds, in acts, in progress, but it will be slow after all."

eight o'clock, and passed into the four proscenium boxes and a part of the front row of the dress circle. The orchestra then played the Russian National Anthem, which took the visitors by surprise, as at a signal from the Admiral they all arose, and remained standing until the piece was performed. . . . It was followed by a storm of applause, and when silence was restored, "Hail Columbia" and "Yankee Doodle," were given—the Russians applauded with might and main, and evidently appreciating the national sentiment embodied in the latter. The evening passed off very pleasantly and the occasion was as gratifying to the spectators as to the recipients of the courtesies.[181]

Though such events and ceremonies were no longer rare or isolated, direct cultural exposure was still relatively restricted. The great black Shakespearean Ira Aldridge played Othello and Shylock in St. Petersburg, but with, according to one source, mixed results:

The worst is that Mr. Aldridge is accompanied by a German Troupe, who perform the parts assigned to them in their vernacular, and the effect produced by their German answers to his English speeches is the most comical imaginable, and puts all illusion out of the question. . . . Fortunately, to the majority of our Petersburg audiences, both English and German are 'heathen Greek,' so that comparatively small portion of the spectators are acquainted with the two languages.[182]

A young Bostonian, John P. Groves, was hired by the Golitsyn family to direct a provincial opera company in Saratov, but very little is known about his experiences there, except that he soon got into trouble with the local authorities. And Russia was also treated to some of the more popular types of American diversions: for example, Theodore Leut's "American Comic Opera Troop"; Frederick Billing and his performing horses; an "American" photographic shop in St. Petersburg; and a "medium" named Hume who was reported to have impressed the tsar with his mystic performances.

The Russian View of the United States

In general, the reporting from Russia and the gathering of information about that country was unorganized and amateurish, at least in comparison with the other side of the coin—the Russian effort to learn about the United States. As

[181]"Reception of the Russian Officers," *Alta California*, 16 December 1859. Capt. Alexander Butakov (future admiral and naval reformer) was publicly entertained by Gen. John E. Wool in 1857. San Francisco *Evening Bulletin*, 17 January 1857.

[182]"Russia—A Capital Company," *Frank Leslie's Illustrated Newspaper*, 5 February 1859; Herbert Marshall and Mildred Stock, *Ira Aldridge, The Negro Tragedian* (Carbondale and Edwardsville: Southern Illinois University Press, 1968), pp. 220-28.

"Mark Random" observed: "When we take into consideration how little Americans know of Russia, we can more readily appreciate the industry with which the intelligent classes of this country [Russia] have collected exact information in relation to us, and the eagerness with which they listen to any facts tending to give them a still wider and more intimate knowledge of the United States."[183] The unpopularity of Britain and France after the Crimean War, a rising public interest in reform and technological progress, a freer and more liberal atmosphere in Russia, and greatly increased direct contacts between the two countries inspired Russians to seek more information after 1856. Russians had one distinct advantage: There were infinitely more educated Russians well versed in English than Americans literate in Russian, so that many Russians could and did receive their knowledge from original sources. The availability of American books in Russia is indicated by the following report of 1859: "The New York *Evening Post* observes that few people have any idea of the extent to which some of our book publishers are interested in the Russia trade. Last week the Appletons filled an order for three hundred dozen American works, chiefly of American authors, with a few reprints, for St. Petersburg. These American books go to stock a circulating library in the Russian capital."[184]

American literature was gaining in popularity, thanks to its own growth and greater repute. Among authors, James Fenimore Cooper, Washington Irving, and Edgar Allen Poe continued to head the list, the latter especially promoted by Fedor Dostoevsky, but Nathaniel Hawthorne, Herman Melville, Ralph Waldo Emerson, and Henry Wadsworth Longfellow were also widely read and translated into Russian during these years. The appearance of *The House of Seven Gables* and *The Scarlet Letter* in the journal *Sovremennik* [Contemporary] in 1852 and 1856, respectively, attracted much attention. In fact, Hawthorne is credited with having considerable influence on Ivan Turgenev and the literary and social critics, Nicholas Chernyshevsky and Nicholas Dobroliubov, who edited that journal and raised the awareness of American literature. The leading expert on Hawthorne in particular and American literature in general was Mikhail Mikhailov, a close friend of Chernyshevsky's and a fellow member of the new generation of Russian radical intelligentsia. Mikhailov especially singled out the theme of women's rights in *The Scarlet Letter*.[185]

Undoubtedly the best-known American work in Russia in the immediate pre-

---

[183]"Saint Petersburg," New York *Times*, 2 September 1858.

[184]"Russian Demand for American Books," Baltimore *Sun*, 18 August 1859.

[185]A. N. Nikoliukin, *Literaturnye sviazi Rossii i SShA: Stanovlenie literaturnykh kontakov* (Moscow: Nauka, 1981), p. 374; M. L. Mikhailov, "Amerikanskie poety i romanisty," *Sovremennik*, no. 10 (October 1859): 217–32; and no. 12 (December 1859): 305–24. A Mikhailov essay on Hawthorne, from an 1860 issue of *Sovremennik*, is in Nikoliukin, *A Russian Discovery of America* (Moscow: Progress Publishers, 1986), pp. 234–49.

emancipation period, however, was Harriet Beecher Stowe's *Uncle Tom's Cabin*, a book that was not easy to publish in Russian because of concern about provoking peasant disturbances. As the American consul in Moscow reported:

> The fear is freely expressed and appears to be generally entertained that serious troubles may arise and blood may be shed; as an indication of this feeling, remonstrances have been made that a translation into Russ of "Uncle Tom's Cabin" now in press should not be permitted to be published, for as a French translation has for a long time been in the hands of the educated classes, the issue of the one in question is looked upon as purposely incendiary and calculated to mislead the peasantry into the idea that they are no better circumstanced and treated than the slaves in America.[186]

Additionally, Russia took the initiative in the expansion of publication exchanges between official agencies and educational institutions. Though access to resources on the United States was naturally much greater than American exposure to Russian language materials, it was still limited to those who could read English or French and who resided in, or visited frequently, St. Petersburg, Moscow, or western cities.

Russia was well served in the 1850s by the level of expertise of its own reporters on the United States, most of whom were professionally trained in their field and went overseas expressly to find information or on temporary assignment. This was also an especially open time for publishing in Russia, because censorship was fairly relaxed and curiosity about the outside world was more intense. And in the concern with technical modernization, observers focused on the United States, which, as every traveling Russian must have known, had already contributed significantly to mechanical progress—railroads, bridges, ships—in Russia. A fairly large number of Russian naval officers were on hand for the building of ships, went aboard war vessels, or were, like Pavel Golovin, just passing through; several wrote articles for the naval journal *Morskoi Sbornik*. But more important were five rather different "Russians," whose descriptions of the United States were widely distributed in Russia at the time—Vladimir Bodisko, Aleksandr Lakier, Adam Gurowski, Eduard Zimmerman (Tsimmerman), and Dmitri Zhuravskii.

As a diplomat on courier assignment, Bodisko (nephew of the late minister) described in detail his sojourn in New York and Washington and his trip by steamer to Central America.[187] He concentrated on the peculiarities of Ameri-

---

[186]Francis Claxton (Moscow) to Cass, 1 January 1858, DUSC, Moscow, vol. 1 (roll 1, M 456), RG 59, NA.

[187]Vladimir Bodisko, "Iz Ameriki," *Sovremennik*, no. 3 (1856): 114–40; no. 4 (1856): 237–58.

can public and private dress and behavior, stressing the great variety and the refreshing lack of conformity. Though obviously not enraptured of all American tastes and manners, Bodisko portrayed a generally flattering and intriguing picture to the reader, especially regarding the talents and beauties of American women. He was also impressed by the practical education of children and their early exposure to politics through playing in bands on patriotic holidays and participating in election parades.

Lakier was not only well educated (University of Moscow) but fluent in English. He resigned his administrative post in the Imperial Ministry of Justice in 1857 to follow in the footsteps of Ivan Golovin in making a systematic tour of the country. He began in Boston, then proceeded to New York and up the Hudson and to Buffalo before returning to Baltimore, Philadelphia, and Washington. Striking west through the Ohio Valley and Indiana and Illinois, he went as far as Dubuque, Iowa, from where he went up the Mississippi to St. Paul, stopping off to visit a Dakota Indian reservation. He sailed down the Mississippi to New Orleans and returned to Washington to see Congress in session. The account of his trip appeared in a series of articles in *Sovremennik* and was published in more complete form in a book in 1859.[188] The result was a colorful, accurate, detailed view of the United States at an interesting time, with a special emphasis on prisons because of the author's professional background.

As a perceptive reporter of the American scene, Lakier compares well with other foreign observers of the United States. The following passages are representative of a work that has the capacity to engage both Russians and Americans, now as then:

[188]Robert V. Allen, *Russia Looks at America: The View to 1917* (Washington, D. C.: Library of Congress, 1988), pp. 27–28, 292. The sections of Lakier's work dealing with Congress and New York were published in the April, September, and October 1858, issues of *Sovremennik*, and the April issue of 1859 contained a twenty-five-page review of his book by Dobroliubov. For a useful guide to the contents of this important and popular periodical, see V. Bograd, *Zhurnal "Sovremennik," 1847–1866—ukazatel' soderzhaniia* (Moscow-Leningrad: Gosizkhudozhlit, 1959).

The impact of Lakier's *Puteshestvie po severo-amerikanskim shtatam, Kanade i ostrovu Kube*, 2 vols. (St. Petersburg: Vul'fa, 1859), was noted in "Our St. Petersburg Correspondence," the New York *Herald*, 1 September 1859: "An eminent Russian author, Mr. Lacquiers, has published a description of his travels in the United States, in which he gives a very flattering picture of your republic, and which is read with great avidity, everything American being quite popular in this country. The works of the best American writers, such as Cooper, Irving, Hawthorne, etc., are all translated into Russian, as are the historical writings of Prescott, down to the 'History of Phillip II,' the last volumes of which are now in press." For a professionally edited but abridged translation of Lakier's book, see Arnold Schrier and Joyce Story, eds. and trans., *A Russian Looks at America: The Journey of Aleksandr Borisovich Lakier in 1857* (Chicago and London: University of Chicago Press, 1979).

The American does not become completely attached to any one occupation: today a farmer, tomorrow an official, then a merchant and a seafarer. This is not because he is fickle but because he is adroit enough, or as the people themselves say, "smart" enough, to accustom himself to any occupation he chooses, either from inclination or necessity. He will finally stay in the one that seems to him the most lucrative.[189]

Lakier was especially impressed by the pace and progress of American life in contrast with that of Russia.

But why is it, I thought, as I bid farewell to New York, that while much in individual Americans is not personally pleasing and offends our senses, yet from a distance one looks at these lively, clever, practical people and begins to have a reverential attitude for their boldness, their activity, and their realistic views of things? One may not love certain particulars in America, but one cannot help loving America as a whole or being amazed at what it has that Europe cannot measure up to—a people who know how to govern themselves and institutions that, unaided, give a person as much happiness and well-being as he can accommodate . . . a foreigner who does not understand and cannot respect the concepts and new attitudes of a country that does not recognize caste and feudal distinctions may disapprove of America. But when your elbows no longer hurt from the blows of Americans on the run, and when you are no longer seated at the dinner table next to an American in a hurry, it is another matter. Then you love and marvel at him![190]

He concluded his observations with an emphasis on the American ability to recognize their own failings and to deal with their own problems.

If the shortcomings [such as slavery] are rectifiable or considered worthy of correction, there are all sorts of means readily available to the practical patriot-American: the press, the public meeting, the magazine, the state legislature and the federal Congress. Europeans, either because they know very little about the internal life of a distant country or because they purposely misinterpret the meaning of what they see and read, proclaim the disintegration of the Union as a consequence of the excessively mercantile bent of its inhabitants, their immorality, and the decline of a sense of honor. If there were any basis in truth for these dangers, a terrible fate indeed would threaten the United States.[191]

[189]Schrier and Story, *A Russian Looks at America*, p. 75.
[190]Ibid., p. 98.
[191]Ibid, p. 260.

Lakier may have underestimated the danger of dissolution, but he believed in the potential power of Americans: "They will have an influence on Europe but they will use neither arms nor sword nor fire, nor death and destruction. They will spread their influence by the strength of their inventions, their trade, and their industry. And this influence will be more durable than any conquest."[192] This must have been impressive to the Russian reader.

Zimmerman, a prominent Baltic-German merchant who had resettled in Moscow, covered much the same ground as Lakier and in the same year. His reports were published in several issues of *Russkii Vestnik* in 1858 and 1859 and also in book form. However, he was less of an analyst and confined himself mainly to detailed description. For example, he was as impressed as Lakier with the rapid development and new sophistication of the United States and used the assembly-line processing of pork and the prefabrication of wooden houses in Cincinnati as illustrations.[193]

Another important reporter of the American scene for the Russian audience was Adam Gurowski, a Polish Pan-Slavist who had lived in the United States since 1850. Prominent as a spokesman-writer on both sides of the Atlantic, he was also the subject of an excellent biographical study by an American scholar, and, as a result, his time in the United States is better known to historians. While serving on the editorial staff of Horace Greeley's New York *Tribune* during the Crimean War, Gurowski's principal feat was in rewriting the articles of Marx and Engels on Pan-Slavism to fit his own views. Still employed on the *Tribune* staff in 1857, he wrote *America and Europe*, which contrasted the liberty of the United States with the authority that governed Europe, much to the advantage of the former: "The American world . . . is not circumscribed by the narrow, blind, fatalistic physical laws of race. Amidst ups and downs, in smooth and in thorny paths, at times overshadowed and then brilliantly luminous, the American world has been the bearer of the all-embracing, truly human manifestation of principles."[194] Gurowski also contributed to Appleton's *New American Cyclo-*

---

[192]Ibid., pp. 261–62.

[193]S. Frederick Starr, "The Ohio Valley through Russian Eyes, 1857," *Bulletin of the Cincinnati Historical Society* 24, 3 (July 1966): 211–20; Allen, *Russia Looks at America*, pp. 28, 310.

[194]Adam Gurowski, *America and Europe* (New York: Appleton and Co., 1857), p. 58. See also LeRoy H. Fischer, *Lincoln's Gadfly, Adam Gurowski* (Norman: University of Oklahoma Press, 1964). In the rough manuscript notes, apparently taken for the book, Gurowski allowed his thoughts to ramble further: "An American signifies already, and will do it more and more, not a special descendant of this or that peculiar race, not one distinguished by an exclusive and limited feeling of nationality, but . . . free man governing himself. Regulating his actions by the only compass in which consist his likeness to god. Yet this is reason—common sense. Can they be separated from the *thought*, or are they not rather the brightest expression of it?" "America," box 1, Gurowski Papers (Ac. 1463), Manuscript Division, LC.

pedia, but he lost this job and the newspaper position in 1858 for his criticism of the poor quality of the encyclopedia. Always a colorful but irascible and eccentric figure, Gurowski socialized with Walt Whitman, Longfellow, Emerson, and many other American notables of the day, but this only seemed to add to his continual financial difficulties.

In 1858 Gurowski began a series of "Letters from America" and a number of separate articles for *Vestnik Promyshlennosti* [Bulletin of Industry], edited by Fedor Chizhov in St. Petersburg. Writing at least as many pages as Lakier or Zimmerman and covering more subjects, Gurowski drew upon his political and social connections, his various travels around the country, and insights gained during his residency, and he himself considered the articles much superior to his previous book on the United States.[195] He dealt with finances, slavery, westward expansion, commerce, industry, communications and transportation, education, religion and culture, and, especially, the meaning of the American constitution, which should have been of keen interest to Russian liberals on the eve of internal reforms.

Gurowski emphasized the economic determinism and freedom of the United States: "The present union was brought about on the political side for the most part by commercial demands. . . . Neither the union, nor the separate states, nor communities can interfere in the free function of industrial activity; in the United States no one rules it, no one prescribes laws for it."[196] He also remarked on the similarity of New England to northern Russia as suitable for industry but not agriculture and reminded his readers that Russia could learn from the United States in striving for economic and technological advances.[197] Gurowski believed that although the United States had produced "a huge mountainous reservoir of practical thought" that could assist the "social and intellectual revolution now being completed in Russia," it did not provide American life with a real foundation, which he thought accounted for the vast number of cheap novels and religious polemics circulating throughout the country. "The minds of America cannot produce a single good scientific, literary, or critical review."[198] He contrasted this situation, however, with the great progress in mass education. As an ardent abolitionist, Gurowski also saw the contradiction in the substantial freedom allowed and the existence of slavery. Though he predicted the end of the latter in a Republican national victory, he thought it was unfortunate that there was no Washington or Hamilton on the horizon to lead the country

---

[195]Gurowski (New York) to Chizhov (St. Petersburg), 15 August 1860, f. 111 (Chizhov), 22.30, Manuscript Division, Lenin Library, Moscow.

[196]*Vestnik Promyshlennosti*, no. 2 (August 1858): 87–89.

[197]Ibid., no. 5 (November 1858): 66.

[198]Ibid., no. 4 (April 1860): 15–16.

through a difficult time.[199] He would become a vehement and pesky critic of the Lincoln administration, while supporting and actually working for it.

Though it is not possible to gauge adequately the impact in Russia of Gurowski's writings about the United States, they did appear in almost every issue of a popular and progressive journal during a three-year period (1858–60) when critical reforms were being cast in Russia. Moreover, the influence of Alexis de Tocqueville's *Democracy in America* is clearly evident in the works of both Lakier and Gurowski. In fact, one might describe their efforts as an updating and reshaping of Tocqueville for a Russian audience.

While Gurowski geared his writings to Russia's educated progressives and radical intelligentsia—and Lakier and Zimmerman, to the general public—Col. Dmitri Zhuravskii reported from the United States on technical topics for a more restricted but nonetheless important professional group. As a trained engineer, Zhuravskii had assisted Whistler and Mel'nikov in the construction of the St. Petersburg–Moscow railroad and won acclaim for designing a large bridge using the American Howe system of wooden trestles on stone pillars. He wrote books and articles about this system and about railroad construction in general. Zhuravskii was even better known for having rebuilt the spire on the church in the Peter and Paul Fortress, one of the landmarks of St. Petersburg and a symbol of westernization.[200]

In 1859 he was sent to the United States by the Ministry of Ways and Communications to inspect new developments there. His articles for the ministry's journal covered a wide range of technical subjects such as snowplows, heating systems, iceboats, and new steam engines.[201] Most significant for the Russian context was his "Notes about the Grain Trade in America and about the Relationship between Production and the Conditions of Transportation," in which he reported firsthand from Chicago, Cincinnati, and Toledo on marketing, price structures, elevator design and operations, and the importance of efficient water and rail transportation for the grain export business.[202] Though underscoring American progress in the competition for world grain markets, the articles had little immediate effect on the stubborn backwardness of Russian agriculture and grain handling. However, when Russians did attempt to modernize this sector of the economy, they used American models.

Other Russians sought American shores for more personal reasons, marking the beginning of a genuine emigration to the United States from Russia that

---

[199]Ibid., no. 3 (March 1860): 139–40.

[200]*Dmitrii Ivanovich Zhuravskii* (St. Petersburg: Erlikh, 1897), pp. 2–3.

[201]Zhuravskii (New York), 10/22 February 1860, *Zhurnal Gravnago Upravleniia Putei Soobshcheniia* (Journal of the Russian Ministry of Ways and Communications), no. 31 (1860): 96–103.

[202]*Zhurnal . . . Putei Soobshcheniia*, no. 34 (1860): 1–25.

would slowly gather momentum through the remainder of the century. In early 1857 Prince Mikhail Khilkov arrived with Zimmerman and obtained rather ordinary employment on the railroads.[203] He would return to Russia many years later to put his skills to work as minister of transportation. Ivan Turchaninov, a disillusioned Don Cossack cavalry officer, came to the United States after conferring with Alexander Herzen in London. Though at first unhappy, he later achieved success in land and settlement promotion and railroad administration in the Midwest and served with distinction as a regimental commander in the Union army during the Civil War under the name Turchin.[204]

The leading Russian dissident writers, who were rapidly gaining influence and recognition during this period, also considered the "American alternative." Alexander Herzen, now settled more or less in permanent exile in London, published comments on American society, comparing its unity, opportunity, and democratic character with the moribund, stagnant Old World—by now, hardly an original theme. In an 1857 article in his journal *Kolokol* [The Bell], Herzen praised the simple, direct way by which Americans approached political and economic questions.[205] At one point, Herzen had even written, "If I were not a Russian, I should long ago have gone away to America."[206] But he stayed in Europe and took Swiss citizenship over the only other one he would consider— that of the United States. Clearly, Russian dissidents, forced by circumstances to remain outside of Russia, always hoped to return to lead a new Russia; they thus tended to congregate in congenial, free environments with good communications with Russia, such as London, Paris, Geneva, and Zurich.

One leader of this generation of the Russian intelligentsia, Michael Bakunin, did visit the United States, though not exactly by choice. Still restricted to a Siberian exile in the relatively open period following the Crimean War, he was actually employed by the Amur Company. Under the benevolent care taking of Murav'ev-Amurskii and General Korsakov, who both happened to be related to him, Bakunin decided to escape to a freer, more active life with better opportunity of contact with his fellow ideologists. He had no difficulty fleeing Nikolaevsk in 1861 aboard an American ship and in October of that year reached San Francisco, where he declared his intention to obtain American citizenship. According to a report in a local paper, he planned to tour eastern American cities, then to visit London before returning to the United States. He journeyed east by Panama steamer in company with the outgoing California senator, Wil-

<hr>

[203]*National Intelligencer*, 31 March 1857.

[204]Robert F. Ivanov, *Diplomatiia Avraama Linkol'na* (Moscow: Mezhdunarodnye Otnosheniia, 1987), pp. 141–42.

[205]Iskander [Herzen], "Amerika i Sibir," *Kolokol*, no. 29 (December 1858): 234–35.

[206]David Hecht, *Russian Radicals Look to America, 1825–1894* (Cambridge, Mass.: Harvard University Press, 1947), pp. 33–39.

liam Gwin.[207] He followed his announced itinerary and impressed his various American hosts with his knowledge of the United States, but once in Europe, Bakunin became engrossed in continental political and intellectual battles and remained there.

Many of the Russians who wrote about the United States during the 1850s were still influenced by Tocqueville's well-known opus, which circulated widely in Russia in its numerous French editions. Finally, in 1860 a rather poor Russian translation was published in Kiev. Nicholas Chernyshevsky reviewed it for *Sovremennik* and took the occasion to compose a lengthy essay on Tocqueville's philosophy and American society. As a radical democrat-populist, Chernyshevsky naturally found fault with that author's aristocratic liberalism and his tendency to slant his description of the United States to fit his view of a French future. Chernyshevsky also stressed that the book was now considerably out of date, thus giving the reader a misleading impression of contemporary America. Above all, he condemned Tocqueville's simplistic insistence on equating democracy with decentralized institutions. Chernyshevsky agued that the real basis of American society was the adaptability of its institutions, and he foresaw the possibility that central power could save democracy, having the slavery issue particularly in mind.[208] Coming as it did just after the proclamation of serf emancipation, Chernyshevsky's review probably attracted more attention in Russia than any of the direct reports from the United States then available, including Tocqueville's.

An Englishwoman, Mary Anne Pellew Smith, provided an interesting, outside perspective on Russians and Americans from her experiences during an extended stay in Russia. She thought Americans had a great advantage over the British in cultivating Russian friendships, for

> it is quite easy to perceive that they are very popular in that country. . . . A Russian nobleman with whom I am sufficiently acquainted to pass a joke, a man of great shrewdness and high attainments, in comparing the British and Americans, remarked:—"Ah! They!—alluding to the latter—"are the people for us; they possess all that we admire in the English, without that unapproachable hauteur, that impenetrable barrier with which you surround yourselves;" . . .
>
> The Americans certainly comprehend the Russians better than we do; they know more of them, and a lively sympathy exists between them. This may be traced to many causes—for there is much in common—and not the least

[207]"A Distinguished Russian Refugee," *Alta California*, 21 October 1861; Anthony Masters, *Bakunin: The Father of Anarchism* (New York: Saturday Review Press/E. P. Dutton & Co., 1974), pp. 131–33.

[208]"Nepochtitel'nost' k avtoritetam," *Sovremennik*, no. 6 (June 1861): 312–36.

prominent one perhaps may be found in the physical similarity of their climates, and the internal habits and necessities induced thereby; as well as by the magnitude of their respective geographical possessions. Both young, fresh and vigorous in body and mind, unprejudicial, and unshackled by conformity to precedent, the acquired acuteness of the one may be said to be an inherent ingredient in the character of the other. Extravagant in their tastes and habits to an unprecedented degree, both seem equally desirous of outstripping the old nationalities of the world; these young "go-aheads" never look back, and a remarkable feature common to both—the chief attribute of hopeful youth—is, that in conversation they rarely allude to the past; while we, with the habit peculiar to age, sit brooding over the relics of time, gone never more to return, they stride on, on, on, with every sense and muscle at work, growing in the knowledge, and power, and wealth.[209]

Much of that youth and vigor sensed in this and so many Russian and American accounts would soon be consumed by civil war and reform and by the accompanying political and social battles over continuity and change in both countries.

[209]Mary Ann Pellew Smith, *Six Years Travels in Russia, by an English Lady*, 2 vols. (London: Hurst & Blackett, 1859), 1: 159–61.

6

Emancipation
and Reform

In the 1860s, Russia and the United States both
experienced a major transformation of institutions; both also undertook a new
search for national identity. In part because of the harmonious relations of the
preceding years, the two countries gave each other important mutual support
during these difficult adjustments. In Russia the abolition of serfdom spearheaded a series of reforms that restructured the autocracy but also fostered the
growth of the radical intelligentsia, while in the United States the regional conflict aroused by the slavery issue brought forth a bloody civil war. Both having
survived the worst of these times, they made a congenial territorial adjustment
in the transfer of Alaska in 1867.

These pivotal events in the annals of both countries have inspired a variety of
historical investigations and approaches. In fact, because of the obsession of
contemporaries and later historians with upheavals and turning points, this is
one of the most examined and written-about periods in the history of either
country. In retrospective examinations, Soviet historians have focused much attention on the American Civil War, while American historians have weighed
the successes and failures of the Russian reform era. And though the most visible contemporary episodes in the relations between the two countries have received a number of treatments, controversy remains.[1] Why did Russia support

[1]Most secondary works on nineteenth-century Russian-American relations—both
Soviet and American—emphasize the Civil War period and the sale of Alaska but are
dated. Belonging in the "vintage" category is one study devoted entirely to the period:
Albert A. Woldman, *Lincoln and the Russians* (Cleveland and New York: World Publishing Company, 1952). The most thorough is M. M. Malkin, *Grazhdanskaia voina v SShA
i Tsarskaia Rossiia* (Moscow-Leningrad: OGIZ, 1939). More recent studies in article form
will be cited appropriately below. The very large number of general works about the

the North from the beginning? Why did the "progressive" North fail to back the revolt for Polish independence? What was the real purpose behind the sending of the Russian squadrons to the United States in 1863? What was the extent and nature of the Russian role in mediating the American conflict? How much did Russian policy affect French and British attitudes about the United States? And finally, what were the circumstances of the Russian sale of Alaska?

Serfdom and Slavery

Clearly a parallel exists in the experience of the two countries in dealing with servile systems. They were the only remaining western Great Powers that sanctioned such conditions of life for a substantial portion of their populations through the 1850s. Both almost simultaneously eliminated the formal, legal aspects of involuntary servitude, at least technically, while maintaining the essential dual character of their socio-political institutions. Yet both the Russian and American nations emerged from the costly upheavals strengthened internally and externally.

Another similarity can be found in their respective abolitionist movements, which were produced by a humanistic concern gradually developing among especially the urban middle class and "enlightened" aristocrats and were propelled by the power of ideas and literature. The strength of a relatively new, nationalistic intellectual community was key to the awakening of political crusades, or, perhaps more accurately, to the abandonment of traditional compromise. Commercial and industrial development and the perception of the need for continued and increased growth accompanied the spread of opinion in "official" circles for abolition. The results, however, were far from what many people wished and certainly far from the aspirations of the servile people themselves. Both countries were left with a residue of trouble, unrest, and social-political embarrassment.

Similarities should not be overstressed, because there were critical distinctions in the situations of the two countries.[2] Most obviously, the American slaves were of a different color, culture, and origin from most of the surrounding populace and were confined to a particular region and economy, mainly the cotton plantations of the South. In Russia the serfs shared the same culture, language, and religion as the basic population of the country, except Ukrainians and Belorussians

Civil War and contemporary international affairs deal with Russian-American relations in a perfunctory manner and rely on the older studies. Exceptions are those of a Soviet scholar, Robert F. Ivanov, *Diplomatiia Avraama Linkol'na* (Moscow: Mezhdunarodnye Otnosheniia, 1987) and a long chapter by Hans Rogger, "Russia and the Civil War," in *Heard Round the World: The Impact Abroad of the Civil War*, ed. Harold Hyman (New York: Knopf, 1969), pp. 177–255.

[2]For a detailed examination of American slavery and Russian serfdom, see Peter Kolchin, *Unfree Labor: American Slavery and Russian Serfdom* (Cambridge, Mass., and London: Harvard University Press, 1987).

with Polish landlords. But another difference was the much greater degree of autonomy in the social and economic life of the serfs, in contrast to the usual restrictions in the slave quarters of the Old South. Simply put, the Russian villages provided a cohesion largely absent on the American plantations.

Politically and administratively, the dissimilarities were also considerable. In the United States the crisis was finally precipitated by the electorate after decades of intense debate and political compromises. The Russian emancipation of the serfs was dictated by a central authority, prodded by military defeat, and was accomplished through its bureaucratic machinery in every province and locality with the backing and power of a large army and police force. Its opponents, the conservative landholders, were scattered and bound by allegiance to the tsar, whereas the strength of local government, regional loyalties, and the democratic process in the United States made a bloodless solution much less likely. While the Russian manumission was carried out painstakingly and gradually over several years with a generally compromised result, the United States proclaimed an emancipation in the middle of a costly military conflict, the outcome of which was still very much in doubt. This in turn gave rise to one more significant difference: Russian emancipation had virtually no impact outside of the country or on its foreign relations, while the Civil War affected American international relations and had marked repercussions in other parts of the world.[3]

The most important parallel of all, however, was that both "solutions" were incomplete—one offering some land without freedom, the other presenting some freedom without land. Future generations would be left with the difficult economic and civil-rights issues that remained.

The United States and the Serf Emancipation

American observers of Russia viewed the emancipation of the serfs as a natural component of the modernization and liberalization that Russia was pursuing

[3]Useful sources on the international dimensions of the American Civil War are: Ephraim Douglass Adams, *Great Britain and the American Civil War*, 2 vols. (London: Longmans, Green and Co., 1925); Donaldson Jordan and Edwin J. Pratt, *Europe and the American Civil War* (Boston and New York: Houghton Mifflin, 1931); Ernest N. Paolini, *The Foundations of the American Empire: William Henry Seward and U.S. Foreign Policy* (Ithaca, N. Y., and London: Cornell University Press, 1973); Norman Ferris, *Desperate Diplomacy: William Seward's Foreign Policy, 1861* (Knoxville: University of Tennessee Press, 1976); D. P. Crook, *The North, the South, and the Powers, 1861–1865* (New York: John Wiley and Sons, 1974); Lynn M. Case and Warren F. Spencer, *The United States and France: Civil War Diplomacy* (Philadelphia: University of Pennsylvania Press, 1970); James Morton Callahan, *The Diplomatic History of the Southern Confederacy* (Springfield, Mass.: Walden Press, 1957); and Frank Lawrence Owsley, *King Cotton Diplomacy: Foreign Relations of the Confederate States of America*, 2d ed. (Chicago: University of Chicago Press, 1959).

with American support and assistance. This was implied in the perception of Russia as a young nation, like the United States, expanding and developing along the path of its own manifest destiny—a path basically complementary to the United States and opposed by the same forces, mainly British. It should not be surprising, then, that the preparations for change in Russia received a particular coloration in American eyes.

One of the first to report on the impending emancipation was the American consul in Moscow, Francis Claxton, who saw behind it the growth of Russian liberalism:

> The nobles and proprietors who are opposed to this measure are loud in their denunciations whilst the mercantile class and the literary men, who are the partizans of the peasantry and may be called the liberal party, have adopted the English and American custom of speech making at public dinners, [but] these "reform banquets" have by order of the Emperor ceased, and the Grand Master of Police has *notified* the more prominent of the Liberals, that this *mode* of displaying their patriotism is not agreeable.[4]

He also noted that the nobility were yielding to pressure and agreeing to give serfs liberty but that they wanted to keep the land. Both Claxton and John Appleton, the American minister, highlighted the role of Grand Duke Constantine, a committed friend of the United States, in the process.

Meanwhile, in the United States the obsession with internal issues, relating particularly to "Bleeding Kansas," distracted American attention away from the Russian moves toward emancipation. In their separate lectures, Andrew Dickson White and Bayard Taylor juxtaposed the liberal progress in Russia with the impasse in the United States.[5] Typical of the press reports in the North was an article entitled "Russia and America" from the New York *Times*, ironically extracted from the city's French language newspaper. While emphasizing the "sympathy that inheres in kindred circumstances, opportunities and temptations, . . . already springing up between the great Eastern autocracy and the great democracy of the West," the author made one pointed contrast: "The emancipation of the Russian serfs, liberating twenty millions of men from the control of 900,000, launches Russia upon a career of political ideas exactly opposite to that in which the party which has long controlled the domestic movement of the United States seems inclined to move."[6]

The manifesto issued by Alexander II on 19 February/3 March 1861 (at the

[4]Claxton to Cass, 12 February 1859, DUSC, Moscow, vol. 1 (roll 1, M 456), RG 59, NA.
[5]New York *Times*, 26 September 1860.
[6]Ibid., 3 April 1861; *National Intelligencer*, 13 April 1861.

beginning of Lent) received favorable notices in the American press. The *National Intelligencer* printed the full text, and the New York *Times* labeled it a "grand act of enfranchisement" that would, by liberating the peasant commune, lead to a great alteration of Russian society. That it would probably take Russia in a socialist direction was "an event not unlikely when we consider that communism is a product of the most ancient Slavic life. . . . The religion, the politics, the habits and the morals of the Russians are all destined to undergo a transformation, and how far the expanding circles of growth may go no man now living can tell."[7]

Fortunately, the United States happened to have a quiet, prudent pro-Union minister in St. Petersburg to report back to the new besieged and divided American government in March 1861. John Appleton, having already resigned his commission but awaiting his successor, reflected:

> The plan has undergone so many changes in the hands of different committees, and finally, in the revision by the Imperial Council, that no one seems to know exactly what it is. We can only imitate the long-suffering serfs, and wait patiently for its publication. . . .
>
> The nobles claim, that if the freedom of those below is to be enlarged, the freedom of the upper classes ought to be regarded at the same time; and they ask for a constitution. It is probable that a constitution will be eventually granted; and the Emperor may be quite willing to divide his responsibility. This is the tendency of the age.[8]

And, though cautious about the costs involved, Appleton remained generally optimistic:

> Under the old system, with no constitution, no parliament, no courts of justice properly so-called, no people, a few nobles exhausting the resources of the country by luxury and extravagance, education confined to a small class, . . . and all powers civil and religious, centered absolutely in one man; under this system, I say, Russia could scarcely keep its place much longer in Europe as a civilized power. The first movement has now been made towards a better condition of things, and whatever may be the difficulties, I hope the reform will advance steadily to its consummation.[9]

[7]New York *Times*, 3 April 1861.
[8]Appleton to Seward, 22 February/6 March 1861, DUSM, Russia, vol. 18 (roll 18, M 35), RG 59, NA.
[9]Appleton to Seward, 22 May/6 June 1861, ibid.

To replace Appleton, Abraham Lincoln picked Cassius Marcellus Clay, a radical Kentucky abolitionist famous for his skills in both oratorical and hand-to-hand combat. The choice of this ill-tempered, rough-hewn (but Yale-educated) personality seemed an odd and illogical one at the time, but it turned out well for Russian-American relations in the long run. Clay had provided crucial support for Lincoln at the Republican convention and deserved some position in the new government, but obviously the president preferred not to have him in Washington, where he hoped saner heads could prevail. It may also have saved Clay's life, since he had already been a target of assassins. Awkwardly, however, Clay would have to serve under Secretary of State William H. Seward, whom he despised and had opposed at the convention.[10] But Clay also accepted the post on condition that he be recalled for a military command when needed.

The new minister descended on St. Petersburg in June 1861 with his family and three secretaries—Francis Williams and nephews William Goodloe and Green Clay. In his lengthy epistles from Russia, Clay preached to Seward and Lincoln on a great variety of topics, not least of which was his estimation of the Russian conditions. He also displayed a wide spectrum of his contrary views. Long a Southern abolitionist, Clay was also an economically-minded, protariff internationalist from the lower Middle West. In August he wrote to Seward:

> The Russians are advancing rapidly in the arts, and are very rapidly throwing off their dependence upon foreign talent. . . . I find not only her leading men very shrewd, but her masses which have been denounced through all Europe as very stupid, not at all deficient in shrewdness and ingenuity. In my opinion there is in the great millions of Russian serfs, an excellent material for future progress. The great reason why Russia has not advanced in civilization is because of her isolation. . . . But railroads and steamships are now obviating all of this. The liberation of the slaves, will not only set into activity an immense mass of muscle and mind heretofore inactive, but her educated class will have to cease being nonresidents and consumers—and devote themselves to the culture of the soil—to the mines and to commercial pursuits, and to manufactures. . . .
>
> I think ourselves fortunate then in having this great power now our sincere friend. We should in our tariffs, etc. keep up this friendly feeling, which will

[10]Clay's own autobiography is quite useful: *The Life of Cassius Marcellus Clay: Memoirs, Writings, and Speeches*, . . . , 2 vols. (Cincinnati, Ohio: J. Fletcher Brennan, 1886). For more recent biographies, see David L. Smiley, *Lion of Whitehall: The Life of Cassius M. Clay* (Madison: University of Wisconsin Press, 1962), and H. Edward Richardson, *Cassius Marcellus Clay: Firebrand of Freedom* (Lexington: University of Kentucky Press, 1976).

Cassius M. Clay, in uniform of major general, circa 1862.
Courtesy Lincoln Memorial University, Harrogate, Tennessee

give us finally an immense market for commerce: and give us a most powerful ally in common danger. For the American or Monroe ("doctrine") system which was very well, under the old sailing system, is now utterly impossible under "*steam and electricity.*"

We will and must take a common interest in the affairs of Europe: and Europe must and will take a common interest in our affairs. The "balance of power" system must henceforth pervade the world. That Europeans should hold possessions, *still further*, in America is a very different matter—that should not be allowed: as Spain must find out![11]

A few months later, on the first anniversary of the emancipation edict, Clay rhapsodized about the greatness of the tsar while censuring the reaction and un-

[11]Clay to Seward, 3 August 1861, DUSM, Russia, vol. 18 (roll 18, M 35), RG 59, NA.

rest in Poland, which he blamed on the "unbending bigotry of the Catholic clergy":

> The same causes, which have kept the Spanish provinces in America from all stable progress, have kept up the disunity of Poland with the Russian Empire.
>
> Alexander is making steady progress towards liberalism. He *increases* the freedom of the press—the freedom of discussion in the Senate; and the spread of schools; of telegraphs and railroads, and internal steamers—and places the enslaved millions in a new stage of progress—freedom—in order to avail themselves of these new means of civilization. . . . The truth is, in my opinion, that the nobles seek only the overthrow of the Present Ruler, to reestablish *slavery* and their own *despotism*.

About the same time, Clay wrote to his wife (whom he had sent home at the end of the first summer) that he had learned during a private reception that he had much in common with Grand Duchess Elena. They had both freed their slaves early and had instead used their lands for sheep grazing. He added, "Indeed, I have good reason to believe the more I see of Russia, that the people, great and low, are better and wiser and more civilized than we were led to believe by British calumnists, who slander all whom they desire to crush!" Whether Seward or Lincoln or any other contemporary appreciated Clay's commentaries on Russia is not clear, but they make interesting reading for the historian.[12]

This atmosphere of change and breakthrough was repeated by consuls in other parts of the empire. Henry Baldwin Stacy of Vermont reported from Reval in Estonia on the celebrations of the millennium of the Russian state:

> *Russia* has just celebrated with enthusiastic pomp *the thousandth anniversary of her empire*, and enters upon another cycle inspired with new zeal and large hope. Her diverse peoples are well compacted and nationalised, and generally satisfied with a comparative present prosperity which promises so well for the future. The local policy of the government is enlightened, liberal, and eminently *paternal*. The ruling idea of the day seems to be to elevate and improve her people and develop her natural resources. To this end, her schools, her colleges, and her scientific institutions are more liberally endowed and en-

[12]Clay to Seward, 19 March 1862, ibid.; Clay to Mary Jane Clay, 6 March 1862, Clay Papers, Filson Club. The Soviet scholar Robert Ivanov observed that Abraham Lincoln seemed to duplicate Gorchakov's habit, as described by Clay, of remaining in the shadows while speaking to political and diplomatic guests. *Diplomatiia Avraama Linkol'na*, p. 63. Green Clay gave his first impression of Gorchakov as plainly dressed, slightly bald, six feet tall but slightly stooped, over middle-aged, "an intelligent face with some marks of severe thought, and with pleasing manner." Green Clay Journal, 1861–1862, State Historical Society of Missouri (hereafter SHSM), Columbia.

couraged; new rights and privileges are conferred upon the people; a new system of jurisprudence has just been established which secures to every citizen a public hearing and trial by jury; the revenue system is being remodelled, because it is found to bear disproportionably upon the poorer classes; her system of railroads and internal improvements is urged judiciously forward; her extensive mineral resources, her manufactures, and her commerce, are receiving increased attention; and more important still, the great interest of agriculture and its million masses, seems to be the speciality of the present Emperor. . . . Every individual of these millions has now new hopes, new desires, and new necessities.[13]

And from Odessa, Timothy Smith reported:

Russia is beginning to change. The old fashioned stand-still of the autocracy and serfdom is beginning to give place to the more enlightened advance of amelioration and emancipation. A new stimulus is given to industry, a new purpose and a better hope to life. Her new born men are better friends to the government . . . , are better supporters of law and order, are more industrious, more intelligent, and therefore better subjects, and the Emperor of Russia today is rendered safer and stronger upon his throne than was his August father . . . with all his bayonets and all his concentrated Imperial will and power.[14]

Both Smith and Stacy followed up their general analyses by predicting a great future for sales of American agricultural implements and other tools of economic progress.

Clay's counterpart in the United States, Eduard Stoeckl, was so engrossed in reporting the kaleidoscope of American events that he gave little regard to how the United States was viewing the Russian changes. He did, however, make one revealing remark in commenting on the spirit of hospitality attending the Russian fleet visit in 1863: "The bases of good entente, and I would say of sympathy, which have at all times existed between the two Governments and the two peoples have their origin in the nature of things, and it would be superfluous to repeat them here." But, he added, two new linkages had developed in recent years—the hostile attitude and actions of France and Britain toward both coun-

---

[13]Stacy to Seward, 20 November 1862, DUSC, Reval, vol. 1 (roll 1, M 484), RG 59, NA. The secretary of state was apparently quite impressed with Stacy's report, because he wrote him a rare special commendation for it. David Read, "Henry Baldwin Stacy," in *Vermont Historical Gazetteer* (edited and published by Abby Maria Hemenway, Burlington) 2 (1871): 966–67.

[14]T. C. Smith to Seward, 1 July 1864, DUSC, Odessa, vol. 4 (roll 2, M 459), RG 59, NA.

tries, "and the grand act of serf emancipation which finds here, more than in Europe, its true appreciation."[15]

Clearly the changes in Russia were received positively in the United States and increased the sense of common bonds during the period of civil turmoil. Americans, in the North at least, responded quickly and easily to the liberal shift in direction in Russia, not only because they needed an ally but also simply out of a belief in humanitarian progress, in civil rights, and in common causes. Russia seemed to be removing an autocratic embarrassment from the quasi-alliance between the two countries—and perhaps the United States and its abolitionist propaganda had something to do with it.

The Russian View of American Disorder

Although Americans could take heart from the apparent stability that accompanied emancipation and reform in Russia, Russians were dismayed by the upheaval and disorder into which the United States plunged in pursuit of a similar cause. Many Russians had perceived the threat; most who wrote about the United States condemned slavery while praising other aspects of American life. Others, especially among the Slavophiles, viewed the existence of slavery in a country that purported to be a democratic republic as proof that the United States had had its values indelibly corrupted by old Europe—or, in another version, distorted by economic and territorial greed. Yet Russians also recalled a century-old legacy of friendly relations, reinforced especially by the Crimean War detente, and emphasized their affinity with the United States. Some such as Golovin saw division as the only solution—the way to "purify" at least part of the country—but most abhorred the idea of a weakening and declining United States. An American disaster, moreover, would be a sharp blow to liberal causes in Russia. Possibly only those conservative, soon to be serfless, landlords could cherish such a thought.

Perhaps also reflecting his own dismay, John Appleton was nevertheless astute in assessing the Russian response to the news of the secession of South Carolina in response to Lincoln's election:

> I think the general belief here is still favorable to some amicable adjustment. . . . They cannot understand . . . how a great government like ours, whose career has been eminently prosperous, can be suddenly destroyed, without any apparent cause, by the very people who are themselves a part of it and who are daily receiving its benefits. They have never seen an American citizen abroad who did not glory in the American name and boast

[15]Stoeckl to Gorchakov, 18/30 November 1863, f. kants. Vashington 1863, d. 103, AVPR.

with honest pride of our popular institutions. They have never seen an American journal either, where this same spirit was not manifested of satisfaction with the American institutions and of attachment to the American form of government. Under this government they have seen our country advance in population and territory and wealth and honor, as no nation on earth was ever before permitted to do, and this progress, instead of exhausting its energies, has seemed to them to inspire it with new vigor for its future growth. . . . They cannot persuade themselves that a government, thus idolized apparently by its citizens, under which these great results have been already worked out, and under which still greater results may fairly be anticipated, is really about to be destroyed in the midst of its usefulness, and by the hands of its own people. . . . They have no sympathy with the idea of state secession any more than with the system of Negro slavery, and they will be slow, therefore, to give back their old confidence in the United States, even if the present difficulties there should be happily surmounted, unless indeed they can understand at the same time, that the right of secession which is now so earnestly claimed, has been substantially abandoned throughout the country and is not likely to be again insisted on in any practical form. If, however, the existing difficulties shall not be surmounted, and under the influence of this doctrine the Union shall be broken up, the result will be hailed undoubtedly by the cabinets of Europe, as conclusive proof of the instability of popular institutions; and the destruction of the American government will be a calamity, therefore, not only to those who enjoy its benefits at home, but to those oppressed peoples, also, in the old world whose hearts are now cheered by the knowledge of its existence and whose eyes are turned daily towards it for support and consolation.[16]

In Washington, Stoeckl, too, watched with deepening chagrin and sorrow the breaking up of the Union. He saw its roots, however, in the unrelenting abolitionist pressure of the Puritan clergy of New England, who were "always ready to confound politics with religion." Their extreme doctrines had spread to other states, even to the South, which was "no less fertile in demagogues than the North." He thought that Lincoln would have received only half as many votes had the election been held in December rather than November, but for the moment he was still optimistic about a compromise solution:

During my long stay in the United States I have had the occasion to study in depth the character of America, and . . . it is impossible to believe that a people so practical, so devoted to its interests, and so prosperous could let

[16]Appleton to Black, 31 December 1860/12 January 1861, DUSM, Russia, vol. 18 (roll 18, M 35), RG 59, NA.

their passions go to the point of sacrificing everything and precipitating themselves into an abyss that no one could foresee the depth, that at the last moment an unpredicted event will save the country. I desire this cordially because in regard to the political considerations we can view only with regret the fall of a great nation with which our relations have always been friendly and intimate and which, on a memorable occasion, was nearly the only Power that sympathized sincerely with our cause.[17]

This statement would appear to contradict sources that accused Stoeckl of hostility toward the United States, though it is certainly true that he became increasingly exasperated with the course of events and the apparent weakness and vacillation of the federal government.

In January 1861 Stoeckl reiterated the consequences of a division: "The fall of the great American republic will not be of less importance for our era than the first American revolution, and it would prevent these once isolated States which are bound in federal pact from forming a Power of the first rank." The approaching war was a sad alternative but the only one. The North, he added, could exist without the South (although it would not be so wealthy or powerful) whereas the South would have to depend on outside protection, thus inviting foreign intervention and a European presence for some time to come. The Monroe Doctrine would essentially be destroyed, and North America would again become the arena of European conflict. Stoeckl also believed that a new constitution would be necessary—one that would strengthen the remaining central government and eliminate the evils associated with universal suffrage and free elections, which foster anarchy and "the revolutionary and socialist spirit" spread by European immigrants. Stoeckl advised that Russia recognize the Richmond government only after it had regularized its own relations with the North; in the meantime, Russia should avoid offending the "disunionists." This position was applauded by both Gorchakov and Alexander II.[18]

Nor did the Russian minister simply stand by and watch. As soon as the Lincoln administration was installed, Stoeckl attempted to bring about direct negotiations between Southern emissaries and William H. Seward, the new secretary of state, in early April. In fact, he had Seward's agreement to a meeting with Ramon, a Confederate delegate, at his own house, but Seward suddenly changed his mind and became adamant against compromise. Stoeckl then had to referee an intense and hostile encounter at the British ambassador's residence, where

---

[17]Stoeckl to Gorchakov, 11/23 December 1860, f. kants. Vashington 1861, d. 162, AVPR. Photostat copies of much of the Russian diplomatic correspondence during the Civil War are in the Manuscript Division, LC.

[18]Stoeckl to Gorchakov, 9/21 January 1861, ibid. Notations of approval by Gorchakov and Alexander II are on the margins of the reports.

Seward declared to the French and British representatives, Henri Mercier and Lord Lyons, "that if civil war breaks out all commercial relations with the ports of the South will be interrupted."[19] Despite this warning, both almost immediately recommended to their governments the full recognition of the Confederacy. Stoeckl now recommended that Russia remain strictly impartial but recognize Confederate independence after Britain and France had done so.

Stoeckl became more alarmed about the American situation in late April, after listening to the report of Charles Arnaud, a countryman who had just made an extensive tour through the South and was convinced that Confederate military capabilities should be taken seriously. According to Arnaud, Stoeckl asserted that Russia "would not permit, under any circumstances, the disruption of the Union." And he followed this up by dispatching Arnaud on a mission that led to Cincinnati and Louisville, from where he made several intelligence sorties into the South for Gen. John C. Fremont. While serving on the staff of Fremont during the summer of 1861, Arnaud helped plan the Tennessee River campaign that shifted some of the focus of the war to the West.[20] Wounded in September, Arnaud returned for treatment to Russia, where he continued to assist the Northern cause. He and John Turchin (Ivan Turchaninov), who commanded a regiment of Illinois volunteers, were the most renowned of the active Russian participants in the war.

Meanwhile, in St. Petersburg, Appleton had several interviews with Gorchakov on the state of American affairs. At one in April he handed the Russian chancellor a copy of Lincoln's inaugural address with the hope that the American government might receive "at this crisis a renewed manifestation of that friendly disposition which had always marked the intercourse between the United States and that Empire."[21] Gorchakov responded that the emperor was not considering the question of recognizing the Confederacy. As Appleton reported: "I might assure you, he said, that His Majesty was not unmindful of the friendly relations which had so long subsisted between the two countries, and that he sincerely desired the harmony and prosperity of the Union. It was the only commercial counterpoise in the world, he added, to Great Britain, and Russia would do nothing, therefore, to diminish its just power and influence."

---

[19]As quoted by Stoeckl to Gorchakov, 28 March/9 April 1861, ibid. See also Ferris, *Desperate Diplomacy*, pp. 19–20, and Case and Spencer, *United States and France*, p. 46.

[20]Col. Charles A. de Arnaud, *The Union, and Its Ally, Russia: An Historical Narrative of the Most Critical and Exciting Period of Our Late War* (Washington, D.C.: Gibson Bros., 1890), p. 3, passim. Arnaud also credits Stoeckl with pointing out—earlier than most people—the importance of the western theater of war.

[21]As quoted by Appleton to Seward, 8/20 April 1861, DUSM, Russia, vol. 18 (roll 18, M 35), RG 59, NA.

Gorchakov concluded by saying that "no nation would witness the restoration with more satisfaction than Russia."[22]

The words of Stoeckl and Gorchakov expressed more than simple sympathy for the predicament of the United States. They were also concerned that a weakened and divided country across the Atlantic would be of little value to Russia in its continuing rivalry with Great Britain and in restoring Russia's place in the European balance of power, the chief goal of Russian foreign policy since the Crimean War. This was critical especially because of the instability and conflict then occurring in central Europe involving the unification and rise of Germany and Italy and the decline of Austria. Russia was also somewhat vulnerable as a result of its own internal reforms. Thus any lessening of the potential of the United States to act as a counterbalance to France and Britain was a concern to Russian officials.

So, aristocratic, semifeudal Russia, which, even after emancipation, resembled much more the South, unhesitatingly cast its lot with the North and the preservation of the Union. In his first substantive dispatch from Russia, Cassius Clay quoted with added emphasis a remark of Ivan Tolstoy, the assistant minister of foreign affairs, *"that the Confederate States would not venture an embassy here."*[23] And after his first reception by Gorchakov on 16 June, Clay noted that the chancellor sounded very "American" in expressing his hopes that the rebellion would be "crushed out" and "speedily done."[24] The new minister and his secretaries were then received by Alexander II at his Peterhof summer palace on 14 July. The emperor's friendly welcoming speech was in Russian, but when Clay in his response compared Alexander's reforms with those of Peter the Great, Alexander was apparently so moved that he replied directly in English—"so much the more had he hopes of the perpetuity of the friendship between the two nations, now that in addition to all former ties we were bound together by a common sympathy in the common cause of emancipation."[25]

Already, on 10 July, Gorchakov had sent Stoeckl a remarkable letter making clear Russia's support for the Union cause but deploring the deepening of the conflict:

> The Emperor profoundly regrets that the hope of a peaceful solution is not realized, and that American citizens, already in arms against each other, are ready to let loose upon their country the most formidable of the scourges of political society—civil war.

[22]Ibid.

[23]As quoted and underlined in Clay to Seward, 7 June 1861, DUSM, Russia, vol. 19 (roll 19, M 35), RG 59, NA.

[24]Clay to Seward, 21 June 1861, ibid.

[25]As quoted in ibid. This was apparently a "running" diary of events through July, since the next dispatch was dated 3 August.

For the more than eighty years that it has existed the American Union owes its independence, its towering rise, and its progress, to the concord of its members, consecrated, under the auspices of its illustrious founders, by institutions which have been able to reconcile union with liberty. This union has been fruitful. It has exhibited to the world the spectacle of a prosperity without example in the annals of history.

While deliberately never mentioning slavery, Gorchakov called for a peaceful resolution of the rift:

The American nation would . . . give a proof of high political wisdom in seeking in common such a settlement before a useless effusion of blood, a barren squandering of strength and of public riches, and acts of violence and reciprocal reprisals, shall have come to deepen an abyss between the two parties to the confederation, to end definitely in their mutual exhaustion, and in the ruin, perhaps irreparable, of their commercial and political power.

Although Russian concern about the international effects of the Civil War could not have been plainer,

this Union is not simply in our eyes an element essential to the universal political equilibrium. It constitutes, besides, a nation to which our August Master and all Russia have pledged the most friendly interest; for the two countries, placed at the extremities of the two worlds, both in the ascending period of their development, appear called to a natural community of interests and of sympathies, of which they have already given mutual proofs to each other.[26]

This letter caused an enormous stir after it was translated for the president, circulated around Washington, and published in all the prominent Northern newspapers in September. The inspiration for it has generally been credited to Stoeckl's alarmist dispatches and Clay's ardor, but three other persons may have been at least as influential. Baron Ungern-Sternberg of Estonia, whose admiration for American technology had already been demonstrated, left the United States after a tour of the North in May carrying dispatches from Stoeckl, and he probably conferred personally with Gorchakov or other members of the foreign ministry about American affairs when he reached St. Petersburg. Also, a veteran secretary and longtime resident in the United States, Vladimir Bodisko, was sent home in early June with a special message from Stoeckl that described the atmosphere of desperation in Washington and with instructions to commu-

[26]Gorchakov to Stoeckl, 28 June (O.S.) 1861, f. kants. Vashington 1861, d. 162, AVPR; the full text (which translation is used here) is in Woldman, *Lincoln and the Russians*, pp. 127–29.

nicate verbally the international implications of the American conflict. Ungern-Sternberg and Bodisko would have been the first Russians to report directly on the beginning of the war, and they arrived shortly before the date of Gorchakov's dispatch.[27] Gorchakov's skillfully honed language also bears the likely imprint of Alexander Jomini, the son of a French-Swiss general in Napoleon's army who defected to the Russian side in 1813 and who subsequently became a famous military historian and theorist. Jomini is known to have taken a special interest in American affairs. Moreover, as a highly regarded stylist, he composed many of Russia's diplomatic documents of this period in his position as senior counselor in the Ministry of Foreign Affairs.[28]

Another young Russian diplomat, Konstantin Katakazi, was also close to Jomini and probably influential on policy toward the United States, since he had served as secretary of legation in Washington for several years and was married to an American from New York. He was reassigned to Portugal in the 1850s and formed a friendship with George W. Morgan, the American minister in Lisbon. Returning to the United States, Morgan soon donned a general's uniform and served in William T. Sherman's western campaign. In January 1862, Morgan wrote to Katakazi expressing the '*universal* satisfaction which the letter of your great Gortchakoff gave to our people without distinction of party." "In

[27]Stoeckl to Gorchakov, 11/23 May and 23 May/3 June 1861, f. kants. Vashington 1861, d. 162, AVPR. These dispatches carried by Ungern-Sternberg and Bodisko, respectively, were both logged in at the ministry in St. Petersburg on 23 June, Old Style (5 July by the western calendar), five days before the date on Gorchakov's famous message. Bodisko reached the Winans estate at Aleksandrovsk to help conclude a Fourth of July party with a joke about Southern ladies not wanting Washington to cut off their mail deliveries. Green Clay Journal, 4 July 1861, SHSM. Moreover, in another dispatch of the same date, Gorchakov acknowledged receipt of Stoeckl's communications via Ungern-Sternberg. The return mail was probably carried by Col. Dmitri Romanov, an army communications expert who was also instructed to survey the military situation. His subsequent report on the Army of the Potomac was enclosed in Stoeckl to Gorchakov, 4/16 December 1861, f. kants. Vashington 1862, d. 152, AVPR. Clay naturally tried to claim the credit. To his friend Senator Rollings of Missouri he wrote, "Russia has thrown all her vast European power and prestige openly in our favor in the two celebrated letters of Prince Gortchacow . . . [thanks to my] 'undiplomatic' diplomacy." To James S. Rollins, Rollins Papers, box 2, f. 80, SHSM.

[28]Jomini requested, and received directly, in-depth analyses of American affairs from the secretary of legation, and later consul general, Robert Osten-Sacken. See Osten-Sacken (Washington) to Jomini, 1/13 September 1861, f. kants. Vashington 1861, d. 162, AVPR; and Osten-Sacken to Jomini, 3 June 1862, Jomini-Onou Papers, Eg. 3174, British Library (hereafter BL), London. Another person in the equation may have been Grand Duke Constantine, who was at the height of his influence as a leading promoter of liberal reform, and whose aide-de-camp, a Captain Malinovskii, was also dispatched to the United States at about this time. Malinovskii's main mission, however, was to convince Czech immigrants in the United States to resettle in the Amur region. Stoeckl to Gorchakov, 28 August/9 September 1861, f. kants. Vashington 1861, d. 162, AVPR.

fact," Morgan emphasized, "Russia and the United States are natural allies, and the day will come when they will act together in advancing the cause of civilization and in counteracting the arrogant and insolent interference of Great Britain in the affairs of other nations."[29] Katakazi forwarded Morgan's letter to Jomini and was soon summoned (coincidentally?) to St. Petersburg to be a special adviser to Gorchakov.

During the summer and fall of 1861, the Russian legation in Washington continued to bombard St. Petersburg with baleful descriptions and dire predictions about the surrounding political and military chaos, reflecting the general panic in the capital. After the Battle of Bull Run in July, Stoeckl remarked, "The Administration and the Congress have entirely lost their heads," and secretary Robert Osten-Sacken wrote unofficially to Jomini that everything could be summed up in two words—"confusion and stupidity. Mr. Lincoln's government is essentially a government of parties, while it throws up the pretense of being an independent power."[30] This turmoil led Stoeckl and Osten-Sacken to claim that a "revolution" was under way. For Stoeckl, however, this meant the triumph of "demagogues" over honest but weak leaders like Lincoln, which should be "a salutary lesson for the anarchists and visionaries of Europe." He was careful to add that "the disintegration of the United States as a Power is an event that we must regret. The American confederation is a counterweight to English power and as such its existence constitutes an element of equilibrium in the world."[31]

As the war progressed into 1862, with no sign of an end, the Russian minister could sympathize with the Union leaders, as he saw no way out of the dilemma, nor could he see a purpose or result from abolishing slavery and occupying the South. "The great difficulty of the abolition of slavery in this country is the incompatibility of the races," a situation different from that in the Spanish and Portuguese territories of the New World.[32] He also observed that blacks were "a degraded class" throughout the country, scarcely tolerated in the North. Osten-Sacken, while trying to find a parallel between American and European institutional development, privately advised Jomini that it was impossible to predict

[29]George W. Morgan (Mount Vernon, Ohio) to Katakazi (Lisbon), 6 January 1862, Jomini-Onou Papers, Eg. 3170, BL. Also, Edward Everett to Clay, 5 January 1862, Clay Papers, Lincoln Memorial University.

[30]Osten-Sacken to Jomini, 1/13 September 1861, f. kants. Vashington 1861, d. 162, AVPR. Karl (or Carl or Charles) Robert Osten-Sacken usually signed his diplomatic correspondence as "Robert." As consul-general in New York beginning in 1862 he was quite socially active and best known as an entomologist whose four-volume work on North American diptera became a classic. His father was a high-ranking Russian foreign ministry official of German Estonian background.

[31]Stoeckl to Gorchakov, 12/24 February 1862, f. kants. Vashington 1862, d. 151, AVPR.

[32]Ibid.

the course of "the revolution we are now witnessing," because "nothing is definite, nothing is certain."[33]

The growing liberal-radical fringe of Russian society also watched American events and varied strikingly in their reactions. Though almost all applauded the antislavery movement, most regretted the coming of war. Nicholas Chernyshevsky optimistically predicted a Union victory and, in its aftermath, the evolution of the United States along an egalitarian, socialistic path. Alexander Herzen, on the other hand, more accurately feared an increase in centralized political and economic authority emerging from this "second American revolution."[34] The comments of the Russian intelligentsia, however, were overshadowed by their natural obsession with what was then happening in their own country.

Diplomatic Repercussions

From the beginning of the upheaval in the United States, international relations were very much affected. Steam power, the telegraph, and integrated commerce were making the countries of the world more interdependent at the same time that nationalism was fostering distinction and rivalry. A series of conflicts that began in Mexico in the 1840s had extended around the globe through Italy, the Crimea, Iran, Afghanistan, India, and China. As a result, governments and peoples alike were sensitized to internal crises and military solutions that often involved intervention by "Great Powers." Even in the relatively isolated North American states, people in town and country were very much aware of the outside world—the outgrowth of their immigrant backgrounds, inexpensive ship, rail, and telegraphic communications, the prevalence of literacy, and the spread of competing daily newspapers.

However cognizant of world affairs Americans might be, the nature of the political system handicapped the conduct of foreign policy. The new government that came to Washington in March 1861 forced a clean break in what continuity did exist. Neither Lincoln, Seward, Chase, nor Stanton had any real experience in the diplomatic field, in contrast to their predecessors. And many of the older generation of American diplomats were Southerners, had passed from the scene,

[33]Stoeckl to Gorchakov, 23 April/5 May 1862, ibid.; Osten-Sacken to Gorchakov, 3 June 1862, Jomini-Onou Papers, Eg. 3174, BL. Gorchakov also received firsthand reports from Arnaud in March 1862. Arnaud, *The Union and Its Ally*, p. 21, gives the date as February, but he was apparently remembering by the Russian calendar, since Clay pinpointed the date of the first interview as 7 March and indicated that Arnaud returned to the United States almost immediately as a courier. Clay to Seward (private), 7 and 8 March 1862, DUSM, Russia, vol. 19 (roll 19, M 35), RG 59, NA.

[34]Rogger, "Russia and the Civil War," pp. 235–36; Max Laserson, *The American Impact on Russia, Diplomatic and Ideological, 1784–1917* (New York: Collier Edition, 1962), pp. 277–88.

or were swept aside by the Republican tidal wave. The clamor for spoils meant that there would be almost no possibility of retaining those with diplomatic expertise. Gone were Buchanan and Dallas, Cass and Marcy, Appleton and Seymour. In contrast, the other leading players on the international scene—Britain, France, Russia, and even Spain—had ministers in Washington any one of whom boasted more diplomatic experience than the whole Lincoln administration.

An early test of the Union's diplomatic skills was the Trent affair, a tense entanglement with Britain over the North's interception and forced removal of two Southern envoys to Europe from a British packet ship in November 1861. After much posturing in Washington and inflammation of public opinion on all sides, counsels of restraint, including those from Russia, prevailed, and Seward agreed to their release and safe passage to Europe. Instrumental in preventing war with Britain was practically the only Lincoln diplomatic appointment of some repute—Charles Francis Adams, the new envoy to Britain. A vocal antislavery New Englander with an illustrious ancestry, Adams had spent several years with his family in St. Petersburg as a youth. Thus, despite its want of experience, the Lincoln administration, thanks to Seward and Adams, demonstrated a degree of shrewdness and initiative in the handling of the Trent affair.

More the norm were the appointments to St. Petersburg beginning with Cassius Clay, the Kentucky brawler, and his motley assortment of secretaries. Once the war was in full swing, Clay itched to fight and managed to secure his own recall in the spring of 1862 to command a brigade at home. Rumors circulated that Carl Schurz was next in line, but Clay was instead replaced by Simon Cameron of Pennsylvania, whose only qualification seemed to be his demonstrated incompetence as secretary of war and the resultant need to get him out of Washington as quickly and gracefully as possible. But his tenure was expected to be short. As Clay recalled, "It was understood that Cameron was to slide down to his old level, using the mission to St. Petersburg as a parachute."[35]

Though obviously hampered by the circumstances of his appointment, Cameron brought with him to Russia in the spring of 1862 a sophisticated traveler, writer, and lecturer, Bayard Taylor, to serve as secretary. Expecting to succeed Cameron as minister, Taylor at least had the advantages of familiarity with foreign cultures, including previous exposure to Russia, and of social connections, since his wife's sister was married to a well-known Russian astronomer. He also had a genuine desire to study Russian society and the Russian language, writing to James T. Fields of the *Atlantic*, "I am studying Russian (a thing no other Diplomat does), and making myself thoroughly acquainted with everything relating to the country and the people."[36] With the diplomatic appointment, Taylor also

[35]Clay, *The Life of . . .* , 1:299.
[36]Taylor to James T. Fields, 18 August 1862, Bayard Taylor Papers, box 5 (indexed correspondence), Cornell. In another letter, Taylor wrote Fields, "In Russian, I begin to

hoped to finance a trip to Central Asia, where Russian sovereignty was expanding rapidly.

The reception of Cameron and Taylor in Russia was overtly friendly. In his first conversation with Alexander II on 25 June, Cameron found that the emperor "exhibited not only his profound interest in every thing relating to our country, but his accurate knowledge of her present situation . . . [and] that he was very anxious the United States, as a nation, should suffer no diminution of power or influence; our interests and those of Russia were in many respects identical, and he was desirous to hasten, by all the means in his power, the progress of that telegraphic enterprise which will enable the two Governments to communicate directly with each other."[37] In his few substantive reports from Russia, Cameron reiterated this theme of Russian support: "There is no capital in Europe where the loyal American meets with such universal sympathy, as St. Petersburg—none where the suppression of our unnatural rebellion will be hailed with more genuine satisfaction."[38] In fact, the American minister found the tranquil summer atmosphere of Russia boring in comparison with the storms of Washington: "At this court . . . I am spared the necessity of advocating our cause. I find a constant desire to interpret everything to our advantage."[39] Prodded by self-interested "friends" such as Clay and Taylor, Cameron begged Seward for a leave of absence to reenter the fray at home by running for the Senate in the fall of 1862. Obtaining no response, he simply abandoned his post in September, leaving Taylor in charge.

An imbroglio then developed concerning Cameron's successor. Clay had become dissatisfied because he had not received a major army command. Having suffered financial losses in the war, he wanted to regain the appointment and believed he had both Lincoln's and Cameron's promises on the matter.[40] Taylor, on the other hand, had won the support of his literary and journalistic friends at home, of the American community in St. Petersburg, of Cameron and Vice-

read with tolerable facility—even poetry. It is a tough language, though, I assure you." One difficulty was that "one rarely hears anything but French in society," though Taylor noted that "the tone of the higher Russian society is quite free and agreeable, with a certain democratic air." To Fields, 23 January 1863, ibid. See also Taylor's letters to Horace Greeley, 5 July 1862, Greeley Papers, and to William Cullen Bryant, 20 June 1862, Bryant-Godwin Collection, Manuscript Division, NYPL.

[37]Taylor to George P. Smith, 18 August 1862, in John Richie Schultz, ed., *The Unpublished Letters of Bayard Taylor in the Huntington Library* (San Marino, Calif.: Huntington Library, 1937), p. 55.

[38]Cameron to Seward, 23 July 1982, DUSM, Russia, vol. 19 (roll 19, M 35), RG 59, NA.

[39]Cameron to Seward, 9 September 1862, ibid.

[40]Clay to Cameron, 13 August and 6 September 1862, Simon Cameron Papers, reel 9, Manuscript Division, LC (originals in Pennsylvania History and Museum Commission, Harrisburg).

president Hamlin, and of the Russian court. In private letters Taylor pressed his desire for the appointment and vilified his opponent, "whose incredible vanity and astonishing blunders are still the talk of St. Petersburg." Yet he still feared that Clay "will probably be allowed to come back to his ballet-girls (his reason for coming) by our soft-hearted Abraham."[41] The prim and proper Taylor seemed genuinely horrified by the court gossip about Clay—that "he cut Kentucky pigeon wings in dancing the court quadrilles," which was expertly imitated by Grand Duke Michael to the great amusement of Alexander II. Taylor suspected another reason that Clay wanted so desperately to return to Russia was to make money from a gas-lighting contract with an intriguer named Laslo Chandor.[42]

Cameron's opinions about who should succeed him were hampered by his failure to win the Senate seat and charges of bribery connected with the race. Joseph Casey offered a "patriotic" basis for the decision: "Clay should be sent back to Russia where *he can do no harm at least.*" And Clay himself pressured Cameron: "General, you got the place which I *was promised*—the war department—when I was set down in Russia for the Presidential term you crowded me from there."[43] Taylor, however, believed Clay's story that Seward's opposition to him was the main factor in the selection: "Clay tells me that Seward is hostile to me, which I have all along suspected to be the case. Seward is hostile to everyone who will not burn incense under his nose. . . . He is the Chief Eunuch at the Court of our feeble Sultan."[44] Thus, an ardent pro-Unionist, influential publicist, and promising diplomatic talent was cast aside. Since Seward detested Clay as much as anybody, it was Lincoln who finally made the decision, on Cameron's somewhat reluctant advice, to send Clay back to Russia.

In the eight-month interim between Cameron's departure and Clay's return, Taylor cultivated a more respectable American presence in Russia. He faced,

[41]Taylor to Edmund Clarence Stedman, 23 February 1863, Stedman Papers, Columbia University Manuscript Collection.

[42]Taylor to Cameron, 27 January 1863, Cameron Papers, reel 9, Manuscript Division, LC.

[43]Joseph Casey to Cameron, 3 November 1862; Clay to Cameron, 13 December 1862; and Lincoln to Cameron, 14 December 1862, Cameron Papers, reel 9, Manuscript Division, LC.

[44]Taylor to Cameron, 3 August 1863, Cameron Papers, reel 7, Manuscript Division, LC. Taylor hoped to secure the mission to Persia as consolation but was convinced—by Lincoln—that Seward prevented it. Taylor to his mother, 11 May 1863, in Marie Hansen-Taylor and Horace E. Scudder, eds., *Life and Letters of Bayard Taylor*, vol. 1 (Boston: Houghton Mifflin, 1884), pp. 411–14.

The New York *Times* commented on Clay's return to Russia: "We hope the Emperor will not get the impression that we confound his dominions with Siberia, and regard them as penal colonies for the banishment of uneasy politicians." As quoted in Smiley, *Lion of Whitehall*, p. 195.

however, a growing Russian exasperation with the course of American affairs. At the end of October 1862, after more Union reverses and stronger signs of British and French efforts to intervene in the war, Taylor met with Gorchakov, ostensibly to deliver Lincoln's letter of thanks for Russian support. He found the chancellor quite upset, reflecting the current frustration in Washington that was expressed in Stoeckl's dispatches. Gorchakov thought "the chances of preserving the Union were growing more and more desperate" and added, "Can nothing be done to stop this dreadful war?" He did not hide his fears of American exhaustion and loss of world power that could result from the continuing division. And when Taylor tried to paint a brighter picture, Gorchakov quickly interrupted:

> I am tired of predictions. I have heard nothing else from Mr. Clay, who still sends them to me—but they are never fulfilled. Let me be perfectly sincere with you. You know that the Government of the United States has few friends among the Powers. England rejoices over what is happening to you: she longs and prays for your overthrow. France is less actively hostile: her interests would be less affected by the result; but she is not unwilling to see it. She is not your friend. Russia, alone, has stood by you from the first, and will continue to stand by you. We are very, *very* anxious, that some means should be adopted—that *any* course should be pursued, which will prevent the division that now seems inevitable. One separation will be followed by another: you will break into fragments.

Gorchakov then made the policy of Russia perfectly clear:

> We desire, above all things, the maintenance of the American Union as one indivisible nation. We cannot take any part, more than we have done. We have no hostility to the southern people. Russia has declared her position, and will maintain it. There will be proposals for intervention: we believe that intervention could do no good at present. *Proposals will be made to Russia, to join in some plan of interference. She will refuse any invitation of the kind.* Russia will occupy the same ground, as at the beginning of the struggle. *You may rely upon it, she will not change.* But we entreat you to settle the difficulty. I cannot express to you how profound an anxiety we feel—how serious are our fears.[45]

The Russian court continued to follow events in the United States closely through the winter of 1862–63. At the New Year's Day diplomatic reception, Alexander II made a special point of asking Taylor for war news. At a ball two days

---

[45]Taylor to Seward, 29 October 1862, DUSM, Russia, vol. 19 (roll 19, M 35), RG 59, NA. This dispatch reached Washington not long before Lincoln's decision to issue the Emancipation Proclamation; the underlining represents Taylor's emphasis.

later, they discussed the Union defeat at Fredericksburg but agreed that the Emancipation Proclamation was the equivalent of several victorious engagements. Still, Taylor felt compelled to submit a detailed private communication to Gorchakov listing the advantages on the Union side.[46] Through March, Taylor was sought out regularly by Alexander II for discussion of the Civil War: "The Emperor manifests a steady and eager interest in the progress of our national cause. The effect of the President's Proclamation of Emancipation and the trial of our new ironclads by the test of actual warfare seem especially to occupy his mind."[47] It was at about this time that the decision was made to send a squadron of the Russian Baltic fleet to American waters.

Mediation

While Taylor manned the Union's ramparts in St. Petersburg, the first serious public offer of mediation was tendered. Since the beginning of the conflict, Henri Mercier, the French minister in Washington, had been urging his government to take a more active stance and had even engaged in direct conversations with Confederate leaders. He was anxious to have Britain and Russia participate but was always a little too insistent and faulty in his timing. In May 1862 Stoeckl refused Mercier's invitation to join him on a private mission to Richmond, "because I did not see any chance that this project would succeed."[48] The Russian minister, however, promoted the idea of a French initiative behind the scenes, because his own hands were tied by the clearly enunciated Russian policy of nonintervention and because he was convinced that any British overture would be automatically rejected. Stoeckl's pessimism regarding the consequences of prolonging the conflict seemed substantiated in the summer of 1862; after the brutal fighting appeared to dim the prospects of Union success, rumors mounted of even more moves toward intervention and possible formal recognition of the Confederacy by the European powers.

Despite the tentative initiatives, Stoeckl and the Russian government were unprepared for the public call issued by Napoleon III in November for a three-power (France, Britain, and Russia) mediation, with representatives of the two American sides to meet at a neutral site. Stoeckl was surprised that this proposal came when it did and that it was not done in concert with Britain. But he also would not have predicted the latter's refusal to join, a sign of the disunity of the European powers.[49] Just as France moved aggressively, Britain became cau-

---

[46]Taylor to Seward, 21 January 1863, ibid.

[47]Taylor to Seward, 3 March 1863, ibid.

[48]Stoeckl to Gorchakov, 23 April/5 May 1862, f. kants. Vashington 1862, d. 152, AVPR.

[49]Stoeckl to Gorchakov, 19 November/1 December 1862, ibid.

tious, somewhat appeased by the Union's backing down from its initial *Trent* position and releasing the Southern envoys to resume their voyage.

Gorchakov was quick to react to the French entreaty. Noting to Stoeckl that the apparent French desire to establish peace was also Russia's, he added, "We attach too much value to the reports you have sent on the probable effect of this offer of collective mediation to be ready to join this project of *entente* suggested by the French government." Gorchakov stipulated that Russia would lend its assistance only when the two sides were definitely ready to negotiate. He gave Stoeckl a relatively free hand to determine the appropriate time but emphasized, "Be circumspect!"[50] In November the minister conferred with Democratic party leaders in New York after their election gains. Stoeckl thought there was a chance that a joint Franco-Russian mediation (sans Britain) might be accepted, but then he saw these hopes dashed by the Emancipation Proclamation, which he considered "impolitic and impractical" and aimed to incite a slave uprising in the South.[51] Stoeckl's wish to be the strategic peace-broker between France and Britain on one side and between the North and the South on the other was left unfulfilled. One reason for this was the new mood in St. Petersburg, where the more decisive and militant policy of the Lincoln administration was greeted enthusiastically as veering away from any compromise settlement that would leave the North weak and vulnerable. Military victory now only seemed a matter of time. Another reason was the failure of the Confederacy to exploit the mediation sentiment in Europe.

Confederate Diplomacy

The complicated foreign situation of the Lincoln administration and the disarray of the European powers left the door open for Southern action. Considering the significant role that Southerners had assumed in the prior diplomatic relations of the United States, it is perplexing that so little was accomplished. The taking of James Mason and John Slidell from the *Trent* in 1861 seems to have paralyzed Confederate foreign policy and made it a hostage to Britain and France. That no steps were taken to establish a relationship with Russia is even more surprising, since Russia was a major consumer of Southern products and especially since Francis Pickens, the new governor of South Carolina and an influential voice in the South, had recently earned widespread respect there.

Almost two years into the conflict, in November 1862, Confederate Secretary of State Judah Benjamin finally designated Lucius Q. C. Lamar for a mission to

[50]Ibid.; Gorchakov to Stoeckl, 27 October 1862, ibid.
[51]Stoeckl to Gorchakov, 24 December 1862/5 January 1863, f. kants. Vashington 1863, d. 160, AVPR.

St. Petersburg.[52] In making this appointment, the South passed up another ex-cellent opportunity—using the services of Matthew Fontaine Maury, the emi-nent hydrographer from Virginia who had resigned his commission in the navy when the war began. Learning of this, Grand Duke Constantine offered him political asylum and a position in Russian service.[53] Instead, he spent most of the war years in Britain, attempting, largely in vain, to bolster the Confederacy's commerce-raiding capability.

Confusion reigned among the Confederate agents in Europe. Maury arrived in Liverpool in November 1862 and apparently was on his way to Russia, since John Slidell reported that he viewed Maury's "selection for St. Petersburg a very happy one." The Confederate commissioner added, "We should have had an agent there long since."[54] Then, after learning of the other appointment, Slidell asked James Mason in London if he knew which Lamar this was. Regardless, no Lamar ended up in Russia, either because such a mission seemed a lost cause, on account of illness, or both.[55] Taliaferro Shaffner was another old Russia hand who at first strongly sympathized with the Southern cause and who "wasted" the war years in Britain.[56] These missed opportunities might not have swayed Russia from its path of support for the Union, but the South never had a chance to test directly the firmness of Russian pro-Unionism. A sophisticated Confederate diplomat, respected by the Russian court, might have made mince-meat of Cassius Clay and his Kentucky "pigeon-wing" dancing.

The Civil War and the Polish Revolt

If it is true that the best chance for European mediation of the conflict rested with a joint effort of France and Russia, that option was essentially closed by the Polish revolt that began in January 1863. After the abortive uprising of 1830–31, the case for an independent Poland remained very much alive among Polish na-

[52]Callahan, *Diplomatic History*, p. 95; Owsley, *King Cotton Diplomacy*, p. 489.

[53]Patricia Jahns, *Matthew Fontaine Maury and Joseph Henry: Scientists of the Civil War* (New York: Hastings House, 1961), pp. 193–94; Warren F. Spencer, *The Confederate Navy in Europe* (University: University of Alabama Press, 1983), pp. 127–35; Stoeckl to Gorchakov, 6/18 November 1861, f. kants. Vashington 1861, d. 162, AVPR; Charles Francis Adams to Bayard Taylor, 26 November 1862, Taylor Papers, box 8, Cornell.

[54]Slidell (Paris) to Mason (London), 28 November 1862, vol. 3, James Murray Mason Papers, Manuscript Division, LC.

[55]Slidell to Mason, 15 March 1863, vol. 4, ibid. In October, Mason reported that La-mar was in Paris but had been ill. Mason to Jefferson Davis, 2 October 1863, vol. 6, ibid.

[56]For his proslavery, anti-Lincoln diatribe: Taliaferro P. Shaffner, *The War in America: Being an Historical and Political Account of the Southern and Northern States . . .* (London: Hamilton, Adams, 1862). A contemporary periodical commented on Shaffner: "We al-ways thought him a humbug, but too 'smart' to be a traitor." *Frank Leslie's Illustrated Newspaper*, 12 April 1862.

tionalists, both in the territories of former Poland and in the hearts and minds of exiles and liberals who identified with the Poles and/or were hostile to Russia. A brief rebellion in Galicia (Austrian Poland) in 1846 and the Revolution of 1848 spurred and revived these hopes. The Crimean defeat and the reforms in Russia further inspired the Poles but also illuminated the split between those who wanted to work within the context of a liberally oriented Russian program of reform and those who strove for complete independence from Russia.[57]

A substantial number of the Poles who had fled after 1830 and in the 1840s settled in the United States. By 1860 the Polish-American population was about twenty-five thousand. The majority, however, were from non-Russian Poland, that is, from Galicia and Prussian Poland, primarily from the Poznan (Posen) area. As many as twenty-five hundred Poles fought in the American Civil War on both sides.[58] Although some may have been motivated by ideology, most apparently joined up for money, for advancement, and perhaps because of a military calling, many having come from a noble, martial background. Some Polish volunteers, especially in the North, received officer commissions and made distinguished contributions to the military cause, often sacrificing their lives. For example, Aleksandr Bielawski, who was from Lithuania and had been trained as an engineer at a Russian military academy in St. Petersburg, served as a captain on the staff of the First Illinois Brigade and was killed in his first battle at Belmont, Missouri, in November 1861.[59] Those Poles who fought for the Confederacy were often responding to circumstances, a number having settled in New Orleans, but many of these later deserted to the Northern side.

The greatest Polish contribution to the Northern cause was probably that of Wlodzimierz Krzyzanowski, from the Poznan region. He had moved to Washington, D. C., in the early 1850s, married an American, and was an early supporter of the Republican party and the campaign of Abraham Lincoln. One of the first volunteers for the Army of the Potomac, Krzyzanowski was detached by Secretary of War Cameron to raise a regiment of foreign-born volunteers in New York. This Fifty-eighth Regiment—the "Polish Legion," as it was commonly called, although only about one hundred in the regiment were Polish—was made up prominently of recent emigrés, mostly "forty eighters," or exiles from the 1848 revolts in Europe. It had an honorable military record under Krzyzanowski's command and as part of a foreign corps commanded by the Prussian exile Franz Sigel at the Second Battle of Bull Run, Chancellorsville, and Gettys-

[57]For the background and details of the Polish revolt, see R. F. Leslie, *Reform and Insurrection in Russian Poland, 1856–1865* (London: University of London, Athlone Press, 1963).

[58]Bogdan Grzelonski, *Poles in the United States of America, 1776–1865* (Warsaw: Interpress, 1976), pp. 137, 146–47.

[59]Ibid., pp. 157–58.

burg.[60] Krzyzanowski himself finally attained general rank at the end of the war and later settled in San Francisco.

Many of the most militarily active and competent Poles in the United States thus did not participate in events in Poland but chose for various reasons to commit themselves to the service of their new homeland. This no doubt weakened any Polish-American response to the revolution of 1863 in Poland. Though a Polish Central Committee was formed in New York under the leadership of Henryk Korwin-Kalussowski and others in March, it made virtually no contribution to the overseas struggle. Its efforts were, nevertheless, watched closely by Stoeckl, and he even made a short trip to New York specifically to investigate Polish activities.[61]

The Polish cause in the United States was thus hampered by a single political fact: The Russian Empire and the Lincoln administration were friends and were drawing especially close in 1863. Although the Republican press in the North voiced initial outrage about the events in Russian Poland and sympathy for the Poles, it soon quieted in the face of strong French and British support for Polish independence. Another handicap was that the most vocal and visible Pole in the United States, Adam Gurowski, was a firm supporter of Russia as well as of the Northern cause. Ironically, therefore, a liberal and progressive North fighting against an oppressive system in the South was ultimately indifferent to the Polish cause in 1863—in contrast to its support of Poland in 1831 or Hungary in 1849.

After France formally asked for American support for the Poles in Russia, Seward remarked to the Russian minister, "This is a request to which we can never accede, especially when our own affairs are so embarrassing." To this report Alexander II appended a cryptic "Bravo!"[62] Seward was obviously pleased that the Polish rebellion was diverting European attention from the American conflict. This was seconded by his minister in London, Charles Francis Adams: "It is a shame to find relief in the troubles of our neighbors, especially such a friendly one as Russia has been to us, but there is no denying that the Polish troubles have done something to take off continental pressure from us."[63]

The American representatives in St. Petersburg seconded Seward's anti-

[60]Ibid., pp. 176–194; see also, Mieczyslaw Haiman, *Polish Past in America, 1608–1865* (Chicago: Polish Museum of America, 1974), pp. 108–49.

[61]Stoeckl to Gorchakov, 12/24 March and 26 March/7 April 1863, f. kants. Vashington 1863, d. 160, AVPR.

[62]Stoeckl to Gorchakov, 29 April/11 May 1863, ibid.

[63]Charles Francis Adams (London) to Taylor, 14 March 1863, Taylor Papers, box 8, Cornell. William Dayton, the American minister in France, was also relieved by the Polish diversion: "The Polish affair has even here taken possession for the time being of the public mind to the exclusion of our matters. It lets me up a little." To Bayard Taylor, 7 April 1863, ibid.

Polish, pro-Russian policy. Bayard Taylor, after a series of briefings by Gorchakov on the Polish situation, commented simply, "History teaches no truer lesson than that there is no resurrection for a nation once dead."[64] However, it is not true, as a Polish historian has claimed, that Taylor campaigned across the United States that year against the Polish cause.[65] Cassius Clay was especially biased, depicting in his official dispatches a liberal Russia opposing "*reactionary* Catholic and despotic Poland!"[66] Clay revealed his clearly political slant in a private letter to his wife: "My sympathies are all on her [Russia's] side—for Poland is Catholic and of course antiliberal, and would be the tool of France in her European wars; and as Napoleon has avowed himself our enemy—his enemies are our friends and the reverse."[67]

Obviously, anti-Catholicism was an important part of the American apathy toward Poland in 1863. Clay even saw this as one more reason for friendly relations with Russia. To Robert Walker he wrote: "The Russians are our friends—tolerant in religion, and progressive in civil administration. We know what Catholicism is, and that we have nothing in common with it. You see they have crowded out the *democratic* party from any control in the revolution [in Poland]. So I say once more what folly our press is guilty of in denouncing our liberal friend, the Emperor, for the sake of our *conservative enemy*, the New Poland."[68] Interestingly, Clay found his relations with the British ambassador, Lord Napier, suddenly improved in May 1863, and he attributed this to their common view of a Catholic plot developing between France and Poland.[69] From that point Clay mollified considerably, but did not entirely cease, his anti-British rhetoric.

Visits of Russian Squadrons to the United States

As in the case of the American Civil War, the issues raised by the insurrection in Russian Poland were not easily or quickly resolved. The Polish rebellion ended any possibility of Russian participation in a joint mediation of the American conflict, while Britain stepped up its involvement in both situations after April 1863, joining France in a call for arbitration in Poland and allowing the Confederacy to

[64]Taylor to Seward, 1 April 1863, DUSM, Russia, vol. 19 (roll 19, M 35), RG 59, NA.
[65]Haiman, *Polish Past*, p. 147. Taylor did not leave Russia until mid-May and then spent the summer in Germany, awaiting an expected appointment to Persia until he learned that his brother had died at Gettysburg.
[66]Clay to Seward, 23 July 1863, DUSM, Russia, vol. 20 (roll 20, M 35), RG 59, NA.
[67]July 1863 (no day given), Clay Papers, box 2, Filson Club.
[68]As quoted in James P. Shenton, *Robert John Walker: A Politician from Jackson to Lincoln* (New York and London: Columbia University Press, 1961), p. 204, citing Walker papers in private hands.
[69]Clay to Seward, 29 May 1863, DUSM, Russia, vol. 20 (roll 20, M 35), RG 59, NA. Clay's disposition toward Britain may also have been influenced by the arrival of a new secretary, Henry Bergh, who had just sojourned there.

purchase ships to serve as corsairs against Union merchant shipping. In the aftermath of these events, the decision was made in St. Petersburg to dispatch a squadron of the Baltic fleet to American waters. The motivations behind the preparation to send eight of Russia's best warships to New York (only six actually arrived) have been debated by historians and remain a complex question.

Frank Golder and others have persuasively argued that the primary purpose was to avoid having these ships bottled up in Baltic ports in case a European war should break out over Poland.[70] More to the point, a Russian commerce-raiding capability on the high seas would make Britain and France think twice about initiating military action on behalf of the Poles. The other leading explanation, accepted by American contemporaries and some later commentators, is that the action was essentially a show of strength on behalf of the Union, that is, purely out of friendship and Russian interest in a strong United States. Some claim that the ships would have been committed militarily to the North if either France or Britain had expanded their support of the South. According to this analysis, the Russian navy played an important role in preventing France and Britain from fully recognizing the Confederacy.[71] The grand welcome to the Russian ships was, therefore, quite justified. A middle view is that the Russian squadrons were merely on routine cruises, but the Union was able to use their presence to good effect. Whatever their original purpose, they prevented modern, new ships (Laird rams) from being placed in Confederate hands.[72] These interpretations are not, of course, mutually exclusive, but there are some problems with them.

The project of sending the squadron to American waters was handled by Adm. Nikolai Krabbe, director of the ministry and acting minister during Grand Duke Constantine's absence in Poland. His instructions to the desig-

[70]Malkin, *Grazhdanskaia voina*, pp. 282–305; Frank Golder, "The Russian Fleet and the Civil War," *American Historical Review* 20, 4 (July 1915): 801–12; Thomas A. Bailey, "The Russian Fleet Myth Re-examined," *Mississippi Valley Historical Review* 38 (June 1951): 81–90; Howard I. Kushner, "The Russian Fleet and the American Civil War: Another View," *Historian* 34 (August 1972): 633–49; William E. Nagengast, "The Visit of the Russian Fleet to the U.S.: Were Americans Deceived?" *Russian Review* 8 (January 1949): 46–55; Earl S. Pomeroy, "The Visit of the Russian Fleet in 1863," *New York History* 24, 4 (October 1943): 512–17.

[71]In subsequent decades, whenever the subject of Russian-American friendship came up, invariably the aid of the Russian navy to the Union cause was mentioned. For one later memoir of this kind, see Frederick W. Seward, *Reminiscences of a War-time Statesman and Diplomat, 1830–1915* (New York and London: G. P. Putnam's, 1916), p. 218. See also Gen. Rush C. Hawkins, "The Coming of the Russian Ships in 1863," *North American Review*, no. 569 (April 1904): 539–44. For centennial reflections by Russian émigré historians in the United States, see *Stoletniaia godovshchina pribytiia russkikh eskadr v Ameriku, 1863–1963* (Washington, D.C.: Victor Kamkin, 1963).

[72]Henry Clews, "England and Russia in Our Civil War, and the War between Russia and Japan," *North American Review* 178 (June 1904): 813.

Adm. Stepan Lesovskii. Engraving by H. B. Hall from
Loubat's Mission to Russia, *1866*

nated commander of the Baltic squadron, Adm. Stepan Lesovskii, in July clearly committed the squadron to action against the maritime commerce of any declared enemy of Russia. Lesovskii was to use New York or other American ports as his bases. Utmost secrecy was to be maintained in the preparation for and during the voyage.[73] Poland was not mentioned directly in this written order, but Minister of War Dmitri Miliutin recalled in his memoirs that Lesovskii was instructed, perhaps verbally, not to bring his squadron back to Russia until the threat of foreign intervention over the Polish situation had passed.[74]

An important factor in the background of these diplomatic-naval intrigues was the modern capability of the Russian navy. Developed under the management of Grand Duke Constantine and his chief lieutenants, this new generation of naval officers was schooled in the latest tactics and strategy. The limitation

[73]John E. Jessup, "Alliance or Deterrence: The Case of the Russian Fleet Visit to America," *New Aspects of Naval History*, ed. Craig L. Symonds et al. (Annapolis, Md.: Naval Institute Press, 1981), pp. 244–45. The text of the instructions to Lesovskii is in an appendix in Alexandre Tarsaidze, *Czars and Presidents* (New York: McDowell, Obolensky, 1958), pp. 353–58.

[74]Miliutin, "Moi starcheskie vospominaniia za 1816–1873," 1863 and 1864, f. 169, Manuscript Division, Lenin Library.

imposed by the Treaty of Paris on a Black Sea navy, a growing interest in the Pacific, and technological developments led them to focus on faster and more maneuverable steam-assisted and screw-propelled vessels with excellent commerce-raiding abilities.[75] Practical training had also been stressed with regular summer cruises by Baltic squadrons into the Atlantic and Mediterranean. In one sense, then, the dispatch of squadrons to the United States *was* part of a normal training exercise, since at least some Russian naval ships would have left their Baltic bases for a long-distance cruise that summer in any event. Furthermore, Grand Duke Constantine's involvement in the concept of a modern, more active navy and in restoring order in Poland points to him as the originator of the plan. His frequently expressed admiration of the United States could thus have influenced the destination of the 1863 Baltic squadron.

Russian war vessels would most likely have visited American ports in 1863 regardless of Polish events and threatened foreign intervention. Orders already issued in January 1862 to Adm. Andrei Popov, commander of the Pacific squadron, underscored the importance of long-range cruises and visits to principal Pacific ports, including San Francisco. Consequently, Popov sailed to San Francisco in the summer of 1862 with three of his ships, and because of the war, they were accorded an even grander reception than Californians customarily lavished on visiting Russians.[76]

Also motivating the 1863 cruises was an instructional factor. In the course of 1862, Stoeckl had called attention to the desirability of having Russian naval ships and officers in American waters to observe the new style of iron-vessel warfare then taking place. Noting that the British and French already had a naval presence along the Atlantic coast, he suggested that the frigate *Osliaba*, wintering in the western Mediterranean, be sent to the United States—and, in fact, it was, preceding Lesovskii's squadron to New York.[77]

The Russian Baltic fleet was not in any danger of being bottled up in port in the event of war over Poland. The new, rapidly expanding fleet was quite capable of dealing with anything the French and British could have spared on the open waters of the Baltic, thanks to the dispersion of those forces because of the American conflict and the secure support and friendship of Prussia and Denmark for Russia. Nor could the British navy have easily blockaded the exit from the Baltic—although winter and the freezing of the Gulf of Finland could have

---

[75]For details and analysis of Grand Duke Constantine's new navy, see Jacob W. Kipp, "Consequences of Defeat: Modernizing the Russian Navy, 1856–1863," *Jahrbucher fur Geschichte Osteuropas*, n.s. 20, 2 (June 1972): 210–25.

[76]A. Efimov, "Posylka dvukh russkikh eskadr v Severnuiu Ameriku," *Istorik-Marksist* 3 (1936): 102.

[77]Stoeckl to Gorchakov, 26 February/10 March 1863, d. 160, and 27 February/11 March 1863, d. 152, f. kants. Vashington 1863, AVPR.

the same effect. Regardless, the emphasis should be less on fears of entrapment and more on the dramatic demonstration of new Russian naval capability in the Atlantic itself.

The Polish situation made its impact felt in the secrecy that surrounded the expedition and in the numbers of ships and men sent. Of particular importance is that most of Lesovskii's ships carried double crews—twice as many officers and men as normal—to provide Russia with the potential of doubling the size of its Atlantic forces by the purchase or "borrowing" of additional ships. This was a primary reason for basing the squadron initially in New York—and it was clearly a major concern of Adm. Alexander Milne, commander of the British North Atlantic squadron based at Halifax, whose ships visited New York in October with the apparent purpose of spying upon the Russians.[78] The British minister in Washington also noted (with some disquiet) the American reaction to the Russian navy: "Their presence is exciting much attention and comment, and is generally attributed to the desire of Russia to have an efficient Squadron at sea and within reach of Friendly Ports, instead of being frozen or blockaded in the Baltic in the event the complications in Europe resulted in war."[79]

That the Russian ships may have been sent mainly to aid the Union cannot be as easily dismissed as Golder and most other historians have done, since that was the contemporary sense of many people, not only in the United States but in France, Britain, and even Russia. The British ambassador in St. Petersburg, Lord Napier, uncovered details of the expedition soon after it left Kronstadt: "It is said that unusual secrecy was observed in preparing the Instructions under which this force has sailed. It is reputed that it is destined to cruize in the Atlantic and speculation naturally adds that in case of a war with England, its duty would be to prey upon British commerce in that Sea. The supposed destination of the Squadron is associated with the report of an offensive and defensive alliance supposed to have been negotiated with the United States."[80] Moreover, Le-

[78] Milne (Halifax) to Admiralty, 18 October 1863, Admiralty Records (hereafter ADM) 1/5821 (Letters from Admirals), PRO. Confirmed in Hammond (Washington) to Secretary of Admiralty, 2 November 1863, ADM 1/5852, PRO. The British commander was also concerned about the desertion of several of his own sailors in New York. Milne to Admiralty, 26 October 1863, ADM 1/5821, PRO.

[79] Stuart to Russell, 27 September 1863, FO 5/893, PRO.

[80] Napier (St. Petersburg) to Lyons (Washington), 29 August 1863, FO 181/416 (St. Petersburg drafts), PRO. Napier also discounted the possibility of war: "I cannot credit that the Russian and U.S. governments have been so precipitant as to conclude any formal engagements in anticipation of eventualities still so remote as war between France and England on one side against Russia or the United States on the other. Nevertheless Russia and the United States have undoubtedly some interests in common. The Imperial Cabinet has always affected a particular deference and favor for that of Washington." Lyons, however, was more circumspect: "But a war with a European Power, and especially a war with Great Britain is a contingency never absent from the

sovskii's instructions to his commanders specifically directed them, in case of war, to interdict commerce with the Confederacy. Thus, the North would have been a direct beneficiary of Russian military assistance had a European war ensued over either Poland, the United States, or both. Cassius Clay believed that the fleet's presence in American waters had expressly warded off French and British intervention. Upon receiving Grand Duke Constantine's personal thanks a year later for the friendly reception given the squadrons, Clay replied "that the debt of gratitude was from us to his Imperial Majesty, who, we believed, had by his friendly course, prevented England and France from hostile intervention in our affairs. That our people fully appreciated this fact, and though we could not rival Europe, perhaps in the magnificence of our public fetes—we trusted that we had not been wanting in heart."[81]

Not surprisingly, rumors of a political alliance between Washington and St. Petersburg circulated around Europe and the United States in advance of the Russian squadron. Seward suspected Clay might be behind this and wrote Stoeckl, asking him to check with Gorchakov and disavow any such overture. Seward added, "The identity of our interests commits us to a friendship so secure that it does not matter if there is an alliance," to which Gorchakov appended *"tres juste"* but "I do not think he has ever made such proposals."[82]

In retrospect, however, the fact remains that military action or greater political intervention by France or Britain in American affairs was becoming more and more remote before the Russian ships ever left the Baltic. French involvement in Mexico and British suspicion of French motives militated against any joint action in Europe of the United States. Spain, a part of any projected European alliance with the Confederacy, was even more uneasy about possible retribution by a victorious North against its remaining American colonies. Growing worldwide sympathy for the Northern cause, now committed to the abolition of slavery, the shifting tide of battle after Vicksburg and Gettysburg, and the triumph of saner heads, particularly in Britain, were already damaging the French-sponsored case for mediation, intervention, or recognition. Even so, a sense of tension and uncertainty prevailed in Washington in the late summer of 1863.

Veteran Russian diplomats such as Stoeckl and Ambassador Philipp Brunnow (in London) saw no point in the Russian naval presence in American waters,

minds both of the men in power and the public at large; and the source of the measures taken, such as those for the defence of the Northern Ports, have little reference to the present struggle with the Southern States." And he gave the initial advantage in such a conflict to the United States. Lyons to Russell, 3 November 1863 (confidential), FO 5/895, PRO.

[81]Clay to Seward, 22 November 1864, DUSM, Russia, vol. 20 (roll 20, M 35), RG 59, NA. See also Efimov, "Posylka," p. 108.

[82]As quoted in Stoeckl to Gorchakov, 11/23 September 1863, f. kants. Vashington 1863, d. 160, AVPR.

were annoyed that they had not been consulted or informed about it, and feared that it would reagitate an already calming international situation. And Brunnow's views that a conflict with Britain was very much against Russia's interests, especially in securing British assistance for building railroads, were seconded by Americans in Russia who had witnessed a considerable recovery of British business in Russia since the Crimean War. Stoeckl was even worried about the increased vulnerability and cost of Russian ships operating so far from home and asked Brunnow to warn him of any British naval moves in that direction.[83]

Actually, the easing of international tensions in the summer of 1863 was probably an important precondition for the dispatch of the squadron. Not really needed in the Baltic, it could be sent to demonstrate peacefully Russia's new naval capability; to strengthen Russia's strategic position in case any new crisis developed over Poland, the Black Sea, the Far East, or elsewhere in the near future; and, as a bonus, to bolster ties with the reuniting American states. It is interesting to note that at the very time this squadron was being readied for sea, Russia was negotiating with a British shipbuilder for the acquisition of a new type of ramming warship.[84]

Whatever its causes, the invasion of New York by over three thousand officers and men of the Russian imperial navy was a great moment in the history of the Civil War. Americans everywhere could "see" the clean lines and impressive armament of the Russian ships as depicted in the illustrated weeklies, while the daily press recounted in detail the various official and unofficial ceremonies. The first to arrive at New York, on 11 September, was the *Osliaba* from the Mediterranean. Lesovskii's Baltic squadron, led by the flagship *Alexander Nevsky*, a new 51-gun, 800-horsepower, 4,500-ton steam frigate patterned after the *General-Admiral*, came in over the next several days.[85] Somewhat worse for the wear after the transatlantic passage, the Russian ships were given access to repair facilities at the Brooklyn Navy Yard by Secretary of Navy Gideon Welles.[86] Accompanying

[83]Stoeckl to Brunnow, 11/23 September 1863, and Brunnow to Stoeckl, 5/17 October 1863, f. kants. Vashington 1863, d. 160, AVPR.

[84]The British government pressured the Laird Company to reject the Russian bid. Frank J. Merli, *Great Britain and the Confederate Navy, 1861–1865* (Bloomington and London: Indiana University Press, 1965), p. 193. But there were also reports at about the same time, believed by an American consul, that British agents were purchasing ships from Russia to use as blockade runners. William Edwin Phelps to Seward, 12 June 1863, DUSC, St. Petersburg, vol. 11 (roll 6, M 81), RG 59, NA.

[85]*National Intelligencer*, 26 September 1863.

[86]Stoeckl to Gorchakov, 11/23 September 1863, f. kants. Vashington 1863, d. 160b, AVPR. Welles, who was in a better position than most to form an opinion about the Russian ships, wrote in his diary: "They are not to be confined in the Baltic by a northern winter. In sending them to this country at this time there is something significant. What will be the effect on France and the French policy we shall learn in due time. It

Russian squadron in New York harbor, Frank Leslie's Illustrated Newspaper, *October 24, 1863*

the squadron to assist in such matters was the newly designated consul-general for New York, Robert Osten-Sacken.

The following two months were filled with Russian-American social events. The first, a more or less private dinner for thirty of the Russian officers, was hosted by Capt. James Buchanan Eads, a river-warship builder from St. Louis, on 28 September at the Metropolitan Hotel. In attendance were Lesovskii and his staff, headed by Capt. Alexander Butakov, a future naval leader, and, on the American side, admirals William Radford and David Farragut, naval engineer Columbus Delano, and generals John Dix and Stewart Van Vliet. From interviews on this occasion, the press reported, "While the Russians disclaimed any political object in their visit to this port, they did not seek to disguise their open and decided sympathy with the nation, and their earnest desire to see it restored, by its own efforts, and in the face of European opposition, to all of its former integrity and power."[87] And the president's wife also honored the Russian squadron with a visit at this time.

may moderate; it may exasperate. God bless the Russians." 25 September 1863, *Diary of Gideon Welles,* 3 vols. (Boston and New York: Houghton Mifflin, 1911), 1: 443.

[87]*National Intelligencer,* 3 October 1863. The special New York correspondent of the *Daily Picayune* (New Orleans) noted, "There is, indeed, a very ancient belief here that

On 1 October, the Russians were presented with an official welcome to the city. The ceremony began with the steamer *Andrews* conveying a formal commission, deliberately circling by the quiescent British and French ships to the Russian flagship, where Lesovskii apologized for not having yet rendered a formal salute for fear of causing some injury to nearby ships. After being reassured by the welcoming party and carefully noting that Admiral Milne's squadron was anchored at a safe distance, he ordered a signal shot fired from the *Alexander Nevsky*. "Suddenly the guns from all the Russian fleet simultaneously broke forth into an explosion so loud that the terrific thunder fell upon the ear as a continuous and unbroken roar. Immense columns of luminous and silver edged smoke rose to a vast height, and then expanding into a canopy, pausing for a while over the harbor and fleet, eventually furled away and drifted slowly up the Hudson."[88] Thus awakened, the New Yorkers outdid themselves in greeting the Russian officers and sailors who disembarked at Pier 1. The parade along Twenty-third Street and down Fifth Avenue and Broadway to City Hall featured a band playing "God Save the Tsar," a huge Russian flag suspended over the street at Tiffany's (550 Broadway), a military review of fifteen regiments numbering three hundred to eight hundred men each, and official greetings from Mayor George Opdyke. On this beautiful fall day, the streets were thronged with the citizenry, and descriptions of the gala event competed for space in the newspapers with grim accounts of defeat at Chickamauga. The North needed some good news.

Receptions and dinners on shore and visits to the Russian ships followed. There was a private dinner at the Astor House on 12 October presided over by James T. Brady, a prominent local attorney and unsuccessful candidate for governor in 1860; a larger gathering at the same location a week later hosted by municipal authorities for three hundred guests (mostly ward politicians); and a six-day excursion at the end of October to Niagara Falls, organized by Watts Sherman on behalf of the Hudson River Steamboat Company and the New York Central and Erie railroads.[89]

The visit culminated in a lavish dinner and ball on 5 November at the Acad-

there is to be a sort of general war, in which Russia and the United States are to hold by each other against all creation." Letter dated 3 October in issue of 13 October 1863.

[88]New York *Times*, 2 October 1863. The *Times* carried four columns of front-page description of the day's proceedings, matched by the other city papers. Under the heading "The New Alliance Cemented," the *Herald* (same date) commented, "We have seldom seen so many people in the streets of this city as poured in from every direction yesterday . . . and we never remember to have seen the city present a more picturesque aspect." See also Pomeroy, "Visit of the Russian Fleet," pp. 512–17, and Robin Higham, "When the Russians Conquered New York," *Mankind* 3, 8 (August 1872): 10–18.

[89]New York *Herald*, 13, 14, and 20 October 1863; Watts Sherman Papers, Miscellaneous Manuscripts, NYHS.

"The Grand Procession of the Russian Visitors through Broadway," Harper's Weekly, October 17, 1863

emy of Music at Fourteenth Street and Irving Place. Theodore Roosevelt, Sr., whose young son was suitably impressed by the affair, was in charge of arrangements, which featured two bands of fifty pieces each, a giant model of the *General-Admiral* suspended from the ceiling, and huge portraits of Peter the Great, George Washington, Alexander II, and Abraham Lincoln. On a large canopy suspended out from the stage was depicted "the genius of America," dressed as an Indian maiden, clasping the hand of "the genius of Russia," wearing furs and bearing a resemblance to Catherine the Great. Food and drink were served in another hall, connected by a 125-foot overhead passageway: "The tables were loaded with all that culinary science could furnish, and as Delmonico was not stinted, the result was a collection of delicacies such as seldom tempt an epicure."[90] The American secretary of state led the toasts on this occasion, and the New York *Times* concluded its narration with "the repertoire of hospitality has been exhausted."[91] And Bennett's *Herald*, to Stoeckl's chagrin, grumbled about excessive catering to prolonged Russian freeloading on American goodwill.

[90]*Frank Leslie's Illustrated Newspaper,* 7 November 1863. According to the New York *World* (as cited by Tarsaidze, *Czars and Presidents,* p. 206), 12,000 oysters, 1,200 game birds, 250 turkeys, 400 chickens, a dozen 30-pound salmon, and 1,000 pounds of steak, as well as 3,500 bottles of wine were consumed.

[91]New York *Times,* 6 November 1863. See also Pomeroy, "Visit of the Russian Fleet,"

*The ball for the Russian squadron at the Academy of Music, New York, November 1863,
from* Frank Leslie's Illustrated Newspaper, *November 21, 1863*

To the probable relief of many New Yorkers, Lesovskii accepted invitations to call on Philadelphia, Baltimore, and then Washington. Moving his squadron southward to Annapolis, the four smallest ships then entered the Potomac and anchored at Alexandria in early December. The Russians hosted on the twelfth a grand reception aboard their ships for members of the cabinet and Congress and other dignitaries and a separate one a few days later for the general public. President Lincoln could not attend because of illness, but he was represented by the secretary of state and reciprocated with a state dinner and reception for the Russian officers at the White House. Among those enthusiastically toasting the Russian presence in Washington was none other than Cong. Henry Winter Davis, whose anti-Russian book had caused such a stir ten years earlier. More important, Seward adroitly made use of the presence of the Russian squadron in

pp. 115–17; New York *Tribune* (most complete coverage), 6 November 1863; and, for double-page sketches of the event, *Frank Leslie's Illustrated Newspaper*, 21 November 1863. A special correspondent of a New Orleans paper viewed the whole episode as a "vulgar display" that was especially inappropriate in wartime and, emphasizing the ostentatious finery, added: "There were many beautiful and some refined ladies, but a great many who were neither, and some in respect to whom it was asked how they got there, or being there, why they remained, as their faces were well known to the police." New Orleans *Daily Picayune*, 18 November 1863.

Symbolic representations of Russia and the United States at the Russian ball in New York, from Frank Leslie's Illustrated Newspaper, *November 21, 1863*

the United States to pressure Britain to prohibit any more ships from being built for the Confederacy.[92]

[92]Kushner, "The Russian Fleet and the American Civil War," pp. 646–49; "Our Russian Guests," *National Intelligencer*, 15 December 1863; Stoeckl to Gorchakov, 11/23 November 1863, f. kants. Vashington 1863, d. 160b, and 19/31 December 1863, f. kants. Vashington 1864, d. 150, AVPR. Upon receiving the personal appreciation of Alexander II for the reception given his sailors, President Lincoln assured Stoeckl that "the appearance of our [Russian] flag on the coasts of the United States and the exchanges of courtesies that have taken place form a new bond of friendship between the two countries." 19/31 December 1863, f. kants. Vashington 1864, d. 150, AVPR.

Benjamin Brown French, a keen observer of the Washington scene, described the atmosphere surrounding the promenade to and from the Russian ships on 12 December: "We could see from our windows the flashes of guns which saluted the party when they left, considerably after dark. The Russians were exceedingly polite and, at a time so fearful in our history when we hardly know who are and who are not our friends among the nations of the world, it is truly gratifying to have a powerful Empire like Russia able, with us, to cope with all the world besides, exhibit for us such marked friendship. I have always regarded the Russians as a noble people, and I trust we shall not permit them to outdo us in courtesy." *Witness to the Young Republic: A Yankee's Journal, 1828–1870*, ed. Donald B. Cole and John J. McDonough (Hanover, N. H., and London: University Press of New England, 1989), p. 441. The reception at the White House on 20 December was "the most brilliant I ever attended, because it was the only one where the mudstained people did not mingle with the court dresses." Ibid., p. 442.

Sailors on the Russian frigate Osliaba *at Alexandria, Virginia, 1863, from the collections of the Library of Congress*

Leaving part of his squadron at Annapolis, Lesovskii sailed on to Hampton Roads (Norfolk) for supplies and then cruised to Havana and other ports in the West Indies before returning to New York for a few months in early 1864. The Russian naval visit to American waters in 1863 had certainly elicited an outpouring of amicable sentiments on both sides. Its effect on the military situation is difficult to measure, but some positive impact on Northern morale and corresponding damage to the Southern can be claimed. The expedition, moreover, was not without wider political meaning, as both Britain and France were quite wary of this new sign of an "unholy alliance." A report from Paris emphasized this concern:

In one word, the enthusiastic reception, the kind of popular ovation, which has been given to the officers of the Russian squadron in that city [New York] has fixed the attention of France upon American policy and public feeling in a way in which perhaps no other event could have commanded it. . . . Thus, you see, Russian and American affairs necessarily react upon each other and produce a mutual independence and sympathy between the two nations. France is shackled in her European actions by the consequences, both present and apprehended, of her policy in the West, and she is restrained and impeded from pushing that policy further, perhaps even to a joint alliance between herself and her Sovereign of Mexico . . . by her desire to enter upon a new course of aggression in the north of Europe. The interests of America and Russia thus become identical, and the reports which reach us of an *entente cordiale* between the Cabinets of St. Petersburgh and Washington are felt to be both natural and credible.[93]

With Mexico in mind, even the relatively tranquil winter excursion to the Caribbean by Lesovskii would not be taken lightly in France.

Meanwhile, the visit by the Russian Pacific squadron to San Francisco was off to a bad start when the first ship, the steam corvette *Novik*, wrecked on the rocks off Point Reyes on 27 September 1863. Fortunately, alert action by American sailors saved all of the crew. Two weeks later Admiral Popov safely brought in his flagship, the frigate *Bogatyr*, followed by the corvettes *Gaidamak*, *Kalevala*, *Abrek*, and *Rynda*. Their arrival in San Francisco Bay differed in one important respect from the Russian naval expedition to New York—it came as no surprise. The *Kalevala* was a familiar sight, having called at the port in the two previous years. The *Abrek* had also been there with Popov in 1862, and the *Rynda* had made a three-week visit the preceding June to prepare for the stay of the whole squadron.[94] At least three other features distinguished the Pacific coast visit: The ships were smaller, though they carried officers and crews totaling over twelve hundred (counting those of the *Novik*); the duration was much longer, since the squadron made San Francisco (or more accurately, Sausalito and the Mare Island Navy Yard) its base until the following August; and the honors and hospitality were more evenly distributed.

The Russians took the lead with a celebration for the officers and sailors of the revenue-cutter *Shubrik* for rescuing the crew of the *Novik* and a banquet for the officers of the *Lancaster* aboard the *Bogatyr* on 25 October.[95] San Franciscans, however, learning of the plans for the big affair in New York, outdid their previous fetes for Russians with a gala "Russian ball" on 17 November. Limited by the size of the largest hall in the city to twenty-five hundred guests (though over ten thousand wanted to attend), it was apparently more widely acclaimed than its New York counterpart.

[93]*National Intelligencer*, 29 October 1863.

[94]*Daily Alta California*, 29 June and 17 July 1863; a description of the visit by an officer on the *Rynda* is in K. Zelenoi, "Iz zapisok o krugosvetnom plavanii (1861–1864): Ot Shankhaia do San-frantsisko," *Morskoi Sbornik* 80, 9 (September 1865): 60–71.

[95]*Daily Alta California*, 2 and 26 October 1863; see also Benjamin F. Gilbert, "Welcome to the Czar's Fleet: An Incident of Civil War Days in San Francisco," *California Historical Society Quarterly* 26, 1 (March 1947): 13–19.

The ovation to our Russian naval officers, which proved to be so triumphant a success, was the theme of universal conversation on the streets, yesterday, in social gatherings, and in the passing compliments of the day. Many loyal citizens, who failed to receive invitations, instead of feeling chagrined, rejoiced that our Muscovite visitors had so superb an entertainment given them, and the more, that the guests were pleased with the civilities extended to them. Such persons considered that this entertainment was given not only out of compliment to our Russian visitors, but for the purpose of cementing still stronger those bonds of good will, amity and sympathy now existing between our Government and people and the Government and subjects of the Emperor Alexander.[96]

Other notable events involving the Russians included their assistance in putting out a major fire in the city (23 October), a reception for Commodore Thomas Selfridge, Jr., on the *Rynda* (4 February), a festive "bombardment" celebrating Washington's birthday (22 February), a formal dinner for San Francisco officials on the *Bogatyr* (23 February), a joint affair commemorating the anniversary of the Russian serf emancipation (2 March), and a grand salute from the *Bogatyr* to start the Independence Day fireworks display.[97] The squadron finally set sail with much fanfare on 13 August 1864, but without Admiral Popov, who made his way homeward via Panama and Washington—the fast way—leaving a number of large expense accounts behind.[98]

The practical intent behind the concentration of Russian naval power in the Pacific on the North American coast for almost a year is somewhat puzzling. There was certainly no threat of the fleet being blockaded anywhere. Honolulu would have been strategically better positioned, and Russia had recently cemented good relations there—but it did lack the repair facilities of San Francisco Bay. The best conclusion is that this Russian presence in San Francisco was an even more obvious show of support for the Union cause and of increased Russian naval potential than the Atlantic coast visit. This, at least, is how it was interpreted at the time.

The Pacific squadron had also come closer to action. In early 1864 rumors circulated that San Francisco and the ships in its weakly defended harbor might come under attack from Confederate raiders cruising the Pacific. Admiral Popov

[96]*Daily Alta California*, 18 November 1863.

[97]Ibid., various issues for 1863 and 1864, especially 23 and 24 February, 29 June, 6 July, and 14 August 1864; Stoeckl to Gorchakov, 25 October/6 November 1864, f. kants. Vashington, d. 150, AVPR.

[98]In August alone, Admiral Popov paid over $40,000 for supplying his ships to Rowland, Walker and Company, which also handled the business of the Russian America Company in San Francisco. Account books, Rowland, Walker and Company, California Historical Society (hereafter CaHS), San Francisco.

asked Stoeckl how to respond to such an eventuality. The minister, alarmed at the prospect of Russian ships firing at the Confederate flag, telegraphed his response: "Received your letter. The matter is grave. If the contingency takes place, you may use your influence to prevent what you fear. But it is urgent to avoid a collision as much as possible."[99] The fact remains that had a Confederate raider ventured into the bay during the visit, Russian guns would most likely have been discharged. The presence of the squadron thus definitely added to the security of this important Pacific port.

Business as Usual?

The extended visits of ten Russian warships and approximately forty-five hundred Russian officers and sailors in American ports generated considerable business in supplies and repairs. Though precise figures are not available, it probably amounted to a substantial sum (as good as a war loan), especially in San Francisco, where services involved not only thorough ship overhauls but also the making of new uniforms for the crews. In general, however, Russian-American commerce and business enterprise passed through a period of upheaval and adjustment.

The biggest change, of course, was the complete interruption in the direct shipments of cotton, which had shown such promise of expansion through the employment of the new, larger Yankee clippers after the Crimean War. Of what was available from open ports or smuggled out of the Confederacy, little apparently found its way to Russia, at least not in unfinished form. One result was a rapid increase in cotton cultivation in Central Asia for the Russian market. Stimulated by the demand of Moscow merchants and industrialists, the price of Turkestan cotton rose by five or six times during the American war. Securing this trade was an important motive for the Russian conquest of the independent khanates of that region between 1864 and 1868. Bayard Taylor, who had a special interest in Central Asia, predicted to Seward further enlargement of this source of cotton:

> It may interest you to know that a new field for the supply of cotton is being developed in Central Asia. The Tartar Khanates of Bokhara and Khokand appear to be very well adapted to the production of the plant, and the amount of cotton imported from those regions into Russia, though still comparatively inconsiderable, is rapidly increasing. The bales, of convenient size for transportation on the backs of camels, are brought across the Kirghiz steppes to Orenbourg, and thence find their way to the great market of Nijni-

[99]Copy of telegram in Stoeckl to Gorchakov, 10/22 March 1864, f. kants. Vashington 1864, d. 150, AVPR.

Novgorod. . . . The staple is of good length and fine quality, and when mixed with American cotton, produced a superior manufactured article. When an organized line of transportation, by way of the Volga and the Caspian Sea, shall be established, Russia can draw an important proportion of her supply from those regions.[100]

Many of the large American ships formerly employed in the cotton trade found other cargoes, and some of these went to Russia, transporting coal from England, salt, sugar, and other raw materials. One, the *Emperor*, made the long voyage from the East Indies carrying teak but was wrecked in a storm near Helsingfors on its way to Kronstadt. This received more than the usual publicity because a Russian steam frigate, the *Grimashchyi*, went to its rescue but also fell victim to the stormy, rocky Finnish coast.[101]

New and more unusual items of import from the United States were the result not so much of the war but of industrial development: sewing machines, clocks, reapers and other agricultural machinery, and petroleum. Although Ropes and Company imported some sewing machines directly from Boston and New York, many more entered Russia through third countries, especially Britain and France. This was even more true of the farm implements. However, considerable quantities of petroleum, beginning in 1863, were imported straight from the Pennsylvania fields as fuel for the American-inspired street lighting of St. Petersburg and Moscow.[102] Though oil was already being pumped from Russia's own sources in the Caucasus, inefficient and expensive transportation to the northern cities remained a stumbling block.

Outgoing cargoes in American ships from the Baltic ports were more familiar—hemp, iron, cordage, red leather, sailcloth and other rough linens, and wool—and were now approximately equal to the volume of incoming goods. In the south, from Odessa and Taganrog, wool exports for the Northern states increased considerably during the war, most likely because of military demands. An occasional American ship was chartered to carry grain to European markets. Overall, however, the number of American vessels calling at Russian ports decreased by about half after 1860, to the lowest level since the War of 1812.

---

[100]Taylor to Seward, 1 October 1862, DUSC, St. Petersburg, vol. 11 (roll 6, M 81), RG 59, NA. For an analysis of Russian expansion in the area, see Martin Sicker, *The Strategy of Soviet Imperialism: Expansion in Eurasia* (New York and London: Praeger, 1988), pp. 62–63.

[101]Wilkins to Taylor, 3/15 October 1862, and Taylor to Seward, 4 November 1862, DUSC, St. Petersburg, vol. 11 (roll 6, M 81), RG 59, NA.

[102]Clay to Seward, 4 November [but actually 4 December] 1863, DUSM, Russia, vol. 20 (roll 20, M 35), RG 59, NA; and Phelps to Seward, 6 January 1865, DUSC, St. Petersburg, vol. 12 (roll 7, M 81), RG 59, NA.

Though it is difficult to estimate, indirect trade appeared to be growing rapidly in the 1860s and represented a greater variety of goods. Timothy Smith, the American consul in Odessa, noted in 1865 that

> in many shops articles from the United States are offered for sale, almost invariably as very superior as indeed they generally are. It is a great recommendation to say of such articles that they are "Americanskoiee." American petroleum, lamps, sewing machines, reaping machines, clocks, India rubber goods, oil cloths, codfish, rice, starch and maize are some of the articles which I now think of as having seen for sale here. It would be a good speculation for some wide awake Yankee or company to open here an exclusively American store with everything of American growth or production to sell, from adzes to ox yokes, from gum to gimblets, sweet potatoes, brooms, and pea nuts.[103]

A few months later, Smith reported, "The trade with the United States has been but very little by direct invoice. . . . [But] American goods by way of England and France are to be found here in many places."[104] By 1866 the popularity of American-made articles led to widespread counterfeiting of trademarks by Europeans, a problem that would plague the American trade with Russia for many years.[105] Other American business endeavors in Russia, as well as trade, had mixed success in the 1860s because of the war and increased European competition.

Although the United States had a full complement of regular consuls on the scene in Russia during the Civil War—William Phelps in St. Petersburg, John Hatterschiedt in Moscow, Timothy Smith in Odessa, and Henry Stacy in Reval—they all remarked on the growing number of other foreign enterprises in their areas. British Ambassador Napier also observed that investors and contractors from his country were actively pursuing opportunities in Russia, since they had been "thrown out of their usual line of business by the American difficulties, or suffering a plethora of capital. . . . It is a remarkable fact that while the political relations of the two countries are not in a perfect state of harmony, English capitalists are embarking on speculation founded on Peace."[106] He was, however, concerned about the number of British companies selling armaments

---

[103]Timothy Smith to Seward, 11 November 1865, DUSC, Odessa, vol. 4 (roll 2, M 459), RG 59, NA.

[104]Smith to Seward, 1 December 1865, ibid. Smith estimated that in 1864 enough wool was shipped to the United States from Odessa and Taganrog by various means "to make sixteen to twenty cargoes for ordinary sized sailing vessels." To Seward, 2 January 1865, ibid.

[105]Clay to Seward, 22 December 1866, DUSM, Russia, vol. 21 (roll 21, M 35), RG 59, NA.

[106]Napier to Russell, 5 October 1863, Reports from St. Petersburg, FO 65/638, PRO.

to Russia at the very time that relations were strained over Poland. The paradox was that the Civil War, which brought the United States and Russia into a very close political bond, was seriously damaging the long-standing economic connections between the two countries and was enhancing those of their rivals. Commercially and industrially, Britain and France gained at American expense.

The Winans brothers of Baltimore were among the leading foreign businesses in Russia in 1861, having already expanded their construction and repair of railroad cars and engines (now under the supervision of George William Whistler) to naval armaments. Their plans to build large, fast, and powerful warships with heavy armor-plating and large breech-loaded guns, powered hydraulically, impressed Cassius Clay, who kept Seward informed of their progress.[107] Experiments were conducted at Kronstadt through a contract with the Russian naval ministry and under the direction of James Murray but especially with the prospect of Union naval requirements in mind.[108] The company also hoped to obtain a fifteen-year lease on the St. Petersburg–Moscow railroad as a result of the Russian government's privatization program.

Despite support from railroad administrator Pavel Mel'nikov, not only did the Winans fail to win this lease, but they also lost, in 1862, their main repair and management contract after a lower bid was tendered by a consortium of French capitalists.[109] With their manufacturing base at Aleksandrovsk thus taken from them, the Winans moved their naval construction operations to England. In 1866 their experimental "cigar-ship"—part monitor, part submarine, and part ram—was successfully launched, flying American, Russian, and British flags.[110] The Russian government, meanwhile, became unhappy with the French contractors because they made no effort to increase the traffic on the railroad, and the Winans were invited to resubmit their bid in 1865, before the expiration of the four-year agreement with the French.[111] This time the Americans negotiated an eight-year contract and were able to buy out most of the last year of the French one. Thus, after a few years interruption, the Winans railroad equip-

[107]Green Clay Journal, 19 July 1861, SHSM; William L. Winans to Clay, 10/22 August 1861, and Clay to Seward, 10 January 1862, DUSM, Russia, vol. 19 (roll 19, M 35), RG 59, NA.

[108]James Murray to Clay, 29 December 1861, and Winans to Clay, 15/27 January 1862, ibid.

[109]William L. Winans to Thomas Winans, 15 December 1861, William L. Winans Letterbook, box 18 (Letterbooks and Diaries), Winans Papers, MaryHS.

[110]Clay to Seward, 14 October 1864, DUSM, Russia, vol. 20 (roll 20, M 35), RG 59, NA; Clay to Seward, 5 December 1866, DUSM, Russia, vol. 21 (roll 21, M 35), RG 59, NA; and *Frank Leslie's Illustrated Newspaper*, 7 April 1866.

[111]Thomas Winans (St. Petersburg) to Prescott Smith, 2 August 1865, Thomas Winans Letterbook no. 2, box 18, Winans Papers, MaryHS.

ment industry in Russia was back in business at an even more lucrative level.[112] The "cigar-ship," however, never became more than a naval curiosity.

Another American, Robert O. Williams, who had been connected with the original Harrison, Winans, and Eastwick firm, became a partner of a Moscow manufacturer named Bukhterev in the iron and copper business and was reported in 1866 to be "immensely rich."[113] He had married a Russian woman of noble ancestry and had several children. A cousin visiting in 1867 reported that Williams "had only to complain of numerous Royal favors and frequent courtesies on the part of the Russian Government. He is wonderfully popular with Russians, Germans, Prussians, Americans and English, and his home is a *rendezvous* for all nationalities in *Moscow*."[114]

Judging from fragmentary evidence, other American business ventures in Russia were less successful. John E. Gowen completed his contract for raising the sunken vessels at Sevastopol in 1862 and the following year became an oil prospector in the Caucasus.[115] After some initial difficulties, his company was reported in 1866 to have a well in the Kuban Valley that was producing up to five thousand gallons a day.[116] Another "American" oil company began drilling in the Kerch region on the Sea of Azov in 1864 under the direction of Green Clay, the minister's nephew, and St. John Constant. This operation was linked to Laslo Chandor's schemes to light the streets of St. Petersburg and Moscow with distilled petroleum (kerosene) lamps. Clay became involved in this novel business through his uncle's connections with Chandor and because he feared that Kentucky was not "safe" for a Clay. Chandor soon found himself in financial straits and sold his share to a Russian nobleman, Naryshkin; Green Clay continued to oversee the Clay share through the Civil War, also serving as secretary of legation in Turin.[117]

Another American project in the south ran afoul of the vagaries of both international commerce and Russian bureaucracy. D. C. Pierce, who had supplied Gowen's salvage crews at Sevastopol, formed a partnership with another Ameri-

[112]Thomas Winans (Baltimore) to John H. B. Latrobe, 1 October 1865, ibid.

[113]Timothy Smith (Odessa) to Lewis Meacham, 13 June 1865, Hoyt and Meacham Papers, NYHS.

[114]M. D. Landon (Moscow) to Eliza Meacham, 17/29 August, 1867, ibid. Landon also noted that his cousin seldom wrote letters, which may account for the paucity of information available about Williams's Moscow business.

[115]Smith to Seward, 18 October 1862 and 17 October 1863, DUSC, Odessa, vol. 3 (roll 2, M 459), RG 59, NA.

[116]Smith to Seward, 1 December 1866, vol. 4, ibid.

[117]Smith to Seward, 12 March and 29 October 1864, ibid.; Cassius Clay to Mary Jane Clay, July 1863 and 26 December 1863; Green Clay (Tamara) to Mary Jane Clay, 17 July 1864; and Cassius Clay to Green Clay, 22 April 1865, Clay Papers, Filson Club. In the letter to Mary Jane, Green Clay commented, "I do not think that I will make anything by staying in this place, but just to please you and Pa, I will try to do so."

can, T. P. Harward, and they signed a contract with a French firm, represented by Michel Trone, to ship wooden railroad ties (known as "sleepers") from the Caucasus to Marseilles. Unfortunately, Harward accidentally drowned, the French reneged on payment, and Pierce was left with a great many sleepers on his hands and bills to pay to the owners of the Mingrelian forests. The result was the seizure of his ships and other properties at Chura in 1864 by local authorities. For several years Pierce attempted in vain to obtain redress and damages through Clay and officials in St. Petersburg.[118]

Laslo Chandor was an unlikely entrepreneur in Russia. A Hungarian emigré to the United States, he managed to cultivate favors from various American and Russian officials and dabbled in numerous business ventures—including plans to construct railroads and a partnership with Cassius Clay for street lighting. The "partners" had trouble importing American oil without excessive duties and ran behind schedule, but apparently they did make money on the deal. Clay and Chandor quarreled and severed their relationship in 1866 (which Clay blamed on his secretary, Jeremiah Curtin), but they later reconciled.[119] The whole affair only added to the eccentric and somewhat shadowy reputation of the American minister at the Russian court. Several resident Americans complained openly about Clay's conduct, but "conflict of interest" was not a serious issue in nineteenth-century American civil service.

Theodore Rosenstraus, an Austrian Jew who had emigrated to the United States and obtained citizenship, came to Russia in 1862 to establish an optical business in Voronezh; the next year he moved to Kharkov, where he immediately got into trouble with local officials.[120] His offense was that he was operating a business outside of the Jewish Pale. Since his Amerikanskii Magazin [American Store] also allegedly sold materials considered obscene in this provincial

[118]Smith to Seward, 19 April 1863, DUSC, Odessa, vol. 3 (roll 2, M 459), RG 59, NA; Clay to Seward, 22 November 1865, DUSM, Russia, vol. 20 (roll 20, M 35), RG 59, NA. The "Pierce case" generated a lot of internal correspondence, for example: Clay to Valuev (Minister of Interior), 22 May 1863, and Clay to Gorchakov, 18/30 August 1865, DPR, Russia, vol. 4534, Notes Sent, RG 84, NA; Clay to Nikolai Muchanov (Deputy Foreign Minister), 1/13 April 1865, copy, DUSM, Russia, vol. 20 (roll 20, M 35), RG 59, NA.

[119]Most of the details of Chandor's affairs also come from "internal" sources: Clay to Gorchakov, 29 July 1863 and 10 March 1864, DPR, Russia, vol. 4534, Notes Sent, and Maltsov to Clay, 22 August/3 September 1863, and Westman to Clay, 3/15 September 1865, DPR, vol. 4501, Notes Received, RG 84, NA. Apparently fearing a reaction at home, Clay was reticent about his involvement with Chandor in his official correspondence; but see Clay to Seward (confidential), 3 August 1866, DUSM, Russia, vol. 21 (roll 21, M 35), RG 59, NA, and Clay to Schuyler Colfax (private), 30 September 1868, Clay Papers, box 1, Filson Club.

[120]Clay to Westmann, 28 June/10 July 1866, DPR, Russia, vol. 4534, Notes Sent, and John P. Groves to Clay, 12 June 1866, DPR, Russia, vol. 4501, Notes Received, NA.

town (French postcards?) he found himself periodically under arrest, but he used bribes and the influence of the American minister in St. Petersburg to secure his release and to preserve his business. This continued for some twenty-five years, drawing attention to one of the thorniest problems in Russian-American relations after 1880—Russian discrimination against Jews.

Several other Americans worked independently in Russia. John P. Groves continued to direct an opera company in Saratov but had difficulty obtaining his salary, the countercharge being that he had not fulfilled his contract.[121] George Prince continued to handle the Ropes business, which, however, was much reduced in scope, and Gaun Hutton maintained his hardware trade, now primarily wholesale. William Dunster superintended the imperial mint, and Thomas Evans made regular trips from his Paris base to fix imperial teeth. The newest and most successful of these "free-lancers" was Lewis Broadwell, a former Mississippi River steamboat captain who was suspected by some of the American community of Confederate leanings. He was employed at the gun foundry at Kronstadt, where he developed a new type of breech-loading cannon and received for his efforts many monetary and other rewards from the Russian government. Clay was convinced that Broadwell's invention warranted trial by the Union navy, so, ever mindful of profit potential, he acquired the American rights for himself.[122]

The Collins Overland–Western Union Telegraph Project

The largest new business project directly involving the United States and Russia was the building of a telegraph line that would connect Europe and North America by way of Siberia, the North Pacific, and Alaska. The stage for this was set by the unsuccessful first attempt to lay a transatlantic cable, by the completion of telegraph lines across the United States to San Francisco in October 1861, and by the Russian effort to extend their wires across Siberia. Russia and the United States, furthermore, were already aware of their respective telegraphic endeavors: In Russia, several Americans (in particular, Taliaferro Shaffner) had proposed the construction of such networks, while in the United

[121]Theodore Rosenstraus (Kharkov) to Clay, 2/14 December 1865, and 29 September 1867, DPR, Russia, vols. 4501 and 4502, Notes Received, RG 84, NA.

[122]Clay to Hiram Sibley, 26 March 1865, Hiram Sibley Papers, box 1, Rochester; Miliutin (Minister of War) to Clay, 26 August/7 September 1865, DPR, Russia, vol. 4501, Notes Received, RG 84, NA, conferring the Order of Stanislas Third Class on Broadwell. The Ropes and Company agent, who was very anti-Clay, commented, "Broadwell—the rampant secessionist—is now a frequenter of the Legation along with some other chap who lodges in Paris at the Grand Hotel! These sorts of things are past endurance. . . . My nationality I look upon as insulted and degraded and should dearly like to tell Mr. Seward so." G. H. Prince to Bayard Taylor, 19/31 May 1865, Taylor Papers, box 3, Cornell.

States, Russian army officers Col. Dmitri Romanov and Maj. Sergei Abaza had made an extensive study of American wire communications during the Civil War. Meanwhile, the Russian line pushed forward to Omsk in Western Siberia in the spring of 1862 and reached Irkutsk and Kiakhta on the Chinese border in 1864, while Romanov, with supplies from San Francisco, began extending the line westward from Nikolaevsk at the mouth of the Amur.[123]

The chief promoter of this new Russian-American telegraph project was Perry McDonough Collins, the youthful pioneer of American-Amur development a few years earlier. He had sounded out Russian officials on the idea as early as 1859. Though President Lincoln at first wanted to settle a political debt by naming Richard Hannah of Indiana as the new "commercial agent" for the Amur region, Collins, with the help of Seward, was finally reappointed in September 1861, allowing him to retain a diplomatic character that would be useful leverage in pressing his plans.[124] Collins also conferred with Shaffner, who was adamantly opposed to Cyrus Field's Atlantic cable enterprise and, after its initial failure, advocated the Bering Sea route. In 1861, however, Shaffner decided to devote his energies to promoting the Confederate cause in Britain. As the remaining American torchbearer for the Pacific line, Collins approached Seward for official backing: "Russia progressing from the west towards the east proposes to reach the Pacific at the Amoor; thus the two great powers Russia and America will soon stand, telegraphically, face to face, looking across the intervening ocean."[125] By early 1862 he had received encouragement from the expansion-minded Seward, from Stoeckl, and from Senator Latham of California, and financial backing from Hiram Sibley, whose Western Union Company had pioneered the first transcontinental route.

Collins arrived in St. Petersburg in September 1862, ostensibly to carry out his diplomatic assignment but really to obtain Russian agreement to a joint telegraph construction project. He first discussed it with Gen. Konstantin Chevkin, the minister of ways and communications, who was a cautious, conservative bureaucrat, and with Gen. Mikhail Korsakov, who had recently succeeded Murav'ev as governor general of Eastern Siberia. Simon Cameron also urged Gorchakov to render assistance, but the usual delays ensued. When Chevkin was replaced by Pavel Mel'nikov in October, there was a surge of optimism about

---

[123]Collins to Seward, 31 December 1861, DUSC, Amoor, vol. 2 (roll 2, T 111), RG 59, NA. Shaffner, who claimed to have originated the idea of an Atlantic cable, was, by 1858, firmly convinced of its impracticality. Shaffner (St. Louis) to Sibley, 30 September 1858, Sibley Addition (uncataloged), Rochester.

[124]Seward to Collins, 18 September 1861, and Collins (New York) to Seward, 13 and 18 September and 10 October 1861, DUSC, Amoor, vol. 2 (roll 2, T 111), RG 59, NA.

[125]Collins to Seward, 31 December 1861, ibid. For a good sketch of the enterprise, see Phillip H. Ault, "The (almost) Russian-American Telegraph," *American Heritage* 26, 4 (June 1975): 12–15, 92–98.

Russian support for the project. Then the direction of telegraphs was transferred to the jurisdiction of Ivan Tolstoy, who was already very familiar with American business affairs.[126] Apparently these officials were divided as to the propriety of a new and perhaps permanent American presence in Alaska and Eastern Siberia, so the matter was referred to the Siberian Committee, an interministerial advisory body, as well as to the Asiatic department of the Ministry of Foreign Affairs, headed by Nikolai Ignat'ev. All of this, of course, took time, exasperating the usually patient Collins, who complained to Sibley that "our cat has a very long tail and paper is cheap when the government pays for it."[127]

After nine months of negotiation, Collins received preliminary Russian agreement in June 1863. He believed Mel'nikov was responsible for the delay, and perhaps the new minister was being painstakingly cautious even though he was sympathetic to the endeavor.[128] However, Collins had not attended to some essential groundwork. Russian officials wanted evidence of solid financial backing on the American side and of the organization specifically for this purpose of a company supported by the United States government; they had learned from experience about grandiose American schemes that turned out to have weak, if any, capital foundation. Another unresolved issue was the vital right-of-way through British Canada, especially problematic considering the status of Russian and American relations with Britain.

[126]Collins (St. Petersburg) to Hiram Sibley, 31 October 1862, Sibley Papers, box 1, Rochester; Collins to Seward, 31 October 1862, DUSC, Amoor, vol. 2 (roll 2, T 111), RG 59, NA; Cameron to Seward, 9 September 1862, and copy of Cameron to Gorchakov, 5/17 September 1862, enclosed in Cameron to Seward, 18 September 1862, and Taylor to Seward, 29 October and 19 December, DUSM, Russia, vol. 19 (roll 19, M 35), RG 59, NA.

[127]To Hiram Sibley, 20 November 1820, Sibley Addition, Rochester. Collins had a way with words. To Sibley he wrote, "The Emperor has gone to Moscow, consequently St. Petersburg is like the play of the Prince of Denmark, with Hamlet left out. . . . I have piped, and piped, and done all the dancing myself." And on Mel'nikov: "I hope by spring to tap him, yet it is a question whether this high northern maple yields much, if any, suchharine matter." To Sibley, 4 December 1862, ibid.

See also Collins (St. Petersburg) to Seward, 20 January 1863, enclosing Mel'nikov to Collins, 30 November 1862, DUSC, Amoor, vol. 2 (roll 2, T 111); and Collins to Seward, 30 March 1863, DUSC, St. Petersburg, vol. 11 (roll 6, M 81), RG 59, NA. Since Collins was performing simultaneously as commercial agent for the Amur and consul in St. Petersburg—as well as a joint-venture entrepreneur—his "official" dispatches are divided between two sets of records.

[128]Collins (London) to Seward, 18 August 1863, DUSC, Amoor, vol. 2 (roll 2, T 111), RG 59, NA. Collins continued to press for a subsidy; in a letter to General Ignat'ev, he wrote, "But above all, capitalists are ever distrustful of government management of financial matters, in all countries; and would prefer a fixed sum to an uncertain one. Without reiterating arguments already offered, the undersigned fears that, unless such change is made, the enterprise may . . . fall through altogether." 17 June 1863, DPR, Russia, vol. 4534, Notes Sent, RG 84, NA.

Before a final, operative agreement could be signed, Collins had to show proof that these obstacles were overcome. Then Russia would provide access to the territory and labor assistance, and the American company would send materials and supervisors. The line would be extended from Nikolaevsk on the Amur northeast to the Bering Strait and then through Alaska and along the north-west Pacific coast to San Francisco. Two Russian supply ships would also be made available to the American company. Meanwhile, Russia would push rapidly the completion of the transsiberian line from Irkutsk to the mouth of the Amur (Nikolaevsk), where the connection would be made with the American-built line. Other provisions of the agreement required that construction begin within two years and be completed in five and stipulated that the company would have exclusive rights for thirty-three years. Russia balked at the American suggestion that it pay a construction subsidy, on grounds that the most of the transmissions on the line would be for other countries, such as messages from New York to London or Paris. However, officials did agree to a 40 percent rebate to Collins's company on the Russian charges for international messages carried over Russian lines.[129]

Collins spent the next year acquiring the funding and permission to extend the line through British Columbia, which was not easy to secure because of the natural British preference for the Atlantic route. With the help and influence of Seward, who was quite interested in promoting an American-controlled North Pacific line over the Atlantic cable, Sibley agreed to issue up to $10 million in stock (100,000 shares) for a new company that was essentially a Western Union subsidiary. Western Union stockholders bought most of the stock and provided a 5 percent assessment for operating costs, while Collins gave up to Sibley and Western Union all rights he had obtained in return for 30,000 of these shares and a $5,000 annual salary as a new member of the board of directors. Seward and Senator Latham secured congressional support in the form of a land grant—forty acres for each fifteen miles of line across government lands in the West—and the use of at least one naval vessel.[130]

[129]Mel'nikov to Collins, 23 May/4 June 1863, enclosed in Collins (St. Petersburg) to Seward, 18 June 1863, DUSC, Amoor, vol. 2 (roll 2, T 111), RG 59, NA; also in Sibley Papers, box 1, Rochester.

[130]Ault, "The (almost) Russian-American Telegraph," p. 15; Seward's communications with congressional committees are included in DUSC, Amoor, vol. 2 (roll 2, T 111); on negotiations in London, see Collins (London) to Seward, 30 December 1863, ibid. In his annual message to Congress in December 1863, President Lincoln prematurely announced, "Satisfactory arrangements have been made with the Emperor of Russia, which, it is believed, will result in effecting a continuous line of telegraph through that Empire from our Pacific coast." Edward McPherson, *The Political History of America during the Great Rebellion*, 4th ed. (Washington, D.C.: James J. Chapman, 1882), p. 142.

Collins made one more trip to St. Petersburg with Sibley in tow in October 1864. Although very cordially received—even as guests at a private dinner with Alexander II—there were again aggravating delays regarding rates and terms, with Tolstoy suggesting at one point that he might turn the whole venture over to another company. Sibley especially was impatient with Russian bureaucratic procedures and threatened to pull his company out: "Nothing discourages me so much as the impracticable habits of the Russians. It takes forever to get anything done."[131] The main obstacle was the 40 percent net rebate stipulation, which the Russian officials interpreted as applying to all telegraphic business in the empire (which had not yet shown a profit because of increased construction costs). The Americans argued that it was meant to cover only the transcontinental message traffic, but recognizing the difficulty of calculating net profits on Russian government lines, they countered with a 20 percent gross rebate. The Russians insisted on a net calculation and won, thus effectively eliminating any payments to the American company for at least several years. Western Union, of course, expected handsome dividends on their end of the line. Finally, in March 1865 the Russian-American Telegraph Charter was signed, but not without a formal protest from Collins and Sibley over the rebate that greatly annoyed the Russians. Regardless, it was a kind of binational, joint-venture arrangement unusual for the time.[132]

The Expedition

In the meantime, the company, now awkwardly labeled the Collins Overland–Western Union Extension but more generally known as the Russian-American Telegraph of Collins Overland, had begun operations. Col. Charles S. Bulkley, a former chief of Union military telegraphs in the South, was named overall direc-

[131]Sibley to his wife, 24 December 1864, Sibley Papers, box 1, Rochester. Much official correspondence also relates to the negotiations, for example: Collins (Washington) to Seward, 25 May 1864, ibid.; Clay to Seward, 14 November 1864 and 12 March 1865, DUSM, Russia, vol. 20 (roll 20, M 35), RG 59, NA; Gorchakov to Clay, 31 October 1864, DPR, Russia, vol. 4501, Notes Received, RG 84, NA; Collins to Seward, 1 December 1864, DUSC, St. Petersburg, vol. 12 (roll 7, M 81), RG 59, NA; Clay to Gorchakov, 21 March/2 April 1865, DPR, vol. 4534, RG 84, NA.

For an outline of the involvement of Western Union, see Robert Luther Thompson, *Wiring a Continent: The History of the Telegraph Industry in the United States, 1832–1866* (Princeton, N. J.: Princeton University Press, 1947), pp. 427–34.

[132]Clay to Seward, 12 March and 5 April 1865, DUSM, Russia, vol. 20 (roll 20, M 35), RG 59, NA; Collins to Hunter, 10 May 1865, DUSC, Amoor, vol. 2 (roll 2, T 111), RG 59, NA; Clay to Sibley, 8 April and 3 June 1865, Sibley Papers, box 1, Rochester. Clay was apparently the one who advised accepting the Russian terms: "With the Russians, we must make up our minds to be *satisfied*; and encourage the best feeling, whilst by a firm and manly course we can win their confidence." To Sibley, 22 March 1865, Sibley Papers, box 1, Rochester.

tor of construction, while Capt. Charles M. Scammon signed on as "chief of marine." In March 1865 they departed from San Francisco on the revenue-cutter *Shubrik* to coordinate construction plans at Victoria and Sitka. They left Dr. Henry P. Fisher, the expedition surgeon, at Sitka to complete local arrangements with the Russian authorities.[133]

During the summer Bulkley and Scammon assembled ships, supplies, and personnel in San Francisco. Since the *Shubrik* was considered too small and inadequate for an extended voyage (probably having poor cabin space), it was replaced by the *Golden Gate*, an aging Panama steamer with four mounted cannon, in case it should encounter a still-active Confederate privateer. The *George S. Wright*, a well-worn Columbia River steam tugboat, was adapted as an auxiliary vessel.[134] For supplies the company depended upon the sailing barks *Olga* and *Clara Bell*, purchased by Russia for this purpose, and on the schooners *Palmetto*, a veteran of the Amur trade, and the *Milton Badger*. The latter brought a crew of workers from New York that included George Kennan, an employee of Western Union who had volunteered for this duty and so began his career as one of the leading American authorities on Russia. The other recruits were mostly demobilized Union officers with good service records or naturalists designated by the Smithsonian Institution—neither group having much (or any) telegraphic experience or knowledge of Russia. They were all to rely heavily on Maj. Sergei Abaza, a Russian expert on both the telegraph and Siberia, who was named overall supervisor of the Siberian sector.[135]

In July 1865, after receiving word of the final agreement and at least a month later than anticipated, this motley squadron set sail to reconnoiter the territory. The *Olga*, with Abaza, Kennan, Richard J. Bush, and civil engineer James A. Mahood aboard, made a long and stormy trip directly to Petropavlovsk on the Kamchatka coast, which was to serve as the base for the Abaza-Kennan exploring party. At Petropavlovsk they were joined by a Russian-speaking American named James Dodd, who had been in business in the area for several years. The group was to make its way by horseback, reindeer, and dogsled up the rugged

[133]*Daily Alta California* 8 March and 14 and 19 April 1865; George Kennan, *Tent Life in Siberia* (New York and London: G. P. Putnam's Sons, 1910), pp. 1–6.

[134]*Daily Alta California*, 14 and 19 April 1865; Charles S. Bulkley Journal, microfilm P-K 212, pp. 4–7, UCB, Bancroft Library (original in Oregon Historical Society); George Russell Adams, "First American Exploring Expedition to Russian America," microfilm of typescript, P-K 215, pp. 36–45, UCB, Bancroft Library. Adams (p. 38) commented after his interview with Bulkley for a job, "It looked to him as if all the young men of the city were anxious to take the chances of losing their lives in exploring the unknown."

[135]Abaza (San Francisco) to Sibley, 1 July 1865, Sibley Addition, Rochester; George Kennan (San Francisco) to his father, 29 June 1865, box 10, Kennan Papers, Manuscript Division, LC.

Kamchatka Peninsula with the assistance of native guides. Then, at the intersection of the proposed route of the line, they would split off in two directions, Kennan and Dodd heading northeast to meet Bulkley at the mouth of the Anadyr River and Abaza heading southwest to meet Bush, who had been transported on the *Olga* to Nikolaevsk on the Amur to explore the route northward on the west side of the Okhotsk sea. These small, valiant parties struggled through the winter over uncharted and largely untouched territory, risking life and limb, and the details of their adventures were vividly described in Kennan's *Tent Life in Siberia*, Bush's *Reindeer, Dogs, and Snow-Shoes*, and in various reports and letters.[136] Their success (and survival) obviously depended greatly on helpful and friendly natives.

Meanwhile, the *Golden Gate*, commanded by Scammon, and the *George S. Wright*, carrying Bulkley, William H. Dall (a reluctant surgeon-naturalist), and artist Frank Whymper, sailed along the American northwest coast. The *Clara Bell* brought a small river steamer directly from New York and met them at Sitka. They then searched along the Alaskan coast for suitable coal supplies until they reached Fort St. Michael on Norton Sound where a party disembarked to explore up the Yukon River into the interior of Alaska. This group was headed by twenty-one-year-old "Major" Robert Kennicott of the Smithsonian and assisted by the local Russian commander Sergei Stepanov, and it also endured severe hardships during the winter.[137]

The *Palmetto* and *Milton Badger* were sent ahead with the coal the steamers needed to make their way to Petropavlovsk. Arriving in mid-October, Bulkley then sailed northeast to the mouth of the Anadyr to land belatedly another survey crew under Capt. Charles Macrae, which was to track westward along the Anadyr River. The telegraph fleet finally reassembled in San Francisco in December after rough passages from Siberia and Alaska, leaving the exploring parties to their own devices. The Macrae party, which suffered the most, spent sixty-five days holed up through terrible winter storms with Chukchi villagers before being rescued by Kennan.[138]

[136]Kennan, Notebook, box 19, Kennan Papers, Manuscript Division, LC; William H. Dall Papers, box 2 and 20, and Western Union Telegraph Expedition Papers (hereafter WUTE), Smithsonian Institution Archives (hereafter SI); Richard J. Bush, *Reindeer, Dogs, and Snow-Shoes: A Journal of Siberian Travel and Explorations Made in the Years 1865, 1866, and 1867* (New York: Harper & Bros., 1871).

[137]*Daily Alta California*, 16 September and 15 November 1865; Private Journal, Correspondence, and Papers of George Melville Scammon, P-K 205, UCB, Bancroft Library. Kennicott reported from Fort St. Michael, "My outfit and equipment for telegraph work is abominable and absurd—my men are splendid—But we are sent on a forlorn hope with miserable equipment." To Spencer Baird, 16 September 1865, WUTE, SI.

[138]Kennan, *Tent Life*, p. 4; "Letters from Russia," *Daily Alta California*, 22 November 1866; Scammon Papers, p. 55, UCB, Bancroft Library. A typical diary entry by Dall on

In 1866 the serious job of construction began. In early May the *Clara Bell* left San Francisco for Petropavlovsk with telegraphic materials and coal. It was followed in June by the supply barks *Palmetto*, *Onward*, and *L. H. Rutgers*. After unexplained delays, the *George S. Wright* cleared San Francisco with Bulkley, Count Pavel Anosov as a Russian liaison, and Thomas W. Knox, a reporter for the New York *Herald*.[139] Scammon followed in July with a new, much bigger flagship, the *Nightingale*. His cargo included large quantities of blankets, tents, clothing, and food, as well as 432 tons of coal, 356 packages of telegraphic instruments, and 1,031 coils of wire. Although additional American supervisors headed to the sites on these ships, most of the work crews were Siberian natives, especially Yakuts, recruited by Abaza some distance inland from the actual workplace. The more mundane job of cutting and erecting poles and stretching wire could now begin; all of these activities drew the attention of the American press. Even examples of the portable transmission stations, specifically designed for the project, were on display in San Francisco.[140]

This largely overland route was expected to be more reliable and more easily repaired than one that needed extensive submarine cable, but given the distances involved and the terrain covered, difficulties could be expected. Fortunately, few lives were lost, though Major Kennicott's tragic death on the Yukon was a disheartening blow.[141] The whole enterprise was poorly planned and managed, however. Why so much time and effort were expended exploring Kamchatka when no line was intended to be erected there is a mystery. Going through the sparsely inhabited and rugged interior of Alaska rather than along the coast also did not make good sense. The delays in the shipment of supplies and the poor condition of the vessels forced much of the work to be done in fall and winter; that in turn probably contributed to the wreck of the *Golden Gate* on a late supply run in 1866 to the mouth of the Anadyr. Abaza complained bit-

30 September records an example of the human misery of the expedition in Alaska: "Fisher [the doctor] drunk as a fool sleeps in my room all night. Stepanoff has just raped the only virtuous girl in the fort." Dall Papers, box 20, SI.

[139]*Daily Alta California*, 2 and 24 May, 6 and 30 June 1866; Thomas W. Knox, *Overland through Asia: Pictures of Siberian, Chinese, and Tartar Life* (Hartford, Conn.: American Publishing Co., 1870; New York: Arno Reprint, 1970), pp. 30–34; Scammon Papers, p. 81, UCB, Bancroft Library. The *Clara Bell* and the *Milton Badger* also carried 1,200 miles of wire and 35,000 insulators from New York. O. H. Palmer (Rochester) to Sibley, 16 January 1865, Sibley Papers, box 1, Rochester.

[140]*Daily Alta California*, 12 July 1866 and 15 December 1865.

[141]Ibid., 4 October 1866; Adams, p. 151, UCB, Bancroft Library. Though Kennicott's death was attributed to a heart attack, Dall believed that he had really succumbed to tension and depression especially as a result of the machinations of William Ennis, one of his party. Dall diary, 25 September 1866, box 20, and Dall to his mother, 7 March 1867, box 2, Dall Papers, SI.

terly that the dearth of population and development on the Siberian side hindered surveying and construction.[142]

Overall direction was also a serious problem. Collins, who had invested so much in getting the enterprise started, seemed to drop out of sight. Publicity about the project raised Western Union stock for a time to record levels, but Sibley lost interest and chose to remain in Europe "for reasons of health"—more likely because the Western Union directors opposed his liberal dispensing of free stock. The scientific orientation of the operation through the involvement of the Smithsonian is to be admired and did produce impressive results in Alaska, but it was not conducive to harmony and cooperation among the staff. Nor was the choice of the military-minded Bulkley as director a wise one. Captain Scammon quarreled with Bulkley over rules about trading with natives for furs and then was accused of dereliction of duty on account of drunkenness and smuggling. No one seemed to be able to tolerate the second in command, William Hyde, whom Dall termed "a red headed, arrogant, ungentlemanly ass."[143] Even Kennan became distressed about Bulkley's direction; in a private letter to Abaza in December 1866, he wrote,

> It looks just as if Col. Bulkley deliberately intended to 'cripple' us here, and kept the "Golden Gate" at Plover Bay two weeks in order to accomplish his object as completely as possible! He has done it. I believe I cannot be accused by anyone of prejudice against Col. Bulkley. Never a word against him or his management has passed my life before; but the leaving of the Bush party to starve at the mouth of the Anadyr, and the detention of the "Golden Gate" until winter set in, are things which would make a saint indignant. He may explain these to the satisfaction of the Company but he never can to mine. I have lost confidence in him entirely.[144]

In any event, a new base was established at Gizhiga at the far northern tip of the Sea of Okhotsk, and Dall took Kennicott's place in Alaska. As construction continued through the winter of 1866–67, expectations were high that the line would be finished on schedule by the end of 1869. But in late March 1867, Kennan was one of the first of the Siberian crew chiefs to learn from a passing whaler the news of the successful completion of the Atlantic cable the previous

[142]Dall to his father, 19 September 1865, Dall Papers, box 2, SI. More officially, Dall reported that "Col. B. has been under the control of a parcel of swindlers sots and toadies whose advice he has followed to the detriment of the objects of the Company." Dall to Spencer Baird, 18 September 1866, WUTE, SI.

[143]Abaza (Petropavlovsk) to Bulkley, 15 February 1866, WUTE, SI.

[144]Kennan (Ghizhiga) to Major Abaza, 4/16 December 1866, box 6 (Letters Sent), Kennan Papers, Manuscript Division, LC. See also W. A. Howard to Scammon, 19 March 1867, Scammon Papers, pp. 22–24, UCB, Bancroft Library.

summer. Not only were telegraphic communications now in service between Europe and the United States, connecting Siberia with California from the other direction, but the first Atlantic cable had also been repaired. Kennan considered this latter feat an even greater blow to their enterprise, since it demonstrated an ability to maintain service.[145] As they later discovered, Western Union, which now stood to profit from the Atlantic cable, had ordered in October 1866 the cancellation of the whole Pacific enterprise and the return of crews and equipment. For six months they had been setting obsolete poles, a few of which may still be in place.

Kennan and Abaza remained in Eastern Siberia for several months to supervise the liquidation of the company property, selling the stock of food, clothing, and other supplies to pay off local obligations (mostly wages to native workers), while the wire, insulators, and telegraphic equipment were shipped back to the United States. They still ran short and left unsettled claims behind. Those who had purchased stock suffered losses, though not as much as might have been expected. Western Union offered a liberal trade of stock for regular company bonds, expecting to profit immensely from the Atlantic cable. Kennan hoped to reduce some of his own personal losses by traveling across Siberia to St. Petersburg to gather more material for a book on his adventures—and others followed his example.[146]

Whether a Siberian-Alaskan telegraph line would ever have been practical is an interesting question. It would have been extremely tenuous at best. Already doubts had been raised, chiefly by Dmitri Romanov, about the feasibility of a line extending along the generally uninhabited and rugged western Okhotsk coast, which was especially vulnerable to fierce winter storms. As a result, an alternative route from the Bering Sea to Yakutsk, then south to Irkutsk, was being considered, even though it would bypass Collins's much-revered Amur region.[147] The news of the cancellation only reached St. Petersburg in March 1867, shortly before the sale of Alaska was announced. Russian officials were naturally very disappointed and thought the action precipitate—as did Cassius Clay, who had been given three hundred shares in the enterprise for his "assistance."[148]

[145]Kennan, *Tent Life*, pp. 414–18. Kennan at first expected the Atlantic cable to fail and bought more stock in the company, raising his total to around eighty shares. Kennan to Bush, 1 April 1867, box 6, Kennan Papers, Manuscript Division, LC.

[146]Clay to Sibley, 8 December 1867, box 1, Sibley Papers, Rochester.

[147]Clay to Sibley, 20 February 1867, and James Thal (St. Petersburg) to Sibley, 4/16 March 1867, Sibley Addition, Rochester. The issue had first been raised a year earlier by Romanov and Alexander Phillipeus, a Finnish merchant in Petropavlovsk. Thal to Sibley, 26 March/7 April 1866, and Sergei Abaza (Okhotsk) to Vasily Abaza, 14/26 January 1866, translation enclosed in Vasily Abaza to Sibley, 14/26 April 1866, ibid. For a more positive view of the enterprise, see Frederick Travis, *George Kennan and the American-Russian Relationship* (Athens: Ohio University Press, 1989).

[148]Clay to Sibley, 26 December 1866 and 18 March 1867, ibid. Clay had remarked a

But the Russian-American telegraph project had accomplished three important things: It had drawn public attention to the North Pacific and Siberia just before the purchase of Alaska; vast new territory was explored and described; and it served as an example of friendly and potentially beneficial Russian-American collaboration. Although unintentional, it probably also spurred the work on the Atlantic cable. The Americans involved in surveying and construction may have quarreled among themselves, but they were united in their respect and admiration for Russian hospitality and regional cooperation.

American Naval Visits

Meanwhile, the Civil War was brought to a close by Union military superiority in April 1865, much to Russian satisfaction and surprise, at least about its suddenness. Little occurred diplomatically in connection with the end of the war, since peace terms were an internal matter. In other, contemporary affairs, Seward was perturbed at Stoeckl's refusal to apply pressure on Britain and France to end Maximilian's reign over Mexico.[149] Official and public remorse over the assassination of President Lincoln was genuinely expressed throughout the Russian empire and by Minister Stoeckl in Washington, despite his long-standing criticism of Lincoln's conduct of the war; and the president's picture was displayed prominently throughout Russia beside that of the tsar's oldest son, Grand Duke Nicholas, who had died about the same time.[150]

   Almost a year after the murder of the president, there was an unsuccessful attempt on the life of Alexander II engineered by disenchanted Russian radicals, leading Congress to approve a joint resolution congratulating the emperor on his escape. To deliver it to Russia on board a warship, Pres. Andrew Johnson se-

few months before, "Besides my private interest in the Collins line, I felt as you indicate a desire to see in my term here a work accomplished of which I was a cofather with friend Collins: and which, without disparagement to him, I believe unaided he would have abandoned in despair." To Sibley, 21 December 1866, ibid. Stoeckl also received a "payoff" of three hundred shares. Collins to Sibley, 27 August 1865, ibid.

   [149]Stoeckl to Gorchakov, 26 April/8 May 1865, f. kants. Vashington 1865, d. 183, AVPR.

   [150]In another dispatch of the same date, Stoeckl, who had been a frequent critic of the late president, commented, "The more time passes, the more one has reason to regret the death of Mr. Lincoln." Ibid. On the prevalence of Lincoln's picture in Russia, see Cleveland Abbe (Pulkovo) to his mother, 21 July 1865, box 2, Abbe Papers, Manuscript Division, LC. Timothy Smith forwarded a typical letter he received. This one was from Abraham Rudich, a Russian Jew living in Rostov-on-Don, and was written in English. It read in part: "The blow to America is as heavy as the war itself that spilled so much blood and riches. Poor America! Abraham Lincoln! Thou shouldest have been invulnerable to iron and fire; the blood should not have flown when iron cut thee, for thou belongedst not to thyself and America only, but to the whole world!" Enclosure, Smith to Seward, 13 May 1865, DUSC, Odessa, vol. 4 (roll 2, M 459), RG 59, NA.

The U.S. monitor Miantonomoh *on its way to Russia, 1866, from Loubat's* Mission to Russia, *1866*

lected Assistant Secretary of Navy Gustavus Fox, whom Stoeckl considered the true architect of Union naval successes and "one of our best friends in America." The real purpose, however, was to reciprocate the visit of the Russian naval squadrons three years earlier and to extend thanks for friendship during the war.

The "Fox mission" was unusual in several respects. It was the first time in American history that a resolution of this kind had been passed and then carried to its destination by a high-ranking government official. And by pointedly and publicly going through both Britain and France, it highlighted a continuing political connection between Russia and the United States. Fox, received warmly in Britain, was warned in Paris, "Do not be too friendly with Russia,"[151] which he, of course, ignored. In Copenhagen the roving "ambassador" was dazzled by the beautiful Danish princess Dagmar, who was soon to be married to the new heir to the Russian throne, Grand Duke Alexander (and who would later become empress and the mother of the last tsar, Nicholas II). Also at Copenhagen, Joseph Loubat of New York and E. H. Green of Boston joined the delegation as recording secretaries.

The mission was also memorable in naval history. To Fox was assigned a new American monitor, the *Miantonomoh* (from a river named after a Narragansett Indian chief), which was accompanied by an older steam frigate, the *Augusta*. The *Miantonomoh* was wooden-hulled but heavily clad in iron; though only 1,200 tons, it rode unusually low in the water, weighed down by the 450-pound Dahlgren cannon mounted in the turrets.[152] It was the first time that a monitor-

[151]Joseph F. Loubat, *Narrative of the Mission to Russia, in 1866, of the Hon. Gustavus Vasa Fox* (New York: D. Appleton and Company, 1873), pp. 46–47.
[152]Ibid., p. 28.

type vessel had crossed the Atlantic, and it did so with much initial trepidation from crew members. The crossing was uneventful and comfortable, although the deck was continually awash. The unique design of the *Miantonomoh* attracted considerable attention, especially in Britain. There the press complained about the Admiralty's backwardness in ship design, guessing that the heavily armed American ship could easily dispose of the much larger but lightly armed British ships. Fox, however, later expressed privately his view that Swedish and Russian monitor-type vessels were superior.[153] His leisurely progress over the Baltic and digressions to Stockholm and Helsingfors were due, at least in part, to worries about a cholera epidemic in St. Petersburg.

American hospitality to the Russian squadron's visit to New York had already been celebrated upon its return and again at a lavish reception for Cassius Clay and other Americans in Moscow in February 1866. Even so, the Fox mission was eagerly anticipated in St. Petersburg. The New York *Herald* quoted its St. Petersburg correspondence: "Our naval men are on the tiptoe of expectation to see the *Miantonomoh*, which has caused such excitement in England and promises to inaugurate a new era in maritime warfare. We have a fleet of iron-clads, too, which has been cruising the Baltic for the last three or four weeks; but it is doubted whether one of them would stand a voyage across the Atlantic, and we fear they would have a poor chance if pitted against one of your American sea monsters."[154] Clay had even implored a friend to send all of the most popular American songs for welcoming bands to play, and Heinrich Furstnow, musical director at the Pavlovsk pleasure gardens outside the capital, composed the "Miantonomoh Gallop" for the occasion.[155] Finally, escorted by a Russian fleet of eleven first-rate ships, the unusual American squadron made its way from the Finnish shores to Kronstadt on 6 August. Among the high-ranking naval officers greeting it were admirals Gorkovenko, Lesovskii, Butakov, and Popov, all veterans of extended visits to the United States.

Almost at once, on the eighth, Fox was received by Alexander II at his Peterhof summer palace near Kronstadt. Accompanying him were Clay, the commanders of the two ships (Alexander Murray and John Beaumont), the two secretaries, and John Van Buren, the former president's son, who had traveled separately to St. Petersburg with his daughter Anna to participate in the festivities.[156] The congressional resolution was formally presented to the tsar (and the

[153]Ibid., pp. 41–44; Fox (Kiel) to Henry Augustus Wise, 30 September 1866, Wise Papers, Letters from Gustavus Fox, Manuscript Division, NYPL.

[154]"St. Petersburg Correspondence," 13 July, in New York *Herald*, 30 July 1866.

[155]Clay to Benjamin Moran, 16 July 1866, Clay Papers, Filson Club. The music for the "Miantonomoh Gallop" can be found in Loubat, *Mission to Russia*, app. C, pp. 430–35.

[156]Clay did not report details of these ceremonies, since he felt Fox covered them am-

report of the ceremony was the first transmission on the new Atlantic cable from Russia). Afterwards, Gorchakov himself translated Alexander's friendly response, which promised never to forget the occasion and the future interests of friendship between the two countries.

The next morning the emperor and a retinue of grand dukes and high officials toured the American ships and then hosted a lunch on the imperial yacht. A number of gala events around the city ensued, including the launching of a ship named *Fox* by Miss Van Buren, who apparently had many Russian naval officers under her spell. One of the high points of the many, inevitable dinner toasts was a poem written specially for the mission by Oliver Wendell Holmes. It suitably sentimentalized the occasion:

Though watery deserts hold apart
  The worlds of East and West,
Still beats the self-same human heart
  In each proud nation's breast.
. . . .
She comes! she comes! her banner dips
  in Neva's flashing tide,
With greeting on her cannon's lips,
  The storm-god's iron bride.

Peace garlands with the olive-bough
  Her thunder-bearing tower,
And plants before her cleaving prow
  the sea-foam's milk-white flower.
. . . .
When darkness hid the stormy skies
  In war's long winter night,
One ray still cheered our straining eyes,
  The far-off Northern light.
. . . .
A nation's love in tears and smiles
  We bear across the sea;
O Neva of the hundred isles,
  We moor our hearts in thee![157]

On 23 August, Fox, Clay, secretary of legation Jeremiah Curtin, the entourage

ply in his official report: Fox (Kiel) to Gideon Welles, 30 September 1866, copy, DUSM, Russia, vol. 21 (roll 21, M 35), RG 59, NA. See also Loubat, *Mission to Russia*, pp. 86ff., which includes speeches, menus, etc.
[157]Loubat, *Mission to Russia*, pp. 180–81.

of officers, diplomats, and hangers-on entrained for Moscow, where they were treated to an even more elaborate reception staged by city and province officials and local businessmen. They toured the Kremlin, the Novodeivichi Convent, and the zoo; dined at Prince Nikolai Golitsyn's country estate, along with groups of merchants; and visited Zagorsk, the monastery city outside Moscow. Jeremiah Curtin impressed the assemblages at the various dinners by giving long, flowery toasts in Russian, which he had first begun to learn from the Russian officers visiting New York in the winter of 1863–64.

Then came another train ride to Nizhni Novgorod, the great market city on the Volga, where they were met by a large crowd at the station, huge illuminations, a band playing "Hail, Columbia," and the sight of American flags flying all over the city. A steamboat took the company up the Volga to Kostroma, Rybinsk, and Tver, from where they returned to St. Petersburg. Everywhere, the American party, joined by admirals Lesovskii and Gorkovenko, were greeted with cheers, curiosity, and obvious affection from masses of people. Fox and the naval officers were repeatedly forced to sit for photographs because of the great demand for their pictures, with Beaumont's black servant subject to special attention. And during all this touring, the ships at Kronstadt were plagued by visitors (while crew members on liberty often became drunk and unruly).[158]

The climax of the remainder of the visit in the capital was a dinner hosted by Gorchakov at the English Club for 250 guests and Russian dignitaries. The speech of the foreign minister raised Russian-American relations to a new rhetorical high—if indeed higher it could go:

> I need not insist upon the manifestations of sympathy between the two countries. They shine out in broad daylight. It is one of the interesting facts of our day—a fact which creates between two peoples—I will venture today, between two continents—the genus of good will and reciprocal friendship; which will bear fruit; which create traditions; and which tend to consolidate between them relations based upon a true spirit of Christian Civilization. That understanding does not rest upon geographical neighbourhood: the sea's abyss divides us. Nor does it rest upon parchments, I find no trace of it in the archives of the ministry confided to myself. It is instinctive: from this time I venture to call it Providential. I approve of that good understanding ("en-

[158]Ibid., pp. 282–91; logbook, *Miantonomoh*, 1866, Records of the Bureau of Naval Personnel, RG 24, NA. Fox's wife, who from home kept tabs on her husband's journey, reported that ten thousand photographs of her husband were supplied for Nizhni Novgorod alone. Virginia Woodbury Fox Diary, 18 September 1866, box 34, Woodbury Family Papers, Manuscript Division, LC. Van Buren to Clay, n.d., Clay Papers, Lincoln Memorial University.

tente"). I have faith in its duration. In my political policy, all my cares will tend to its consolidation. I say cares ("soins") and not efforts ("efforts") when we have to do with a reciprocal and spontaneous attraction.

One motive which leads me to proclaim aloud that "entente," is, because it is not a menace or a peril to any body. It inspires me with no covetousness, with no afterthought. The Lord has made the existence of the two countries upon such conditions, that their great interior life is for them enough. The United States are at home invulnerable. That state of things does not alone depend upon the fact that an Ocean-rampart defends them from European conflicts, but upon the public spirit, which there reigns—upon the personal character of their citizens. America can experience no other evil than what she may inflict upon herself. We have veiled in black the melancholy pages of these latter times. We have seen with profound regret the struggle between the brothers of the North and the brothers of the South; but we have always had faith in the final triumph of the Union: and we hope for its durable consolidation from the efforts of the actual President; whose policy breathing at the same time firmness and moderation, has all our sympathies.

I allow myself to find also a certain analogy between the two countries. Russia by her geographical position can be drawn into European complications. The chances of war may make us submit to reverses. Nevertheless I think that the same invulnerability exists equally for Russia: which she would at all times prove when the dignity and honor of the country should be seriously threatened: for then, as in all crises of her history the true power of Russia would be manifest. It does not consist only in the territorial vastness, or in the number of her population; it is in the intimate and indissoluble tie which binds the nation to the sovereign, and which consigns to his hands all the material and intellectual forces of the Empire, as it concentrates in Him today all the sentiments of love and devotion.[159]

Clay, miffed as usual by being upstaged by his Russian-speaking secretary, still managed to strike a different, more practical note in his brief response:

Russia can treat with indifference the petty questions of the balance of power in Europe: and devote all her energies to the development of her civil, social, and material well-being. I propose as a sentiment then: Commerce, agriculture, education, and manufactures, more powerful than arms to maintain the independence and liberties of a people.[160]

[159]Clay to Seward, 13 September 1866, DUSM, Russia, vol. 21 (roll 21, M 35), RG 59, NA. This translation, probably by Curtin, is less polished but more literal than the one in Loubat, *Mission to Russia*, pp. 342–46.
[160]Clay to Seward, 13 September 1866, DUSM, Russia, vol. 21 (roll 21, M 35), RG 59, NA.

An interesting thought for that time and later.

After taking leave of the emperor and enduring a few more formalities, the mission departed on 15 September, again with a Russian naval escort. Strangely, Grand Duke Constantine, who had done so much to advance Russian-American relations and Russian naval development, was absent during the entire episode. Although he was in the Caucasus, there would have been plenty of time for him to return. His position at court had waned somewhat because of his liberal views, and Alexander II no doubt feared that he might dominate the whole proceeding. Nevertheless, he would be back in St. Petersburg within weeks to play an important role in another Russian-American undertaking.

Publicity about the Fox excursion through Russia, which demonstrated once again Russian-American amity, reached many more of the Russian people and, concurrently, thanks to newspapers and the Atlantic cable, the entire United States. The New York *Tribune* had its own reporter covering the scene, while the *Herald* competed with space but also quoted a sarcastic story from the London *Times* on the visit to Moscow:

> The burden of the whole business seems to have been, "Let us swear eternal friendship!" The speech making was interminable, and every speech overflowed with compliments. "Hail Columbia!" was inscribed in letters of fire on a temple of glory, and the band at the Moscow station played "God Save America"—probably some new national air.
>
> At a magnificent banquet, given at the hotel of Prince Dolgoroukoff, the feast of sentiment was only to be equalled by the flow of champagne, Mr. Fox, returning thanks for a toast, declared that if the hearts of the Americans could open, there could be seen within them what he there saw, the union of the Russian and American flags. "May that union of the banners be sealed by the blood of our hearts!"
>
> Captain Murray was still more eloquent and figurative. "In the extracts we have given," says the *Temps*, "will be found a series of manifestations which resemble the transports of a violent passion during the happy days of the honeymoon." And the writer marvels, as well he may, at the strange coupling of the most free and active people in the world with a nation having but a *varnish of civilization, with despotism for its political regime, and communism for its social state.*[161]

One of the American party most responsible for cultivating this air of harmony and understanding was Jeremiah Curtin. However, the secretary had

[161]New York *Herald*, 27 September 1866, quoting the London *Times* of 10 September. Fox's toast is rendered "May these two flags in peaceful embrace be thus united forever!" by Loubat, *Mission to Russia*, p. 233.

aroused a fit of jealousy in Cassius Clay for flaunting his Russian at the various social functions and, even worse, receiving much praise for it from the Russian hosts. In retaliation, the paranoid-prone minister accused Curtin of insubordination, drunkenness, fomenting a rift with Chandor, and, worst of all, being a spy for Seward.[162] Whereupon Curtin, unfortunately, left Russia forever.

Russia in the American Mind

By the time the *Miantonomoh* had weighed anchor for home, the American public had been exposed to an avalanche of news about Russia. There seemed to be a yearning to catch up on foreign lands after so long an obsession with domestic affairs, and especially to learn about the "far-off Northern light" that had been so helpful to the Union cause. And Americans were prepared as never before to provide expert descriptions and interpretations. The United States now had the advantage of a respectable number of long-term residents in Russia—Winans, Whistler, Pierce, Prince, Ropes, Hiller, Hutton, Murray, Williams, Dunster, Ames—and members of the diplomatic colony—Clay, Smith, Croswell, Hatterscheidt, Collins, Chase, and Phelps—with substantial tenure and a good knowledge of the country.

Though these Russian "experts" rarely returned home or reached the American public through publications, they wrote many letters and were valuable resource people to the parade of American visitors to Russia. A number of these Americans had taken the trouble to study the language systematically. At least six by 1866 were fairly fluent: Bayard Taylor, Jeremiah Curtin, Henry Hiller, Joseph Ropes, George Prince, and George Kennan. Several others could manage simple conversations, and they had all traveled extensively in Russia. This represented a fundamental shift away from American parochialism regarding that country.

It was opportune for Benjamin Moran, the North's chief arms agent in Europe, to write to Taylor about the need to know Russian: "And I like your purpose of studying the language and the people. The fact is, we know too little really of Russia, just as the world knows too little really of ourselves."[163] Taylor himself was especially conspicuous in disseminating information about Russia as

---

[162]"I have regarded him [Curtin] for a long time as Seward's tool and spy." Clay to Sibley, 19 January 1867, Sibley Papers, box 1, Rochester. But to Seward, Clay wrote, "I regard him [Curtin] as my secret enemy and you must not place any confidence in him. He is the protege of Mr. Sumner." 26 April 1867 (private), Seward Papers, indexed correspondence, reel 100, Rochester. Curtin was apparently not aware of Clay's animosity until after his return from a tour of the Caucasus late in 1867. *Memoirs of Jeremiah Curtin*, ed. Joseph Schafer (Madison: State Historical Society of Wisconsin, 1940), p. 14.

[163]Benjamin Moran (London) to Taylor, 13 October 1862, box 2, Taylor Papers, Cornell. For an example of Taylor's descriptions, see "Winter Life in St. Petersburg," *Atlantic Monthly* 16 (July 1865): 34–46.

he resumed his rounds of public lecturing at home in 1865 and wrote articles for the popular press, yet he did not fulfill his goal of a return visit in 1866.[164] Also, both Taylor and Curtin were well connected with American literary circles, although it is uncertain what those linkages may have offered in terms of transmitting impressions.

Of by far the greatest importance in stimulating interest in Russia among Americans were the Western Union telegraph enterprise and the Fox mission. In fact, few foreign countries were covered as well as Russia in the American popular press, thanks to the space devoted to these ventures. Russia and Russians became more accessible to the "officer-class," socially conscious American as well as the ordinary worker-seaman. The two projects also, however, dramatically illustrated a problem that all people had in interpreting Russia—the blind men and the elephant. The sophistication of St. Petersburg and western Russia contrasted sharply with the wilderness of Eastern Siberia, but this was a duality that Americans especially might comprehend.

One example of this higher level of contacts is the experience of Cleveland Abbe, who was invited by the noted Russian astronomer Otto Struve to study at the Pulkovo observatory early in 1865, thus becoming one of the first American "exchange" students in Russia.[165] Struve had died while Abbe was en route, but the American found the new director, Auguste Wagner, quite congenial. He stayed for a year and a half, during which time he described candidly the passing Russian scene in a series of letters to his parents. Upon seeing that his first letter from home was addressed to "National Observatory," Abbe wrote to correct his parents: "In these parts of the world the nation is kept out of sight. The Royal Family represent it at all times—consequently we have imperial." Life at the self-contained observatory was pleasant enough, but he found Pulkovo, though "the best of Russian serf villages, . . . had no signs of life and energy compared with what we should expect in an American place of one quarter the size."[166]

Free to come and go as he pleased, Abbe spent a lot of time in nearby St. Petersburg in the company of Prince, Phelps, and Curtin and met Collins and Sib-

---

[164]George Prince (St. Petersburg) to Taylor, 19/31 May 1865, box 3, Taylor Papers, Cornell.

[165]Otto Struve (Pulkovo) to Cleveland Abbe, 25 June 1864, box 2, Abbe Papers, Manuscript Division, LC. A friend and mentor at the U. S. Naval Observatory encouraged Abbe to go: "A term of study at such a place will doubtless mark you as an astronomer for life, and it cannot but be profitable and pleasant." He also noted that astronomy was in a poor state in the United States and that Abbe would be able to import knowledge from Russia: "What we need is good *astronomers, and a system of practical astronomy which will tend to produce them.*" A. Hall (Washington) to Cleveland Abbe, 6 September 1864, ibid.

[166]To Parents, 1 February 1865, ibid.

ley during their stay. He had praise for the appearance of the city, commenting that "in Berlin the stucco is poor, of a dismal color and shabby. In St. Petersburg it is excellent new and of a warm color *very pleasing* after once the novelty wears away. I dislike stucco but it really is charming in St. Petersburg."[167] Later, after witnessing the Easter celebrations, he noted, "St. Petersburg seems to me to be a city bent on amusements and excitement—there is always something to see hear or do, and though we find the same in every city, yet not everywhere does one feel a pressure urging him to join the crowd."[168] But Abbe was especially revolted by the prevalence of drunkenness on the day after Easter:

As the day wore on it became more and more painfully evident that the common people consider themselves truely happy only when they are drunk. . . . Adding together all that I have ever seen have I ever seen so many men tipsy and reeling or else dead drunk. Really the whole city had gone on a drunken spree. . . . The police seemed to have no orders to arrest tipsy men nor to prevent them going where they would. On the pleasantest promenades where were gentlemen and ladies of at least exterior decency—were intermingling the tipsy reelers as freely as though they were all on the same level. And indeed I began to think they were when men appeared not in the least pained at this to me distressing exhibition of animal nature. Gentle ladies looked on with as much unconcern as the Spanish ladies look on a bull fight. And where all were so much hardened by having frequently seen such spectacles—I thought all must be essentially equally lowered.[169]

About the same time that Abbe entered Russia, another American scientist, Raphael Pumpelly, crossed the border from China at Kiakhta. Traveling through Siberia to St. Petersburg, he examined mineral and plant collections, conferred with leading Russian scientists, and formed general impressions similar to Abbe's: "The two great evils of the country, which run through all classes, are gambling and drinking to excess. I know of no nation in which drunkenness assumed such frightful proportions as in this eastern section of the Russian Empire."[170] He was, however, enthusiastic about the postal service and Siberian development, and concerning Russian hospitality he observed: "I could not

[167]To Parents, 17 January 1865, ibid.

[168]To Mother, 11/23 June 1985, ibid.

[169]To Mother, 14/26 April 1865, ibid. To a friend Abbe confided that he was much shocked by "the lewdness in society": "In all my life I never saw so much drunkenness as on last Sunday." However, on Pulkovo he wrote, "Especially am I pleased with the warm spirit of cooperation that is fostered." To Charles Hyatt, 21 April 1865, Hyatt Papers, MaryHS.

[170]Raphael Pumpelly, *My Reminiscences*, 2 vols. (New York: Henry Holt and Company, 1918), 2: 517.

help thinking that this was extended to me quite as much in my character of an American as individually. It was pleasant to meet everywhere an expression of the most cordial feeling toward the United States, and I was often surprised to hear, in this distant part of Asia, a very just appreciation of the causes and probable results of the war which was going on at home."[171]

Many other, more anonymous Americans visited Russia in the immediate postwar years, some attending special events (such as the wedding of Princess Dagmar and Grand Duke Alexander), others traveling with the Fox mission. Some penned very frank observations. A woman identified as "R," who was accompanying her husband and two other Americans as a tourist in 1866, wrote about Moscow for a hometown audience: "I cannot see the *"magnificence"* of this ancient metropolis, of which people and the Guide Books speak; but its *grotesqueness* is everywhere apparent, not only in the style of the buildings, but in the strolling mendicants and pilgrims who meet you at every step. Moscow seems to me today to be an extensive site, with streets wider than some of our widest squares, ill-paved, dusty, hot and disagreeable."[172] Obviously the exotic, Eastern flavor of the city did not suit her, but she was more favorably impressed with St. Petersburg—by the squares, wide streets, fine horses, the Neva, and St. Isaacs—although it was terribly expensive.[173]

Another visitor was even more shocked at the quality received for these high prices in Russia:

> There is not a single cafe or restaurant in the capital equal to what you would find in any third-rate provincial town in France. At the very best and most expensive you must put up with soiled tablecloths, dirt-begrimed floors, and unwashed waiters. . . . The dinners they provide for the ordinary customers are miserably bad. In fact, it is a mystery to me how people of moderate incomes live at St. Petersburg. My explanation is, that there are very few people there with moderate incomes; and that these few live wretchedly. I was never in a city in which the millions seemed so little cared for.[174]

About a year later Nathan Appleton, traveling with Gen. Benjamin Stone Roberts, made a tour of western Russia. Though finding the people agreeable, he repeated a frequent American complaint about border formalities: "There is probably no part of the civilized world where the annoyances about passports and baggage are greater than in conquered Poland. Everyone who enters the

[171]Ibid., p. 519.
[172]"Letter from Russia," Boston *Evening Transcript*, 28 June 1866.
[173]"The Sights of St. Petersburg," ibid., 12 July 1866.
[174]San Francisco *Daily Evening Bulletin*, 16 January 1867.

land is looked upon with suspicion, and the difficulty is not by any means over when you get in, for there is the same trouble to get out again, sometimes even worse."[175] Most Americans did not enter Russia wearing blinders but, on the contrary, tended to be blunt observers.

A typically American concern about efficiency, cleanliness, and convenience only slightly tainted the generally flattering pictures of Russia that predominated in the American press. The rhetoric of Russian-American friendship prevailed: "It may indeed be said of Russia and America, with the same truth as sometimes of individuals, that extremes meet, and that nothing tends more to produce sympathy than the existence of strong contrasts, coupled with the same national likes and dislikes, and the total absence of rivalry or the possibility of collision."[176]

Other views, however, expressed a commonality of interests in antipathy to the other European powers, in a social, political, and economic restructuring to eliminate servility and slavery, and in simultaneous and comparable communication and industrial progress. Much of this was a repetition of prewar sentiments but was given an added boost by the "cleansing" military victory for the Union and the continuation of western-style progressive reforms in Russia.

The United States in Russian Eyes

During the war and after, the Russian public was similarly inundated with information about the United States from the periodical press. Some articles were copied from the European papers, while others were original accounts or interpretations based on various sources. Inventiveness and ingenuity were still the attributes that dominated the Russian perception of Americans, even though they had had great difficulty managing armies and winning a war. Although Chernyshevsky lauded the ideals of the abolitionists, the American character in his famous 1864 novel, *What Is to Be Done*, symbolized practicality and technical progress. A notable emphasis in Russian publications was to portray the bustling character of American city life and modern means of transportation, which seemed to have special appeal to Russians.[177] And as a result of the fleet visits, many more Russians decided to see the United States for themselves.

The war and its progress were also followed closely in the Russian press. There was, first of all, a natural interest in the slavery issue, complemented by the rise

[175]Nathan Appleton, *Russian Life and Society* (Boston: Murray and Emery, 1904), p. 75.

[176]"Russia in 1866," Chicago *Tribune*, 20 March 1866.

[177]Dmitri Zavalishin, the old Decembrist, commenced a series on American cities based on his 1866 tour, but apparently only one appeared: Dmitrii I. Zavalishin, *Primery bystrago razvitiia gorodov v Soedinennykh Shtatakh*, vol. 1, *Chikago* (Moscow: Univ. tip., 1868).

of the populist ethos of concern for the downtrodden masses. In addition, many in official Russian society possessed a military background and training, so that the strategy of American campaigns and the leadership qualities of its commanders were frequent topics of conversation. Judging from the written records and oral testimonies to Americans, Russians were universally elated with the outcome of the war and the prospect of the increased power of the new American Union, which they expected to support Russia against Britain. The triumph of the North would also bolster the expansionist and reformist movements in Russia. Emancipation, political and social reform, economic progress, territorial aggrandizement, and government centralization seemed to be occurring at once in both countries, which balanced the still-considerable differences in societies and institutions.[178]

Not all Russians, of course, supported this general assessment—or agreed among themselves. In fact, within the radical and liberal movements there was a great deal of confusion and disagreement about the meaning and interpretation of recent American events, though most analysts at least put them in a revolutionary context. Summarization is not easy because individual opinions shifted in response to new developments, especially the Polish uprising of 1863 and the assassination attempt on Alexander II in 1866. For example, Mikhail Katkov, an influential editor, well-known liberal "emancipator," friend of Gurowski's, and admirer of the United States, turned decidedly in a conservative, nationalist direction after these events and became a vocal opponent of republican ideals. He remained convinced that the Russian-American "understanding" was more than a matter of convenience, but his rationalization was now political rather than liberal or ideological. The Washington and St. Petersburg governments were fighting a common battle against internal rebellion and sedition and opportunism by other European powers.

Likewise, the leading literary and political journal of this period, *Sovremennik*, went through a transformation after the death of Dobroliubov in 1861 and the arrest and imprisonment of Chernyshevsky in 1862. Though its political commentary still emphasized the American scene under the editorship of Ernest Watson, it was less concerned with interpretation and speculation. Then the journal ceased publication completely in 1866. Filling the vacuum and meeting the demand for American news were more conservative periodicals such as *Russkii Vestnik* [Russian Messenger], *Delo* [Cause], *Epokha* [Epoch], *Vremia* [Times], and *Zagranichnyi Vestnik* [Foreign Messenger].

Clearly, then, the course and result of the American Civil War provoked a

[178]For an overview of the Russian view of the United States during the Civil War, see Robert V. Allen, *Russia Looks at America: The View to 1917* (Washington, D.C.: Library of Congress, 1988), pp. 30–33; and Hans Rogger, "America in the Russian Mind—or Russian Discoveries of America," *Pacific Historical Review* 47, 1 (February 1978): 36–38.

lively debate in the Russian public press during what was still a fairly liberal period relatively free from the usual strict government censorship. One popular retrospective view was that what had happened in the United States was inevitable: that slavery like serfdom was an inherently doomed vestige of the past and that the triumph of national power and reunification was a good, positive development. The cruel war was the concomitant price that had to be paid. Herzen and his friend and colleague Nicholas Ogarev optimistically heralded the Northern victory as proving the strength and vitality of democratic institutions, which must eventually succeed everywhere.

Others took a less sanguine view. Some had opposed the violence of war, even believing that the North would be better off without the South, and at its end they feared that brutal retribution and the abuse of central power would prevail, that the United States would essentially follow the ruthless European path in dealing with dissent and revolt. An even more pessimistic view was that the lives of the American blacks, though now freed from formal bonds of slavery, would not improve but might worsen, unprotected by the benevolent aspects of that system. The clear contrasts between the Russian and American situations were the race discrimination in the United States that did not exist in Russia and the awards of land to the peasants in Russia as part of the emancipation process. But disenchantment with the limits of reform in Russia extended to American Reconstruction as well. Ultimately, some said, there were no victors, no amelioration of conditions for the masses; the revolutions had failed. More hopeful commentators would argue that it was still too soon to draw that conclusion, or, like Herzen, would continue to idealize the United States for the sake of beating old Europe with it.

One view of the United States shared by Russians of various political persuasions was strengthened by the fuller details available in the 1860s. This was the picture of greed and materialism and harsh, inhumane conditions for a large number of the lower strata of the population, especially in the cities of the North and the war-torn countryside of the South. Here the Slavophile and populist idealism and rising Russian religious nationalism clashed with the image of a crass, uncultured, and materialistic America. Though still overshadowed by the aura of cooperation and friendship during the war and immediate postwar years, this perception would sharpen and develop in Russia in the 1870s.[179]

A brooding disenchantment with the United States is reflected in the dispatches of Russia's chief representative in Washington, Eduard Stoeckl. Though "Americanized" by his marriage and long tenure, Stoeckl seems to have been

[179]The foregoing is based on an examination of the leading Russian journals and on David Hecht, *Russian Radicals Look to America, 1825–1894* (Cambridge, Mass.: Harvard University Press, 1947); Laserson, *American Impact*; and especially Rogger, "Russia and the Civil War," in *Heard Round the World*, pp. 231–46.

thrown off balance by the sudden change in administrations and the demise of Washington's traditional Southern political orientation. The new rabble-rousing radicals who seemed to dominate Congress, the incompetence of Northern commanders, and, above all, a cautious, temporizing president clearly upset the minister. But the overall tenor of his reports, taking into account the entire spectrum from 1854 to beyond 1867, was not nearly as anti-American as most secondary authorities (Albert Woldman and M. M. Malkin, for example) claim. Even so, there was a definite sense in both St. Petersburg and Washington that his views were not entirely to be trusted. This may also explain the Russian government's frequent sending of couriers and special agents and the curious "end runs" executed by his two top assistants, Robert Osten-Sacken and Konstantin Katakazi. Katakazi quite pointedly forwarded a letter he had received from an American to Jomini, a high foreign ministry official, that voiced the fear that Stoeckl was pro-South and urged his transfer, "for such a suspicion would paralyze his influence at Washington, although it would not change the cordial sentiments of our government and people for the Czar and for Russia."[180] In fact, Stoeckl was a loyal but critical supporter of the Northern cause who would have jumped at the chance to help Seward become president. Through the trials of war and peace, Stoeckl and Seward had formed a cautious common bond, self-interested though it might be.

Like many Russians, Stoeckl considered what was happening in the United States truly revolutionary. Recapping the war in April 1865, he wrote, "The battle has ended, but it has created in the institutions and even in the manners of this country a situation entirely new." Yet it was incomplete as far as the former slaves were concerned. "They have given them civil rights but are forcing them to work. . . . The presence of enfranchised Negroes will be an embarrassment for them. The Negro will be tolerated only as long as he is useful to Americans, who, like all Anglo-Saxons, are always ready to declaim the rights of man but are slow to put them into practice." Stoeckl also wisely noted that "the effect of the revolution most difficult to erase will be the animosity of the South."[181] Reiterating that theme later, the Russian minister warned his government of a reliable report that Lincoln intended to weld the Union by uniting the armies of the North and South in foreign wars and by the conquest of Canada and Mexico and that these aggressive moves would be popular in both North and

[180]George W. Morgan (Mount Vernon, Ohio) to Katakazi, 6 January 1862, Jomini-Onou Papers, Eg. 3170, BL.

[181]Stoeckl to Gorchakov, 2/14 April 1865, f. kants. Vashington 1865, d. 183, AVPR. The perspective of the American Civil War as revolutionary was followed by later Soviet historians who applied a Marxist analysis to show the completion of the bourgeois revolution by eliminating a "Prussian-style" serf-slave system and by centralizing power in Washington. See especially G. P. Kuropiatnik, *Vtoraia amerikanskaia revoliutsiia* (Moscow; Nauka, 1961).

South.[182] "One must live among Americans to get an idea of their vanity and illusions. They believe blindly that after the conquest the men of the South will submit willingly to the dominion of the North and return to be peaceful and devoted brothers. They are persuaded that what they call "the best government that God ever saw" [in English] is destined to exist forever and they forget that in this world nothing is eternal." And, he added, "Today they are going too far and will repent it."[183]

Russia and the United States in the North Pacific

In the Far East, the Western Union project had literally tried to wire the two countries together, and though it was in vain, the activity had greatly raised the profile of the region in 1865 and 1866. The cumulative American impact was thus notable, considering the ice business in Alaska, the handling of Russian business in China by the Augustine Heard Company, whaling in the Sea of Okhotsk, and the dominance of American traders in the Amur region. Moreover, American sightseers and reporters were no longer a rarity in Eastern Siberia.

Americans might even have settled there in large numbers. In the closing weeks of the war, Stoeckl received from a delegation of Baltimore businessmen a grand proposal for Amur colonization: "Must not the Amoor country be built up for Russia as California was by the United States? . . . If Russia institutes a plan of the same sort for her possessions on the Amoor, will she not do more for that country in ten years, by water, than can be done in one hundred years (if ever done at all) by land?"[184] They proposed using clipper ships to transport large numbers of able-bodied Civil War veterans of both North and South. All that Russia had to do was to provide a generous tract of free land, which in turn would be divided up into equal-size farms à la the Homestead Act.[185] Although the scheme received the backing of Thomas Winans, as well as that of an emissary of Grand Duke Constantine's named Harrowitz in New York, Stoeckl took a dim view of the whole idea, observing shrewdly that suitable American colonists were unlikely to be found, since there was already ample free land available in the United States itself. These types of adventurers would, moreover, prove to be as dangerous and volatile an element in Russia as they had been in California and on the Fraser River.[186]

On that front and despite Collins's continuing exertions, the Amur region

---

[182]Stoeckl to Gorchakov, 12/24 January 1865, in code, ibid.

[183]Stoeckl to Gorchakov, 2/14 April 1865, ibid.

[184]Thomas Buchler, George T. Coulter, and William Prescott Smith to Stoeckl, undated, enclosed in Stoeckl to Gorchakov, 29 November/10 December 1865, ibid.

[185]Ibid.

[186]Stoeckl to Gorchakov, 29 November/10 December 1865, ibid.

was stagnating economically. By 1862 only one important American company was active at Nikolaevsk and Petropavlovsk—that of Bostonian William Boardman. His chief agent, Charles Gordon Chase, also served as the American "vice-commercial-agent" during the extended and, as it happened, permanent absence of Perry McDonough Collins. At least two other Americans were long-term residents of the area: Henry Winans Hiller, who also worked for Boardman, and Enoch Emory, who concentrated on trade upriver at Blagoveshchensk.

Chase was extremely dubious about commercial expansion in the area. Reviewing the activity of 1862, he wrote: "The *export trade* of this place and this country (via this Port) up to the present time is of so very little importance as not to call for and hardly suffice for a detailed report, and what little trade of that kind that there has formerly been appears to have actually decreased for a year or two last past [sic] in comparison with former years."[187] He did note that a new item of export, ice, had been shipped to Shanghai. Alcoholic beverages, one of the biggest imports had declined owing to the inroads of Siberian production. Other reasons Chase cited for the lack of progress were internal tariffs, the severity of the climate, the unsuitability of Nikolaevsk as an ocean port, and government mismanagement.

But Collins, viewing affairs from London, spoke of "great and steady progress" in Amur development and blamed the American merchants themselves for failing to respond: "Some of our earlier merchants there by a monopolizing and timid policy did not develop commerce in our favor as rapidly as I conceived they should have done. By holding their imports at high rates, and keeping down supplies to mere necessaries for a local population, they have allowed much of the trade which should have almost exclusively belonged to us to slip into other channels."[188] His friend Chase, reporting from the scene in 1864, presented a more discouraging picture: "It can be safely said, that no perceptible, favourable progress had been made in increasing, or extending the mercantile, or trade intercourse of our countrymen, with the inhabitants of the Amoor country, and the adjacent provinces and regions and the more distant parts of the Maritime Province of East Siberia"—the result, in part at least, of "the nature of the country being in the main an unbroken wilderness of rugged, precipitous, and lofty hills, with intermediate valleys."

> The *great* difficulty in this trade now is, that the extension, and increase of it, by no means keeps pace, or has done so, with the increased supply of foreign imported merchandise received at this place, and the result is, that the

[187]Charles G. Chase to Seward, 15/27 January 1863, DUSC, Amoor, vol. 2 (roll 2, T 111), RG 59, NA.
[188]Collins (London) to Seward, 18 August 1863, ibid.

very limited business is entirely over done. No better proof of the insignificance of the trade here, considered as mercantile or commercial operations, can perhaps be presented, than simply to state, that it does not yet permit of particular branches of business being engaged in exclusively, for instance, exclusive Dry Good, Hardware, Crockery Ware, or other separate establishments, all branches of business, being united in one concern, and conducted in one establishment.[189]

Additional factors depressed the Amur economy in the mid-1860s: the disappearance of promotional leadership after Murav'ev-Amurskii's departure from office; the costs of the domestic reforms, which limited development; the collapse of the salmon fishing—vital to the coastal economy—in 1866; the liquidation of the Amur Company, which dumped warehouses of supplies on the market at half-price; and the similar outcome from the stoppage of telegraph operations in 1867. A crowning blow came early in 1867 when the naval administration announced the withdrawal of all naval ships and facilities from the Okhotsk area in order to concentrate them at Vladivostok, where they would be supplied directly by the navy itself.[190] By 1867 Boardman was sending only one ship a year to the Russian ports, and the business ceased completely after his death in 1872. The American agency in Nikolaevsk closed down soon afterwards.[191]

While opportunities on land diminished, the seas continued to provide an immense booty for hardy American ship captains. Whaling, of course, was still the primary business of the Okhotsk region, although a turning of the tide in the demand for whale oil was signaled by the rapid development of the American petroleum industry. Whalers typically brought all the supplies they needed and more to trade with coastal villages for a few luxuries—women and furs. In 1866 codfish suddenly loomed in importance in response to a new demand for salted fish and cod oil and the discovery a few years earlier of rich Okhotsk fishing grounds by Matthew Turner. Knowledge of the location of the bank, stretching one hundred miles off the west side of Kamchatka, fueled a veritable cod rush. In 1865 seven ships carried 249,000 fish, averaging two-and-a-half pounds each,

[189]Chase to Seward, 18/30 March 1864, ibid.

[190]"A great reduction, or withdrawal of the fleet, and considerable decrease of the population of the port in the naval service, would be a severe blow to the commercial interests, and if some other equal support should not be soon substituted most of the foreign houses in the trade would probably speedily abandon it." Chase (Nikolaevsk) to Seward, 1 February 1867, ibid.

[191]George Cushing (Boston) to Henry Hiller, 8 December 1873, Hiller Papers, box 1, folder 2, Mystic Seaport. And the American diplomatic post was closed in 1874, leaving the archives with Hiller's father-in-law. Enoch Emory to Secretary of State, 30 June 1874, DUSC, Amoor, vol. 2 (roll 2, T 111), RG 59, NA.

to San Francisco from Russian waters, but in 1866 fifteen vessels brought in 773,000 fish and a less precise amount of processed cod oil.[192] This saturated the Pacific Coast fish market, severely limiting the opportunity for the Russian America Company to expand its fish exports.

The Sale of Alaska

The purchase of Alaska from Russia by the United States has gripped the popular imagination like few events in the history of either country. Consequently, there is a very extensive literature examining the causes and circumstances of the transfer of this large territory from one government to the other. Thanks to the earlier work of historians such as Frank Golder, Anatole Mazour, and Thomas Bailey and the more recent analyses of Howard Kushner, Oleh Gerus, James Gibson, and Nikolai Bolkhovitinov, many angles have been usefully explored.[193] But why Russia sold remains more complicated and more subject to varying interpretations than why the United States bought. The following are the main reasons historians have proposed for Russia's decision: a response to American manifest destiny, the economic problems of the Russian America Company, the inability to defend properly the territory against attack, the liberal reforms sweeping Russia at the time, a military-territorial rationalization, and out of simple friendship for the United States.

It should first be recalled that the sale/purchase did not come completely out of the blue. The concept of such an exchange originated at the beginning of the Crimean War with a proposal for a fictitious sale of the territory by the Russian America Company to its California business partner, the American Russian Commercial Company. As we have seen, the idea received little notice at the time, since it was obviated by the company's neutrality agreement with the Hudson's Bay Company. The Crimean War situation may also have instigated conversations in Washington between Sen. William Gwin and Russian envoy Stoeckl, although the evidence is not conclusive. The rumors that Thomas

---

[192]*Daily Alta California*, 7 December 1866.

[193]Frank A. Golder, "The Purchase of Alaska," *American Historical Review* 25, 3 (April 1920): 411–25; Reinhard H. Luthin, "The Sale of Alaska," *Slavonic and East European Review* 16, 2 (July 1937): 168–82; Anatole G. Mazour, "The Prelude to Russia's Departure from America," *Pacific Historical Review* 10, 3 (September 1941): 311–19; Ronald J. Jensen, *The Alaska Purchase and Russian-American Relations* (Seattle and London: University of Washington Press, 1975); Oleh Gerus, "The Russian Withdrawal from Alaska: The Decision to Sell," *Revista de Historia de America*, nos. 75–76 (1973): 157–75; James R. Gibson, "The Sale of Russian America to the United States," *Acta Slavica Iaponica* (Sapporo, Japan) 1 (1983): 15–37; N. N. Bolkhovitinov, "How It Was Decided to Sell Alaska," *International Affairs* 8 (August 1988): 116–25. The most thorough analysis is the latter's *Russko-Amerikanskie otnosheniia i prodazha Aliaski* (Moscow: Nauka, 1990).

Cottman's return from Russia in August 1854 involved a project concerning the sale of Alaska did, however, receive much publicity, thus first planting the notion in the public mind. And most likely, conversations on the subject occurred around that time between other Americans and Russians, especially Grand Duke Constantine.

In April 1857, as the fiscal damage of the Crimean War in the Pacific was being assessed, the grand duke first proposed within the Russian government circles the sacrifice of the territory to the United States. The response was weak, in part because the charter guarantee to the company extended until 1862 and there was a twenty-year contract commitment to the American Russian Commercial Company, and also because Foreign Minister Gorchakov was opposed to the idea.[194] But the grand duke continued to attack the company for its monopolistic privileges and mismanagement. In his famous letter of December 1857, written while on cruise in the Mediterranean, Constantine presented a more sophisticated argument: "Russia must endeavor as far as possible to become stronger in her center, in those fundamentally Russian regions which constitute her main power in population and in faith, and Russia must develop the strength of this center in order to be able to hold those extremities which bring her real benefit." Serious, direct discussions with Stoeckl occurred in Washington on the initiative of Gwin, President Buchanan, and acting Secretary of State John Appleton in 1860, but the embroilment of the administration in domestic affairs and then the outbreak of the Civil War prevented further negotiations. After the war ended the country was exhausted and lacked much of its earlier zeal for territorial expansion—especially since the most sought-after areas, Canada, Mexico, and Cuba, had eluded the American grasp and seemed indefinitely out of reach. Secretary of State William Seward, however, was still in an expansionist mood.

Though a buyer now seemed ready, selling Alaska was not so easy for a country accustomed to territorial conquest. One argument in support of such a move, which came especially from Stoeckl, was that the course of American expansion in North America was invincible and inevitable and that sooner or later American "manifesters" would be knocking on the door of Alaska; his attitude no doubt reflected his many conversations with Seward. Shortly before the final decision was made, the minister summarized forcefully his often-expressed

[194]Gerus, "Russian Withdrawal," pp. 166–67; texts of Constantine's letters of 1857 arguing for the sale are in Documents Relating to the Transfer of Alaska, 1857–68, Manuscript Division, LC, and Papers Relating to the Cession of Alaska, annexes 3–5, RG 59, NA. A Soviet historian also stresses Grand Duke Constantine's "political" campaign against the company as a prime cause of the sale. R. V. Makarova, "K istorii likvidatsii Rossiisko-Amerikanskoi Kompanii," in *Problemy istorii i etnografi Ameriki* (Moscow: Nauka, 1979), p. 270.

appreciation of the power of American aggrandizement and his conviction that Russia would stand in its way at the cost of close, friendly relations: "Our role is to dominate the East. The one of the United States is to exercise an absolute control over the American continent. In the march of progress that destiny has bequeathed to Russia and the United States, the two nations will advance without their paths being blocked, without exciting jealousies, without their interests conflicting."[195] More specifically, Stoeckl was haunted by the image of Americans swarming to a Russian Alaska—like Mormons seeking private space or prospectors seeking gold.[196] American expansionism, or "imperialism" to later Soviet historians,[197] was thus certainly a key factor in the mind of Stoeckl. To the extent that the minister played a role in the Russian decision, manifest destiny was indeed a contributing cause of the sale.

Stoeckl, however, did not have a particularly good record of evaluating the American scene, nor did he have much direct influence in St. Petersburg. Clearly, he was overawed by rumors, expansionist rhetoric, and especially by William Seward's ambitious schemes. He had already predicted an American invasion of Canada and Mexico, and those two eventualities were rapidly diminishing by the end of 1866, as the French withdrew from Mexico, Canada moved toward dominion status, and the ardor for territory was cooled by the problems of Reconstruction. Moreover, at no time had the United States been as attracted to Alaska as to other areas, such as Cuba and Central America. The manifest destiny threat to Alaska would seem to come more naturally from Canada, whose Hudson's Bay Company already leased some of the Russian territory. Finally, those Americans most involved in Alaska preferred to deal with an ongoing Russian administrative organization, as opposed to operating in a wide-open, unstable American frontier. But this situation only created a secondary consideration in selling Alaska to the United States—to prevent Britain from getting it.

Just as the Spanish remained in Cuba, Russians might have stayed in Alaska for many more years, if the Russian America Company had been a flourishing

[195]Stoeckl to Gorchakov, 29 September/11 October 1866, f. kants. Vashington 1866, d. 221, AVPR. This was the minister's last dispatch before departing for St. Petersburg.

[196]Gibson, "Sale of Russian America," pp. 28–29; Mazour, "Prelude to Russia's Departure," pp. 317–19.

[197]Soviet historians in recent years place special stress on American expansion in the North Pacific: Bolkhovitinov, "How It Was Decided," p. 124; M. Belov, "O prodazhe Aliaski," *Nauka i zhizn'*, no. 1 (1967): 72; T. M. Batueva, "Prokhozhdenie dogovora o pokupke Aliaski v kongresse SShA v 1867–1868 gg.," *Novaia i Noveishaia Istoriia*, no. 4 (July–August 1971): 117; A. I. Alekseev, *Sud'ba Russkoi Ameriki* (Magadan: Magadanskoe knizhnoe izd., 1975), p. 291. In fact, the United States at the time was in rapid retreat with the cancellation of the telegraphic enterprise, the collapse of the Amur trade, and even the decline of whaling—though, of course, in the long look back, the United States had certainly been expanding toward the Pacific.

economic success. Overhunting, combined with a decline in the market for furs, had long ago damaged the company's profitability and undermined its original reason for existing. The Crimean War had an especially crippling effect because it forced an expensive dependency on the company for American shipping and supplies, resulting in a very unfavorable balance of trade and stoking the public criticism of the company that followed.

Yet the Russian America Company under more efficient and open direction, especially that of Johann Furuhjelm, showed a surprising amount of initiative, much more than its critics would allow, in seeking other sources of revenue: ice, coal, lumber, fish, and whaling. Above all, with the help of the Augustine Heard Company and favorable government tariff treatment, it became a very successful importer of tea from China for the Russian market. The animal population and hunting potential also improved, thanks to better management. The supply picture was improved by developing commerce with Vancouver and chartering ships for European voyages, thus relying less on California. And even the living conditions of the natives showed gains. Many of these endeavors were still not as profitable as had been expected, mainly because of insufficient capital for investment and simply bad luck. The business record of the company was thus somewhat mixed but certainly not all negative.

Still, as the date for charter renewal approached and passed, the company had to endure awkward short-term extensions of its 1842 charter. The review committee designated to make a recommendation on the charter was stacked against the company by the combined opposition of Grand Duke Constantine and the new minister of finance, Michael Reutern. An investigation by Golovin and Kostlivstev produced biased, critical reports for the committee, although they concluded by recommending charter renewal. Even so, the company, led by Ferdinand Wrangel, waged a strong defense, showed a willingness to compromise, and, because of the government's reluctance to assume full responsibility for the territory, was offered a twenty-year renewal in 1865.[198]

By the new charter, the company would continue to administer the territory and would retain most of its resource and trading privileges. At the company's insistence, its growing debt to the state was forgiven and it gained a 200,000-ruble annual subsidy to cover administrative costs. The company's future appeared to be secure, but the new regulations provided for close supervision by a

---

[198]"Po proektu novago ustava Rossiiskoi-Amerikanskoi Kompanii," f. 398, op. 24, no. 9196, TsGIA. This contains the texts of the charges and refutations of the Russian America Company in the 1861–63 discussions. The attack on the company was led by the naval journal *Morskoi Sbornik*, for example, K. Zelenoi, "Is zapisok o krugosvetnom plavanii (1861–1864)," pp. 51–88. The main defense was commissioned by the company: Petr Tikhmenev, *Istoricheskoe obozrenie obrazovaniia Rossiisko-Amerikanskoi Kompanii i deistvii eia do nastoiashchago vremeni*, 2 vols. (St. Petersburg, 1861–63).

government agency, this time the naval ministry. Another controversy arose over the directors' demand for either a one-time substantial capital-improvement grant or a free hand in charting the company's future economic course, including borrowing needed funds, if necessary from British banks. Government officials were naturally alarmed by the prospect of a "mortgage foreclosure" that could leave Alaska in British hands. The finance ministry, already upset by the subsidy arrangement, opposed the new demands. The company was left in a situation of government restriction that only worsened its financial condition and depressed its stock to record lows. The government was also concerned about the cost of defense, which was to be its responsibility under the new charter. This expense was bound to increase, as the company had rendered very little military protection, certainly not that commensurate with Russia's status as a great power.[199]

Hence, another reason for selling Alaska that was much discussed at the time was that the territory was vulnerable to attack and seizure, that neither the company nor the Russian government was providing adequate defense, and that to do so would have been prohibitively expensive. During a time of crisis or war the territory might be occupied by an unfriendly power, which generally meant Britain. The best course, then, would be to unload the territory on a friendly power while the moment was ripe.

This argument, though undoubtedly useful in convincing the military-minded Alexander II to approve the sale, was somewhat illogical. The most likely time for Alaska to have been lost by conquest was during the Crimean War, but the threat evaporated almost immediately. The best protection for Alaska was, in fact, the friendly disposition of the United States, which was most secure in 1867. Even under the company's management, Alaska was no less defended and open to attack than Kamchatka or other parts of the Siberian coast. Additionally, the territory might be a useful card to play in evading military or diplomatic reverses elsewhere. As will be seen shortly, however, continued Russian possession would have demanded a better defense for honor alone, and that would indeed have been expensive.

The decision to sell Alaska coincided, and not accidentally, with an era of liberal reforms in Russia. Emancipation of the serfs was the keystone, and with some accuracy, the Russian America Company was viewed by the liberal emancipators who dominated government policy as one more servile estate. Another powerful influence at the time was the doctrine of free trade. State-owned railroads were being offered up for sale, and Winans had lost his protected business in open bidding to a French firm. There was simply no room in the new, re-

---

[199]Gibson, "Sale of Russian America," pp. 20–23; "Po proektu novago ustava Rossiiskoi-Amerikanskoi Kompanii," f. 398, op. 24, no. 9196, TsGIA.

formed Russia for monopoly or for dictatorial treatment of "employees," of which the Russian America Company was the best example. Ultimately, the company was in a no-win situation with reformers: It was attacked for its illiberal, monopolistic status as well as for what it could become under the operation of free trade (for example with its China tea business)—a multinational company dependent upon foreign capital.

However, denying the Russian America Company its monopoly position in its administrative responsibilities meant that the region would have to be opened to all and sundry, including foreigners, and the central government would have to shoulder the burden of administrative costs at a time of severely strained finances; hence the finance ministry's advocacy of the sale. In fact, it could be argued that the Civil War almost delayed the Alaska treaty out of existence; by 1866–67, a more conservative Russian national sentiment was rising against reform and the surrender of territory. Even a high-placed foreign ministry official, Fedor Osten-Sacken, objected strongly to the arguments for selling, while a chorus of complaints followed the announcement of the sale in the Russian conservative press.[200]

"Selling the sale" would thus have been very difficult for the liberal cabal if Russia had not been gaining other, compensatory territory at the same time—in Central Asia and the Far East. Murav'ev-Amurskii for years had opposed the company's involvement in Alaska as a diversion of resources that would be better employed administratively and economically by a concentration on Siberia and especially the Amur region. Grand Duke Constantine had a similar view but focused on a new naval program of stationing fast, steam-powered warships in the Far East at a good, strategically situated harbor, which led to the buildup of Vladivostok as a modern naval base in 1866–67. This was even farther to the south than the Amur, where the fleet could be a factor in the geopolitical struggle for dominance in the Far East. To prepare for an expanded role in the region, Russia occupied the southern half of Sakhalin Island late in 1866 and was making aggressive moves in Korea.

The grand duke, ever mindful of expenses, naturally opposed the costs of a naval commitment to defend far-off Alaska or even routine cruises to Sitka. An important but little-mentioned factor here is the promotion of a modern navy that relied much more on steam power and thus depended upon coal, readily accessible from Sakhalin. Steaming greatly escalated the costs of long voyages to

[200]"Po proektu novago ustava Rossiiskoi-Amerikanskoi Kompanii," f. 398, op. 24, no. 9196, TsGIA; Gerus, "Russian Withdrawal," pp. 172–73; Osten-Sacken's memorandum defending a reorganized colony was written just hours after the crucial meeting on 16/28 December under the misperception that it was scheduled for the following day. For the text, see David Hunter Miller, "Russian Opinion on the Cession of Alaska," *American Historical Review* 48, 3 (April 1943): 523–25.

the northeast, and the rocky Alaskan and Aleutian coasts added other hazards that were known only too well to Russians. The company similarly was handicapped by technological change, since regular incoming supplies and mail could best be handled by new but expensive steamers, while outgoing cargoes such as furs, ice, fish, and lumber were best carried on large clippers. Strong, sound arguments for rationalizing Russia's political, military, and economic focus in the Far East thus left Alaska out of the picture. And the campaign waged against the company and government administration of Alaska by Grand Duke Constantine and his circle of progressive officers was crucial in preparing the way for the sale.

Finally, Russia's buyer, the United States, must be considered. The outwardly friendly relations, especially as manifested in the fleet visits, were an important precondition of the treaty that was signed at Seward's home in Washington at the end of March. In fact, it was in the wake of the Fox mission, on 28 December 1866, that the decision was actually made. Before this an exchange of notes between Russian officials had stressed the financial burdens, the advantage of avoiding future conflict with the United States, and the opportunity to seal off the North Pacific from the British by an American pincering of British Columbia. These arguments won the support of Alexander Gorchakov, whose ministry would be in charge of the negotiation.[201]

The conference on 28 December at Gorchakov's office in the foreign ministry included the tsar, Stoeckl, and four high officials—Constantine, who was now chairman of the State Council; Reutern, armed with fresh financial data about the company; Gorchakov; and Adm. Nikolai Krabbe, head of the naval ministry. Though no transcript was apparently kept of the meeting, it lasted no more than an hour and featured only arguments for selling.[202] Alexander II simply agreed with the recommendation to send Stoeckl back to Washington with authorization to sell for not less than $5 million, with the stipulation that the rights of natives and employees to leave and to retain their religion if they stayed must be specified.

Despite the previous rumors and open discussions, the actual process of the sale was successfully kept secret and hurried to a conclusion at the end of March 1867, and agreement to the terms on both sides was facilitated by the new Atlantic cable. The result was a surprise to all but the small inner circles of officials—treaty by cabal. Such important Russian officials as Minister of War Dmitri Miliutin and Minister of Interior Petr Valuev were not informed about the negotiations. Even an activist at the Russian court like Cassius Clay was

[201]Batueva, "Prokhozhdenie dogovora," p. 118; Golder, "Purchase of Alaska," pp. 417–18.

[202]For details and results of the December meeting, see Bolkhovitinov, "How It Was Decided," pp. 116–25.

caught unawares—and Clay was chagrined at Seward's coup. Andrew Buchanan, the British ambassador in St. Petersburg, was understandably upset that his government had no opportunity to present a bid. After considering all the reasons for the sale and listening to Gorchakov's vague explanations about mutual best interests, Buchanan concluded that the main reason was to cement the Russian-American accord.[203]

Almost everyone seemed to gain by the deal: Russia for liquidating a financial and strategic embarrassment for $7,200,000; frustrated American expansionists; newspapers on both sides, whose circulations jumped in the debate over the pros and cons; and even the Russian America Company, whose stock soared to 300 rubles a share after the news broke that it was entitled to a portion of the purchase price and was shorn of all its debts and liabilities.[204] Seward took great pride in this "cheap" acquisition of an enormous territory, though the political uproar about it caused delays in ratification and payment. In fact, he is probably better known for his signature on the Alaska treaty than for his difficult but largely successful job of overseeing American foreign policy during the Civil War.[205] About the future of those most directly affected and least considered—the natives and residents of Alaska—only time would tell.

The bureaucratic process was, needless to say, complicated but effective in arranging the sale. To recap the arguments and their proponents, the reasons for

[203]Andrew Buchanan (St. Petersburg) to Lord Stanley, 4 April 1867, FO 5/638, PRO. His counterpart in Washington reported Stoeckl's explanation that Alaska had been sold because of the "little value and unproductive nature of the territory, the expence of the force needed to protect it and preserve order, and the desire of getting rid of a possession which may ultimately involve them in questions with the United States," but he believed the real reason was to neutralize Britain in the East. Wright-Bruce to Stanley, 2 April 1867, ibid.

[204]Secondary sources are quite confused about the price of the company stock. It had probably never reached 500 rubles a share, as Golder and others claim, and certainly not in 1866, as Gerus states. At the beginning of 1867 shares were selling for 100 rubles, then dropped to a low of 75 on 1/13 March before edging back up to 100 on the day the Alaska treaty was announced. The price of a share then quickly jumped to 165, gradually rose, and topped out at 300 in December 1867, reflecting in part the remaining earnings potential from the sales of tea. *Birzheviia Vedomosti*, the financial newspaper, issues for 1866 and 1867, University of Helsinki Library. A smart stockholder would have sold then, since the company followed a long downhill road toward liquidation, finally received only 73,000 of its claim of 4,043,882 rubles for its lost property, and paid out at 3.95 rubles per share in 1881. Makarova, "K istorii likvidatsii," p. 272.

[205]The historical marker in front of the Seward house in Auburn, New York, emphasizes the secretary of state's role in the purchase of Alaska. Gideon Welles, who dined with Seward the night the treaty was negotiated, was put off by his boasting: "I was somewhat amused and not a little disgusted with the little arts and overpowering egotism he exhibited. The last is a growing infirmity." *Diary of Gideon Welles*, 3:75. "Seward's icebox" happened to be based on fact: A valuable commodity of the territory for the West Coast of the United States was indeed ice.

the sale boiled down to the financial burden of keeping Alaska and the monetary gain from disposing of it (Reutern); the poor management and archaic nature of the Russian America Company (Constantine); an American destiny to possess it (Stoeckl and Seward); an inability to defend the territory (Constantine and Gorchakov); strategic-territorial reorientation (Constantine, Murav'ev-Amurskii, and Alexander II); enhancing a harmonious Russian-American relationship for the future (Gorchakov). Some of these may have been pure rationalizations or based partly on misinformation; the last two made perhaps the most sense, but even they did not pay off for Russia in the long run.

The transfer of Alaska to the United States was a fitting climax to a period of generally close and amicable relations between the two countries. Both the United States and Russia had gained substantially from each other, in terms of their own national interests, from the Crimean War through the American Civil War. The fleet visits symbolized and dramatized the accord, especially for the public. The other, less obvious aspects of the mutually beneficial relationship ranged from commerce and technological assistance to a higher level of cultural and national understanding and appreciation, fostered by a perceived kinship in the passage through emancipation, reform, and reconstruction.

A sign of this expanded American perception of Russia as an essential friend among the great powers was a book—circulated widely, especially in the Middle West—that emphasized the U.S. destiny to lead all of the Americas. In its revised edition of 1866, Charles Brandon Boynton, then serving as chaplain of the House of Representatives, stressed the importance of Americans' appreciation of the progressiveness of the Russian reforms and of welcoming Russia into a firm, natural alliance that would safeguard an expanded Monroe Doctrine and the future of both peoples.

When Europe has been taught that these Americas are the rightful and exclusive domain of Americans, the theater for an American civilization, which will brook no foreign dictation, the United States, as the leader of a grand alliance of American States, may present to all nations the type and model of a Christian Republic, while Russia, let us hope, will exhibit to Europe and the East, a Christian monarchy and a national Church administered so as to bless, instruct, and elevate the people.

If so, America and Russia will be the two great powers of the future.[206]

Close friends in separate spheres.

[206]*The Four Great Powers: England, France, Russia and America; Their Policy, Resources, and Probable Future* (Cincinnati, Chicago, and St. Louis: C. F. Vent and Company, 1866), pp. 512–13.

7

Conclusion

That the inhabitants of two large land masses and their governments should have contact in an increasingly interconnected world should come as no surprise. The history and development of the two countries were, of course, quite different. Russia was a deeply rooted Eurasian sovereignty that matured through a long socio-political struggle into a major world power in the eighteenth century. The core of its empire was Russian, but it had become, in the course of its advance, a large multinational empire. The united colonies of North America, on the other hand, were the result of an age of expansion and of western European settlement of a new continent, a wilderness obstructed only by relatively defenseless Indians. Distant as these two areas might be around the globe, the twain would meet, east to west and west to east.

Though Russia bore eastward and the United States westward, it would be across old Europe that the two would really join hands—in Russia's assistance to the American war for independence and, more important and naturally, in commerce. An active trade in commodities preceded diplomatic relations and contributed to their initiation. The United States needed the mainsprings of seaborne commerce—hemp, iron, and sailcloth—and in return, American ships, to the benefit of their owners, carried to Russia a broad assortment of colonial merchandise—coffee, sugar, spices, rice, and dye goods. This symbiotic relationship grew and developed amid European political tempests and flourished especially during the 1809–12 critical gap in the Napoleonic Wars.

Interrupted by the War of 1812, commerce between the two revived, thanks to Yankee fortitude, ambition, and simple self-interest and with the support of the merchant-banker houses of St. Petersburg. A thriving trade required ships and their sustenance. A particular lift was given to trade by the sugar boom of the 1830s and 1840s, when mainly New England ships poured Cuban sugar into Russian ports. But then American commercial fleets became less dependent on

Russian naval stores because of the substitution of jute and sisal for rope and tackle, of cotton canvas for sails, and native iron. Though trade continued, the balance shifted in favor of the United States in the cotton revolution and away from the triangular routes that had been the boon of the New England and St. Petersburg economies. However, the problem with cotton was that it customarily passed through British hands, except for the period during and just after the Crimean War when Yankee clippers carried thousands of bales directly to Russian Baltic ports. Stunted by the Civil War, the commercial exchange between the two countries, long a crucial factor in their relationship, began to decline.

Or rather it became more diversified and less direct. By the middle of the century, machinery and consumer goods ranging from stoves to clocks entered the Russian market from the United States. Yet the total after the American Civil War was relatively much lower and less essential to their respective economies than in earlier years. The exchange was now more important to Russia because of its technological needs for modernization. Russia had already sought to emulate the American model, especially in transportation and communications, and now it would move forward in a variety of areas, from petroleum development to dentistry and photography, with the help of American expertise. The United States very definitely held most of the cards in this deal and had the most advantage in the economic relations between the two countries. But third parties were usurping that advisory role and providing a conduit for equipment and knowledge, presenting a problem that would grow in significance.

Although both countries had military and defense needs, Russia's were greater because of its geopolitical situation, its traditions, and from a real sense of insecurity. As a safe, distant, and emerging power, the United States could and did render developmental assistance, especially in naval engineering. Thus vital warships were built in the United States for Russia, and Russian military leaders kept abreast of American military equipment and observed carefully their tactical employment in the Mexican and Civil wars. A driving force behind the pursuit and support of these mutually beneficial endeavors was a common hostility toward other powers, especially Britain and France—hence the especially friendly relations during the Crimean War and Civil War periods.

The exchange of products and technology was mainly an Atlantic affair—between Kronstadt-St. Petersburg and the principal port cities of the eastern and southern United States. The much-discussed opening to the South from the Black Sea through the Mediterranean never materialized, except for the substantial quantities of wool exported from there during the Civil War. The Far East, however, was another area where real mutual self-interest was indicated, with Americans furnishing shipping and supplies to the Russian colonies and outposts around the perimeter of the North Pacific. The speculative projection of vigorous advances in the area for both sides was realized only in the profitable but one-dimensional whaling industry centered in Russian waters. In such other North Pacific activities as the Amur trade and the Alaskan ice industry, cooperation triumphed over friction, but the results were disappointing. Finally, in a combined effort at accommodation and in the absence of serious conflict, the large Russian territory in North America was transferred to the United States.

Diplomacy and politics initially and literally followed the sails, beginning with the establishment of consular relations and then regular diplomatic relations in 1809. But these representatives were quickly embroiled in related political questions, such as tariffs, the rights of neutrals at sea, the presence and influence of other European powers, and territorial jurisdiction. Still, Russian-American relations were comparatively calm and free from schism during this period. For example, cases involving the illegal coastal activities of American ships in the North Pacific caused tension but, perhaps because of their remoteness to the centers of authority, never developed into serious disputes.

The Russian Empire and the American Republic were drawn steadily closer politically by their unconflicting courses of expansion and the opposition and threats of other nations, especially Great Britain. There is no question that the "friendship" of the two continental powers was generated to a large extent by mutual Anglophobia. By the middle of the century, this was strengthened by a somewhat contradictory Francophobia that was based primarily on a rising anti-Catholicism in both countries. These antagonisms crystallized during the Crimean and Civil wars and spawned especially close and congenial feelings of sympathy and support between the two countries. The sentiments were far from universal, however, since a free American press and an active Russian dissent were continually pointing out fallacies and contradictions in the relationship, especially the contrast and real or potential conflict between autocratic and republican institutions.

Besides economics and politics, the two countries developed a surprising degree of cultural affinity. Here the credit belongs to the Russian side, which seemed to crave literary as well as technical information about the United States. This enthusiasm may be due, at least in part, to the ferment within literate Russian society in the first half of the nineteenth century. In any event Cooper, Irving, Poe, Longfellow, Emerson, and Hawthorne, not to mention Harriet Beecher Stowe, were far better known and appreciated in Russia than Pushkin or Gogol were in the United States. This is somewhat ironic, for a common criticism leveled by Russians against the United States was that it was a cultural wasteland inhabited by people concerned only with business and material goods.

Americans may have been either ignorant of Russian history and literary and artistic creativity or simply culturally chauvinistic, but they made considerable effort to become informed about Russia. Though it is true that there was much

misinformation and bias in the reporting about Russia, Americans were generally understanding and objective, certainly in comparison with their western
European counterparts. Moreover, as the relationship matured and expanded,
natural curiosity about that distant, unusual friend increased.

Without doubt, many more Americans traveled to Russia than Russians came
to the United States. This was partly spurred by economic opportunities but
also stemmed from inquisitiveness and a sense of adventure and challenge,
which attracted Americans to the exotic world of Siberia, to the capitals of St.
Petersburg and Moscow, to the market center of Nizhni Novgorod, and to the
missionary service of religion or medicine. Reactions varied enormously to the
land, its people, and its institutional frustrations, just as some American diplomats could not get away fast enough while others, like Middleton, Seymour,
and Clay, merged comfortably into Russian society. Although few put their experiences into print, many letters circulated and talks proliferated. As a result
Americans probably had as objective a view of the country as any outsiders.
Certainly, despite individual impressions, a sense of kinship, friendship, and
sympathy emerged and developed between Russians and Americans.

On the whole the diplomats, businessmen, and tourists or adventurers held
favorable opinions of the other country, because of their fascination with the
different and exotic, the generally gracious and friendly hospitality, and the perceived opportunity to learn something that might be personally useful or in
their country's interest. With the exception of strange characters such as John
Randolph, these experiences were positive and tended to attract others. The
Russians in the United States were predominantly diplomats and military officers, at least until the 1850s, while the Americans in Russia were more often independent travelers, seekers of profit and adventure, or amateur diplomats. Still,
contacts were limited in number and duration by distance, climate, and the
greater cultural and historical attractions of western Europe.

Nor were Americans—or Russians—generally deluded by show or propaganda. Their descriptions were amazingly frank and critical, considering the
quasi-alliance that existed between the two countries. It was always clear to both
sides that fundamental political and social differences existed between them.
They also perceived that it was the circumstantial world-power situation that
drew them together in their own self-interests. Yet there was something else acting as a magnet: a common sense of destiny, of kindred psychological make-up,
of space and soil, of romance and soul—perchance of dreams—underlying the
political rhetoric, the economic gains, and the critical commentaries.

This was a hundred years of general harmony and optimism in the Russian-
American relationship, albeit fraught at times with elements of conflict and dis-
content. Some difficulties could naturally be expected between two countries of
such different origins and development, between two contrasting societies span-

ning a large portion of the earth—from St. Petersburg and Washington to Sitka and Nikolaevsk. What is surprising is that the relationship was so mutually beneficial and friendly. Although credit must go to the two governments and their leaders, more must be given to the individuals, both Russian and American, who devoted their lives, or at least a substantial portion, to the furtherance of the relationship. Unfortunately, over the next fifty years the conditions for friendship and goodwill would be altered dramatically in a more complex and violent world.

Appendix A

U.S. Ministers to Russia, 1809–1867

Name	State	Tenure	Prior Political Position	Later Political Position
John Quincy Adams (1767–1848)	Mass.	1809–15	Senator	Minister to Britain Secretary of State President
William Pinkney (1764–1822)	Md.	1816–18	Senator Attorney General	None
George W. Campbell (1768–1848)	Tenn.	1818–20	Senator Secretary of the Treasury	None
Henry Middleton (1770–1846)	S.C.	1820–30	Congressman Governor	None
John Randolph (1773–1833)	Va.	1830–31	Senator	None
James Buchanan (1791–1868)	Pa.	1831–33	Congressman	Senator Secretary of State President
William Wilkins (1779–1865)	Pa.	1834–36	Senator	Congressman Secretary of War
George M. Dallas (1792–1864)	Pa.	1837–39	Senator	Minister to Britain Vice-President
Churchill Cambrelling (1786–1862)	N.Y.	1840–41	Congressman	None
Charles S. Todd (1791–1871)	Ohio	1841–46	Army officer	None
Ralph Ingersoll (1789–1872)	Conn.	1847–48	Congressman	None
Arthur Bagby (1796–1858)	Ala.	1848–49	Senator	None
Neill Brown (1810–1886)	Tenn.	1850–53	Governor	None

Thomas H. Seymour (1807–1868)	Conn.	1854–58	Governor	None
Francis Pickens (1805–1869)	S.C.	1858–60	Congressman	Governor
John Appleton (1815–1864)	Mass.	1860–61	Asst. Secre- tary of State	None
Cassius Clay (1810–1903)	Ky.	1861–62 1863–69	None	None
Simon Cameron (1799–1889)	Pa.	1862–63	Senator Secretary of War	Senator

Appendix B

Russian Ministers to the United States, 1808–1867

Name	Tenure	Former Position	Later Position
Andrei Dashkov (1775–1831)	Chargé 1808–10 Minister 1811–17	None	None
Fedor (Friedrich) Pahlen (1780–1863)	1810–11	None	Minister to Portugal-Brazil
Petr Poletika (1778–1849)	1817–22	None	Foreign Ministry adviser
Fedor (Diderick) Tuyll van Serooskerken (1772–1826)	1823–25	Minister to Portugal-Brazil	None
Paul Krudener (1784–1858)	1828–37	None	Minister to Switzerland
Alexander Bodisko (1786–1854)	1837–54	Consul General, Stockholm	None
Eduard Stoeckl (1814–1869)	1854–68	Secretary of Legation U.S.	None

Bibliography

Manuscripts and Unpublished Sources

Abraham Lincoln Museum, Lincoln Memorial University, Harrogate, Tennessee
  Cassius Clay Papers
Alabama Department of Archives and History, Montgomery
  Bagby Papers
Arkhiv Vneshnoi Politiki Rossii [AVPR], Moscow
  fond kantselariia Vashington (Diplomatic correspondence between Washington and
    St. Petersburg)
Boston Public Library, Manuscript and Rare Book Department [BPL]
  John Quincy Adams letter
  James Buchanan letter
  Bowditch Correspondence
  Letter of Dana to Lovell
  Ward Papers
British Library, London [BL]
  Egerton 3170–3174, Jomini-Onou Papers
Brown University, John Hay Library, Providence
  Jonathan Russell Papers
University of California, Berkeley, Bancroft Library [UCB]
  George Adams
  American Russian Commercial Company By-laws
  Charles Bulkley Journal
  Scammon Papers
California Historical Society, San Francisco [CaHS]
  Moss letters
  Rowland, Walker and Company
Cincinnati Historical Society [CinHS]
  Todd Papers
Columbia University Manuscript Collection, New York
  Stedman Papers
Connecticut Historical Society [ConnHS]
  Barnard Papers
  Hoadley Papers
  Seymour Papers
Cornell University, John M. Olin Library, Department of Manuscripts and University
    Archives
  Bayard Taylor Papers
  Andrew Dickson White Papers
Duke University, William R. Perkins Library, Manuscript Department
  Bourne Papers
  Francis Calley Gray Diary
  John Knight Papers

407

Francis Pickens Letters
Essex Institute, Salem
  Czarina logbook
  Endicott Family Papers
  Martha Ropes Papers
Filson Club, Louisville
  Samuel Brown Papers
  Cassius Clay Papers
  Taliaferro Shaffner Papers
  Charles S. Todd Papers
Harvard Business School, Baker Library, Boston
  Dexter Papers
  Heard Collection I and II
  Locks and Canals Company Papers
  Ropes Papers
Harvard University, Houghton Library, Cambridge
  Autograph file: Pierce, Irving
  Jeremiah Curtin letter
Harvard University, Pusey Theatre Library, Cambridge
  Edwin Forrest Diary
Historical Society of Pennsylvania, Philadelphia [HSP]
  Buchanan Papers
  Cadwalader Collection
  Edward Coles Correspondence
  Gilbert Cope Collection
  Joseph Harrison, Jr., Letterbook
  Lewis-Neilson Papers
  Joel Poinsett Papers
Johns Hopkins University, Milton Eisenhower Memorial Library, Baltimore
  Gilman Papers
University of Kansas Spencer Research Library
  Robert Ker Porter Papers
Lenin Library, Manuscript Division, Moscow
  fond 111 Chizhov
  fond 41 Svin'in Papers
  fond 169 Miliutin Diary
Library of Congress, Manuscript Division [LC]
  Cleveland Abbe Papers
  Simon Cameron Papers
  George Washington Campbell Papers
  Documents Relating to the Transfer of Alaska
  Adam Gurowski Papers
  Hale Family Papers
  George Kennan Papers
  Nicholas King Papers
  George McClellan Papers
  William Marcy Papers
  James Murray Mason Papers
  Alfred Mordecai Papers
  Samuel Morse Papers
  Ross Parke Diary

Pennell-Whistler Papers
John Randolph Papers
Woodbury Family Papers
Maryland Historical Society, Baltimore [MaryHS]
Hyatt Papers
Latrobe Papers
Mayer-Roszel Papers
Oliver Papers
Pinkney Papers
Winans Papers
Massachusetts Historical Society, Boston [MassHS]
Adams Papers
Bancroft Papers
Dabney Papers
Dana Papers
Everett-Noble Papers
Everett-Peabody Papers
William Steuben Smith Diary and Letterbook
State Historical Society of Missouri [SHSM]
Green Clay Journal
James Rollins Papers
Mystic Seaport, George W. Blount Library, Mystic, Connecticut
Burrows Papers
Miers Fisher letter
Hiller Papers
National Archives and Records Service, Washington, D. C. [NA]
Despatches from United States Consuls [DUSC], Record Group [RG] 59, St. Petersburg (M 81), Odessa (M 459), Reval (M 484), Moscow (M 456), Amoor [Amur] River (T 111)
Despatches from United States Ministers [DUSM], Record Group 59, Russia (M 35), Sweden and Norway (M 45)
Diplomatic Instructions Department of State [DIDS], Record Group 59 (M 77)
Diplomatic Post Records [DPR], Russia, Moscow, Record Group 84
Domestic Letters of the Department of State, Record Group 59 (M 40)
Letters Received by the Office of the Adjutant General, Record Group 94 (M 567)
Miscellaneous Letters of the Department of State, Record Group 59 (M 179)
Notes from the Russian Legation in the United States to the Department of State, Record Group 59 (M 39)
Notes to Foreign Legations in the United States from the Department of State, Record Group 59 (M 99)
Papers Relating to the cession of Alaska, Record Group 48 (T 495)
Records of the Bureau of Naval Personnel, Record Group 24 (logbooks)
Records of the Russian America Company, Correspondence of the Governors General [RRAC, CGG], Record Group 261 (M 11)
New-York Historical Society [NYHS]
James Barnes Papers
Henry Bergh biographical sketch
George Bliss Autobiography
Gallatin Papers
Hoyt and Meacham Papers
Maxwell Papers

Miscellaneous Papers
Osgood Papers, Dana correspondence, 1786
Watts Sherman Papers
Wyer Letterbook
New York Public Library, Manuscript Division [NYPL]
Bryant-Godwin Collection
Greeley Papers
Madigan Collection
Peyton Letters
Anna Whistler Journals
Whistler report to Kleinmichel
Whistler-Swift Papers
Wise Papers
Yevstafiev (Evstaf'ev) Papers
University of North Carolina, Southern Historical Collection, Chapel Hill
James Gwyn Papers
Randall MacGavock Papers
Mordecai letter
Wood Trist Papers
Peabody Museum, Salem
Joseph Peabody Journal
Logbooks
Public Record Office, London [PRO]
Foreign Office Papers [FO] 5/590–653; 5/893–896; 5/904; 97/34; 65/128; 65/272–75;
65/462; 65/476; 65/504; 65/638; 65/688; 115/160; 181/416
Admiralty Records [ADM], 1/5821, 1/5852, 50/304
Private Collection
Sanders Papers
Rhode Island Historical Society
Champlin Papers
University of Rochester, Rush-Rhees Library [Rochester]
Seward Papers and Seward Addition
Hiram Sibley Papers and Sibley Addition
Rutgers University Archives
John D. Lewis Papers
Saltykov-Shchedrin State Public Library, Leningrad
Poltoaratskii fond
University of South Carolina, South Caroliniana Library, Columbia
Bonham Papers
Holt Papers
William Lowndes Papers
Henry Middleton Collection
Pickens Papers
Watts Papers
Smithsonian Institution Archives [SI]
William H. Dall Papers
Secretary Files—Incoming and Outgoing
Western Union Telegraph Expedition Papers [WUTE]
Tsentral'nyi Gosudarstvennyi Arkhiv Drevnikh Aktov [Central State Archive of An-
cient Acts], Moscow
fond 19 Kronstadt Reports

Tsentral'nyi Gosudarstvennyi Istoricheskii Arkhiv [Central State Historical Archive—
    TsGIA], Leningrad
  fond 18 Sanders "treaty"; Russian America Company materials
  fond 198 Mel'nikov memoirs
  fond 206 Ways and Communications
  fond 398 Russian America Company Charter Review
  fond 446 Russian Railroads
  fond 1265 Siberian Committee
  fond 1272 Shaffner negotiations
  fond 1325 Norton award
University of Virginia Library, Manuscripts Department
  Coles Collection
  McGregor Collection
  John Randolph Correspondence
University of West Virginia Archives
  Ambler Papers

Published Documents and Reference Resources

Alaska Boundary Tribunal: The Case of the United States. Washington, D. C.: Government
    Printing Office, 1903.
The American Image of Russia. Edited by Eugene Anschel. New York: Frederick Ungar, 1974.
Annuaire diplomatique de l'Empire de Russie. St. Petersburg: F. Bellizard, 1860s.
Arkhiv kniazia Vorontsova. Edited by Petr Bartenev. 40 vols. St. Petersburg: tip. Mamon-
    tova, 1870–95.
The Correspondence of John Lothrop Motley. Edited by George William Curtis. 2 vols. Lon-
    don: John Murray, 1889.
"Correspondence of the Russian Ministers in Washington, 1818–1825, Part 2." *American
    Historical Review,* 18, 3 (April 1913): 537–62.
Diary and Autobiography of John Adams. Vol. 2. Edited by L. H. Butterfield. Cambridge,
    Mass.: Harvard University Press, 1961.
"Diary and Memoranda of William L. Marcy." *American Historical Review* 24, 4 (July
    1919): 641–53.
*Diplomatic Correspondence of the United States concerning the Independence of the Latin-
    American Nations.* Vol. 3. Edited by William R. Manning. New York: Oxford Univer-
    sity Press, 1925.
Documents on the History of the Russian-America Company. Edited by Richard A. Pierce.
    Kingston, Ont.: Limestone Press, 1976.
Documents on Russian-American Relations: Washington to Eisenhower. Edited by Stanley S.
    Jados. Washington, D. C.: Catholic University of America Press, 1965.
Entsiklopedicheskii Slovar'. 82 vols. St. Petersburg: Brokgauz-Efron, 1890–1904.
*Graf Nikolai Nikolaevich Murav'ev-Amurskii—po ego pis'mam, offitsial'nym dokumentam,
    razckazam sovremennikov i pechetnym istochnikam (materialy dlia biografii).* Vol. 2. Edited
    by Ivan Barsukov. Moscow: Sinodal. tip., 1891.
Guide to Materials for American History in Russian Archives. Compiled and edited by Frank
    A. Golder. 2 vols. Washington, D. C.: Carnegie Institution, 1917, 1937.
"Letters from Russia, 1802–1805." Edited by George C. Rogers, Jr. *South Carolina Maga-
    zine* 60, 2 (April 1959): 94–105.
"Letters from St. Petersburg, 1850–1851." *Proceedings of the New Jersey Historical Society*
    82, 2 (April 1964): 75–100.
Life and Correspondence of Rufus King. Edited by Charles R. King. 4 vols. New York: Put-
    nam, 1897.

Life and Letters of Bayard Taylor. Vol. 1. Edited by Marie Hansen-Taylor and Horace E. Scudder. Boston: Houghton Mifflin, 1884.

Modern Encyclopedia of Russian and Soviet History. Edited by Joseph L. Wieczynski. 46 vols. Gulf Breeze, Fla.: Academic International Press, 1976–87.

New Letters of Abigail Adams, 1788–1801. Edited by Stewart Mitchell. Boston: Houghton Mifflin, 1947.

Neizdannye pis'ma inostrannykh pisatelei XVIII–XIX vekov iz Leningradskikh rukopisnykh sobranii. Edited by M. P. Alekseev. Moscow-Leningrad: Nauka, 1960.

Otchet Rossisko-Amerikanskoi Kompanii glavnago pravleniia za odin god, ... St. Petersburg: tip. Fishera, 1838–1867.

The Papers of James Madison: Secretary of State Series. Vol. 1. Charlottesville: University Press of Virginia, 1986.

The Papers of James A. Bayard, 1796–1815. Edited by Elizabeth Donnan. New York: Da Capo Press Reprint, 1971. Originally published as *Annual Report of the American Historical Association for the Year 1913,* vol. 2.

The Papers of Joseph Henry. Vol. 4. Edited by Nathan Reingold. Washington, D. C.: Smithsonian Institution Press, 1981.

Pushkin in English: A List of Works by and about Pushkin. Edited by Avrahm Yarmolinsky. New York: New York Public Library, 1937.

Records of the Russian-American Company 1802, 1817–1867. Edited by Raymond H. Fisher. Washington, D. C.: National Archives and Records Service, 1971.

Russia and the United States: An Analytical Survey of Archival Documents and Historical Studies. Edited by N. N. Bolkhovitinov. Translated and edited by J. Dane Hartgrove. Armonk, N.Y.: M. E. Sharpe, 1986.

The Russian American Colonies, 1798–1867: A Documentary Record. Vol. 3 of *To Siberia and Russian America: Three Centuries of Russian Eastward Expansion.* Edited and translated by Basil Dmytryshyn, E. A. P. Crownhart-Vaughan, and Thomas Vaughan. Portland: Oregon Historical Society, 1989. Cited as *RAC.*

Russkii biograficheskii slovar'. 25 vols. St. Petersburg: Lissner i Sovko, 1896–1914.

Treaties and Other International Acts of the United States of America. Edited by David Hunter Miller. 8 vols. Washington, D. C.: Government Printing Office, 1913–48.

"Tsar Alexander and Jefferson: Unpublished Correspondence." Edited by N. Hans. *Slavonic and East European Review* 32 (December 1953): 215–25.

The United States and Russia: The Beginning of Relations, 1765–1815. Washington, D. C.: Department of State and Government Printing Office, 1980. Cited as *USR.*

The Unpublished Letters of Bayard Taylor in the Huntington Library. Edited by John Richie Schultz. San Marino, Calif.: Huntington Library, 1937.

Vneshniaia politika Rossii XIX i nachala XX veka: Dokumenty Rossiiskogo ministerstva inostrannykh del. Ser. 1, 8 vols. Moscow: Nauka, 1960–72. Ser. 2, 9 vols. Moscow: Nauka, 1974.

The Writings of Albert Gallatin. Vol. 1. Edited by Henry Adams. Philadelphia: J. B. Lippincott, 1879.

The Writings of James Monroe. Edited by Stanislaus Murray Hamilton. 7 vols. New York and London: G. P. Putnam's, 1898–1903.

The Writings of John Quincy Adams. Edited by Worthington C. Ford. 7 vols. New York: Macmillan, 1913–17.

Published Memoirs, Diaries, and Other Primary Materials

Adams, Charles Francis. *Diary of Charles Francis Adams.* Edited by Aida DiPace Donald and David Donald. Cambridge, Mass.: Harvard University Press, 1964.

_____, ed. *Memoirs of John Quincy Adams Comprising Portions of His Diary from 1795 to 1848.* 12 vols. Philadelphia: J. B. Lippincott, 1874. Cited as *Memoirs.*

Afanas'ev, D. "Amurskii krai i ego znachenie." *Morskoi Sbornik* 69, 11 (November 1863): 3–87.

_____. "Nikolaevsk na Amure." *Morskoi Sbornik* 75, 12 (December 1864): 91–147.

Appleton, Nathan. *Russian Life and Society.* Boston: Murray and Emery, 1904.

Baird, Robert. *Visit to Northern Europe: or Sketches Descriptive, Historical, Political and Moral, of Denmark, Norway, Sweden and Finland, etc.* 2 vols. New York: John S. Taylor & Co., 1842.

Barrow, John. *A Memoir of the Life of Peter the Great.* New York: Harper & Bros. 1839.

Bigelow, John. *Retrospections of an Active Life.* Vols. 1–3. New York: Baker and Taylor Co., 1909. Vol. 4. New York: Doubleday and Company, 1913.

Bodisko, Vladimir. "Iz Ameriki." *Sovremennik,* no. 3 (1856): 114–40; no.6 (1856): 137–62.

Bograd, V. *Zhurnal "Sovremennik," 1847–1866—ukazatel' soderzhaniia.* Moscow-Leningrad: Gosizkhudozhlit, 1959.

Boynton, Charles B. *Address before the Citizens of Cincinnati: Delivered on the Fourth Day of July, 1855.* Cincinnati, Ohio: Cincinnati Gazette Company, 1855.

_____. *The Four Great Powers: England, France, Russia and America; Their Policy, Resources, and Probable Future.* Cincinnati, Chicago, and St. Louis: C. F. Vent and Company, 1866.

_____. *The Russian Empire: Its Resources, Government, and Policy by a "Looker-On" from America.* Cincinnati, Ohio: Moore, Wilstock, Kemp & Co., 1856.

Buchanan, James. *James Buchanan's Mission to Russia, 1831–1833: His Speeches, State Papers and Private Correspondence.* New York: Arno Press and New York Times, 1970.

Burrows, Silas E. *America and Russia: Correspondence, 1818 to 1848.* N. p. c. 1848.

Choules, John Overton. *The Cruise of the Steam Yacht North Star.* London: James Blackwood, 1854.

Clay, Cassius. *The Life of Cassius Marcellus Clay: Memoirs, Writings, and Speeches . . . .* 2 vols. Cincinnati, Ohio: J. Fletcher Brennan, 1886.

Coggeshall, George. *Thirty-Six Voyages to Various Parts of the World, Made between the Year 1799 and 1841.* 3d ed. New York: George P. Putnam, 1858.

Collins, Perry McDonough. *A Voyage Down the Amoor: with a Land Journey through Siberia, and Incidental Notices of Manchooria, Kamschatka, and Japan.* New York: D. Appleton and Company, 1860.

Cooper, James Fenimore. *Gleanings in Europe: England.* Introduction and Notes by Donald A. Ringe and Kenneth W. Staggs. Albany: State University of New York Press, 1982.

Curtin, Jeremiah. *Memoirs of Jeremiah Curtin.* Edited by Joseph Schafer. Madison: State Historical Society of Wisconsin, 1940.

Dallas, George Mifflin. *Diary of George Mifflin Dallas.* Edited by Susan Dallas. Philadelphia: J. B. Lippincott, 1892.

_____. *Letters from London, Written from the Year 1856 to 1860.* Edited by Julia Mifflin. 2 vols. London: Richard Bentley, 1870.

Darby, William. *The Northern Nations of Europe, Russia and Poland.* Chilicothe, Ohio: by author, 1841.

Davis, Henry Winter. *The War of Ormuzd and Ahriman in the Nineteenth Century.* Baltimore: James S. Waters, 1852.

Dearborn, Henry A. S. *A Memoir on the Commerce and Navigation of the Black Sea, and the Trade and Maritime Geography of Turkey and Egypt.* Boston: Wells and Lilly, 1819.

Delafield, Major Richard. *Report on the Art of War in Europe in 1854, 1855 and 1856.* Washington, D. C.: George W. Bowman, 1860.

Ditson, George Leighton. *Circassia or a Tour to the Caucasus*. New York: Stringer and Townsend, 1850.

D'Wolf, Captain John. *A Voyage to the North Pacific and a Journey through Siberia*. Cambridge, Mass.: n. p., 1861.

Eustaphieve (Evstaf'ev), Alexis. *Resources of Russia in the Event of a War with France with a Short Description of the Cozaks*. 2d ed. Boston: n. p., 1813.

————. *Memorable Predictions of the Late Events in Europe, Extracted from the Writings of Alexis Eustaphieve, Esquire*. Boston: n. p., 1814.

Everett, Alexander Hill. *Europe: or a General Survey of the Present Situation of the Principal Powers with Conjectures*. Boston: O. Everett, 1822.

Fremont, Jessie Benton. *Souvenirs of My Time*. Boston: D. Lothrop and Company, 1887.

French, Benjamin Brown. *Witness to the Young Republic: A Yankee's Journal, 1828–1870*. Edited by Donald B. Cole and John S. McDonough. Hanover, N. H., and London: University Press of New England, 1989.

Gallatin, James. *The Diary of James Gallatin: Secretary to Albert Gallatin, a Great Peace Maker, 1813–1827*. Edited by Count Gallatin. New York: Charles Scribner's Sons, 1916.

Golder, Frank. *John Paul Jones in Russia*. Garden City, N. Y.: Doubleday, 1927.

Golovin, Ivan. *Stars and Stripes, or American Impressions*. New York: Appleton and Co., 1856.

Golovin, P. N. *Civil and Savage Encounters: The Worldly Travel Letters of an Imperial Russian Navy Officer, 1860–1861*. Edited and translated by Basil Dmytryshyn and E. A. P. Crownhart-Vaughan. Portland: Oregon Historical Society, 1983. Originally published as "Iz putevykh pisem P. N. Golovina." Edited by Voin Rimskii-Korsakov, *Morskoi Sbornik* 66, 5 (May 1863): 101–82; 6 (June 1863): 275–340.

————"Obzor russkikh kolonii v Severnoi Amerike." *Morskoi Sbornik* 57, 1 (January 1862): 19–192. (Also published separately)

Griffin, Gilderoy Wells. *Memoir of Col. Chas. S. Todd*. Philadelphia: Claxton, Remson, and Haffelfinger, 1873.

Gurowski, Adam. *America and Europe*. New York: Appleton and Co., 1857.

————. *Russia As It Is*. New York: Appleton and Co., 1854.

Habersham, A. W. *My Last Cruise: Where We Went and What We Saw . . . .* Philadelphia: J. B. Lippincott, 1878.

Hamilton, James A. *Reminiscences of . . . or Men and Events, at Home and Abroad during Three Quarters of a Century*. New York: Charles Scribner & Co., 1869.

Harrison, Joseph, Jr. *The Iron Worker and King Solomon*. 2d ed. Philadelphia: Lippincott, 1869.

Harrison, Robert. *Notes of a Nine Years' Residence in Russia, from 1844 to 1853 with a Notice of the Tzars Nicholas I and Alexander II*. London: T. Cautley Newby, 1855.

Heco, Joseph. *The Narrative of a Japanese: What He Has Seen and the People He Has Met in the Course of the Last Forty Years*. 2 vols. Yokohama: n. p., n. d.

Henderson, Thulia S. *Memorials of John Venning, Esq. with Numerous Notices from His Manuscripts Relative to the Imperial Family of Russia*. London: Knight and Son, 1861; Newtonville, Mass.: Oriental Research Partners Reprint, 1975.

Holdcamper, Forrest R., comp. *List of American-Flag Merchant Vessels that Received Certificates of Enrollment or Registry at the Port of New York*. Special Lists, no. 22. 2 vols. Washington, D. C.: National Archives and Records Service, 1968.

Kennan, George. *Tent Life in Siberia*. New York and London: G. P. Putnam's Sons, 1910.

Knox, Thomas W. *Overland through Asia: Pictures of Siberian, Chinese, and Tartar Life*. Hartford, Conn.: American Publishing Co., 1870; New York: Arno Reprint, 1970.

Kohl, Johann Georg. *Russia and the Russians in 1842*. Philadelphia: Carey & Hart, 1843.

Kostromitinov, A. "Dva sobytiia v San-Frantsisko v 1855 i 1856 godu." *Russkii Vestnik* (July 1866): 47–56.

Lakier, Aleksandr. *Puteshestvie po severo-amerikanskim shtatam, Kanade i ostrovu Kube.* 2 vols. St. Petersburg: Vul'f, 1859.

Ledyard, John. *Journey through Russia and Siberia, 1787–1788: The Journals and Selected Letters.* Edited by Stephen D. Watrous. Madison: University of Wisconsin Press, 1966.

Lewis, William David. *The Bakchesarian Fountain, by Alexander Pooshkeen, and Other Poems, by Various Authors, Translated from the Original Russian by William D. Lewis.* Philadelphia: by author, 1849.

Lord, Louisa. *Miss Louisa Lord's Diary of a Voyage on the Ship 'St. Petersburg' in the Year 1840.* Edited by Winifred Trask Lee. New York: Ivy Press, 1875.

Loubat, Joseph F. *Narrative of the Mission to Russia, in 1866, of the Hon. Gustavus Vasa Fox.* New York: D. Appleton and Company, 1873.

Maak, R. *Puteshestvie na Amur sovershennoe po rasporiazheniu Sibirskago otdela imperatorskago geograficheskago obshchestva v 1855 godu.* St. Petersburg: Vul'f, 1859.

McClellan, George B. *Report of the Secretary of War Communicating the Report of Captain George B. McClellan . . . .* Washington, D. C.: A. O. P. Nicholson, 1857.

MacGavock, Randal W. *A Tennessean Abroad or Letters from Europe, Africa, and Asia.* New York: Redfield, 1854.

Markov, A. I. "Russkie na Vostochnom okeane." *Moskvitianin,* no. 8 (April 1849): 205–22; no. 9 (May 1849): 17–60; no. 10 (May 1849): 91–111; no. 14 (July 1849): 63–96; no. 16 (Agusut 1849): 147–70.

Maxwell, John S. *The Czar, His Court and People: Including a Tour in Norway and Sweden.* 3d rev. ed. New York: Baker and Scribner, 1850.

Mayo, Richard Southwell Bourke. *St. Petersburg and Moscow: A Visit to the Court of the Czar.* London: Henry Coburn, 1846.

Michi, A. *Puteshestvie po Amuru i Vostochnoi Sibiri . . . .* St. Petersburg: Vol'f, 1868.

Mordecai, Major Alfred. *Military Commission to Europe in 1855 and 1856. Report of Major Alfred Mordecai of the Ordnance Department.* Washington, D. C.: George W. Bowman, 1860.

Nazimov, N. "O puti po reke Amur v 1857 godu." *Vestnik Imperatorskago Russkago Geograficheskago Obshchestvo* 5 (1857): 25–29.

Nevel'skoi, G. "Obzor rezul'tatov deistviia russkikh na severo-vostochnykh predelakh Rossii i uchastiia ofitserov nashego flota v dele vosprisoedinneniia pri-amurskago kraia k Rossii." *Morskoi Sbornik* 72, 6 (June 1864): 21–45.

Niemcewicz, Julian Ursyn. *Under Their Vine and Fig Tree: Travels through America in 1797–1799, 1805 with Some Further Account of Life in New Jersey.* Edited by Metchie J. E. Budka. Vol. 14, *Collections of the New Jersey Historical Society at Newark.* Elizabeth, N. J.: Grossman, 1965.

Nolte, Vincent. *Fifty Years in Both Hemispheres: Reminiscences of the Life of a Former Merchant.* New York: Redfield, 1854.

Perry, Matthew C. *A Paper by Commodore M. C. Perry, U. S. N. Read before the American Geographical and Statistical Society, at a Meeting held March 6th, 1856.* New York: D. Appleton and Company, 1856.

[Poletika, P. I.] *A Sketch of the Internal Condition of the United States of America and of Their Political Relations with Europe, by a Russian. Translated from the French by an American with Notes.* Baltimore: E. J. Coale, 1826.

Polk: The Diary of a President, 1845–1849. Edited by Allan Nevins. New York: Capricorn Edition, 1968.

Poore, Benjamin Perley. *Perley's Reminiscences of Sixty Years in the National Metropolis.* Vol. 1. Philadelphia: Hubbard Bros., 1886.

Prince, Nancy. *Narrative of the Life and Travels of.* Boston: by author, 1850.
Pumpelly, Raphael. *My Reminiscences.* 2 vols. New York: Henry Holt and Company, 1918.
Roehm, Marjorie Catlin, ed. *The Letters of George Catlin and His Family: A Chronicle of the American West.* Berkeley and Los Angeles: University of California Press, 1966.
"Recollections of St. Petersburg." *Harper's New Monthly Magazine* 4, 22 (March 1852): 447–57.
Romanov, Dmitrii. "Amur." *Morskoi Sbornik* 47, 2 (May 1860): 173–87.
Schrier, Arnold, and Story, Joyce, eds. and trans. *A Russian Looks at America: The Journey of Aleksandr Borisovich Lakier in 1857.* Chicago and London: University of Chicago Press, 1979.
Schmidt-Phiseldek, C. F. von. *Europe and America or the Relative State of the Civilized World at a Future Period.* Translated by Joseph Owen. Copenhagen: Bernhard Schlesinger, 1820. Facsimile reprint, with postcript by Thorkild Kjaergaard. Copenhagen: Royal Danish Ministry of Foreign Affairs 1976.
Schuyler, George L. *Letter to the Hon. W. Gwin, Member of Congress from Mississippi, concerning the Steam Ship Kamschatka.* New York: Charles S. Francis, 1843.
Seward, Frederick W. *Reminiscences of a War-time Statesman and Diplomat. 1830–1915.* New York and London: G. P. Putnam's, 1916.
Shaffner, Taliaferro P. *Shaffner's Telegraph Companion, Devoted to the Science and Art of the Morse American Telegraph.* New York: Pudney and Russell, 1855.
———. *The War in America: Being an Historical and Political Account of the Southern and Northern States . . . .* London: Hamilton, Adams, 1862.
Smith, Mary Ann Pellew. *Six Years Travels in Russia, by an English Lady.* 2 vols. London: Hurst & Blackett, 1859.
Smith, Richard. *Reminiscences of Seven Years of Early Life.* Wilmington, Del.: Ferris Bros., 1884.
Southgate, Horatio. *The War in the East.* New York: Pudney and Russell, 1854.
Stephens, John Lloyd. *Incidents of Travel in Greece, Turkey, Russia and Poland.* 2 vols. New York: Harper & Bros., 1838.
Strong, George Templeton, *The Diary of George Templeton Strong.* Vols. 1–2. Edited by Allan Nevins and Milton Thomas. New York: Macmillan, 1952.
Stuart-Wortley, Lady Emeline. *Travels in the United States.* London: Richard Bentley, 1851.
Svenin (Svin'in), Paul. *Sketches of Moscow and St. Petersburg Ornamented with Nine Coloured Engravings, Taken from Nature.* Philadelphia: Thomas Dobson, 1813.
Svin'in, Pavel. *Opyt' zhivopishago puteshestviia po Severnoi Amerike.* St. Petersburg: F. Drekhsler, 1815.
———. *Vzgliad na respubliku Soedennykh Amerikanskikh oblastei.* St. Petersburg: F. Drekhsler, 1814.
Talvj [Therese Albertina Louisa von Jakoban]. *Historical View of the Languages and Literature of the Slavic Nations; with a Sketch of Their Popular Poetry.* New York: Putnam, 1850.
Taylor, Bayard. "Winter Life in St. Petersburg." *Atlantic Monthly* 16 (July 1865): 34–46.
———. *Greece and Russia.* New York: Putnam, 1859.
Taylor, Marie Hansen. *On Two Continents: Memories of Half a Century.* New York: Doubleday, Page and Company, 1905.
Tocqueville, Alexis de. *Democracy in America.* rev. ed. 2 vols. New York: Colonial Press, 1900.
Vevier, Charles, ed. *Siberian Journey Down the Amur to the Pacific, 1856–1857, by Perry McDonough Collins.* Madison: University of Wisconsin Press, 1962.

Welles, Gideon. *Diary of Gideon Welles*. 3 vols. Boston and New York: Houghton Mifflin, 1911.

Whittingham, Captain Bernard. *Notes on the Late Expedition against the Russian Settlements in Eastern Siberia*. London: Longman, Brown, Green and Longmans, 1856.

Wikoff, Henry. *The Reminiscences of an Idler*. New York: Fords, Howard & Hulbert, 1880.

Zavalishin, Dmitrii I. *Primery bystrago razvitiia gorodov v Soedinennykh Shtatakh*. Vol. 1, *Chikago*. Moscow: Univ. tip., 1868.

Zelenoi, K. "Iz zapisok o krugosvetnom plavanii (1861–1864): Ot Shankhaia do Sanfrantsisko," *Morskoi Sbornik* 80, 9 (September 1865): pp. 51–88.

Newspapers and Journals

Alta California and *Daily Alta California*, San Francisco
Baltimore *American and Commercial Advertiser*
Baltimore *Sun*
Birzhevnaia Vedomosti [Stock Exchange News], St. Petersburg
Boston *Daily Journal*
Boston *Evening Transcript*
Boston *Post*
Charleston *Mercury*
Chicago *Tribune*
Cincinnati *Daily Enquirer*
Daily Cincinnati Gazette
Dukh Zhurnalov [Soul of Journals], St. Petersburg
Edgefield, South Carolina, *Advertiser*
Frank Leslie's Illustrated Newspaper
Harper's Weekly
Hartford *Daily Courant*
Hartford *Daily Times*
Istoricheskii, Statisticheskii i Geograficheskii Zhurnal [Historical, Statistical, and Geographical Journal], Moscow
Kommercheskaia Gazeta [Commercial Gazette], St. Petersburg
Literaturnaia Gazeta [Literary Gazette], St. Petersburg
London *Times*
Moskovskii Telegraf [Moscow Telegraph], Moscow
Moskovskiia Vedomosti [Moscow News], Moscow
Moskvitianin [Moscovite], Moscow
Nashville *Whig*
National Intelligencer, Washington
New Orleans *Commercial Bulletin*
New Orleans *Daily Picayune*
New York *Advertiser and Express*
New York *Commercial Advertiser*
New York *Daily Tribune*
New York *Evening Post*
New York *Herald*
New York *Times*
Norfolk *Beacon* and *American Beacon*
North American Review
Otechestvennyia Zapiski [Fatherland Notes]
Philadelphia *Evening Bulletin*

Philadelphia *Public Ledger*
Providence *Journal*
Russkii Vestnik [Russian Herald]
San Francisco *Daily Evening Bulletin*
Sankt Peterburgskiia Vedomosti [St. Petersburg News]
Sovremennik [Contemporary], St. Petersburg
Saturday Evening Post, Philadelphia
Vestnik Evropy [Herald Of Europe], St. Petersburg
Vestnik Promyshlennosti [Herald of Industry], St. Petersburg
Zagranichnii Vestnik [Foreign Herald], St. Petersburg

Secondary Sources: Background Studies

Abrahams, Robert D. *The Uncommon Soldier: Major Alfred Mordecai.* New York: Farrar, Staus and Cudahy, 1958.
Adams, Ephraim Douglass. *Great Britain and the American Civil War.* 2 vols. London: Longmans, Green and Co., 1925.
Albion, R. G. *Forests and Seapower: The Timber Problem of the Royal Navy.* Cambridge, Mass.: Harvard University Press, 1926.
Alekseev, A. I., Argentov, I. N., and Grigorov, A. A. *Kostromichi na Amure.* Iaroslavl: Verkhne-volzhskoe izd., 1979.
Alexander, John T. *Catherine the Great: Life and Legend.* New York and Oxford: Oxford University Press, 1989.
Amburger, Erik. *Geschichte der Behördenorganisation Russlands von Peter dem Grossen bis 1917.* Leiden: E. J. Brill, 1966.
Bailey, Thomas A. *A Diplomatic History of the American People.* 10th ed. Englewood Cliffs, N. J.: Prentice-Hall, 1980.
Bayley, Charles Calvert. *Mercenaries for the Crimea: The German, Swiss, and Italian Legions in British Service, 1854–1856.* Montreal and London: McGill-Queen's University Press, 1977.
Barratt, Glynn. *Voices in Exile: The Decembrist Memoirs.* Montreal and London: McGill-Queen's University Press, 1974.
Belohlavek, John M. *George Mifflin Dallas: Jacksonian Politician.* University Park and London: Pennsylvania State University Press, 1977.
————. *"Let the Eagle Soar!": The Foreign Policy of Andrew Jackson.* Lincoln and London: University of Nebraska Press, 1985.
Bemis, Samuel Flagg. *John Quincy Adams and the Foundations of American Foreign Policy.* New York: Knopf, 1949.
Blackwell, William L. *The Beginnings of Russian Industrialization. 1800–1860.* Princeton, N. J.: Princeton University Press, 1968.
Blakely, Allison. *Russia and the Negro: Blacks in Russian History and Thought.* Washington, D. C.: Howard University Press, 1986.
Boand, Nell Holladay. *Lewis Littlepage.* Richmond, Va.: Whittet & Shepperson, 1970.
Bolkhovitinov, N. N. *Doktrina Monro: Proiskhozhdenie i kharakter.* Moscow: Nauka, 1959.
Brant, Irving. "Joel Barlow, Madison's Stubborn Minister." *William and Mary Quarterly,* 3d ser. 15, 4 (October 1958): 438–51.
Brebner, J. Bartlett. "Joseph Howe and the Crimean War Enlistment Controversy between Great Britain and the United States." *Canadian Historical Review* 11, 4 (December 1930): 300–27.
Brighton, Ray. *Clippers of the Port of Portsmouth and the Men Who Built Them.* Portsmouth, N. H.: Portsmouth Marine Society, 1985.

Bryan, Wilhelmus Bogart. *A History of the National Capital from its Foundations through the Period of the Adoption of the Organic Act.* 2 vols. New York: Macmillan, 1914, 1916.

Caffrey, Kate. *The Twilight's Last Gleaming: Britain and America, 1812–1815.* New York: Stein and Day, 1977.

Callahan, James Morton. *The Diplomatic History of the Southern Confederacy.* Springfield, Mass.: Walden Press, 1957.

Carter, Samuel, III. *Cyrus Field: Man of Two Worlds.* New York: Putnam's, 1968.

Case, Lynn M., and Warren F. Spencer. *The United States and France: Civil War Diplomacy.* Philadelphia: University of Pennsylvania Press, 1970.

Clarke, Dwight L. *William Tecumseh Sherman: Gold Rush Banker.* San Francisco: California Historical Society, 1969.

Clews, Henry. "England and Russia in Our Civil War, and the War between Russia and Japan." *North American Review* 178 (June 1904): 812–19.

Coatsworth, John H. "American Trade with European Colonies in the Caribbean and South America, 1790–1812." *William and Mary Quarterly,* 3d ser. 24, 2 (April 1967): 243–66.

Croffut, William Augustus. *The Vanderbilts and the Story of Their Fortune.* Chicago and New York: Bedford, Clarke and Company, 1886.

Crook, D. P. *The North, the South, and the Powers, 1861–1865.* New York: John Wiley and Sons, 1974.

Curti, Merle Eugene. *The American Peace Crusade, 1815–1860.* Durham, N.C.: Duke University Press, 1929.

Curtiss, John Shelton. *Russia's Crimean War.* Durham, N.C.: Duke University Press, 1979.

————. "Russian Diplomacy in the Mid-nineteenth Century." *South Atlantic Quarterly* 72 (Summer 1973): 396–405.

Davis, Curtis Carroll. *The King's Chevalier: A Biography of Lewis Littlepage.* Indianapolis and New York: Bobbs-Merrill, 1961.

Dearborn, H. A. S. *The Life of William Bainbridge, Esq., of the United States Navy.* Edited by James Barnes. Princeton, N. J.: Princeton University Press, 1931.

Dennett, Tyler. *Americans in Eastern Asia: A Critical Study of United States' Policy in the Far East in the Nineteenth Century.* New York: Barnes and Noble Reprint, 1963.

Dupuy, Richard Ernest. *Silvanus Thayer: Father of Technology in the United States.* West Point: U.S. Military Academy, 1958.

Edmunds, John B., Jr. *Francis W. Pickens and the Politics of Destruction.* Chapel Hill and London: University of North Carolina Press, 1986.

Egan, Clifford L. *Neither Peace nor War: Franco-American Relations, 1803–1812.* Baton Rouge and London: Louisiana State University Press, 1983.

Elliott, Charles Winslow. *Winfield Scott: The Soldier and the Man.* New York: Macmillan, 1937.

Emden, Paul H. *Money Powers of Europe in the Nineteenth and Twentieth Centuries.* London: Sampson Low, Marston & Co., 1937.

Fanger, Donald. *The Creation of Nikolai Gogol.* Cambridge, Mass.: Harvard University Press, 1979.

Ferris, Norman. *Desperate Diplomacy: William Seward's Foreign Policy, 1861.* Knoxville: University of Tennessee Press, 1976.

Field, James A., Jr. *America and the Mediterranean World, 1776–1882.* Princeton, N. J.: Princeton University Press, 1969.

Fisher, Charles E. *Whistler's Railroad: The Western Railroad of Massachusetts.* Railway and Locomotive Historical Society Bulletin no. 69. Boston, 1947.

Forbes, John D. "European Wars and Boston Trade." *New England Quarterly* 9 (December 1938): 709–30.

Fox, Frank. "Negotiating with the Russians: Ambassador Segur's Mission to Saint-Petersbourg, 1784–1789." *French Historical Studies* 7 (1971): 47–71.

Franklin, Fabian. *The Life of Daniel Coit Gilman.* New York: Dodd, Mead, 1910.

Fry, Joseph A. *Henry S. Sanford: Diplomacy and Business in Nineteenth Century America.* Reno: University of Nevada Press, 1982.

Gatrell, Peter. *The Tsarist Economy, 1850–1917.* New York: St. Martin's Press, 1986.

Giesinger, Adam. *The Story of Russia's Germans from Catherine to Khrushchev.* Battleford, Sask.: Marian Press, 1974.

Gleason, John Howes. *The Genesis of Russophobia in Great Britain: A Study of the Interaction of Policy and Opinion.* Cambridge, Mass.: Harvard University Press, 1950.

Goldenburg, Joseph A. *Shipbuilding in Colonial America.* Charlottesville: University of Virginia Press, 1976.

Golder, Frank. *Russian Expansion on the Pacific, 1641–1850.* New York: Paragon Reprint, 1971.

Goodfellow, Donald M. "The First Boylston Professor of Rhetoric and Oratory." *New England Quarterly* 19, 3 (September 1946): 372–89.

Gower, Herschel. *Pen and Sword: The Life and Journals of Randal W. McGavock.* Nashville: Tennessee Historical Commission, 1959.

Green, Constance McLaughlin. *Washington: Village and Capitol, 1800–1878.* Princeton, N. J.: Princeton University Press, 1962.

Greer, Jack Thorndyke. *Leaves from a Family Album (Holcombe and Greer).* Edited by Jane Judge Greer. Waco: Texian Press, 1975.

Griffiths, David M. "The Rise and Fall of the Northern System: Court Politics and Foreign Policy in the First Half of Catherine II's Reign." *Canadian Slavic Studies* 4, 3 (Fall 1970): 547–69.

Grimsted, Patricia Kennedy. *The Foreign Ministers of Alexander I: Political Attitudes and the Conduct of Russian Diplomacy, 1801–1825.* Berkeley and Los Angeles: University of California Press, 1969.

Haberly, Lloyd. *Pursuit of the Horizon: A Life of George Catlin, Painter and Recorder of the American Indian.* New York: Macmillan, 1948.

Haiman, Miecislaus. *Kosciuszko: Leader and Exile.* New York: Kosciuszko Foundation and Polish Institute of Arts & Sciences in America, 1977.

Halicz, Emanuel. *Danish Neutrality during the Crimean War (1853–1856): Denmark between the Hammer and the Anvil.* Odense: Odense University Press, 1977.

Haywood, Richard Mowbray. *The Beginnings of Railway Development in Russia in the Reign of Nicholas I, 1835–1842.* Durham, N. C.: Duke University Press, 1969.

———. "The Question of a Standard Gauge for Russian Railways, 1836–1860." *Slavic Review* 28, 1 (March 1969): 72–80.

———. "The 'Ruler Legend': Tsar Nicholas I and the Route of the St. Petersburg-Moscow Railway, 1842–1843." *Slavic Review* 37, 4 (December 1978): 640–50.

Herlihy, Patricia. *Odessa: A History, 1794–1914.* Harvard Ukrainian Research Institute Monograph Series. Cambridge, Mass.: Harvard University Press, 1986.

Holbo, Paul S. *Tarnished Expansion: The Alaska Scandal, the Press, and Congress, 1867–1871.* Knoxville: University of Tennessee Press, 1983.

Howard, Leon. "Joel Barlow and Napoleon." *Huntington Library Quarterly* 2, 1 (October 1938): 37–51.

Hulley, Clarence C. *Alaska: Past and Present.* 3d ed. Portland, Ore.: Binfords and Mort, 1970.

Hutson, James H. *John Adams and the Diplomacy of the American Revolution*. Lexington: University of Kentucky Press, 1980.

Jahns, Patricia. *Matthew Fontaine Maury and Joseph Henry: Scientists of the Civil War*. New York: Hastings House, 1961.

Jelavich, Barbara. *A Century of Russian Foreign Policy, 1814–1914*. Philadelphia and New York: J. B. Lippincott, 1964.

Jomini, Baron A. G. *Diplomatic Study of the Crimean War*. 2 vols. London: W. H. Allen, 1882.

Jones, W. Gareth. *Nikolay Novikov, Enlightener of Russia*. Cambridge: Cambridge University Press, 1985.

Jordan, Weymouth T. *George Washington Campbell of Tennessee, Western Statesman*. Tallahassee: Florida State University Press, 1955.

Kahan, Arcadius. *The Plow, the Hammer, and the Knout: An Economic History of Eighteenth-Century Russia*. Chicago and London: University of Chicago Press, 1985.

Kennan, George F. *The Marquis de Custine and His "Russia in 1839."* Princeton, N. J.: Princeton University Press, 1971.

Key, Mary Ritchie. *Catherine the Great's Linguistic Contribution*. Carbondale, Ill., and Edmonton, Alberta: Linguistic Research, 1980.

Kimball, Marie Goebel. "William Short, Jefferson's Only 'Son,' " *North American Review*, no. 223 (September–November 1926): 471–86.

Kiniapina, N. S. *Politika Russkogo samoderzhaviia v oblasti promyshlennosti (20-50-e gody XIX v.)*. Moscow: MGU, 1968.

Kipp, Jacob W. "Consequences of Defeat: Modernizing the Russian Navy, 1856–1863." *Jahrbucher fur Geschichte Osteuropas*, n. s. 20, 2 (June 1972): 210–25.

Kolchin, Peter. *Unfree Labor: American Slavery and Russian Serfdom*. Cambridge, Mass., and London: Harvard University Press, 1987.

LaFeber, Walter. *The American Age: United States Foreign Policy at Home and Abroad since 1750*. New York and London: W. W. Norton & Company, 1989.

Lensen, George. *Russia's Japan Expedition of 1852 to 1855*. Gainesville: University of Florida Press, 1955.

Ley, Francis. *La Russie, Paul de Krüdener et les soulèvements nationaux, 1814–1859 (d'après de nombreux documents inédits)*. Paris: Hachette, 1971.

Lincoln, W. Bruce. *Nicholas I: Emperor and Autocrat of All the Russias*. Bloomington and London: Indiana University Press, 1978.

Liss, Peggy K. *Atlantic Empires: The Network of Trade and Revolution, 1713–1826*. Baltimore and London: Johns Hopkins University Press, 1983.

Lobanov-Rostovsky, Andrei A. *Russia and Europe, 1789–1825*. New York: Greenwood Press, 1968.

McDonald, Forrest. *The Presidency of Thomas Jefferson*. Lawrence: University Press of Kansas, 1976.

Madariaga, Isabel de. *Russia in the Age of Catherine the Great*. New Haven, Conn., and London: Yale University Press, 1981.

Malone, Dumas. *Jefferson and His Time*. Vol. 5, *Jefferson the President, Second Term, 1805–1809*. Boston: Little, Brown, 1974.

Marshall, Herbert, and Stock, Mildred. *Ira Aldridge, The Negro Tragedian*. Carbondale and Edwardsville: Southern Illinois University Press, 1968.

Martin, John M. "The Senatorial Career of Arthur Pendleton Bagby." *Alabama Historical Quarterly* 42, 3–4 (Fall and Winter 1980): 155–56.

May, Ernest R. *The Making of the Monroe Doctrine*. Cambridge, Mass., and London: Harvard University Press, 1975.

May, Robert E. *The Southern Dream of a Caribbean Empire, 1854–1861.* Baton Rouge: Louisiana State University Press, 1973.

Mazour, Anatole G. *The First Russian Revolution, 1825.* 1937. Reprint. Stanford, Calif.: Stanford University Press, 1961.

Merli, Frank J. *Great Britain and the Confederate Navy, 1861–1865.* Bloomington and London: Indiana University Press, 1965.

Miller, Martin A. *The Russian Revolutionary Emigrés, 1825–1870.* Baltimore and London: Johns Hopkins University Press, 1986.

Morison, Samuel Eliot. *The Maritime History of Massachusetts, 1783–1860.* 2d ed. Boston: Houghton Mifflin, 1961.

————. *"Old Bruin" Commodore Matthew C. Perry, 1794–1858.* Boston and Toronto: Little, Brown, 1967.

Moses, Montrose J. *The Fabulous Forrest: The Record of an American Actor.* Boston: Little, Brown, 1929.

Mumford, Elizabeth. *Whistler's Mother.* Boston: Little, Brown, 1939.

Nichols, Roy Franklin. *Franklin Pierce: Young Hickory of the Granite Hills.* Philadelphia: University of Pennsylvania Press, 1931.

Niven, John. *Martin Van Buren: The Romantic Age of American Politics.* New York and Oxford: Oxford University Press, 1983.

Oeste, George I. *John Randolph Clay: America's First Career Diplomat.* Philadelphia: University of Pennsylvania Press, 1966.

Okun', S. B. *Ocherki po istorii kolonial'noi politiki tsarizma v Kamchatskom krae.* Leningrad: Sotsekgiz, 1935.

Owsley, Frank Lawrence. *King Cotton Diplomacy: Foreign Relations of the Confederate States of America.* 2d ed. Chicago: University of Chicago Press, 1959.

Paolini, Ernest N. *The Foundations of the American Empire: William Henry Seward and U. S. Foreign Policy.* Ithaca, N. Y., and London: Cornell University Press, 1973.

Parton, James. *Life of Andrew Jackson.* Vol. 3. Boston: James R. Osgood, 1876.

Pintner, Walter McKenzie. *Russian Economic Policy under Nicholas I.* Ithaca, N. Y.: Cornell University Press, 1967.

Porter, Kenneth Wiggins. *John Jacob Astor Business Man.* 2 vols. New York: Russell and Russell, 1966.

Pratt, Edwin J. *Europe and the American Civil War.* Boston and New York: Houghton Mifflin, 1931.

Price, Jacob M. "The Tobacco Adventure to Russia: Enterprise, Politics, and Diplomacy in the Quest for a Northern Market for English Colonial Tobacco, 1676–1722." *Transactions of the American Philosophical Society,* n.s. 51, pt. 1 (1961).

Proctor, John Clagett. *Proctor's Washington and Environs.* Washington, D. C.: by author, 1949.

Ragsdale, Hugh. *Detente in the Napoleonic Era: Bonaparte and the Russians.* Lawrence: Regents Press of Kansas, 1980.

Ransel, David L. *The Politics of Catherinian Russia: The Panin Party.* New Haven, Conn., and London: Yale University Press, 1975.

Read, David. "Henry Baldwin Stacy." *Vermont Historical Gazetteer* (edited and published by Abby Maria Hemenway, Burlington) 2 (1871): 961–68.

Reinoehl, John H. "Post-Embargo Trade and Merchant Prosperity: Experiences of the Crowninshield Family, 1809–1812." *Mississippi Valley Historical Review* 42, 2 (September 1955): 229–49.

Rich, Norman. *Why the Crimean War?: A Cautionary Tale.* Hanover, N. H., and London: University Press of New England, 1985.

Richardson, H. Edward. *Cassius Marcellus Clay: Firebrand of Freedom*. Lexington: University of Kentucky Press, 1976.

Rieber, Alfred J. *Merchants and Entrepreneurs in Imperial Russia*. Chapel Hill: University of North Carolina Press, 1982.

Rippy, J. Fred. *Joel R. Poinsett: Versatile American*. Durham, N. C.: Duke University Press, 1935.

Rozhkova, M. K., ed. *Ocherki ekonomicheskoi istorii Rossii pervoi poloviny XIX veka: Sbornik statei*. Moscow: Sotseklit, 1959.

Ryan, A. N. "The Defense of British Trade with the Baltic, 1808–1813." *English Historical Review* 292 (1959): 443–66.

Saab, Ann Pottinger. *The Origins of the Crimean Alliance*. Charlottesville: University of Virginia Press, 1977.

Sawyer, Lemuel. *Biography of John Randolph of Roanoke with a Selection from His Speeches*. New York: William Robinson, 1844.

Schroeder, John H. *Shaping a Maritime Empire: The Commercial and Diplomatic Role of the American Navy, 1829–1861*. Westport, Conn., and London: Greenwood Press, 1985.

Schroeder, Paul W. *Austria, Great Britain, and the Crimean War: The Destruction of the European Concert*. Ithaca, N. Y.: Cornell University Press, 1972.

Semenov, A. *Statisticheskiia svedeniia o manufakturnoi promyshlennosti v Rossii*. St. Petersburg: Glazunov, 1857.

Shenton, James P. *Robert John Walker: A Politician from Jackson to Lincoln*. New York and London: Columbia University Press, 1961.

Shepelev, L. E. *Aktsionernye kompanii v Rossii*. Leningrad: Nauka, 1973.

Shepherd, Jack. *Cannibals of the Heart: A Personal Biography of Louisa Catherine and John Quincy Adams*. New York: McGraw-Hill, 1980.

Smiley, David L. *Lion of Whitehall: The Life of Cassius M. Clay*. Madison: University of Wisconsin Press, 1962.

Spencer, Donald. *Louis Kossuth and Young America: A Study of Sectionalism and Foreign Policy, 1848–1852*. Columbia: University of Missouri Press, 1977.

Spencer, Ivor Debenham. *The Victor and the Spoils: A Life of William L. Marcy*. Providence, R. I.: Brown University Press, 1959.

Spencer, Warren F. *The Confederate Navy in Europe*. University: University of Alabama Press, 1983.

Spivak, Burton, *Jefferson's English Crisis: Commerce, Embargo, and the Republican Revolution*. Charlottesville: University Press of Virginia, 1979.

Stanislavskaia, A. M. *Russko-angliiskie otnosheniia i problemy sredizemnomor'ia, 1798–1807*. Moscow: Nauka, 1962.

Steele, Robert V. [Lately Thomas]. *Between Two Empires: The Life Story of California's First Senator, William McKendree Gwin*. Boston: Houghton Mifflin, 1969.

Steers, Don. *Silas Enoch Burrows, 1794–1870: His Life and Letters*. Chester, Conn.: Pequot Press, 1971.

Steiner, Bernard C. *Life of Henry Winter Davis*. Baltimore: John Murphy, 1916.

Stillé, Charles J. "The Life and Services of Joel R. Poinsett." *Pennsylvania Magazine of History and Biography* 12, 2 (1888): 129–64.

Struve, B. "Vospominaniia o Sibiri." *Russkii Vestnik*, no. 195 (April 1888): 145–84.

Tarle, Evgenyi. *Krymskaia voina*. 2d ed. 2 vols. Moscow: Nauka, 1950.

Tegoborski, M. L. de. (Ludwig Tengoborskii). *Commentaries on the Productive Forces of Russia*. 2 vols. London: Longman, Brown, Green, and Longmans, 1956; New York: Johnson Reprint, 1972.

Thompson, Robert Luther. *Wiring a Continent: The History of the Telegraph Industry in the United States, 1832–1866*. Princeton, N. J.: Princeton University Press, 1947.

Tønnessen, J. N. *Kaperfort og Skipsfart, 1807-1814*. Oslo: J. W. Cappelans Forlag, 1955.

Urodkov, S. A. *Peterburgo-Moskovskaia zheleznaia doroga: Istoriia stroitel'stva (1842-1851)*. Leningrad: LGU, 1951.

Varg, Paul A. *New England and Foreign Relations, 1789-1850*. Hanover, N. H., and London: University Press of New England, 1983.

Vose, George L. *A Sketch of the Life of and Works of George W. Whistler*. Boston: Lee and Shepard, 1887.

Walters, Raymond, Jr. *Albert Gallatin: Jeffersonian Financier and Diplomat*. New York: Macmillan, 1957.

Walworth, Arthur Clarence. *Black Ships Off Japan: The Story of Commodore Perry's Expedition*. New York: Alfred A. Knopf, 1946.

Wilkinson, Norman B. *Lammot Du Pont and the American Explosives Industry, 1850-1884*. Charlottesville: University Press of Virginia, 1984.

Zlotnikov, M. F. *Kontinental'naia blokada i Rossiia*. Moscow-Leningrad: Nauka, 1966.

Secondary Sources on Russian-American Relations

Adamov, E. A. "Soed. Shtaty v epokhu grazhdanskoi voiny i Rossiia." *Krasnyi Arkhiv* 38 (1930): 148-64.

Alden, John R. *Stephen Sayre, American Revolutionary Adventurer*. Baton Rouge: Louisiana State University Press, 1983.

Alekseev, A. I. *Sud'ba Russkoi Ameriki*. Magadan: Magadanskoe knizhoe izd., 1975.

Allen, Robert V. *Russia Looks at America: The View to 1917*. Washington, D. C.: Library of Congress, 1988.

Anderson, M. S. "The Continental System and Russo-British Relations during the Napoleonic Wars." In *Studies in International History Presented to W. Norton Medlicott*, edited by Kenneth Bourne and D. C. Watt, 68-80. London: Longmans, 1967.

Arnaud, Colonel Charles A. de. *The Union, and Its Ally, Russia: An Historical Narrative of the Most Critical and Exciting Period of Our Late War*. Washington, D. C.: Gibson Bros., 1890.

Ault, Phillip H. "The (almost) Russian-American Telegraph." *American Heritage* 26, 4 (June 1975): 12-15, 92-98.

Babey, Anna. *Americans in Russia, 1776-1917: A Study of the American Travelers in Russia from the American Revolution to the Russian Revolution*. New York: Comet Press, 1938.

Bailey, Thomas A. *America Faces Russia: Russian-American Relations from Early Times to Our Day*. Ithaca, N. Y.: Cornell University Press, 1950.

Barraclough, Geoffrey. "Europa, Amerika und Russland in Vorstellung und Denken des 19. Jahrhunderts." *Historische Zeitschrift* 203, 2 (October 1966): 280-315.

Barratt, Glynn. *Russia in Pacific Waters, 1715-1825: A Survey of Russia's Naval Presence in the North and South Pacific*. Vancouver and London: University of British Columbia Press, 1981.

————. *Russian Shadows on the British Northwest Coast of North America, 1810-1890: A Study of Rejection of Defence Responsibilities*. Vancouver: University of British Columbia Press, 1983.

Bartley, Russell H. *Imperial Russia and the Struggle for Latin American Independence, 1808-1828*. Latin American Monographs, no. 43. Austin: University of Texas Press, 1978.

Batueva, T. M. *Ekspansiia SShA na Severe tikhogo okeana v seredine XIX v. i pokupka Aliaski v 1867 gg.*. Tomsk: TGU, 1976.

————. "Iz istorii ekspansii amerikanskogo kapitala na russkom dal'nem vostoke (50-60-e gg. XIX v.)." *Trudy Irkutskogo gos. univ. im. A. A. Zhdanova* (seriia istoricheskaia) 59, 2 (1970): 168-77.

Belov, M. "O prodazhe Aliaski." *Nauka i zhizn'*, no. 1 (1967): 69–73.

Berquist, Harold E., Jr. "Russian-American Relations, 1820–1830: The Diplomacy of Henry Middleton, American Minister at St. Petersburg." Ph.D. diss., Boston University, 1970.

Bishop, J. Leander. *A History of American Manufactures from 1608 to 1860.* 2 vols. Philadelphia: Edward Young & Co., 1838. Reprint. New York: Augustus M. Kelley, 1966.

Bolkhovitinov, N. N. "V arkhivakh i bibliotekakh SShA: Nakhodki, vstrechi, vpechatleniia." *Amerikanskii Ezhegodnik 1971.* Moscow: Nauka, 1971.

———. *The Beginnings of Russian-American Relations, 1775–1815.* Translated by Elena Levin. Cambridge, Mass., and London: Harvard University Press, 1975. Original Soviet edition: *Stanovlenie russko-amerikanskikh otnoshenii 1775–1815.* Moscow: Nauka, 1966.

———. "How It Was Decided to Sell Alaska." *International Affairs*, no. 8 (August 1988): 116–25.

———, and Polevoi, B. P., "Obshchestvennost' SShA i oborona Sevastopolia v 1854–1855 godakh." *Novaia i Noveishaia Istoriia*, no. 4 (1978): 35–52.

———. *Russia and the American Revolution.* Translated and edited by C. Jay Smith. Tallahassee, Fla.: Diplomatic Press, 1976.

———. "Russia and the Declaration of the Non-Colonization Principle: New Archival Evidence." Translated by Basil Dmytryshyn. *Oregon Historical Quarterly* 72, 2 (June 1971): 101–26.

———. "Russian-American Rapprochement and the Commercial Treaty of 1832." Edited by J. Dane Hartgrove. *Soviet Studies in History* 19, 3 (Winter 1980–81): 3–92.

———. *Russko-amerikanskie otnosheniia, 1815–1832.* Moscow: Nauka, 1975.

———. *Russko-Amerikanskie otnosheniia i prodazha Aliaski, 1834–1867.* Moscow: Nauka, 1990.

———. "Vydvizhenie i proval proektov P. Dobella (1812–1821)." *Amerikanskii Ezhegodnik 1976.* Moscow: Nauka, 1976.

Bradley, Joseph. *Guns for the Tsar: Technology Transfer and the Small Arms Industry in Nineteenth-Century Russia.* DeKalb: Northern Illinois University Press, 1990.

Cabot, Harriett Ropes. "The Early Years of William Ropes and Company." *American Neptune* 23, 2 (April 1963): 131–39.

Carson, Gerald. "God Bless the Russians." *Timeline* 3, 4 (August–September 1986): 2–17.

Chevigny, Hector. *Russian America: The Great Alaskan Venture, 1741–1867.* New York: Viking Press, 1965.

Cresson, William Penn. *Francis Dana: A Puritan Diplomat at the Court of Catherine the Great.* New York: Dial Press, 1930.

Crosby, Alfred W., Jr. *America, Russia, Hemp, and Napoleon: American Trade with Russia and the Baltic, 1783–1812.* Columbus: Ohio State University Press, 1965.

Dolgova, S. R. *Tvorcheskii put' F. V. Karzhavina.* Leningrad: Nauka, 1984.

Dowty, Alan. *The Limits of American Isolation: The United States and the Crimean War.* New York: New York University Press, 1971.

Dulles, Foster Rhea. *The Road to Teheran.* Princeton, N. J.: Princeton University Press, 1943.

Dvoichenko-Markov, Eufrosina. "Americans in the Crimean War." *Russian Review* 13, 2 (April 1954): 137–45.

———. "Benjamin Franklin, the American Philosophical Society, and the Russian Academy of Science." *Proceedings of the American Philosophical Society* 96, 3 (August 1947): 250–58.

————. "A Russian Traveller to Eighteenth-Century America." *Proceedings of the American Philosophical Society* 97, 4 (September 1953): 350–55.

Efimov, A. "Posylka dvukh russkikh eskadr v Severnuiu Ameriku." *Istorik-Marksist* 3 (1936): 93–103.

Fauchille, Paul. *La Diplomatie française et la ligue des neutres de 1780 (1776–1783)*. Paris: A Durand et Padone Lauriel, 1893.

Fedorova, Svetlana G. *Russkoe naselenia Aliaski i Kalifornii: Konets XVIII veka-1867 g.* Moscow: Nauka, 1971.

Fischer, LeRoy H. *Lincoln's Gadfly, Adam Gurowski*. Norman: University of Oklahoma Press, 1964.

Fisher, Raymond H. *Bering's Voyages: Whither and Why*. Seattle and London: University of Washington Press, 1977.

Gaddis, John Lewis. *Russia, the Soviet Union, and the United States: An Interpretive History*. New York: John Wiley and Sons, 1978.

Gerus, Oleh. "The Russian Withdrawal from Alaska: The Decision to Sell." *Revista de Historia de America*, nos. 75–76 (1973): 157–75.

————. *Feeding the Russian Fur Trade: Provisionment of the Okhotsk Seaboard and the Kamchatka Peninsula, 1639–1856*. Madison: University of Wisconsin Press, 1969.

————. "The Sale of Russian America to the United States." *Acta Slavica Iaponica* (Sapporo, Japan) 1 (1983): 15–37.

Gilbert, Benjamin F. "Welcome to the Czar's Fleet: An Incident of Civil War Days in San Francisco." *California Historical Society Quarterly* 26, 1 (March 1947): 13–19.

Golder, Frank A. "The Purchase of Alaska." *American Historical Review* 25, 3 (April 1920): 411–25.

————. "Russian American Relations during the Crimean War." *American Historical Review* 31, 3 (April 1926): 462–76.

Griffiths, David M. "American Commercial Diplomacy in Russia, 1780 to 1783." *William and Mary Quarterly*, 3d ser. 27, 3 (July 1970): 379–410.

————. "An American Contribution to the Armed Neutrality of 1780." *Russian Review* 30, 2 (April 1971): 164–72.

————. "Catherine the Great, the British Opposition, and the American Revolution." In *The American Revolution and "A Candid World,"* edited by Lawrence S. Kaplan, 85–110. Kent, Ohio: Kent State University Press, 1977.

————. "Nikita Panin, Russian Diplomacy, and the American Revolution." *Slavic Review* 28, 1 (March 1969): 1–24.

Grossman, Joan Delaney. *Edgar Allan Poe in Russia: A Study in Legend and Literary Influence*. Wurzburg: Jal-Verlag, 1973.

Grzelonski, Bogdan. *Poles in the United States of America, 1776–1865*. Warsaw: Interpress, 1976.

Haiman, Mieczyslaw. *Polish Past in America, 1608–1865*. Chicago: Polish Museum of America, 1974.

Hawkins, Rush C. "The Coming of the Russian Ships in 1863." *North American Review*, no. 569 (April 1904): 539–44.

Hecht, David. *Russian Radicals Look to America, 1825–1894*. Cambridge, Mass.: Harvard University Press, 1947.

Herber, Elmer C. "Spencer Fullerton Baird and the Purchase of Alaska." *Proceedings of the American Philosophical Society* 98, 2 (April 1954): 139–43.

Higham, Robin. "When the Russians Conquered New York." *Mankind*, 3, 8 (August 1872): 10–18.

Hildt, John C. *Early Diplomatic Negotiations of the United States with Russia*. Johns

Hopkins University Studies in Historical and Political Science, vol. 24, nos. 5-6. Baltimore: Johns Hopkins University Press, 1906.

Howe, George. "The Voyage of Nor'west John." *American Heritage* 10, 3 (April 1959): 78-80.

Ivanov, Robert F. *Diplomatiia Avraama Linkol'na*. Moscow: Mezhdunarodnye Otnosheniia, 1987.

Ivanchenko, Ia. A. "Promyshlennoe razvitie SShA v 20-30e gody xix v. v otsenke russkoi pechati." *Amerikanskii Ezhegodnik 1982*. Moscow: Nauka, 1982.

Jensen, Ronald J. *The Alaska Purchase and Russian-American Relations*. Seattle and London: University of Washington Press, 1975.

Jessup, John E. "Alliance or Deterrence: The Case of the Russian Fleet Visit to America." *New Aspects of Naval History*. Edited by Craig L. Symonds et al. Annapolis, Md.: Naval Institute Press, 1981.

Jones, Horace Perry. "Southern Opinion on the Crimean War." *Journal of Mississippi History* 29, 2 (May 1967): 95-117.

Khalfin, N. A., and Muradian, A. A. *Ianki na Vostoke v XIX veke, ili kolonializm bez imperii*. Moscow: Mysl', 1966.

Kirchner, Walther. *Studies in Russian-American Commerce, 1820-1860*. Leiden: E. J. Brill, 1975.

Kozlovskii, V. M. "Tsar' Aleksandr I i Dzhefferson: Po arkhivnym dannym." *Russkaia Mysl'*, no. 10 (1910): 79-95.

Kushner, Howard I. " 'Hellships': Yankee Whaling along the Coasts of Russian-America, 1835-1852." *New England Quarterly* 45, 1 (March 1972): 81-95.

———. *Conflict on the Northwest Coast: American-Russian Rivalry in the Pacific Northwest, 1790-1867*. Westport, Conn.: Greenwood Press, 1975.

———. "The Russian Fleet and the American Civil War: Another View." *Historian* 34 (August 1972): 633-49.

Laserson, Max. *The American Impact on Russia, Diplomatic and Ideological, 1784-1917*. New York: Collier Edition, 1962.

Lensen, George Alexander. *The Russian Push toward Japan, Russo-Japanese Relations, 1697-1875*. Princeton, N. J.: Princeton University Press, 1959.

Lerski, Jerzy Jan. *A Polish Chapter in Jacksonian America: The United States and the Polish Exiles of 1831*. Madison: University of Wisconsin Press, 1958.

Luthin, Reinhard H. "The Sale of Alaska." *Slavonic and East European Review* 16, 2 (July 1937): 168-82.

McPherson, Hallie M. "The Interest of William McKendree Gwin in the Purchase of Alaska, 1854-1861." *Pacific Historical Review* 3, 1 (March 1934): 28-38.

Madariaga, Isabel de. *Britain, Russia and the Armed Neutrality of 1780*. New Haven, Conn.: Yale University Press, 1963.

Maggs, Barbara. "Fedor Karzhavin and Vasilii Baranshchikov: Russian Travellers in the Caribbean and Colonial America." In *Russia and the World of the Eighteenth Century*, edited by R. P. Bartlett. Columbus, Ohio: Slavica, 1988.

Makarova, R. V. "K istorii likvidatsii Rossiisko-Amerikanskoi Kompanii." In *Problemy istorii i etnografii Ameriki*, 264-74. Moscow: Nauka, 1979.

Malkin, M. M. *Grazhdanskaia voina v SShA i Tsarskaia Rossiia*. Moscow-Leningrad: OGIZ, 1939.

Mazour, Anatole G. "The Prelude to Russia's Departure from America." *Pacific Historical Review* 10, 3 (September 1941): 311-19.

———. "The Russian-American and Anglo-Russian Conventions, 1824-1825: An Interpretation." *Pacific Historical Review* 14, 3 (September 1945): 303-10.

Mikhailov, M. L. "Amerikanskie poety i romanisty." *Sovremennik*, no. 10 (October 1859): 305–24.

Miller, David Hunter. *The Alaska Treaty*. Kingston, Canada: Limestone Press, 1981.

Mohrenschildt, Dmitri von. *Toward a United States of Russia: Plans and Projects of Federal Reconstruction in the Nineteenth Century*. Rutherford, N. J.: Fairleigh Dickinson University Press, 1981.

Morison, Samuel Eliot. *John Paul Jones: A Sailor's Biography*. Boston and Toronto: Little, Brown, 1959.

Narochnitskii, A. L. "Ekspansiia SShA na Dal'nem Vostoke v 50-70-e gody XIX veka." *Istoricheskie Zapiski* (Moscow) 44 (1953): 130–76.

Neunherz, Richard Emerson. "The Purchase of Russian America: Reasons and Reactions." Ph.D. diss., University of Washington, 1975.

Nichols, Irby C., Jr. "The Russian Ukase and the Monroe Doctrine: A Re-evaluation." *Pacific Historical Review* 36, 1 (February 1967): 13–26.

———— and Ward, Richard A. "Anglo-American Relations and the Russian Ukase: A Reassessment." *Pacific Historical Review* 41, 4 (November 1972): 447–56.

Nikoliukin, A. N. *Literaturnye sviazi Rossii i SShA: Stanovlenie literaturnykh kontaktov.* Moscow: Nauka, 1981.

————. *A Russian Discovery of America*. Moscow: Progress Publishers, 1986. Okun, S. B. *The Russian-America Company*. Translated by Carl Ginsburg. Cambridge, Mass.: Harvard University Press, 1951.

————. *Vzaimosviazi literatur Rossii i SShA: Turgenev, Tolstoi, Dostoevskii i Amerika*. Moscow: Nauka, 1987.

Oliva, L. Jay. "America Meets Russia: 1854." *Journalism Quarterly* 40, 1 (Winter 1963): 65–69.

Parry, Albert. *America Learns Russian: A History of the Teaching of the Russian Language in the United States*. Syracuse, N. Y.: Syracuse University Press, 1967.

————. "American Doctors in the Crimean War." *South Atlantic Quarterly* 54, 4 (October 1955): 478–90.

————. *Whistler's Father*. Indianapolis and New York: Bobbs-Merrill, 1939.

Pattock, Florence Bangert. "American Russian Relations, 1861–1869: A Period of Calculated Coexistence." Ph.D. diss., University of Minnesota, 1973.

Petrov, V. P. *Russkie v istorii Ameriki*. Washington, D.C.: Izd. Russ.-Amer. Ist. Ob., 1988.

Pierce, Richard A. *Builders of Alaska: The Russian Governors, 1818–1867*. Kingston, Ont.: Limestone Press, 1986.

————. *Russia's Hawaiian Adventure, 1815–1817*. Kingston, Ont.: Limestone Press, 1976.

Polevoi, B. P. "Popytka amerikanskogo posrednichestva v krymskoi voine." In *Problemy istorii etnografii Ameriki*, 43–54. Moscow: Nauka, 1979.

Pomeroy, Earl S. "The Visit of the Russian Fleet in 1863." *New York History* 24, 4 (October 1943): 512–17.

Ponomarev, V. N. "Russko-amerikanskie otnosheniia v gody krymskoi voiny, 1853–1856." *Istoricheskie Zapiski* (Moscow) 110 (1984): 232–81.

Popova, I. M. "F. Kuper v otsenke V. G. Belinskogo." *Pisatel' i literaturnyi protsess: Sbornik nauchnykh statei*. Vol. 6. Dushanbe: Tadzhikskii gos. univ., 1979.

Radovskii, M. I. "Iz istorii russko-amerikanskikh nauchnykh sviazei." *Vestnik Akademii Nauk SSSR* 26, 11 (November 1956): 93–99.

————. *Veniamin Franklin i ego sviazi s Rossiei*. Moscow-Leningrad: Nauka, 1958.

Reid, Virginia Hancock. *The Purchase of Alaska: Contemporary Opinion*. Long Beach, Calif.: Press Telegram, 1939.

Rhoads, James Barton. "Harris, Lewis, and the Hollow Tree." *American Archivist* 25, 3 (July 1962): 295–314.

Robertson, James Root. *A Kentuckian at the Court of the Tsars: The Ministry of Cassius Marcellus Clay to Russia, 1861–1869* (Berea, Ky.: Berea College Press, 1935).

Robertson, William Spence. "Russia and the Emancipation of Spanish America, 1816–1826." *Hispanic American Historical Review* 21, 2 (May 1941): 196–221.

Rogger, Hans. "America in the Russian Mind—or Russian Discoveries of America." *Pacific Historical Review* 47, 1 (February 1978): 27–51.

_____. "Russia and the Civil War." In *Heard Round the World: The Impact Abroad of the Civil War*, edited by Harold Hyman, 177–255. New York: Knopf, 1969.

Saul, Norman E. "America's First Student of Russian: William David Lewis of Philadelphia." *Pennsylvania Magazine of History and Biography*, 96, 4 (October 1972): 469–79.

_____. "An American's Siberian Dream." *Russian Review* 37, 4 (October 1978): 405–20.

_____. "The Beginnings of American-Russian Trade, 1763–1766." *William and Mary Quarterly*, 3d ser. 26, 4 (October 1969): 596–601.

_____. "Beverley C. Sanders and the Expansion of American Trade with Russia, 1853–1855." *Maryland Historical Magazine* 67, 2 (Summer 1972): 156–70.

_____. "Jonathan Russell, *The President Adams*, and Europe in 1910." *American Neptune* 30, 4 (October 1970): 279–93.

Savurenok, A. K. "Roman Fenimora Kupera 'Bravo' v otsenke russkoi kritiki 1830-kh godov." *Russko-evropeiskie literaturnye sviazi: Sbornik statei k 70-letiiu so dnia rozhdeniia akademika M. P. Alekseeva.* Moscow-Leningrad: Nauka, 1966.

Shaw, J. Thomas. "Puskin on America: His 'John Tanner,'" In *Orbis Scriptus: Dmitrij Tschizewskij zum 70. Geburtstag*. Edited by Dietrich Gerhardt et al., 738–56. Munich: Wilhelm Fink Verlag, 1966.

Slezkin, Lev Iur'evich. *Rossiia i voina za nezavisimost' v ispanskoi Amerike.* Moscow: Nauka, 1964.

Sorokin, Pitirim A. *Russia and the United States.* New York: E. P. Dutton and Company, 1944.

Starr, S. Frederick. "The Ohio Valley through Russian Eyes, 1857." *Bulletin of the Cincinnati Historical Society* 24, 3 (July 1966): 211–20.

_____, ed. *Russia's American Colony.* Durham, N. C.: Duke University Press, 1987.

Startsev, A. I. *Amerika i russkoe obshchestvo: Korni istoricheskoi druzhby russkogo i amerikanskogo narodov.* Tashkent: Gosizdat, 1942.

_____. "F. V. Karzhavin i ego amerikanskoe puteshestivie." *Istoriia SSSR*, no. 3 (1960): 132–39.

Stoletniaia godovshchina pribytii russkikh eskadr v Ameriku, 1863–1963. Washington, D.C.: Victor Kamkin, 1963.

Tarsaidze, Alexandre. *Czars and Presidents.* New York: McDowell, Obolensky, 1958.

Thomas, Benjamin Platt. *Russo-American Relations, 1815–1867.* Johns Hopkins University Studies in Historical and Political Science, vol. 48, no. 2. Baltimore: Johns Hopkins University Press, 1930.

Tikhmenev, Petr A. *A History of the Russian American Company.* Edited by Richard A. Pierce and Alton S. Donnelly. 2 vols. Kingston, Ont.: Limestone Press, 1979. Originally published as: Petr Tikhmenev, translator. *Istoricheskoe obozrenie obrazovaniia Rossiisko-Amerikanskoi Kompanii i deistvii eia do nastoiashchago vremeni.* 2 vols. St. Petersburg, 1861–63.

Travis, Frederick F. *George Kennan and the American-Russian Relationship, 1865–1924.* Athens: Ohio University Press, 1989.

Tumarkin, D. D. *Gavaiskii narod i amerikanskie kolonizatory, 1820–1865 gg.* Moscow: Nauka, 1971.

Vaughan, Thomas, ed. *The Western Shore: Oregon Country Essays Honoring the American Revolution.* Portland: Oregon Historical Society, n. d. [1976?].

Völkl, Ekkehard. *Russland und Lateinamerika, 1741–1841.* Wiesbaden: Otto Harrassowitz, 1968.

Walicki, Andrzej. "Adam Gurowski: Polish Nationalism, Russian Panslavism and American Manifest Destiny." *Russian Review* 38, 1 (January 1979): 1–26.

Weiner, Leo. "The First Russian Consul in Boston." *Russian Review* 1 (April 1916): 131–40.

Wieczerzak, Joseph W. "The Polish Insurrection of 1830–1831 in the American Press." *Polish Review* 6 (Winter–Spring 1961): 53–72.

Wheeler, Mary E. "Empires in Conflict and Cooperation: The 'Bostonians' and the Russian-American Company." *Pacific Historical Review* 40 (1971): 419–41.

Woldman, Albert A. *Lincoln and the Russians.* Cleveland and New York: World Publishing Company, 1952.

Yarmolinsky, Avrahm. *Picturesque United States of America, 1811, 1812, 1813.* New York: Rudge, 1930.

———. "A Rambling Note on the 'Russian Columbus,' Nikolai Petrovich Rezanov." *Bulletin of the New York Public Library* 31, 9 (September 1927): 707–13.

Yatsunsky, V. K. "The Industrial Revolution in Russia." In *Russian Economic Development from Peter the Great to Stalin.* Edited by William L. Backwell. New York: New Viewpoints, 1974.

Zavalishin, Dmitri. "Kaliforniia v 1824 godu." *Russkii Vestnik* 60, 6 (November 1865): 322–68.

Zonin, S. A. "Russkie eskadry v Soedinennykh Shtatakh (1863–1864 gg.)." *SShA,* no. 7 (1974): 58–63.

Index

431